Working with Microsoft Dynamics™ CRM 3.0

Mike Snyder
Jim Steger

Microsoft Press
A Division of Microsoft Corporation
One Microsoft Way
Redmond, Washington 98052-6399

Library of Congress Control Number 2005939238

Printed and bound in the United States of America.

3 4 5 6 7 8 9 QWT 1 0 9 8 7 6

Distributed in Canada by H.B. Fenn and Company Ltd.

A CIP catalogue record for this book is available from the British Library.

Microsoft Press books are available through booksellers and distributors worldwide. For further information about international editions, contact your local Microsoft Corporation office or contact Microsoft Press International directly at fax (425) 936-7329. Visit our Web site at www.microsoft.com/mspress. Send comments to *mspinput@microsoft.com*.

Acquisitions Editor: Ben Ryan
Project Editor: Valerie Woolley
Technical Editor: Joe LeBaron
Copy Editor: Crystal Thomas
Production: Elizabeth Hansford
Indexer: Ginny Munroe

Body Part No. X11-89442

Table of Contents

Acknowledgments

We want to thank all of the people that assisted us in writing *Working with Microsoft Dynamics CRM 3.0*. If we accidentally missed anyone, we apologize in advance. On the Microsoft Dynamics CRM product team, special thanks to the following people:

- **Bill Patterson** Bill sponsored the book project, and helped make sure that all the pieces fell into place correctly, such as the trial version of the software bundled with this book. He also agreed to help us by writing the book's foreword.
- **Irene Pasternack** Irene was an unbelievable resource who acted as our point person tracking down and following up on various questions and details related to the book's content.
- **Amy Langlois** Amy provided great feedback and comments on the SDK-related chapters, and helped verify the sample code.
- **Dave Porter** Dave originally invited us to participate in the Microsoft CRM 3.0 Technology Adoption Program and helped connect us with the appropriate resources on the product team.
- **Jim Daly** Jim shared beta-versions of all the Microsoft CRM training materials with us which we used to help learn all the ins and outs of the new version of the software.

In addition, we want to thank these members of the Microsoft CRM product team that helped us at one point or another during the book project:

Mike Bishoff
Rich Dickinson
Min Fan
Tony Frink
Dave Garner
Barry Givens
Corey Hanson
Kate Harper
Lisa Higginbotham
Scott Kostojohn
Debbie Larson
Jesse Leatherman
Matt Magness
Todd Merrell
Terry Morris
Greg Nichols
Michael Ott
Matt Peart
Neelu Ramisetty
Wilfred Schmidt
Alex Simons
Ilana Smith
Karen Smith
Norma Smith
Crystal Smithwick
John Song
Betsy Stadick
Derik Stenerson
David Thacher
Brad Wilson
Tao Yue
Lan Zhang
Wan Li Zhu

Of course, we also want to thank the folks at Microsoft Press who helped support us throughout the book writing and publishing process:

- **Ben Ryan** Ben championed the book project, and was gracious enough to approve a larger page count than we originally estimated!
- **Valerie Woolley** Valerie helped us navigate the entire writing process and provided great support for us. As first-time authors for Microsoft Press, we really appreciated the incredible amount of patience that Valerie displayed with us.
- **Crystal Thomas** Crystal did a great job reviewing and editing the text for consistency and conformity, a very detailed and demanding task.

We also would like to thank Tess McMillan, Robert Lyon, and Charlotte Bowden for their assistance with packaging the sample download code. Linda Engelman also helped drive the marketing and promotions for the book.

In addition, we want to thank Microsoft Program Manager Brad McCabe who helped connect us with the appropriate people at Microsoft Press.

Last but not least, we want to thank Joe LeBaron. As the technical editor for the book, Joe worked around the clock to confirm the technical accuracy of the book. This included reviewing and testing all of our code samples and double-checking our facts.

Mike Snyder's Acknowledgments

I want to thank my lovely wife Gretchen who tolerated all the long nights and weekends that this book consumed over the past six months. Despite my frequent absence around the house, she supported me 100 percent from start to finish. Even though my kids won't be able to read this thank-you for years, I want to thank my children who provided me with the motivation to undertake this project. I also want to recognize my parents and my wife's parents who assisted my family with various babysitting stints. My mom Ann Snyder, a technical writer, also reviewed several of the chapters and provided great feedback from an outsider's perspective. In conclusion, I want to thank all of my coworkers at Sonoma Partners who helped pick up the slack created by my time commitment to this book.

Jim Steger's Acknowledgments

First and foremost, I wish to thank my loving wife Heidi for her unbelievable patience during this long and hectic process. I could not have completed this endeavor without her unwavering support, understanding, and encouragement. I want to thank my one-year-old son, Calvin, who was on his best behavior for his Mom during these past few months which allowed me the extra time required to write! I would also like to personally thank Amy Langlois of Microsoft who took the time to review code and answer my numerous questions. I know she received input from numerous members of the Microsoft CRM development team, and I want to extend my thanks to them as well. I wish to express my gratitude to my associates at Sonoma Partners who really stepped up their effort and understanding while I was forced to prioritize my writing over some of my day-to-day duties.

Foreword

What a difference a few years can make in the world of customer relationship management (CRM). Rewind the market just three short years, and you would find every one of the leading CRM software providers proclaiming the death of CRM. Failed implementations, unhappy customers, and the backlash of the dot-com burst led even the most faithful to question whether the customer would ever be right in the world of business applications. In yesterday's market, CRM was hard: hard to deploy, customize, implement, manage, upgrade–and most importantly, hard to use. CRM vendors appeared to have followed the path of Henry Ford and the Model T when constructing their offerings, essentially proclaiming that you could have CRM any way you needed it, so long as it worked how we intended it to work.

That was then and this is now.

Today, we find a rebirth in the world of CRM applications centered on the core tenets of simplicity, flexibility, and adaptability. CRM was never dead. It was, however, being beaten down by those who failed to understand the core challenges for successful CRM deployment: a simplified system that works by and with existing applications that end users know and trust; a system that adapts quickly and easily to the way that each unique business interacts with customers; and a system that is fast to deploy, simple to manage, and easy to maintain, without causing unnecessary workload for an already constrained IT organization.

At Microsoft, we have internalized these core tenets, and we offer today's businesses Microsoft Dynamics CRM 3.0, the third release in our flagship customer relationship management software package. With Microsoft CRM 3.0, organizations around the world can finally realize the benefits of CRM, experiencing a faster, more flexible, and more affordable way of deploying customer relationship management tools and technologies.

For end users, Microsoft CRM offers a seamless, native Microsoft Office Outlook experience that provides enhanced productivity when communicating with customers.

For systems implementers and customizers, Microsoft CRM offers unmatched customization, process automation, and development, enabling exceptionally quick and powerful customization to meet the unique needs of businesses.

And for IT administrators, Microsoft CRM offers an incredibly stable and reliable business system that businesses can rely on when managing their all-important customer relationships.

Working with Microsoft Dynamics CRM 3.0 is a detailed guide that will lead your exploration, evaluation, and learning of Microsoft CRM 3.0. Mike Snyder and Jim Steger provide you with an informative and easy-to-follow guide to help you learn and understand all of the new features and enhancements in this release. This book is full of detailed product overviews, combines practical, real-world experiences from the authors' very successful Microsoft CRM implementation practice, and offers guidance and insight for successful deployment of Microsoft CRM.

I hope you find this text as informative and fun to read as I have. I wish you success with your implementation of Microsoft CRM 3.0.

Sincerely,

Bill Patterson
Senior Product Manager
Microsoft Corporation

Introduction

We love Microsoft Dynamics CRM 3.0. And hopefully by the time you finish reading this book, you'll love Microsoft CRM too. We understand if you're skeptical about the possibility of falling for a piece of software, but we want you to know right up front that our goal is to show you all of the wonderful and amazing benefits that Microsoft CRM can provide for your business.

Who Is This Book For?

We wrote *Working with Microsoft Dynamics CRM 3.0* for the people who implement Microsoft CRM in their organizations. If you're the person responsible for setting up or configuring Microsoft CRM software on behalf of other users at your company, this book's for you. You might be an IT professional or simply a "power user" from the sales or marketing department. You should be comfortable with technical concepts and understand the role of Microsoft technologies such as Microsoft Exchange Server, Active Directory directory service, and Microsoft SQL Server. You don't have to be a coding expert to benefit from this book, but you should be able to edit an XML file and understand how relational databases work.

Project managers and software developers looking to extend and customize Microsoft CRM will enjoy our deep review of the Microsoft CRM client-side and server-side software development kit (SDK). We included a large number of code samples that software developers can immediately build and deploy to their own Microsoft CRM installations. And of course, you can extend our code examples to include your own unique modifications specific to your business.

This book can also help prospective customers with their software selection process as they evaluate the customization options that Microsoft CRM offers. You get two 90-day trial versions of Microsoft CRM (both Small Business Edition and Professional) on two CDs that you can use to work with the examples included in this book. The trial versions of Microsoft CRM are fully functioning, so you must meet the system requirements listed on the product Web site to install the software: *http://www.microsoft.com/dynamics/crm/product/systemrequirements.mspx*. If you like the trial version of Microsoft CRM and you decide to purchase the software, you can simply upgrade from the trial key to a production key without having to uninstall and reinstall the software. In addition, the trial version of the software includes a sample database for a fictional company called Adventure Works Cycle. You can refer to the Microsoft CRM Implementation Guide for detailed instructions on using the Sample Data Wizard to install the sample data.

Who is this book *not* for? It's not for end users interested in learning how they could use Microsoft CRM on a day-to-day basis because their company just started using the software. If you don't have System Administrator rights, you won't be able to perform most of the steps in this book, so it probably won't provide much benefit for you. If you're not sure whether you have System Administrator rights, this book probably isn't for you!

This book will also not tell you how to install the Microsoft CRM software and troubleshoot any installation-related issues. We don't cover upgrading an existing Microsoft CRM 1.2 installation to Microsoft CRM 3.0. The Microsoft CRM Implementation Guide gives excellent and detailed advice on the installation and upgrade processes, so there's no need for us to repeat that information here.

Organization of This Book

We divided *Working with Microsoft Dynamics CRM 3.0* into three parts and eleven chapters. The three parts are:

- **Part I: Configuration and Settings** Provides a quick overview of the components of Microsoft CRM, and explains how to configure some of the more frequently used parts of the software.
- **Part II: Customization** Provides deep coverage on modifying Microsoft CRM to match the way your business works. This includes adding new data fields, revising the user interface, creating reports, and automating business processes with workflow.
- **Part III: Extending Microsoft CRM** Explains how to create custom code that will integrate with Microsoft CRM through its predefined software interface. This section includes lots of code samples and examples that you can implement in your organization immediately.

Obviously, software developers and development managers will get the most benefit from Part III, but we tried to explain the coding and extensions concepts so that anyone can understand the examples, even if you don't understand the coding syntax.

Microsoft CRM 3.0 includes over 1,500 pages of product documentation in resources such as the Implementation Guide, the SDK, the Report Writers Guide, the User Interface Style Guide, and the online Help. Our goal is to focus on the key needs that most companies will have when setting up, customizing, and extending the software, while providing plenty of examples and real-world advice. If you want to learn more about using the software (as opposed to setting up and customizing it), we recommend that you take advantage of the many training options that Microsoft offers, such as E-Learning, classroom training, and the Foundation Library. Because of the book's space constraints, we decided not to repeat any information or samples already covered in the product documentation. Therefore, you'll find that we will frequently refer you to the SDK and the Implementation Guide.

A final point about the organization of this book is that we tried to eliminate any "marketing fluff" so that we can cram as much information as possible into the book. So you're not going to read about why other CRM projects fail, for example, or a discussion about the future of

CRM software. We're straight-forward and direct people, so we appreciate it when books present information in the same manner. Hopefully you like this style too.

Prerelease Software

We reviewed and tested this book using the final release of Microsoft CRM 3.0 (build number 3.0.5300.0). However, at the time that this book went to print, Microsoft had not yet released some utilities and tools related to Microsoft CRM, such as the Data Migration Framework, Microsoft CRM 3.0 Mobile, and integration with Microsoft Dynamics GP (formerly Microsoft Business Solutions–Great Plains). Consequently, we were not able to include those topics in the book.

Note In the back of *Working with Microsoft Dynamics CRM 3.0*, there is a 90-day trial version for both the CRM Professional Edition and the CRM Small Business Edition

System Requirements

You'll need the following hardware and software to run the code samples for this book:

Client

- Microsoft Windows XP with Service Pack 2 (for the client)
- Microsoft Internet Explorer 6 Service Pack 1
- Microsoft Visual Studio 2003 Standard Edition or Professional Edition

Server

- Microsoft Windows Server 2000 or Windows Server 2003, or Microsoft Windows Small Business Server 2003
- Microsoft SQL Server 2000 Standard Edition with Service Pack 4 or SQL Server 2005
- Dual 700-MHz or higher Intel Pentium (Xeon PIII) or compatible CPU Recommended: Dual 1.8-GHz Pentium (Xeon P4)
- 512 MB of RAM, 2 GB or more of RAM recommended
- SCSI hard disk with hardware RAID 5
- 10/100-megabit network card

Technology Updates

As technologies related to this book are updated, links to additional information will be added to the Microsoft Press Technology Updates Web page. Visit this page periodically for updates on Microsoft CRM and other technologies:

http://www.microsoft.com/mspress/updates/

Code Samples

All of the code samples discussed in this book can be downloaded from the book's companion content page at the following address:

http://www.microsoft.com/mspress/companion/0-7356-2259-0/

Creating a Virtual Web in IIS

Many of the code samples in this book require you to create and use a virtual Web in Internet Information Services (IIS). Here are the steps for creating a virtual Web named workingwithcrm that we reference throughout the book. These steps assume a default IIS configuration and Microsoft CRM installation.

1. Log on to the Microsoft CRM server.
2. Create a directory called **workingwithcrm** at C:\Inetpub. If necessary, you can create this directory anywhere on the file system *except* where you install the Microsoft CRM Web files. Microsoft CRM recommends that you do not alter the Web directory structure of the Microsoft CRM application.
3. On the taskbar, click **Start**, point to **All Programs**, point to **Administrative Tools**, and then click **Internet Information Services (IIS) Manager**.
4. Expand the local computer, and then expand **Web Sites**.
5. Right-click **Microsoft CRM 3.0**, and on the menu that appears, point to **New**, and then click **Virtual Directory**. Click **Next**.
6. In the **Alias** box, type **workingwithcrm**, and then click **Next**.
7. In the **Path** box, enter the full directory path of the previously created directory (C:\Inetpub\workingwithcrm), and then click **Next**.
8. Select the **Read** and **Run scripts (such as ASP)** check boxes, and then click **Next**.
9. Click **Finish**. You have created a virtual directory in IIS.

Support for This Book

Every effort has been made to ensure the accuracy of this book and the companion content. As corrections or changes are collected, they will be added to a Microsoft Knowledge Base article. To connect directly with the Microsoft Learning Knowledge Base and enter a query regarding an issue, go to *http://www.microsoft.com/learning/support*.

Microsoft Press provides support for books and companion content at the following Web site:

http://www.microsoft.com/learning/support/books/

Questions and Comments

If you have comments, questions, or ideas regarding the book or the companion content, or questions that are not answered by visiting the sites mentioned previously, please send them to Microsoft Press via e-mail to

mspinput@microsoft.com

Or via postal mail to

Microsoft Press
Attn: Working with Microsoft Dynamics CRM 3.0 Editor
One Microsoft Way
Redmond, WA 98052-6399

Please note that Microsoft software product support is not offered through these addresses.

Part I
Configuration and Settings

No two businesses are alike, each uses a unique set of tools and processes to manage their customers. Therefore, companies need to make sure that their customer management software can easily adjust and conform to their needs. Microsoft Dynamics CRM 3.0 offers powerful configuration tools so that customers can modify and customize the software, yet administrators can use these tools through a simple and easy-to-learn Web interface.

The first three chapters of this book will cover Part I, "Configuration and Settings." We will give you some background on Microsoft Dynamics CRM 3.0 and then we'll introduce some of the key Microsoft CRM terminology and concepts you'll use throughout the entire book. After the overview, we'll jump right into the details of how to set up and configure common areas of the application. Before you read Chapters 2 and 3 you should install Microsoft CRM 3.0, increase your comfort level navigating through the user interface, and have a rough idea of how your company wants to implement your CRM strategy. For the most part, you'll find the configuration and settings administration tools we cover in Part I located under the Settings section of Microsoft CRM. Of course, you'll need the appropriate security privileges to access the Settings area. In Chapter 3, we'll go into the details of configuring information security and data access in Microsoft CRM.

Part II of this book will explain how you can customize Microsoft CRM. The last part of this book, Part III, will review how you can create custom code for more complex Microsoft CRM implementation and integration needs.

Chapter 1
Microsoft Dynamics CRM 3.0 Overview

In this chapter:

We know you're eager to get into the details of how Microsoft Dynamics CRM 3.0 works and learn more about its great customization capabilities. Before we can jump into those details, we need to cover a little background information about Microsoft Dynamics CRM 3.0 and introduce some of the core concepts and terminology you'll use throughout this book.

Life Without CRM

Think back to a particularly bad customer service experience. Maybe you called a customer service phone number and were transferred to five different people, and every single person asked you the same questions, so you had to keep repeating the same answers over and over again. Or perhaps a salesperson pulled together a proposal for you but forgot to include your preferred-customer pricing in the quote. Or maybe a credit card company mailed you an application for a new account, even though you've had an account with that company for 10 years. You probably thought to yourself, "Why doesn't this company know who I am?" Does this sound familiar?

As its name implies, the goal of *customer relationship management* (CRM) is to enable businesses to manage each and every customer experience better. More importantly, CRM strategy recognizes that customer experiences span over time and that a typical customer might interact with your business 50 to 100 times in the course of your relationship. Ideally, your company could provide each customer a personalized experience based on the customer's unique history of interactions with you. For example, you wouldn't ask long-standing customers if they would like to open an account; when customers call your customer service department, you wouldn't have to ask them to answer the same questions over and over again; and your most valuable customers would always receive preferred pricing.

Important The purpose of CRM is to enable businesses to track and manage all of their customer interactions over the lifetime of the customer relationship. CRM is a business strategy, and companies typically use a CRM software system as a technology platform to help implement their CRM strategy, processes, and procedures.

In today's competitive business environment, mistreated customers can easily find other vendors or suppliers that are eager to replace you. However, if you give your customers a personalized experience, they're more likely to value their relationship with you and continue to patronize your business. The CRM philosophy makes so much sense, so why do so many companies force good customers to suffer through bad experiences every day?

As you probably know, it's very difficult for companies to embrace a CRM strategy and create consistently great customer experiences. Some of the factors that make a CRM strategy difficult to implement include:

- **Multiple customer management systems** Almost every company uses more than one system (such as sales tracking, warehouse management, or financial accounting) to run its business. Most of these systems can't easily communicate with each other to seamlessly share data. Therefore, you can imagine how salespeople using a sales tracking system might not know that a customer just opened an urgent customer service issue in your customer service system.
- **Remote workers** Even if your company is lucky enough to use a single system to track all of your customer interactions, remote and offsite workers might not have the ability to access data in the customer management system.
- **Rapidly changing business processes** You might recognize the saying, "The only thing constant in life is change," by French author François de la Rochefoucauld. This expression really hits home regarding the business processes of our Internet-enabled world. No sooner does a company finalize a customer management process than it must reconsider how that methodology will change in the next month, quarter, or year. Rapidly changing business processes challenge employees to adjust quickly, but most CRM systems can't react and adjust as quickly as the business needs it to.
- **Multi-channel customer interactions** Customers expect to be able to work with your company using any communication channel that they prefer. With the proliferation of different technologies, these customer communication channels might include Web sites, phone, fax, e-mail, mail, and instant messaging. If a company wants to track all of a customer's interactions, its customer management system must work with each of these technologies.
- **Difficult and rigid systems** Adopting a CRM strategy usually requires a company to select a technology system as its customer management platform. Earlier CRM systems earned the reputation of being difficult to use and complex to install. Even worse, companies could customize their CRM systems to their business needs only if they invested large sums of money and time in consultants who would customize the software for them.

CRM isn't a particularly new concept and it's earned something of a bad reputation among businesses. These are just some of the reasons responsible for its less-than-stellar track record over the years.

So what would happen if a company *could* successfully implement a CRM strategy and software? What types of benefits might the company receive?

- CRM could track customer interests and purchase history over time and then proactively generate new marketing initiatives for customers based on their unique histories.
- CRM could log a history of a customer's service requests so that a service technician could easily view all of those requests when the customer called with a new issue. Reviewing a customer's service history might help the technician resolve a customer's new issue much more quickly.
- A manager could view all of the interactions with a customer across various functional areas such as sales, marketing, and customer service. People typically refer to this cross-functional history as a *360-degree view* of the customer.
- Marketing managers could analyze and report on the effectiveness of their marketing lists and campaigns to determine how they should re-allocate future marketing investments.
- An analyst could use business intelligence tools to segment customers and prospects to identify trends and create predictive models for sales and customer service planning.

This list doesn't include all of the benefits of CRM, but it's clear that a successful CRM implementation can provide many short-term and long-term benefits for any business.

Introducing Microsoft CRM

Microsoft saw the need for a better CRM software platform and created a solution called Microsoft Dynamics CRM ("Microsoft CRM"). They designed this software for companies of all sizes to use as their technology platform for implementing CRM strategies. Microsoft first released Microsoft CRM (version 1.0) in late 2002 and has continued to update the software over the past few years with new releases and feature packs. This book covers the latest release of the software, Microsoft Dynamics CRM 3.0. This chapter will give you a brief overview of the Microsoft CRM 3.0 software to explain how it helps companies implement CRM strategies. We'll discuss the following overview topics:

- Software design goals
- Front office vs. back office
- Editions
- Licensing
- Requirements

After we cover Microsoft CRM from a high-level perspective, the subsequent chapters will explain how you can configure, customize, and extend the software to meet your company's unique business needs.

More Info This book explains how to configure and customize the Microsoft CRM software, but we will not instruct you on CRM strategies because they can vary widely by industry and company size. If you're interested in learning more about the philosophies and methodologies behind CRM, we suggest that you purchase one of the many books that discuss these topics in a non-software-specific manner. We wrote this book for people who are responsible for managing and deploying Microsoft CRM.

Software Design Goals

Microsoft CRM is designed to resolve the common issues that historically caused problems during CRM implementations. Some of the issues we've already reviewed include: offsite workers needing remote access to data, multi-channel customer communications, and rigid software design. To solve these problems, Microsoft CRM targeted three software design themes:

- Works the way you do
- Works the way your business does
- Works the way Information Technology (IT) expects it to

Works the Way You Do

Earlier CRM systems forced users to track information in multiple systems because the CRM software didn't include all of the functionality, such as e-mail, calendaring, task management, and spreadsheets, needed for users to complete their jobs. People performed their work with productivity tools such as Microsoft Office Outlook, Microsoft Office Excel, and Microsoft Office Word, but then they had to copy customer data into their CRM system! This extra step caused negative user feedback because it slowed users down, created additional work, and forced them to learn an entirely new tool.

To address this problem, Microsoft CRM works directly within Office and Outlook so that users can perform their normal job functions *and* track data in Microsoft CRM at the same time. Microsoft CRM is a server-based product that you install and run on a Web server, and users can install the Microsoft CRM client for Outlook software to work directly within Outlook, as shown in Figure 1-1. You can see that Microsoft CRM adds a toolbar to Outlook and adds Microsoft CRM folders to the Outlook folder list.

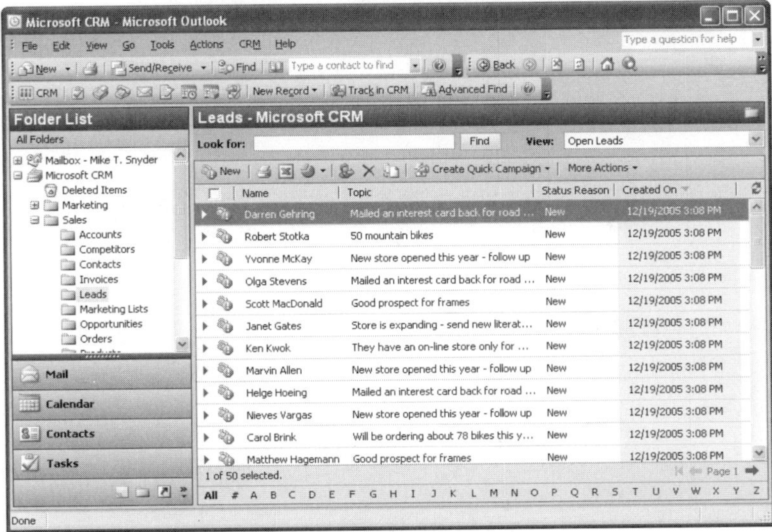

Figure 1-1 Tracking Microsoft CRM data in Outlook

If your users know how to use Outlook, they already know how to use the key customer management tools in Microsoft CRM such as contacts, tasks, appointments, and e-mail. Figure 1-2 shows the Microsoft CRM toolbar that allows a user to compose an e-mail message in Outlook and then simply click the Track In CRM button to save a copy of the message to the Microsoft CRM database.

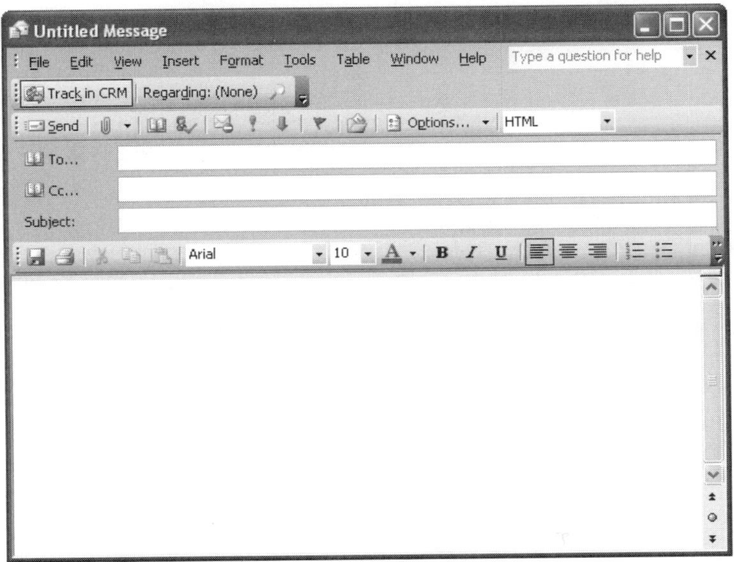

Figure 1-2 The Track In CRM button for saving data to Microsoft CRM

This tracking concept applies not only to e-mail messages, but also to calendar items, contacts, and tasks. By offering this native Outlook experience to users, Microsoft CRM lets users work with their normal tools *and* easily track and manage CRM data.

Real World Believe it or not, many companies still require their employees to copy information from their Outlook e-mail messages and paste it into their CRM systems. It sounds crazy, but we've seen this process implemented at many companies, both big and small. The native Outlook integration of Microsoft CRM eliminates the need for this extra work.

Even if your company doesn't use Outlook, or if you use Microsoft Office Outlook Web Access, Microsoft CRM provides you with additional user interface options:

- Microsoft Internet Explorer Web browser
- Personal Digital Assistant (PDA) using Microsoft mobile technology

Microsoft CRM also integrates directly with additional business productivity tools such as:

- Microsoft Excel
- Microsoft Word
- Microsoft Exchange Server
- Microsoft SharePoint Products and Technologies

By providing a tight integration with tools that your users already know, Microsoft CRM provides an extremely rapid learning curve to ensure maximum user adoption. More important, it's designed to work the way your users work.

More Info We explain the details of the integration of Microsoft CRM with these other products in later chapters.

Works the Way Your Business Does

So you've seen how Microsoft CRM works hard to make life easier for the people who use the system on a day-to-day basis. Microsoft CRM also offers several benefits designed to accommodate the way businesses work. In particular, these benefits include:

- **Web-based customization tools** Because your business processes change rapidly, you can quickly and easily customize Microsoft CRM by using Web-based customization tools. In addition to customizing forms and adding fields, you can create entirely new types of data to track and manage in CRM without writing a single line of code.
- **Robust security model** Microsoft CRM uses a role-based security model to provide you with incredibly detailed and flexible security configuration options. You can structure the system so that users access and edit only the information they need for their jobs. Yet, the security model remains agile enough to allow users to create ad hoc teams for collaborative work on projects and customer accounts.

- **Open programming interfaces** Because businesses use more than one system for their operations, Microsoft CRM offers you an open programming interface that enables you to connect Microsoft CRM with almost any type of external application, such as your company Web site, a financial system, or a company intranet. The Microsoft CRM programming interface uses Web services, so you can use almost any integration technology or platform that meets your needs.
- **Business process automation** Microsoft CRM offers you a Workflow feature to automate business processes and repetitive tasks such as automatically creating follow-up tasks for new leads or escalating overdue customer service issues to a manager. You set up these business workflows by using a graphical user interface, so you can easily customize and revise them without programming code when your business needs to shift quickly.
- **Multiple deployment options** You can choose how you want to deploy the Microsoft CRM software for your business. You can purchase the software and install it onsite in your local network, or you can rent the software on a monthly basis from a Microsoft partner who will manage all of the hardware, software, network, and security issues on your behalf. You can also switch from one deployment model to another if your business needs to change over time. Regardless of the deployment option you select, you can always configure the security settings so that your remote and offsite workers can log on and access the system with no problems.

More Info Part II, "Customization," and Part III, "Extending Microsoft CRM," explain how you can customize Microsoft CRM to match your business process and procedures.

Works the Way IT Expects It To

If you're in the Information Technology (IT) department, we're sure you've worked with some difficult systems. Maybe the software used some proprietary database format that only three people in the world understand, or maybe the software was so fragile that you didn't want to upgrade it for fear of breaking it! Microsoft CRM is designed to work with the existing tools, applications, and infrastructure that IT professionals use every day. Some of the Microsoft CRM benefits specific to IT include:

- **Industry standard technologies** Microsoft CRM uses industry standard network management technologies for its foundation. It uses Microsoft Active Directory directory service and Integrated Windows authentication for user and password management. Microsoft CRM stores all of its data in Microsoft SQL Server for easy backups, restores, and failovers. It also uses the SQL Server Reporting Services platform as its main reporting engine, and it works directly with Exchange Server for sending and tracking e-mail.

- **Wizard-driven deployment** When you install Microsoft CRM, the software checks for all of the system prerequisites and tells you which adjustments you might need to make. Depending on your network environment, it's possible to install the Microsoft CRM software with 10 clicks or fewer!
- **Failover and disaster recovery** Microsoft CRM supports clustering for Web, database, and e-mail server environments, so you can feel confident about the safety of your mission-critical data.
- **Zero-footprint clients** Users can access Microsoft CRM by using Internet Explorer and still use the software's rich functionality. In addition, you can deploy the Microsoft CRM desktop client for Outlook so that you can use the software if your organization uses thin-client technology for your users.
- **Automation support** You can install Microsoft CRM from a command line or via Terminal Services.

In light of these benefits (and many more that we didn't list), you'll find that Microsoft CRM works the way IT would expect it to.

> **More Info** This book focuses on configuring and customizing Microsoft CRM, but we do not cover the software installation and related troubleshooting because the Microsoft CRM 3.0 Implementation Guide provides all the information that you need on those topics. You can learn more by downloading the latest version of the Implementation Guide from *http://go.microsoft.com/fwlink/?LinkId=55129*.

Front Office vs. Back Office

Because CRM strategies revolve around tracking and managing customer interactions, CRM applications typically focus on customer touchpoints in departments such as sales, customer service, and marketing. Some people refer to these customer interfacing departments as the *front office* of a company. Consequently, you can refer to the departments that help support a business's operations but don't interact directly with customers as the *back office*. Typical back office departments include information technology, human resources, manufacturing, distribution, and accounting. Most people refer to software applications that help companies manage back office operations as Enterprise Resource Planning (ERP) applications. Just like CRM systems, implementing ERP applications requires a very careful and well-planned process to maximize the project's success.

The Microsoft CRM functionality focuses mostly on front office features, so it doesn't really include any back office functionality as part of its default installation. Of course, you could customize the Microsoft CRM software to include your own back office functionality, but developing ERP functionality can prove extremely complex and expensive. Fortunately, Microsoft offers several ERP applications from the same division that created Microsoft CRM.

Important In addition to Microsoft CRM, the Microsoft Dynamics division—formerly known as Microsoft Business Solutions—offers several ERP software products in its lineup.

Some of the current Microsoft Dynamics ERP products include:

- Microsoft Dynamics GP (formerly known as Microsoft Business Solutions–Great Plains)
- Microsoft Dynamics SL (formerly known as Microsoft Business Solutions–Solomon)
- Microsoft Dynamics NAV (formerly known as Microsoft Business Solutions–Navision)
- Microsoft Dynamics AX (formerly known as Microsoft Business Solutions–Axapta)

Each of these products provides rich functionality, and choosing the right ERP product for your business requires careful consideration well beyond the scope of this book.

The reason we mention these ERP products is to let you know that Microsoft already offers software for these back office departments if you're interested in automating that part of your business. In addition, Microsoft offers software integration between Microsoft CRM and Microsoft Dynamics GP, so that you can synchronize customer records, orders, and invoices between your front office and back office systems, as Figure 1-3 illustrates.

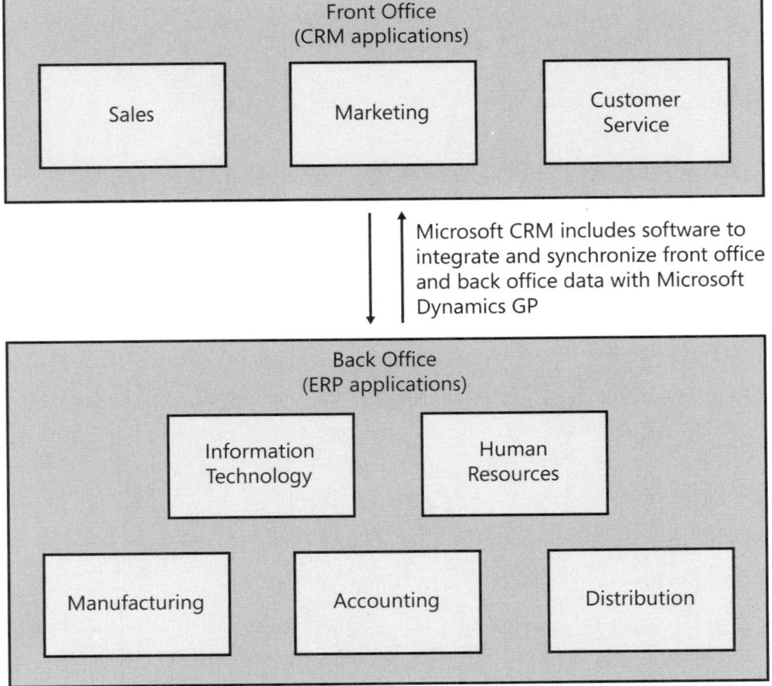

Figure 1-3 Microsoft CRM synchronization and integration with Microsoft Dynamics GP

More Info Microsoft CRM includes software to integrate with Microsoft Dynamics GP so that you can synchronize front office and back office data. This integration software includes its own software development kit (SDK) so that you can customize the synchronization. The official name, pricing, and functionality of this integration software wasn't released at the time that this book was written. However, Microsoft CRM 1.2 included the Microsoft CRM 1.2 Integration for Great Plains 8.0 software for no charge if you purchased the Professional edition of the software.

Editions

You can obtain Microsoft CRM 3.0 in one of two editions:

- Microsoft Dynamics CRM 3.0 Small Business Edition
- Microsoft Dynamics CRM 3.0 Professional

As the names of the editions imply, the Small Business Edition targets smaller companies, and Professional is more appropriate for medium and large companies.

Some of the key differences between the two editions include:

- You must deploy the Small Business Edition on a Microsoft Windows Small Business Server, but you can install Professional on various Microsoft Windows Server operating systems.
- You can accommodate a maximum of 75 users in the Small Business Edition, but Professional allows you to deploy as many users as necessary. After you factor in performance considerations, a recommended maximum number of users for the Small Business Edition might range from 40 to 50 users, depending on their usage and the system hardware.
- The Small Business Edition includes all of the functionality that Professional includes, in addition to features unique to Small Business Edition such as CRM integration with the Small Business Server Shared Fax Service.
- The Small Business Edition provides less flexibility in regard to custom third-party system integration and external user access because you cannot purchase and deploy an External Connector license with this edition. We explain the External Connector license in the next section of this chapter.

Note Small Business Server is a specialized operating system version that bundles Windows Server 2003, Exchange Server 2003 technology, and Microsoft Windows SharePoint Services so they can be deployed on a single piece of hardware. Small Business Server 2003 Premium Edition also includes Microsoft SQL Server 2000 and ISA Server 2004 in the bundled software. You must deploy Microsoft CRM with Small Business Server 2003 Premium Edition, because Microsoft CRM requires a SQL Server database.

Although deploying Microsoft CRM with Small Business Server includes several great benefits, it does include some notable restrictions:

- Small Business Server 2003 supports only two physical CPUs and up to four virtual CPUs.
- Each domain can contain only one installation of Small Business Server 2003.
- Small Business Server 2003 does not support trusts between domains, and you must install the server at the root of the Active Directory forest.
- A Small Business Server 2003 domain cannot have any child domains.
- You cannot run Terminal Services in Application Server mode on Small Business Server 2003.

Microsoft CRM Small Business Edition software licenses cost less than Microsoft CRM Professional licenses, but you can see that some constraints exist in regard to configuration of the underlying network.

Licensing

Microsoft CRM requires two types of software licenses for each deployment: server licenses and user licenses. Every deployment must include at least one server license, and you must have a user license for every active user in the system. User licenses are also referred to as *Client Access Licenses*. When you add a user to Microsoft CRM, you specify his or her Active Directory account, so you must also create an Active Directory account for every Microsoft CRM user.

Important The number of user licenses that you need depends on the number of *named users* in your system. Every active user in Microsoft CRM will consume a license, regardless of how often he or she accesses the system or how many users log on at the same time. Named user licensing is different from other software programs that base their licensing on the number of concurrent users. A system administrator can easily transfer user licenses from one user to another when necessary.

If your company deploys a Web farm with multiple Microsoft CRM Web servers, you must have a server license for every Web server running Microsoft CRM.

If you want to share Microsoft CRM data with external users such as your customers or partners, you can purchase an *External Connector license* that allows you to share Microsoft CRM data with an unlimited number of third-party users and systems. By using the External Connector License, you do not need to purchase a user license (create an Active Directory account) for each external user. For example, you can create an extranet Web site that lets customers log on and retrieve Microsoft CRM data in real time. You could also create a special Web site for your partners to enter and update Microsoft CRM data. You need an External Connector license for every server required to support external access.

In summary, Microsoft CRM offers the following software licenses:

- Small Business Edition server license
- Small Business Edition user license
- Professional edition server license
- Professional edition user license
- External Connector license (compatible with Professional only)

As you might guess, you cannot mix and match Small Business Edition licenses with Professional licenses in a single deployment. Of course, you can purchase these licenses through various Microsoft licensing programs such as Open Business, Open Value, Select, Enterprise Agreement, and Full-Package Product. We won't go into the details of these programs, but the key point is that you can purchase the software using whatever licensing program makes the most sense for your business.

Important When you purchase Microsoft CRM licenses, you will receive software updates and new version rights at no charge for a period of time after your initial purchase. The length of time that you receive software updates depends on the licensing program that you used to purchase the licenses, but it ranges from one to three years. You can continue to receive software updates by purchasing Software Assurance for additional years. If you choose not to renew updates, you will still own the Microsoft CRM software licenses in perpetuity.

As we mentioned earlier, Microsoft CRM 3.0 also includes the option for you to rent your software licenses and hosting through Microsoft partners. You must contact the hosting partners to understand the terms of their pricing, support levels, licensing, and so on.

Requirements

Microsoft CRM uses industry standard technologies such as Windows Server, Active Directory, and SQL Server for its platform. You have great flexibility in designing and configuring your Microsoft CRM environment, and your final system design will depend on several variables such as:

- Number of servers available and server hardware specifications
- Number of Microsoft CRM users and their expected system usage
- Hardware specifications of your servers and your local area network performance
- Your network structure and security configurations, including firewalls and virtual private network (VPN) connections
- Amount of disaster recovery and failover systems needed in your deployment

The Microsoft CRM 3.0 Implementation Guide lists some recommended deployment configurations based on these variables. However, as a general rule of thumb, the Microsoft CRM server environment requires the following components:

- Windows Server (2000 or 2003) or Small Business Server 2003 Premium Edition
- SQL Server (2000 or 2005) with SQL Server Reporting Services
- Exchange Server (if you want to integrate e-mail with Microsoft CRM)

Of course, users accessing Microsoft CRM must also meet certain minimum hardware and software requirements on their computers. These requirements range from minimal for Web interface users (Windows 98 or later with Internet Explorer 6.0 with Service Pack 1, for example) to more restrictive for Microsoft CRM client for Outlook users (Windows 2000 Professional with Service Pack 4 and Office 2003 with Service Pack 1, for example).

More Info We don't include the exact hardware and software specifications in this book because they vary over time as Microsoft releases new versions of its software. Please consult the Microsoft CRM Web site at *http://www.microsoft.com/crm* for the latest hardware and software requirements.

Core Concepts and Terminology

Now that you understand some of the background on Microsoft CRM, let's get into the details of the actual software! We will cover the Microsoft CRM core concepts and terminology in the following areas:

- User interfaces
- Entities
- Microsoft CRM customizations

We'll explain these areas, but it will be a quick tour because we want to dedicate as much space as possible in the book to cover how you can customize and extend Microsoft CRM.

User Interfaces

Microsoft CRM is a Web-based application built using the Microsoft .NET technology platform. Because of its native Web architecture, users can access Microsoft CRM through the Internet Explorer Web browser. Figure 1-4 shows what the interface looks like.

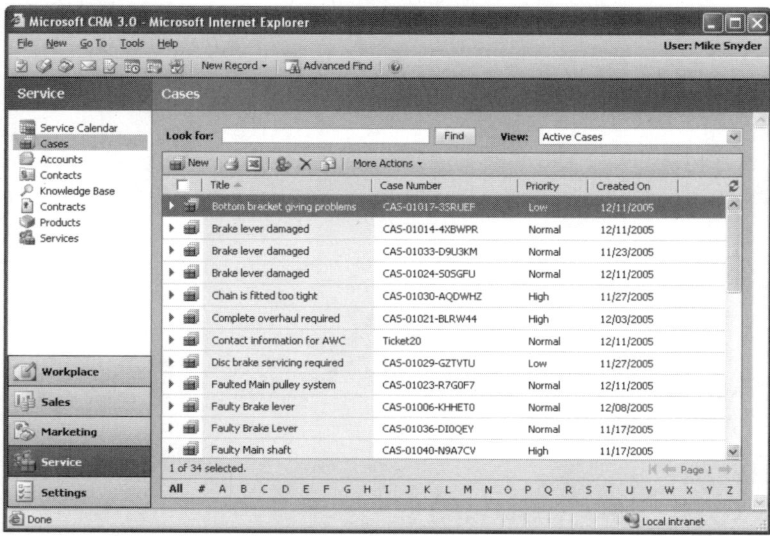

Figure 1-4 Internet Explorer interface to Microsoft CRM

In addition to the Web interface (also known as the *Web client*), users can access Microsoft CRM by installing the Microsoft CRM client for Outlook on a computer running Outlook. Figure 1-1, earlier in this chapter, shows a sample screenshot of the Microsoft CRM client for Outlook. The Microsoft CRM client for Outlook offers two versions:

- **Microsoft CRM 3.0 desktop client for Microsoft Office Outlook** Designed for use with desktop computers that will remain connected to the Microsoft CRM server at all times. Use this client for "online only" scenarios and when multiple users log on to the same computer with different profiles.
- **Microsoft CRM 3.0 laptop client for Microsoft Office Outlook** Designed for users of laptop computers who must disconnect from the Microsoft CRM server but still need to work with CRM data when they're offline. The software copies data from the Microsoft CRM server to a Microsoft SQL Server Desktop Engine (MSDE) database installed on the user's computer so that the user can work while disconnected. When the user reconnects to the server, the Microsoft CRM laptop client bidirectionally synchronizes data between the Microsoft CRM server and the user's MSDE database. The laptop client can be used by only one user on a single machine. Microsoft CRM refers to the process of connecting and disconnecting from the server as *go online* and *go offline*.

Note When we reference the Microsoft CRM client for Outlook in this book, we're referring to *both* the laptop and the desktop versions. They offer nearly identical functionality, except that the laptop version can be used offline.

Users can access the vast majority of Microsoft CRM system functionality from either the Web client or the Microsoft CRM client for Outlook. Therefore, you can decide whether you want to deploy the Web client, the Microsoft CRM client for Outlook, or if you want to offer both options to your users. A few notable differences in functionality exist between the Web client and the Microsoft CRM for Outlook clients:

- Users can access the Mail Merge feature in the Microsoft CRM client for Outlook only.
- You must use the Web client to access the administration section of the Microsoft CRM software to change settings and access the system customizations.
- The Microsoft CRM client for Outlook can synchronize a user's Microsoft CRM contacts, tasks, and appointments between the Microsoft CRM server and a user's Outlook data. You can configure how often this synchronization occurs and you can also filter the data that you want the software to synchronize on each user's behalf.
- Users can access the Service Calendar and Workplace Calendar in the Web client only.
- When working offline, Microsoft CRM laptop client for Outlook users cannot use some of the Microsoft CRM functionality such as running reports.

More Info In addition to the Web client and the Microsoft CRM client for Outlook, Microsoft CRM includes a mobile edition that supports handheld devices using Pocket PC and Windows Mobile operating systems. The mobile edition of Microsoft CRM 3.0 was not yet released at the time that this book went to press.

Using the Web Client with Outlook Running

It might appear that certain portions of Microsoft CRM "disappear" from the Web client user interface from time to time. In reality, Microsoft CRM hides certain areas of functionality in the Web client if the Microsoft CRM client for Outlook is open and running on a computer. Some of these areas include:

- Settings
- Customizations
- Service Calendar
- Workplace Calendar

To access these areas in the Web client, simply close Outlook and refresh the Internet Explorer window. Voilà! The hidden sections will appear again.

If you *really* need to access these hidden areas in the Web client with Outlook open, you can trick the software by browsing to the Microsoft CRM server using a different alias than the one you used to install Microsoft CRM client for Outlook. For example, if you used the server NETBIOS name (such as http://crm) when you installed Microsoft CRM client for Outlook, you could use the Web client to browse to the IP address of the Microsoft CRM Web server (such as http://192.168.0.1). Even though both resolve to the same Microsoft CRM installation, the Microsoft CRM client for Outlook will not hide the Settings and Customization links in the Web client.

Entities

Microsoft CRM uses the term *entities* to describe the record types it uses throughout the system. The concept of entities is easily one of the most important concepts to understand before you can customize Microsoft CRM. Some people use the term *objects* to describe the concept of entities.

The default installation of Microsoft CRM includes almost 115 different entities for tracking and managing different types of data. We don't have the space to list all of the default entities, but some of the more frequently used entities include:

- **Lead** A potential customer that users can qualify or disqualify as a sales opportunity. When you qualify (convert) a Lead, Microsoft CRM can automatically create an Account, Contact, and Opportunity record for you.
- **Contact** A person who interacts with your organization. Contact records might be customers, but you can also track any type of Contact, such as partners, suppliers, vendors, and so on.
- **Account** A business or organization that interacts with your company. You can link an Account's employees as Contacts related to the Account. In addition, you can create parent and child relationships between Accounts to reflect divisions or departments within a single large Account.
- **Case** A customer service problem reported by a customer that your organization wants to track and manage until it's successfully resolved.
- **Activity** An action or follow-up item that your users must complete, such as tasks, phone calls, letters, and e-mail messages. You can link Activities to an entity to specify what the follow-up item is regarding.

- **Note** Short text annotations that you can link to various entities throughout Microsoft CRM.
- **Opportunity** A potential sale for your organization. After a customer decides whether he or she will purchase from your company, you can mark the Opportunity as won or lost.

Microsoft CRM uses a *form* to display the attributes of a single entity record, as shown in Figure 1-5. Users can view and update entity records by editing the data that appears on its form.

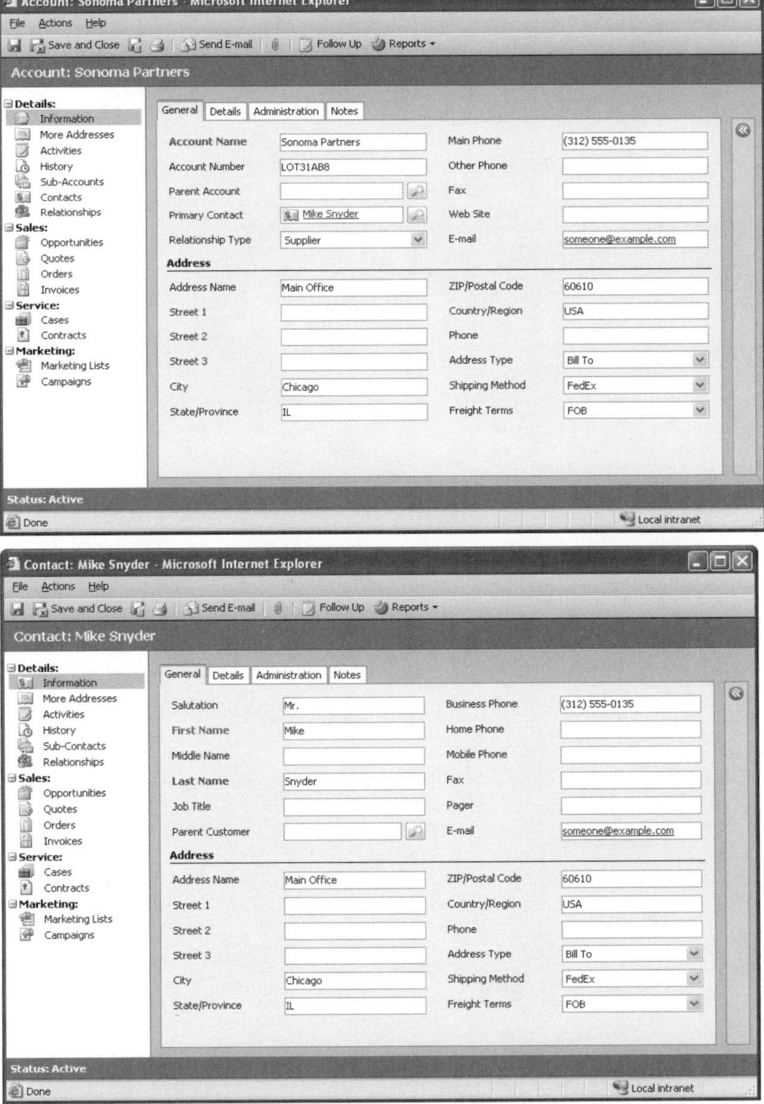

Figure 1-5 Account and Contact forms

In addition to an entity form that displays one record at a time, users can retrieve data for multiple entity records at the same time by using a *view*. Figure 1-6 shows the Open Opportunities view (in the Web client).

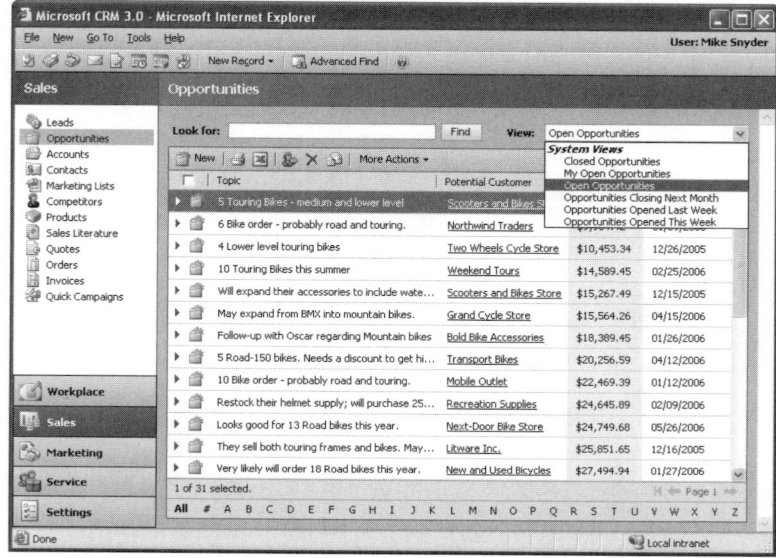

Figure 1-6 The Open Opportunities view

> **Important** Entities can have only one form, but you can create as many views as you want for each entity. Forms and views are two of the most important user interface components in the system, and you'll probably invest a lot of time customizing the forms and views for the entities in your Microsoft CRM system.

Microsoft CRM categorizes entities into four user interface areas: Workplace, Sales, Marketing, and Service. Table 1-1 summarizes the entities that appear in the various areas by default.

Table 1-1 Entities by Area

Workplace area	Sales area	Marketing area	Service area
Accounts	Accounts	Accounts	Accounts
Contacts	Contacts	Contacts	Contacts
Activities	Leads	Leads	Service Calendar
Calendar	Marketing Lists	Marketing Lists	Cases
Queues	Quick Campaigns	Quick Campaigns	Knowledge Base
Articles	Products	Products	Products

Table 1-1 Entities by Area

Workplace area	Sales area	Marketing area	Service area
Announcements	Sales Literature	Sales Literature	Contracts
	Opportunities	Campaigns	Services
	Competitors		
	Quotes		
	Orders		
	Invoices		

Note You can create new areas in the user interface and change where entities appear by editing the site map. For example, you could edit the site map so that the Announcements entity appears in the Sales and Marketing area in addition to the Workplace area. Refer to Chapter 6 for more information about editing the site map.

Your users will work with entity records mostly by using the various forms and views throughout the system. However, as a system administrator, you can review all of the configuration data related to an entity, such as its data attributes, its form, its views, and any relationships an entity might posses with other entities in Microsoft CRM. Figure 1-7 shows the entity editor for the Account entity.

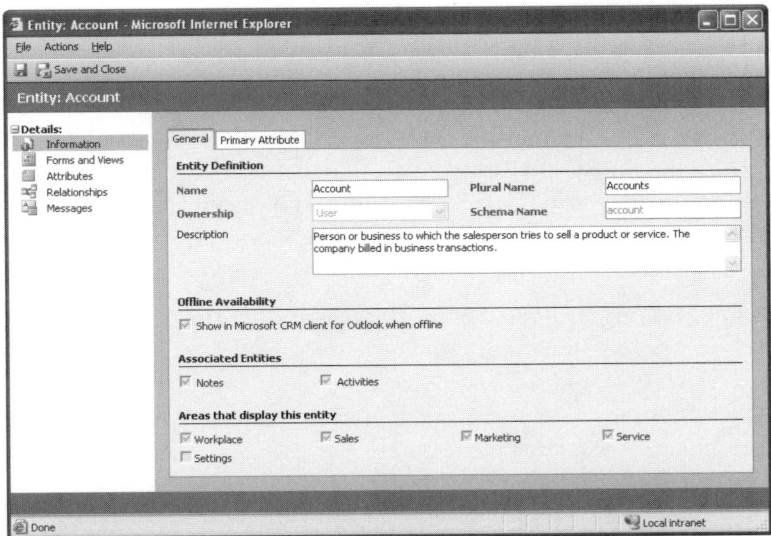

Figure 1-7 Entity editor for the Account entity

Important Microsoft CRM allows you to customize entities, but you can also create entirely new entities that you can use to store additional types of data. System administrators use a Web-based interface to create new entities and customize existing entities, without having to create a single line of programming code.

You can customize about half of the default entities that Microsoft CRM creates, but there are some entities that you cannot customize because Microsoft CRM uses them to manage the inner workings of the software. Chapters 4, 5, and 6 go into great detail about how to customize existing entities and create new entities to meet your business's needs.

Microsoft CRM Customizations

Microsoft CRM offers great out-of-the-box functionality, but in our opinion one of its biggest benefits is the ease with which you can customize and revise the software to make it fit your business perfectly. Microsoft CRM includes some of the most powerful, yet flexible, customization options available for any CRM program on the market. Some of the customization highlights include:

- **Entity customization and creation** Customize entities by adding, modifying, or deleting their various properties, such as attributes, forms, views, relationships, mappings, and system messages. You can also create entirely new custom entities.
- **Custom reports** Use SQL Server Reporting Services to modify the default reports or create entirely new reports. Reporting Services includes powerful reporting functionality such as data caching, report snapshots, and automated report delivery.
- **Workflow rules** Use the Workflow Manager to create rules that help automate business processes. Workflow rules can reference and incorporate data from your own custom .NET workflow assemblies. A sample workflow might accomplish something like, "Make sure a salesperson calls and introduces himself to every new account by automatically creating a phone call Activity due one day after an account is created."
- **Client-side customization** Tap into client-side events such as *onLoad*, *onSave*, and *onChange*. You can attach your custom scripts to these client events, and Microsoft CRM will trigger them for you. Client-side events will help improve your users' experience because you can add advanced data validation and automatic formatting when they're entering data on forms. Automatically formatting a phone number is an example of a client-side customization.
- **Server-side integration** Programmatically access and update Microsoft CRM data through Web services by creating your own custom code. By adhering to the Microsoft CRM published APIs, your custom code can upgrade smoothly to future versions of Microsoft CRM. You can create two-way integration between Microsoft CRM and other systems, such as your company Web site or extranet, by leveraging the server-side integration tools.
- **Pre- and post-callouts** Create custom business logic with .NET assemblies that you can link directly to the Microsoft CRM application logic.
- **Site map and ISV.config** You can revise the user interface and application navigation by adding new areas, links, and buttons to areas throughout the application.

- **Filtered views** Use filtered views in the Microsoft SQL Server database so that you (or your users) can retrieve raw data for additional manipulation, reporting, or analysis. Although users access the database directly with filtered views, the filtered views still respect security and configuration settings so that users can access only the data they have privileges for.

Supported vs. Unsupported Customizations

Although Microsoft CRM provides almost limitless customization options, you might encounter scenarios in which you want to customize the software in a manner not described in this book or in the product documentation. You might hear that these types of undocumented customizations are "unsupported," but what does that really mean? Unsupported customizations could fall into one of three categories:

- Microsoft has not tested the change and can't confirm whether it will cause problems.
- Microsoft has tested the change and knows that it will cause problems.
- The change might not cause problems now, but it might cause problems if you update your software with hot fixes, patches, or new releases of Microsoft CRM.

Unfortunately, you can't really know which of these categories a particular customization might fall into. Therefore, you might make an unsupported change and never experience a problem. However, it's more likely that unsupported customizations will cause problems sooner or later, potentially even months after the change! If you do experience a problem with an unsupported customization and you call Microsoft technical support, guess what they'll say? "That's unsupported, so we can't assist you." Of course they're quite friendly people and they might give you a tip or two related to your request, but you should not expect any assistance from Microsoft technical support if you implement unsupported customizations. Some of the most obvious unsupported customizations include:

- Manually or programmatically interacting directly with the SQL Server database (other than filtered views)
- Modifying any of the .aspx or .js files
- Installing or adding files to the Microsoft CRM folders
- Referencing or decompiling any of the Microsoft CRM .dll files

Even though many "unsupported" customizations are technically possible to implement, you should carefully consider the risk/reward tradeoff of doing so. You should anticipate that your unsupported customizations could *possibly* break with Microsoft CRM 3.0 hot fixes and that they will *probably* break with future versions of Microsoft CRM.

Summary

CRM is a strategy that businesses implement to improve the quality of all their customer interactions. For companies using industry standard technologies such as Active Directory, SQL Server, and Exchange Server, Microsoft CRM is an excellent choice as the technology platform for implementation of their CRM strategies. Microsoft designed the Microsoft CRM software to address the common user and IT complaints related to earlier CRM applications. In particular, Microsoft CRM uses all of the common tools that employees already use every day, such as Outlook, Internet Explorer, and Excel. It also uses industry standard network technologies such as Active Directory, SQL Server, and Exchange Server to help minimize the time required by IT professionals to deploy and administer the software.

Microsoft CRM uses entities as the data storage mechanism for the record types in the software. System administrators can customize the default system entities, including modifying their forms and views. You can also create entirely new custom entities to capture data about new record types unique to your business. In addition to entity customization, Microsoft CRM offers a variety of customization and integration options.

Chapter 2

Setting Up Your System

In this chapter:

Now that you understand some of the background, benefits, and architecture of Microsoft Dynamics CRM 3.0, let's delve into the details of setting up and configuring the software for your use. Because companies of varying sizes and industries use Microsoft CRM, we will concentrate on the setup information that typically applies to most businesses. At this point, we assume that you have already installed the software and that you can access it from the Web client or through the Microsoft CRM client for Microsoft Office Outlook. In addition, we also assume that you're at least a little familiar with using the Microsoft CRM user interface and you understand how to work with records to add activities, notes, and so on.

Tip Installing your Microsoft CRM software is a topic beyond the scope of this book. The Microsoft CRM 3.0 Implementation Guide provides excellent information on this topic. You can download the guide at *http://go.microsoft.com/fwlink/?LinkId=55129*.

As a system administrator, you'll need to know how to set up and customize the software to fit the exact business needs of your organization. As you might expect, you must have System Administrator or System Customizer rights to perform almost all the setup and configuration tasks covered in this chapter.

When you browse to the Settings area of Microsoft CRM, you'll see the options shown in Figure 2-1.

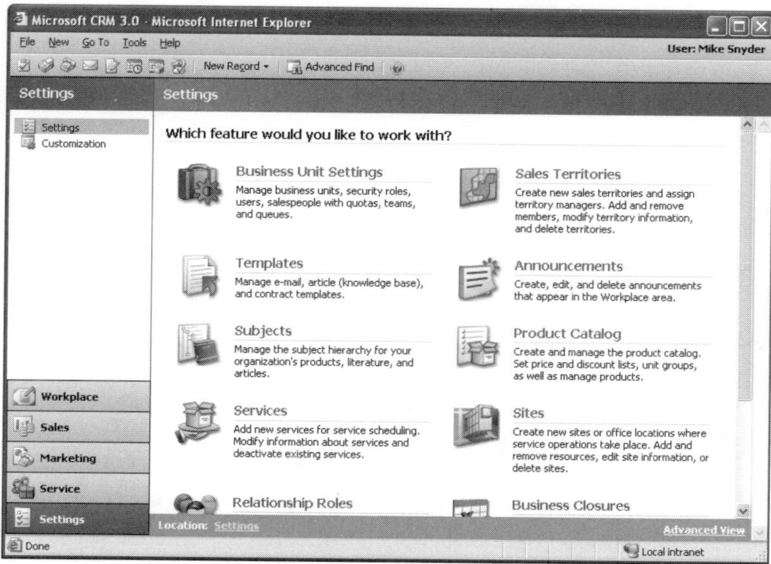

Figure 2-1 Microsoft CRM Settings

You can see that Microsoft CRM provides a short description of each feature that you can set up. We'll explain how to set up the following features in detail:

- Templates
- Subjects
- Announcements
- Relationship Roles
- Queues (part of Business Unit Settings)

In addition, we'll cover additional information related to setting up your system, such as e-mail tracking tokens, mail merge, and mass mailings.

In Chapter 3, "Managing Security and Information Access," we'll explain additional settings information related to the security configuration features found in Business Unit Settings.

> **Tip** Setting up Microsoft CRM 3.0 is extremely convenient because you can set up and configure the various areas of the software in any order that you choose. You can even go back and change your settings later when your business requirements change. One of the few settings that you can not modify later is your Fiscal Year Settings, so make sure you select those values carefully when you get started.

Templates

Templates allow you a convenient means of standardizing the content and layout of similar documents in Microsoft CRM. You can use three types of templates:

- Contract
- Article
- E-mail

Because they're all templates, you might expect the setup of these three types to be similar. In reality, their functionality and usage in the application is quite different.

Contract Templates

In the Microsoft CRM Service area, companies can track and manage data related to customer service requests such as Cases, the Service Calendar, and the Knowledge Base. When a customer contacts your company with a problem or a service request, you create a Case and link it to that customer. Most companies require their customers to maintain a valid service agreement before they can open new Cases. Microsoft CRM uses the Contract entity to save data related to these types of customer service agreements.

Warning By default, the Contract field on the Case form has a requirement level of No Constraint. Therefore, users can create a Case even if a customer does not have a valid service contract. You can require a Contract for all Cases by modifying the Contract attribute of the Case entity. Chapter 4, "Entity Customization: Concepts and Attributes," explains in detail how to modify entity attributes.

Microsoft CRM offers three types of Contract allotments:

- **Number of Cases** Allows you to specify a specific number of Cases that a customer can create. Each new Case request counts against a customer's Contract allotment.
- **Time** Allows you to specify a specific amount of time for which a customer can receive service. For example, you might create a Contract for 1,000 minutes; the time required to resolve each Case accumulates and counts against the customer's Contract allotment.
- **Coverage Dates** Allows you to specify a start and end date for the customer's Contract. You can create new Cases for customers, as long as they're within their Contract coverage dates.

Of course, each customer (Account or Contact) can have multiple valid Contracts open at any given time, depending on the structure of your agreements. Users can create a new Contract for a customer by clicking the New button on the toolbar of the Contract grid. Microsoft CRM prompts users to select which Contract template they want to use to create the new Contract, as shown in Figure 2-2.

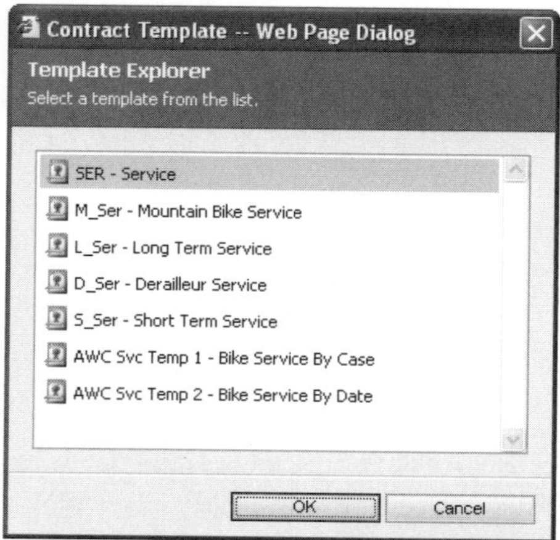

Figure 2-2 Selecting a Contract template (sample data templates shown)

Therefore, you must create Contract templates if you want to use the Contract entity to track your customer service agreements. You can create a Contract template by browsing to the Templates section of the Settings area and then clicking Contract Templates. Then click the New button on the Contract Template grid toolbar. Microsoft CRM launches the window shown in Figure 2-3.

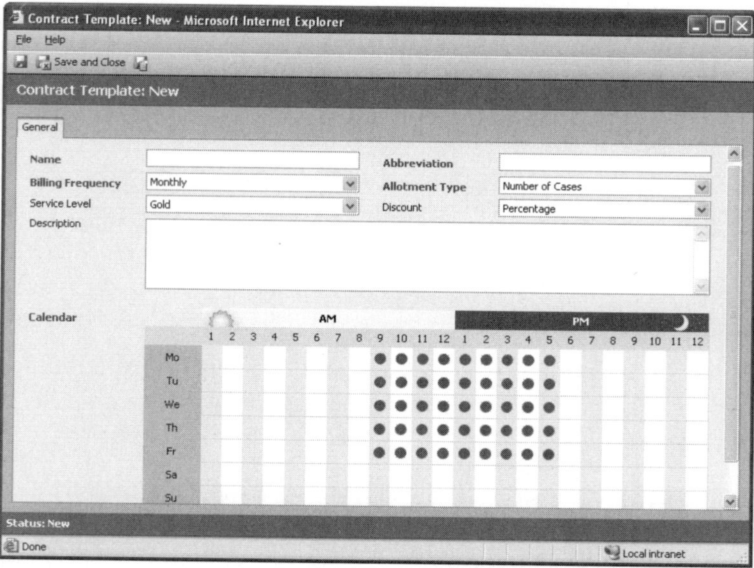

Figure 2-3 Creating a new Contract template

In addition to the allotment type that we discussed, you can also specify the Contract template service calendar by clicking the boxes in the Calendar section to indicate the time and days of the week supported by the Contract.

> **Important** When users select a Contract for a Case, they can choose only Contracts with a status of Invoiced. New Contracts default to a Draft status until you invoice them. To invoice a Contract, select Invoice Contract from the Actions menu on the Contract's menu bar.

Article Templates

Microsoft CRM uses the Knowledge Base entity to capture information about a company's products, services, or support techniques. A Knowledge Base allows users to discover solutions to problems that someone else has already solved. A Knowledge Base consists of many different Articles, and Figure 2-4 shows a sample Article for buying a properly sized bicycle.

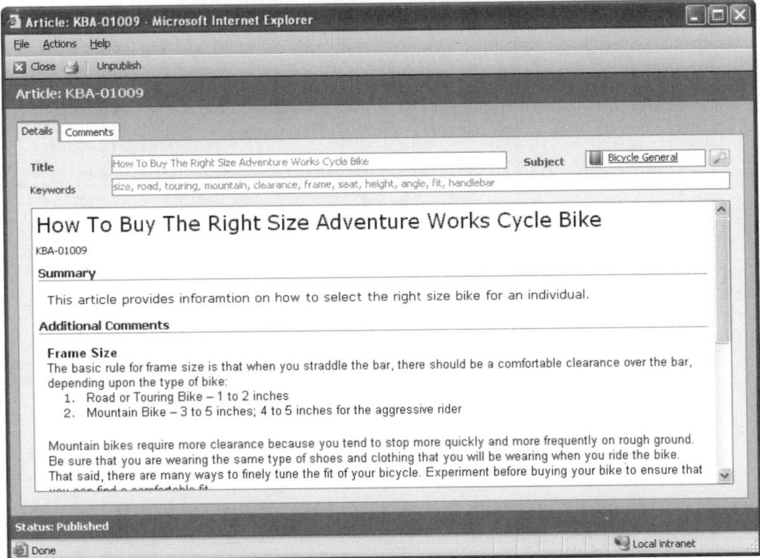

Figure 2-4 Sample Knowledge Base Article

When users create a new Article, they must first select an Article template that specifies the structure of the information that should be contained in the Article. You can create an Article template by browsing to the Templates section of the Settings area, clicking Article Templates, and then clicking the New button on the grid toolbar. Figure 2-5 shows the Article template for the sample Article displayed in Figure 2-4.

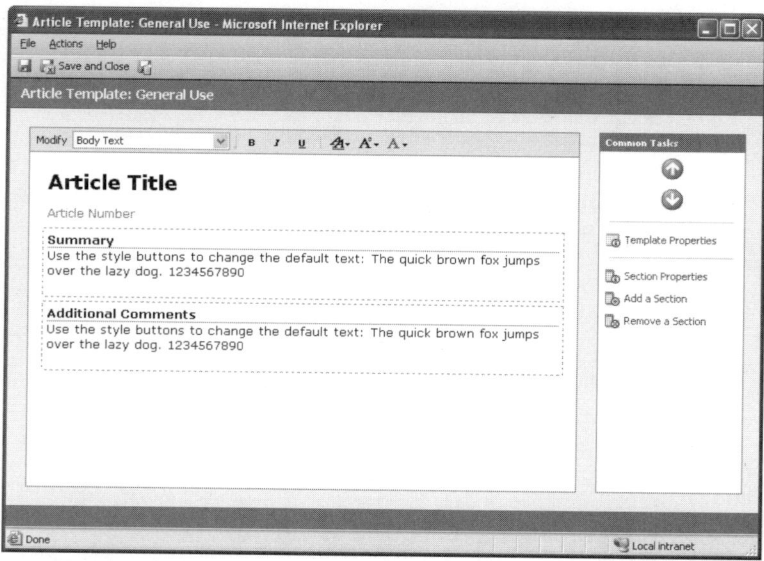

Figure 2-5 Sample Article template

In this example, every Article using this template will include a Summary section and an Additional Comments section. Of course, you can create multiple Article templates and structure them with as many different sections as you deem necessary. In addition, you can control the formatting of the text that appears in each Article by using the buttons that appear above the Article Title text. Some typical types of Knowledge Base Articles include:

- General use
- Simple procedure
- Detailed procedure
- Question and answer / frequently asked questions
- Troubleshooting sequence

You might want to create a unique Article template for each type of Knowledge Base content that your organization uses.

Important New Articles must go through an approval process before users can access them. In the Knowledge Base area of the user interface, users submit Articles for approval. Then administrators and managers with the correct security privileges can approve the unapproved Articles so that they become published.

E-Mail Templates

If E-mail templates behaved exactly like Contract and Article templates, you might expect to select an E-mail template when you create a new e-mail. However, E-mail templates provide much more functionality than the Contract and Article templates. You can use E-mail templates in the following ways:

- **Insert templates into e-mail messages** Instead of selecting an E-mail template to create a new e-mail message, you can insert an E-mail template into the body of an e-mail message that a user is composing. This allows you to insert multiple E-mail templates into a single e-mail message if necessary.
- **Send direct e-mail by using templates** You can use E-mail templates to send the same e-mail message to multiple records. For example, you could use the Direct E-mail feature (which uses E-mail templates) to send the same message to 500 Contacts.
- **Reference E-mail templates in workflow rules** You can reference E-mail templates within Microsoft CRM workflow to accomplish many types of business process automation techniques. Chapter 8, "Workflow," describes in detail how to set up and create workflow rules.

Microsoft CRM uses E-mail templates primarily for external communications to Contact and Account records, but you can also use E-mail templates for internal e-mail between users.

In addition to being accessible from different areas of the Microsoft CRM application, E-mail templates have the following unique features:

- **Data fields** You can insert data fields into E-mail templates that Microsoft CRM will dynamically populate on usage. For example, if you wanted to send an e-mail message to 20 people and address each recipient by his or her first name, you would insert a first name data field into the E-mail template. When Microsoft CRM sends the message, it would automatically populate the correct first name value in the data field for each of the 20 recipients.
- **User and organization ownership** All the Contract and Article templates are owned by the organization, but users with the appropriate security privileges can create their own personal E-mail templates for their exclusive use. Of course, you can also create organization E-mail templates for use by all users. Chapter 3 explains more about organization and user ownership of records.
- **Template types** For each E-mail template that you create, you must specify to which single entity (such as Lead or Opportunity) the template applies. You can also create a Global template for use with multiple entities.

Let's get into the details of working with E-mail templates. In this chapter, we will examine accessing E-mail templates by using the Direct E-mail feature and by inserting E-mail templates into an e-mail message. Chapter 8 explains the use of E-mail templates in workflow rules.

Sending Direct E-Mail

If you want to send an e-mail message to multiple records in your database, the Direct E-mail feature allows you to select recipients in a grid and then choose an E-mail template that you want to send. As we mentioned, you can also include data fields in E-mail templates that Microsoft CRM dynamically populates with information specific to each recipient. You can create and use E-mail templates for each of the following types of entity records:

- Lead
- Opportunity
- Account
- Contact
- Quote
- Order
- Invoice
- Case
- Contract
- Service Activity

You can access the Direct E-mail feature from the grid toolbar for these types of entities. Figure 2-6 shows the Direct E-mail button for the Leads entity. You will not see the Direct E-mail button in the Web client if you have Microsoft Outlook opened with the Microsoft CRM client for Outlook installed.

When you click the Direct E-mail button, Microsoft CRM opens a dialog box, shown with sample data in Figure 2-7.

In this dialog box, you can choose which E-mail template to send. Because E-mail templates are defined with an entity type, you can select only templates specific to the entity that you're working with or one of the global templates. In our example, you could not send an Account or Contact template from this page because we clicked the Direct E-mail button from the Leads grid toolbar. To select an E-mail template, simply click its name in the selection box.

Tip If you move your mouse cursor over the description text, CRM will display the entire text of the E-mail template description.

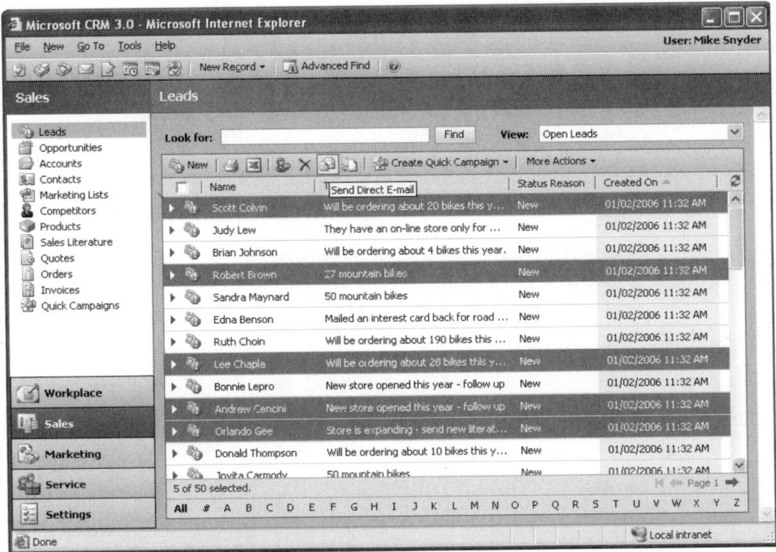

Figure 2-6 Accessing the Direct E-mail feature from the grid toolbar

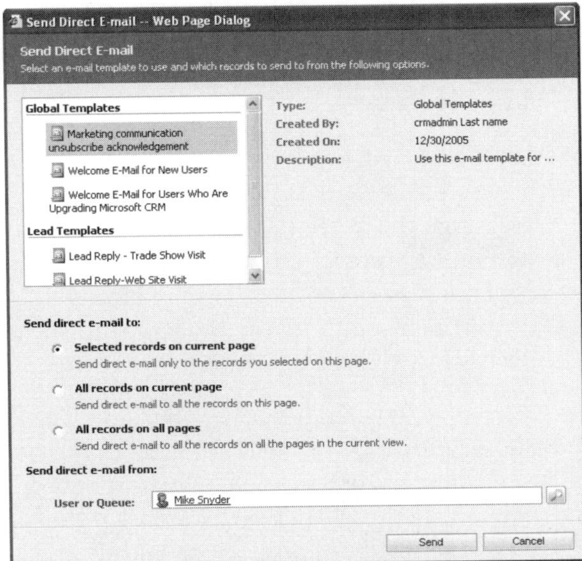

Figure 2-7 Direct E-mail dialog box

After you select the E-mail template that you want to send, you can specify to which records you want to send the message. As the dialog box explains, you can send the message to just the selected records, to all the records on the current page, or to all the records in the selected view.

Regardless of the value that you select here, Microsoft CRM will not send Direct E-mail messages to any Account or Contact record if the Do Not Allow Bulk E-mails or Do Not E-mail attributes for the record are set to Do Not Allow.

By default, Microsoft CRM sends the e-mail message as coming from the user who is currently logged on. You can change this value by clicking the lookup button and selecting a different user or queue.

> **Caution** Be very careful when using the Direct E-mail feature! When you click the Send button, Microsoft CRM sends the message immediately. There is no "preview" or "cancel" option, so make sure that your message is ready to send.

When you use the Direct E-mail feature, Microsoft CRM sends messages through Microsoft Exchange Server. Therefore, use some discretion when sending a very large number of messages at one time. Some factors that come into play include the hardware specifications on your servers, your network performance, your Internet bandwidth, and the amount of load on the server. Although no published specifications exist and the numbers can range widely depending on your infrastructure, if you need to send more than 10,000 to 20,000 e-mail messages in one hour, we recommend that you explore the option of using third-party e-mail engines instead of Exchange Server.

Inserting Templates into E-Mail Messages

Sometimes you will not want to use the Direct E-mail feature because you can't edit or add content to the e-mail message before Microsoft CRM sends it. Fortunately, you can insert an E-mail template into an individual e-mail message that you're composing so that you can modify it before you send it. When you're writing a message in the Web client, you can click the Insert Template button (shown in Figure 2-8) to open the dialog box shown in Figure 2-7. You must select at least one e-mail recipient before you can insert a template, because Microsoft CRM must know which template types apply to the message (based on the entity type of the recipients).

After you select an E-mail template, Microsoft CRM automatically populates the template content in the body of the message and fills out any data fields that the E-mail template might contain. This is a convenient feature if you want to edit or add additional content to an e-mail before you send it (something you can't do with the Direct E-mail feature). If your e-mail message includes multiple recipients, you must select one of them as the E-mail template target when you insert a template into the message.

> **Warning** Each time you insert an E-mail template into the body of an e-mail message, Microsoft CRM updates the subject line of the e-mail message to match the subject of the E-mail template. So if you insert multiple templates, the subject will be determined by the last template inserted. This is very convenient for writing new e-mails, but you should be aware of this behavior if you insert E-mail templates when you reply to messages.

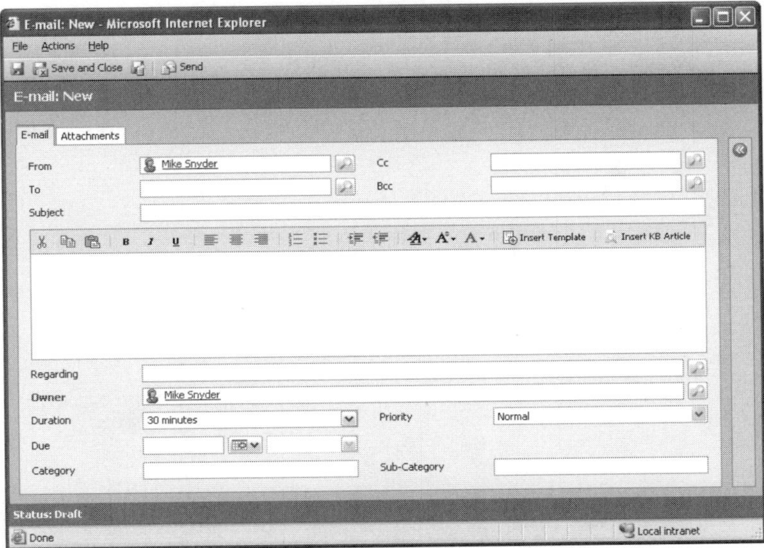

Figure 2-8 Inserting an E-mail template into an e-mail message

You cannot insert an E-mail template into an Outlook e-mail message if you are using the Microsoft CRM client for Outlook.

Creating or Modifying E-Mail Templates

Now that you understand some of the ways in which you can use E-mail templates in Microsoft CRM, let's discuss how you can create and set up new E-mail templates. Microsoft CRM includes 18 E-mail templates in the default installation, including:

- Lead Reply – Web Site Visit
- Lead Reply – Trade Show Visit
- Closed Case Acknowledgement
- Marketing Event Notification
- Order Thank You

You can modify these default templates or create entirely new E-mail templates that meet your needs. To view the E-mail templates that are currently in your system, browse to the Settings area of Microsoft CRM, click Templates, and then click E-mail Templates. A grid displays all the E-mail templates and their types. Simply double-click any record to view a template, such as the Follow-Up to Our Meeting template shown in Figure 2-9.

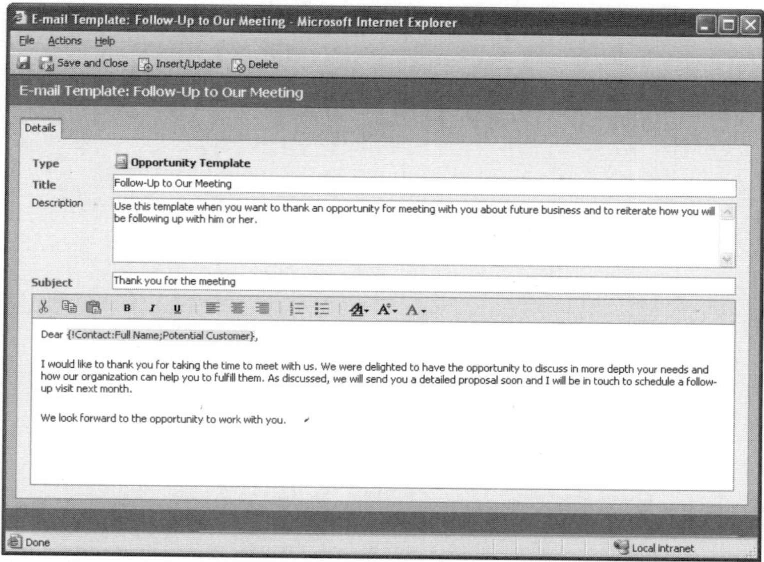

Figure 2-9 Follow-Up to Our Meeting template

You can see that a template contains several attributes, such as:

- **Type** Whether the template is global or applies only to an individual entity.
- **Title** Short title of the E-mail template that appears when users select a template.
- **Description** Additional descriptive text that explains the function of the E-mail template. Users can access the description when they select a template.
- **Subject** The subject line of the e-mail message.
- **Body** The body of the e-mail message. It isn't labeled on the form, but this is the large text box below the subject.

You can also see in Figure 2-9 that the E-mail template includes a highlighted data field that contains data such as the following:

```
{!Contact:Full Name;Potential Customer}
```

Microsoft CRM automatically converts this data field to the full name of the Contact for this record. The text before the colon refers to the entity, and the text after the colon specifies the attribute name. If an Opportunity record does not have a Contact Full Name value, you can include a default value for the data field by entering text after the semicolon. In this example, Microsoft CRM would insert the following text in the e-mail message if there were no data in the Opportunity record for the Contact Full Name value:

```
Potential Customer
```

To add a new data field to an E-mail template, click the Insert/Update button on the form toolbar. The dialog box shown in Figure 2-10 appears.

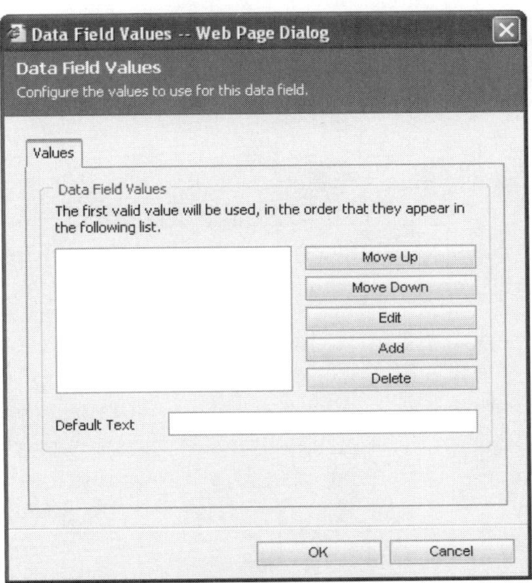

Figure 2-10 Data Field Values dialog box

When you click the Add button, another dialog box prompts you to select the Record Type and Field for the data field. Depending on the entity you selected for the E-mail template type, you can add fields from different related entities. For example, on Lead E-mail templates, you can only add fields from the Lead and User entities. However, for Opportunity E-mail templates, you can add fields from the Account, Contact, Opportunity, and User entities. After you select the field that you want to add and click OK, the field appears in the Data Field Values list. Then you can specify the default value text (optional) by entering it in the Default Text box. When you click OK, Microsoft CRM adds the data field to the E-mail template.

> **Tip** You can add data fields to both the subject and body of an E-mail template.

If you want to add multiple data fields to an E-mail template, you must add them one at a time, as in this example:

```
{!Contact : Salutation;} {!Contact : Last Name;}
```

These data fields would insert the following text into an e-mail message for a sample Contact, Mr. Bill Gates:

```
Mr. Gates
```

However, if you added both data fields at the same time by using the Data Field Values dialog box, Microsoft CRM would create one data field in the template, like this:

```
{!Contact : Salutation;Contact : Last Name;}
```

This data field would insert the following text for the same Contact:

```
Mr.
```

As you can see, Microsoft CRM allows you to enter a dynamic data field for the default value of a different data field. In this example, Contact: Last Name is the default value for the Contact: Salutation data field. However, because the Contact record included a value for the salutation, it didn't need to output the default value of Contact: Last Name.

Creating a new E-mail template is straightforward enough. Just click the New button on the grid toolbar, select the entity type for the E-mail template, and then enter the appropriate information in the template fields. After you set up your new template with the attributes and data fields that you want, simply click Save on the E-mail template toolbar. Microsoft CRM immediately applies your changes to the E-mail template and users can access it.

> **Tip** When you enter and edit text in the E-mail template body, pressing Enter on your keyboard adds an extra line. If you want a single carriage return (instead of a new paragraph), simply press Shift+Enter instead.

Creating and Sharing Personal E-Mail Templates

The process we just explained will create an E-mail template that the entire organization can view and use. Users can also create personal templates for their own use. To create a personal E-mail template, follow these steps:

1. On the application menu bar, click **Tools**, and then click **Options**.
2. On the **E-mail Templates** tab, click **New** on the grid toolbar, and then follow the steps for creating an organization E-mail template.

If a user decides that he or she wants to share an E-mail template with the entire organization, he or she can convert a personal template to an organization template at any time. To do this, open the E-mail template that you want to convert, and then click Make Template Available To Organization on the Actions menu. Microsoft CRM immediately updates the E-mail template. If necessary, you can undo this conversion by clicking Revert To Personal Template on the Actions menu.

> **Tip** E-mail templates follow the security settings and privileges related to the E-mail template entity and its user ownership (Chapter 3 explains security and privileges in detail). Therefore, you can configure the user security roles and E-mail template ownership however you choose, such as allowing users to see only the templates for their specific business units.

Inserting Graphics and HTML into E-Mail Templates

After you create a few E-mail templates, you'll probably notice that the editing tools for the e-mail message body are somewhat limited. For example, you cannot use the available buttons to add a hyperlink or an image to the message. If you want to develop a more sophisticated E-mail template with multiple images, links, and so on, you will probably want to create HTML code with a development tool such as Microsoft Visual Studio .NET. However, if you try to copy and paste your HTML code into the E-mail template, it is displayed as plain text; your recipient would receive a bunch of HTML code instead of the nice formatted version of your message! Fortunately, with just a little trick you can easily copy and paste your custom HTML code into the E-mail template and still maintain the correct formatting.

First, let's assume that you want to send a simple company newsletter to contacts in your database by using an E-mail template with the following requirements:

- Display the company logo in the message.
- Address the customers by their first names.
- Add a hyperlink that readers can click to get more information.

We created some sample HTML code in Visual Studio .NET that will meet these requirements, as shown in Figure 2-11.

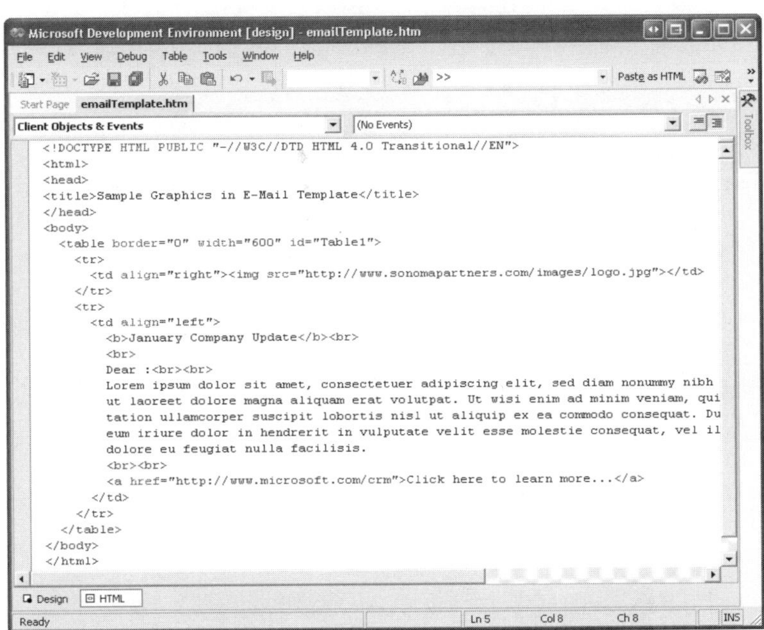

```
<!DOCTYPE HTML PUBLIC "-//W3C//DTD HTML 4.0 Transitional//EN">
<html>
<head>
<title>Sample Graphics in E-Mail Template</title>
</head>
<body>
  <table border="0" width="600" id="Table1">
    <tr>
      <td align="right"><img src="http://www.sonomapartners.com/images/logo.jpg"></td>
    </tr>
    <tr>
      <td align="left">
        <b>January Company Update</b><br>
        <br>
        Dear :<br><br>
        Lorem ipsum dolor sit amet, consectetuer adipiscing elit, sed diam nonummy nibh
        ut laoreet dolore magna aliquam erat volutpat. Ut wisi enim ad minim veniam, qui
        tation ullamcorper suscipit lobortis nisl ut aliquip ex ea commodo consequat. Du
        eum iriure dolor in hendrerit in vulputate velit esse molestie consequat, vel il
        dolore eu feugiat nulla facilisis.
        <br><br>
        <a href="http://www.microsoft.com/crm">Click here to learn more...</a>
      </td>
    </tr>
  </table>
</body>
</html>
```

Figure 2-11 Sample company newsletter template

Next, we want to create a new E-mail template for the Contact entity and insert our sample code into the template. Browse to the Settings area of Microsoft CRM, click Templates, and then click E-mail templates. Click the New button on the grid toolbar, select the Contact entity from the drop-down list, and then click OK. The new E-mail template form appears, and you can use any title, description, and subject that you want.

If you just typed the sample HTML code from Figure 2-11 into the body of the message, it would appear as plain text. Therefore, we want to copy (Ctrl+C) the sample newsletter and paste (Ctrl+V) it into the e-mail message body. You can accomplish this in a few ways, such as:

- Copy and paste the HTML code from Visual Studio .NET HTML view
- Copy and paste the formatted message from Visual Studio .NET Design view
- Copy and paste the formatted message from Microsoft Office FrontPage 2003 Design view

Important You cannot copy and paste HTML code from a text editor program such as Notepad into the E-mail template. In addition, you cannot copy and paste HTML code from FrontPage 2003 Code view.

After you copy and paste the contents of the message into the E-mail template body, you will see the properly formatted e-mail message, complete with an image and a hyperlink. After we pasted the code into the message, we added a data field to display the contact's first name in our newsletter, to satisfy our original requirement. Figure 2-12 shows the finished e-mail message.

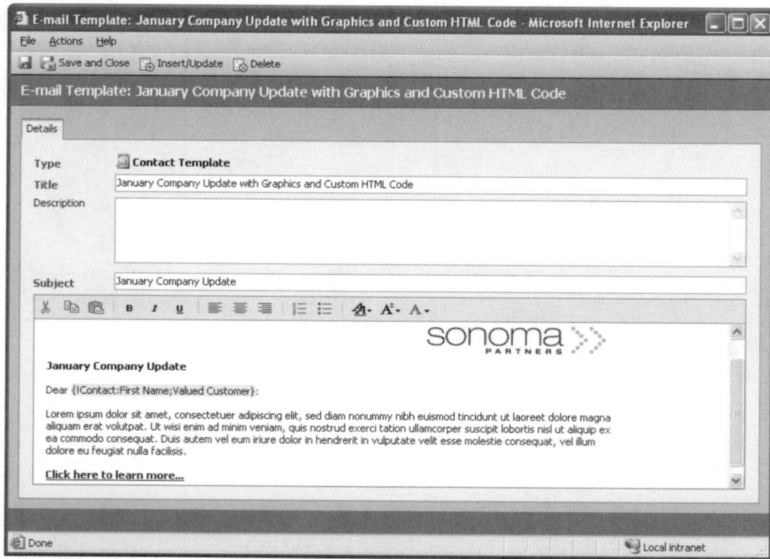

Figure 2-12 E-mail message with graphics and HTML

If you try this copy-and-paste technique but it does not work, confirm that you have the following element at the top of your HTML code.

```
<!DOCTYPE HTML PUBLIC "-//W3C//DTD HTML 4.0 Transitional//EN">
```

You can also try using the copy and paste technique with other applications, such as Microsoft Internet Explorer. The success of this technique varies depending on the format that different applications use to copy data to the clipboard.

Subjects

Microsoft CRM provides the Subjects feature so that you can hierarchically categorize various entities such as Products, Cases, Sales Literature, and Knowledge Base Articles under a common topic structure. Figure 2-13 shows a sample subject tree for the fictional Adventure Works Cycle database.

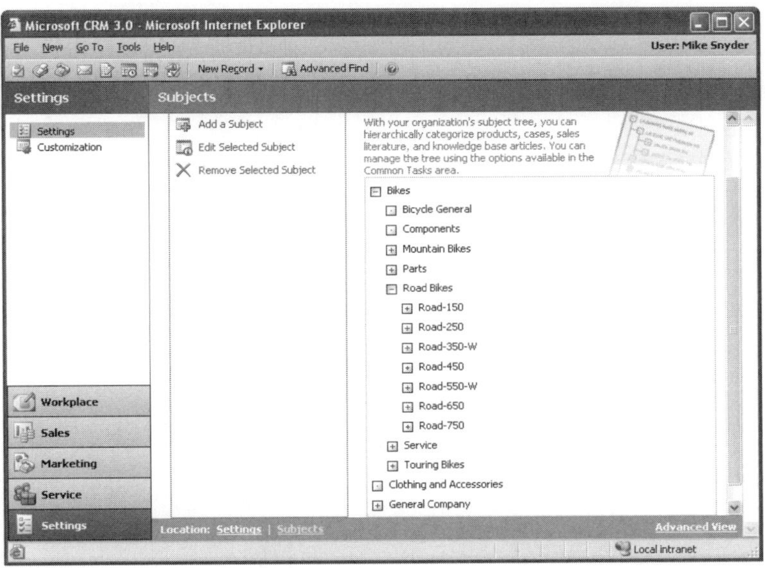

Figure 2-13 Sample subject tree

By creating a subject tree such as this one, you could link a product category, such as Road-150, with all its related Products, Cases, Sales Literature, and Knowledge Base Articles. To create your own subject tree, browse to the Settings area and click Subjects. Then use the tools in the Common Tasks pane to structure the subject tree for the different types of areas related to your organization, such as products, services, business operations, and anything else that you need to categorize in Microsoft CRM. After you establish your subject tree, you can assign entity records to one of the subjects, as shown in Figure 2-14.

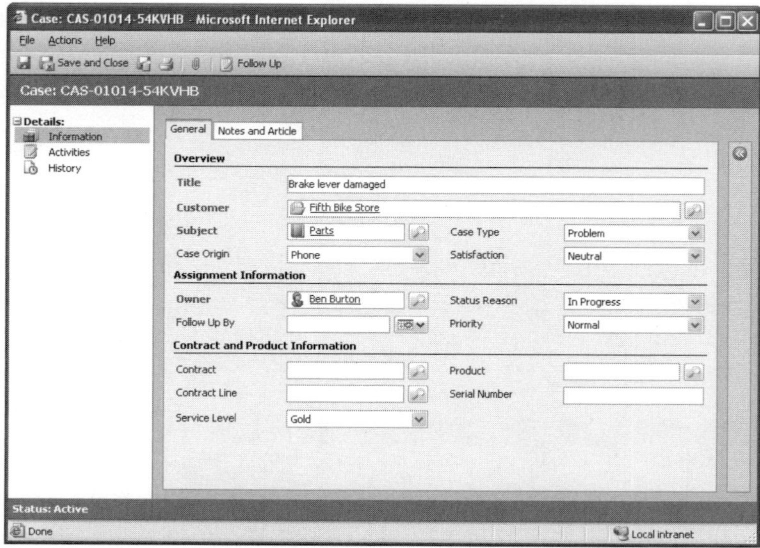

Figure 2-14 Assigning a subject for a Case record

Categorizing your entity records by their correct subjects offers the following benefits:

- Users can browse Knowledge Base Articles by subject.
- You can create new views, using subject values as filter criteria. For example, you can create a view that shows only the open cases for the Road-150 subject.
- You can create workflow rules that automatically route or assign cases to specific individuals based on the Case subject.

When designing your subject tree, keep the following in mind:

- You can easily adjust and modify the subject tree at any time, so don't fret too much over the initial layout.
- When you modify subjects, Microsoft CRM applies your changes immediately throughout the system.
- You should avoid creating subjects that have only one child subject.
- Although there is no fixed limit on how deep you can make your subject tree, we recommend that you keep it between four and five levels deep, with a maximum of seven levels. If you go much deeper, it might become difficult for users to select the correct subject in the user interface, particularly if they use the form assistant.

Announcements

As you might guess, you can use the Announcements feature to create and post information to the entire organization. For example, you can post information about scheduled system downtime or a list of new customizations that you recently published to the system. Users can view announcements by clicking the Announcements subarea in the Workplace area of the user interface, as shown in Figure 2-15.

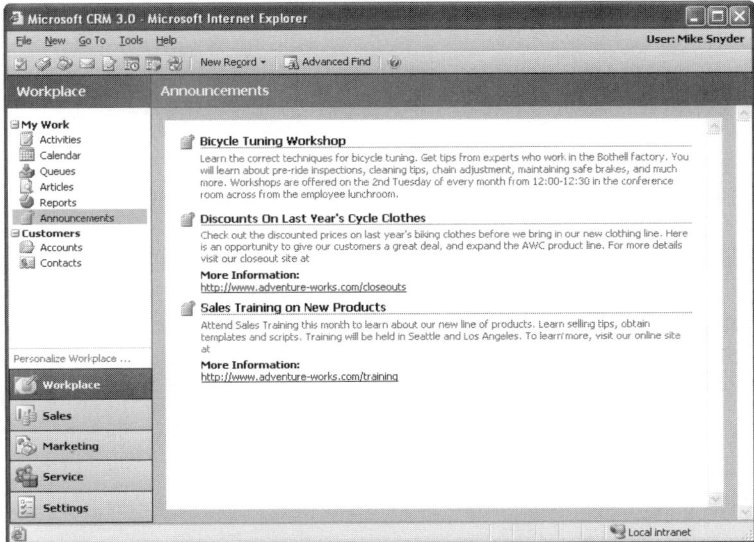

Figure 2-15 Viewing announcements in the Workplace area

When you create announcement posts, you can include a URL that Microsoft CRM will display as a clickable hyperlink. You can use this feature to link to additional information regarding the announcement. To create an announcement, browse to the Settings area of Microsoft CRM, click Announcements, and then click New on the grid toolbar. You can enter up to four attributes for each announcement:

- **Title** The text that appears above the line in a bold font
- **Body** The body text that appears below the line
- **More Information URL** An optional address that users can access for more information about the announcement
- **Expiration Date** The date on which the announcement will be automatically removed from the Announcements list

Note that when the expiration date passes, Microsoft CRM automatically removes the announcement from the grid. You cannot update the expiration date after an announcement expires; if you want to display an expired announcement, you must create it again.

Also note that announcements are displayed to all the users in the system. You cannot create an announcement specific to a particular business unit.

Tip You can't force users to check the Announcements list every day, so they might miss a new posting. If users want to make sure that they always see new announcements, they can configure the Announcements list to be their default start page by clicking Tools and then Options on the application menu bar, and then specifying the default page on the General tab. Microsoft CRM will direct them to the Announcements list every time they log on to the system.

Relationship Roles

Of course, you already know that tracking the relationships between your company and your customers is the primary goal of any CRM application. However, what about tracking the relationships between the customers in your database? The Relationship Roles feature allows you to create and capture the relationships between your Accounts, Contacts, and Opportunities. Let's consider an example of how relationship roles can provide great benefits to your organization. Assume that you're a salesperson who has just discovered a potential sale opportunity with a fictional company named Coho Vineyard & Winery. If you examine the Account and Contact hierarchy in your Microsoft CRM database, you see that Coho Vineyard & Winery includes two child Accounts and two Contact records, as shown in Figure 2-16.

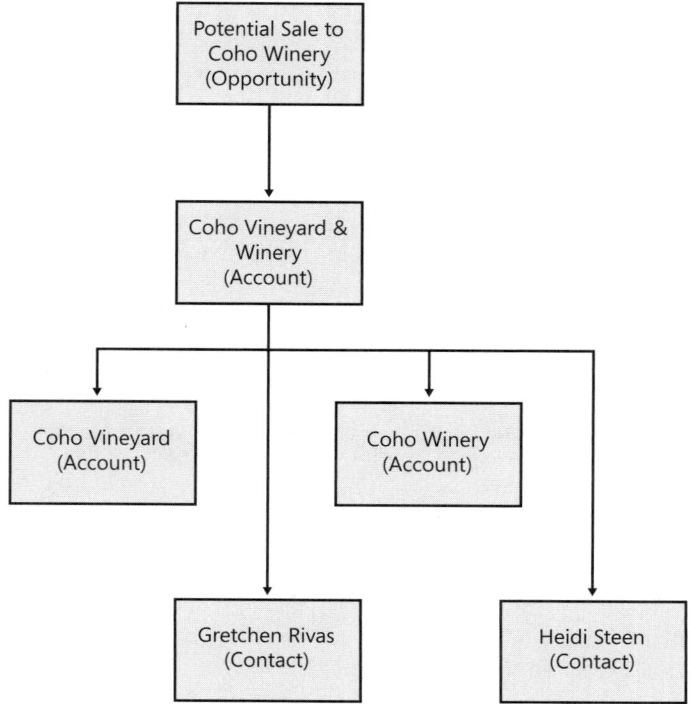

Figure 2-16 Account hierarchy without relationship roles

This information does help you understand the Account, but consider how much more information about the Opportunity you would possess if your company used the Relationship Roles feature (as shown in Figure 2-17).

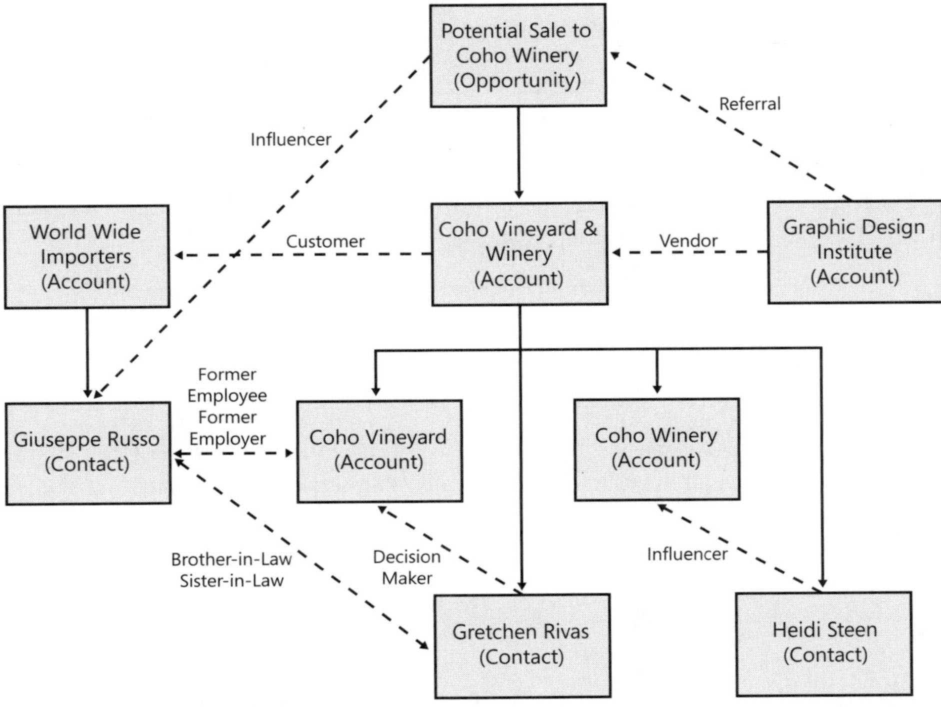

Figure 2-17 Relationship roles, which help you better understand the relationships between your customers

The dotted lines in Figure 2-17 show the relationship roles between the Coho Vineyard & Winery account and additional Account and Contact records in your Microsoft CRM database. Using relationship roles would give you additional information about this Opportunity, such as:

- Giuseppe Russo (who works for Wide World Importers) is an influencer on this Opportunity because he used to work for Coho Vineyard.
- The decision maker for Coho Vineyard, Gretchen Rivas, is the sister-in-law of Giuseppe Russo.
- Wide World Importers purchases products from Coho Vineyard & Winery.
- You learned about this Opportunity from the Graphic Design Institute, and their firm supplies design services for Coho Vineyard & Winery.
- Heidi Steen's role is an influencer for the Coho Winery Account.

Tip One great benefit of relationship roles illustrated in this example is that you can specify a Contact's true role in the decision-making process. Sometimes you can determine a Contact's authority based on his or her title, but a title doesn't necessarily translate to actual decision-making authority. You've probably worked with a company that seems to have an endless supply of vice presidents, but you know that they do not all possess the same decision-making authority.

As a salesperson, you could take the additional information provided by relationship roles to craft an entirely new sales strategy for this Opportunity! For example, you might leverage these relationships to get some personal introductions to the true decision makers for the Coho Vineyard & Winery Account.

Important You can create your own custom relationship roles to track and manage the detailed links between your Accounts, Contacts, and Opportunities. However, you cannot create a relationship role that links to a Microsoft CRM user.

To configure relationship roles, browse to the Settings area and click Relationship Roles. Microsoft CRM lists all the relationship roles configured in your system. Figure 2-18 shows some example relationship roles and how you can filter the view based on the type of entity relationship for each role.

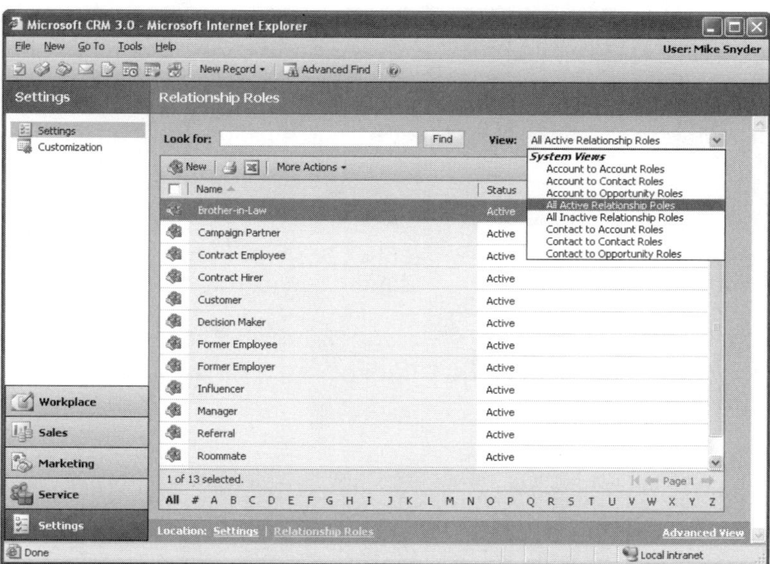

Figure 2-18 Sample relationship roles

To create a new relationship role, click the New button on the grid toolbar to open the Relationship Role editor. On this page, you can enter the role name and configure which types of entity relationships the role supports. You might want to restrict the relationships between entities depending on the nature of your data. For example, if you wanted to track a husband-and-wife relationship role between two Contacts, you would not select the Account or Opportunity entities because they don't apply to this type of relationship. Figure 2-19 shows a sample configuration that manages an attorney relationship.

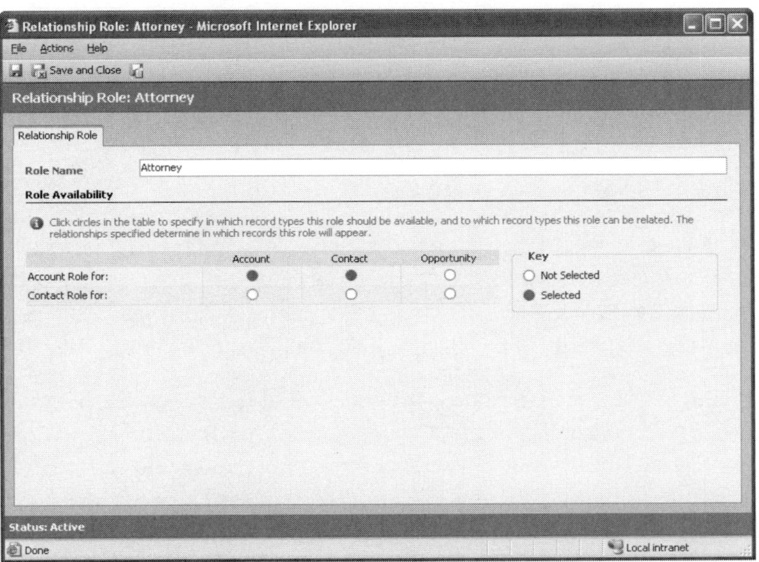

Figure 2-19 Configuring an attorney relationship role

Because an attorney might be a law firm (an Account) or a single practitioner (a Contact), we selected both the Account and Contact entities in the Account Role For row. This means that we can create an attorney relationship for an Account and select either an Account record or a Contact record. However, because we didn't select any entities in the Contact Role For row, we could not specify an attorney relationship for Contact records. Likewise, we could not specify an attorney relationship for an Opportunity, because we did not select that entity for either Account Role For or Contact Role For.

Now that we've created the attorney relationship role, users can add this relationship between two records in the user interface by clicking Relationships on the Account and Contact forms and then clicking New on the grid toolbar. A window appears that allows the user to select two different records to create the relationship, shown in Figure 2-20.

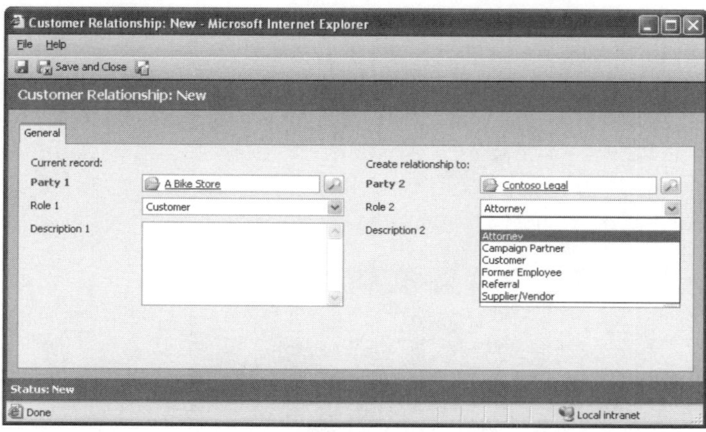

Figure 2-20 Adding a relationship between two records

As the figure shows, you can also specify two relationship roles for each of the records in a single relationship. In this example, the A Bike Store Account uses Contoso Legal as its attorney, so we set the A Bike Store role as "Customer" and Contoso Legal's role as "Attorney." After you save this record, users can view the relationships by clicking Relationships in the entity navigation pane.

You can get very creative with the setup and configuration of the business relationships that you want to capture between your Accounts, Contacts, and Opportunities. Microsoft CRM provides great reporting and analysis on these relationships, because you can use relationship roles as filter criteria in your views and advanced find searches. Also, you can automate business processes by using the workflow module and using relationship roles as part of your workflow rule criteria and conditions.

More Info Microsoft Dynamics CRM Small Business Edition uses a Configuration Wizard that creates some predefined relationship roles upon installation. However, the Professional Edition does not include any default relationship roles.

Queues

Imagine that a sample organization, Adventure Works Cycle, has created the e-mail address bikesupport@adventure-works.com to handle all incoming customer support requests. The goal of this support alias is to allow the Adventure Works customer service representatives to monitor incoming support requests in a single location to make sure that everything gets resolved in a timely manner. Microsoft CRM uses the Queue feature to track and hold pending work items until they are assigned to a user. Adventure Works Cycle could create a queue called Bicycle Cases; then every e-mail sent to bikesupport@adventure-works.com would create a queue item in the Bicycle Cases queue. In addition to activities such as E-mails and Tasks, you can also assign Cases to a queue. Users can access the queues for your organization by browsing to the Queues subarea of the Workplace area, as shown in Figure 2-21.

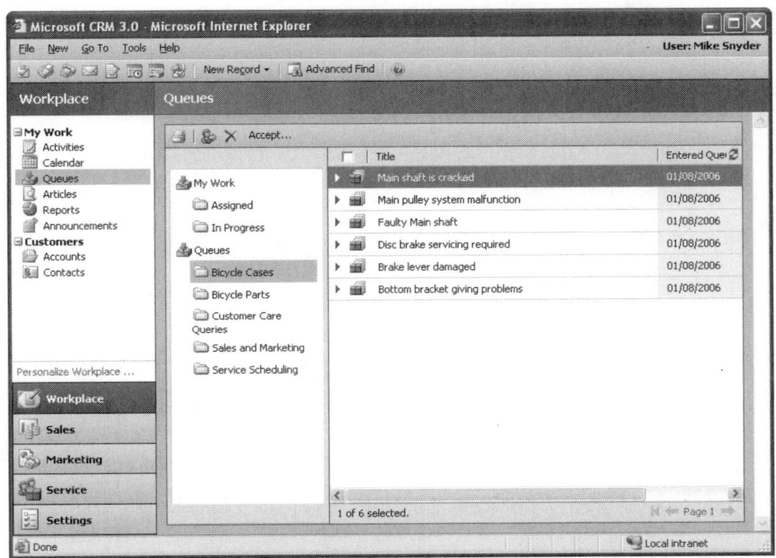

Figure 2-21 A sample queue with Cases assigned to the Bicycle Cases queue

Microsoft CRM removes items from a queue when they're assigned to a user, or when a user accepts an item currently in the queue. If you assign a queue item to a user, the item will move to the Assigned folder until the user accepts it. When a user accepts an item, it moves to the user's In Progress folder until he or she completes the item. Microsoft CRM automatically removes Cases and Activities from the In Progress folder when you complete them, except for completed E-mail activities. To remove a completed E-mail item from your In Progress folder, you must delete it. This does not delete the item, it just removes the item from your In Progress folder. Figure 2-22 shows the queue flow chart.

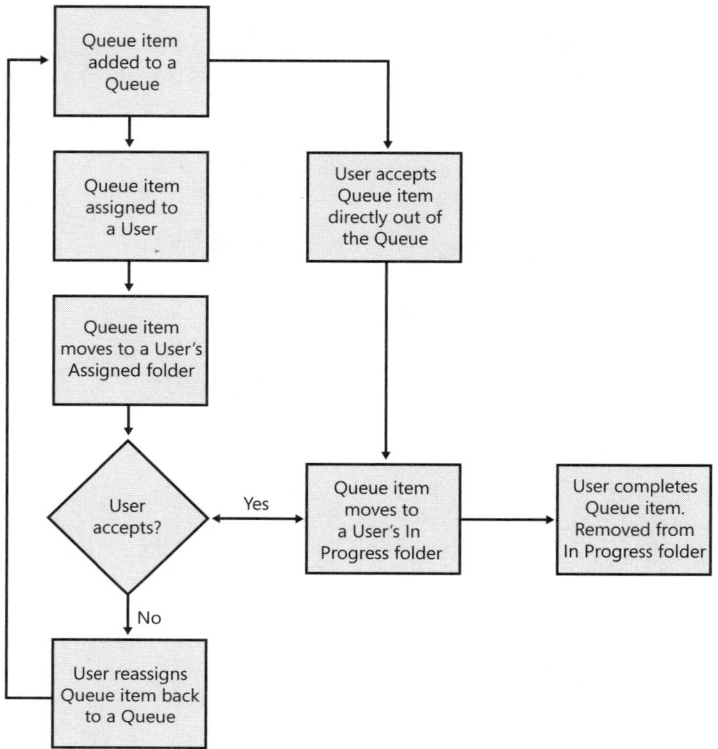

Figure 2-22 How items move through a queue

You can set up and manage your queues by browsing to the Settings area, clicking Business Unit Settings, and then clicking Queues. You don't have to use an e-mail address for each queue, but you can configure this functionality by following the detailed instructions included the Microsoft CRM Implementation Guide.

The following are additional important points to consider regarding queues:

- You can use queues for any type of business activity that uses activities, including incoming sales requests and marketing tasks. You should not consider queues as strictly a customer service tool.
- Queues do not own records, so assigning an item to a queue will not change its ownership (or trigger the workflow assign event), but it will add the item to the queue.
- Although assigning an item to a queue will not change ownership, assigning a queue item to a user will change the ownership of the item.

- Items listed in the queue respect the Microsoft CRM security settings regarding which records each user can read, write, delete, and so on. However, all users can view all the queues and all the items in the queue (even though Microsoft CRM won't allow them to open a record for which they don't have access).
- You can configure multiple queues to suit various business needs.
- If you set up an e-mail alias to automatically create queue items, Microsoft CRM will not automatically create Cases for each e-mail message sent to the alias. You must do this manually or with custom programming code. Chapter 9 includes sample code on how to automatically create a Case for each e-mail message sent to a queue.
- Queues are not a customizable entity, so you cannot modify the columns that appear for the queue folders (as shown in Figure 2-21).

Although queues do involve a few minor constraints, they provide a great tool to help your organization streamline and automate many business operations.

E-Mail Tracking

If you deploy Microsoft CRM and you use Exchange Server 2000 or 2003 for your corporate e-mail, you have the option of installing the Microsoft CRM-Exchange E-mail Router (also called the Router), which you can configure to provide the following benefits:

- Users can create and send e-mail messages by using the Web client interface.
- You can automatically create copies of all incoming messages (to Microsoft CRM users) in the Microsoft CRM database.
- Microsoft CRM can automatically track e-mail conversations and threads by using a tracking code appended to the message subject line.
- You can manually track individual e-mail messages in the Microsoft CRM database on an ad hoc basis in the Microsoft CRM client for Outlook.

You receive the Router software with the purchase of Microsoft CRM, so there's no additional cost. When you install the Router, Microsoft CRM also installs the Rule Deployment Wizard, which you can use to help administer and manage e-mail tracking configuration. If you're using Exchange Server at your organization, you should absolutely plan on using the Router with your Microsoft CRM deployment.

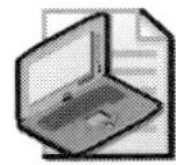

Note You do not need Exchange Server to use Microsoft CRM. If you don't want to use Exchange Server, you can still send e-mail messages through the Web client with any Simple Mail Transfer Protocol (SMTP) mail server. However, without Exchange Server and the Router, you won't be able to track inbound and outbound messages automatically.

In this section, we'll address the following topics related to e-mail tracking in Microsoft CRM:

- Tracking overview
- E-mail tracking tokens

If you want to use the e-mail tracking features, you must confirm that the e-mail tracking option is activated for your deployment. You can verify this by browsing to the Settings area, clicking Organization Settings, clicking System Settings, and then clicking E-mail Tracking.

Tracking Overview

First let's discuss the technical details of how the Router works in conjunction with Microsoft CRM, Outlook, and Exchange Server. The e-mail tracking feature works differently depending on whether a message is inbound or outbound, so we'll discuss the two topics separately.

Inbound Messages

When you install the Router on your server, you must create a dedicated Exchange Server mailbox to process all the Microsoft CRM e-mail messages. Then you'll enter that mailbox as the forward e-mail address for the Router to use. You'll use the Rule Deployment Wizard to create a server-side rule for each of your Microsoft CRM users to forward copies of all incoming mail to this dedicated mailbox.

> **Note** When you run the Rule Deployment Wizard, you can select some of, none of, or all your Microsoft CRM users to create the server-side rules, depending on your needs.

This dedicated mailbox creates a holding bin with copies of all incoming e-mail messages for all Microsoft CRM users with the forward rule attached. The Router processes all the messages in this holding bin to determine which should be tracked as E-mail activities in Microsoft CRM and which it should ignore. Figure 2-23 shows the components and the process used for tracking inbound messages as E-mail activities in Microsoft CRM.

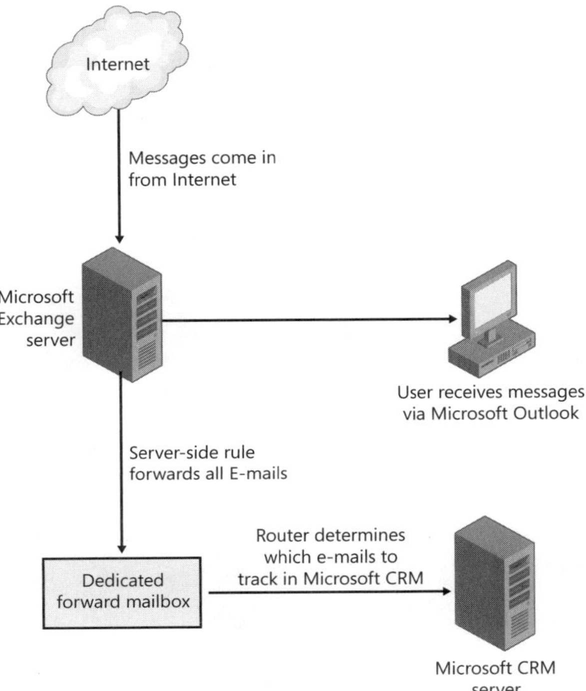

Figure 2-23 Inbound e-mail message tracking process and components

The Router reviews each message in the forward mailbox and determines whether it was *solicited*, by looking for a valid tracking token in the message. If a valid tracking token does not exist, the Router considers the message *unsolicited* and defers to the individual user settings (click Options on the Tools menu in the Web client, and then click the Activities tab) to determine whether to track all e-mail messages or just those with a tracking token. The flowchart in Figure 2-24 shows the decision-making process used by the Router.

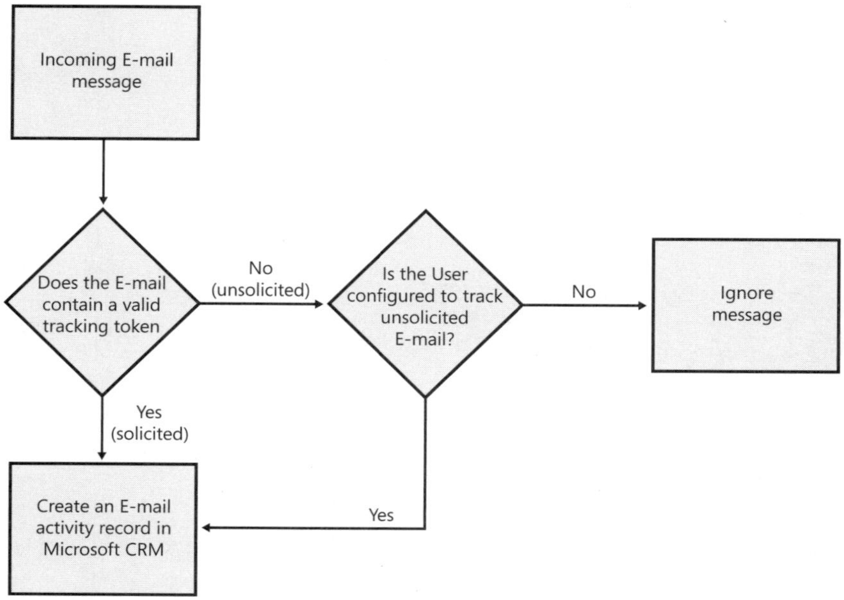

Figure 2-24 The Router decision flowchart for incoming messages

If you don't want to configure automatic e-mail tracking for all (or some of) your users, users can manually track individual e-mail messages by using the Microsoft CRM client for Outlook (both the laptop and desktop versions). When users receive messages that they want to save in Microsoft CRM, they can click the Track In CRM button in the toolbar of the e-mail message, and then set the Regarding value.

Warning If a user accidentally clicks the Track In CRM button in an e-mail message, he or she can't "untrack" the message. If the user does not want to save a copy of the message in Microsoft CRM, he or she should simply browse to Microsoft CRM Activities and delete the E-mail activity record from the system. Likewise, after you have set the Regarding value for an e-mail message, you cannot change it, so make sure that you get it accurate the first time.

Outbound Messages

Now let's discuss how Microsoft CRM tracks outbound messages sent from the Web client or the Microsoft CRM client for Outlook. Microsoft CRM automatically creates an E-mail activity record for any e-mail message created and sent in the Web client. However, users of the Microsoft CRM client for Outlook can decide whether they want to create an E-mail activity in Microsoft CRM for each e-mail message they create in Outlook. If they do want to create an

Activity record, they can click the Track In CRM button in the toolbar of the e-mail message and then send the message they normally do in Outlook. With either client, Microsoft CRM automatically appends the tracking token to the subject line of the outbound message (assuming that this option is activated). Figure 2-25 shows the components and the process of sending and tracking outbound messages in Microsoft CRM.

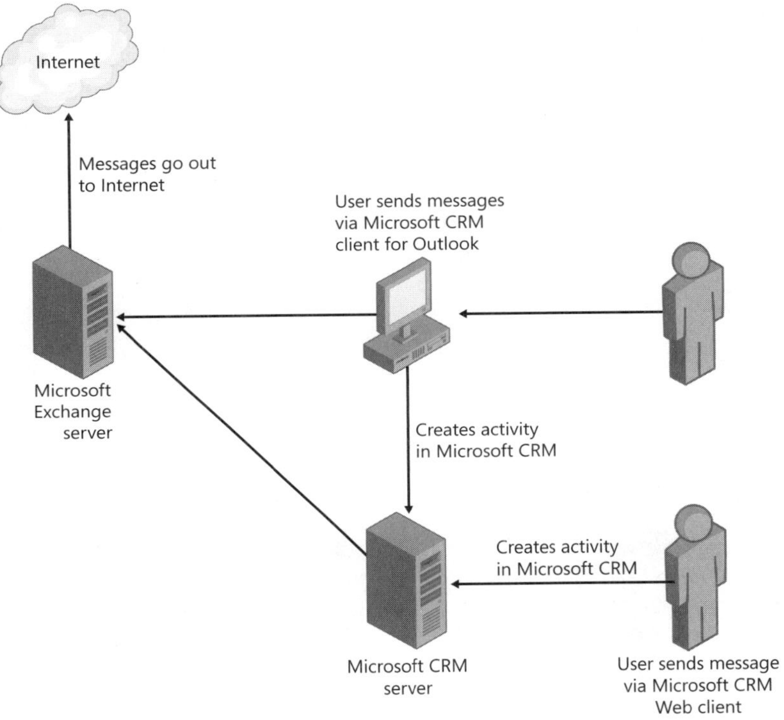

Figure 2-25 Outbound e-mail message tracking process and components

E-Mail Tracking Tokens

Microsoft CRM uses a unique identifier known as a tracking token to link e-mail messages with the appropriate records in Microsoft CRM. Figure 2-26 shows how the tracking token appears in an e-mail message.

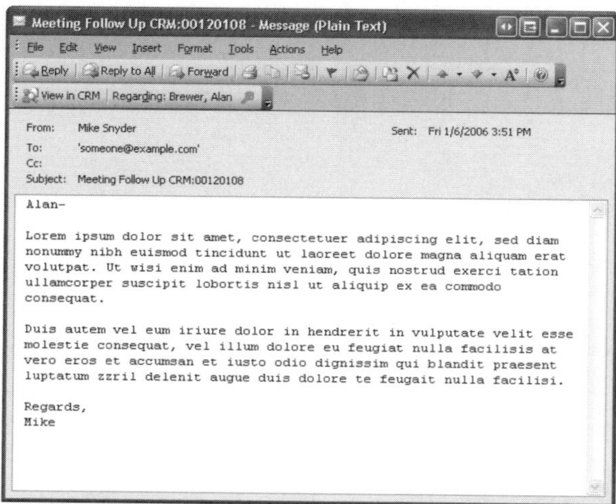

Figure 2-26 Tracking token in the subject line of an e-mail message

You can see that Microsoft CRM automatically appended the tracking code "CRM:00120108" at the end of the e-mail subject line in Figure 2-26. This tracking code uniquely identifies the E-mail activity in the database. If a customer were to reply to this message, the Router would automatically recognize the tracking token in the message and set the Regarding field of the E-mail activity to the correct record. For example, if a user sent an outbound e-mail message regarding a specific Case, when the customer replied, Microsoft CRM would automatically create an E-mail activity and link it to the correct Case! For even more functionality, you can combine the Microsoft CRM Campaign and Quick Campaign features with the tracking token to automatically capture e-mail responses and record them against their originating marketing campaign.

Important The tracking token in Microsoft CRM allows the Router to automatically link e-mail messages (and entire conversation threads) to a specific record, such as an Opportunity, a Case, a Campaign, a Quote, or an Order. It does this by examining the tracking token and then updating the Regarding field of the E-mail activity to the appropriate record.

If you don't care for the default tracking token format, you can specify your own unique tracking token configuration. To change the token configuration, browse to the Settings area and click Organization Settings. Then click System Settings, and click the E-mail Tracking tab, shown in Figure 2-27.

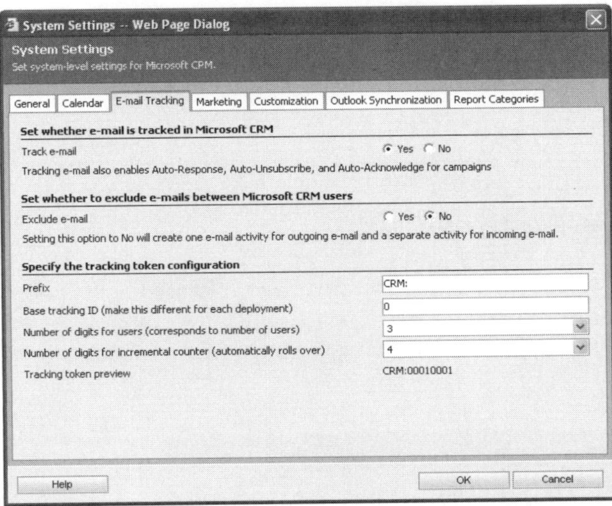

Figure 2-27 Altering the tracking token configuration

On this page, you can alter the token's appearance by modifying the prefix and adjusting the number of digits for the components of the tracking token.

Mail Merge and Mass Mailings

Earlier in this chapter, we discussed creating and using E-mail templates to send information to multiple records in your Microsoft CRM database. But suppose that you wanted to create printed letters, envelopes, or labels for a large number of records? Clearly, using an E-mail template isn't an appropriate choice for this type of printed (non-e-mail) task. Microsoft CRM offers you several options for mass mailing activities, including the following:

- Use the Microsoft CRM mail merge feature in the Microsoft CRM client for Outlook.
- Use the mail merge feature in Microsoft Office Word, using Microsoft CRM filtered views as a data source.
- Use the mail merge feature in Word, using Microsoft CRM data exported to Microsoft Office Excel as a data source.
- Write a Microsoft SQL Server Reporting Services report.
- Use the Microsoft CRM Campaign and Quick Campaign features.
- Create a custom mass mailing application.

Although using the mass mailing and mail merge features of Microsoft CRM doesn't necessarily fall under the chapter title "Setting Up Your System," we've received so many questions on the topic that we felt the need to cover it in this book. Therefore, the remainder of the chapter examines the benefits and drawbacks of these options to help you decide which one provides the best fit for you.

Note Explaining the details of setting up and using the Word mail merge feature is beyond the scope of this book. We assume you're already familiar with the concepts and techniques related to using Word mail merge.

Microsoft CRM Mail Merge Feature

Within the Microsoft CRM client for Outlook, users can access the mail merge feature to generate mass mailings for records in their databases. The mail merge feature can be accessed on the More Actions menu on the grid toolbar for the Lead, Account, and Contact entities, as shown in Figure 2-28.

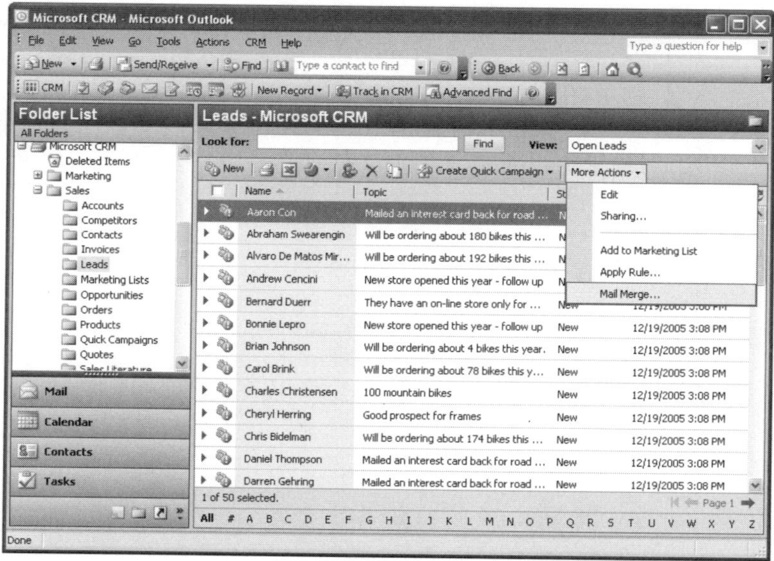

Figure 2-28 Accessing the Mail Merge feature in the Microsoft CRM client for Outlook

When you click mail merge on this menu, Microsoft CRM automatically launches Word with the records you selected in the grid as your mass mailing data source. This feature makes it very easy for users to quickly create mail merges because it simplifies the mail merge data source selection in Word. In Word, the mail merge behaves identically to the standard Word mail merge feature, in which you can select templates, insert mail merge fields, preview your letter, and so on. However, when you complete your mail merge, Microsoft CRM automatically creates a completed Letter activity for each of the records in your mail merge. Some of the constraints related to using this feature include:

- You cannot include custom attributes as Mail Merge fields.
- You can only create mail merges for Leads, Accounts, and Contacts (no custom entities).
- If you're using Word 2002 or 2003, Microsoft CRM automatically creates a completed Letter activity for each recipient.
- Word uses the records selected in the grid as the mail merge data source. Therefore, if you have five pages of records that you want to include in your mail merge, you must repeat this process five times, once for each page of records. You can change your user settings to display as many as 250 records at one time on a single page by clicking Options on the Tools menu.
- You cannot configure the subject and body of the completed Letter activity that Microsoft CRM creates for each record in the mail merge. The subject will always be "Word Mail Merge," and the body will always be "Mail Merge document created in Microsoft Word."
- You can access the Microsoft CRM Mail Merge feature using the Microsoft CRM client for Outlook only; you cannot use the Web client.

Word Mail Merge Using Filtered Views

The mail merge feature in Word (different from launching the mail merge feature in Microsoft CRM) lets you choose from a variety of data sources, such as Microsoft Office Access files, HTML files, XML files, and text files. In addition, you can connect directly to a database that supports an OLE DB or ODBC connection. Because SQL Server supports OLE DB connections, you can connect directly to the Microsoft CRM filtered database views and use those records as the data source for your mail merge. To do this, simply create a new data source connection pointing at the SQL Server database that your Microsoft CRM installation uses, and then select the filtered view that you want.

> **More Info** Chapter 7, "Reporting and Analysis," explains the details of working with Microsoft CRM filtered views.

After you select your filtered view, you will probably want to further refine the records included in your mail merge. You can do this by using the advanced filter tools that Word offers, shown in Figure 2-29.

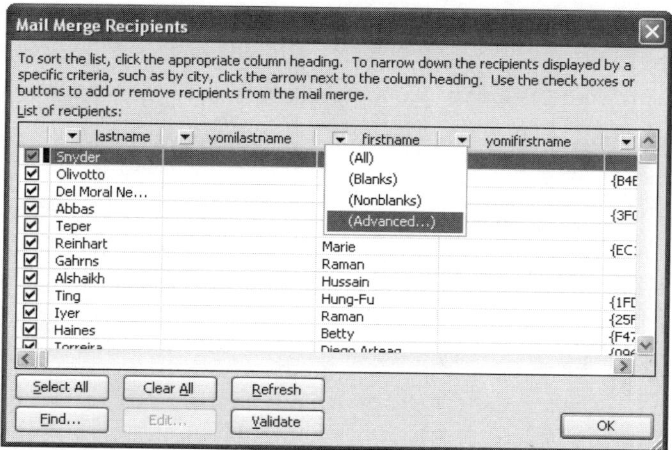

Figure 2-29 Accessing the advanced filter menu for mail merge recipients

After you filter the records that you want to include in your mail merge, you can set up and create your letters just as you can with any other Word mail merge. Some of the benefits and restrictions of using this technique include:

- You can access all the custom attributes by using the filtered views.
- You can access all the Microsoft CRM entities, including any custom entities that you create.
- You can use the advanced filter tools in Word to limit the records included in your mail merge.
- Microsoft CRM will not automatically create completed Letter activities for each of the records in your mail merge.
- You can select records from only one filtered view for each mail merge. For example, you could not include records from the FilteredOpportunity and FilteredOpportunityProduct views in the same mail merge file.

Word Mail Merge Using Microsoft CRM Exported Excel Data

As an alternative to using Microsoft CRM filtered views as your mail merge data source, you could use an Excel data file exported from Microsoft CRM to create the recipient list for your mail merge. By combining the powerful Microsoft CRM Advanced Find feature with the ability to export data to Excel, users can quickly search and target the records that they want to include in a mail merge. They can use the Advanced Find feature to create their mail merge criteria, export the record set to Excel, and then use the exported Excel file as their mail merge data source. Some of the benefits and restrictions of this technique include:

- You can access all the custom attributes in the filtered views.
- You can access all the entities, including any custom entity that you create.
- Users can create the recipient list by using the Web-based Advanced Find feature in Microsoft CRM and save the Advanced Find view for later use with future mass mailings.
- You can save the list of mailing recipients in an Excel file for later reference, and you can programmatically import this mass mailing data into Microsoft CRM to create completed Letter activities with a custom script.
- Microsoft CRM will not automatically create completed Letter activities for each of the records in your mail merge.

SQL Server Reporting Services Report

Another clever method for creating mass mailings in Microsoft CRM is to create a custom report using SQL Server Reporting Services. You can format reports however you want, so instead of including typical report items such as charts or graphs, you could simply include the text and formatting of your mass mailing letter. Then you would add the data fields such as first name, last name, and so on to the appropriate mass mailing report fields. When you wanted to create your mass mailing, you would run the report and then simply print out the report results for use in your mailing. Some of the benefits and restrictions of this technique include:

- You can access all the custom attributes in the filtered views.
- You can access all the entities, including any custom entities that you create.
- You can schedule reports to run on a specific interval (such as every Monday or once a month).
- You can easily export the report results into other formats such as PDF, Excel, and XML.
- You can include multiple data sources in a single report, so you could include different types of data in one mass mailing. For example, if you wanted to send a letter to all your contacts, you could include their five most recent Orders and their five most recent Cases.
- You can launch reports from multiple places in the user interface, including the grid toolbar of various entities.
- Developing complex reports with multiple data sources typically requires a more experienced report writer.
- Microsoft CRM will not automatically create completed Letter activities for each of the records in your mail merge.

More Info Chapter 7 explains creating and administering SQL Server Reporting Services reports in detail.

Microsoft CRM Campaign and Quick Campaign Features

Microsoft CRM includes sophisticated Campaign and Quick Campaign features that allow you to create mass mailings as part of a marketing initiative. Campaigns and Quick Campaigns behave a little differently, but conceptually they both accomplish the same goal of bulk-generating Activity records (such as mass mailings) for a list of records. Both of these features use the Microsoft CRM Mail Merge feature. Some of the benefits and constraints involved with using these features are summarized here:

- You cannot include custom attributes as Mail Merge fields.
- You can create Campaigns and Quick Campaigns for Accounts, Contacts, and Leads only.
- For Campaigns, you can include multiple members in a Marketing List, and then automatically generate letters by using the Mail Merge feature. Marketing Lists can contain thousands of member records. For Quick Campaigns, you can choose to include just the selected records in a grid, or you can include all the records on all the pages in a view. Therefore, both Campaigns and Quick Campaigns prevent you from having to repeat the mail merge process for every page of records.
- Microsoft CRM creates a completed Letter activity for each record. However, unlike the regular Microsoft CRM Mail Merge, the name of the document that you used for the Mail Merge template will be included the subject line of the activity.

Custom Mass Mailing Application

If none of the preceding mass mailing options suits your particular needs, you can create your own custom mass mailing application with the Microsoft CRM 3.0 Software Development Kit (SDK). By using the SDK, you can create entirely new types of mass mailing functionality, such as:

- Automatically creating closed Letter activities populated with the exact subject and body values that you want.
- Automatically saving copies of the actual letter (in Word format) that you sent to recipients.
- Electronically transmitting your letters to a third-party mail fulfillment center for bundling with additional marketing materials.

- Creating follow-up activities for each of the letters in your mass mailing, based on custom parameters that you establish.
- Contacting a third-party address verification Web service to standardize (and confirm) the mailing address of each letter's recipient.

The SDK opens almost unlimited customization possibilities for setting up and configuring your mass mailings.

More Info Chapter 9, "Microsoft CRM Server-Side SDK," explains creating custom applications by using the Microsoft CRM SDK.

Summary

Microsoft CRM includes multiple setting and configuration options for various functionality areas. We could not review all the Microsoft CRM settings in detail because there are so many, so we chose the most commonly used areas of the application. We explained how you can change the settings to use Contract, Article, and E-mail templates, including using the Direct E-mail feature in Microsoft CRM. We also summarized Subjects, Announcements, Relationship Roles, and Queues. Then we went into the details of how Microsoft CRM uses tracking tokens for automatically capturing customer responses and e-mail conversation threads. Finally, we described several options to consider when preparing mass mailings for your customers.

Chapter 3

Managing Security and Information Access

In this chapter:

If you've deployed software systems in the past, you already know that you must design your CRM solution to appropriately restrict information based on individual user permissions. Controlling how your users access customer data is a mission-critical component of any business application. Microsoft designed the Microsoft CRM security model to support the following goals:

- Provide users with only the information they need to perform their jobs; do not show them data unrelated to their positions.
- Simplify security administration by creating security roles that define security privileges, and then assign users to one or more security roles.
- Support team-based and collaborative projects by enabling users to share records as necessary.

Microsoft CRM provides an extremely granular level of security throughout the application. By customizing the security settings, you can construct a security and information access solution that will most likely meet the needs of your organization. The process to customize the Microsoft CRM security settings requires you to configure your organization structure, decide which security roles your system users (employees) will have, and then define the security privileges associated with each security role.

Although you might not expect to, you will find yourself constantly tweaking and revising the security settings as your business evolves. Fortunately, the Microsoft CRM security model makes it easy for you to update and change your security settings on the fly.

More Info Although the security settings user interface appears similar to Microsoft CRM 1.2, Microsoft completely revamped the technical security structure in the Microsoft CRM 3.0 database to eliminate the use of security descriptors. Because of this, you can change and modify your security settings without the performance issues that some Microsoft CRM 1.2 users experienced if their system contained a large number of records.

In this chapter, we'll review the following security topics:

- Mapping your needs
- Security concepts
- Users and licenses
- Security roles and business units
- Sharing records

Mapping Your Needs

For the first step in planning security settings for your deployment, we recommend that you create a rough model of your company's current operational structure (by using a tool such as Microsoft Office Visio). For each section of your organization layout, you should identify the approximate number of users and the types of business functions those users perform. You will need this rough organization map to plan how you want to set up and configure security in your Microsoft CRM deployment.

To put this type of organization mapping into a real-world context, let's consider an example organization. Figure 3-1 shows the business structure for the Microsoft CRM sample company, Adventure Works Cycle.

Each box in the figure represents a business unit in Microsoft CRM, and you can structure parent and child relationships between business units. *Business units* represent a logical grouping of business activities, and you have great latitude in determining how to create and structure them for your implementation.

Tip Sometimes people refer to business units with the abbreviation BU.

One constraint of configuring business units is that you can specify only one parent for each business unit. However, each business unit can have multiple child business units. Also, you must assign every Microsoft CRM user to one (and only one) business unit.

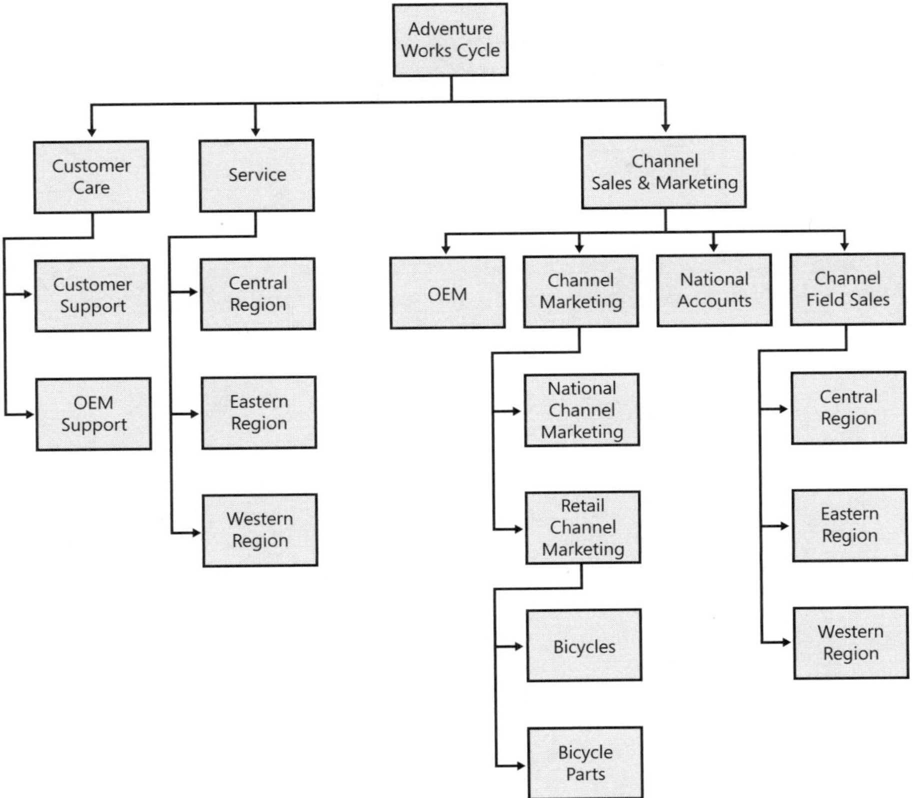

Figure 3-1 Organization structure for the sample company, Adventure Works Cycle

For each user in your organization structure, you should try to determine answers for questions such as the following:

- To which areas of Microsoft CRM will the users need access (such as Sales, Marketing, and Customer Service)?
- Do users need the ability to create and update records, or will read-only access suffice?
- Will you need to structure project teams or functional groups of users that work together on related records?
- Can you group users together by job function or some other classification (such as finance, operations, and executive managers)?

After you develop a feel for how your organization and users will use Microsoft CRM, you can start to configure the Microsoft CRM application to meet those needs.

Real World For smaller organizations, mapping out your Microsoft CRM organization model might take only 15 minutes. However, you might want to budget several days to map out the security model for enterprise organizations with hundreds of users spread geographically throughout the country. You should also not expect to get the security model *done*, because it will constantly change over time.

Don't spend too much time trying to perfect your organizational model right now. The goal of the exercise is to research and develop more details about how your organization intends to use Microsoft CRM so you can configure the security settings correctly. This organizational model won't be your final version, but it can help you think through and consider the ramifications of the security settings you choose.

Security Concepts

After you've developed a rough organization model with information about the different types of users in your system, you must translate that information into Microsoft CRM security settings. Before we explain how to configure the security settings in the software, let's explain two of the key topics related to Microsoft CRM security:

- Security model concepts
- Integrated Windows authentication

Once you understand these concepts, we'll get into the details of configuring the software to meet your specific needs. Because of the many security customization options offered in Microsoft CRM, very rarely do we see an organization structure that Microsoft CRM's security settings can't accommodate.

Security Model Concepts

The Microsoft CRM security model uses two main concepts:

- Role and object-based security
- Organization structure

Role-Based and Object-Based Security

Microsoft CRM uses security roles and role-based security as its core security management techniques. A *security role* describes a set of access levels and privileges for each of the entities (such as Leads, Accounts, or Cases) in Microsoft CRM. All Microsoft CRM users must have one or more security roles assigned to them. Therefore, when a user logs on to the system, Microsoft CRM looks at the user's assigned security roles and uses that information to determine what the software will allow that user to do and see throughout the system. This is known as *role-based security*.

The security model also allows you to define different security parameters for the various records (such as Lead, Account, Contact, and so on) because each record has an owner. By comparing the business unit of the record owner with the security role and business unit of a user, Microsoft CRM determines that user's security privileges for a single record. You can think of configuring access rights on the individual record level (not the entity level) as *object-based security*. Figure 3-2 illustrates this concept.

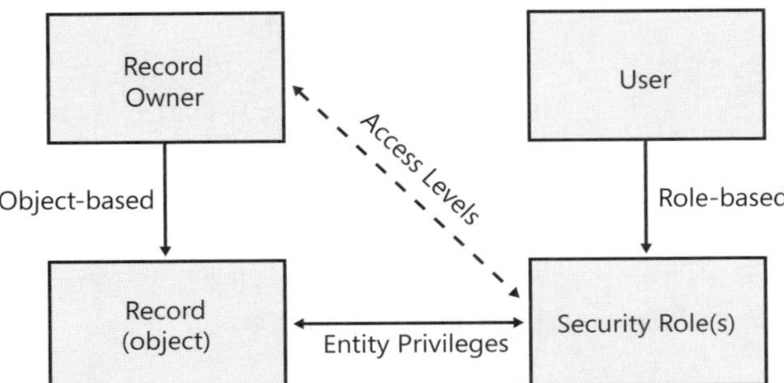

Figure 3-2 Role-based security and object-based security combine to determine user privileges

In summary, Microsoft CRM uses a combination of role-based and object-based security to manage access rights and privileges throughout the system.

Organization Structure

In addition to security roles, Microsoft CRM uses an organization's structure as a key concept in its security model. Microsoft CRM uses the following definitions to describe an organization's structure:

- **Deployment** A single installation of Microsoft CRM.
- **Organization** The company that owns the deployment. The organization is the top level of the Microsoft CRM business management hierarchy. Microsoft CRM automatically creates the organization based on the name that you enter during the software installation. You cannot change or delete this information. You can also refer to the organization as the *root business unit.*
- **Business unit** A logical grouping of your business operations. Each business unit can act as parent for one or more child business units. In the sample organization in Figure 3-1, you would describe the Customer Care business unit as the parent business unit of the Customer Support and OEM Support business units. Likewise, you would refer to the Customer Support and OEM Support business units as child business units.
- **User** Someone who typically works for the organization and has access to Microsoft CRM. Each user belongs to one (and only one) business unit, and each user is assigned one or more security roles.

Later in this chapter, we'll explain how these terms relate to setting up and configuring security roles.

Integrated Windows Authentication

Microsoft CRM uses Integrated Windows authentication (formerly called NTLM, and also referred to as Microsoft Windows NT Challenge/Response authentication) for user security authentication in the Web browser and Microsoft Office Outlook interfaces. By using Integrated Windows authentication, users can simply browse to the Microsoft CRM Web site and Internet Explorer automatically passes their encrypted user credentials to Microsoft CRM and logs them on. This means that users log on to Microsoft CRM (authenticate) by using their existing Microsoft Active Directory directory domain accounts, without having to explicitly sign in to the Microsoft CRM application. This integrated security provides great convenience for users, because there's no need for them to remember an additional password just for the CRM system. Using Integrated Windows authentication also helps system administrators, because they can continue to manage user accounts from Active Directory services. For example, disabling a user in Active Directory prevents him or her from logging on to Microsoft CRM, because the user's logon and password will not work anymore.

> **More Info** Disabling or deleting users in Active Directory prevents them from logging on to Microsoft CRM, but it does not automatically disable their user records in Microsoft CRM. Because all active users count against your licenses, make sure that you remember to disable their user records in Microsoft CRM to free up their licenses. Also, if you change a user's name in Active Directory, you must manually update it in Microsoft CRM.

Most companies install Microsoft CRM on their local intranet in the same Active Directory domain to which users log on. By default, the User Authentication security settings in Microsoft Internet Explorer 6.0 automatically log users on to any intranet site to which they browse, including Microsoft CRM. This default setting will work fine for almost all of your users.

However, you might find that you want to alter the default security settings to change how the Internet Explorer browser handles user authentication. Typical reasons to modify the Internet Explorer security settings include:

- You want to log on to Microsoft CRM impersonating one of your users during setup and development.
- Your Microsoft CRM deployment resides in a different Active Directory domain (or on the Internet) and you want to change the log on settings.
- You want to explicitly trust the Microsoft CRM Web site to allow for pop-up windows.

To view your Internet Explorer 6 security settings, click Internet Options on the Tools menu in Internet Explorer. The Security tab in the Internet Options dialog box displays Web content zones, including Internet, Local Intranet, Trusted Sites, and Restricted Sites, as shown in Figure 3-3.

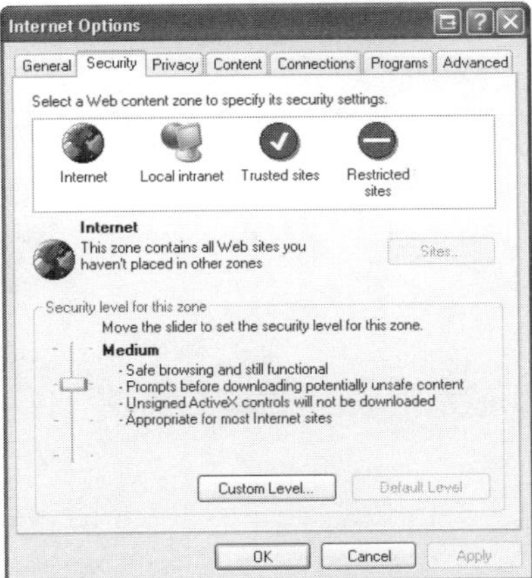

Figure 3-3 Web content zones in Internet Explorer

By altering the security settings, you can change how Internet Explorer passes your logon information to various Web sites, such as your Microsoft CRM Web site.

Turning off automatic logon in the Local intranet zone

1. On the **Security** tab, click **Local intranet**, and then click **Custom Level**.
2. In the **Security Settings** dialog box, scroll down until you see the **User Authentication** section, and then select **Prompt for user name and password**.

When you disable automatic logon, Internet Explorer does not automatically pass your user credentials to Microsoft CRM (or any other Web site on your local intranet). Instead, it prompts you to enter your user name and password when you browse to the Microsoft CRM server. This prompt gives you the opportunity to enter any user credentials that you want, including user credentials from a different domain. As an administrator, you might want to log on as a different user during your setup and configuration phase to confirm that your security settings are correct.

Warning The Microsoft CRM client for Outlook requires automatic logon, so you should not set this value to **Prompt for user name and password** if you need to use the Microsoft CRM client for Outlook.

In addition to disabling automatic logon, you might want to add Microsoft CRM as a trusted site in Internet Explorer or list it as part of your Intranet zone. The steps and benefits of either are almost identical, but we'll review adding Microsoft CRM as a trusted site.

Adding a trusted site to Internet Explorer

1. On the **Security** tab, click **Trusted sites**, and then click **Sites**.
2. In the **Trusted sites** dialog box, enter the address of your Microsoft CRM server (include the http:// portion of the address), and then click **Add**. You might need to clear the **Require server verification** check box if your Microsoft CRM deployment does not use https://.
3. Click **OK**.

Adding a trusted site to Internet Explorer will accomplish two things in regard to Microsoft CRM:

- Internet Explorer will automatically pass your user credentials to the Web site and attempt to log you on. You might want to set this up for your Microsoft CRM users who are not located on your local intranet (such as offsite or remote users) so that they do not have to enter a user name and password each time they browse to Microsoft CRM.
- The Internet Explorer Pop-up Blocker allows pop-up windows for any Web site listed in your Trusted Sites zone.

Caution Intranet sites and trusted sites in Internet Explorer 6 become quite powerful, so you must use caution when deciding which sites you will trust. For example, the default security settings for trusted sites in Internet Explorer 6 automatically install signed Microsoft ActiveX controls on your machine.

Microsoft CRM and Pop-up Blockers

Many users install a pop-up blocker add-in for Internet Explorer in an attempt to limit the number of pop-up advertisements they see when browsing the Internet. Unfortunately, some of these pop-up blockers might also block some of the Web browser windows that Microsoft CRM uses. Consequently, you'll probably need to let your users know how to configure their pop-up blockers to allow pop-up windows from the Microsoft CRM application.

The most common problem caused by pop-up blockers manifests itself when users initially log on to Microsoft CRM. If your users say something like, "the window just disappeared," you can pretty safely assume that pop-up blocker software caused the problem. When users log on to Microsoft CRM, a new browser window pops up, and the original browser window closes. However, if the user's pop-up blocker stops the new window from appearing, it appears to the user that the original window simply disappeared, because Microsoft CRM closed their original browser window.

Internet Explorer 6.0 on Microsoft Windows XP SP2 includes a pop-up blocker, but the default setting allows sites in the Intranet and Trusted Sites zones to launch pop-up windows. If Internet Explorer doesn't recognize Microsoft CRM as an intranet site, or if you don't want to add it as a trusted site, you can configure the pop-up blocker to allow pop-up windows form the Microsoft CRM Web site (on the Tools menu, point to Pop-Up Blocker, and then click Pop-up Blocker Settings to enter the Microsoft CRM address).

Some pop-up blockers do not allow you to manually enter a trusted address like the Internet Explorer pop-up blocker. Therefore, you have to browse to the Web site you want to allow and then click some sort of "Allow Pop-ups" button. However, because the Microsoft CRM window disappears on initial log on, you might wonder how you could ever open the Web site to allow pop-ups. A simple trick is to browse to *http://*<crmserver>*/loader.aspx,* and then Microsoft CRM will launch in the same Internet Explorer window instead of popping up a new one. From this page, you can click the Allow Pop-ups button to always allow pop-ups for your Microsoft CRM Web site. Here's another trick related to pop-up windows: you can reference the same Microsoft CRM Web site by using several different URLs. For example, you could access Microsoft CRM by using any of the following:

- NetBIOS name (Example - http://crm)
- IP address (Example - http://127.0.0.1)
- Fully qualified domain name (Example - http://crm.domain.local)
- A new entry in your Hosts file (add by editing C:\WINDOWS\system32\drivers\etc\hosts)

Although all of these URLs take you to the same Microsoft CRM server, Internet Explorer 6 treats each of these as different Web sites. Therefore, you could configure different security settings in Internet Explorer for each of these URLs. For example, you might browse to the NetBIOS name by using Integrated Windows authentication to log on as yourself, but configure Internet Explorer to prompt for a log on when you browse to the IP address to impersonate a user.

Users and Licenses

A user is someone with access to Microsoft CRM and typically works for your organization. Before you can add and configure users, you must add user accounts to Active Directory. To manage users in Microsoft CRM, browse to Business Unit Settings in the Settings area, and click Users. For each user, you must complete the following security-related tasks:

- Assign one or more security roles to the user.
- Assign the user to one business unit.
- Assign the user to one or more teams.

The combination of these three settings determines a user's access to information in Microsoft CRM.

Note Although most of your users will be employees of your organization, you can create user accounts for trusted third-party vendors or suppliers if you want to grant them access to your system. Obviously, you should carefully structure the business units and security roles to make sure that third-party users don't see information that you don't want them to view.

Every user that you add to Microsoft CRM automatically counts against the number of Microsoft CRM licenses that you purchased, with one exception. If you select the Restricted Access Mode check box on a user record, that user can perform administrative functions within Microsoft CRM such as changing settings and customizations, but the user will not count as an active licensee because he or she cannot access any of the sales, service, or marketing functions.

When a user stops working with your Microsoft CRM deployment, you should disable the user's record by clicking Actions, and then clicking Disable on the user record menu bar. To maintain data integrity, Microsoft CRM does not allow you to delete users. Disabling a user will not change his or her record ownership because disabled users can still own records.

Tip If you change a user's business unit, Microsoft CRM removes all of that user's security roles because roles vary by business unit. In such a situation, remember to grant the user security roles again; otherwise, he or she won't be able to log on to Microsoft CRM.

If you want to view a summary of your current active licenses, launch the Microsoft CRM Deployment Manager on the Microsoft CRM Web server, and then click License Manager. Right-click a license and select License Summary (shown in Figure 3-4).

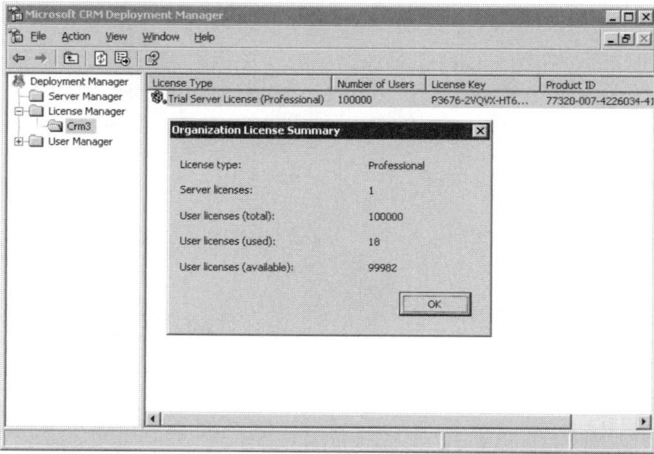

Figure 3-4 License summary in Microsoft CRM Deployment Manager

Security Roles and Business Units

As we explained earlier, Microsoft CRM uses a combination of role-based security and object-based security to determine what users can see and do within the deployment. Instead of configuring security for each user one record at a time, you assign security settings and privileges to a security role, and then you assign one or more security roles to a user. Microsoft CRM includes the following 13 predefined security roles:

- **CEO-Business Manager** A user who manages the organization at the corporate business level
- **CSR Manager** A user who manages customer service activities at the local or team level
- **Customer Service Representative** A customer service representative (CSR) at any level
- **Marketing Manager** A user who manages marketing activities at the local or team level
- **Marketing Professional** A user engaged in marketing activities at any level
- **Sales Manager** A user who manages sales activities at the local or team level
- **Salesperson** A salesperson at any level
- **Scheduler** A user who schedules appointments for services
- **Schedule Manager** A user who manages services, required resources, and working hours
- **System Administrator** A user who defines and implements the process at any level
- **System Customizer** A user who customizes Microsoft CRM records, attributes, relationships, and forms
- **Vice President of Marketing** A user who manages marketing activities at the business unit level
- **Vice President of Sales** A user who manages the organization at the business unit level

These default security roles include pre-defined rights and privileges typically associated with these roles, allowing you to save time by using them as the starting point for your deployment. You can edit any of the default security roles, except for System Administrator, to fit the needs of your business.

> **Tip** You can also copy the default security roles by clicking Copy Role on the More Actions menu on the grid toolbar. Copying roles and then modifying the copies greatly reduces the setup time required to create new roles.

When you assign multiple security roles to a user, the privileges are combined so that the user can perform the highest-level privilege associated with any of his or her roles. In other words, if you assign two security roles with conflicting security rights, Microsoft CRM grants the user the least-restrictive permission of the two. For example, consider a fictional Vice President of Sales named Connie Watson. Figure 3-5 shows that Connie has two security roles assigned to her: Salesperson and Vice President of Marketing.

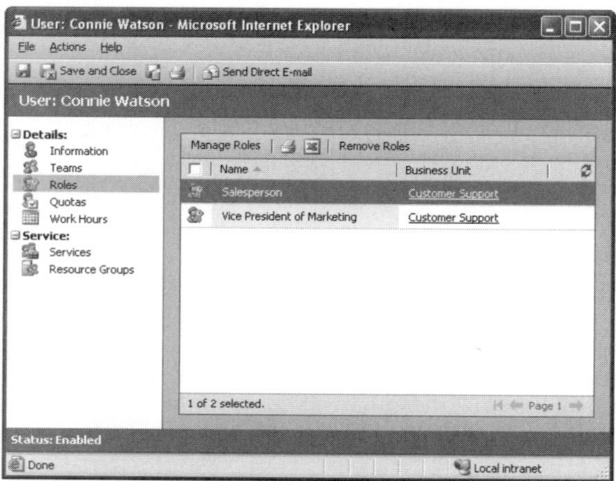

Figure 3-5 Multiple security roles assigned to a user

Using the Microsoft CRM default security roles, a user with the Salesperson security role cannot create new announcements, but the Vice President of Marketing security role can. Because Microsoft CRM grants the least-restrictive privilege across all of a user's roles, in this example, Connie would be able to create announcements because of her Vice President of Marketing security role.

> **Important** Security roles combine together to grant users all of the privileges for all of their assigned security roles. If one of a user's security roles grants a privilege, that user *always* possesses that privilege, even if you assign him or her another security role that conflicts with the original privilege.

Security Role Definitions

Before we explain how to modify security roles, let's quickly cover the terminology related to security roles. To view and manage the settings for a security role, browse to Business Unit Settings in the Settings area, and click Security Roles. Then double-click one of the roles listed in the grid. Figure 3-6 shows the Salesperson default security role settings.

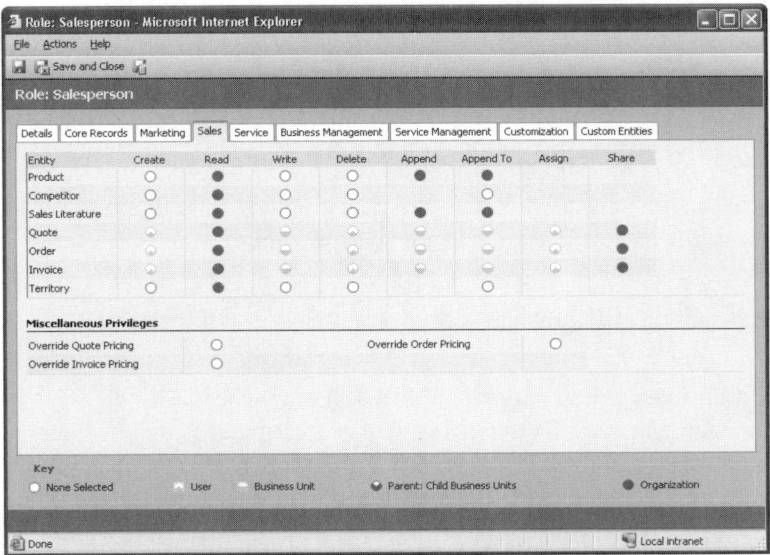

Figure 3-6 Salesperson security role settings

The columns in the top table represent entity privileges within Microsoft CRM. *Privileges* give a user permission to perform an action within Microsoft CRM such as Create, Read, or Write. The bottom table lists additional miscellaneous privileges such as Override Quote Pricing and Override Invoice Pricing. Microsoft CRM divides the privileges of a security role into subsets by creating tabs for the functional areas, such as Marketing, Sales, Service, and so on. Each tab in the security role editor lists different entity privileges and miscellaneous privileges for entities in Microsoft CRM.

The colored circles in the security role settings define the access level for that privilege. *Access levels* determine how deep or high in the organization business unit hierarchy the user can perform the specified privilege. For example, you could configure access levels for a security role so that a user could delete any record owned by someone in his or her business unit, but only read records owned by a user in a different business unit.

Important The actions that privileges grant to users (such as Create and Delete) do not vary by access level. For example, the Read privilege for the User access level offers the same action (functionality) as the Read privilege with Organization access level. However, the different access levels determine on which records in Microsoft CRM the user can execute the privilege.

Let's explore configuring access levels for a security role in more detail.

Access Levels

As you can see in the key (located at the bottom of Figure 3-6), Microsoft CRM offers five access levels:

- **None Selected** Always denies the privilege to the users assigned to the role.
- **User** Grants the privilege for records that the user owns, in addition to records explicitly shared with the user and records shared with a team to which the user belongs. We explain sharing records later in this chapter.
- **Business Unit** Grants the privilege for records with ownership in the user's business unit.
- **Parent: Child Business Units** Grants the privilege for records with ownership in the user's business unit, in addition to records with ownership in a child business unit of the user's business unit.
- **Organization** Grants the privilege for all records in the organization, regardless of the business unit hierarchical level to which the object or user belongs.

> **Note** The User, Business Unit, and Parent: Child Business Unit access levels do not apply to some privileges, such as Bulk Edit and Print (found in the Business Management tab under Miscellaneous Privileges), because the concept of user ownership or business units doesn't apply to those privileges. No user or business unit owns Bulk Edit or Print because they're just actions. Therefore, these types of privileges offer only two access levels: None Selected and Organization. In these scenarios, you can think of None Selected as "No" and Organization as "Yes" in regard to whether the user possesses that privilege.

Let's consider an example scenario to illustrate access levels in a real-world context. Figure 3-7 shows five business units, six users, and six Contact records.

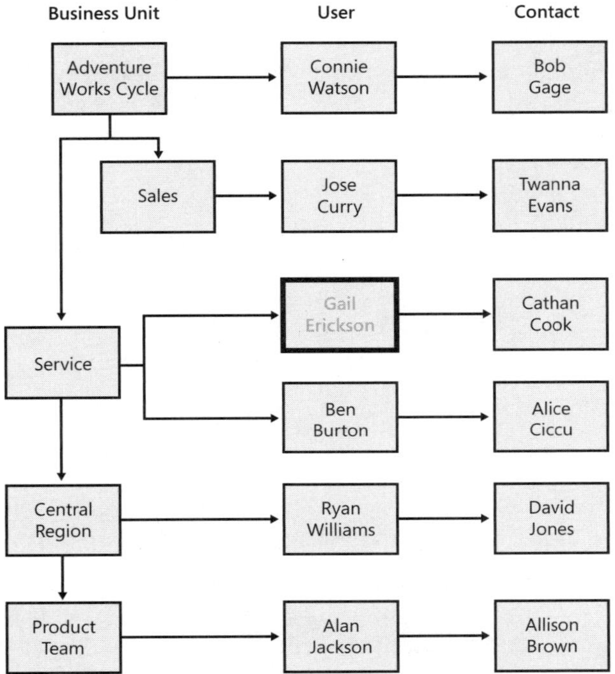

Figure 3-7 Access levels example

We will examine the impact of configuring different access levels for a single privilege (Contact Read) in the context of a fictional user named Gail Erickson. Gail belongs to the Service business unit, which is a child of the Adventure Works Cycle business unit and is also a parent of the Central Region business unit. Each of the Contacts shown is owned by the user record that it is linked to. Table 3-1 shows which Contact records Gail could read for each of the five possible access level configurations.

Table 3-1 Read Privileges for Gail Erickson by Access Level

Read privilege access level for the Contact entity	Bob Gage	Twanna Evans	Cathan Cook	Alice Ciccu	David Jones	Allison Brown
None	No	No	No	No	No	No
User	No	No	Yes	No	No	No
Business Unit	No	No	Yes	Yes	No	No
Parent: Child Business Unit	No	No	Yes	Yes	Yes	Yes
Organization	Yes	Yes	Yes	Yes	Yes	Yes

For the Business Unit access level, Microsoft CRM would grant Gail the Read privilege for the Alice Ciccu contact because Ben Burton owns that record and he belongs to the same business unit as Gail. For the Parent: Child Business Unit access level, Microsoft CRM would grant Gail the read privilege for the David Jones and Allison Brown records because the Central Region and Product Team business units are children of the Service business unit that Gail belongs to, and both the David Jones and Allison Brown records are owned by users that belong to these child business units.

As this example illustrates, configuring access levels for a security role requires that you understand and consider the following parameters:

- The organization and business unit hierarchy
- Record ownership and the business unit to which the record owner belongs
- The business unit of the logged-in user

Table 3-2 summarizes how Microsoft CRM grants and denies privileges based on these parameters.

Table 3-2 Privileges Granted Based on Access Level and Record Ownerships

Privilege access level	Record owned by user	Record owned by different user in same business unit	Record owned by user in any child business unit	Record owned by user in any non-child business unit
None	Deny	Deny	Deny	Deny
User	Grant	Deny	Deny	Deny
Business Unit	Grant	Grant	Deny	Deny
Parent: Child Business Unit	Grant	Grant	Grant	Deny
Organization	Grant	Grant	Grant	Grant

By now you should have a good understanding of how Microsoft CRM determines whether to grant security privileges to users based on access levels. Now we'll discuss what each of the privileges means and the actions that they allow users to perform in the system.

Privileges

Privileges define what users can view and do within Microsoft CRM, and you bundle privileges together within a security role definition. Some of the privileges describe actions that users can take against entity records such as delete or create, and other privileges define features in Microsoft CRM such as Mail Merge and Export to Excel. In this section, we will explore:

- Entity privileges
- Miscellaneous privileges
- Privilege impact on application navigation

Entity Privileges

As Figure 3-6 showed, some privileges such as Create, Read, and Write apply to the entities within Microsoft CRM. For each entity type and privilege, you can configure a different access level. The following list describes the actions that each privilege allows:

- **Create** Permits the user to add a new record
- **Read** Permits the user to view a record
- **Write** Permits the user to edit an existing record
- **Delete** Permits the user to delete a record
- **Append** Permits the user to attach another entity to, or associate another entity with, a parent record
- **Append To** Permits the user to attach other entities to, or associate other entities with, the record
- **Assign** Permits the user to change a record's owner to a different user
- **Share** Permits the user to share a record with another user or team
- **Enable/Disable** Permits the user to activate or deactivate records

More Info Not all of the entity privileges apply to all of the entities in Microsoft CRM. For example, the Share privilege does not apply to any of the entities on the Service Management tab. The Enable/Disable privilege only applies to the Business Unit and User entities.

The Append and Append To actions behave a little differently than the other privileges because you must configure them on two different entities to work correctly. To understand the Append and Append To actions better, consider the analogy of attaching a sticky note to a wall. To configure the sticky note concept using Microsoft CRM security privileges, you would need to assign Append privileges to the sticky note and then configure Append To privileges to the wall. Translating that concept to Microsoft CRM entities, if you want to attach (or append) a Contact to an Account, the user would need Append privileges for the Contact and Append To privileges for the Account record.

Microsoft CRM also allows you to configure entity privileges for any custom entities that you create in your deployment. You can configure all five access levels for each custom entity for all of the entity privileges, except the Enable/Disable action.

Miscellaneous Privileges

In addition to entity privileges, Microsoft CRM includes additional miscellaneous privileges on each tab of the security role editor. The privilege name often provides enough information about what it does, but sometimes the description might leave you guessing. This is especially true for miscellaneous privileges that relate to areas of the application that you might not use often. In the following list, we provide a little more description about what each of the miscellaneous privileges means and, in some cases, where to find the related feature.

- **Publish E-mail Templates** Permits the user to make a personal E-mail Template available to the organization. Users can access this feature by browsing to Templates in the Settings section, and opening a personal E-mail Template by double-clicking it. Then they can click Make Template Available to Organization located under the Actions menu.
- **Override Quote Pricing** Permits the user to override a quote's calculated price (based on products added to the quote) and manually enter new quote pricing. Users can access the Override Price button when they're editing a Quote Product attached to a Quote.
- **Override Invoice Pricing** Permits the user to override an invoice's system-generated price and manually enter new invoice pricing. Users can access the Override Price button when they're editing a Invoice Product attached to an Invoice.
- **Override Order Pricing** Permits the user to override an order's system-generated price and manually enter new order pricing. Users can access the Override Price button when they're editing an Order Product attached to an Order.
- **Publish Articles** Permits the user to publish unapproved Knowledge Base articles. Users access the Approve (publish) button in the grid toolbar of the Unapproved Article Queue located within the Knowledge Base area.
- **Assign Role** Permits the user to add or remove security roles from user records in the Settings section.
- **Bulk Edit** Permits the user to edit multiple records at the same time. Users with this privilege can access the feature from an entity's grid toolbar. The bulk edit action does not apply to all entities.
- **Print** Permits the user to create a printer-friendly display of a grid. Users with this privilege can access this feature by clicking the Print button on the grid tool bar. You cannot vary this privilege by entity type.
- **Merge** Permits the user to merge two records together into a single record. Users with this privilege can access the Merge feature from the grid toolbar.
- **Go Offline** Permits a user with the Microsoft CRM laptop client for Outlook installed to work in an offline mode. Working offline creates a local copy of the database on the laptop. Because the user can remove the laptop (with the offline data) from your work premises, the offline option raises a potential security question that you must consider.
- **CRM Address Book** Permits a user of the Microsoft CRM clients for Outlook (laptop and desktop) to select CRM records from his or her address book in Outlook.

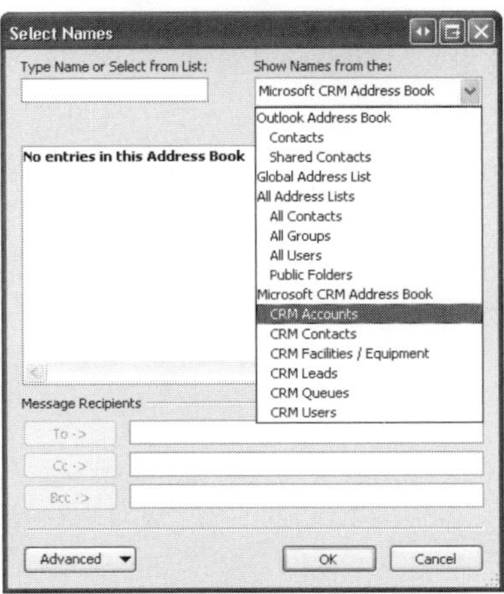

- **Update Business Closures** Permits the user to modify business working hours and closure information. Users access the Business Closures information within the Settings area.
- **Assign Territory to User** Permits the user to add or remove users from a sales territory. Users access the Sales Territories information within the Settings area.
- **Go Mobile** Permits the user to synchronize Microsoft CRM data with Microsoft Windows Mobile-based devices such as Pocket PCs.
- **Export to Excel** Permits the user to export the grid data to Microsoft Office Excel. Users with this privilege access the Export to Excel feature from the grid tool bar.
- **Mail Merge** Permits the user to create mailing items such as letters, envelopes, and labels. Users with this privilege can use the Mail Merge feature in the Microsoft CRM client for Outlook (either version) located under the More Actions menu on the grid toolbar for the Lead, Account, and Contact entities.
- **Sync to Outlook** Permits a user of either Microsoft CRM client for Outlook to synchronize Microsoft CRM data such as Contacts, Tasks, and Appointments to his or her Outlook file.
- **Send E-mail as Another User** Permits the user to select a different user or queue for the From address of an e-mail sent with the Microsoft CRM Send Direct E-mail feature. The Send Direct E-mail button appears on grids only if the user has the following security privileges:
  - Read and Append privileges on the Activity entity.
  - Append To privileges for the entity to which the user is sending direct e-mail (such as Contact or Account).
  - Read privileges on the E-mail Template entity.

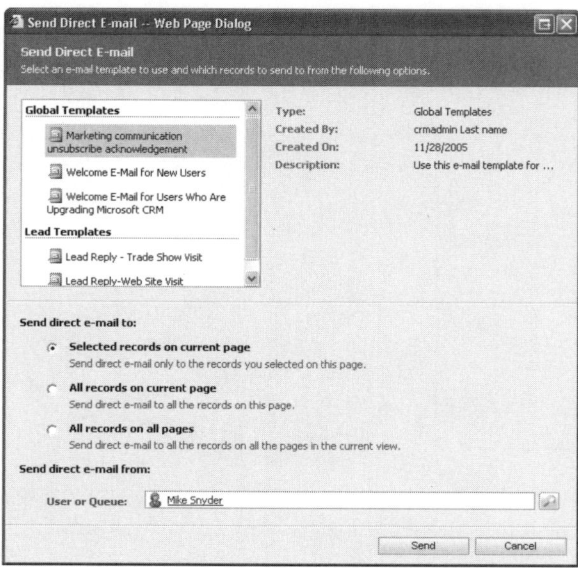

- **Manage Reports** Permits the user to add, modify, or delete reports. Chapter 7 explains managing reports in detail.
- **Search Availability** Permits the user to search for available times when scheduling a Service activity.
- **Browse Availability** Permits the user to view the Service Calendar located in the Service area.
- **ISV Extensions** Determines whether Microsoft CRM displays customizations, such as custom menu items and toolbar buttons, from the ISV.config file to the user. Note that this setting applies to all or none of the ISV extensions–you cannot turn on specific ISV extensions by using this setting.

> **More Info** At the time this book went to press, Microsoft had not yet released the mobile version of Microsoft CRM 3.0 for Pocket PCs and Windows Mobile-based devices. Therefore, we cannot definitively describe how the Go Mobile privilege will behave.

If you're still not sure what a specific privilege does or whether it will do what you want, you can easily test a privilege by enabling it for a security role, saving the role, and then logging on to Microsoft CRM as a user with only that security role. Remember that if your personal account has a System Administrator role, you have organization access level rights for all privileges, so don't log on as a System Administrator to test security privileges. Testing security privileges is a good example of when you might want to impersonate a different user when you log on to Microsoft CRM. We explained earlier in the chapter how you can modify your Internet Explorer security settings so that Microsoft CRM prompts you to enter a user name and password instead of using Integrated Windows authentication.

Note Miscellaneous privileges don't apply to custom entities that you create.

Field-Level Security

You configure privileges and access levels based on entire entity records in Microsoft CRM, not on the individual attributes for each entity. For example, you cannot use security role configurations to specify that users can view a contact's name and phone number but not the social security number or home address. If a user possesses the Read privilege for a Contact record, they can view *all* of the Contact's attributes displayed on the form.

However, you can take advantage of Microsoft CRM's robust programming model to dynamically hide attributes on a form or disable certain attributes based on the user's security role. You would use the form *onLoad* event to execute this type of custom script. Chapter 10, "Client-Side SDK," explains how to use the form *onLoad* event, and it includes sample code.

There's one caveat that you should know about when using the form *onLoad* event to hide attributes on a form: A user could still view the "hidden" data by performing an Advanced Find and adding the hidden column to his or her output result set. Users couldn't edit data with this technique, but they could view all attributes of any entity that they have privileges to read. Users could also potentially view this hidden information by exporting to Excel or running reports that contain this information.

Therefore, using the form *onLoad* event doesn't really provide true field-level security if you need to hide data from users, but you could restrict users from editing specific attributes on the entity form by using this technique.

Privilege Impact on Application Navigation

Microsoft CRM includes over 100 entities and thousands of features within the Sales, Marketing, and Customer Service areas. However, very few organizations will use *all* of the entities that Microsoft CRM offers to track and manage their customer data. Consequently, users commonly request to see only the areas of the application that their organization actually uses. For example, if your organization doesn't use the Sales Literature or Invoices entities, your users won't want to see these entities as they navigate through the user interface.

Although it would be technically possible to use the site map to remove some areas of the navigation (Sales Literature and Invoices, in this example), the better solution would be to modify your users' security roles and privileges, which would also change the user interface.

> **Important** You should modify security roles, instead of modifying the site map, to hide areas of Microsoft CRM that your organization does not use. Modifying security roles also allows you to change the display of the entity navigation pane, which is an area of the user interface that you cannot edit by using the site map. Chapter 6, "Relationships and Custom Entities," explains the site map in more detail and discusses when you should modify it.

If you modify a security role and set the access level of the Read privilege for an entity to None Selected, Microsoft CRM automatically removes that entity from the user interface for users with that security role, including the menu bar, the application navigation pane, and the entity record. Most of the thirteen default security roles include an Organization access level for the Read privilege on all of the entities, so the users will see all of the entities in the application navigation. Therefore, we recommend that you change the Read privilege access level to None Selected for any entity that you're not using in your deployment. By doing so, you'll create a streamlined user interface that will help new users learn the system more quickly and let existing users navigate more efficiently.

> **Tip** To see the updated application navigation after you modify a security role, you might have to refresh your Web browser window or restart Outlook.

Figure 3-8 shows the Account record for a user with the default Customer Service Representative security role assigned. Because that role includes the Read privilege for most of the entities, the user can see all of the links in the entity navigation pane, such as Quotes, Orders, Invoices, Marketing Lists, and Campaigns.

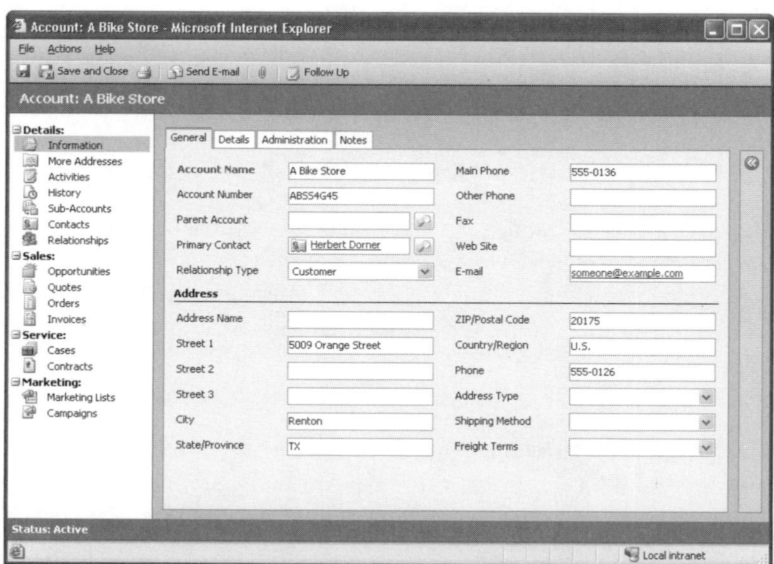

Figure 3-8 Account record as seen by a user with the default Customer Service Representative security role

In reality, most customer service representatives don't need to see all of this information on an Account record. Instead, let's assume that you want your customer service representatives to see only the information shown in the Details and Service groups. By modifying their security roles and setting the Read privilege to None Selected for the entities that you want to hide, the revised Account form might appear like the one shown in Figure 3-9.

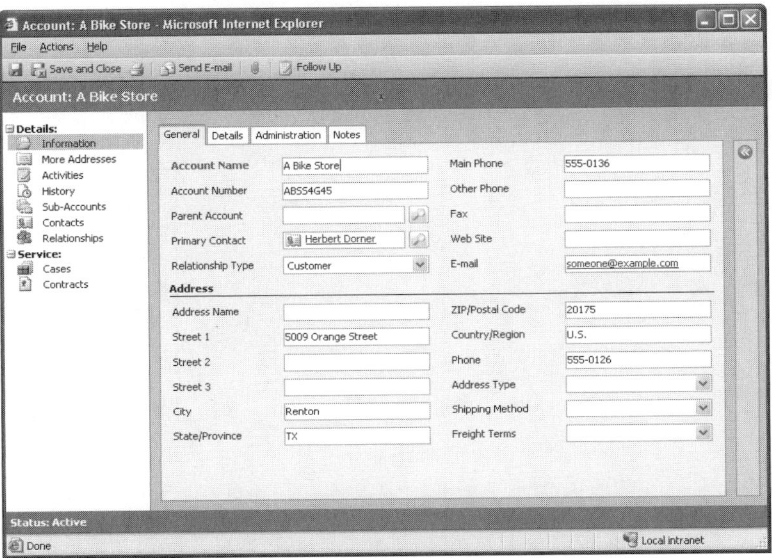

Figure 3-9 Account record as seen by a user with a revised Customer Service Representative security role

This provides a much cleaner user interface that your users will appreciate. Likewise, you could also revise the Salesperson security roles so that salespeople see only entities that they need to perform their jobs.

Security Role Inheritance

If your deployment includes multiple business units, you should understand how Microsoft CRM inherits security roles within the business unit hierarchy. When you create a new security role in a business unit, Microsoft CRM creates an instance (copy) of that security role for every business unit that is a child of the business unit for which you created the new security role. If you try to edit the security role in one of the child business units, you will see a warning message stating, "Inherited roles cannot be modified or updated." You can edit only the parent security role, and then Microsoft CRM automatically copies your changes to all of the security roles in the child business units. Consider the organization hierarchy of the sample organization Adventure Works Cycle, as shown in Figure 3-10.

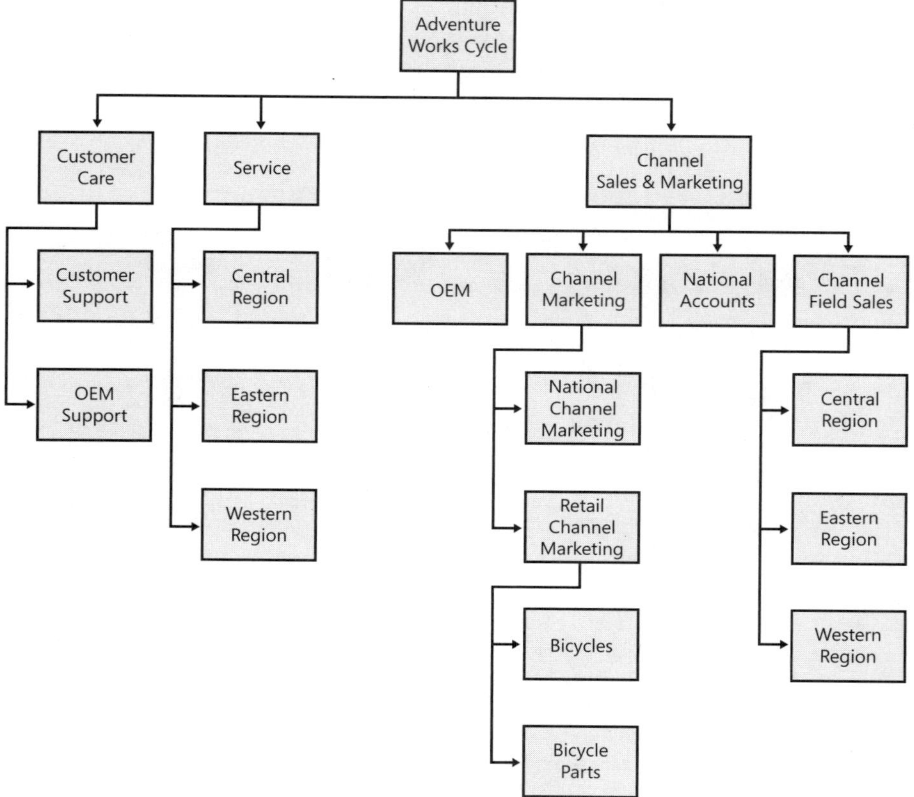

Figure 3-10 Organization structure for the sample company, Adventure Works Cycle

If you create a new security role called Director assigned to the Customer Care business unit, Microsoft CRM automatically creates non-editable copies of the Director security role in the Customer Support and OEM Support business units because they're children of the Customer Care business unit. Any changes you make to the Directory security role are automatically propagated to all of the Director security roles in the child business units. If you viewed the security roles for one of the other business units, such as Service or OEM, you would not see the Director security role listed, because the Service and OEM business units are not children of the Customer Care business unit.

Tip When you a create a new security role, Microsoft CRM assigns the security role to the root business unit by default, so make sure that you remember to change the role's business unit by using the business unit look up if you want to create a role in a non-root business unit.

Every user belongs to only one business unit, and you can only assign users security roles from the business unit to which they belong. Therefore, in this example, you could not assign the Director security role to users who belong to any business unit other than Customer Care, Customer Support, and OEM Support. You can view all of the security roles for a single business unit by using the business unit view filter drop-down list to select a specific business unit.

Because Microsoft CRM inherits security roles to children business units, you cannot vary the privileges of a security role to be different for each business unit. However, you can create a varying number of security roles for each business unit within your deployment. The ability to create unique security roles for each business unit gives you great flexibility to create and configure security roles to meet your organization's needs.

Sharing Records

Despite the numerous security options and configuration choices we've already discussed, you will probably encounter scenarios in which users need to share and collaborate on records that the business unit hierarchy does not support. Consider a fictional company called Coho Vineyard & Winery (the root business unit) with two children business units named Vineyard and Winery. Coho Vineyard & Winery CEO Laura Owen (user assigned to root business unit) owns the Woodgrove Bank account. However, the security roles for Gretchen Rivas (assigned to Vineyard business unit) and Heidi Steen (assigned to Winery business unit) do not have the Write privilege for the Account entity. The CEO decides that she wants Gretchen and Heidi to work on a special project related to Woodgrove Bank for which they will need to edit the record. However, Laura doesn't want them to edit any other Account records that she owns other than Woodgrove Bank. This type of security configuration would not be possible with the security configurations we've covered so far. If Laura gave Gretchen and Heidi privileges to edit Account records for the Organization, they would be able to edit *any* Account, not just the Woodgrove Bank record. Fortunately, Microsoft CRM allows users to share records to accommodate exactly this type of collaboration scenario. *Sharing* records allows a user to grant privileges for a specific record so that other users can work with the shared record, even though they would not normally have the necessary privileges to do so.

To share records, users must have a security role with the appropriate Share privilege. To set up a share like the Woodgrove Bank example, open the entity record and click Sharing... on the Actions menu of the entity menu bar. On the Share dialog page, select the users that you want to share this record with by clicking Add User/Team. Use the Lookup tool to find the records that you want, and then click OK. Microsoft CRM adds the users to the page, as shown in Figure 3-11.

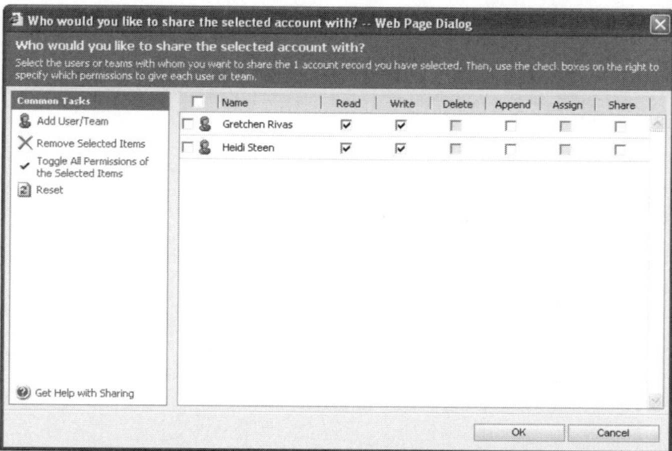

Figure 3-11 Sharing records with users

Next, specify which privileges you want to share with these users. In the Woodgrove Bank example, Laura Owen would select the Read and Write privileges so that Gretchen and Heidi could edit this record. Note that the Delete and Assign privilege check boxes are disabled because Laura doesn't have those privileges for this record, and therefore cannot share them with any other user.

More Info Users can't share a privilege if they do not posses the privilege themselves. For example, a user could not share Delete privileges for a record if he or she did not have the Delete privilege for that record.

With this share in place, Gretchen and Heidi can now read and write just the Woodgrove Bank Account record. Of course, you can revoke a share at any time by simply opening the record and clearing the check boxes for the privileges that you want to revoke.

Teams

In our Coho Vineyard & Winery example, it was easy to set up the share because we needed to select only two users. But what if Laura wanted to share the Woodgrove Bank record with 100 users? What if she wanted to share five different records with those same 100 users? It would be a pretty miserable and time-consuming process to manually share records one user at a time in these examples. Fortunately, Microsoft CRM allows you to set up and configure *teams* of users to expedite the sharing process. By sharing a record with a team instead of individual users, you do not have to manually select user records for each share that you create. Rather, you simply select the team that you want to share with, and all of the users in that team will participate in the share.

You can create and modify teams by browsing to Business Unit Settings in the Settings area and clicking Teams. When you create a team, you specify the Business Unit to which the team belongs, and then you simply add members to the team.

Important Although you assign a team to a business unit, you can add any user in the organization to a team, regardless of his or her business unit. You cannot change a team's business unit once it is created.

If you use a large number of teams, you can configure the security settings so that users only see a subset of all of the teams. To do this, configure the Team entity privilege within a user's security role with an access level appropriate for each team's business unit. For example, if you create a team that belongs to the root business unit but you only grant a security role with a User access level for the team privilege, users with that security role won't see that root business unit team in the user interface unless they personally created that team. This type of configuration allows you to restrict the teams that each user is allowed to view (and share records with) in case you want to hide specific teams (such as executive or financial teams).

Caution Once you create a team, you cannot delete it or disable it. If you no longer want to use a team, all you can do is remove all of its members. Therefore, you should use some discretion when creating teams, or you might end up with a bunch of abandoned teams with no members.

You might wonder if it's possible to have a team own a record, instead of just sharing a record with a team. Unfortunately, you cannot set a team as the owner of a record such as a Lead, Account, or Contact.

Sharing and Inheritance

When you share a record with a team or user, child entities of the shared record can inherit the same sharing settings as the parent record. In the Woodgrove Bank example, Gretchen and Heidi could edit the Account record and its related entities, such as Tasks, Phone Calls, and Notes, because they inherit the same share as their parent record.

More Info For shared records (directly shared or inherited), users receive only the shared privileges for the entity if they have at least a User access level for that entity. For example, if Heidi had an Access Level of None Selected for the Activity entity, she would not be able to view activities related to Woodgrove Bank even if someone shared Read privileges with her for that Account record. Likewise, she would need to have at least a User access level for the Account entity to view the Woodgrove Bank account record after Laura shared it with her.

You can configure how Microsoft CRM shares related records by editing the relationship behavior between two entities. For example, you might want Microsoft CRM to inherit sharing with related entities such as Tasks, but not with a different related entity such as Activities. Chapter 6 explains in detail how to configure relationship behaviors between entities.

> **Note** Microsoft CRM knowledge base article ID #908504 explains that sharing inheritance two levels or deeper might lose its sharing inheritance.

Summary

Microsoft CRM includes a powerful and highly configurable security model that allows you to configure and restrict information access according to your business needs. Microsoft CRM uses Integrated Windows authentication and Active Directory to manage user accounts and authentication. By combining role-based and object-based security settings with your organization's business unit structure, Microsoft CRM allows you to accommodate very complex security and information access needs. Microsoft CRM also supports project-based and collaborative work by enabling users to share records with teams and individual users.

Part II
Customization

Part I of this book gave you a brief overview of Microsoft CRM 3.0 and showed you how to set up and configure some commonly used areas of the software. However, we consider everything we've reviewed so far more as software "configuration" than "customization." Part II of this book will get deep into the details of how you can customize Microsoft CRM and will provide real-world contexts for why you might need to perform these customizations. Just as in Part I, you'll need to have System Administrator rights in your Microsoft CRM system to perform almost all of the customizations we review in Part II. If you're an IT project manager or power user, you have the technical skills necessary to perform all of the customizations we review in this part, even if you're not a programmer or developer.

We highly recommend that you actually log on to Microsoft CRM, if possible, and try to follow along in the user interface as you read the material in these chapters.

Chapter 4

Entity Customization: Concepts and Attributes

In this chapter:

Before we get into explaining how to customize entities in Microsoft CRM 3.0, we want to remind you why you'll need to customize your system. Let's assume your company is considering implementing Microsoft CRM and you've installed the trial version of the software. As soon as you show the company owners or executives the user interface and they look at one of the default forms (like the Account form shown in Figure 4-1), the first words out of their mouth will be something like "That's not the information we track about our customers. We would never use the Shipping Method and Freight Terms fields. And where do we enter the SIC Code and the number of employees each customer has? Also, we don't call customers *Accounts;* we refer to them as *Companies.*"

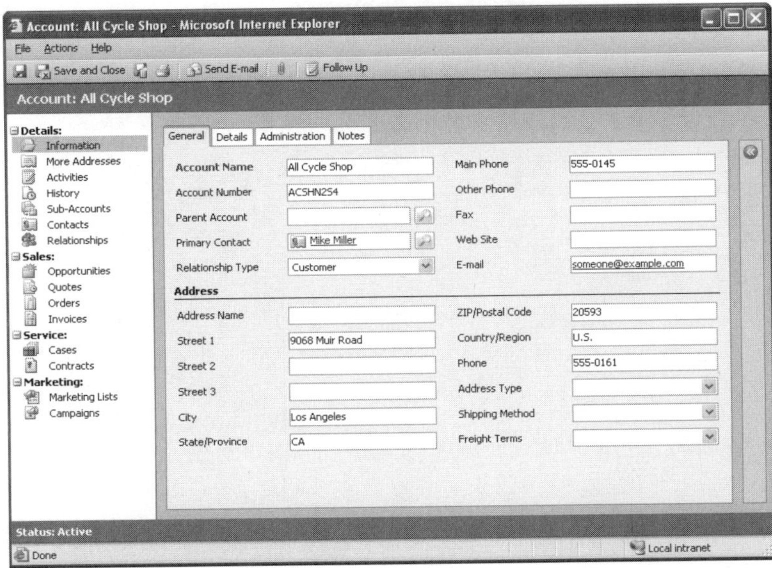

Figure 4-1 Default Account form

Ah-ha! It took only one meeting before users started demanding customizations to the Microsoft CRM system to better match your business's needs. However, within just a few minutes (literally) and without a single line of programming code, you could customize Microsoft CRM so that your new form looks like Figure 4-2.

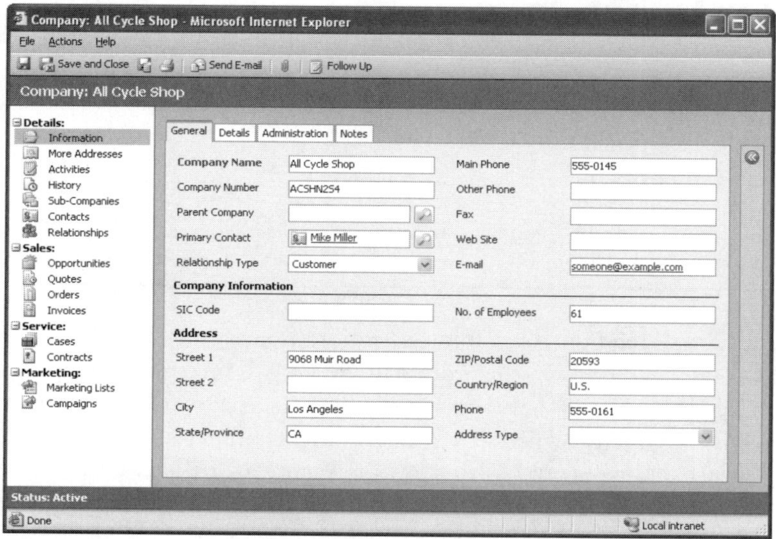

Figure 4-2 Account form revised and renamed as *Company*

Implementing this type of customization in other CRM vendors' applications might take weeks of coding and testing. It might not even be possible to change some of the key system terminology, such as renaming *Account* to *Company*. The Microsoft CRM customization model will make these and other types of customizations seem almost trivial to you.

As we said earlier, Microsoft CRM offers an incredible number of system customization opportunities, and—without any programming expertise—you can complete most of them through a Web-based interface. In fact, Microsoft CRM offers so many customization features that we have to break the entity customization explanation into three separate chapters:

- Concepts and Attributes
- Forms and Views
- Relationships, Custom Entities, and Site Map

In this chapter, we give you an overview of the concepts related to entity customization, and then we start the entity customization explanation with entity attributes.

Customization Concepts

Microsoft CRM is a horizontal platform that can be used by any company, regardless of industry or size. Because no two businesses use the same processes or track the same customer data, Microsoft designed the Microsoft CRM software for easy customization by using a metadata-driven product architecture.

Metadata is defined as data about data. When users look up a customer or prospect, Microsoft CRM runs behind the scenes to retrieve the record data from the metadata, which in turn retrieves information from the actual underlying system data. Microsoft CRM stores its underlying system data in a relational database format by using Microsoft SQL Server. Figure 4-3 illustrates a highly simplified representation of this metadata-driven concept.

Figure 4-3 Metadata product architecture

Of course, your users will never know that Microsoft CRM uses a metadata architecture, but it's important that you know about it for several reasons:

- The metadata makes heavy use of Web services and XML data formats, so you will see terminology (such as *entity* and *attribute*) related to those technologies in the Microsoft CRM documentation and in this book.
- By using a metadata-driven architecture, Microsoft CRM allows you to quickly and easily make customizations that would be extremely difficult (or possibly impossible) to implement in other CRM systems.
- Microsoft CRM automatically manages the extremely complex details of the metadata on your behalf. However, if you attempt to make changes to the underlying system data in SQL Server directly, you run the risk of damaging the metadata and creating irreversible errors in your system. To ensure that the metadata and its underlying data always remain well structured, Microsoft CRM offers a Web-based interface specifically designed for you to make your customizations. The software's administration tools work within the Microsoft CRM predefined framework to correctly update the metadata and the underlying system data.

In addition to helping you protect your software investment, using the Microsoft CRM administration tools for your customizations provides additional benefits, such as the following:

- The Web-based administration tools provide a simple and easy-to-understand interface.
- Microsoft technical support can assist you with any changes that you make using the customization tools.
- Your customizations should upgrade smoothly to future releases and updates of Microsoft CRM.
- You can install third-party software add-ins for Microsoft CRM.

Hopefully, we've convinced you of the benefits of the Microsoft CRM metadata architecture and of using the customization tools that Microsoft CRM provides. Next we'll discuss some of the key concepts and terminology related to customizations:

- Entities and Attributes
- Security and Permissions
- Publishing Customizations
- Importing and Exporting Customizations
- Renaming a Customizable Entity

Entities and Attributes

If you have worked with relational databases such as Microsoft Office Access or SQL Server, you understand the meaning of the terms *table* and *column*. In the Microsoft CRM metadata-driven XML-based terminology, you can mentally translate those concepts to *entity* and *attribute*, as shown in Table 4-1.

Table 4-1 Terminology Comparison

Relational database terminology	XML-based terminology
Table	Entity
Column	Attribute

Microsoft CRM stores data in entities such as Accounts, Contacts, Leads, and Opportunities. The data related to an entity, such as a phone number for a contact, is an attribute of the entity.

Entities

When you install Microsoft CRM, it creates more than 100 *system entities* (also known as *default entities* or *default system entities*) in the software, and of course you will want to customize a lot of these system entities. Microsoft CRM predetermines what types of customizations, if any, it will let you perform on these system entities. For some system entities, you can perform only limited customizations, and other system entities can't be customized at all. In addition to the system entities, you can create entirely new entities, known as *custom entities*, within Microsoft CRM. In summary, there are three types of entities:

- System (non-customizable)
- System (customizable)
- Custom

System (Non-Customizable) Microsoft CRM uses 65 non-customizable system entities (examples include Privilege, License, and String Map) to manage the internal operations of the software. You cannot edit any of these entities' settings, add new attributes to the entities, or delete the entities from the system.

System (Customizable) Microsoft CRM includes 49 customizable system entities. Account, Activity, and User are a few examples. These entities give you extensive customization capabilities, ranging from adding attributes to changing the form layout. You can even rename the customizable system entities. However, you cannot delete any of the customizable system entities.

Custom You can modify custom entities just like you can modify the customizable entities, and you can also delete them. We explain custom entities in detail in Chapter 6.

To view all of the entities in your system, go to the Customization section of Microsoft CRM and click Customize Entities. A grid lists every entity in your deployment.

Tip The terminology used on the entity grid page can be confusing. Entities listed under Type of Customizable are actually customizable system entities, and entities listed with a Type of System are non-customizable system entities.

You can customize the following data for custom and customizable entities:

- Attributes
- Forms
- Views
- Relationships
- Messages

Attributes

Every entity possesses one or more attributes that store data about the entity. Microsoft CRM uses two types of attributes: system and custom.

System As with system entities, Microsoft CRM uses system attributes to manage the internal workings of the software. To ensure that the software always works correctly, Microsoft CRM prevents you from deleting system attributes. However, you can modify some values of system attributes. For example, you can specify the requirement level (Business Required, Business Recommended, or No Constraint) for system attributes.

Custom Microsoft CRM includes the ability to add entirely new custom attributes. You can add or delete custom attributes on both customizable and custom entities, but you cannot add custom attributes to system entities.

Table 4-2 summarizes the customizations that you can perform on each type of entity.

Table 4-2 Customizations Allowed by Entity Type

Entity type	System (non-customizable)	System (customizable)	Custom
Forms			
Add custom form	n/a	Only one form per entity	Only one form per entity
Modify form	n/a	Yes	Yes
Delete form	n/a	No	Yes
Views			
Add custom views	n/a	Yes	Yes
Modify views	n/a	Yes	Yes
Delete views	n/a	Yes	Yes
System attributes			
Add system attributes	No	No	No
Modify system attributes	No	Yes: partial	Yes: partial
Delete system attributes	No	No	No
Custom attributes			
Add custom attributes	No	Yes	Yes
Modify custom attributes	No	Yes	Yes
Delete custom attributes	No	Yes	Yes
Messages			
Add messages	No	No	No
Modify messages	No	Yes	n/a
Delete messages	No	No	n/a

Note that the SQL Server database that Microsoft CRM uses limits the number of custom attributes that you can add to an entity. Most users won't run into a problem with this database limit, but you should recognize that it exists.

Calculating the Maximum Number of Attributes

With Microsoft CRM 1.2, we frequently heard from customers who "ran out of space" in their Account, Contact, Lead, and Opportunity tables. In reality, they had reached the SQL Server limit of 8,060 bytes for any one row. Adding a new custom attribute in Microsoft CRM adds a column in the SQL Server database and Microsoft CRM 1.2 enforced the SQL Server row limit at the column level for newly added columns. Therefore, in CRM 1.2 you could actually run out of space. Because Microsoft CRM 1.2 stores custom fields in the same table as the system fields, many of the available 8,060 bytes in SQL Server were gone before the customer even added one custom field! Compounding the problems, Microsoft CRM 1.2 did not support deletion of custom fields. Consequently, it was pretty easy for customers to add so many custom fields that they reached the byte limit and could not add any more. Thankfully, in version 3.0, Microsoft redesigned the way in which Microsoft CRM handles custom attributes to essentially eliminate the possibility of "running out of space."

Microsoft CRM 3.0 stores custom attributes in a new SQL table that is separate from the system fields so that you get almost all of the 8,060 bytes that SQL Server offers for adding your custom attributes. (Microsoft CRM automatically adds one cross-reference column to link the custom attributes back to the correct entity.) Microsoft CRM 3.0 also supports deletion of custom attributes, so you can remove a custom attribute if necessary.

Because of these enhancements, we don't expect that customers will ever "run out of space" in Microsoft CRM 3.0. However, it is technically possible, so you should be aware of this constraint. The maximum number of bytes for a row (which should provide a guide for you to calculate the maximum number of custom attributes for an entity in Microsoft CRM) depends on the data types of the attributes in your table. Table 4-3 lists the data types and the number of bytes each data type consumes.

Table 4-3 Bytes Required per Data Type

Data type	Bytes required
boolean	1
datetime	8
picklist	4

Table 4-3 Bytes Required per Data Type

Data type	Bytes required
integer	4
float	8
money	8
ntext	16
nvarchar (*n*)	*n* x 2 (where *n* is the length of the *nvarchar* box)

Obviously, the *nvarchar* fields take up the most space, so use some caution when adding these to your CRM data. For example, if you were to add 25 custom *nvarchar* fields with a length of 100 characters each, you would be using 5,000 bytes (25 x 100 x 2) of the 8,060 bytes available (62 percent). But if you added 25 custom *Boolean* fields, you would be using only 25 bytes (25 x 1) of the 8,060 available (0.3 percent).

Microsoft CRM 3.0 also no longer enforces the row byte limit at the column level. Therefore, you can add two custom *nvarchar* attributes, each with a length of 4,000 characters. This would calculate out to 16,000 bytes total (4,000 x 2 + 4,000 x 2), which obviously violates the 8,000-byte SQL limit. Microsoft CRM allows this because SQL Server enforces the byte limit for each row (record), not for the entire table. Therefore, if you added a record and populated the two *nvarchar* fields with 4,000 characters each, you would receive an error message in Microsoft CRM. When we tried this experiment, we received an error message stating, "Duplicate Record -- A record with these values already exists."

Security and Permissions

Users with a System Administrator role can perform all of the functions in the system, including the customizations described in this chapter. However, you might want to let some users customize the system, but you don't want to grant them System Administrator rights. Fortunately, Microsoft CRM allows you to configure security roles to modify who can perform various customizations. Microsoft CRM includes two default security roles with system customization privileges: System Administrator and System Customizer. Figure 4-4 shows the default security settings for the System Customizer role.

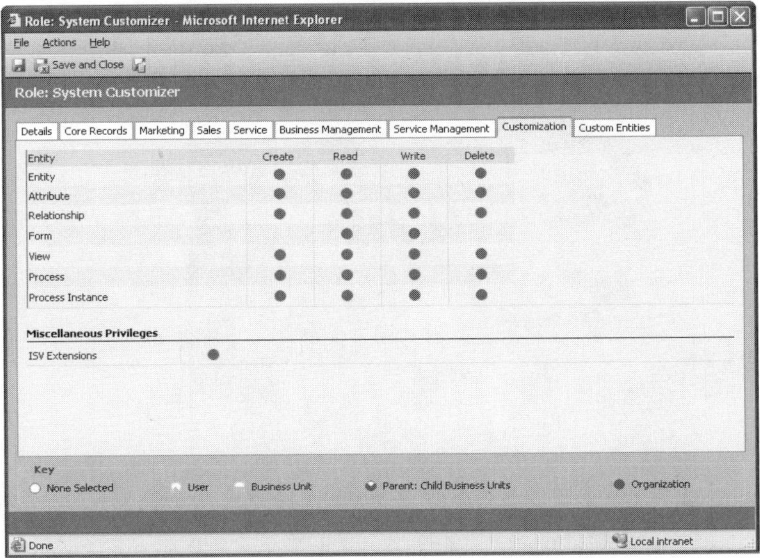

Figure 4-4 Default security settings for the System Customizer role

As you learned in Chapter 3, "Managing Security and Information Access," Microsoft CRM allows you to refine the customization privileges on a more detailed level than just yes or no. For example, you can allow some of your users to create new attributes but not allow the same users to create new entities. You can also remove Delete permissions related to entity customization from a security role. If the person performing your customizations is new to Microsoft CRM, we strongly recommend that you modify the default System Customizer role to remove all of the Delete permissions and that you don't assign him or her to the System Administrator role. Microsoft CRM is very forgiving in regard to mistakes made when you're modifying customizations, but you can't recover a deleted customization. If you spend 40 hours customizing a custom entity and someone accidentally deletes it, your work is gone forever.

Tip Although you cannot undo a deletion, you can avoid an accidental loss of your customizations by proactively backing up your customizations and databases. If someone does mistakenly delete your customizations, you can re-import your customizations from your backup file. You cannot recover any data deleted from the records, but you can save yourself some time by not having to reconstruct your customizations and your databases. We suggest that you back up your customizations after each time you successfully publish your customizations. To back up your customizations, simply export the customizations for all entities and save the file that Microsoft CRM creates. We explain publishing, importing, and exporting customizations in more detail later in this chapter.

To change the security settings of the System Customizer role, simply click the appropriate option and save the security role. Figure 4-5 displays our recommended configuration for the System Customizer security role without Delete permissions.

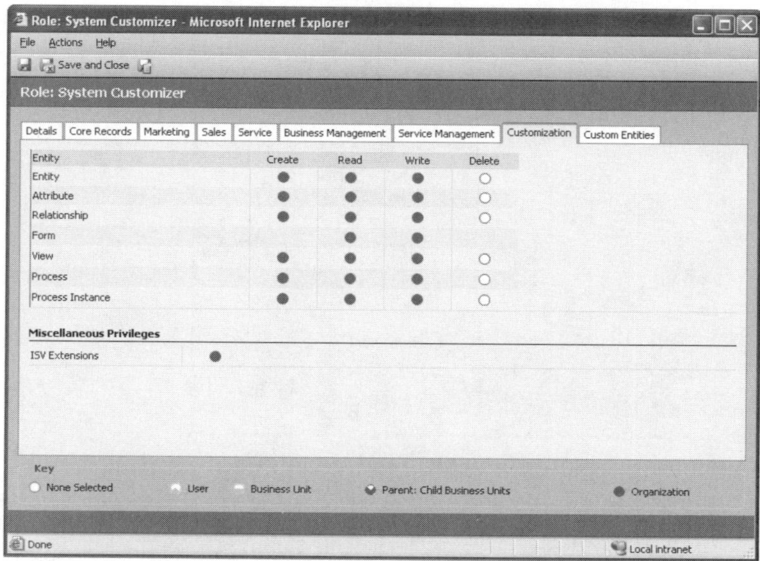

Figure 4-5 Recommended System Customizer role configuration for preventing accidental deletions

Later in this chapter, we review importing and exporting your customizations. Only users with a System Administrator role can perform these import and export actions. Likewise, only system administrators can publish customizations. You cannot assign these import/export and publish rights to any non–system administrator users.

Publishing Customizations

When you perform customizations on Microsoft CRM entities, your users will not immediately see the changes that you make. Rather, you decide when you want to *publish* the customizations to your users. The ability to decide when you want to publish customizations makes your life easier because you can work on a set of interrelated customizations and then make them available to all of your users at the same time. Even more conveniently, Microsoft CRM allows you to select how you want to publish your customizations. You can publish customizations in one of three ways:

- A single entity at a time
- Two or more entities at the same time
- All publishable entities at one time

Microsoft CRM makes publishing customizations a very simple process.

Publishing Process

When you publish an entity, Microsoft CRM publishes all of the changes related to the entity, including all of the attributes, the attribute properties, the form, the views, the relationships, and so on. Next we'll walk you through the steps necessary to publish your customizations to your users.

Publishing customizations for select entities

1. Go to the **Customization** section of Microsoft CRM and then click **Customize Entities**.
2. Select the entities that you want to publish. If you want to select more than one entity, select the first entity, and then hold down the Ctrl key while selecting additional entities.
3. Click **Publish** on the grid toolbar. A message indicates that your customizations are being published.

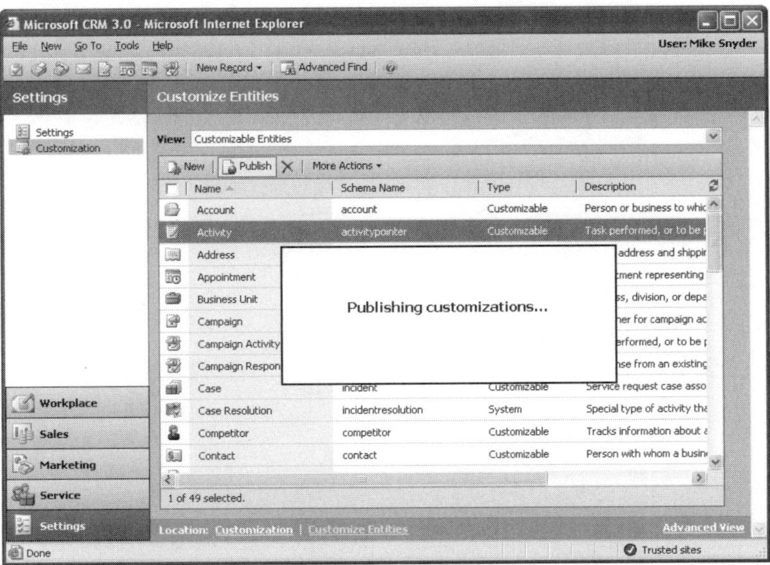

When the publish message disappears, all of the customizations that you just selected to publish will appear to your users. You can also publish customizations for a single entity by clicking Publish on the Actions menu in the entity editor, as illustrated in Figure 4-6.

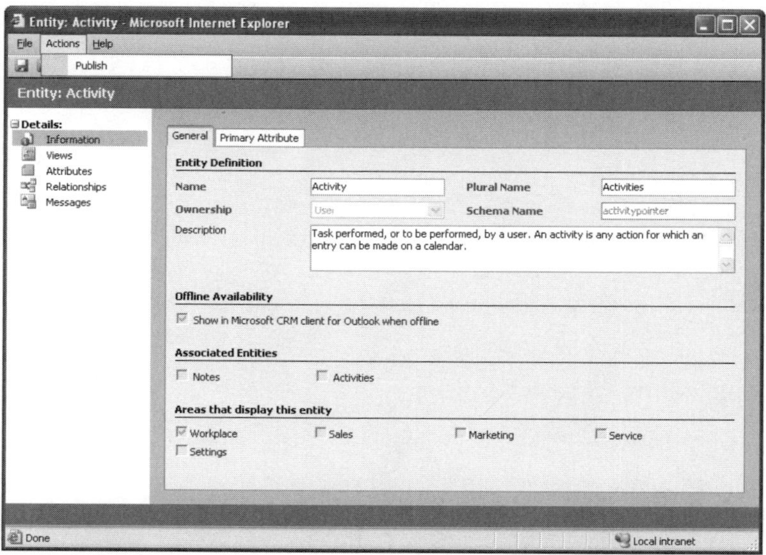

Figure 4-6 Publishing a single entity from the entity editor

Real World Microsoft CRM is a Web application running on Microsoft Internet Information Services (IIS), and a publishing customizations restarts IIS on the Web server. Therefore, some users might experience glitches if they try to access Microsoft CRM in mid-way through publication. If possible, you should try to publish your customizations when you know that users are not using Microsoft CRM.

In addition to publishing select entities, you can also publish all entities at one time.

Publishing customizations for all entities

1. Go to the **Customization** section of Microsoft CRM and then click **Customize Entities**.
2. In the grid toolbar, click **More Actions**, and then click **Publish All Customizations**.

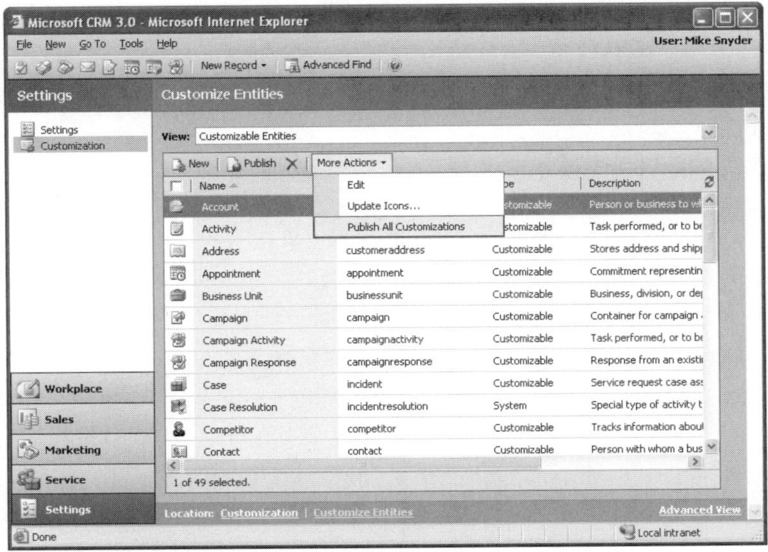

3. A message will appear indicating that your customizations are being published.

Publishing all of the entities takes more time than publishing just a few entities, so you should try to avoid doing this when many users are accessing Microsoft CRM. Another very important factor to consider before you publish all customizations is whether system customizers (other than yourself) have made customizations that they don't want to publish yet. When you publish all customizations, you might unknowingly publish someone else's customizations before they have finished and tested their changes. This type of situation will probably create system errors or user confusion. To play it safe, we encourage you to publish only the entities that you changed. You can't unpublish customizations, so make sure that you're ready before you click that Publish button!

Real World Although Microsoft CRM allows you to publish changes whenever you want and as often as you want, frequent random changes to the system might cause confusion for your users. We recommend that you create a business process in which you queue and publish customizations on a scheduled interval that makes sense for your business (such as weekly, bi-weekly, or monthly). You can also help users understand the changes that you published to the system by creating an *Announcement* in Microsoft CRM. Announcements appear to users within the Workplace; you can use them to provide highlights of changes within the system.

Publishing Customizations to the Microsoft CRM Laptop Client for Outlook

Microsoft CRM offers a laptop version of the Microsoft CRM client for Microsoft Office Outlook that allows users to work offline, totally disconnected from Microsoft CRM. However, what happens when you publish changes and one or more of your Outlook laptop users are not connected to the Microsoft CRM server? Does this cause a problem the next time they connect their laptops with the server? Remarkably, Microsoft CRM queues all of the published customization changes on the Web server and automatically deploys them to the Outlook laptop client the next time the users synchronize their software.

Microsoft CRM can also handle the synchronization if you publish changes multiple times while the Outlook laptop client is disconnected from your network for an extended period of time. Even if your company uses hundreds of Outlook laptop clients, with people connecting and disconnecting from the network at random times unrelated to one another, the Microsoft CRM synchronization engine smoothly manages the process for all of your users.

In summary, you don't need to worry about coordinating the publishing of your customizations when your Outlook laptop users are connected to the network. Simply publish the customizations at your whim, and Microsoft CRM does all the complicated synchronization work for you.

Importing and Exporting Customizations

With all of the customization options available in Microsoft CRM, you could invest anywhere from 30 minutes to several thousand hours customizing the software. Fortunately, Microsoft CRM allows you to export some or all of your customizations and then import them into a different Microsoft CRM system. These import and export features save you valuable time because you don't have to repeat your customization work. You can also export your customizations proactively to make sure you always have a backup copy.

To access the customization export and import features, click Customization in the Settings section. We'll examine exporting customizations first, so click Export Customizations. You'll see a list of the 53 items that you can export (see Figure 4-7).

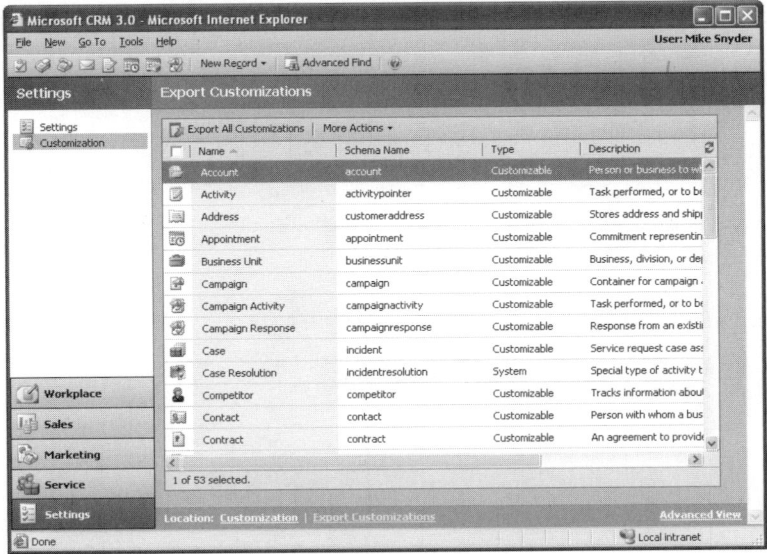

Figure 4-7 List of exportable entities

In addition to all of the custom and customizable entities, you will also notice that you can export the following:

- **Templates** Contains individual article, contract, and e-mail templates
- **ISV.config** Configuration file for customizing the navigation pane, toolbars, and menus
- **Relationship roles** Contains all relationship roles
- **Site map** Describes application navigation structure

Microsoft CRM lists these four items under the type Configuration.

> **Caution** You cannot export or import system settings or business settings such as Services, Sites, Auto-Numbering, and Security Roles. Microsoft CRM also does not export Advanced Find queries or Views created by users. In general, if you don't have to publish a customization, you should assume that you can't export it (templates are one of the exceptions to this rule). In addition, you will use a separate process to export and import Workflow rules, as described in Chapter 8.

Exporting one or more entity customizations

1. Go to the **Customization** section of Microsoft CRM and then click **Export Customizations**.
2. Select the entity (or entities) that you want to export.
3. On the **More Actions** menu, click **Export Selected Customizations**.

4. Microsoft CRM displays the following message.

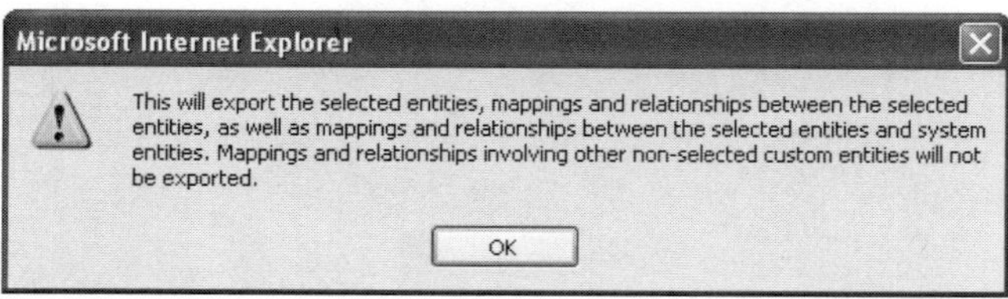

5. Click **OK**.
6. The following dialog box appears.

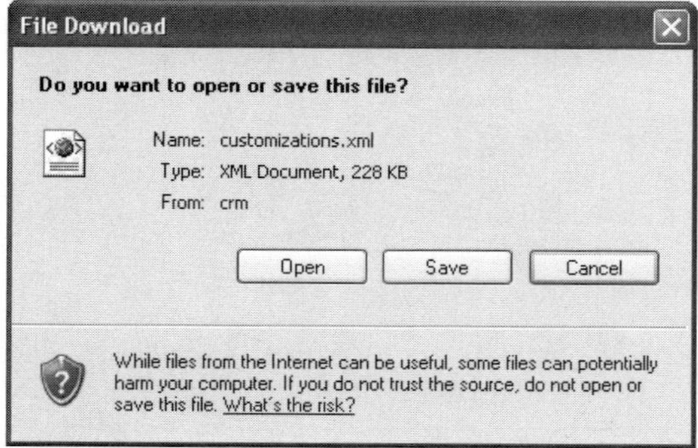

7. Select the destination location to save the Customizations.xml file, and then click **Save**.
8. To export all of the customizations (for all of the items in the list), you can click the Export All Customizations button in the grid toolbar and then proceed to step 7.

> **Important** Microsoft CRM allows only users who are members of the System Administrator role to import or export your customizations. You cannot change the security settings to assign this privilege to non–system administrator users.

If you open the Customizations.xml file with Microsoft Internet Explorer, you will see that this file includes all of the customizations (defined in XML format) related to the entity (or entities) that you selected to export. When you export an entity's customizations, those customizations include (but are not limited to) its attributes, forms, views, mappings, and relationships. However, Microsoft CRM does not export non-modifiable attributes in entities, relationships, attributes, or templates. This does not cause a problem because Microsoft CRM doesn't need this information when it imports the customizations, but don't be surprised if you don't see those items in the Customizations.xml file. Now that you've exported your customizations into the Customizations.xml file, you can import these customizations into a different Microsoft CRM system.

Importing customizations

1. Go to the **Customization** section of Microsoft CRM and then click **Import Customizations**.
2. Click **Browse,** select the Customizations.xml file that you just exported, and then click **Open**.
3. The full path to the Customizations.xml file appears in the **Import File** box. Click **Upload**.
4. Microsoft CRM reads the Customizations.xml file and confirms that it contains a valid structure to import. You will receive an error message if you try to import an invalid file. If the file passes the validation, Microsoft CRM displays a list of entity customizations contained in the Customizations.xml file.

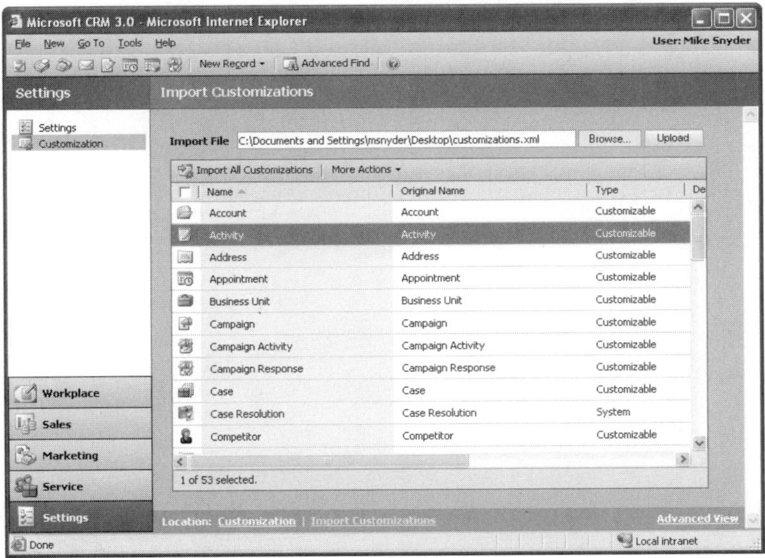

5. Select one or more entity customizations that you want to import. Then on the **More Actions** menu, click **Import Selected Customizations**.
6. A dialog box indicates that customizations are importing.
7. When the dialog box disappears, a message appears that says, “Customizations have been imported successfully.”

Import Customization Conflicts

Microsoft CRM imports customizations by using an additive process. It will add any new customizations to the target system, but it won't remove the customizations that previously existed in the target system. Let's consider the following example to understand how the additive import process works.

Assume that you have a Microsoft CRM system called System A with the following customizations:

- Custom entity B added
- Custom entity C added
- Account entity with custom attributes Y and Z added

Now you want to import the customizations that you set up on another system (called System B) into System A. You configured System B with the following customizations:

- Custom entity B added
- Custom entity E added
- Account entity with custom attributes D and Z added

If you exported all of the customizations from System B and then imported those customizations into System A, System A would have the following final customizations:

- Custom entity B
- Custom entity C
- Custom entity E
- Account entity with custom attributes D, Y, and Z

As Figure 4-8 illustrates, Microsoft CRM examined the customizations import file and determined that custom entity E and the Account custom attribute D needed to be added to the system.

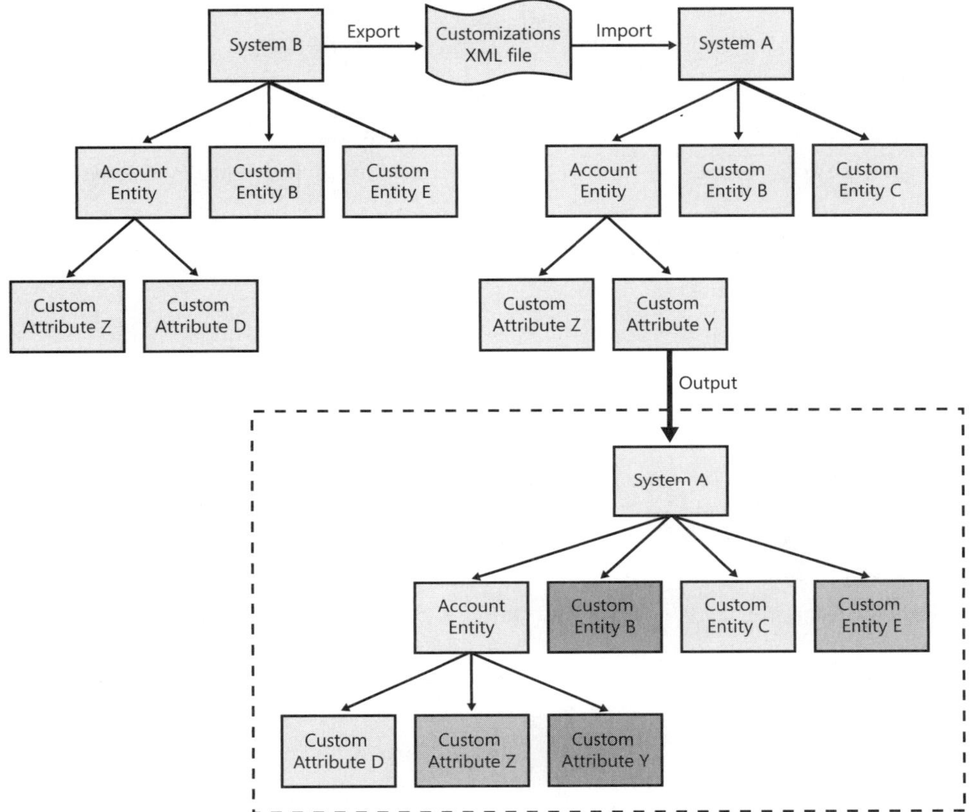

Figure 4-8 Importing customizations, an additive process

However, note that Microsoft CRM did *not* remove the original customizations in System A. In this example, a conflict would occur regarding custom entity B and custom attribute Z because you're trying to import customizations that already exist in the target system. This type of conflict is called a *collision*.

> **Important** Collisions occur when you try to import a customization (such as an entity, attribute, or view) and the schema name of that imported customization already exists in the target system.

Microsoft CRM resolves collisions with one of three actions:

- **Overwrite** The data in the import file overwrites the data in the target system.
- **Error** Microsoft CRM generates an error and aborts the import.
- **New object** Microsoft CRM creates a new object in the target system.

Table 4-4 outlines the import collision conditions and the actions that Microsoft CRM will take for each scenario.

Table 4-4 Import Conflicts and Microsoft CRM Actions

Object	Collision condition	Collision action taken
Modifiable entity property	Same entity name, different property	Overwrite
Non-modifiable entity property	Same entity name	Error
Attribute modifiable property	Same entity name, same attribute name	Overwrite
Attribute non-modifiable property	Same entity name, same attribute name	Error
Form	Same name	Overwrite
Form	Different property	Overwrite
View	Same name	Overwrite
Advanced Find view	Same name	Overwrite
Quick Find view	Same name	Overwrite
Associated view	Same name	Overwrite
Attribute mapping	Different attribute mappings for a source/target pair	Overwrite
Template	Same name	Overwrite
Isv.config	Same name	Overwrite
Custom relationships modifiable property	Same primary/related entity, different property	Overwrite
Customer relationships modifiable property	Same name, different property	New object
Customer relationships non-modifiable property	Same name, different property	Error

Table 4-4 shows that in most cases in which collisions occur, Microsoft CRM overwrites the target system with the values from the import file. When a collision takes place on a non-modifiable property, Microsoft CRM will generate an error during the import process.

Manually Editing Export Files

If you examine the Customizations.xml export file for a single entity, you'll see the customizations for that entity. If you created 30 custom attributes, all 30 of them would be exported into the Customizations.xml file. The Microsoft CRM user interface allows you to choose which entities you want to export, but you can't choose which individual customizations you want to export on each entity. You will get all the customizations for each entity; if you wanted to export just the entity views but not the attributes of the entity, you'd be out of luck.

Fortunately, Microsoft CRM makes it pretty easy to work around this issue if you're familiar with editing .xml files. Since the customizations export is just a standard .xml file, you could manually edit the file to remove any of the customizations that you did not want before importing it into a new system. In our example, you could manually remove 10 of the 30 custom attributes from the Customizations.xml file and then import the edited Customizations.xml file into your target system. The target system would receive just those 20 custom attributes remaining in the customization file, instead of the original 30 custom attributes exported from your parent system. This manual editing concept could also carry over to other customizations related to an entity, including forms, views, and so on.

Warning Do not attempt to manually edit the Customizations.xml file unless you're extremely comfortable working with XML files. If you do manually edit the file, the Microsoft CRM Software Development Kit (SDK) provides an XML schema so that you validate that your edited Customizations.xml file remains well structured.

Manually editing the Customizations.xml file gives you complete control over the customizations that you want to import into a new system. In addition, the Microsoft CRM SDK even allows you to programmatically import customizations if you find a need for that feature.

Renaming Entities

When you implement Microsoft CRM, you might find that the system entity terminology does not exactly match your business terminology. For example, instead of referring to people as Contacts, your business might use the terms *Clients* or *People*. Or you might refer to *Companies* or *Businesses* instead of *Accounts*. The metadata-driven structure of Microsoft CRM offers you an easy method for renaming customizable entities.

To rename an entity, go to the Customization section of Microsoft CRM and click Customize Entities. Find the entity that you want to rename, and then double-click that entity to open the entity editor. You will see a Name field and a Plural Name field in the Entity Definition section of the form, as shown in Figure 4-9.

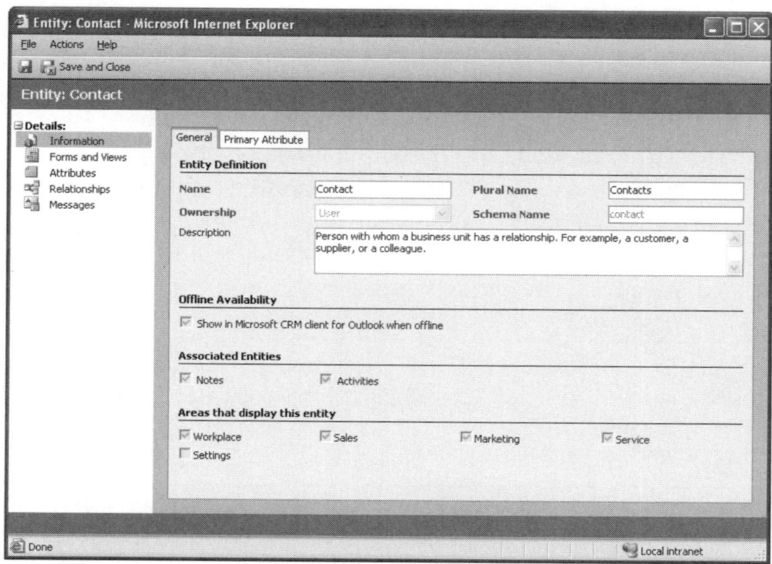

Figure 4-9 General tab for the Contact entity

On this form, simply enter the new name and plural name of the entity and then click Save. Microsoft CRM uses the plural version of the name when referring to multiple records in the system, so make sure that you complete this field.

Important You can rename an entity with almost any value that you want. The only naming requirement that Microsoft CRM enforces is that you cannot use the name of another entity in the system. This might seem obvious enough, but it does cause some confusion. Microsoft CRM contains many system entities, such as Site, Organization, and Unit, but you might forget that these entity names already exist in Microsoft CRM because they're not customizable entities. If you try to use an entity name that already exists, Microsoft CRM will prompt you with an error message.

After you rename the entity, you should also manually update the additional sections of Microsoft CRM that reference the entity name so that the user interface remains consistent with the new name that you just assigned to the entity. You should make the following modifications:

- Rename the entity view names (for example, change *Active Contacts* to *Active Clients*).
- Update form labels (for example, on the Account form, change *Primary Contact* to *Primary Client*).

- Change system messages (explained in the next section).
- Modify any reports that reference the entity name (modifying reports is explained in Chapter 7).
- Update the online Help content to display the new entity name.

After you finish making these changes, remember to publish all of the entities that you customized. Figure 4-10 shows how renaming the Contact entity to *Clients* correctly updates the application navigation pane.

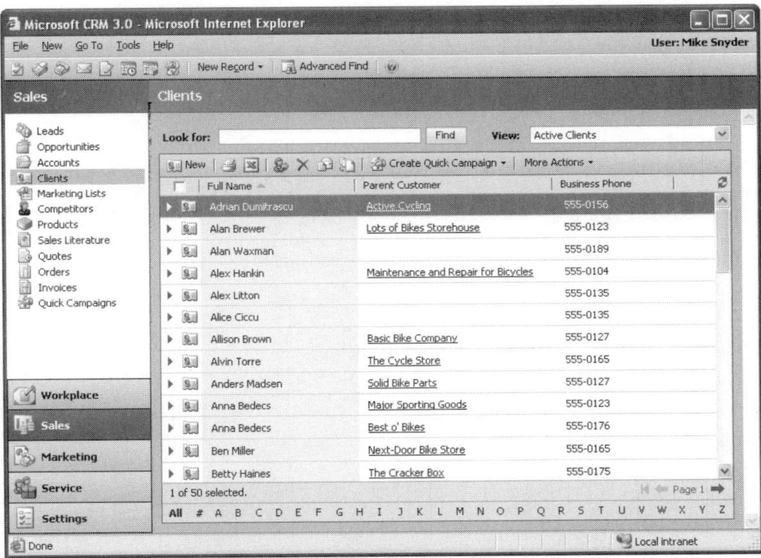

Figure 4-10 Contact entity renamed to *People*

You can use this technique to rename any of the customizable entities, including activity type entities such as Task, Phone Call, Letter, and Appointment.

Changing System Messages

For each entity, Microsoft CRM includes several predefined *system messages* that appear throughout the system. When you rename an entity, we recommend that you update these system messages to maintain consistency. If you do not update the system messages, a user might see an error message that references a *Contact* even though you renamed that entity to *Client*. You can view all of an entity's system messages in the Messages section of the entity editor, as shown in Figure 4-11.

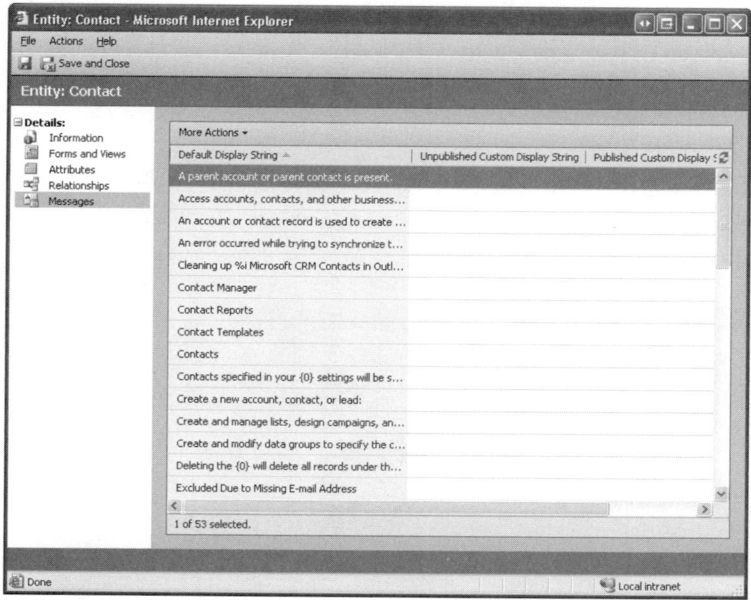

Figure 4-11 System messages for the Contact entity

To edit any one system message, simply double-click a record and enter the updated system message in the Custom Display String field. If you want, you can also add more descriptive information about the system message to help users.

You should note four important things about editing system messages:

1. You cannot include hyperlinks in the Custom Display String field.
2. Some system messages contain data placeholders, such as numbers within braces ({0}) or symbols and letters (%i). You should not remove or edit these data placeholders, because Microsoft CRM populates them with dynamic data when it displays the system message to users.
3. Several entities use a large number of system messages. For example, Account entities use 47 messages, and Contact entities use 53 messages. A single message might be used in several different locations throughout the system. Therefore, rely on your best judgment when you decide what text to enter to update the Custom Display String field.
4. Some areas of Microsoft CRM use messages to display text where you might not normally consider the text a "message." For example, if you decide to rename the Account entity to *Company*, you might also want to change the link in the entity navigation pane of the Account from *Sub-Accounts* to *Sub-Companies*.

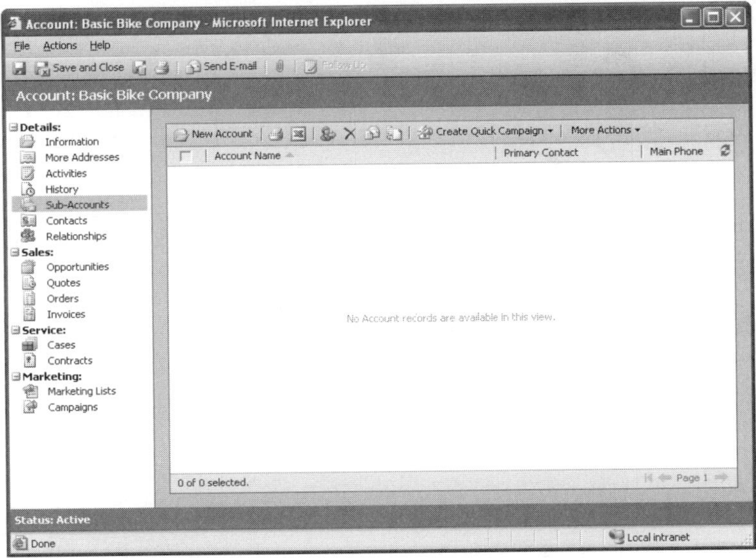

To make this change, navigate to the system messages of the Account entity and then simply change the Custom Display String of *Sub-Accounts* to *Sub-Companies*. Likewise, if you decide to rename the Lead entity to *Prospect*, you would use a message to edit the text that appears on the Convert Lead button of the Lead form.

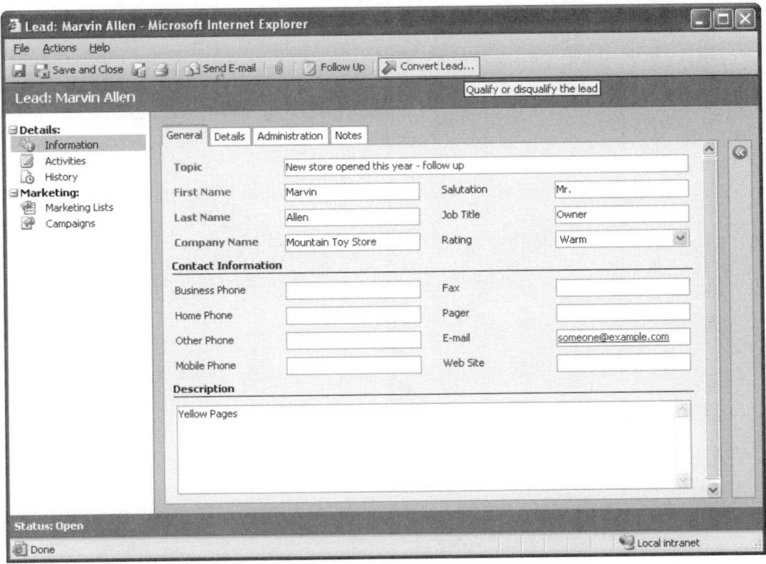

If you rename entities, please carefully review and edit all of the system messages because those messages might appear to users in places where you might not expect them.

Customizing Online Help

Microsoft CRM includes Web-based online Help files that users can access from the Help menu. Of course, the online Help files reference the default entity names such as Account, Contact, Lead, and Opportunity. If you rename entities, the new entity names will not be reflected in the online Help documentation, which might cause confusion for your users. Fortunately, Microsoft CRM allows you to customize the online Help documentation to change the terminology to match your system. If you decide that you want to customize online Help, refer to detailed instructions on the process in the Microsoft CRM SDK.

Advantages of customizing online Help Users can access online Help directly from the Web client or from either of the Outlook clients. By customizing the online Help, you can make the entity name in this documentation consistent with the user interface if you decide to rename entities.

In addition to updating entity names in online Help documentation, you can add entirely new sections of online Help. If your system makes heavy use of custom entities and customization code, your users will benefit from online Help documentation that describes the full functionality of their customized system.

Issues related to customizing online Help Of course, customizing the online Help files seems like a good idea, but there are a few potential issues we want to bring to your attention. Online Help includes two versions:

1. One for the Web client and desktop version (online only) of the Outlook client
2. One for the laptop version (offline capable) of the Outlook client

Changes to the laptop version of online Help must be manually deployed to the laptop computers after each change.

Every time you install Microsoft CRM or upgrade to a new release, the software copies a new version of online Help over the existing online Help files. Therefore, remember to make backup copies of your customized Help files before you re-install or upgrade your system.

Attributes

Attributes provide additional data about entities, and every entity in Microsoft CRM contains multiple attributes. For example, the Contact entity uses attributes such as first name, last name, and phone number. Each attribute has a data type (such as *integer*, *money*, and *bit*) that determines the type of data that you can store in a field.

When you install Microsoft CRM, it creates almost 120 entities, and each entity possesses up to 125 attributes. So we're talking about potentially 15,000 data attributes right out of the box!

But of course you know that even 15,000 attributes won't be enough for your business. Everyone wants a system as highly customized to their business as possible, and Microsoft CRM makes it easy for you to add new attributes or customize the default attributes.

However, before you start customizing attributes, let's review the terminology and concepts related to attributes.

Attribute Properties

Every attribute has multiple *attribute properties* that further define how the attribute behaves within Microsoft CRM. Figure 4-12 shows the attribute editor and the properties of an attribute.

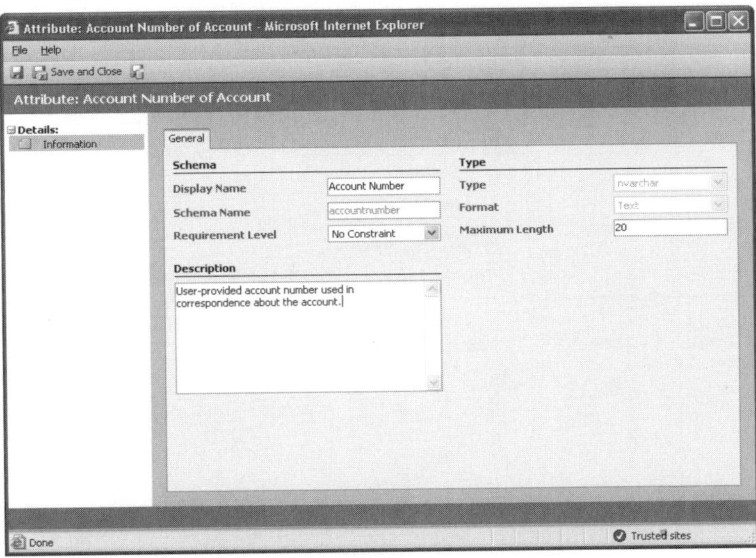

Figure 4-12 Attribute properties for a single attribute

The following attribute properties apply to every attribute:

- **Display name** Sets the text that users see throughout Microsoft CRM, such as on the forms, views, and advanced find feature.
- **Schema name** Displays the metadata schema name. The schema name also correlates to the column name in the underlying SQL Server database.
- **Requirement level** Dictates the type of data validation that Microsoft CRM should enforce when users enter or update data on a form (Business Required, Business Recommended, or No Constraint).
- **Type** Specifies the data type of the attribute. Data types include *integer*, *picklist*, and *bit*, among others.
- **Description** Text that describes the attribute. End users do not see this text, but system customizers can.

Tip When you create a new custom attribute, you might be tempted to skip the description field because it's optional. However, we strongly encourage you to invest an extra 20 to 30 seconds to enter the purpose of this new attribute. This might save you time down the road when you (or someone who takes over the project from you) look at the attribute and wonder, "Why did we add this field?" We suggest that, at a minimum, you enter your name and the date that you created the attribute.

Depending on the data type of the attribute, some attributes include additional properties. Table 4-5 outlines the additional attribute properties and the data types to which they apply.

Table 4-5 Data Type–Specific Attribute Properties

Attribute property	Applicable data types
Format	*nvarchar, int, ntext, datetime*
Maximum Length	*nvarchar, ntext*
List Value	*bit, picklist*
Default Value	*bit, picklist*
Minimum Value	*int, float, money*
Maximum Value	*int, float, money*
Precision	*float, money*

Next, let's review each of these data types in detail to understand how they work within Microsoft CRM.

Data Types

If you've worked with relational databases, you probably already understand data types in great detail, so we'll just review how they relate specifically to Microsoft CRM. If you are not familiar with data types, it's critical for you to develop an understanding of how they work, because data types drastically affect how Microsoft CRM stores, manages, and displays data in the system. For example, Microsoft CRM won't allow users to enter a text value such as *abc* into an attribute with a *money* data type. The attribute data types also determine how Microsoft CRM sorts records and the types of operations that you can perform by using the advanced find feature.

Microsoft CRM uses the following 13 data types to store attribute data:

- *nvarchar* Stores text and numeric data in one field.
- *picklist* Allows you to specify a predefined list of values for the attribute. Users see a drop-down list on the form.
- *bit* Stores data as one of two values: *0* or *1*. In Microsoft CRM, you can relabel the *0* and *1* values so that users see *Yes* and *No*, *True* and *False*, and so on. Many people use the word *Boolean* when referring to *bit* data types.

- *int* Allows you to store only whole numbers, such as *-2*, *-1*, *0*, *1*, and *2*. *Int* is an abbreviation for *integer.*
- *float* Stores numeric values with a configurable number of decimals, such as *1.23* or *3.145*.
- *money* Stores currency amounts.
- *ntext* Stores text and numeric data in one field.
- *datetime* Stores date and time data.
- *status* System data type that stores status information about an entity.
- *state* System data type that stores state information about an entity.
- *primarykey* System data type that stores cross-reference information.
- *owner* System data type that stores the entity's owner.
- *lookup* System data type that stores information about related records.

Microsoft CRM automatically creates and manages the system data types, so you really don't have to worry about too much. However, you should know that they exist, because you will see attributes with system data types listed on every entity.

We'll explain the different data types in more detail later in this chapter when we explain how to add custom attributes to an entity.

Requirement Levels

For every attribute, Microsoft CRM defines a *requirement level.* The requirement level dictates the type of data validation that Microsoft CRM should enforce when users enter or update data on a form. In addition to enforcing data validation, Microsoft CRM automatically formats fields on a form with color codes to indicate the requirement level of the attribute. Table 4-6 explains the three requirement levels and their color coding.

Table 4-6 Requirement Levels

Requirement level	Description	Attribute label formatting on form
Business Required	Users must enter a value for this attribute. If they leave it blank, the system prompts them when they try to save.	Red and bold
Business Recommended	Provides a visual cue to users that your business recommends completion of this field. Users can save the record with no data if necessary. Saving a record with no data in a Business Recommended field does not prompt or warn the user.	Blue and bold
No Constraint	Indicates to users that no constraint exists on the data field.	Black with no special formatting

If you specify an attribute as Business Required, you cannot remove it from the entity form. Likewise, you shouldn't set an attribute as Business Required if it isn't displayed on the form.

Reviewing the Current Schema

Before you start adding or modifying attributes, we recommend that you become familiar with the entity attributes that Microsoft CRM creates upon installation. In other words, you should check the default database schema to determine whether a field already exists in the database before you create a new custom attribute.

> **Warning** Just because you do not see a field on the default forms, do not assume that the field doesn't exist in the database. The default forms contain only some of the attributes for each entity. For example, there are more than 50 Account attributes that do not appear on the default Account form.

Because Microsoft CRM creates up to 15,000 attributes upon installation, we're sure that you're wondering what's the best way to quickly determine which attributes already exist in the system. Microsoft CRM provides two excellent tools to browse the attributes of an entity: the entity editor and the metadata browser.

Entity Editor

To browse the attributes of an entity by using the entity editor, go to the Customization section of Microsoft CRM and click Customize Entities.You'll see a list of all the entities in Microsoft CRM. If you double-click any record, the entity editor appears. Click Attributes to see a list of all the attributes for that entity, as shown in Figure 4-13.

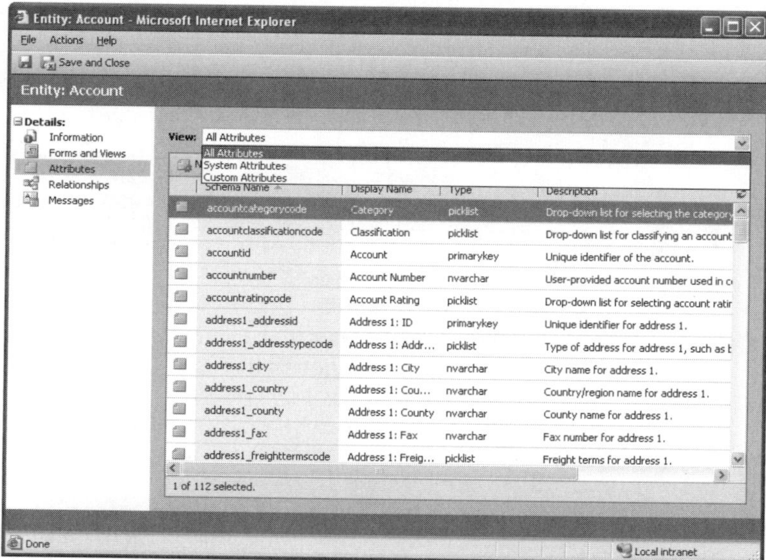

Figure 4-13 Attributes for the Account entity

Before you add a new attribute to an entity, you should review the list of attributes for that entity to make sure that a similar field doesn't already exist. If you want more detail about any one attribute, simply double-click it to open the attribute editor. The attribute editor shows you all of the attribute properties for that attribute, including type, description, schema name, and so on.

Metadata Browser

In addition to the entity editor, you can also use the metadata browser to quickly view all of the attributes for a given entity. To view the metadata browser (as shown in Figure 4-14), use a Web browser to navigate to *http://*<crmserver>*/sdk/list.aspx*, where *<crmserver>* is the name of your server.

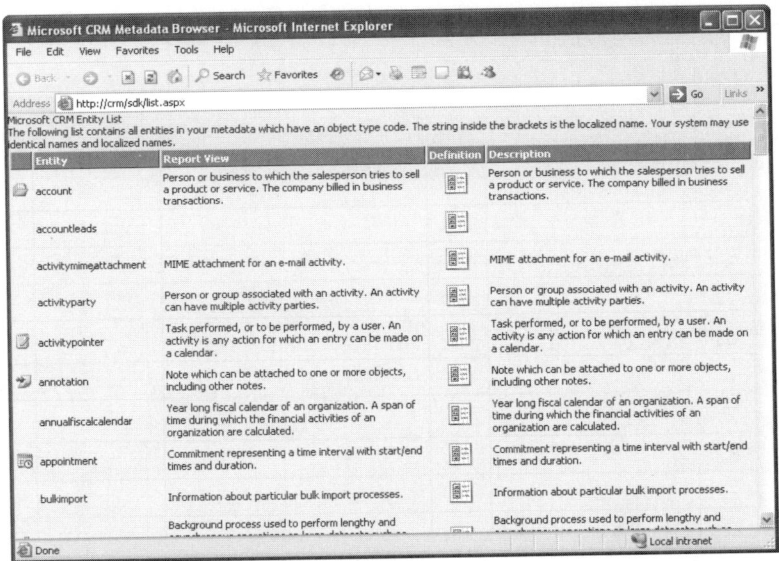

Figure 4-14 Metadata browser

This Web-based metadata browser lists only the entities available through the SDK, so there is not necessarily a one-to-one correlation with the list of entities that you'll see in the Customization section. However, you will find all of the system- customizable and custom entities in the SDK list. If you can't find the entity you're looking for, note that the metadata browser displays the entity schema name instead of the name. For example, the metadata browser displays the Address entity under its schema name of *customeraddress*. To view all of the attributes for an entity, click the icon in the Definition column. The *entity navigator* page for an entity displays all of the attribute and relationship information on one page, as shown in Figure 4-15.

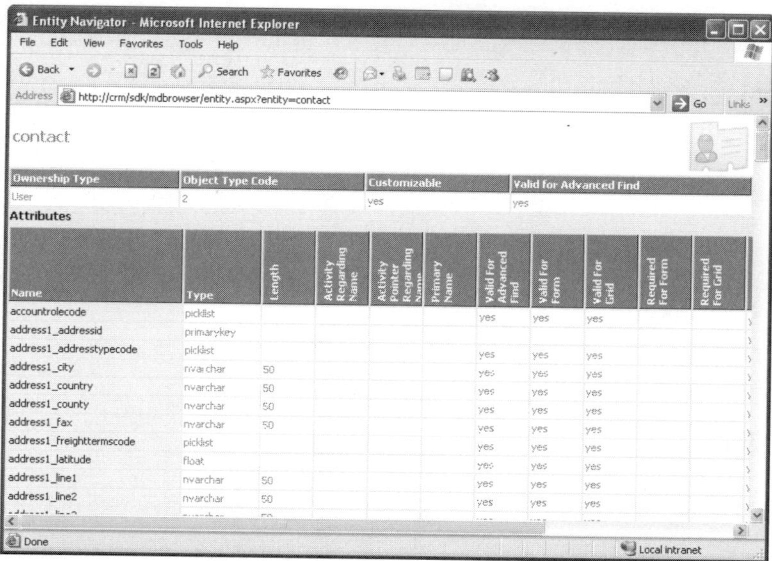

Figure 4-15 Contact entity navigator in the metadata browser

Depending on the type of attribute information you're looking for, this format might be more convenient for you than using the entity editor. We prefer using the metadata browser for several reasons:

- You can view all of the attributes for an entity on one page.
- You can use Internet Explorer to search on the page (by using Ctrl+F) for specific terms that interest you.
- You can easily (and cleanly) copy and paste all of the entity attributes from the definition detail page into a Microsoft Office Excel worksheet if you want to work with them some more.

Although the metadata browser does list all of an entity's attributes, it unfortunately does not display all of the attribute properties. Some of the important attribute properties not shown in the metadata browser include Display Name, Type Format, and Requirement Level.

Caution Because Microsoft CRM stores all of its underlying system data in SQL Server, it is technically possible for you to also view the entity schemas within SQL Enterprise Manager. However, we don't recommend doing this because it creates additional work for you. The entity editor and the metadata browser display the metadata, which automatically consolidates the complex Microsoft CRM data relationships into an easy-to-use format. By viewing the SQL tables directly, you're bypassing the metadata, which means that you have to manually reconstruct where Microsoft CRM stores all of the data, which can be a time-consuming process.

Both the entity editor and the metadata browser give you all of the attributes for an entity, so you simply need to choose the format that you prefer.

Modifying, Adding, and Deleting Attributes

After you've reviewed the entities and you understand their attributes, you're ready to start making some changes. Attribute customizations fall into one of three categories:

- Modifying attributes
- Adding custom attributes
- Deleting attributes

Modifying Attributes

The simplest type of attribute customization you can perform is to modify an existing attribute. When you modify attributes, you actually modify the properties of the attribute. You make changes to the attribute properties in the attribute editor, as shown in Figure 4-16.

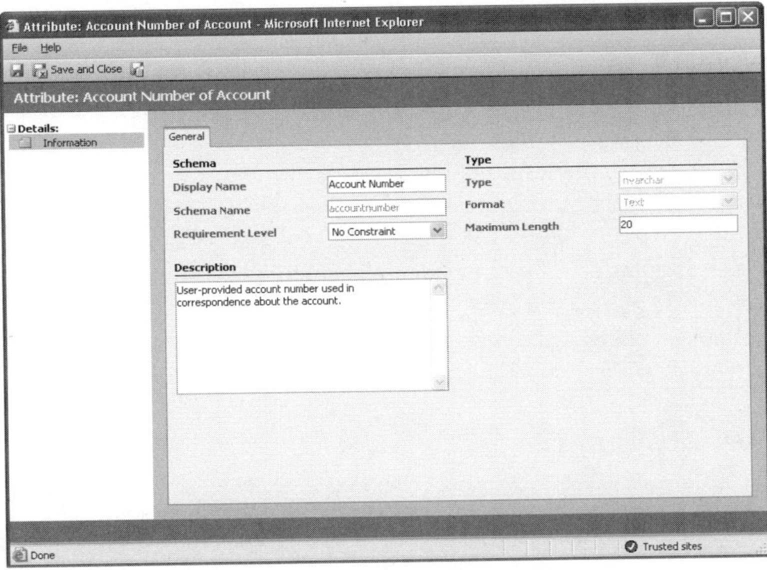

Figure 4-16 Attribute editor for Account Number attribute

To change any one of the attribute properties, simply follow these steps.

Modifying an attribute property

1. Navigate to the entity that you want to customize, and then click **Attributes**.
2. Double-click the attribute that you want to modify. The attribute editor appears.

3. Update a value, and then click **Save**.
4. An "Updating Attribute" message appears. When the message disappears, your change is complete.

As we explained earlier, your users will not see the changes you make until you publish your customizations.

Although Figure 4-16 might not clearly show it, Microsoft CRM shades, or disables, some of the attribute property fields. As you probably expect, the disabled property fields indicate that you cannot edit the attribute properties. You can never edit the schema name or data type for an existing attribute. In addition, Microsoft CRM prevents you from editing attribute properties on the system entities. Of course, these few restrictions help ensure that the software always works correctly and that your system will upgrade smoothly to future releases of Microsoft CRM.

When you're modifying attributes, please take extra care in the following situations:

- **Editing maximum length** Although you can edit the maximum length property for a *nvarchar* or *ntext* attribute, you cannot increase the maximum length value. For example, if the default Microsoft CRM maximum length for an *nvarchar* or *ntext* attribute is 100 characters, you can change the maximum length of that attribute only to a value between 1 and 100; you cannot increase the field length to 200 characters.
- **Deleting *picklist* values** Take extra care when deleting the *picklist* values of existing attributes, because you might permanently lose data. Consider a set of 75 records that uses a custom *picklist*. The *picklist* contains three options: *A*, *B*, and *C* (with 25 records each). If you delete *picklist* value *A*, Microsoft CRM deletes that value from the form so that no new records can select *picklist* value *A*. In addition, Microsoft CRM deletes *picklist* value *A* from the 25 records that used this value. Those records will display a blank *picklist* value when you open them. Fortunately, Microsoft CRM reminds you of this data deletion when you attempt to delete a *picklist*.

Adding Custom Attributes

As you can see, changing the properties of existing attributes really couldn't be any simpler. However, the real customization fun begins when you start adding your own custom attributes. Again, before you add a custom attribute, double check all of the existing attributes for an entity to make sure a similar field doesn't already exist. When you're ready to add a custom attribute, follow these steps.

Adding a custom attribute

1. Go to the **Customization** section of Microsoft CRM and then click **Customize Entities**.
2. Double-click the entity that you want to modify.

3. In the navigation pane, click **Attributes**, and then click **New** in the grid toolbar.
4. Microsoft CRM prompts you to complete the following form.

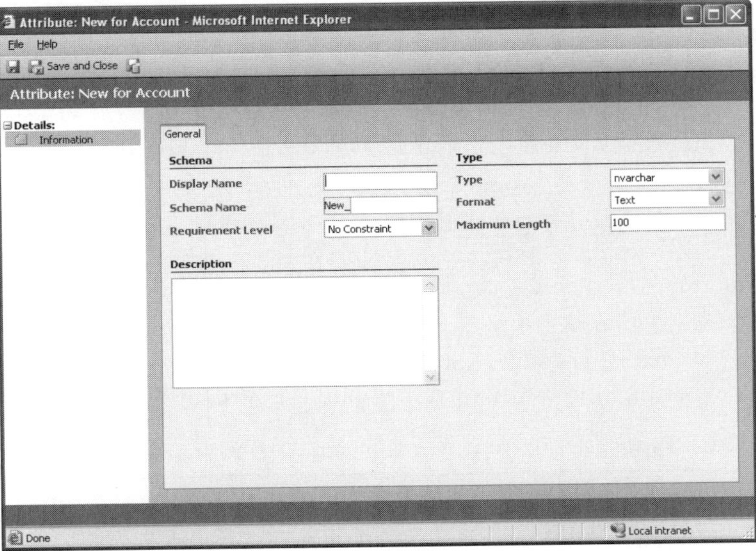

5. Click **Save**.

To create a custom attribute, you must enter the following attribute properties:

- Display name
- Schema name
- Requirement level
- Type
- Description (optional)

We defined each of these properties earlier in this chapter, but now we'll cover the schema name and type in more detail.

Schema Name The schema name represents the name of the attribute in the metadata. Every custom attribute includes a prefix value within the schema name (such as *New_customfield*). Microsoft CRM creates the *New_* default schema prefix. When you're creating a custom attribute, you'll notice that the schema prefix field is read-only, and you can't edit it.

> **Tip** You can change the default schema prefix by navigating to Organization Settings in the Settings section. Click System Settings and then click the Customization tab. The prefix must contain between two and eight alphanumeric characters, and it cannot start with *mscrm*.

When you enter text in the display name field and you lose focus on the field (by pressing the Tab key or clicking elsewhere in the page), Microsoft CRM automatically fills in the rest of the schema name after the prefix. Because the schema name can consist of alphanumeric and underscore characters only, Microsoft CRM removes any inappropriate characters. When you are creating a schema name, keep the following in mind:

1. Your users will never see the schema name.
2. You cannot change the schema name after you create the attribute.
3. Any advanced customizations you create, such as the SDK code, scripting, and reports, will reference the schema name instead of the display name, so save your developers some keystrokes by keeping the name just long enough to describe its function but not so long that it takes forever to type.

Type When creating new attributes, you can choose from one of eight data types, some of which allow you to further specify how Microsoft CRM should format the data. Table 4-7 summarizes the data types and data formatting options available for custom attributes.

Table 4-7 Data Types and Formats for Custom Attributes

Attribute data type	Format	Description
nvarchar	E-mail	Displays text as a clickable mailto: hyperlink.
	Text	Displays text on one line.
	Text area	Displays a multiline text box with scroll bars.
	URL	Displays text as a live hyperlink. Microsoft CRM automatically adds *http://* to whatever the user enters.
	Ticker symbol	Displays text as a live hyperlink that will launch a stock quote request on *http://moneycentral.msn.com*.
picklist	Picklist	Drop-down list control. You can use the additional buttons to add, modify, and delete picklist values. You can also specify a sort order and assign a default picklist value.
bit	Bit	Displays two possible options on the form. You can change *No* and *Yes* to new values such as *True* and *False*, and you can specify the order in which the values appear. You can also specify the default value. On the form editor, you can determine whether you want the text to appear with option buttons, a check box, or a drop-down list.
int	None	Whole numbers only (1, 2, 3, and so on). You can also set a minimum and maximum range for this value.
	Duration	Displays a picklist with 23 predefined duration values ranging from one minute to three days.
	Time zone	Displays a picklist from which users can select one of 75 time zones from around the world.
float	Float	Used to store numeric values with a configurable precision (such as *1.23* or *3.145*). You can also specify a minimum and maximum range.

Table 4-7 Data Types and Formats for Custom Attributes

Attribute data type	Format	Description
money	Money	Used to store currency amounts. You can specify the precision and a minimum and maximum range. If you select this data type, the local currency symbol (for example, $ in the U.S.) appears automatically on the form label.
ntext	None	Displays a multiline text box with scroll bars. You must specify maximum length up to 5,000 characters.
datetime	Date only	Date formatted as MM/DD/YYYY. A calendar control automatically appears on the form.
	Date and time	Date formatted as MM/DD/YYYY HH:MM. A calendar control and time selection drop-down list automatically appear on the form.

Figure 4-17 shows a mockup of how each of these data types would appear to users on the entity form. As you can see, each data type saves and displays information differently, so it's important that you select the appropriate data type for your custom attribute.

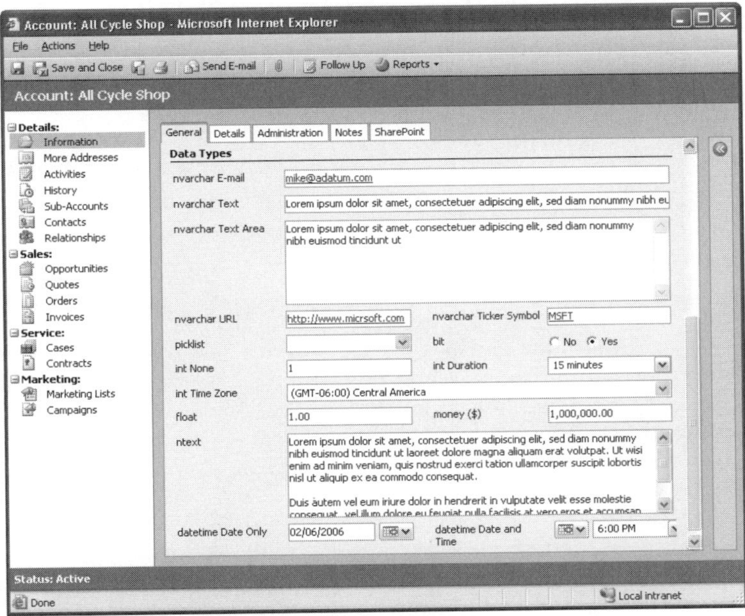

Figure 4-17 How different data types and formats appear on an entity form

> **More Info** Both the *ntext* and *nvarchar* data types store text and numeric data, and both data types format the data on the format by using a text area, so how should you decide which data type to use? For attributes with a length greater than eight characters, the *nvarchar* data type consumes more bytes in SQL Server. However, data stored using the *nvarchar* data type provides better performance than data stored using *ntext*. Therefore, a good rule of thumb is to use the *nvarchar* data type attributes with up to 200 characters and then use *ntext* for attributes with more than 200 characters.

As we explained earlier, you cannot modify the maximum length of the *nvarchar* and *ntext* attributes, so carefully consider the appropriate length of each attribute when you create it.

Attribute Icons When you view a list of attributes for an entity, you can quickly distinguish the custom attributes that you created from the system attributes by looking at the icon in the far left column. Microsoft CRM displays a different icon for custom attributes than for system attributes, as shown in Figure 4-18.

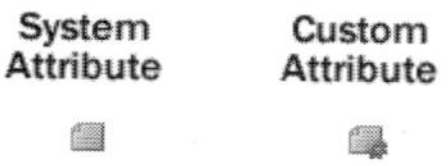

System Attribute | Custom Attribute

Figure 4-18 Custom attribute and system attribute icons

Deleting Attributes

Because it's easy to add to custom attributes, you might find yourself getting a little overzealous and adding more attributes than you need. Of course, you could simply remove any unused attributes from an entity's form, but they will still appear in Advanced Find, SDK, database and filtered views, and so on. If these extra attributes bother you and you decide to delete old or unused custom attributes, you'll find the process very simple.

> **Warning** Deleting a custom attribute also deletes all of the data stored in that field, and you cannot retrieve that data later. Make sure to take the appropriate steps to back up all of your data before deleting an attribute.

Before you delete an attribute, make sure that you remove any existing references to that attribute from Microsoft CRM. To remove references to an attribute, you should remove the attribute from the following:

- The entity's form. Then you can publish the form.
- Any reports that contain the attribute.
- Any filter criteria used in views.
- Any script or code references.

Fortunately, Microsoft CRM does most of the hard work for you by automatically checking all the forms and views in the system. If you miss a reference of an attribute you're trying to delete, you'll see an error message like the one shown in Figure 4-19.

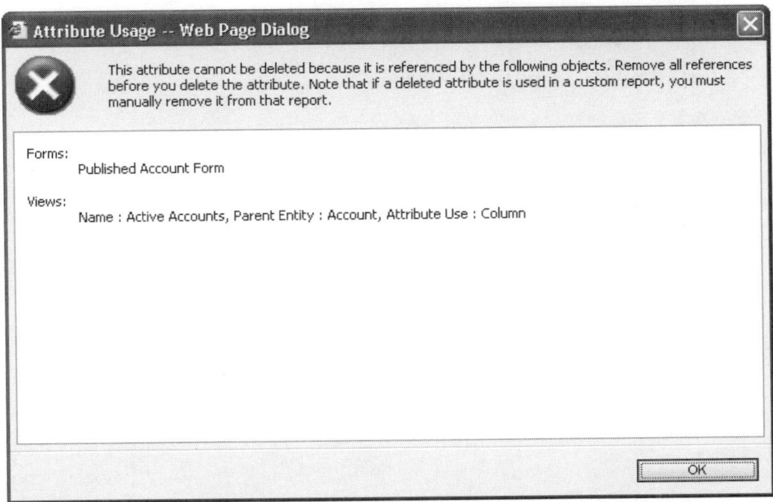

Figure 4-19 Error message shown when you attempt to delete a referenced attribute

Even though Microsoft CRM checks the forms and views for references to deleted attributes, you're on your own to scrub the reports and code to remove any references to the deleted attribute.

After you're certain that you removed all references to the attribute, you can delete the attribute by following these steps.

Deleting a custom attribute

1. Go to the **Customization** section of Microsoft CRM, and then click **Customize Entities**.
2. Double-click the entity of the attribute that you want to delete.
3. Click **Attributes**, and then select the custom attribute to remove.
4. In the grid toolbar, click **Delete**.
5. A warning appears that says, "Deleting this attribute will result in loss of all data stored in it. Continue with the deletion of the attribute?" Click **OK**.

Attributes and Closing Dialogs

Closing dialogs present a special case you need to consider when you're customizing entity attributes. A *closing dialog* is a dialog box that appears when a user takes one of the following actions:

- Closes an activity such as Task or Phone Call

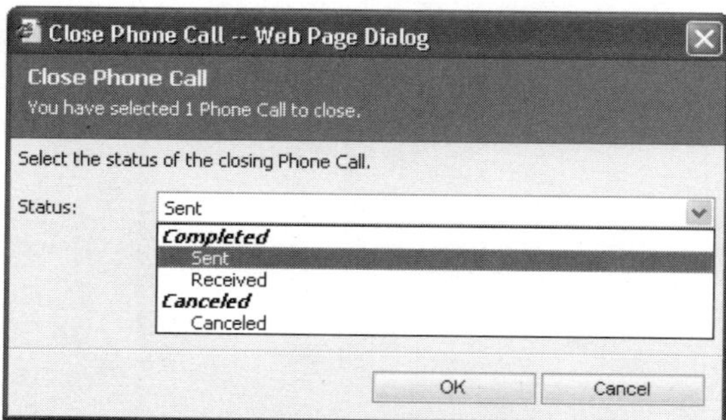

- Converts a Lead

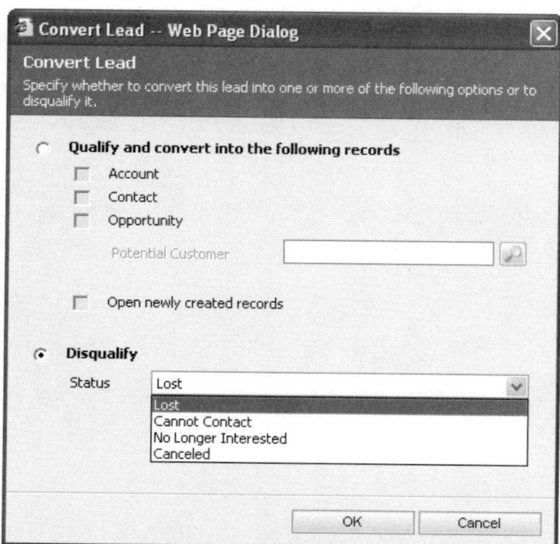

- Closes an Opportunity

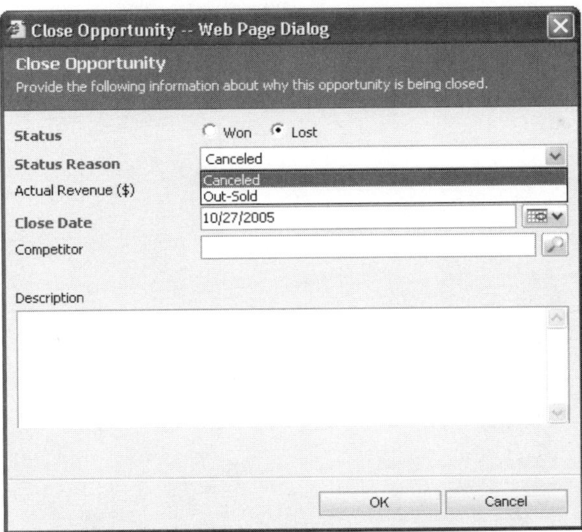

- Resolves a Case

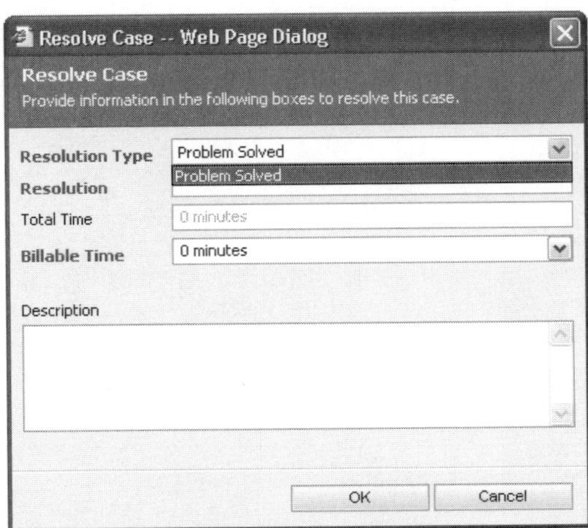

- Converts a Campaign Response

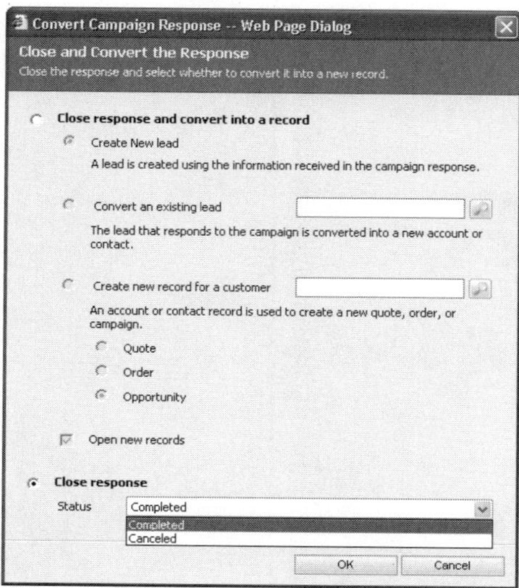

When a user initiates one of these actions, a closing dialog prompts the user to specify how he or she wants to close the entity. It might not be obvious where you should customize the closing dialog picklist values because these closing dialogs aren't entity forms; however, they do display attributes of the entity. To edit the closing dialog picklist values, you must modify the *statuscode* attribute (Status Reason display name) of the entity you're closing. We'll quickly show you how to edit the closing dialog values for the Phone Call entity, and then you can apply the same concept and process to the other closing dialogs referenced in the preceding list.

Important For entities that users can close in Microsoft CRM (such as the Phone Call), the *statuscode* attribute behaves a little differently than a standard picklist attribute. In these examples, you can specify different picklist values for each *statecode* value (Activity Status display name) where most picklists contain only one range of values. You can specify different statuscode picklist values for each of the three *statuscode* values: Open, Completed, and Canceled.

Editing the Phone Call closing dialog values

When you close activities such as Tasks and Phone Calls, a closing dialog appears in which the user determines whether he wants to mark the activity Completed or Canceled. The following procedure explains how to customize those picklist values.

1. Go to the **Customization** section of Microsoft CRM, and then click **Customize Entities**.
2. Double-click the **Phone Call** entity.

3. In the navigation pane, click **Attributes**, and then double-click the **statuscode** schema name. The attribute editor appears.

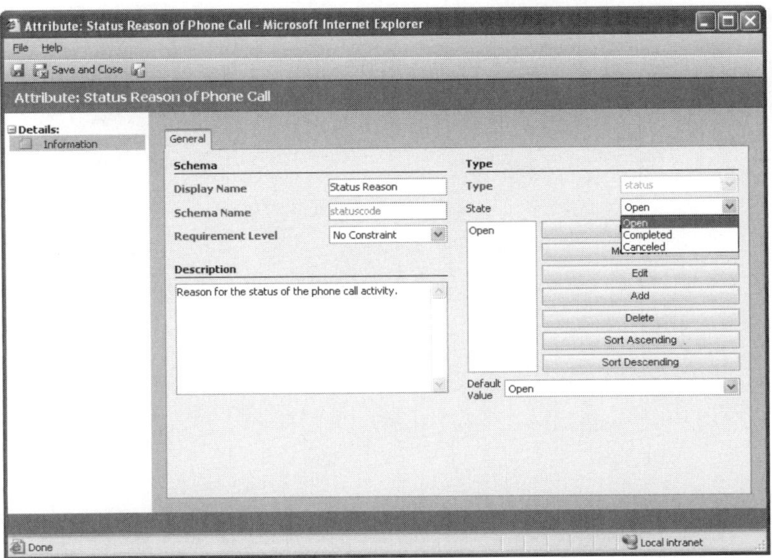

4. In the **State** list, select **Completed**. The picklist values change from the Open value (*Open*) to the Completed values (*Sent*, *Received*).

5. Click **Add**, and then in the **Label** field, type **Left Message**. Click **OK**.

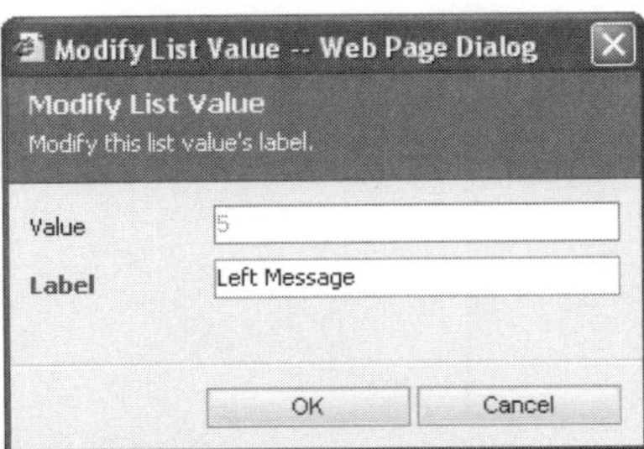

6. In the **State** list, click **Canceled**. Then click **Add**, and in the **Label** field, type **Wrong Number**. Click **OK**. You will see that the *Wrong Number* picklist value is added under the *Canceled* value.

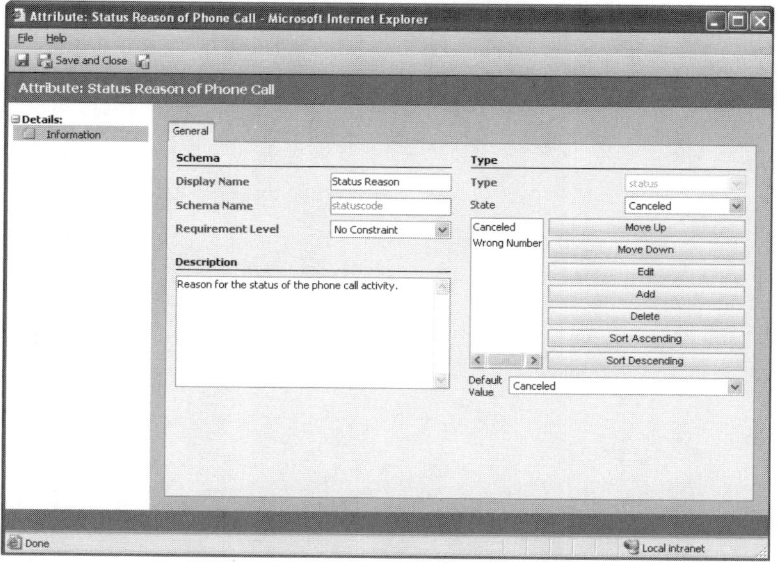

7. In the attribute editor toolbar, click **Save and Close**.
8. In the Phone Call entity editor menu bar, click **Actions**, and then click **Publish**.
9. Now when your users close a Phone Call activity, they will see the following closing dialog that incoporates your new customizations.

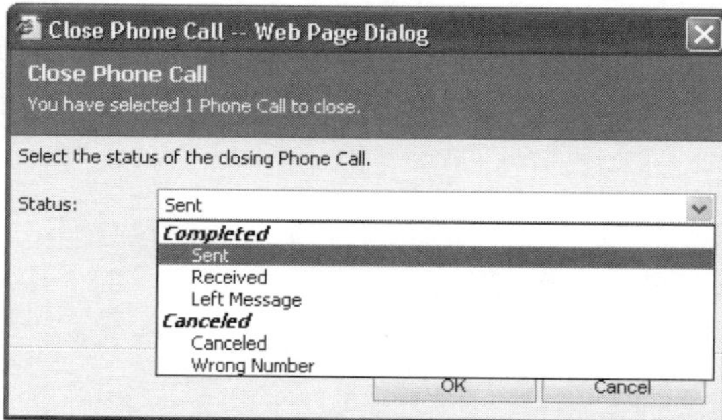

> **Important** If users click the Save As Completed button on the entity toolbar, they will not see the closing dialog. In this case, Microsoft CRM uses the picklist value that you specify as the default value of the Completed state. Because most users will probably click the Save As Completed button, make sure you choose the default value that you want.

Summary

In this chapter, we explained the concepts, terminology, and processes related to customizing entities. Microsoft CRM stores data as entities, and each entity possesses multiple attributes that define its characteristics. The software uses three different types of entities: system customizable, system non-customizable, and custom. Every entity consists of multiple attributes, and Microsoft CRM supports two different types of attributes: system and custom. Only users with the correct security permissions, such as users with the System Administrator or System Customizer security roles, can perform customizations. After you complete your updates, you deploy your customizations to your users by a publishing process. If you need to copy your customizations from one system to another, Microsoft CRM allows you to export your customizations to an XML file that can be imported into a different system. Microsoft CRM also allows you to easily rename the default system entities to terms that better fit your business.

After explaining the basic customization concepts, we explored the details related to entity attributes. Each entity attribute consists of common properties (such as display name and schema name), in addition to properties unique to the data type of the attribute. You can modify existing attributes, in addition to creating or deleting new custom attributes.

Chapter 5

Entity Customization: Forms and Views

In this chapter:

In Chapter 4, "Entity Customization: Concepts and Attributes," you learned the concepts and processes related to customizing entities in Microsoft Dynamics CRM. In this chapter, we'll go deeper into entity customization with detailed explanations of forms, activities, and views.

Customizing Forms

You already know that when a user opens a record, Microsoft CRM displays the form for that record's entity. In addition, Microsoft CRM will display a record's form whenever a user clicks the Information link in the navigation pane, as shown in Figure 5-1.

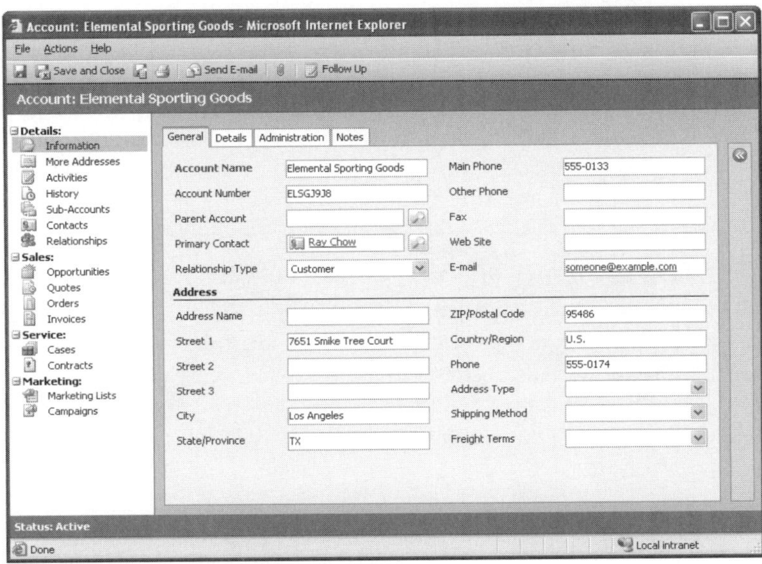

Figure 5-1 The Information link displays an entity's form

Most of the system entities use a form, but some of the non-customizable system entities, such as Case Resolution and Organization, don't use a form because users don't view or update these records directly. There are also a few customizable system entities that don't use a form either, such as:

- Contract Template
- Customer Relationship
- Discount
- Discount List
- E-mail Template
- Opportunity Relationship
- Price List
- Price List Item
- Resource Group
- Team
- Territory
- Unit
- Unit Group

Microsoft CRM uses one unique form per entity, so when you customize an entity's form keep in mind that all users will see the same form. For example, you cannot create one form that displays certain fields for sales users, and then create a second form that displays a different set of fields for customer service users.

Tip One workaround for varying the form by user is to leverage the form *onLoad* event to dynamically hide or disable fields or tabs on a form based on the role of the user viewing a form. See Chapter 10, "Client-Side SDK," for more information on using the form *onLoad* event.

When you view the default Microsoft CRM entity forms, you will notice that most of data fields displayed on the form are just attributes of the entity. Of course, you probably will want to customize the default form layouts to add more than just attributes to meet the requests of your users. Microsoft CRM allows you to customize the following areas of each form:

- Fields
- Field event scripts
- Tabs

- Sections
- IFrames
- Form event scripts
- Form design and layout

In this chapter, we'll explain all of the details related to configuring each of these areas of the form. Form customization follows the same process that you learned in Chapter 4 for attribute customization. After you set up the form exactly how you want it in the Customize Entities section, you must publish the entities you customized before users can see your changes. In addition, you must have the appropriate security permissions to edit forms and publish entities.

To access the entity form editor, follow these steps:

Accessing the Form Editor

1. Go to the **Customization** section of Microsoft CRM and click **Customize Entities**.
2. Double-click the entity that you want to edit to open the entity editor.
3. Click **Forms and Views**.
4. Double-click **Form** to open the form editor.

You will perform all form customizations within the form editor. Figure 5-2 shows the form editor user interface, using the Account form as an example.

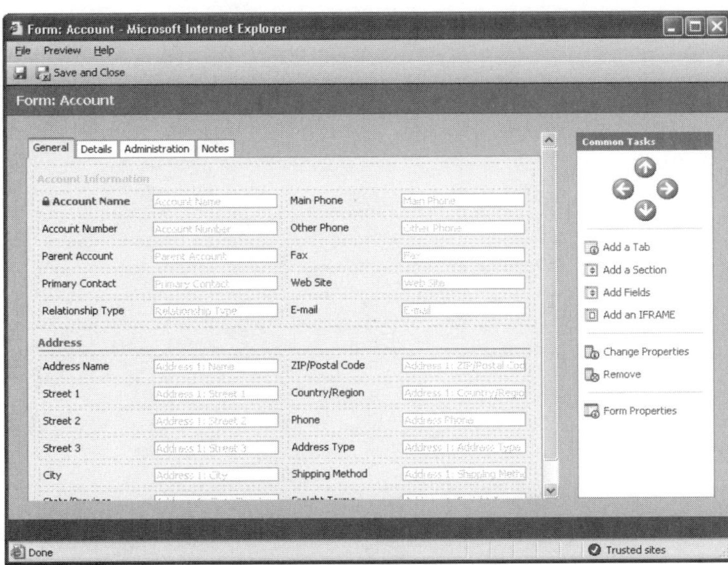

Figure 5-2 Form editor user interface

Forms consist of four components:

- **Tabs** *Tabs* allow you to group and organize the data fields for an entity. The default tabs for an entity typically include General, Details, Administration, and Notes.
- **Sections** On each tab, you can group information into *sections*. For each section, you can specify a section name and decide whether you want to display the section name and a divider on the form. In Figure 5-2, Account Information and Address are sections on the form. Note that Account Information is grayed out indicating that the section name will not display on the form.
- **Fields** *Fields* display the actual data related to an entity. Almost all of the fields on a form are attributes of the entity.
- **IFrames** Microsoft CRM allows you to display an *IFrame* (also known as an *inline frame*) on the form of an entity. You can think of an IFrame as a "window" within the form that allows you to display a different Web page inside the window frame. We'll explain IFrames in more detail and give examples later in this chapter.

In the form editor, you'll notice that dotted lines encapsulate the different areas of the form. These dotted lines indicate the sections, fields, and IFrames. Obviously, the default form for each entity appears a little differently because each entity contains unique attributes. However, all of the entity form editors use these two tools:

- Common Tasks
- Preview

As Figure 5-2 shows, you'll see the Common Tasks tools in the right column of the form editor. You can access the Preview tool from the form editor menu bar. In the following sections, we'll explain how to use both of these tools when you're editing a form. After you understand what the form editor tools do, we will go into greater detail about how to use these tools to set up and configure the following data related to a form:

- Form properties
- Sections
- Fields
- IFrames

Common Tasks

You will use the Common Tasks tools to edit everything on the form, including data fields, event scripts, and form layout. The Common Tasks tools consist of the following:

- **Directional arrows** Four green arrows allow you to move the form components around on the form. The arrows can move fields, sections, tabs, and IFrames. To move a field, section, or IFrame, select it on the form; the dotted line around the area is then highlighted in green. Then click an arrow to move the highlighted item to a new position. To move a tab, select it on the form, and then click an arrow to move it.
- **Add a Tab** The Add a Tab tool allows you to add a new tab to the form. Microsoft CRM adds the new tab to the right of existing tabs. Note that you can add a maximum of eight tabs.
- **Add a Section** This tool allows you to add a new section to a form. Microsoft CRM always adds the new section below the last section on the currently selected tab.
- **Add Fields** The Add Fields tool allows you to select new fields to add to the form. When you click Add Fields, the dialog box only displays fields not already on the form, so if you don't see the field that you're looking for, it's probably already on the form somewhere. If you want to add a field to a specific section, select the section to highlight it, and then click Add Fields.
- **Add an IFrame** This tool allows you to add an IFrame to the form.
- **Change Properties** This tool allows you change the properties of a form component, including tabs, sections, fields, and IFrames. You can also open the Change Properties dialog box by double-clicking a component in the form editor.
- **Remove** This tool allows you to remove a component (including tabs, sections, fields, and IFrames) from the form.
- **Form Properties** This tool allows you to specify scripts to run when Microsoft CRM triggers form events.

You'll use the Common Tasks tools to layout and design almost all of the information that appears on an entity's form. At first it might seem like a lot to learn, but the tools are very intuitive and straightforward, so we're sure you'll learn to use these Common Tasks tools quickly.

Form Preview

When you're done manipulating your form and you have everything where you want it, you can use the convenient form preview tool to evaluate how the form will appear to users before you publish it. Microsoft CRM offers the following three types of form previews:

- **Create Form** Simulates how the form will appear and behave when users create a new record for the entity.
- **Update Form** Simulates how the form will appear and behave when users edit an existing record.
- **Read-Only Form** Shows how the form will appear to users who do not have permissions to edit a record.

The form preview feature does more than just show you the form layout–you can also test any custom scripts that you added to the form. Microsoft CRM offers you three different events for which you can create custom scripts:

- *onLoad* form event
- *onSave* form event
- *onChange* field event

Obviously, being able to test and debug your event scripts using the preview tool will save you time. When you launch the form preview, Microsoft CRM will fire the *onLoad* event which you can use to trigger your custom script. Because the preview doesn't actually save a record, you can use the Simulate Form Save button in the form preview menu bar to triggers the *onSave* form event. You can also fire the *onChange* field event by changing the field focus (by pressing the Tab key to leave a field or by clicking a different field).

Note Sometimes the Microsoft CRM user interface uses different casing for these events, such as *OnLoad* instead of *onLoad*. This book will use the following casing: is *onLoad*, *onSave*, and *onChange*.

We'll explain adding custom scripts to events later in this chapter, and we provide numerous code examples that use these form and field events in Chapter 10.

Form Properties

The Form Properties tool in Common Tasks allows you to add custom scripts to the form's *onLoad* and *onSave* events. The Form Properties dialog box contains two tabs (shown in Figure 5-3):

- **Events** You can add custom scripts to a form that run when Microsoft CRM triggers the *onLoad* or *onSave* event. When you add custom scripts to the form, Microsoft CRM allows you to manually specify which fields those scripts reference (on the Dependencies tab of the event). By indicating the script-dependent fields, Microsoft CRM will prevent other system customizers from removing a field from the form that a script uses. If you don't specify dependent fields and a user unknowingly removes a script-dependent field from a form, the script will fail.

- **Non-Event Dependencies** If you are also using additional external (non-event) scripts, you can manually specify these fields as dependent.

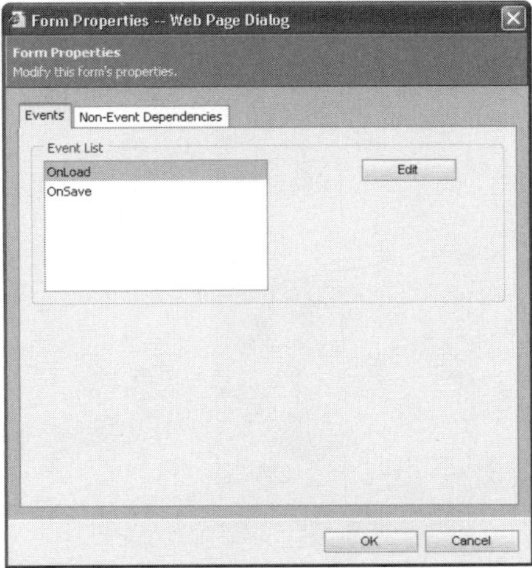

Figure 5-3 The Form Properties page

As we just explained, if you try to remove a field from a form that you specified as dependent (either on an event or a non-event), Microsoft CRM denies your request and displays an error message similar to the one shown in Figure 5-4.

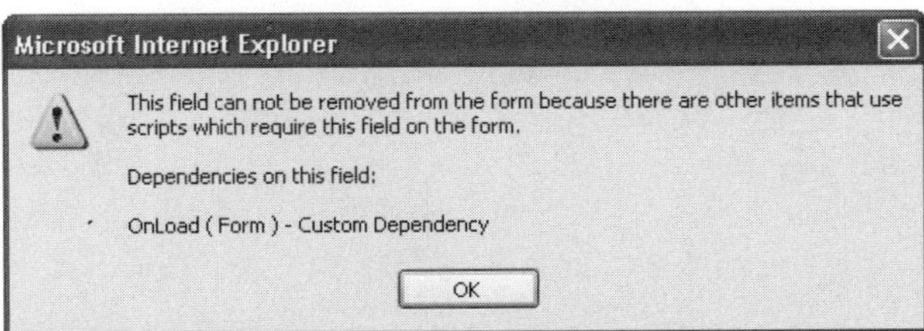

Figure 5-4 Error message displayed when a user tries to remove a dependent field from a form

> **Tip** Microsoft CRM doesn't force you to specify dependent fields, but taking a little extra time to complete this step might save you a headache later. Therefore, we recommend that you always specify script-dependent fields.

Now that you understand how to add scripts by using the Form Properties page, let's walk through a few simple examples to illustrate how and why you might want to use the *onLoad* and *onSave* events.

When users create a new task in Microsoft CRM, the default form appears like the one shown in Figure 5-5.

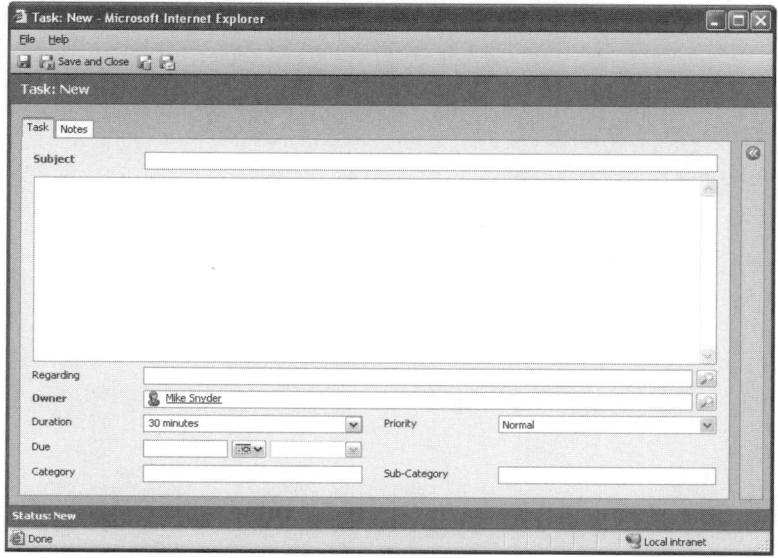

Figure 5-5 Default form for a new task

Because this form in Microsoft CRM 3.0 did not change much from Microsoft CRM version 1.2, we know that customers frequently want to make the following changes to the form:

- Change the default duration from 30 minutes to blank.
- Automatically populate today's date in the Due Date field.

These two changes might seem simple at first, but digging deeper into the details of these fields reveals some issues. Because the Duration field looks like a picklist field, you might expect to be able to simply change the default value by editing the *Duration* attribute of the Task entity. However, even though the Duration field appears to be a picklist, it is actually a special integer field used on a variety of picklist fields in Microsoft CRM. For these special fields, you cannot set a default value (or add picklist values) like you can for normal picklist fields.

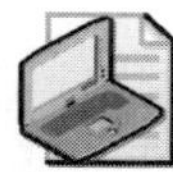

> **Note** The Duration picklists used on activity forms such as Task and Phone Call behave differently than a normal picklist because users can dynamically enter their own values on the form instead of having to select from predefined values like a regular picklist field.

In regards to the Due Date field, you learned in Chapter 4 that *datetime* attribute data types do not have a default value. Because the Due Date field uses the *datetime* data type, we can't use the attribute editor to specify today's date as the default value in the Due Date field. Hence, we now have two issues to solve regarding the customer requests.

Despite the two problems we just outlined, we can easily meet the customer's needs by leveraging the *onLoad* event of the task entity's form. To do this, we will add a simple script to the form's *onLoad* event, and Microsoft CRM will run our script every time a user opens the task form. When our script runs, it will programmatically change the value of the Duration and Due Date fields to the values that we specify. The last issue that we need to address with our script is to make sure that we change the Duration and Due Date values only when users create a *new* task. Obviously, we wouldn't want to change the Due Date and Duration values when a user opened a previously created task. When we're done, every time a user creates a new task, our script will set the Duration field to blank and the current date as the due date.

Now we'll describe how you would set up, test, and deploy this code.

Using the form's *onLoad* event to pre-fill Task Duration and Due Date

1. Go to the **Customization** section of Microsoft CRM and click **Customize Entities**. Double-click the Task entity to open the entity editor.
2. Click **Forms and Views**, and then double-click **Form** to open the form editor for the Task entity.
3. Click **Form Properties**. On this page, you can choose to add a script to the form's *onLoad* or *onSave* event.

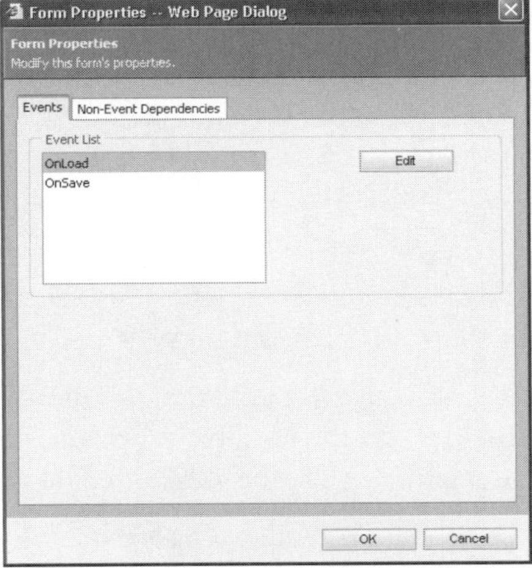

4. As we mentioned previously, we want to use the *onLoad* event so that the script runs when users open a form.

5. Select **OnLoad**, and then click **Edit** to open the **Event Detail Properties** page. On this page, enter the following code:

```
var CRM_FORM_TYPE_CREATE = 1;
var CRM_FORM_TYPE_UPDATE = 2;

switch (crmForm.FormType)
{
        case CRM_FORM_TYPE_CREATE:
                crmForm.all.actualdurationminutes.DataValue = null;
                crmForm.all.scheduledend.DataValue = new Date();
                break;

        case CRM_FORM_TYPE_UPDATE:
                // do nothing
                break;
}
```

6. Now let's quickly review how this JavaScript code will programmatically set the values on the form. This code sets the *actualdurationminutes* field (the schema name for Duration) to *null*, which means blank. It also sets the *scheduledend* field (the schema name for Due Date) to the current date by using the JavaScript *Date( )* function. The *onLoad* event will run this script every time a user opens a form, but remember that we want to set the default values only when users create a *new* task. Therefore, this code includes a *switch* statement so that our script runs only for the form type of 1. Microsoft CRM assigns a form type value to each form (1: Create, 2: Update, 3: Read Only, and so on) so that you can tie this information into your scripts, as we did in this example. In this script, a form type of 2 indicates an Update form, so that the script won't alter the Due Date or Duration field values.

7. After you enter the code, select the **Event is enabled** check box. This check box indicates whether Microsoft CRM should run your script when it fires the *onLoad* event.

8. To set up the dependencies related to our code to ensure that no one accidentally removes the **Duration** or **Due Date** fields from the task form (because our script would generate an error if those fields were missing), click the **Dependencies** tab.

9. The **Available fields** list displays all of the fields that appear on the task form. To make **Due Date** and **Duration** dependent fields, select those values in the left column, and then click the >> button to move them into the **Dependent Fields** list.

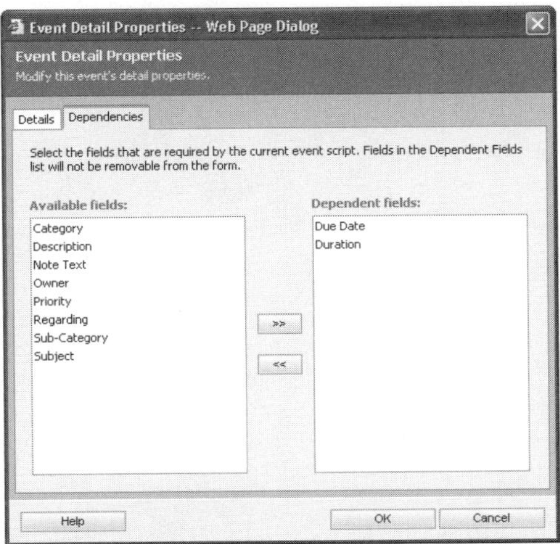

10. Click **OK**.
11. Click **OK** again to return to the task form editor.
12. Before you try to preview this script, save the changes you made by clicking **Save**.
13. To test the script on the create form, click **Preview**, and then click **Create Form**. The form should appear as shown here.

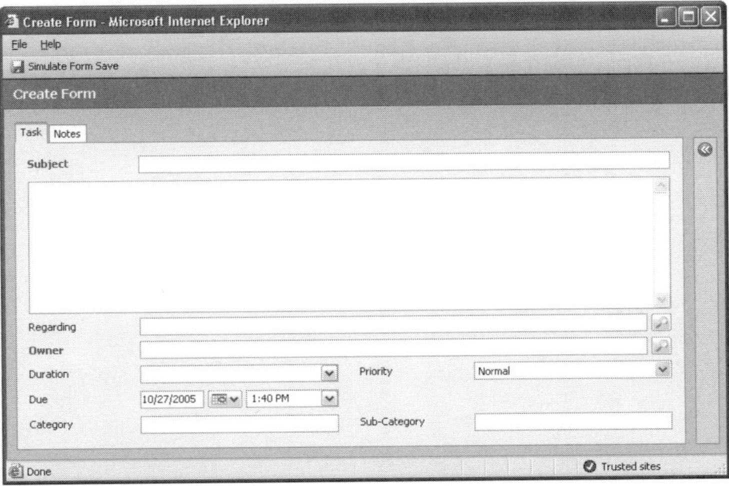

14. You'll see that the **Duration** drop-down list is blank, and the **Due Date** field displays today's date and time. You might need to resize the preview window to make it large enough to display all of the fields correctly.

15. If you test the script on the update form (click **Preview**, and then click **Update Form**), you'll see that the **Due Date** field does not default to today's date as we expect. However, you might notice that the **Duration** field appears blank. When you use the Update Form preview, Microsoft CRM shows you an update of a blank record, so it will always show picklists as blank. The script ran correctly, but the fact that Microsoft CRM shows an update of a blank record might cause some little nuances with the form previews..

16. To publish the task entity, return to the entity editor. Click **Actions**, and then click **Publish** on the top toolbar. That's it, you're done!

This example showed you how to tap into the form's *onLoad* event to manipulate field values before users see the form. Even if you didn't understand the syntax of this code example, you should understand the concepts of customizing your forms by adding custom scripts that tie into Microsoft CRM form events. Figure 5-6 is a flow chart that shows how Microsoft CRM processed the code in our example.

Of course, this example shows a very simple tweak to the Task form, but you can get creative with your own custom code. Chapter 10 goes into more detail on writing code that ties into events and shows you more examples of how you can customize your forms.

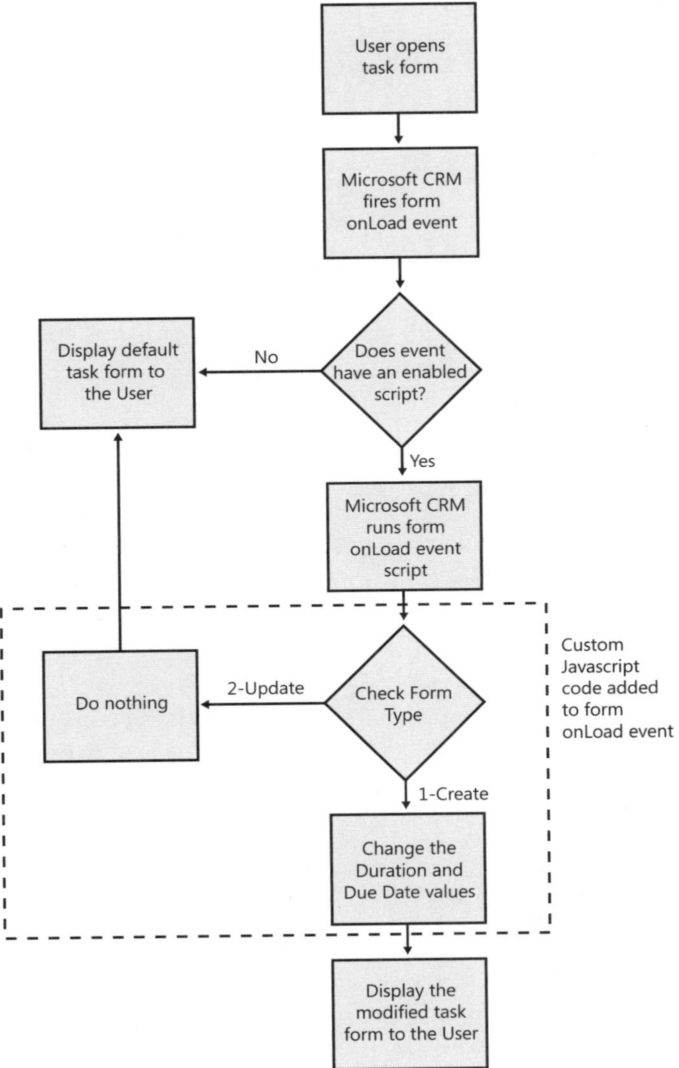

Figure 5-6 Form *onLoad* event flowchart for Task example

Sections

Form sections allow you to group together and organize multiple data fields in a manner that makes the most sense for your users. Every field you add to a form must belong to a section, and you can have as many sections as you need on a form. Each section contains multiple properties:

- **Name** The name of the section. It must be unique for each entity.
- **Label** Specifies whether you want the section name to appear to users on the form. You can also specify whether you want to display a divider line under the section name on the form.
- **Location** Specifies which tab on the form the section should appear on.
- **Layout** Specifies the formatting layout of the fields in the section. After you create a section, you cannot change its layout. You can access the section's layout on the formatting tab when you view a section's properties.

Working with sections is a pretty straightforward process, and only the layout properties require a more detailed explanation.

When you add a new section, you have the option to specify its layout. Microsoft CRM allows you to choose from one of two mutually exclusive section layouts:

- **Variable Field Width** This layout displays all of the fields in the section in two columns. However, you can specify that specific fields (on a field-by-field basis) in the section span the width of both columns on the form.

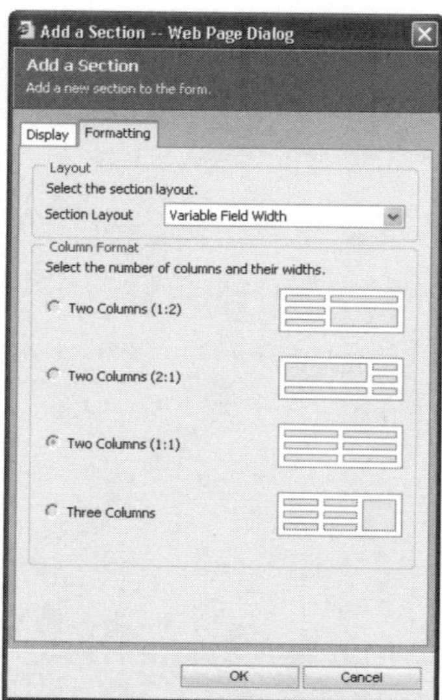

The Variable Field Width layout also allows you to use the auto-expand feature on text area fields (explained in the section titled "Fields," later in this chapter). Microsoft CRM defaults to Variable Field Width for new sections.

- **Variable Field Height** A Variable Field Height section layout gives you the option to specify how the columns and widths should display in a section. You can choose from one of four column formats.

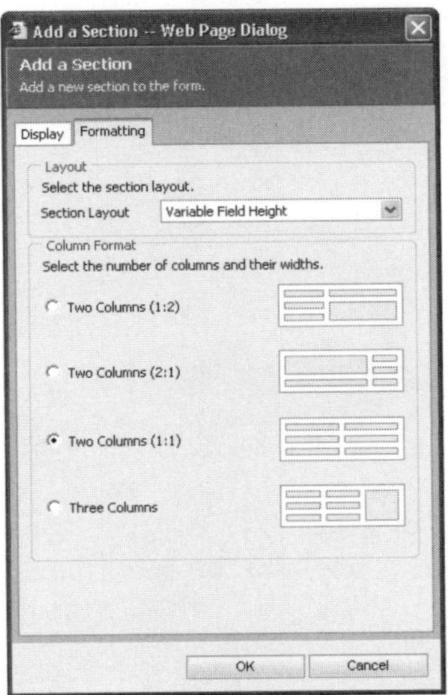

When you select one of these formats, the number of columns in that section remains fixed. So, unlike a Variable Field Width section, you cannot configure a field to span the width of multiple columns. Another way to think of Variable Field Height layout is as a *fixed width* section. All of the fields in a Variable Field Height section will have the width that you specify when you create the section (1:2, 2:1, 1:1, or 3). However, the Variable Field Height layout allows you to include text areas in a column and change the height of the column to meet your needs.

All of the default Microsoft CRM 3.0 forms (and all of the forms in Microsoft CRM version 1.2) use the Variable Field Width layout exclusively. We created a sample section layout that uses the Variable Field Height to illustrate one potential design (Figure 5-7).

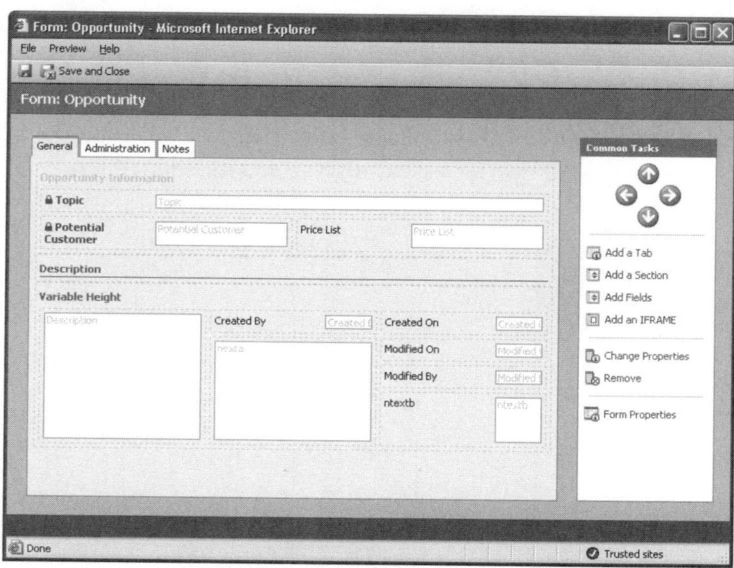

Figure 5-7 Sample form using the Variable Field Height section layout

Another caveat regarding the Variable Field Height section layout is that you can only change the height of text area fields. You cannot change the height of the other data type fields, such as *integer*, *money*, *bit*, or *datetime*.

> **Tip** After you create a section, you cannot change the layout later. If you need to change the section's layout, simply remove the fields from the section and delete it. You can then create a new section with the new desired layout and add all of the fields to the new section.

Fields

Similar to sections, you can add, modify, remove, and change the properties of a field by using the Common Tasks tools. For each field on a form, you can set the following properties related to that field (shown on the tabs in Figure 5-8):

- Display
- Formatting
- Schema
- Events

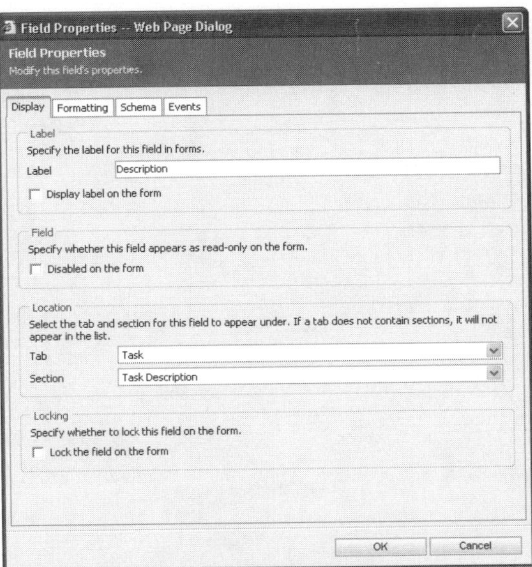

Figure 5-8 The Field Properties page

Display

You can adjust the following display settings for each field:

- **Label** Use this section to set the text that appears on the form to the left of the field. You can hide the field label by unchecking the Display label On the form check box.
- **Field** Selecting the Disabled on the form check box makes the field read-only on the form. This means that users can read the value of the field, but they cannot change it.
- **Location** Use this section to specify the tab and section where the field should appear on the form.
- **Locking** Selecting the check box in this section prevents users (including yourself) from removing the field from the form. A lock icon appears in the form editor next to the field label of a locked field. Of course, a user with customization privileges to customize a form could simply unlock a locked field and then remove it. Therefore, locking a field isn't foolproof, but it should indicate to others that it shouldn't be removed from the form.

Formatting

On the Formatting tab, you can set up additional formatting properties. For a field in a section that uses the Variable Fixed Width layout, you can use the Layout section to toggle between the one-column and two-column displays. If this section is disabled, the field is in a section that uses the Variable Fixed Height layout.

***Bit* Data Types** For fields of the *bit* data type, you can specify the formatting of the data field on the form. By default, Microsoft CRM displays bit options such as yes/no and true/false with two radio (option) buttons. However, you can change this formatting to a check box or drop-down list if you like (see Figure 5-9).

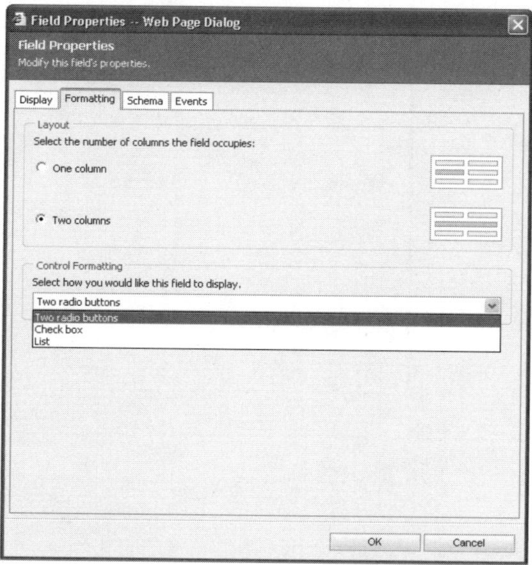

Figure 5-9 Control formatting for *bit* data type fields

***Ntext* and *nvarchar* (text) Data Types** For fields of the *ntext* and *nvarchar* data type, you can also configure the row layout to change the number of rows of the text area to display on the form (see Figure 5-10).

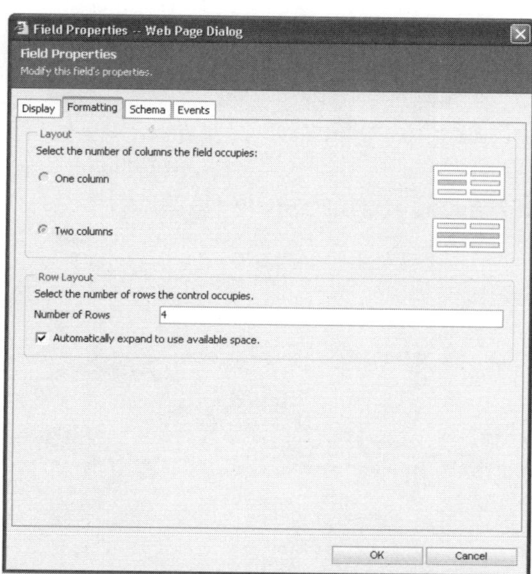

Figure 5-10 Row layout formatting for *ntext* and *nvarchar* (text) data types

For fields within a Variable Fixed Width section only, you can also specify whether the field should automatically expand to use available space. If you select this check box, the form will override the number of rows you specified and expand to include more rows if they will fit in the window. You can use this auto-expand feature on only one field per tab. Figure 5-11 shows two different forms and the benefit of using the auto-expand feature.

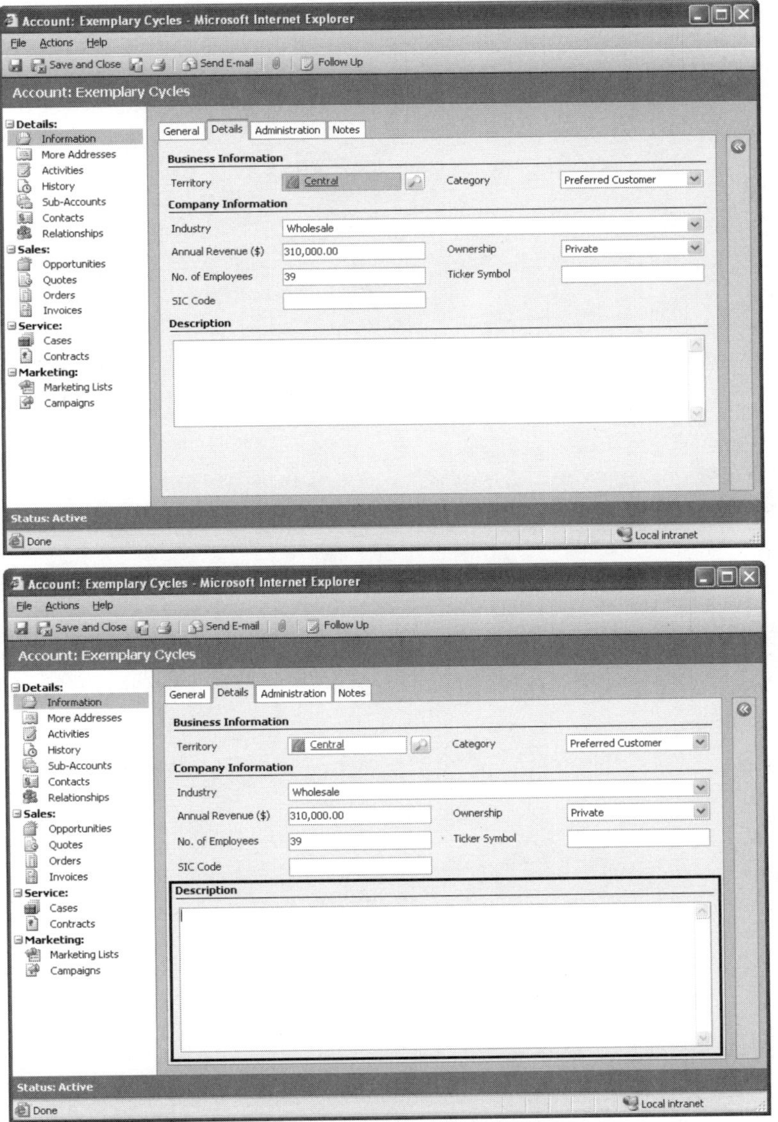

Figure 5-11 Comparing an auto-expand text area with a fixed height text area

As you can see in the figure, the form that uses the auto-expand feature provides the user with more space to enter and view information in the Description field. Therefore, we recommend using the auto-expand option wherever possible.

Schema

The Schema tab displays the schema information for the attribute, including the display name, schema name, and description. To edit the display name and description information, you must update these values using the attribute editor for the entity, as explained in Chapter 4.

Events

As we covered earlier in this chapter, you can include custom scripts that Microsoft CRM triggers on the field's *onChange* event. Let's set up a simple example of an *onChange* event to illustrate how you might use this feature. Many businesses assign a unique account number to each of their customers, and our example customer would like every account number to contain eight digits. Creating a custom *onChange* script that runs on the Account Number field would be a good way to remind users that every account number should be eight digits in length.

Using the field's *onChange* event to enforce account number length

1. Go to the **Customization** section of Microsoft CRM and click **Customize Entities**. Double-click the Account entity to open the entity editor.
2. Click **Forms and Views**, and then double-click **Form** to open the form editor for the account entity.
3. Double-click the **Account Number** field on the form to open the **Field Properties** page. Click the **Events** tab.
4. Select **onChange**, and then click **Edit** to open the **Event Detail Properties** dialog box. Enter the following code:

```
var oField = event.srcElement;

if (typeof(oField) != "undefined" && oField != null)
{
   if (oField.DataValue.length != 8)
         alert("Account Number should be 8 characters.");
}
```

5. Select the **Event is enabled** check box to tell Microsoft CRM to run this script when the field's *onChange* event fires.
6. To add **Account Number** as a dependent field so that our script always runs properly, click the **Dependencies** tab, select **Account Number**, and click the >> button. **Account Number** moves to the **Dependent fields** list. Click **OK**.
7. On the **Field Properties** page, click **OK**.
8. Save the Account form.
9. To test this custom script, click **Preview**, and then click **Create Form**. The preview window appears.
10. Enter **1234567** into the **Account Number** field, and then press the Tab key. The following prompt appears, reminding you that account numbers should contain eight digits.

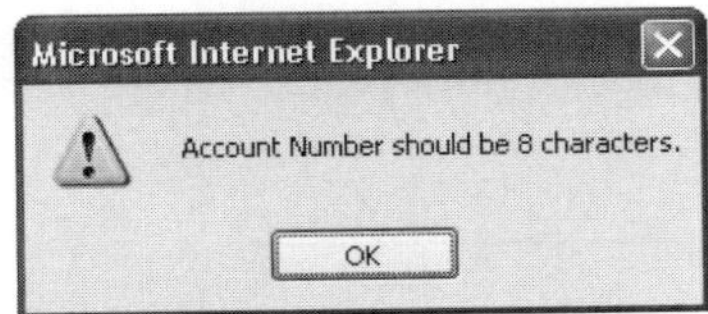

11. To publish the Account entity, simply return to the entity editor, click **Actions** in the menu bar, and then click **Publish**.

Again, don't worry too much about the syntax of the code. The point we're trying to communicate is that you understand how easy it is to add custom scripts to a field's *onChange* event.

More Info In this example, the custom script reminds the user that the account number *should* be eight digits. However, a user could still enter any value for an account number and save the record. A customer might want this behavior. For example, maybe not every Account gets an Account Number immediately, or perhaps some of the old Accounts have Account Numbers from a previous system that contained 10 digits. However, if the customer wanted to always enforce the eight-digit account number requirement, you would have to create a slightly modified custom script and add it to the form's *onSave* event (instead of the field's *onChange* event). By adding a custom script to the form's *onSave* event, you can prevent users from creating or updating records that do not meet your business criteria.

Tweaking the Tab Order of Fields on a Form

When your users enter data on a form, they can use the Tab key to advance from one field to the next field on the form. To move back to the previous field on a form, they can press Shift+Tab. These keyboard functions allow users to enter form data much more quickly than by clicking from field to field with their mouse. As users press the Tab key, Microsoft CRM moves the cursor from field to field down the column of a section and then it moves to the top of the next column (left to right). When users reach the last field in a section, pressing the Tab key advances them to the upper-left field of the next section (see Figure 5-12).

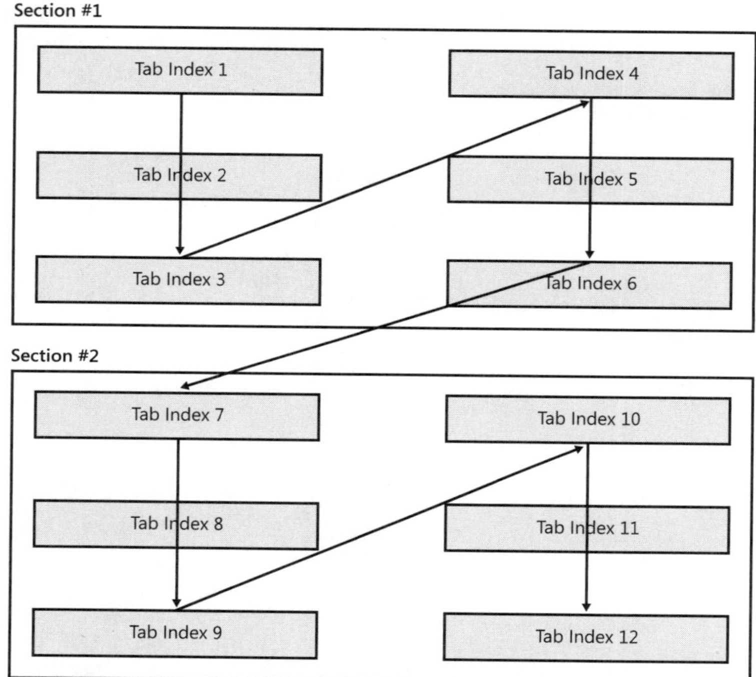

Figure 5-12 Microsoft CRM field tab order on a form

In standard HTML code, you can specify a tab index for each field on a form to control the order in which users move from field to field. Unfortunately, you cannot specify tab indexes on form fields in Microsoft CRM. However, you can easily manipulate the tab sequence that users experience by understanding the Microsoft CRM tab behavior and then getting clever with your use of form sections. Conceptually, you can create *invisible* sections on a form and place the form fields in the appropriate sections, depending on how you want users to proceed. You can make a section invisible by not displaying its name or the divider line on the form. Figure 5-13 shows how to change the tab order from the initial order shown in Figure 5-12.

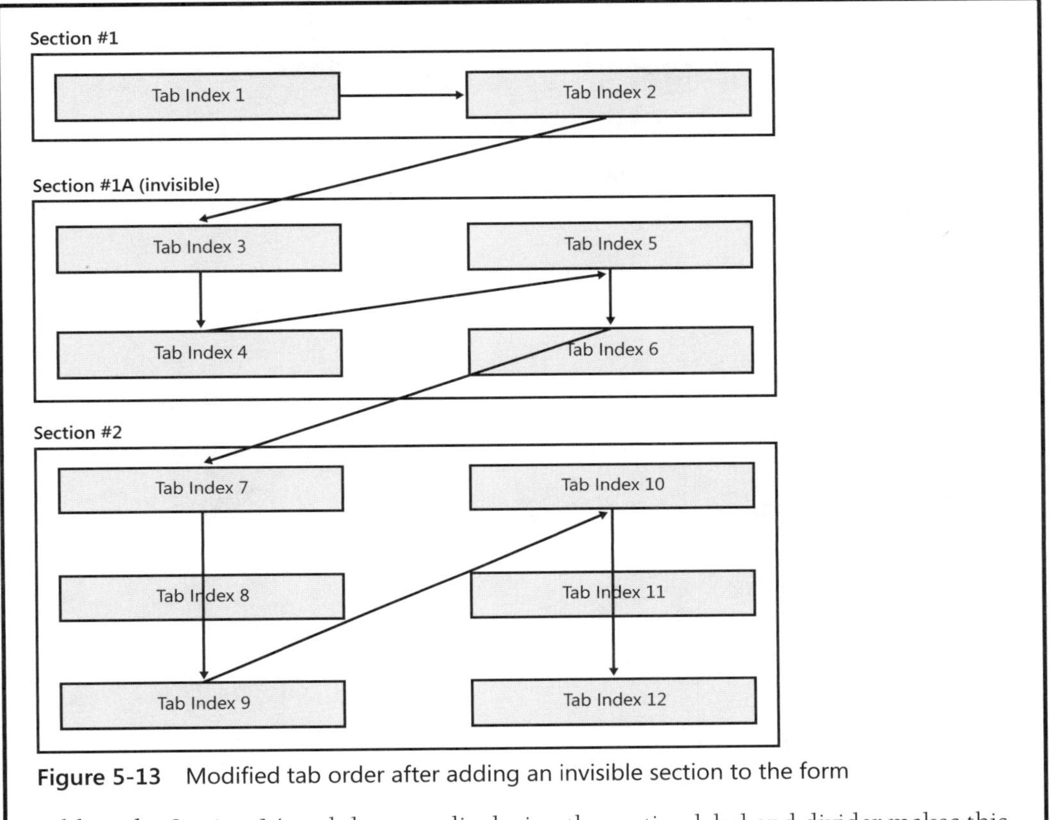

Figure 5-13 Modified tab order after adding an invisible section to the form

Adding the Section 1A and then not displaying the section label and divider makes this section appear invisible to your users. They'll think they tabbed from the left field to the right field (in the top section), but in reality, they tabbed from the bottom of the left column to the top of the right column of Section 1!

IFrames

Microsoft CRM allows you to add IFrames (also known as *inline frames*) to an entity's form. IFrames open the door to almost unlimited customization capabilities within Microsoft CRM forms. Conceptually, an IFrame creates a frame within a Web page that displays a second Web page. The Web page within the IFrame can be any Web page that you want, whether it is hosted on your server or not. In the context of Microsoft CRM, you can add one or more IFrames to any entity's form. Figure 5-14 shows an example of an IFrame on an Account form that references a Sharepoint intranet Web site.

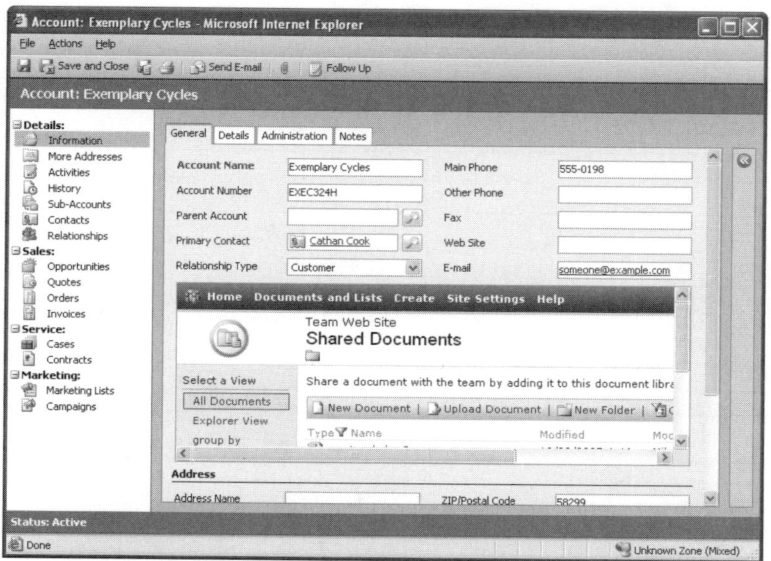

Figure 5-14 An IFrame on an Account form that references a Sharepoint intranet Web site

Although you can see that we need to work out some formatting with the Sharepoint Web site in the IFrame, the concept is that you can reference other non-Microsoft CRM Web sites by using an IFrame. Potential uses for an IFrame on a form include the following:

- Displaying external Web sites
- Displaying your own custom Web pages
- Displaying photos or images related to the record
- Displaying other Web sites on your intranet

The most important feature of the IFrame capability is that Microsoft CRM allows you to programmatically manipulate the Web address (Uniform Resource Locator, or URL) that the IFrame displays. By doing so, you can display Web pages in the IFrame that are unique to the record you are looking at instead of displaying a generic URL such as *http://sharepoint*. So instead of showing the same SharePoint site for every record, you could show the portion of the site that is specific to the record you're looking at. Combining the IFrame display within a form with the ability to dynamically create URLs provides you with amazing customization possibilities.

> **Tip** IFrames reference a URL address. People usually use URLs to reference Web pages, but you can use the IFrame to reference anything that is URL-addressable. For example, you can also use URLs to display images, Microsoft Office Word files, Microsoft Office Excel files, and so on. You can also specify protocols other than HTTP, such as HTTPS or FTP.

Now that you understand the benefits of using IFrames in Microsoft CRM forms, let's review the details related to using an IFrame. When you click the **Add An IFRAME** in the Common Tasks tool on the entity form editor, you are prompted to configure the following IFrame properties on the properties page, shown in Figure 5-15:

- Name
- Label
- Security
- Location
- Layout
- Row Layout
- Scrolling
- Border
- Dependencies

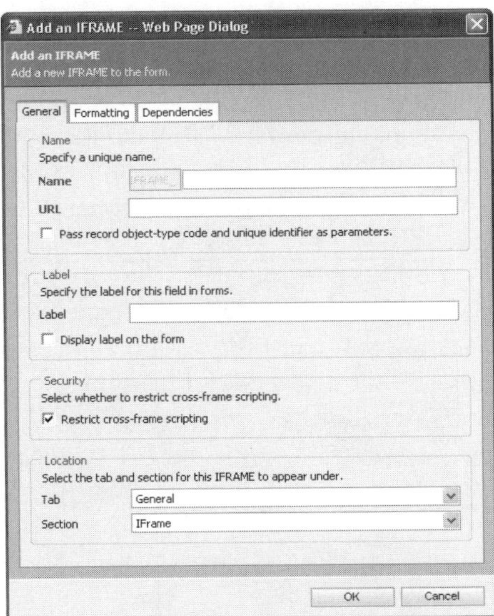

Figure 5-15 IFrame properties page

We'll review each of these properties in detail.

Name

In the Name section on the General tab, you specify the name of the IFrame and its URL.

Name Notice that Microsoft CRM automatically prefixes the value *IFRAME_* to your IFrame name. Unlike the attribute schema prefix that you can configure, you cannot alter this value. After you create an IFrame, you cannot change its name.

URL In the URL field, you enter the address of the Web page or resource that you want to reference in the IFrame. You can specify the full URL (including the *http://*), or a relative URL.

Parameters If you select the Pass record object-type code and unique identifier as parameters check box, Microsoft CRM will append additional querystring parameters to the IFrame URL. Table 5-1 shows how the IFrame URL would appear with and without the parameters check box selected if you entered *http://www.adatum.com* as the IFrame URL.

Table 5-1 Passing Parameters to IFrames

Parameters Passed?	URL displayed in the IFrame
No	*http://www.adatum.com*
Yes	*http://www.adatum.com?type=<objecttypecode>&typename=<schemaname>&<GUID>* *<GUID>* is the globally unique identifier and is the ID of the current record. An example URL with a real GUID would look like this: *http://www.adatum.com?type=112&typename=incident&{948C2AA0-984C-4439-A92A-C015B32DCBA9}*

You can see that passing parameters appends the object type code, the schema name, and the GUID of the record to the querystring. Every Microsoft CRM record has a corresponding object type code such as 1, 2, and so on that references entities (for example, 1 = Account, 2 = Contact, and so on). By including these dynamic parameters in the URL, you can make the Web page in the IFrame behave differently if necessary. The Microsoft CRM SDK lists all of the object type codes for each entity.

Label

Similar to form sections, you can add a label to the IFrame on the form and specify whether to display this label to users.

Security

Because IFrames display content from another Web site, scripts from that alternate Web site could run and perform malicious or unintended behavior within Microsoft CRM. By default, Microsoft CRM blocks cross-frame scripts from the IFrame Web site. Chapter 10 explains cross-frame scripting and related security considerations in detail. For the most part, you should leave the Restrict cross-frame scripting check box selected unless you know that you need to allow cross-frame scripting.

Location

Use these properties to specify the tab and section in which to display the IFrame.

Layout

Figure 5-16 shows the Formatting tab of the IFrame properties page.

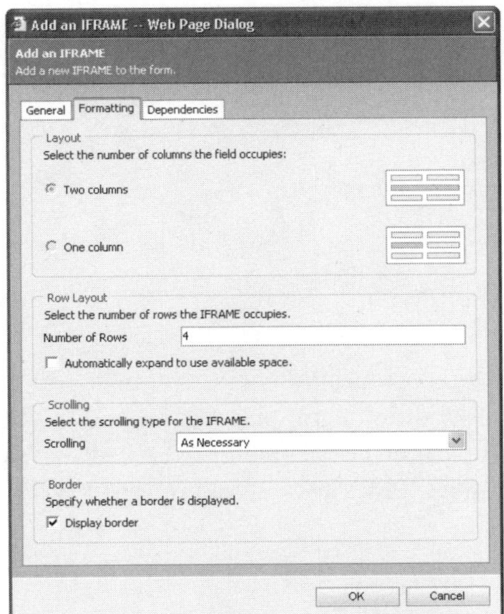

Figure 5-16 Formatting tab of IFrame properties page

Microsoft CRM disables the layout option for IFrames. Consequently, IFrames in a Variable Field Width section will always span both columns, and IFrames in a Variable Field Height section will always remain fixed to the width with the column they occupy.

Row Layout

Use this section to enter the number of rows that the IFrame should occupy. As with fields, you can also set the IFrame to automatically expand to the size of the window.

Scrolling

You can configure the scrolling type for each IFrame. Scrolling refers to adding a scroll bar within the IFrame so that users can move the page up and down within the IFrame. Figure 5-14 shows an example of an IFrame with both horizontal and vertical scroll bars. The three scrolling options are:

- **As Necessary** Microsoft CRM automatically determines whether it needs to add scroll bars. If the content in the IFrame takes more vertical (or horizontal) space than the IFrame offers, Microsoft CRM adds scroll bars.
- **Always** Microsoft CRM always includes horizontal and vertical scroll bars.
- **Never** Microsoft CRM never includes horizontal and vertical scroll bars.

We recommend that you leave the default option, As Necessary, selected.

Border

This IFrame property determines whether Microsoft CRM displays a small, one-pixel blue border around the IFrame. This border matches the style of the border that surrounds each of the data fields on the form.

Dependencies

If you use scripts in your IFrame that reference fields on the form, you can specify those fields as Dependent on the Dependencies tab. This will prevent users from accidentally removing dependent fields from the form.

Being able to add IFrames to forms is one of the most exciting form customization tools available because it opens up so many customization and integration options. You can reference existing Web sites like we just showed you, or you can create entirely new custom Web pages that blend into the form so that users don't even know they're working with a custom Web page.

Customizing Views

Microsoft CRM uses views to display multiple records at one time. You can customize almost all of the views used in Microsoft CRM to display just the data that you want your users to see. In addition, you can also create entirely new views to display different data sets. First, let's define the various components of a view, as shown in Figure 5-17:

- **Quick Find** Users can enter search terms and click Find to search within the view.
- **View Filter** This list shows all of the predefined views available to the user.
- **Grid** The grid displays the records for the view in rows and columns.

- **Grid Tool Bar** The grid tool bar lets users perform additional actions on the records in the grid. Users can select more than one record at a time to perform these grid tool bar actions (such as assigning records or exporting data to Microsoft Office Excel).
- **Columns** Each view consists of one or more data columns. Users can click the column header to sort the view's records in ascending order (A to Z). Clicking the column header a second time sorts the records in the opposite order (descending from Z to A).
- **Index** Users can click an Index letter to quickly filter the records shown in the view.

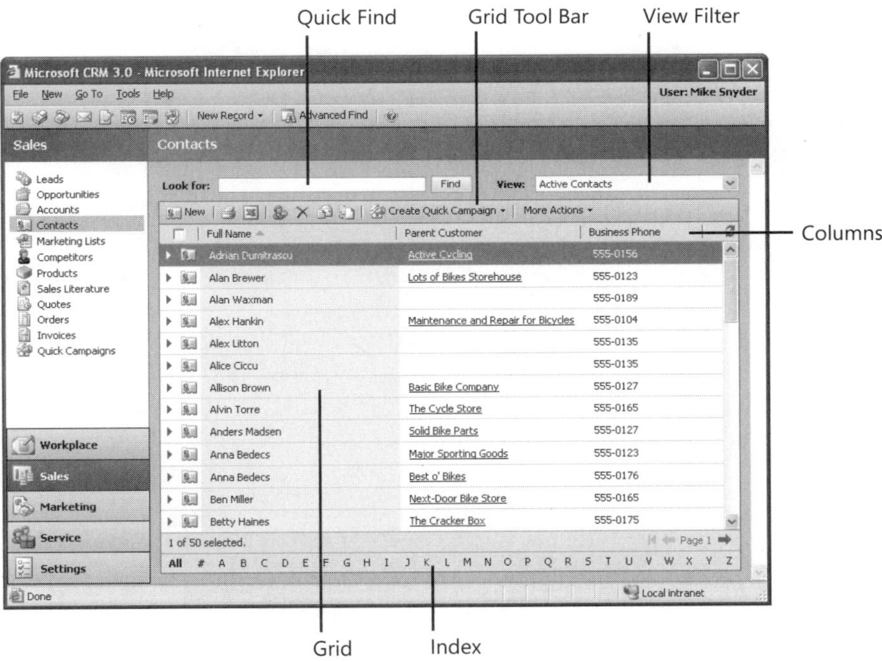

Figure 5-17 View components

To customize views, go to the Customization section of Microsoft CRM and click Customize Entities. Then double-click the entity that you want to modify and click Forms and Views in the navigation pane.

> **Tip** People frequently use the term *grid* interchangeably with the term *view* in regard to Microsoft CRM.

View Types

Microsoft CRM uses four types of views:

- Public Views
- Private Views
- System-Defined Views
- Saved Views

Saved Views are different from the other three views because you do not manage them in the Customization section of Microsoft CRM. Rather, you use the Advanced Find tools to create, modify, and delete Saved Views.

Public Views

Not surprisingly, any Microsoft CRM user can access Public Views for an entity. All of the Public Views appear in the View Filter for each entity. You can also specify a Default Public View for each entity. The Default Public View loads the first time a user browses to an entity area. Therefore, if you want to create a new view for Accounts that every user will see the first time they browse to the Account workspace, create a new view and set it as the Default Public View for the Account entity. You can change the Default Public View in the entity editor by selecting the view that you want to make the default (single click), and then clicking Set Default on the More Actions menu, as shown in Figure 5-18.

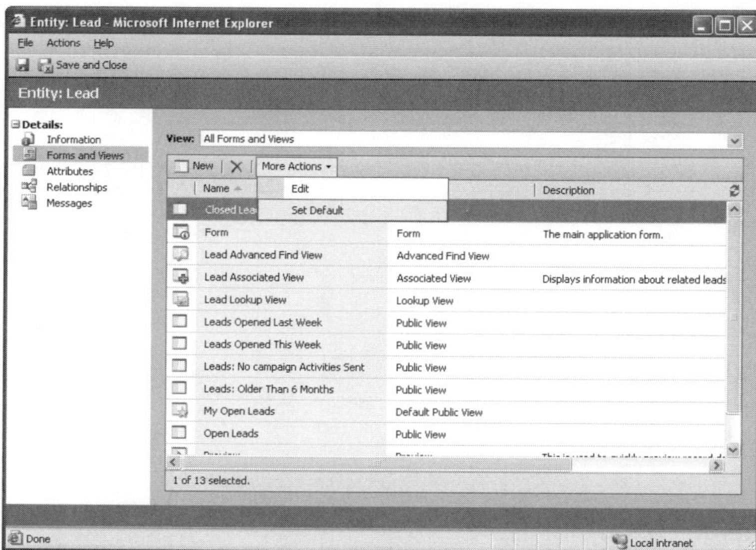

Figure 5-18 Setting a different view as the Default Public View

Private Views

Because you can create as many Public Views as you need, you might find that a large number of views will fill up the View Filter, making it difficult for users to find a specific view. Therefore, Microsoft CRM allows you to utilize Private Views so that only a subset of users will have access to a specific view. Even if you don't have a large number of Public Views, you might want to restrict which views each user can access by using Private Views.

Let's review an example of using Private Views to minimize the number of view names that appear in the View Filter for the Account entity. Consider a fictional company with five sales districts:

- Gulf Coast
- Mid Atlantic
- Midwest
- Rocky Mountain
- West Coast

Each sales district contains sales people who cover Accounts only in their territory. If you created a Public View for each sales district, the View Filter would show all of the views. However, because a sales person in New York doesn't call on West Coast accounts, the West Coast view in the View Filter simply clutters up the screen and reduces usability for users that don't need that view. Fortunately, you can use the Private View feature to streamline the View Filter list for each user. Conceptually, you will make each sales district view a Private View (instead of a Public View) so that each user would only see the view for his or her sales district. Figure 5-19 shows the View Filter two different ways:

- Using just Public Views
- Making each sales district view a Private View

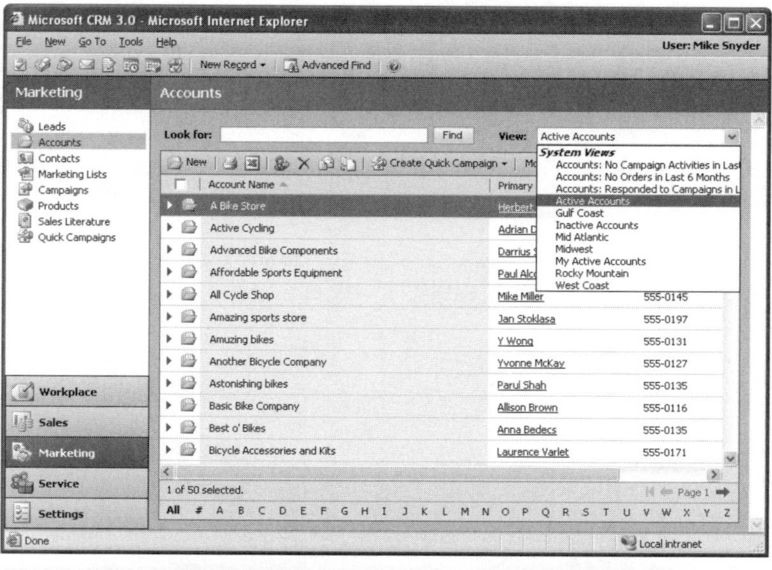

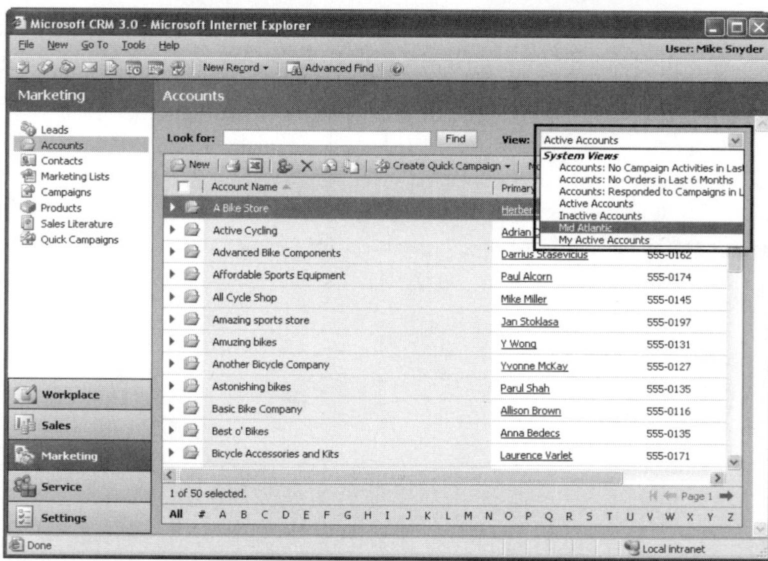

Figure 5-19 Streamlining the View Filter by switching Public Views to Private Views

Obviously, using Private Views will make the user interface much easier for your users to work with. Now let's show you how to set up Private Views.

Converting Public Views to Private Views

1. Go to the **Customization** section of Microsoft CRM and click **Customize Entities**.
2. Double-click the Account entity and click **Forms and Views** in the navigation pane.
3. Double-click the Public View that you want to make private.
4. In the menu bar, click **Actions** and then click **Sharing...** The Share View dialog box will appear.

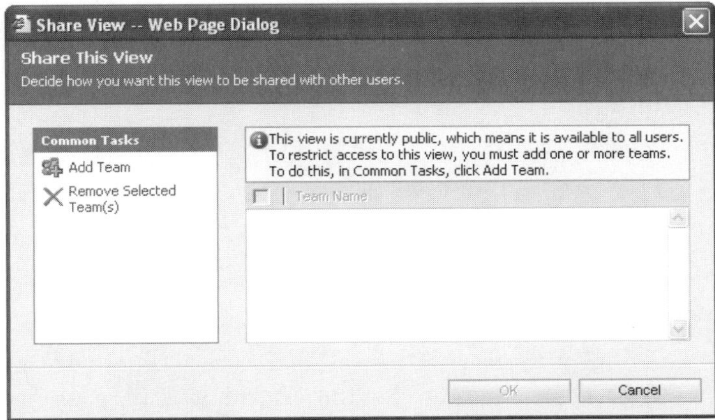

5. In the **Common Tasks** section, click **Add Team**.
6. Select one of the teams and click **OK**. If you don't have any teams created in your system, refer to Chapter 3, "Managing Security and Information Access," for information on creating and using teams.
7. Click **OK** in the Share View dialog box, and then click the **Save and Close** button in the view editor.

You will note that the view type changed from Public View to Private View in the Forms and View grid for the entity (see Figure 5-20).

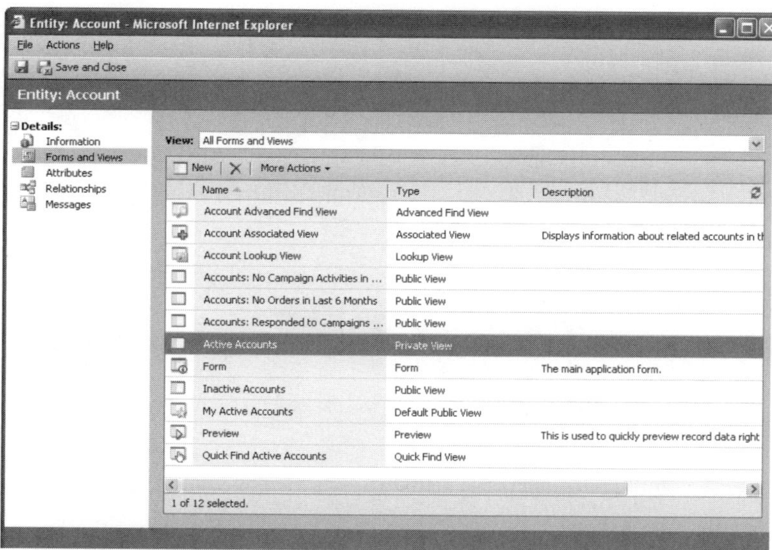

Figure 5-20 Active Accounts updated to a Private View

Now only users who belong to the team you shared the Active Accounts view with can see this view in the View Filter. Of course, you can share a view with multiple teams if you need to do so. Since users can belong to multiple teams, you can get very creative by assigning users to multiple teams or sharing a view with multiple teams. In summary, you can use Private Views to restrict which users have access to a particular view.

> **Important** Somewhat confusingly, you actually make a view private by sharing it with a team. When you share a view with a team, the view becomes private and only users who belong to the team will be able to access it. Users with the System Administrator role will always see all views, regardless of any sharing you set up.

System-Defined Views

Microsoft CRM includes five System-Defined Views:

- Associated View
- Advanced Find View
- Lookup View
- Quick Find View
- Preview

Similar to system entities, Microsoft CRM automatically creates these System-Defined Views upon installation of the software. Each of them serves a unique purpose in the user interface, so the software constrains your ability to modify these System-Defined Views. In particular, Microsoft CRM implements a few notable customization restrictions with all of these views:

- Only one of each System-Defined View can exist for an entity.
- You cannot delete any of the System-Defined Views.
- You cannot configure filtering in the System-Defined Views because the system relationships define the records that Microsoft CRM will display in each view.

Now let's discuss how Microsoft CRM uses each of these views and how you can customize them.

Associated View When you look at the records related to an entity, Microsoft CRM displays the records using the Associated View. For example, when you view the Contacts related to an Account, Microsoft CRM will use the Associated View of the Contact to display the records (Figure 5-21). When you look up the Sub-Accounts of an Account, Microsoft CRM displays the Associated View of the Account entity.

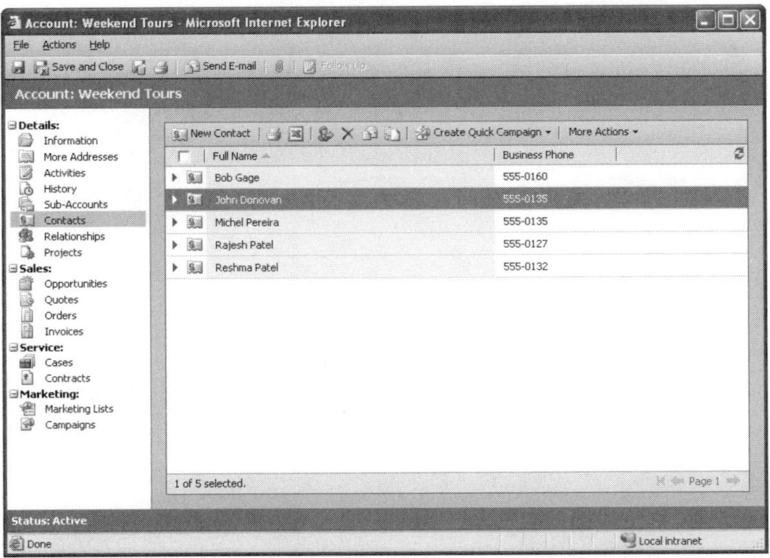

Figure 5-21 Contact Associated View as seen on an Account record

Therefore, if you wanted to add a Contact's title to the view in Figure 5-21, you would edit the Contact Associated View even though you're actually viewing an Account record. Because only one Associated View exists per entity, you cannot display different views based on the related entity. For example, both Lead and Opportunity reference the Activity Associated View. If you change the Activity Associated View, this change appears on both Leads *and* Opportunities, as shown in Figure 5-22.

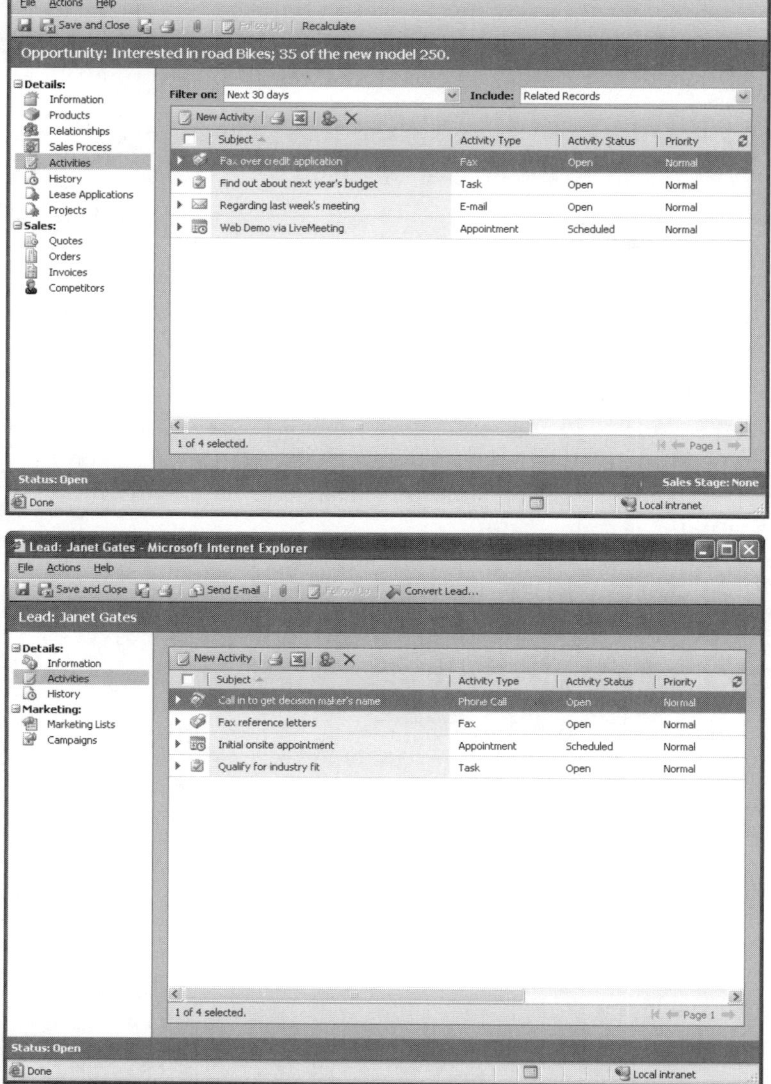

Figure 5-22 Activity Associated View for Lead and Opportunity records

Advanced Find View The Advanced Find View for an entity allows you to define the columns that appear when users use the Advanced Find feature. Figure 5-23 shows the Advanced Find View for Leads.

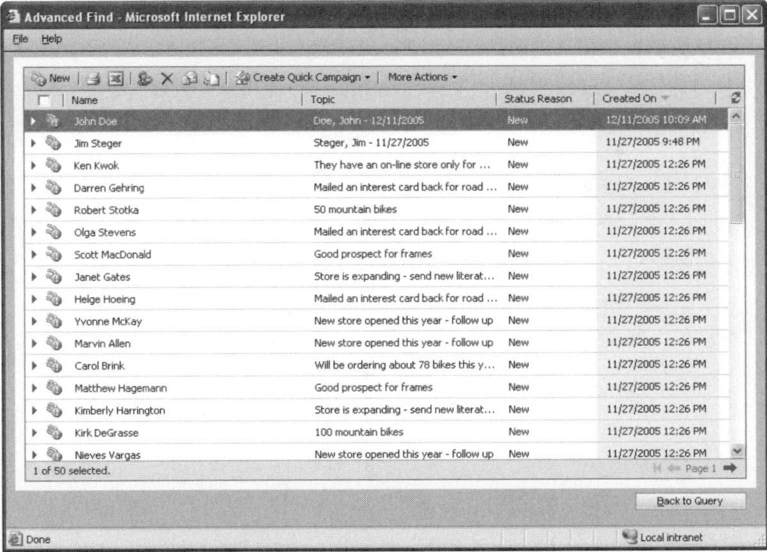

Advanced Find - Microsoft Internet Explorer

Name	Topic	Status Reason	Created On
John Doe	Doe, John - 12/11/2005	New	12/11/2005 10:09 AM
Jim Steger	Steger, Jim - 11/27/2005	New	11/27/2005 9:48 PM
Ken Kwok	They have an on-line store only for …	New	11/27/2005 12:26 PM
Darren Gehring	Mailed an interest card back for road …	New	11/27/2005 12:26 PM
Robert Stotka	50 mountain bikes	New	11/27/2005 12:26 PM
Olga Stevens	Mailed an interest card back for road …	New	11/27/2005 12:26 PM
Scott MacDonald	Good prospect for frames	New	11/27/2005 12:26 PM
Janet Gates	Store is expanding - send new literat…	New	11/27/2005 12:26 PM
Helge Hoeing	Mailed an interest card back for road …	New	11/27/2005 12:26 PM
Yvonne McKay	New store opened this year - follow up	New	11/27/2005 12:26 PM
Marvin Allen	New store opened this year - follow up	New	11/27/2005 12:26 PM
Carol Brink	Will be ordering about 78 bikes this y…	New	11/27/2005 12:26 PM
Matthew Hagemann	Good prospect for frames	New	11/27/2005 12:26 PM
Kimberly Harrington	Store is expanding - send new literat…	New	11/27/2005 12:26 PM
Kirk DeGrasse	100 mountain bikes	New	11/27/2005 12:26 PM
Nieves Vargas	New store opened this year - follow up	New	11/27/2005 12:26 PM

1 of 50 selected.

Figure 5-23 Advanced Find View for Leads

Note that users can easily edit the columns that appear in the Advanced Find results, as shown in Figure 5-24, but their updates will not change the Advanced Find View for the entity.

Advanced Find - Microsoft Internet Explorer

Name	Company Name	City	State/Province	Created On
John Doe	Fabrikam, Inc.			12/11/2005 10:09 AM
Jim Steger	Sonoma Partners			11/27/2005 9:48 PM
Ken Kwok	Largest Bike Store	Boise	ID	11/27/2005 12:26 PM
Darren Gehring	Journey Sporting Goods	Bellevue	WA	11/27/2005 12:26 PM
Robert Stotka	Gift and Toy Store	Dallas	TX	11/27/2005 12:26 PM
Olga Stevens	Maintenance and Repair for Bicycles	Bothell	WA	11/27/2005 12:26 PM
Scott MacDonald	Yellow Bicycle Company	Clearwater	FL	11/27/2005 12:26 PM
Janet Gates	Modular Cycle Systems	Puyallup	WA	11/27/2005 12:26 PM
Helge Hoeing	Little Bicycle Supply Shop	Camarillo	CA	11/27/2005 12:26 PM
Yvonne McKay	Practical Bike Supply Company	La Vergne	TN	11/27/2005 12:26 PM
Marvin Allen	Mountain Toy Store	Federal Way	WA	11/27/2005 12:26 PM
Carol Brink	Outdoor Distributors	New York	NY	11/27/2005 12:26 PM
Matthew Hagemann	Games and Sport Supply Company	Fremont	CA	11/27/2005 12:26 PM
Kimberly Harrington	Exemplary Cycles	Kent	WA	11/27/2005 12:26 PM
Kirk DeGrasse	Outdoor Equipment Store	Reno	NV	11/27/2005 12:26 PM
Nieves Vargas	Exhilarating Cycles	Simi valley	CA	11/27/2005 12:26 PM

1 of 50 selected.

Figure 5-24 Advanced Find columns that have been edited by a user

So every time a user creates a new Advanced Find, the columns from that entity's Advanced Find View will be the default results.

Lookup View When users click the lookup button (the magnifying glass), a Look Up Records dialog box appears that allows users to search for a particular record. Figure 5-25 shows the Contact Lookup View that users see when they select a Primary Contact for an Account.

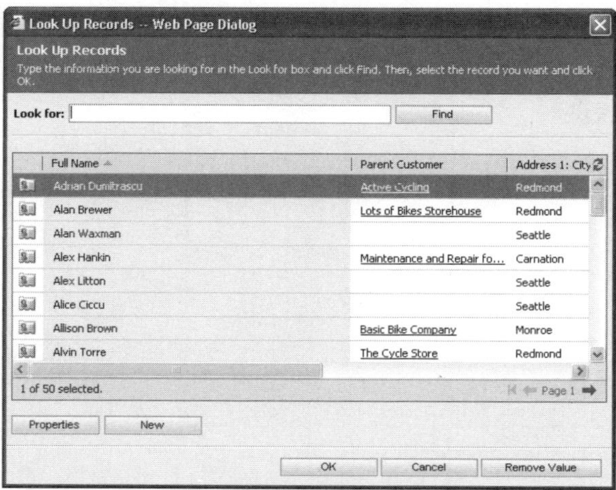

Figure 5-25 Contact Lookup View

You can define the columns that appear in the Look Up Records dialog box by editing the Lookup View for an entity. In addition to modifying the columns in the view, you can also add *Find Columns* to the view. By adding Find Columns, Microsoft CRM will search for data in all of the Find Columns when users enter text to search for. For example, the default Find Columns for Contact are:

- E-mail
- First Name
- Middle Name
- Last Name
- Full Name

When a user searches for a record by entering text into the Look Up Records dialog box, Microsoft CRM will query data in the Find Columns to retrieve matching records. Therefore, if you search for a Contact by entering his or her phone number in the Look Up Records dialog box, Microsoft CRM will not return any records because the phone number field is not one of the Find Columns (Figure 5-26).

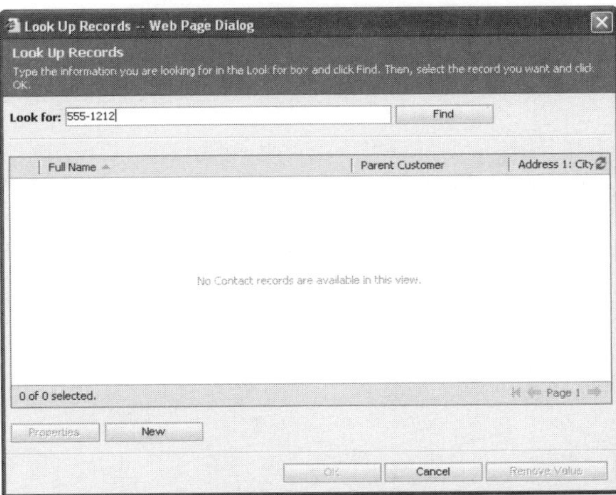

Figure 5-26 Results of a phone number search using the default Find Columns

However, if you edit the Lookup View by adding Business Phone as a Find Column, your users can search for customers by entering their phone number. To add the Business Phone number as a Find Column in the Contact Lookup View, follow these steps:

1. Go to the **Customization** section of Microsoft CRM and click **Customize Entities**.
2. Double-click the Contact entity and click **Forms and Views** in the navigation pane.
3. Double-click the Contacts Lookup View, and then click **Add Find Columns** in the Common Tasks pane. The Add Find Columns dialog box will launch.
4. In the list of attributes for the Contact, select the **Business Phone** check box, and then click **OK**.
5. Click the **Save and Close** button on the view editor tool bar.
6. Now on the entity editor you need to publish the Contact entity by clicking **Publish** under the **Actions** menu bar button.

The next time a user enters a phone number in the Look Up Records dialog box, Microsoft CRM will also search the Business Phone column for matching records. Figure 5-27 shows the search results.

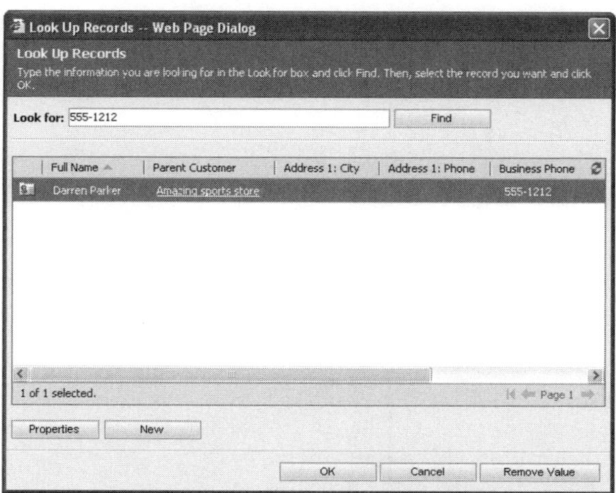

Figure 5-27 Contact record returned after adding Business Phone as a Find Column

In addition to phone numbers, you might also want to add the Contact's Social Security number or a unique customer number (ID) as Find Columns to help users find records more quickly.

Important When users enter search values, please note that Microsoft CRM will search for the value "as is"; it will not search for substrings by default. For example, if you search for "555-1212" and the Contact's Business Phone is "(312) 555-1212" then Microsoft CRM will not find a match. The software tries to find all records that start with "555-1212", but this record doesn't start with that value. To return this Contact record in a search result, you would need to search for "(312) 555-1212" or "(312)". Obviously there might be times when you don't know the exact value of what you're searching for. Therefore, Microsoft CRM allows you to enter an asterisk * as a wildcard character in your searches (both Quick Find and Lookup). So if you didn't know the phone number area code, you could search for "*555-1212" and Microsoft CRM would find the matching record.

Quick Find View On the main entity pages, users can search for records by using the Quick Find feature. To do this, simply type a search value in the Look For box and click Find. Microsoft CRM will then search for matching records and return the results using the Quick Find View of the entity. Note that the Quick Find View in the View Filter appears as "Search Results." Figure 5-28 shows the Leads Quick Find View.

As with the Lookup View, you can customize the Find Columns of the Quick Find View, allowing users to search for records across the entity attributes that you specify.

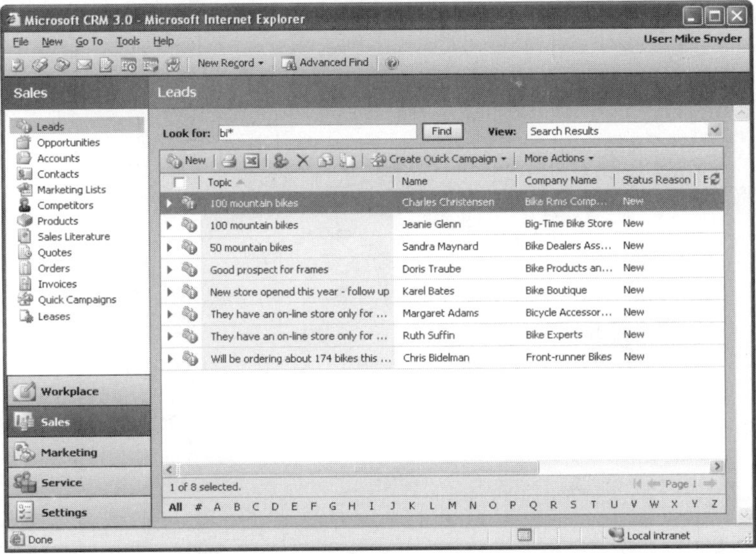

Figure 5-28 Leads search results using Quick Find View and wildcard character

Preview When you are looking at records in a grid, the Preview allows you to show additional information about a record without having to open the record in a new window. Users can display the Preview for a record, shown in Figure 5-29, by clicking the arrow in the far left column.

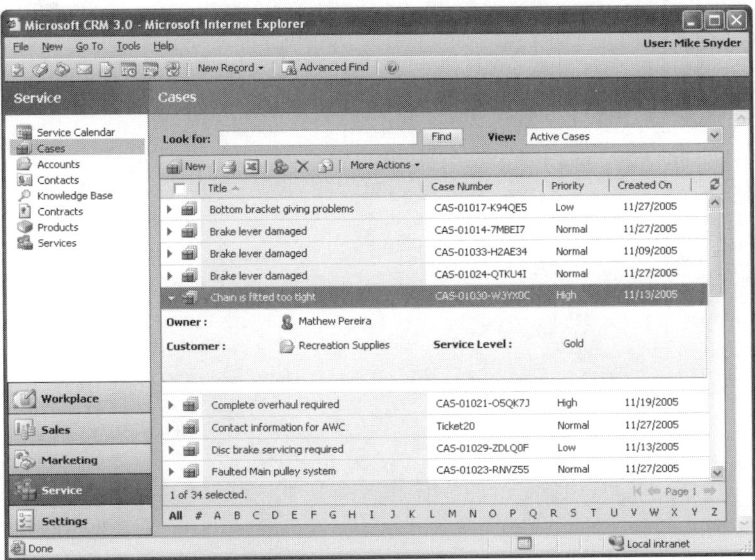

Figure 5-29 Preview of a Case record

If you double-click the Preview record in the **Forms and Views** grid of the entity editor, you'll see the Preview form editor which looks and behaves similarly to the form editor. Editing the Preview will update the information that users will see when they click on the Preview arrow. For the Preview form, you can only add fields, remove fields, and change field properties. Not every entity in Microsoft CRM includes a Preview.

Saved Views

As a reminder, you do not manage Saved Views in the Customization section of Microsoft CRM. When users create new views using the Advanced Find feature, they can save their work as a Saved View. Saved Views have many of the same attributes as the Public, Private, and System-Defined Views, but they also have a couple of unique distinctions.

Saved Views can be activated or deactivated, unlike Public, Private, and System-Defined Views. Only active views will appear in the view name filter. This feature is very beneficial when you are creating a new view but you don't want to see your view name in the view filter until it's complete.

Saved Views also have user ownership. This means that they can be assigned to a specific user, and they will follow the Microsoft CRM security rules. The Saved View privilege is part of the Security Role configuration, so you can specify which security roles can, for example, read, write, or delete the Saved Views. The Saved View ownership and Microsoft CRM security configuration will determine the Saved View records that users can access. However, the Public and System-Defined Views exist across the entire system so that all users can access them. If you create a Saved View that you want to share with everyone, one way to accomplish this is to share the Saved View with a Team that every user belongs to.

Also remember that you can only export (and import) Public and Private views. Unfortunately you can not export Saved Views for use in another Microsoft CRM system.

Customizing Views

Now that you understand the different view types, let's discuss in detail how to customize these views to show the data that you want to see. To edit a view, simply double-click the view name in the Forms And Views grid of the entity editor. All of the views use the same editor tool, shown in Figure 5-30.

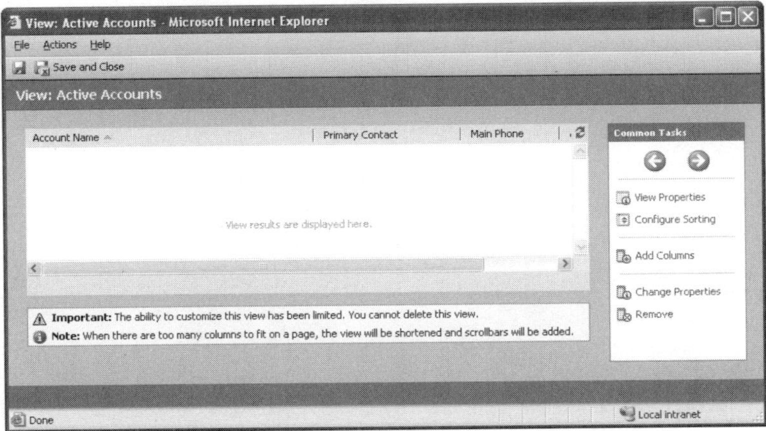

Figure 5-30 Active Accounts view editor

Similar to the form editor, the Common Tasks pane offers several tools to customize a view:

- **Directional arrows** Select a column header, and then use these arrows to move it to the left or right in your view.
- **View Properties** Use this tool to change the name of the view. The view's name appears in the View Filter.
- **Edit Filter Criteria** The Edit Filter Criteria tool gives you the opportunity to create complex criteria that refine the data that each view returns. You can specify view filter criteria only if you create a new view; you cannot use this feature on the System-Defined views installed with Microsoft CRM (like the view shown in Figure 5-30). The Edit Filter Criteria tool uses the same user interface as the Advanced Find feature to create your data query.
- **Configure Sorting** Use this tool to specify the default order in which the view should sort the records. You can choose to sort by any one column in ascending or descending order. If you closely examine the view editor, you might notice that the default sort order column header has a small arrow that points up (for ascending) or down (for descending). Unfortunately, there is no way to add a second or third sort order.
- **Add View Columns** Use this feature to add additional columns to the view. By default, new columns are added to the far right. For views where you cannot Add Find Columns, Microsoft CRM will label this tool as just Add Columns.
- **Add Find Columns** As discussed previously, this feature allows you to specify which columns Microsoft CRM should search for matching records. The Add Find Columns feature does not apply to all views.

- **Change Properties** If you want to change the width of a column in the view, select the column header, and then click Change Properties. You can specify the column's width in pixels (abbreviated as "px" in the user interface).
- **Remove** Use this option to remove a column from the view.

> **Tip** If you select a column header and then add a View Column, Microsoft CRM places the new column to the right of the selected column. This tip might save you some clicks if you have a view with many columns.

When you install Microsoft CRM, the software creates System-Defined Views for each entity. To make sure that the software always functions correctly, Microsoft CRM restricts some of your ability to customize these views. When you edit one of these restricted views, Microsoft CRM displays a warning, as shown earlier in Figure 5-30.

Now let's walk through creating two sample views to show you how to create custom views:

- My Direct Reports' Overdue Activities view
- Opportunity Relationships view

Sample View: My Direct Reports' Overdue Activities

Managers commonly want to view which of their direct reports are falling behind schedule and which are completing their activities on time. We will show you to how to create an Activity view to quickly mine the Microsoft CRM database for this information.

Creating an Overdue Activities custom view

1. Go to the **Customization** section of Microsoft CRM and click **Customize Entities**.
2. Double-click the Activity entity and click **Views** in the navigation pane of the entity editor.
3. Click **New** in the grid tool bar to create a new view.
4. In the properties dialog box, enter the view name **My Direct Reports' Overdue Activities**, and then click **OK**.

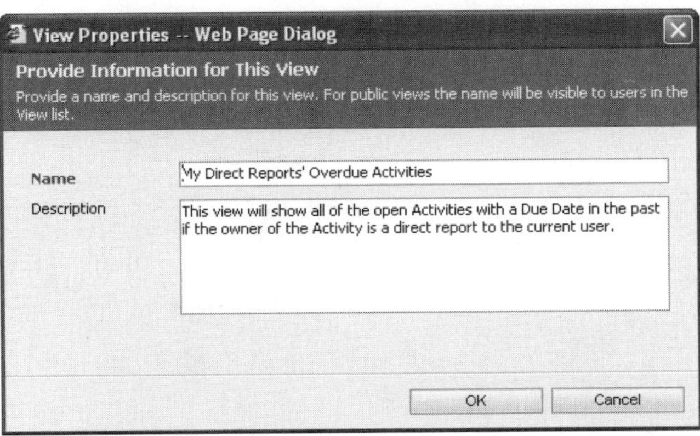

5. Click **Edit Filter Criteria** in the Common Tasks pane and the Edit Filter Criteria dialog box will launch.
6. Hover your cursor (or click) on **Select**. Under the Fields group of the picklist, select **Activity Status**. Next click **Enter Value** and click the ... button that appears.
7. The Select Values dialog box will launch. Under the Available Values section, select **Open** and then click the >> button. Click **Ok** to close the Select Values dialog box. By setting the filter to **Activity Status** of **Open**, the view will select only records that have not been completed or cancelled.
8. Now we want to filter the open Activities to only show those with a Due Date in the past. Hover your cursor (or click) on **Select**, and then select **Due Date**, which is listed under the Fields group.
9. Now click **On** to the right of the Due Date picklist. Microsoft CRM will display a picklist of different date operators that you can select from. However, you will notice that there is no "in the past" or "overdue" option. If you try to choose **On or Before**, Microsoft CRM prompts you to enter a specific date. Therefore, if you use **On or Before** and enter a date value, you would have to update the view every day to show overdue activities. You obviously don't want to do this, so use this simple workaround: Set the Due Date evaluation picklist to **Last X Years** and enter 99 in the Enter Value field. Now Microsoft CRM will display all open Activities with a Due Date in the last 99 years.

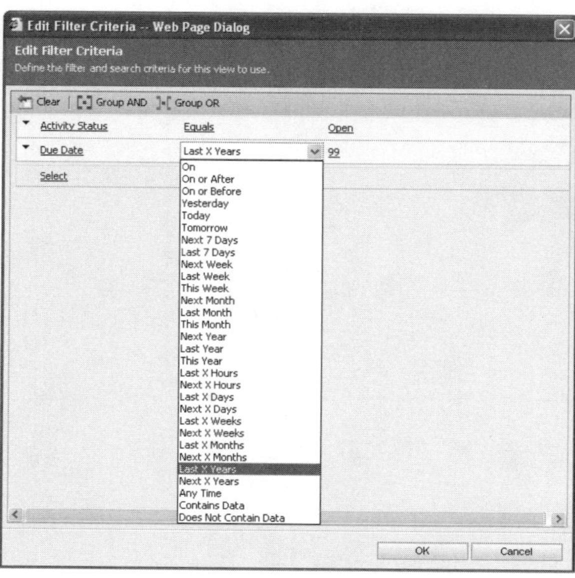

10. So far, the view will return open Activities with a Due Date in the last 99 years, but you want to only see the activities assigned to the manager's direct reports. To add this filter, hover your cursor (or click) on **Select** again. In the picklist, scroll down to the **Related** grouping and choose **Owner**.

11. Now you need to hover your cursor (or click) on the **Select** that appears under **Owner**. Under the Fields group, select **Manager** and leave the default operator value of **Equals Current User**, and click **OK** to close the Edit Filter Criteria dialog box.

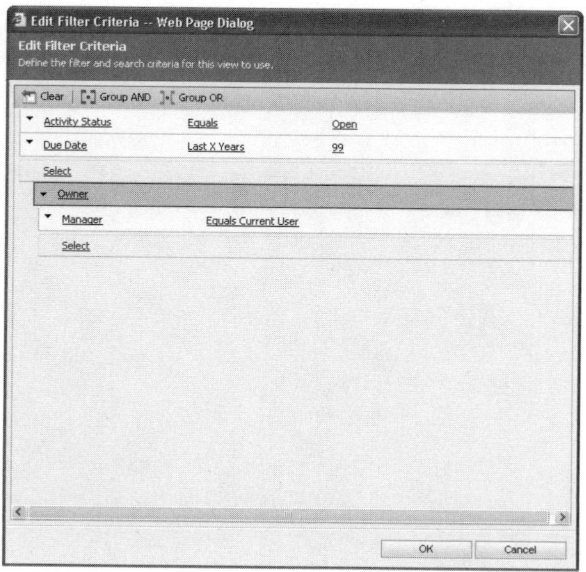

12. Now you should add the columns you want to display in your view. By default, Microsoft CRM includes the Subject in new Activity views, so just add the following columns by clicking **Add Columns** in the Common Tasks pane: Activity Type, Date Created, Due Date, Last Updated, Owner, and Priority.
13. Reorder the columns in the view. Use the left and right arrows to put the columns in the following order from left to right: Activity Type, Subject, Priority, Date Created, Last Updated, Due Date, Owner.

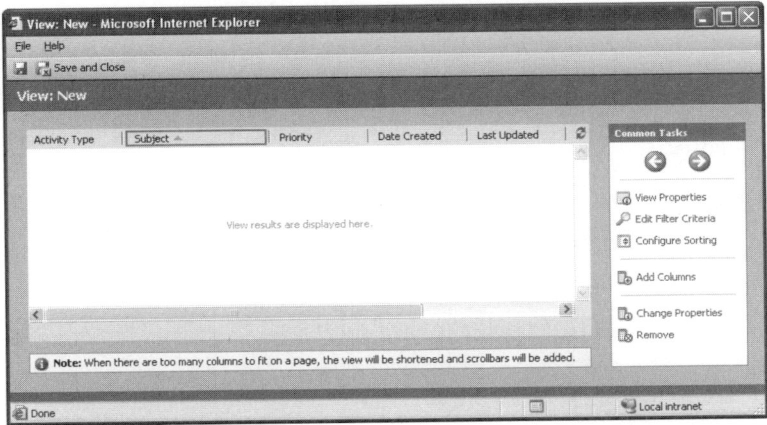

14. When you add a new column, the default column width is 100 pixels (100px). Click **Change Properties** to change the width of the columns so that the width of the **Priority** column is 75 pixels (75px) and the width of the **Due Date** column is 125 pixels (125px).
15. Specify the default sort order to show the most overdue activities first. To do so, click **Configure Sorting** and select **Due Date** in ascending order. Click **OK**.
16. Click **Save and Close** in the view editor tool bar to complete the view customization.
17. To publish the view, click **Activity** in the **Customize Entities** list, and then click **Publish** in the grid tool bar.
18. A "Publishing customizations" message appears. When the message disappears, you can use your new view.
19. Browse to the **Activities** section within the **Workplace** area and select **My Direct Report's Overdue Activities** in the View Filter.

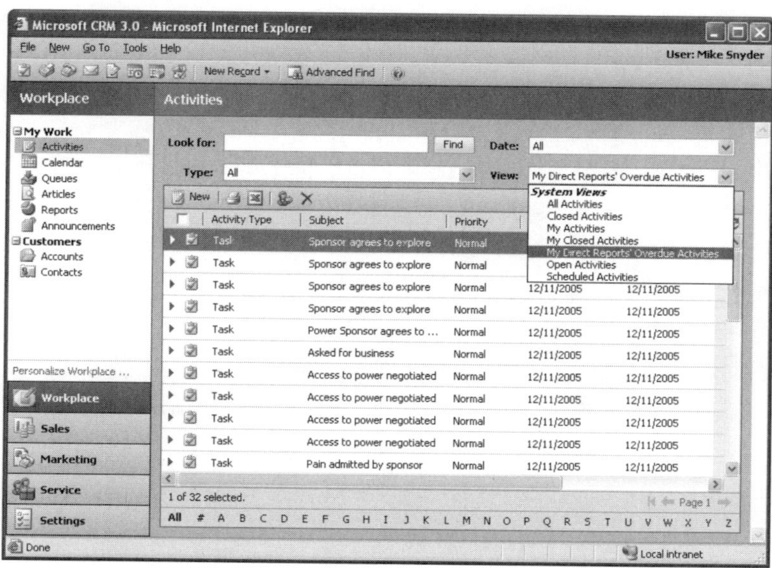

If you don't see the records you expect, confirm that each user's manager record is set correctly. You can view a user's manager on his or her user record. To view a user's record, go to the Settings section of Microsoft CRM and click Users. Then double-click the user's name to open the record and set their Manager by using the Change Manager feature located on the Actions item on the menu bar.

Sample View: Opportunity Relationships

You learned in Chapter 2, "Setting Up Your System," how Microsoft CRM allows users to enter Opportunity relationships to track Accounts and Contacts related to each Opportunity. For example, if an Account referred a potential deal to your company, you could track that Account as a referral by using the Referral Relationship role attached to the Opportunity. If you later wanted to thank the Accounts that referred you a winning deal, a view would be a good way to quickly find the Accounts that meet your criteria.

Creating a Referred Deal custom view

1. Go to the **Customization** section of Microsoft CRM and click **Customize Entities**.
2. Double-click the Account entity and then click **Forms and Views** in the navigation pane.
3. Click **New** in the grid tool bar to create a new view and enter a view name of "Referred Deals that we Won".
4. Click **Edit Filter Criteria** in the Common Tasks pane and the Edit Filter Criteria dialog box will launch.

5. Scroll down the picklist to the Related grouping and select **Opportunity Relationships (Customer)**. Hover your cursor (or click) on the **Select** that appears under **Opportunity Relationships (Customer)** and choose the Customer Role value that appears under the Fields grouping. Leave the default criteria condition of "Equals" and then click on the Lookup button. Use the Lookup dialog box to select **Referral**.

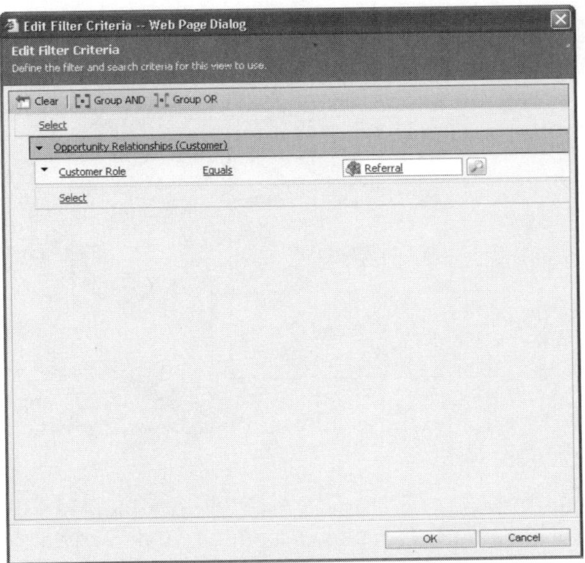

6. Now we will further refine the view to show only those Accounts that referred an Opportunity that turned into revenue. Hover your cursor (or click) on the **Select** that appears under the **Clear** button. Scroll down to the Related grouping values and select **Opportunities (Potential Customer)**. Note that there is also an **Opportunity** under **Fields**, but you want the value listed under **Related**.

7. Hover your cursor (or click) on the **Select** that appears under the **Opportunities (Potential Customer)** and select the picklist value of **Status**. Next, set the criteria to **Won**.

8. Repeat this process and select **Actual Close Date** with a criterion of **This Year**.

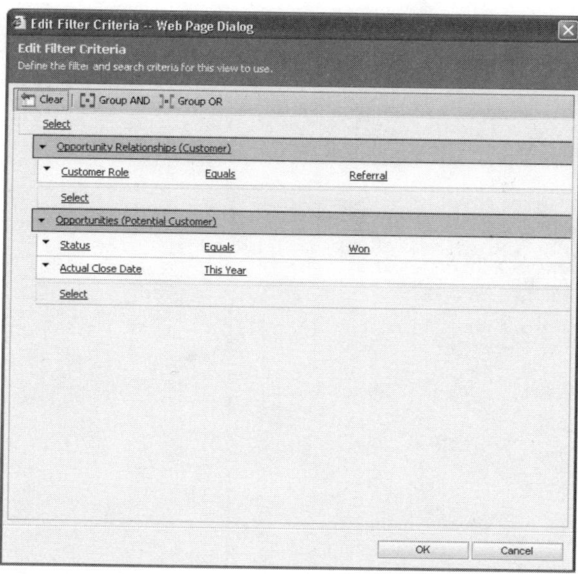

9. When your criteria are identical to those shown in the preceding screen shot, click **OK** to return to the view editor.
10. Now add the **Primary Contact** column to the view by clicking **Add Columns** in the Common Tasks pane. Note that although you can filter on related data (such as Opportunity Relationship, in this example), you cannot add columns from related entities to the view. Therefore, you cannot add a column to the view that displays the name of the Opportunity that this Account referred to the company.
11. Click **Save** in the view editor tool bar, and then publish the Account entity.
12. When you browse to the Account records, you will see the Referred Deals that we Won view in the View Name List. From this view, you could easily click **Create Quick Campaign** to automatically assign Phone Call activities to ensure that each Account is personally thanked.

Customizing Activities

Activities are the heart and soul of any CRM system, including Microsoft CRM. The main purpose of any CRM system is to effectively track and manage all of the sales, service, and marketing data related to your customers, and Microsoft CRM stores the vast majority of this data (also known as *touch points*) as Activities. As with the Lead, Account, Contact, and Opportunity entities, you can perform many of the customizations we've discussed so far on Activities, such as adding attributes, customizing views, and renaming entities.

Important Microsoft CRM uses an entity named Activity (schema name of *activitypointer*) to act as the parent to multiple other entities such as Task, Fax, Phone Call, E-mail, and so on. Microsoft CRM also refers to these sub-entities as Activities because they're children entities of the parent Activity entity.

However, because Activities are so important to Microsoft CRM, we want to explicitly cover some Activity-specific customizations. The default Microsoft CRM installation contains approximately fifteen different types of Activities (child entities of the Activity entity):

- Task
- Fax
- Phone Call
- E-mail
- Letter
- Appointment
- Service Activity
- Campaign Response
- Campaign Activity
- Bulk Import
- Order Close
- Quote Close
- Opportunity Close
- Quick Campaign
- Case Resolution

Microsoft CRM predefines all of the system relationships between the Activity and these related children entities. Since the Activity entities manage many of the software's inner workings, Microsoft CRM restricts your ability to customize itsome of these entities. Consequently, you cannot add any custom attributes to the Activity entity or modify any of the relationships between the Activity entity and its related activity entities. As a matter of fact, the Activity entity doesn't even have a form for you to customize.

Tip Microsoft CRM automatically creates some activities, such as Order Close and Opportunity Close, when users close those records. You can reference these auto-created Activities for reporting purposes and viewing a record's history.

Figure 5-31 summarizes the differences between the Activity entity and its children entities.

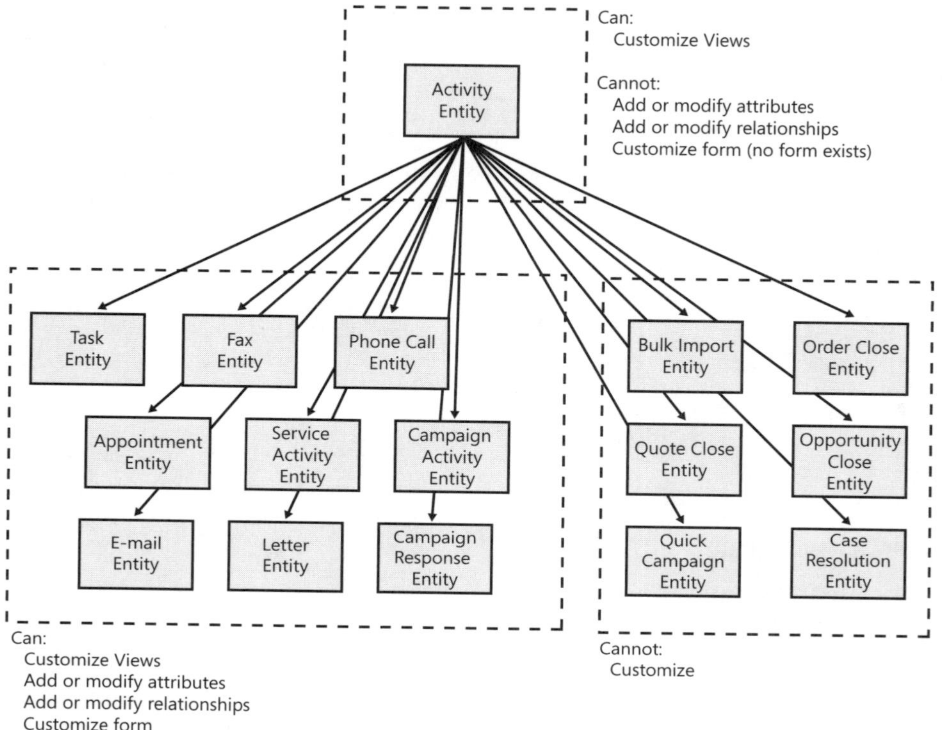

Figure 5-31 Differences between the Activity entity and its related entities

However, just because Microsoft CRM restricts customization of the parent Activity entity, don't make the mistake of thinking that Activities cannot be customized. So even though you cannot add attributes to the Activity entity, you can add attributes to the children Activity entities, such as Task, Phone Call, and Letter.

> **Important** You add custom Activity attributes on the different Activity entities, such as Task, Phone Call, Appointment, and so on, but you cannot add attributes to the Activity entity. Although you cannot add attributes to the Activity entity, you can customize the Activity entity views. In addition, you can not create new types of activity entities. However it is possible to re-purpose an unused activity entity by renaming it and adding new attributes.

Activity Views

You use the same process to customize the views of Activities that you use for the other customizable entities, but there a few view customization nuances that we want to highlight.

Workplace Activities

When users first log on to Microsoft CRM, the default start page is the Activities page in the Workplace.

> **Tip** Each user can specify a different start page by clicking the **Tools** menu, and then clicking **Options**.

From the Activities page, users can quickly and easily filter through all of their Activity records. In addition to the View Filter and the Quick Find features that appear on the other pages, the Activities page also allows users to filter the records by using the Type and Date criteria, as shown in Figure 5-32.

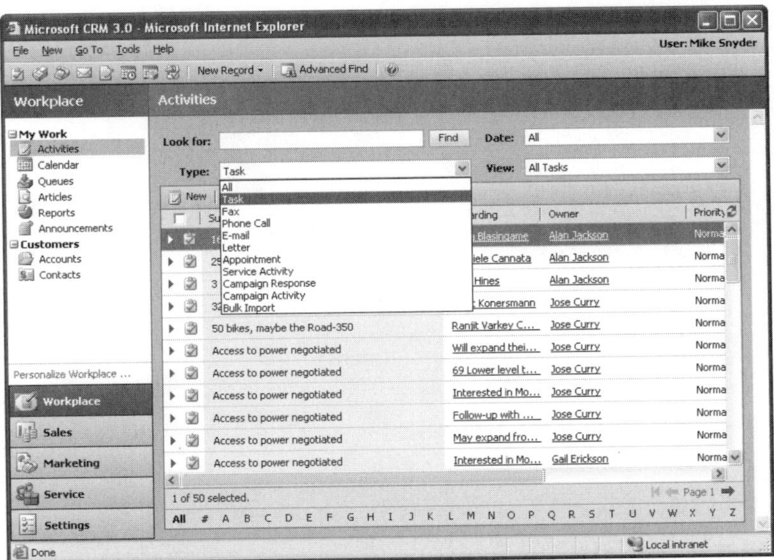

Figure 5-32 The Activities page, showing Type and Date filters

The Type and Date activity filters are hard-coded into Microsoft CRM, so you cannot add your own custom values into these filter picklists. However, you can modify the data columns that Microsoft CRM searches when users use the Quick Find feature. In addition, you can create new views that appear in the View Filter. However, the View Filter behaves differently on the Activities page than it does on other pages in the system: Changing the Activity Type filter changes the list of view names that users can select in the View Filter. Everywhere else in

Microsoft CRM, the View Filter list always contains the same list of views, and it does not update dynamically. Table 5-2 summarizes the default views available for each activity type.

Table 5-2 Default Views for Each Activity Type

Activity type	Views
All	All Activities Closed Activities My Activities My Closed Activities Open Activities Scheduled Activities
Task	All Tasks My Tasks
Fax	All Faxes My Faxes
Phone Call	All Phone Calls My Completed Phone Calls My Phone Calls
E-mail	All E-mails My Draft E-mails My Received E-mails My Sent E-mails
Letter	All Letters My Letters
Appointment	All Appointments My Appointments My Completed Appointments
Service Activity	All Service Activities My Service Activities
Campaign Response	All Campaign Responses My Campaign Responses Open Campaign Responses
Campaign Activity	All Campaign Activities In-Progress Campaign Activities My Campaign Activities
Bulk Import	All Bulk Imports Completed Bulk Imports In-Progress Bulk Imports My In-Progress Bulk Imports

From the Activities page, users can immediately access over 30 different activity views. As you can imagine, this page will be heavily used.

When you want to customize the default Activity views or start creating new views, you need to know that the Activity entity controls the views for the All filter, but all of the other Activity views are contained within their individual entity record. This is important to consider, because the Activity entity only contains attributes that are common to all of the entities. So you could not add a child entity-specific attribute such as Phone Call Phone Number to any of the views that appear in the All filter. The same constraint applies to the Quick Find feature on the Activities page. You can include Find Columns only from an Activity entity that includes common Activity attributes but does not include any of the attributes unique to the individual Activity types.

Entity Activity Views

In addition to the Workplace Activity views, two additional Activity views that contain special features are the Activities and History views that appear for the following entities: Lead, Contact, Account, Opportunity, Quote, Order, Invoice, Case, and Contract. Figure 5-33 shows the Activities views on the Account entity.

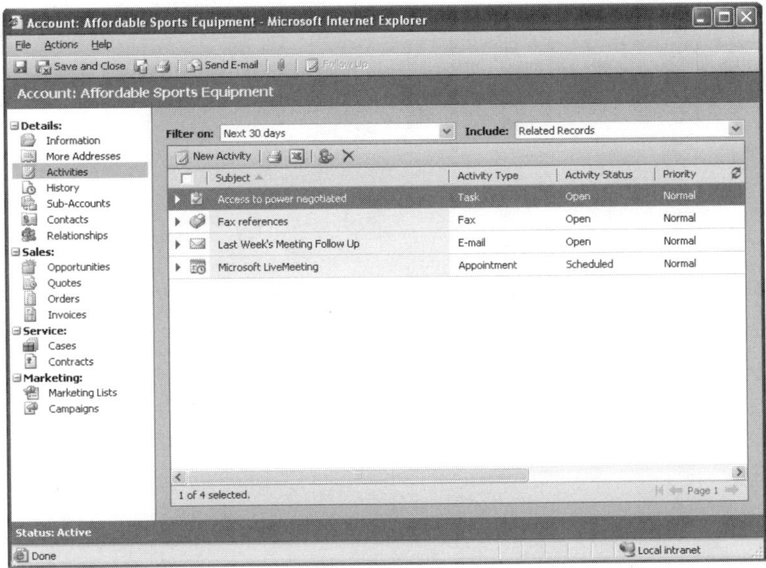

Figure 5-33 Activities views on an Account record

Even though both of these views display Activities related to the entity, clicking History in the navigation pane will show only closed Activities. Clicking Activities in the navigation pane will display only open activities. To customize the columns that appear when users click Activities in the navigation pane, you must edit the Open Activity Associated View of the Activity entity.

To customize the view that appears when users click History in the navigation pane, you must edit the Closed Activity Associated View view of the Activity entity. Again, because these views display different types of Activities entities (Phone Call, Task, Fax, and so on), you can display only the columns from the Activity entity.

Activity Attributes and Forms

As we just explained, some of the Activity views behave a little differently than the non-Activity views in Microsoft CRM. Likewise, customizing the Activity attributes and forms involves a few additional wrinkles that you should be aware of. You can, of course, customize the form for most of the children Activity entities. However, Microsoft CRM uses several special system fields that appear on most of the Activity forms (such as Duration and Due Date Time) that behave differently than regular attributes and forms. The following are some of the Activity attribute and form restrictions:

Adding picklist values to the Duration field

Some of the Activity entities use a special Duration field that appears on their form. This Duration field displays over 20 picklist values such as 1 minute, 5 minutes, and 1 hour. If you wanted to add a new value of 2 minutes, you might expect that you could simply add a new picklist value for the Duration attribute. However, if you browse to the attributes of the Phone Call entity, you will notice that both the *Scheduled Duration* and *Actual Duration* attributes are read-only integers, not a picklist data type, so you cannot add a new value. If this was a standard picklist attribute, you could simply edit the picklist values from this screen, which you obviously can't do here.

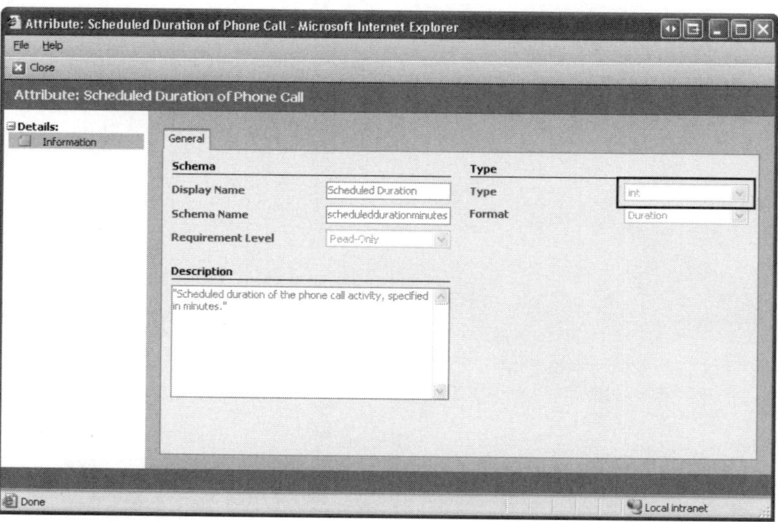

Even though you can't add new picklist values to the Duration attribute, users can simply type a new value in the field when they are entering Activity data. To do so, they would simply select a value in picklist, and then click in the Duration field to enter a new value, such as 2 minutes. This data will be saved correctly in the database as 2 minutes. The database stores the duration in whole minutes, so you can enter 2.25 hours (135 minutes), but you cannot enter 15.25 minutes; Microsoft CRM will automatically convert 15.25 minutes to 15 minutes.

Adding picklist values to Due Date Time

The default picklist values are every 30 minutes for the Due Date Time field, and you cannot add new interval values. However, as with the Duration field, users can simply type their own values (such as 12:15 P.M.) in the Due Date Time field.

Organizing Category and Sub-Category Data

The default data type for the Category and Sub-Category data fields is *nvarchar*, so users can enter any text value in these fields. This free-form text option can make it difficult for companies to track and filter Activities by category, because users might type different values to mean the same thing. For example, one person might type "Sales," and another user might type "Sales Calls." You could enforce a more standardized approach by creating some custom code using the client side SDK (see examples in Chapter 10, "Microsoft CRM Client-Side SDK"). In addition, the Category and Sub-Category fields in Microsoft CRM do not correlate to or link with the Category field for tasks that the Microsoft CRM client for Outlook synchronizes to your Outlook tasks.

Summary

In this chapter, you learned more about entity customization, with a focus on forms and views. Each customizable entity has a form that you can customize by adding fields, tabs, and sections. You also learned how to use the form and field events, *onLoad*, *onSave*, and *onChange*, to add more advanced customizations with scripts. We also went into the details and benefits of adding an IFrame to the form of an entity.

We then reviewed each of the view types that Microsoft CRM uses to display data throughout the system. We covered what each of the system-defined views does, and how you can customize the views to show only the data that you want. Finally, we explained some of the nuances related to activity customization, such as the activity views and attributes.

Chapter 6

Entity Customization: Relationships, Custom Entities, and Site Map

In this chapter:

In Chapters 4 and 5, you learned how to customize entities by modifying their attributes, forms, and views. However, those chapters primarily focused on customizing the entities that Microsoft CRM installs by default. Microsoft CRM also allows you to create entirely new entities to track and manage additional categories of data in your system. The new entities that you create are called *custom entities*. Before you start creating your own custom entities, you should understand how Microsoft CRM uses and manages entity relationships, in addition to knowing the ins and outs of customizing entity attributes, forms, and views that you just learned.

In this chapter, we'll cover all of the details related to entity relationships, including data relationships, relationship behavior, and entity mapping. When you understand entity relationships, you're ready to create custom entities. We'll walk you through the steps and configuration settings necessary to create custom entities, show you how to integrate custom entities with the default Microsoft CRM entities, and highlight some of the tricks we've learned.

Once you start creating custom entities, you will want to tweak and modify where they appear in the Microsoft CRM application navigation. The last topic in this chapter will show you how to use the Microsoft CRM site map to customize and revise the user interface to blend in your custom entities and custom Web pages.

Understanding Entity Relationships

An *entity relationship* in Microsoft CRM defines how two entities interact with each other. A Microsoft CRM entity relationship definition includes three parameters:

- **Data relationship** The nature of the data relationship between two entities (one-to-many, many-to-many, and so on)

- **Relationship behavior** The behavior between two entities, and how Microsoft CRM uses that behavior to manage data when users take actions against one of the entities in the relationship
- **Entity mapping** How Microsoft CRM maps common attributes that two entities share

Microsoft CRM includes hundreds of default entity relationships, and you can modify these default relationships or create entirely new entity relationships. You will almost always create at least one relationship between a custom entity and the Microsoft CRM default system entities. In reality, you will probably create between 5 and 50 custom entity relationships for each custom entity that you create, depending on the complexity of your data model. Consequently, it's critical that you understand entity relationships before you create any custom entities.

> **Important** You won't need a single line of programming code to create custom entities, but you will need a thorough understanding of the different entity relationship types and the custom relationships that Microsoft CRM supports.

You can view all of an entity's relationships by using the entity editor in Microsoft CRM. Figure 6-1 shows the entity relationships for the Lead entity.

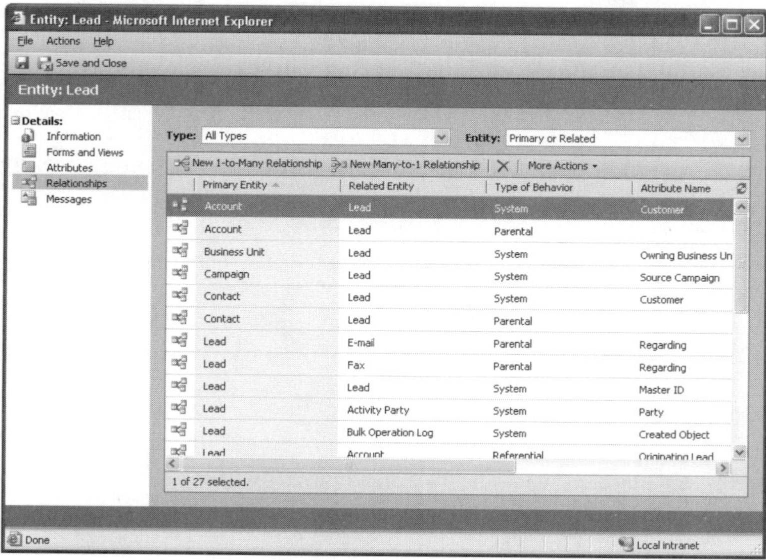

Figure 6-1 Default entity relationships for the Lead entity

This grid lists all of the Lead entity relationships that Microsoft CRM creates by default. To view the details of any one relationship, double-click a record in the grid. For example, double-click the record with the primary entity of Lead and the related entity of Contact, and you'll see the entity relationship editor shown in Figure 6-2.

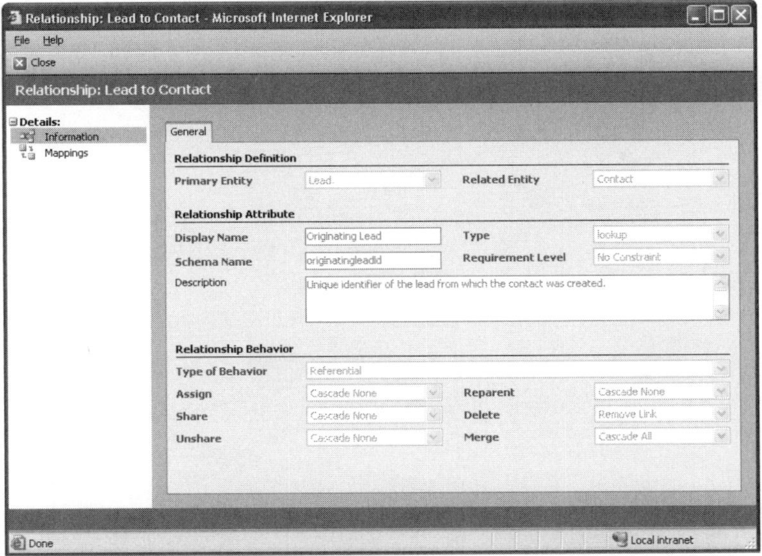

Figure 6-2 Relationship editor

You will use the relationship editor to view and configure all of the entity relationship parameters. Let's review each component of an entity relationship definition, starting with the data relationship.

Data Relationship

One purpose of entity relationships is to define the *data relationship* between two entities in the system. Unlike a traditional database, in which you might configure primary and foreign keys to manage data relationships, you will use entity relationships in Microsoft CRM to manage how data interacts within the system metadata. This metadata design gives you the opportunity to easily customize and manage the data relationships without having to touch the underlying system data (and database keys) in Microsoft SQL Server.

Microsoft CRM uses two types of data relationships:

- One-to-many
- Many-to-many

Let's review both of these concepts in more detail.

One-to-Many

One-to-many describes a relationship between two entities in which a single entity possess one or more (many) related entities. For example, consider the relationship between the Account entity and the Contact entity in Microsoft CRM, as illustrated in Figure 6-3.

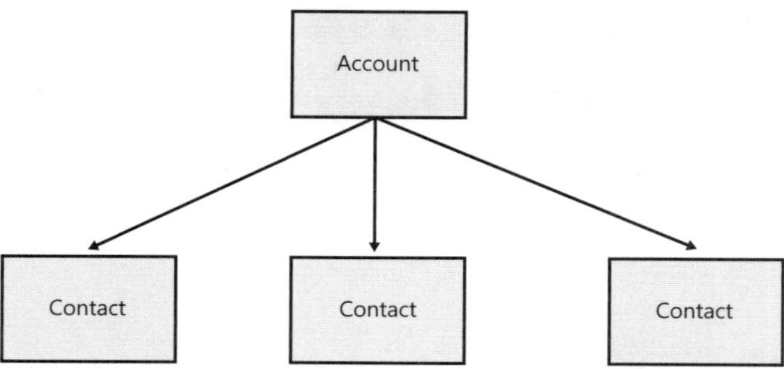

Figure 6-3 Entity relationship between the Account entity and the Contact entity

Figure 6-3 shows that each Account can have many Contacts, but you can assign only one Account to each Contact. You would describe the relationship between these two entities as follows:

- The Account entity has a *primary* relationship to the Contact entity.
- The Contact entity has a *related* relationship to the Account entity.

In other words, the relationship between the Account and Contact entities is *both* primary and related, depending on your perspective when you describe the relationship. Microsoft CRM uses mostly one-to-many relationships between the default system entities (Account to Contact, Account to Opportunity, Lead to Activity, and so on). As you browse through the Microsoft CRM customization section, you might notice that the user interface uses different terminology interchangeably to describe the one-to-many data relationship. Table 6-1 shows frequently used Microsoft CRM terminology that describes a one-to-many relationship between entities.

Table 6-1 Relationship Terminology

Perspective	Example 1	Example 2	Example 3	Example 4
Account	Primary relationship to Contact	One-to-many relationship to Contact	Parent relationship to Contact	Primary entity
Contact	Related relationship to Account	Many-to-one relationship to Account	Child relationship to Account	Related entity

Although Microsoft CRM uses different terminology to describe the one-to-many relationship, the user interface on an entity's form always displays one-to-many entities in a consistent manner. Figure 6-4 shows an example of the relationship between the Account and Contact entities of the Contact form. On the related entity's form (Contact), a *lookup field* appears so that users can select the primary entity (Account).

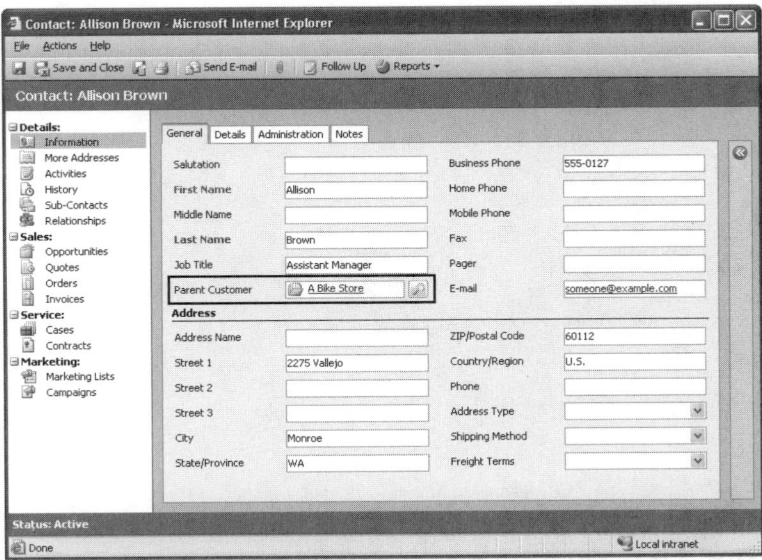

Figure 6-4 The primary entity displayed as a lookup on the related entity's form

Conversely, the related entity (Contact) does not appear on the form of the primary entity (Account). Rather, Microsoft CRM adds a link in the navigation pane of the primary entity to a page that displays all of the related entities in a grid view, as shown in Figure 6-5.

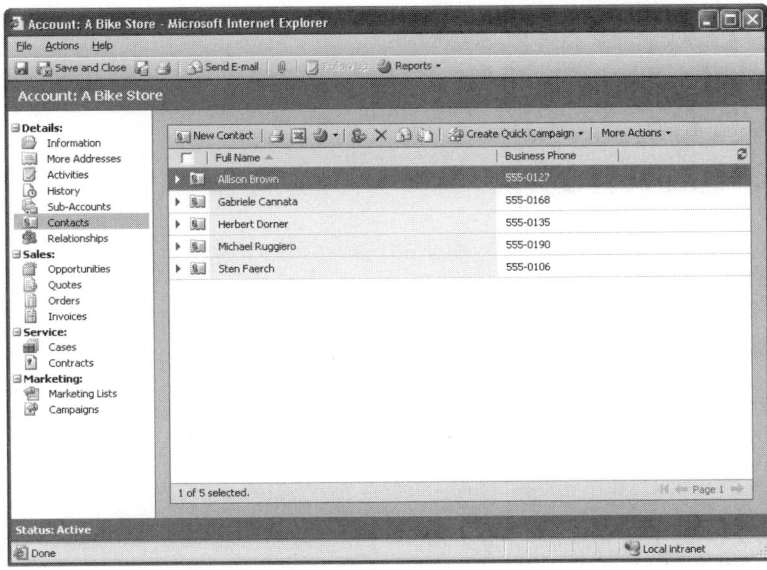

Figure 6-5 Related entities in a grid view

Remembering how Microsoft CRM displays primary and related entities in the user interface might help eliminate some confusion when you try to decide how to set up your custom entity relationships.

Many-to-Many

Now let's discuss another type of data relationship between entities in Microsoft CRM. Consider the relationship between the Marketing List entity and the Marketing List members, as illustrated in Figure 6-6.

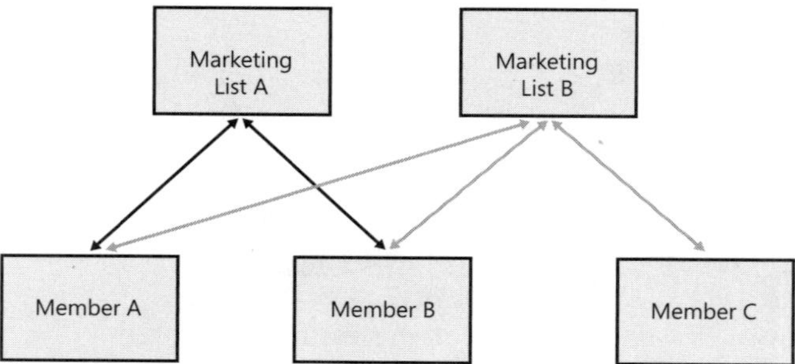

Figure 6-6 Many-to-many relationship between Marketing List and members

Figure 6-6 shows that you can create many marketing lists in Microsoft CRM, and then you can assign multiple members to each list. In addition, you can add members to multiple marketing lists. We would describe this relationship as *many-to-many*. The Microsoft CRM user interface always uses grids to display many-to-many relationships between two entities. Therefore, any time you see a lookup field on a form, you know that a one-to-many relationship exists between the two entities.

More Info Because the Account and Contact entities have a one-to-many relationship, you can assign only one account to each contact. (In a many-to-many relationship, you could assign multiple accounts to a contact *and* multiple contacts per account.) However, Microsoft CRM does allow you to track the relationships between multiple accounts and contacts in a many-to-many environment by using relationship roles as explained in Chapter 2.

Even though Microsoft CRM uses many-to-many relationships between some of its default system entities, you cannot create custom many-to-many relationships. Although you cannot create a custom many-to-many relationship directly between two entities, you can mimic a many-to-many relationship by using an intermediate entity. The final output in the user interface might not appear exactly as you want it to, but it can meet the needs of most people. We'll explain how to do this later in this chapter.

Relationship Behavior

In addition to understanding how Microsoft CRM structures the data relationship between entities, you must understand the *relationship behavior* of entity relationships before you can map out your own custom entities. Entity relationships always exhibit one of two behaviors:

- Parental
- Referential

In the case of parental relationship behavior, actions that you take against the primary entity will also apply to its related entities. With referential relationship behavior, any actions against the primary entity apply only to that entity and to none of its related entities. In Microsoft CRM, only five actions are affected by relationship behaviors:

- Delete
- Assign
- Reparent
- Share
- Unshare

Consequently, if you took any other action against an entity in Microsoft CRM (such as running a workflow rule), that action would not be affected by the entity's parental or referential relationship behavior.

Tip What's the difference between the assign action and the reparent action? When you assign an entity, you change the owner of the record from one user to a different user. When you reparent an entity, you change a record's parent entity by using the lookup tool. Changing the parent account of an account is an example of reparenting an entity.

It's important to understand the differences between parental and referential behavior because you need to specify relationship behavior any time you create a relationship between two entities. We expect that you'll always create at least one entity relationship for every custom entity you create. However, Microsoft CRM also lets you modify the default relationship behavior between the default system entities. Let's review parental and referential behavior in more detail.

Parental Behavior

If the relationship between entities exhibits parental behavior, actions applied to the parent entity will propagate down to all of its children entities. If you deleted an Account record (the primary entity) like the sample record Coho Vineyard shown in Figure 6-7, Microsoft CRM would delete all of that record's related data, such as its Activity, Note, custom entity, and Opportunity, because of those entity records' parental relationships to the Account entity.

Likewise, when Microsoft CRM deletes the custom entity record and the Opportunity record, it determines whether it should also delete their related entities based on the various relationship behaviors.

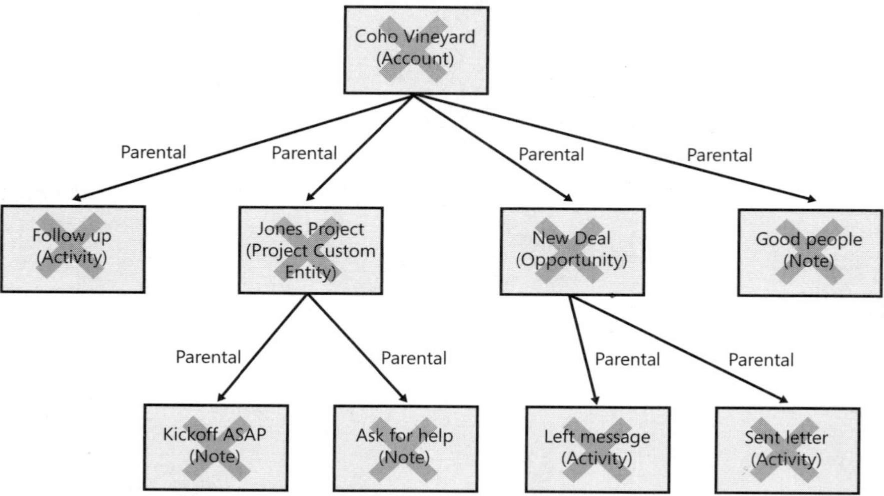

Figure 6-7 Relationship behaviors determine how Microsoft CRM cascades actions

In this Coho Vineyard example, Microsoft CRM would delete the Notes and Activities related to the custom entity record and the Opportunity because a parental relationship behavior exists between the those entities. The software refers to this concept of working down the primary and related entity tree as *cascading*.

More Info All of the default system entities, such as Leads, Accounts, and Contacts, possess a parental relationship with Activities and Notes by default. Therefore, any action you take against the parent entity will cascade down to all of its Activities and Notes. For example, if five active and two completed Tasks exist for an Account and you reassign that Account to a new user, all of the Tasks (active and completed) will also be assigned to the new user. Many customers want to reconfigure this default relationship behavior between system entities because they do not want to change the owner of completed Activity records. We explain how to change this later in the chapter.

You can configure custom entities to have a parental data relationship with system entities, but only if the custom entities have a referential relationship behavior to the default system entities. Custom entities cannot possess a parental relationship behavior to one of the default system entities.

Referential Behavior

In the case of referential relationships, actions taken against the primary entity do not cascade down to its related entities. To demonstrate referential relationship behavior, we modified the previous example by adding a custom entity B with a referential child relationship to the Project custom entity (see Figure 6-8).

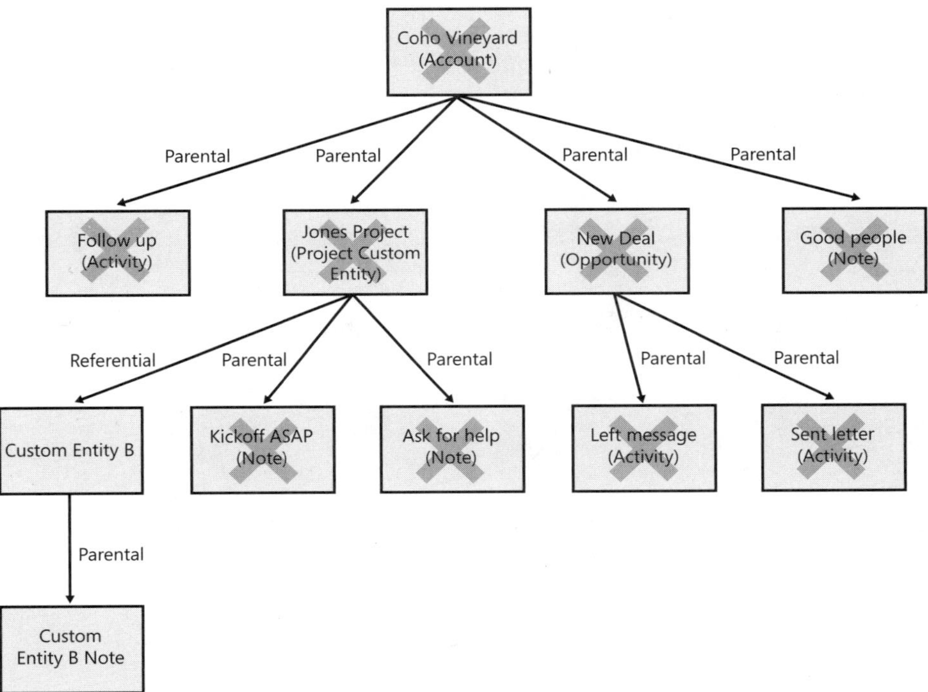

Figure 6-8 Referential behavior example

If you deleted the Coho Vineyard Account in Figure 6-8, Microsoft CRM would delete all of the records except custom entity B and its Note. Microsoft CRM would not delete custom entity B because it contains only a referential relationship to the Project custom entity. Microsoft CRM would delete the Project custom entity because of the parental relationship behavior to its primary entity Account.

Referential, Restrict Delete Behavior

The referential, restrict delete option is a special kind of referential behavior. When you configure this relationship type between a primary entity and a related entity, Microsoft CRM does not allow the user to delete the parent entity if that entity has any related entities. Rather, Microsoft CRM displays the error message shown in Figure 6-9 to the user.

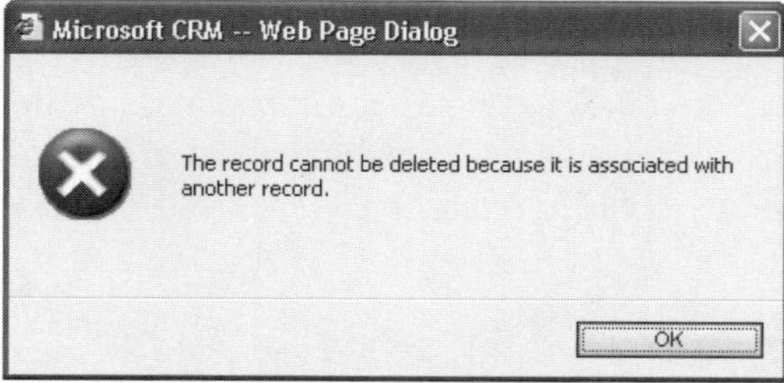

Figure 6-9 Error message displayed when users try to delete a restricted entity that possesses children entities

Behavior Configuration Options

Now that you understand the difference between parental and referential relationship behavior, let's examine how you use the relationship editor to configure these relationships in Microsoft CRM. Figure 6-10 shows the relationship editor when you create a new relationship.

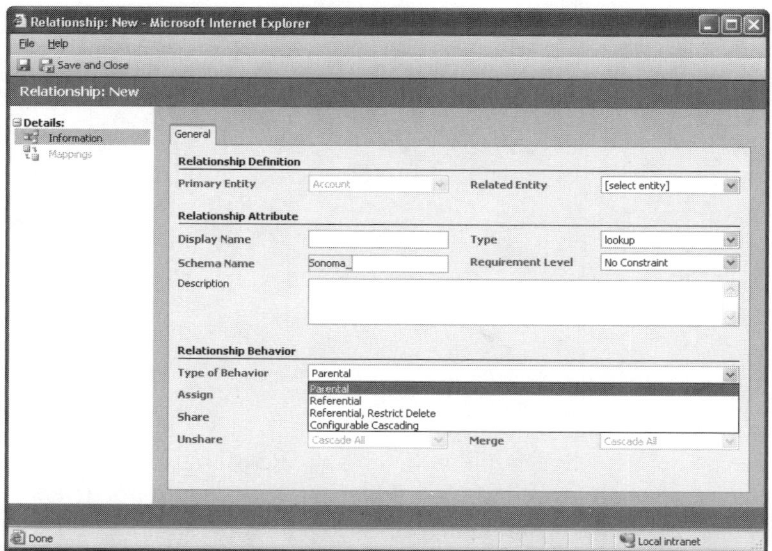

Figure 6-10 Entity relationship editor

In the Relationship Behavior section, you can choose from one of four values in the Type of Behavior list:

- Parental
- Referential
- Referential, Restrict Delete
- Configurable Cascading

If you choose parental or referential behavior, Microsoft CRM applies that relationship behavior to the actions taken against the primary entity.

If you choose Referential, Restrict Delete behavior, Microsoft CRM applies referential behavior to all actions *except* the delete action. As we explained earlier, Microsoft CRM will not allow users to delete an entity with related entities if you choose this behavior. Consequently, the software does not need to know how to cascade the delete action to related entities (because it can't possess any related entities when you delete it).

If you choose configurable cascading, Microsoft CRM allows you to specify different cascading behaviors depending on the action that users take against the parent entity. For example, you could set up parental cascading behavior for delete actions against the parent, but then change the cascading behavior of the assign action to referential behavior. For the assign, share, unshare, and reparent actions, you can configure one of four cascading rules:

- **Cascade All** Perform the action on the parent entity and all of its children entities; equivalent to parental.
- **Cascade Active** Perform the action on the parent entity and all of its children entities where the status is active or open. You might select this option if you want to maintain a history of which users owned the previously completed Activities (Tasks, Phone Calls, and so on).
- **Cascade User Owned** Perform the action on the parent entity and only those child entities for which the entity owner matches the parent entity owner.
- **Cascade None** Perform the action on the parent entity only; equivalent to referential.

A simple example might better illustrate how these cascading rules would work in the real world. Figure 6-11 shows an Account with four Tasks (two active, two completed) attached to it.

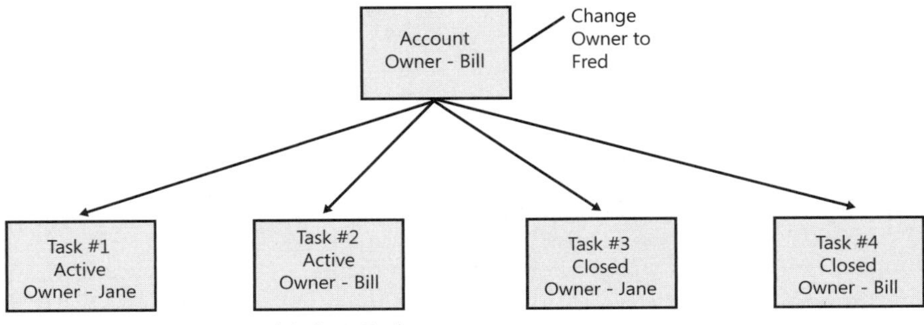

Figure 6-11 Account with four Tasks

If you take an action against the Account (the parent entity), such as changing the Account owner from Bill to Fred, the cascading behavior of the relationship between the Account and Task entities determines how Microsoft CRM applies the same action (assign) to the children entities. Table 6-2 shows how Microsoft CRM would assign the owners of the four tasks for each of the cascading behavior settings.

Table 6-2 Ownership Determined by Cascading Behavior

				Final Owner			
Type	**Entity**	**Status**	**Original Owner**	**Cascade all (parental)**	**Cascade active**	**Cascade owned**	**Cascade none (referential)**
Parent	Account	Active	Bill	Fred	Fred	Fred	Fred
Child	Task 1	Active	Jane	Fred	Fred	Jane	Jane
Child	Task 2	Active	Bill	Fred	Fred	Fred	Bill
Child	Task 3	Closed	Jane	Fred	Jane	Jane	Jane
Child	Task 4	Closed	Bill	Fred	Bill	Fred	Bill

For the delete action, you can configure one of three behaviors:

- **Cascade All** Delete the parent entity and all of its children entities; equivalent to parental.
- **Remove Link** Delete the link between the parent entity and the children entities, but do not delete the children entities; equivalent to referential.
- **Restrict** Prevent the user from deleting an entity that possesses child entities; equivalent to referential, restrict delete.

Although a Merge picklist appears in the Relationship Behavior section, you cannot configure different relationship behaviors for that action. Merge always uses the cascade all (parental) behavior.

Note The merge functionality applies only to the Lead, Contact, and Account entities.

Entity Mapping

Entity mapping is the third component of the relationship definition between two entities. Not every relationship between two entities includes an entity mapping, although every relationship must include a data relationship and relationship behavior. Mapping allows you to specify common attributes that two entities share. Entity mapping provides the benefits of saving your users time and reducing data entry errors by automatically *mapping* data from the primary entity to its related entity at the time that Microsoft CRM creates a related entity.

For example, if you add a related Contact to an Account, the default entity mapping between these entities automatically populates the address of the Contact with the same address as the Account. Without mappings, the user would have to retype the address information into the Contact, even though it's identical to the address of the Account.

Important Microsoft CRM maps entity attributes only at the time that it creates a related entity. Mapping does not continually keep data synchronized. Therefore, if the address of the Account (primary) record changes, Microsoft CRM will not automatically map these changes to the Contact (related) records. This type of synchronization would require additional system customization with custom programming. You could also use the bulk edit feature in Microsoft CRM to update the address of multiple Contact records at one time.

Some of the scenarios in which Microsoft CRM uses entity mappings include:

- Adding a related entity to a primary entity by using actions (such as clicking add Related Activity from Action in the entity menu bar)
- Adding an Activity to an entity by using actions (clicking add Related Activity from Action in the entity menu bar)
- Converting a Lead to an Account, Contact, and Opportunity

To view all of the entity relationships that include a mapping, click the Type list in the Relationships section, and then select Mappable, as shown in Figure 6-12.

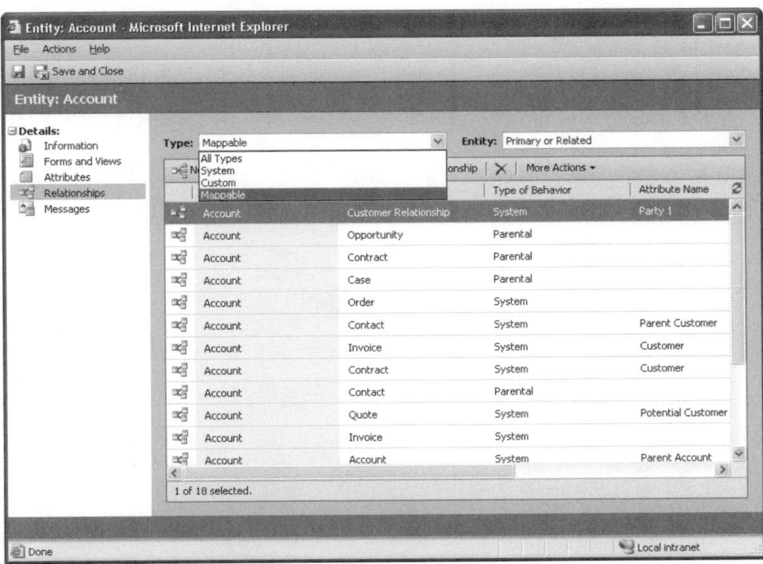

Figure 6-12 Selecting mappable relationships

When you open the relationship editor for any mappable relationship, you see a Mappings link in the left-hand navigation pane. Click the Mappings link to display the mapped attributes for the relationship. Figure 6-13 shows the attribute mappings between the Account and Contact entities.

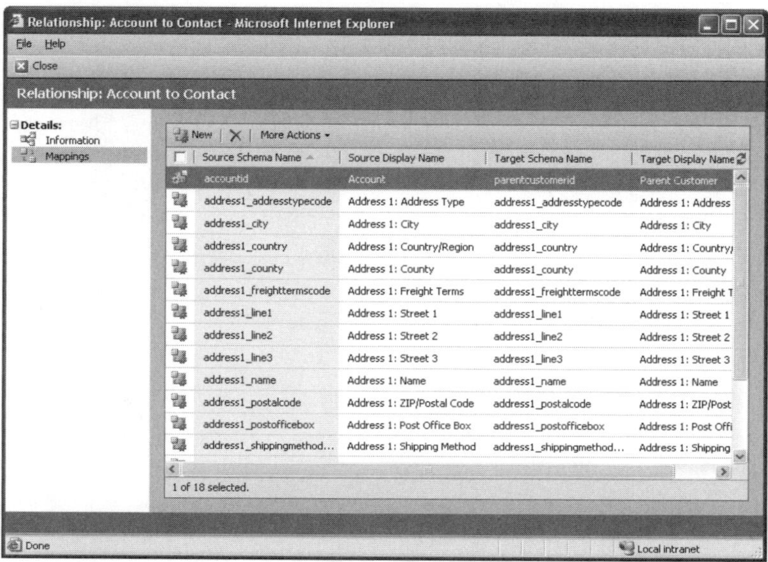

Figure 6-13 Attribute mappings between the Account and Contact entities

Each mapping consists of a source attribute and a target attribute, and you can see that Microsoft CRM already mapped attributes such as the address information between Account and Contact. Therefore, when you create a related Contact for an Account, Microsoft CRM automatically pre-populates the target attributes of the Contact with the values from the source entity (Account). Figure 6-14 shows a graphical representation of the Account and Contact mapping.

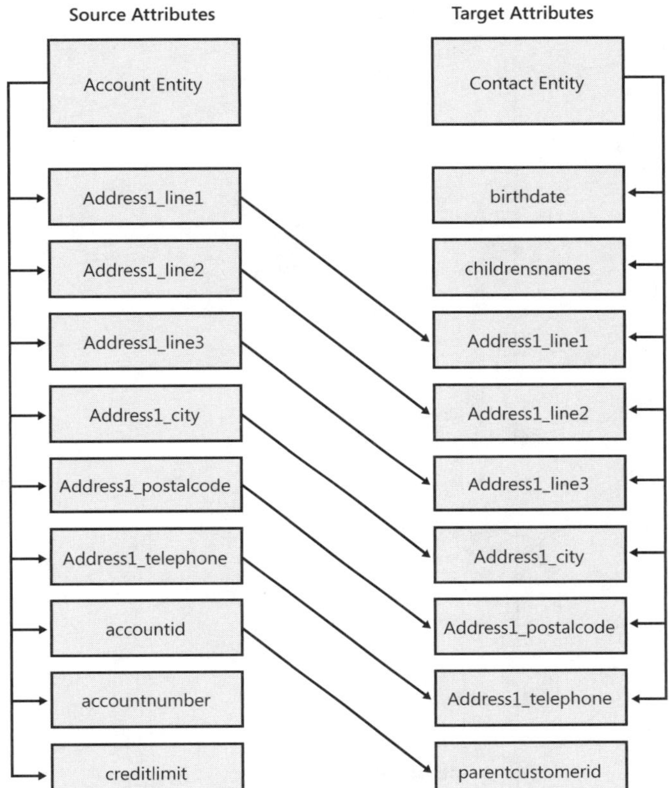

Figure 6-14 Mapping attributes between the Account and Contact entities

We did not include all of the Account and Contact attributes in this figure because of space considerations, but you can see that the Account entity includes attributes (such as accountnumber and creditlimit) that do not map to the Contact entity. Likewise, the Contact entity includes attributes such as birthdate and childrensnames that don't apply to the Account entity. The point we're trying to illustrate is that you don't have to map *all* of the attributes from one entity to another, just the ones that make sense.

Microsoft CRM includes thousands of attribute mappings by default, but you will probably need to create new attribute mappings or modify the default mappings. Consider an example in which you added a custom picklist attribute with a schema name of new_customerrating to both the Account and Contact entities (see Figure 6-15). Although both entities use the same schema name of customerrating, you must still create a mapping between these two attributes if you want Microsoft CRM to automatically populate the customerrating field when you create a related Contact from an Account.

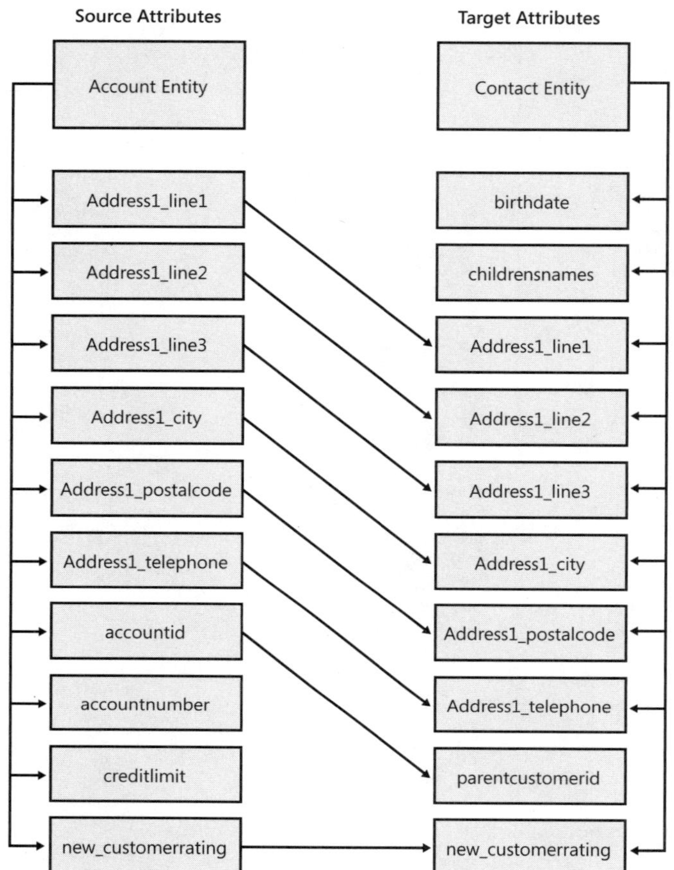

Figure 6-15 Mapping custom attributes between the Account and Contact entities

To create a custom mapping between two attributes, you must meet the following conditions:

- Both attributes must use the same data type.
- The length of the target attribute must be equal to or greater than the source attribute.
- You can specify an attribute as the target value only one time. However, you can map an attribute from the source entity to multiple target schema names.

Microsoft CRM provides two methods for creating mappings. You can manually map attributes one at a time, or you can use the *generate mappings* feature to let Microsoft CRM automatically generate mappings for you. When you use the generate mappings feature, Microsoft CRM creates an attribute map if two attributes share a schema name and a data type.

Manually creating a mapping

1. In the Customization section, double-click an entity record and click **Relationships** in the navigation pane.
2. Double-click the entity relationship that you want to modify the relationship mapping for, including adding a new mapping.
3. The relationship editor window will appear; click **Mappings** in the navigation pane.
4. To add a new mapping, click **New** in the grid toolbar. To modify an existing mapping, double-click the mapping you want to modify.
5. A dialog box appears with the source entity attributes on the left and the target entity attributes on the right.

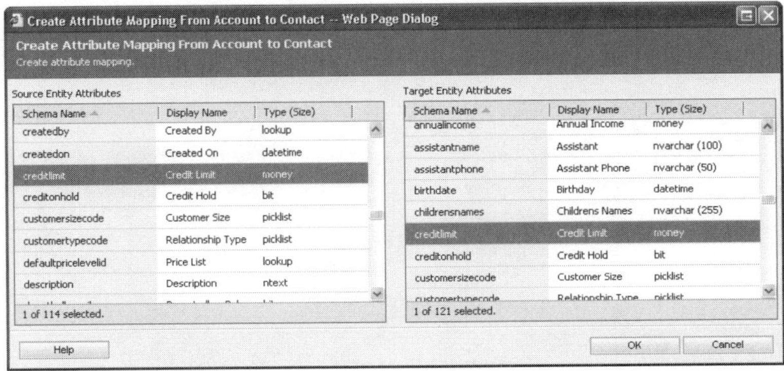

6. Select the source and target attributes that you want to map, and then click **OK**.
7. An "Attribute Mapping" message appears.
8. Save the relationship, and then publish the entities that you customized.

> **Tip** You can map two attributes even if they use different schema names.

To use the generate mappings feature instead of manual mapping, simply click More Actions in the grid toolbar, and then click Generate Mappings. Please note that when you generate mappings, Microsoft CRM removes all of the existing mappings between the entities and creates new mappings.

Mapping Picklist Attributes

Creating mappings for attributes of the picklist data type requires additional steps to ensure that the values map correctly. When you map two picklist attributes together, you must also make sure that the picklist values match up accurately. When a user looks at a drop-down list on a form, Microsoft CRM displays the *picklist label* to the user. However, when Microsoft CRM maps two picklist fields together, it uses the *picklist value*, not the picklist label.

To demonstrate this nuance, let's add a new value to the Industry picklist on the Lead entity. Microsoft CRM includes a default mapping between the Industry attribute of Lead to the Industry attribute of Account. When you convert a Lead and create an Account, Microsoft CRM uses this mapping to automatically populate the Account industry with the same value as the Lead industry.

If you wanted to add a new industry to the picklist called Software, you would add this value to both the Lead and Account attributes to keep the values in sync.

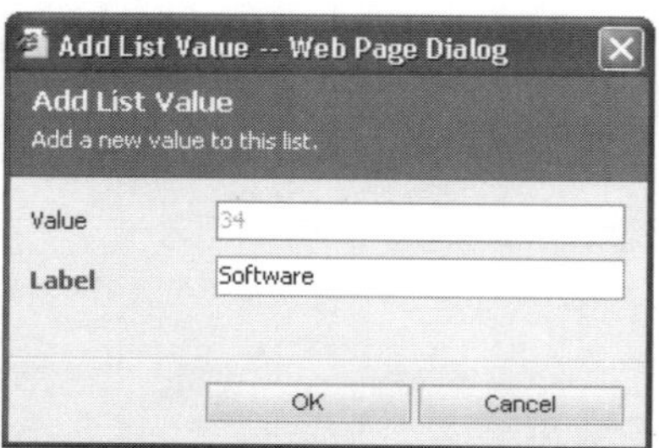

When you click Add, you enter the picklist text "Software" in the Label box. The text in the Label box is what the user will see in the drop-down list on the form. However, note that Microsoft CRM also uses a read-only integer picklist value along with the picklist label. When Microsoft CRM maps the Lead industry to the Account industry, it uses the picklist integer value to set the value on the account. Table 6-3 shows how Microsoft CRM would map different picklist values based on sample picklist values and labels.

Table 6-3 Picklist Mapping Examples

Source picklist value (Lead)	Source picklist label (Lead)	Target picklist attribute value (Account)	Target picklist attribute label (Account)	Match?	Resulting picklist value (Account Record)	Resulting picklist label (Account Record)
1	Consulting	1	Consulting	Yes	1	Consulting
1	Consulting	1	Professional Services	Yes	1	Professional Services
1	Consulting	2	Consulting	No	Blank	Blank
1	Consulting	None	None	No	Blank	Blank

Microsoft CRM always uses the picklist value to determine matches for picklist fields. Consequently, *it is critical that you make sure that the integer values of the picklist always match correctly.*

The picklist integer value is a read-only field that always increments by one when you add new picklist values. Therefore, if you add multiple picklist values at one time, always enter them in the same sequence on both entities. If you get out of sequence or if you accidentally delete a picklist value, you will need some creative reworking to get the picklist values mapping correctly again because you can't edit the picklist integer.

Consider an example in which you added three new Industry picklist values, but you mistakenly entered them in a different order on the Lead and Account entities.

Lead Entity

- Professional Sports (value=34)
- Real Estate (value=35)
- Software (value=36)

Account Entity

- Professional Sports (value=34)
- Software (value=35)
- Real Estate (value=36)

If you entered the three new industry values in the order shown, Microsoft CRM would give them the picklist values listed. However, if you converted a Lead with the Real Estate industry value selected, Microsoft CRM would map that to the Software industry of the Account record because it matched the integer values of 35 on both attributes. Obviously, you would want to modify the system so that the industry values mapped correctly. However, you cannot simply edit the picklists integer values because they are read-only values.

Lead Entity

- Professional Sports (value=34)
- ~~Real Estate (value=35)~~
- ~~Software (value=36)~~
- Real Estate (value=37)
- Software (value=38)

Account Entity

- Professional Sports (value=34)
- ~~Software (value=35)~~
- ~~Real Estate (value=36)~~
- Real Estate (value=37)
- Software (value=38)

To fix this problem, you could delete the existing Real Estate and Software picklist values from both the Lead and Account entities. Then you would create two new picklist values on both entities, making sure to enter them in the same order. Microsoft CRM would assign two new picklist values, which would then map correctly when users converted a lead. If you don't have a lot of records assigned to these picklist values yet, it might be easier to just change the labels and update your lead records accordingly

This same concept of matching picklist values also applies to entities with status reasons and state attributes such as Account, Lead, and Opportunity. Please make sure that you match up the values for all of the status reasons for each of the different states between two entities.

Creating Custom Entities

Microsoft CRM creates over 120 entities when you install the software, and you can add an almost unlimited number of custom attributes to the customizable entities. However, you will most likely want to track business data that does not fit neatly into one of these existing entities. With most other CRM applications (and earlier versions of Microsoft CRM), tracking new categories of data usually required a custom application development project in which consultants would create new custom databases and user interface forms that they tried to blend into the host CRM application.

In addition to the obvious downsides of taking development time and costing money, these customized CRM application projects usually resulted in less-than-ideal functionality for system administrators and end users. Plus, when the host CRM application released an updated version, the consultants had to reprogram the business logic code, update the customized databases, and revise the user interface forms. Add all these factors up and you understand why CRM customization projects in the past required lots of time, money, and effort.

Custom Entity Benefits

Fortunately, Microsoft CRM solves many of the common CRM customzation issues related to tracking new categories of data by allowing you to create custom entities. Even more beneficial, Microsoft CRM allows you to create custom entities and manage their relationships with the Web-based administration interface (so no custom programming is required).

So how might you use custom entities? You have almost unlimited options for setting up and structuring your custom entities. An apartment management company might use custom entities to track its various property locations, leases, and rental applications. A professional services firm might create custom entities to track its various customer projects. A magazine publisher might use custom entities to capture data about its magazines and customer subscriptions. As you can see, how you use custom entities depends on the nature of your business and the types of data that you want to capture in Microsoft CRM.

When you create a custom entity to store a new category of data, Microsoft CRM automatically adds the entity to the metadata and its underlying system data. That means that custom entities behave as "first class" system entities, sharing almost all of the functionality of the default system entities created on installation. Some common benefits of custom entities and the default entities include the following:

- You can customize the custom entity attributes, forms, and views with the same Web-based administration tools that you use to customize the default entities.
- Users can use the Advanced Find feature to create and save custom queries on custom entities.

- You can add client-side events such as *onChange*, *onLoad*, and *onSave* to the custom entity's form.
- You can import and export custom entities and their customizations with the same import/export tool that you use for the default entities.
- Users can access custom entities within the Microsoft CRM client for Microsoft Office Outlook (laptop or desktop).
- Users can work with custom entities offline by using the Microsoft CRM laptop client for Office Outlook.
- You can add relationships and mappings to custom entities, just as you can with the default entities.
- Custom entities fully participate in the Microsoft CRM security framework, so you can set privileges such as Create, Read, and Write on an entity-by-entity basis.
- Developers can programmatically access custom entities through the Microsoft CRM Software Development Kit (SDK), including Create, Retrieve, and Update operations.
- Microsoft CRM supports pre- and post-callouts on custom entities.
- Users can use the batch edit feature on custom entity records.
- Microsoft CRM creates filtered views for custom entities in the SQL database that you can use for creating reports.
- Users can export custom entities to Microsoft Office Excel as a dynamic PivotTable or dynamic worksheet.
- You can modify the Microsoft CRM application navigation and menu structure to seamlessly blend custom entities into the user interface.

This list illustrates that custom entities behave almost identically to the default entities within the Microsoft CRM system.

Custom Entity Limitations

Despite all of the similarities between custom entities and default entities, a few notable limitations exist for custom entities:

- Custom entities support one-to-many and many-to-one relationships only. You cannot create many-to-many relationships directly between two custom entities.
- You cannot merge two custom entity records together.
- The Microsoft CRM Data Migration Framework does not support custom entities. This means that you must export and import custom entity data by using a separate (custom) process.

- The Microsoft CRM system entities include a relationship to Customer in which users can select an Account or a Contact. For custom entities, you can specify a relationship with the Account entity and the Contact entity, but you cannot create a relationship to the composite Customer entity (in which users can select an Account or a Contact on a single lookup).
- You can specify only one parent relationship per custom entity, so you can't add custom entity lookups on non-parent entities.
- Custom entities don't appear in an entity rollup (showing activities from child entities on the parent entity's record).
- Organization-owned custom entities can't participate in Microsoft CRM workflow, but user-owned custom entities can.

As you can see, most of the limitations regarding custom entities revolve around the supported relationships that you can create. We'll explain setting up and configuring custom entity relationships (and their corresponding limitations) next.

Custom Entity Relationships

As you learned earlier in this chapter, Microsoft CRM uses entity relationships to manage how two entities relate to one another. Entity relationships define the nature of the data relationship between entities, the behavior of that relationship, and how to map attributes between the entities. When you use custom entities, you will want to add custom relationships between your custom entities and the default system entities so that users can track and enter data about how the custom entities relate to the other entities. In addition, you will probably want to create custom relationships between custom entities to dictate how the custom entities interact with each other. After we explain how relationships work in the context of custom entities, we'll show you how to set up and create custom entities.

Table 6-4 shows the types of relationships that Microsoft CRM supports.

Table 6-4 Supported Custom Relationships

Primary entity type	Related entity type	Relationship behavior	Create custom relationships?	Create custom mappings?
System	Custom	Parental	Yes	Yes
System	Custom	Referential	Yes	Yes
Custom	Custom	Parental	Yes	Yes
Custom	Custom	Referential	Yes	Yes
Custom	System (Activity and/or Note)	Parental	Only on custom entity creation	No
Custom	System (Activity and/or Note)	Referential	No	No
Custom	System (all other entities)	Parental	No	Yes

Table 6-4 **Supported Custom Relationships**

Primary entity type	Related entity type	Relationship behavior	Create custom relationships?	Create custom mappings?
Custom	System (all other entities)	Referential	Yes	Yes
System	System	Parental	No	Yes
System	System	Referential	No	Yes

In addition, you should be aware of the following nuances:

- You cannot create a custom relationship between an entity and itself. So you could not create a concept similar to the account and sub-account feature that exists in Microsoft CRM.
- Two entities can have only one distinct relationship between them. Therefore, you could not create relationships in such a way that a form has two or more lookups that connect to the same custom entity. However, you can create multiple relationships between a custom entity and other entities; you just can't create multiple relationships to the same entity.
- You cannot create new custom relationships between existing system entities, such as adding additional relationships between the Opportunity and User entities. However, you can use relationship roles to create new opportunity relationships and customer relationships.
- You cannot create many-to-many relationships (custom-to-custom or system-to-custom) between two entities.
- You can create only one parental relationship behavior for each custom entity.
- Custom entities cannot have a parental relationship behavior to system entities.

More Info Although Table 6-4 lists only parental and referential relationship behaviors, you can also use referential, restrict delete, and configurable cascading where appropriate because both of those behaviors are merely sub-types of parental and referential relationship behaviors.

To put these supported relationships and custom entity constraints into context, let's map out a real-world example of creating custom entities and relationships for a fictional property management firm called Litware, Inc.

Litware, Inc. manages 15 apartment buildings on the East Coast. The apartment complexes range in size from 25 to 75 apartments per building, including one-bedroom, two-bedroom, and three-bedroom apartments. As part of the rental process, each prospective tenant must complete a rental application and submit to a credit check. After receiving credit approval, all of the tenants sharing an apartment (roommates) sign a lease. Litware, Inc. will use Microsoft CRM to manage its current tenants and track potential tenants.

Based on this description, we created an initial design proposal in which Litware, Inc. would use the following entities in Microsoft CRM:

- **Building** Custom entity with attributes such as name and address
- **Apartment** Custom entity with attributes such as number of bedrooms, number of bathrooms, square footage, monthly rent, and floor number
- **Lease** Custom entity with attributes such as monthly rent, start date, end date, and security deposit
- **Lease Application** Custom entity with attributes such as employment information and previous addresses
- **Contact** System entity used to track tenants and applicants
- **Opportunity** System entity used to track potential rental opportunities

When you map out an entity design like this one, you should consider different scenarios because no hard rules exist to let you know whether you should create a custom entity or add attributes to an existing entity. We recommend that you try to map out all of the proposed entities and relationships that you think you'll need in your solution before you start entering changes in Microsoft CRM. Making changes to your entity relationships in a modeling tool such as Microsoft Office Visio is much easier and more efficient than making changes in Microsoft CRM. Figure 6-16 shows our proposed entity map for Litware, Inc.

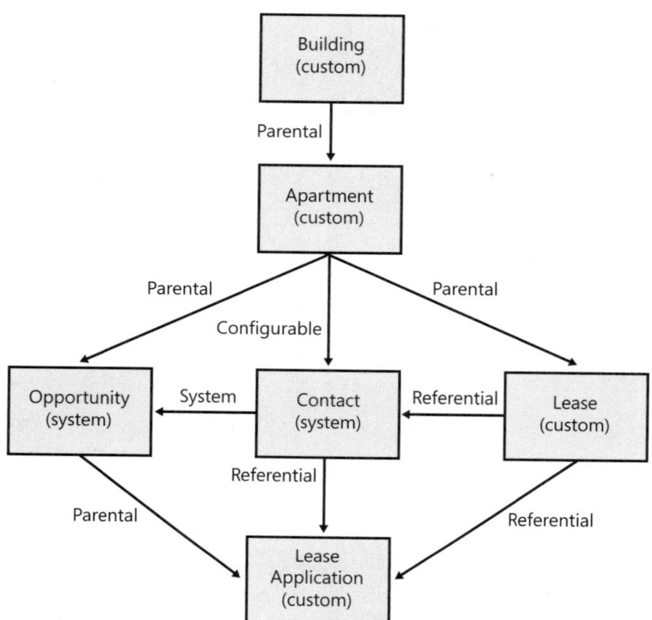

Figure 6-16 Proposed entity relationship map for Litware, Inc.

Based on this initial design, we created visual mockups of the Opportunity and Contact entity forms, as shown in Figure 6-17 and Figure 6-18.

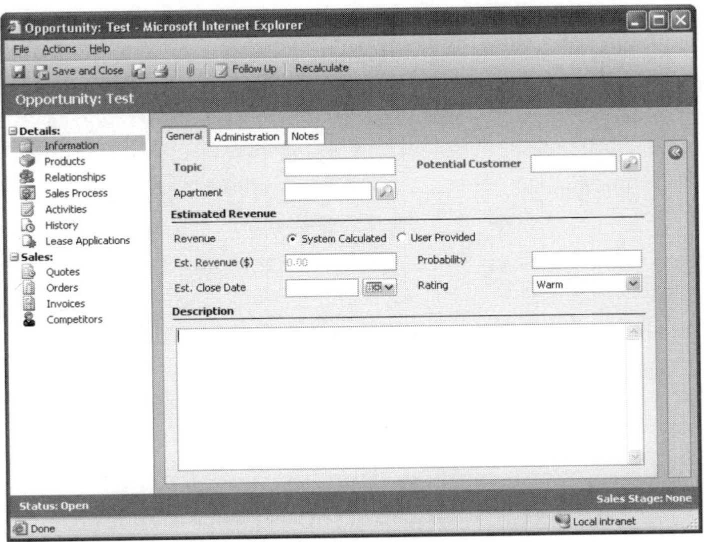

Figure 6-17 Mockup of the Opportunity form

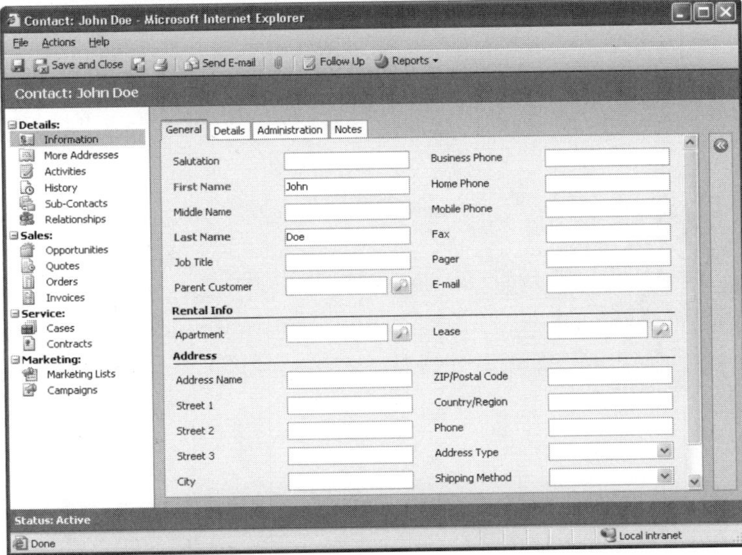

Figure 6-18 Mockup of the Contact form

You can immediately see how some of our proposed entity relationships manifest themselves in the user interface. For example, our proposed design includes the following benefits and caveats:

- We can track multiple Contact records per lease because of the one-to-many relationship between Lease and Contact. However, this relationship also means that each Contact can have only *one* related lease record (as you can see in Figure 6-18). In reality, a tenant might rent from Litware, Inc. for several consecutive years and have multiple leases. However, Microsoft CRM does not support this type of relationship because multiple contacts on a lease *and* multiple leases per contact would constitute a many-to-many relationship.
- For any single apartment, we can view all of the related Opportunities because of the one-to-many relationship between Apartment and Opportunity. However, if a potential tenant were trying to decide between two different apartments, Litware, Inc. could track only one of those apartments. The apartment lookup field on the Opportunity form allows a user to select only one apartment. Again, this constraint appears because Microsoft CRM does not support many-to-many relationships.
- Although you can specify only one lease per Contact, Litware, Inc. can view the entire lease history for any single apartment because of the one-to-many relationship between Apartment and Lease.
- Because we cannot create new relationships between system entities, we could not create a new relationship between Opportunity and Contact. Therefore, on the Opportunity form, we can select only one contact record, even though the apartment might have two or three roommates. Fortunately, opportunity relationships give us an easy workaround for this situation. We can create a new relationship role (in Settings) called Roommate, and then simply add roommates as additional contacts.

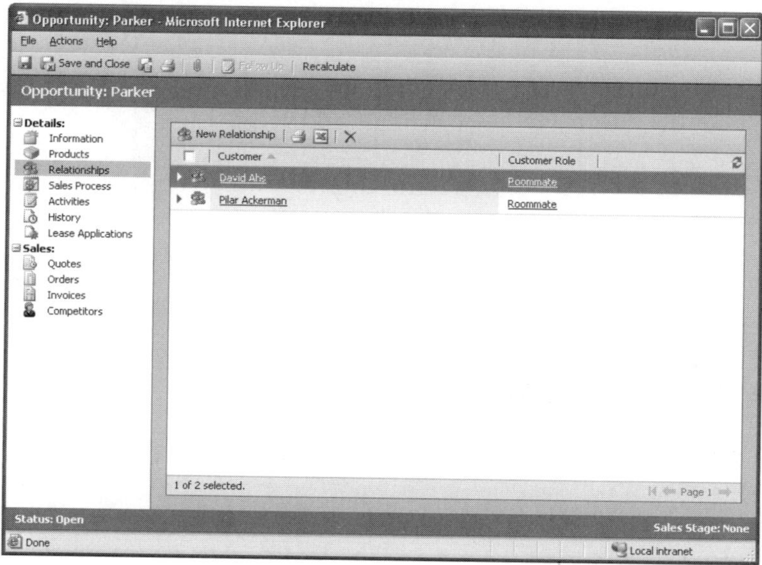

- Our design allows Litware, Inc. to create a unique Contact record for each tenant and add multiple tenants to an apartment. Therefore, the company can quickly and easily find the current tenants for any given apartment with one click from the apartment record.
- The proposed design allows each tenant to complete his or her own lease application independently.

If Litware, Inc. reviewed our proposed relationship design, the reviewers might decide to make changes to the entity relationships based on specific business needs. For example, they might want to change the Contact and Lease Application relationship so that Lease Application becomes the primary entity and Contact becomes the related entity. This change would allow company managers to view multiple Contacts on a single application (our original design allowed them to view multiple lease applications per contact).

Another potential design change might involve eliminating the relationship between Apartment and Contact. At first, this might strike you as strange because it seems intuitive that a relationship should exist between those two entities. However, by eliminating the link between Apartment and Contact in addition to flipping the primary/related entity relationship between Contact and Lease Application, we effectively create a many-to-many relationship between Apartment and Contact! Each apartment can have many leases, and each lease can have many contacts. Therefore, each apartment can have many Contacts and each Contact can have many apartments (through the Lease entity).

Important Although you cannot create a custom many-to-many relationship between two entities in Microsoft CRM, you can effectively create a many-to-many relationship behavior between two entities (A and B) by creating an intermediate entity (C) and then creating two custom one-to-many relationships. Create one relationship between A and C and create a one-to-many relationship between C and B.

Figure 6-19 shows the modified relationship design.

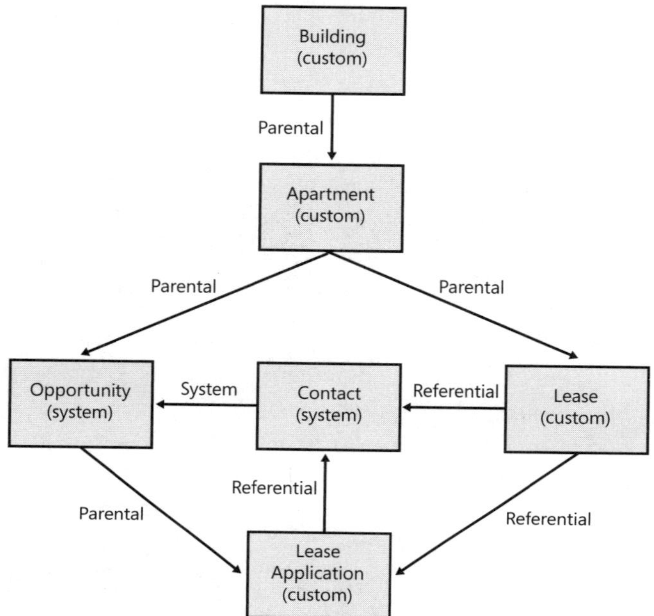

Figure 6-19 Revised entity relationship map for Litware, Inc.

Of course, when you change the entity relationships, you must also update your entity forms. The downside of removing the relationship between Apartment and Contact is that to view the Contacts for an apartment, you must first click the lease record and then click the Contacts link in the navigation pane on the lease record. Figure 6-20 and Figure 6-21 show mock-ups of what the Lease and Apartment forms would look like for the revised design.

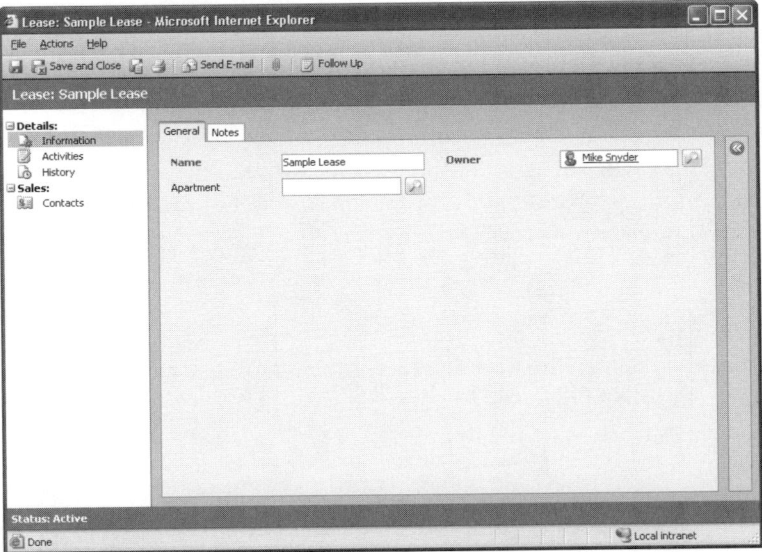

Figure 6-20 Lease form for the revised entity relationship design

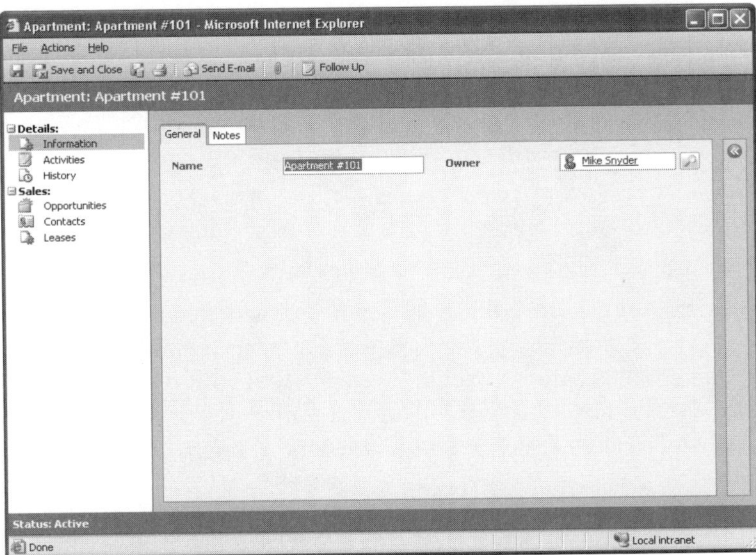

Figure 6-21 Apartment form for the revised entity relationship design

In summary, either of these designs could work perfectly well for Litware, Inc. However, both designs offer unique benefits and drawbacks that you must consider when you create custom entities. Hopefully, this example also convinced you of the benefits of mapping out all of the entity relationships in a tool such as Microsoft Visio.

Ownership

Microsoft CRM assigns an owner to almost all of the records in its database. Records such as Leads, Accounts, Activities, and Contacts have a Microsoft CRM user for their owner. However, Microsoft CRM assigns ownership of records such as products, sales literature, and sites to the organization. These types of records store information that theoretically applies to all of the users in the organization, regardless of their business unit. For each custom entity you create, you must specify one of two ownership types:

- User-owned
- Organization-owned

You must make the entity ownership decision carefully because you cannot change the entity ownership type after you create the entity. Some of the differences between user ownership and organization ownership include the following:

- User-owned entities can be assigned to other users; organization-owned entities cannot.
- User-owned entities can be shared with one or more teams; organization-owned entities cannot.
- Because user-owned entities belong to a user and each user belongs to a business unit, you have more flexibility when configuring security on user-owned entities than you do with organization-owned entities. When you configure a security role regarding organization-owned entities, you can specify only None or Organization access levels. For user-owned entities, you can specify one of five different access levels: None, User, Business Unit, Parent: Child Business Units, or Organization.
- Organization-owned entities can require less work to administer because they belong to the company. However, you must always assign a user-owned entity to a specific user record.
- You can create and run workflow rules on user-owned entities only.

As this list illustrates, making custom entities user-owned provides you with more options and configurability. However, user ownership does require that you carefully assign each entity to the correct owner and configure the security roles correctly. If your users frequently change business units or job functions, you will want to update entity ownership accordingly. In such scenarios, the work of maintaining the correct user ownership might offset the additional configurability and workflow benefits.

Entity Icons

Microsoft CRM uses different icons in the user interface to represent each of the default system entities. These icons appear in the navigation pane, in various views, and on a related entity's form. In addition to improving the visual aesthetics, these entity icons help users navigate the system by providing graphical indicators about each type of record they are working with. By default, Microsoft CRM assigns the icon shown in Figure 6-22 to each new custom entity.

Figure 6-22 Default custom entity icon

When you have more than a few custom entities in your system, using the same default icon for all of the custom entities diminishes the aesthetic benefit of icons and might cause confusion with your users because the same icon appears for multiple entities. Figure 6-23 shows an example of four different custom entities, all using the default icon.

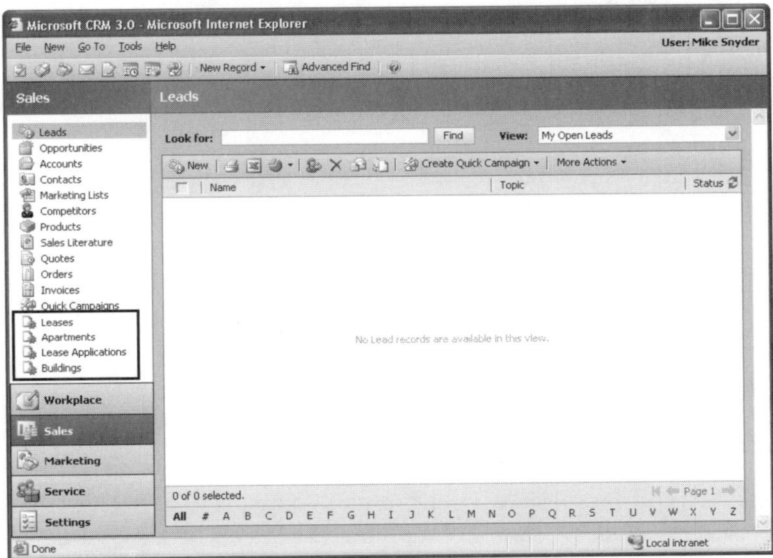

Figure 6-23 Multiple custom entities using the same default icon

Fortunately, Microsoft CRM allows you to upload your own custom icons for each custom entity. We highly recommend that you try to use custom icons for each custom entity in your system. You can upload two types of entity icons for each custom entity, and they must meet the specifications outlined in Table 6-5.

Table 6-5 Entity Icon Specifications

Icon usage	File type	Size (in pixels)	Maximum file size
Web application	.gif	16 x 16	10 kilobytes
Microsoft CRM client for Outlook	.ico (16 colors)	32 x 32	10 kilobytes

In addition, you should use files with transparent backgrounds for both types of entity icon file. When the icons appear on dark backgrounds or when Microsoft CRM highlights the record, failure to use transparency in your images creates an unpleasant effect.

Most graphics editing programs provide the tools to create these icons to the specifications of Microsoft CRM. When you have your icon files ready, uploading them to the custom entity is easy.

Updating Custom Entity Icons

1. In the entity editor, click **Actions**, and then click **Update Icons**. The following dialog box appears.

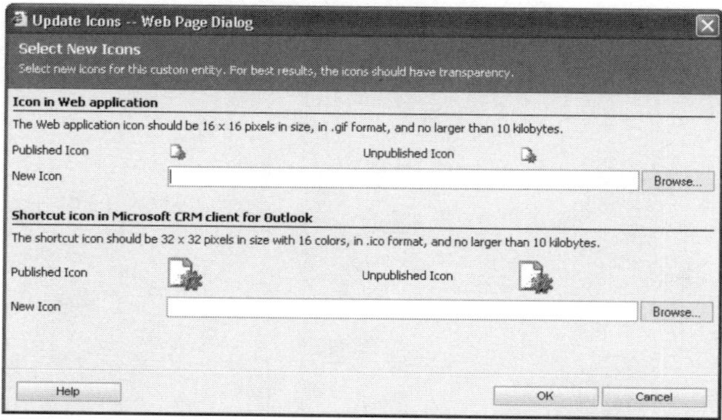

2. For both the Web and Outlook file types, browse and upload the icon files that you want to use, and then click **OK**. A preview of the icon that you uploaded appears, in addition to the current published icon.
3. Publish the entity so that users can see the new icons.

More Info Microsoft CRM allows you to upload icons for custom entities, but you can also change the entity icons by using the site map. The site map allows you to specify new image files for custom entities *and* the default system entities, such as Leads, Accounts, and Contacts. We explain the site map in more detail later in this chapter.

Creating a Custom Entity

By now you should understand the concepts, benefits, and limitations related to custom entities. Now let's go through the steps that you will follow to create a custom entity in Microsoft CRM. For every custom entity you create, you must configure the following parameters:

- Entity definition
- Offline availability
- Associated entities
- Display areas
- Primary attribute

Figure 6-24 shows the user interface for creating a new entity; we'll provide a little more information about each parameter.

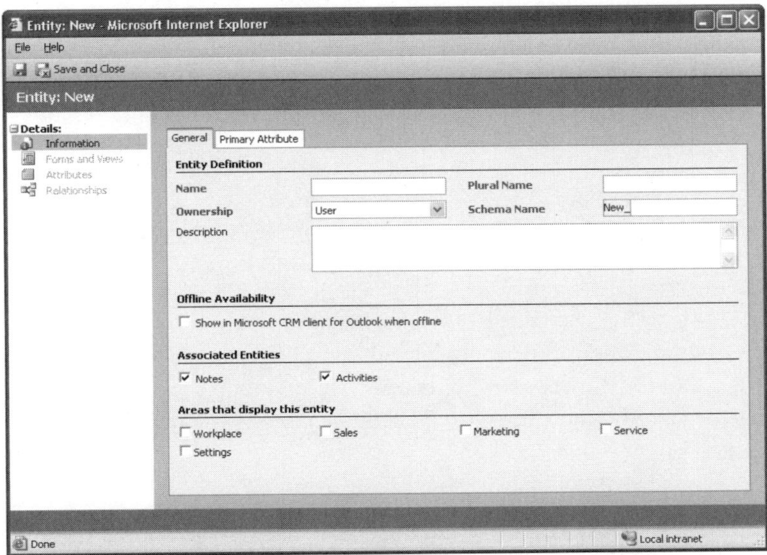

Figure 6-24 Creating a new custom entity

Entity Definition

In the Entity Definition section, you will enter some basic parameters about the custom entity, including:

- Name
- Plural name
- Ownership (user or organization)
- Schema name
- Description (optional)

In Chapter 4, we discussed how the name, plural name, schema name, and description parameters work with regard to renaming entities, so you should be familiar with these concepts. Remember that you cannot change the schema name after you create the entity, but you can modify the name, plural name, and description at any time.

> **Tip** You can change the default schema name prefix from new_ to a different value by configuring the schema-name prefix. To alter this value, browse to Settings, click Organization Settings, click System Settings, and then click Customization.

For the ownership parameter, you must specify whether the entity will be user-owned or organization-owned, as discussed earlier in this chapter.

Offline Availability

Microsoft CRM includes two different Office Outlook clients: Microsoft CRM desktop client for Microsoft Office Outlook and the Microsoft CRM laptop client for Microsoft Office Outlook.

The laptop client allows your users to access Microsoft CRM data if they disconnect from your network. Microsoft CRM refers to this concept of working disconnected from the network as working offline. The desktop client works only when users are connected to the server. You have the option to use one, none, or both of the Outlook clients in your deployment.

When you create a custom entity, you can choose whether you want your users to work offline with custom entities. Obviously, this parameter affects you only if your organization deploys the laptop client because only that client can go offline. The offline availability option has no impact on the desktop client.

> **Tip** Even if you decide to include a custom entity for offline availability, the default synchronization settings for the laptop client will not include any custom entities. Therefore, your users must also manually configure their offline filters to include the custom entity when they go offline.

You have the option to toggle the offline availability feature off or on at any time.

Associated Entities

When you create a custom entity, you can choose whether you want to enable Notes and Activities for the entity. Notes and Activities for custom entities behave just like Notes and Activities for the default system entities. Therefore, if you enable Activities, users can add any type of Activity record (such as Task, Phone Call, or Letter) that their security privileges allow.

You must configure Notes and Activities at the time that you create a custom entity. You cannot change the associated entities settings at a later time.

> **More Info** Because you can't change these settings later, you might be tempted to always include Notes and Activities on your custom entities. Remember that when you include Activities on a custom entity, that entity will appear as an option in the Regarding list for Tasks, Phone Calls, and so on. If you don't want users to select the custom entity as a regarding value, make sure that you do not include Activities.

Display Areas

Microsoft CRM allows you to specify where to display the custom entity to users in the application navigation. The default display area options include:

- Workplace
- Sales
- Marketing
- Service
- Settings

You can choose to display the custom entity in all, some, or none of the areas. When you choose to include a custom entity, Microsoft CRM adds a link in the navigation pane in addition to a link in the application menu bar. You have the ability to toggle the display settings whenever you want, not just during entity creation.

Tip You can further customize the user interface and application navigation with the site map that we will cover later in this chapter. By modifying the site map, you can include additional areas as options for your users to check.

Primary Attribute

Every entity, including the default system entities, has a primary attribute that Microsoft CRM uses to display on the lookup field in related entities. Figure 6-25 shows how Microsoft CRM displays an entity's primary attribute on a related entity's form. In this figure, the schema field *name* is the primary attribute of the apartment entity, so the name of the apartment record appears in the lookup field of its related records.

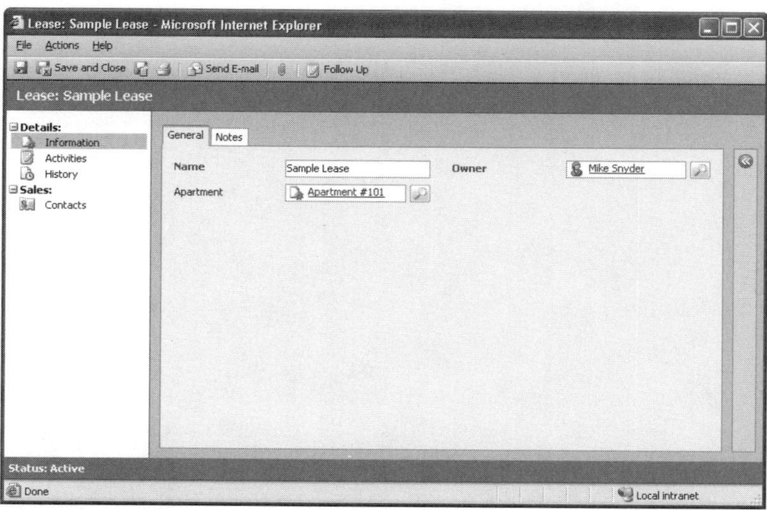

Figure 6-25 An entity's primary attribute appears on a related entity's lookup field

You can probably guess that most custom and default entities use a name field as the primary attribute, but you are not required to do so. However, you will notice that Microsoft CRM does require you to create a primary attribute with a data type of *nvarchar* and a format of text. You can set up a maximum length and business requirement level for the primary attribute that makes sense for your business.

> **Tip** After you create a custom entity, the data fields on the Primary Attribute tab become read-only so it appears that you cannot edit the primary attribute. However, if you navigate to the list of attributes for the custom entity and double-click the primary attribute, you can modify the primary attribute's name, business requirement level, and maximum length in the attribute editor. Although you can edit some of the primary attribute's values, you cannot change the primary attribute of a custom entity.

Other than the data type and data format requirement, the rules and restrictions for creating a primary attribute are the same as they are for creating any attribute for an entity.

Deleting a Custom Entity

If you decide you no longer need to use a custom entity, you can easily delete it from Microsoft CRM. Just like deleting attributes, you must remove all existing references to the custom entity that you want to delete before Microsoft CRM will allow you to delete it. To remove references to an entity, you should do the following:

- Remove references to the entity that you want to delete from the form of any related entities, and then delete any relationships linking to the custom entity.
- Remove the entity from any reports.
- Remove the entity from any script or code references.

> **Warning** Deleting a custom entity also deletes all of the data stored in that entity, and you can never retrieve that data. Microsoft CRM also permanently deletes all of the notes and activities related to that entity. Make sure you take the appropriate steps to back up all of your data before deleting an entity or attribute.

Application Navigation

Because of the flexibility and power of custom entities, you will find yourself creating multiple custom entities in your Microsoft CRM system. Simple deployments might use just a few custom entities, but a complex deployment might contain 25, 50, or 100 custom entities! By default, Microsoft CRM adds custom entities to the user interface and site navigation in the order in which you create them, listing the first custom entity at the top of the list. In addition, Microsoft CRM lists the custom entities together under an *extensions* group in the navigation pane. If you use more than a handful of custom entities, you will want to alter where and how they appear in the user interface. Microsoft CRM uses multiple tools to configure how users access entities and navigate in the application. These application navigation customization tools include:

- Site map
- Entity display areas
- ISV.config

Microsoft CRM combines data from these three tools to create the user interface on a system-wide level. After it determines the system navigation, Microsoft CRM also provides a Personalize Workplace feature in which individual users can customize the groups that appear in their workplaces. Before we discuss what each application navigation tool configures, let's quickly review the Microsoft CRM terminology for the screen region names in the Web application and the Microsoft CRM client for Outlook application. Use the following figures and list to map the screen regions to their names.

Figure 6-26 shows the user interface screen regions.

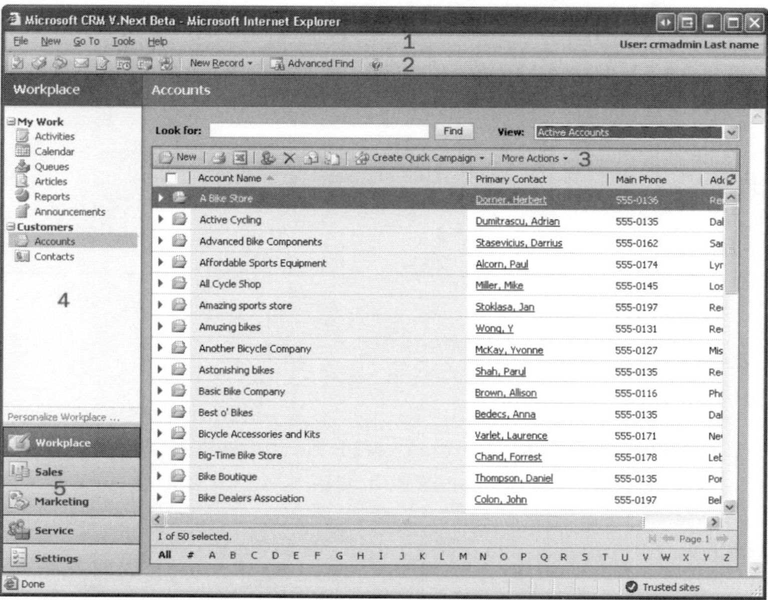

Figure 6-26 Screen regions in the Microsoft CRM user interface

Figure 6-27 shows the entity record screen regions.

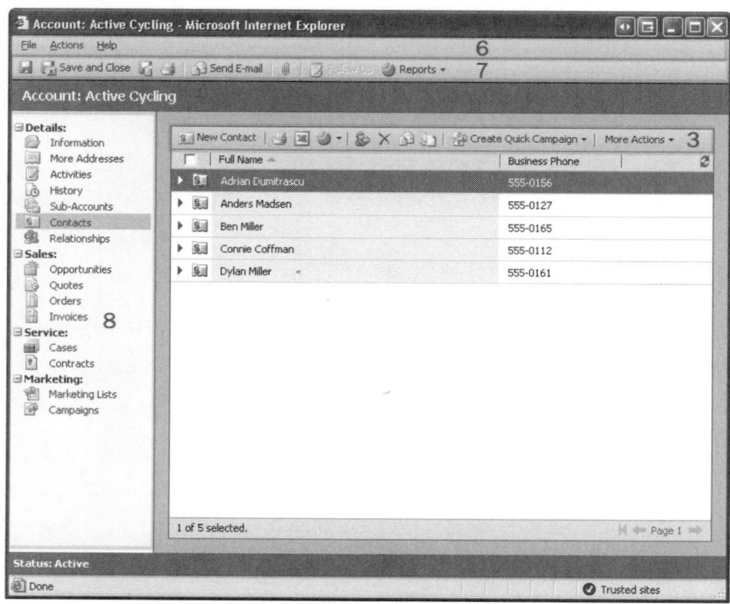

Figure 6-27 Screen regions on a Microsoft CRM entity record

1. Application menu bar
2. Application toolbar
3. Grid tool bar
4. Application navigation pane
5. Wunderbar
6. Entity menu bar
7. Entity toolbar
8. Entity navigation pane

Table 6-6 summarizes which customization tool you should use to modify the Microsoft CRM application navigation, depending on the type of customization that you want to make and where in the application navigation that customization resides.

Table 6-6 Application Navigation Customization Tool Summary

Screen region name	Site map	ISV.config	Entity display areas (custom entities only)	Personalize workplace
Application menu bar	Add, modify, and reorder items on Go To menu	Add new menu items	Choose the areas in which to display an entity	No
Application toolbar	No	Add custom buttons only	No	No
Application navigation pane	Add, modify, and reorder items	No	Choose the areas in which to display an entity	Users can specify the groups in which to display their workplace
Grid toolbar	No	Add custom buttons only	No	No
Wunderbar	Add, modify, and reorder items	No	No	No
Entity menu bar	No	Add new menu items	No	No
Entity toolbar	No	Add custom buttons only	No	No
Entity navigation pane	No	Add custom links only	No	No

These four tools allow you to customize almost every part of the user interface. In general, the site map allows you to add, reorder, and remove items in the application navigation pane and the wunderbar. Use ISV.config to add new links and buttons to the application menu bar and toolbar, in addition to adding new links and buttons to individual entities.

More Info You might be wondering, what does ISV.config mean, anyway? Unlike the site map, the name of the ISV.config feature does not exactly indicate its purpose. Microsoft CRM 3.0 uses the ISV.config terminology as a carryover from earlier versions of Microsoft CRM. The ISV.config file originally allowed independent software vendors (ISVs) to configure their enhancements in the Microsoft CRM interface. The term ISV refers to third-party companies that develop software enhancements and add-ons for the Microsoft CRM platform. Although ISVs do make heavy use of the ISV.config file, customers can also use ISV.config for their own internally developed customizations and enhancements. Because the ISV.config file deals mostly with extending Microsoft CRM, we discuss how to work with it in Chapter 10 along with the other extension features.

Now that you understand which tools to use to customize the navigation components of Microsoft CRM, let's discuss the details of how to edit the site map and Personalize Workplace features.

Site Map

Modifying the site map allows you to customize the user interface of the application navigation pane, the wunderbar, and parts of the application menu bar. As we discussed earlier, if you add more than a few custom entities, you will probably want to modify the site map so that your custom entities appear exactly where you want them in the user interface. Conceptually, the site map is just an .xml file that you edit (with the XML editing tool of your choice) to configure different parts of the Microsoft CRM navigation. Before we explain how to edit the site map, it will help to further define the screen components in the application navigation pane and the wunderbar (as shown in Figure 6-28) because the site map uses new terms to describe these areas of the user interface.

Figure 6-28 Screen components of the application navigation pane and the wunderbar

Microsoft CRM displays five buttons in the wunderbar by default:

- Workplace
- Sales
- Marketing
- Service
- Settings

When you are working with the site map, Microsoft CRM refers to these five buttons as *areas*. When users click an area, Microsoft CRM updates the application navigation pane to show the appropriate links for that area. As the example in Figure 6-28 shows, the Workplace area contains three main elements:

- My Work
- Customers
- Marketing

The site map refers to these elements as *groups*. Microsoft CRM formats groups in the Web client's application navigation pane with bold text and with the expand/collapse control.

Within each group are additional links that the site map refers to as *subareas*. For example, the My Work group in Figure 6-28 includes six subareas:

- Activities
- Calendar
- Queues
- Articles
- Reports
- Announcements

In addition to updating the application navigation pane and the wunderbar, editing the site map concurrently updates the Go To menu on the application menu bar. Figure 6-29 shows the Go To menu for our example.

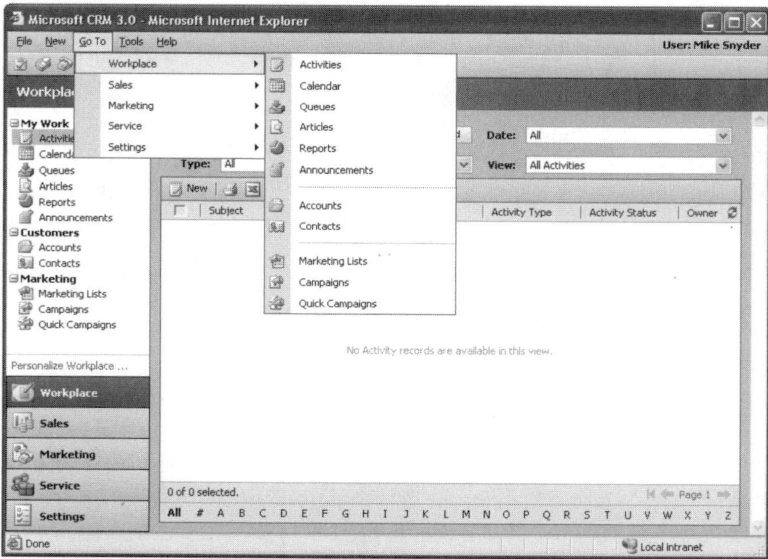

Figure 6-29 The Go To menu for the Workplace area

As you can see, the application menu bar lists the same areas that appear in the wunderbar (and in the same order). In addition, the application menu bar also displays all of an area's subareas nested in the menu. However, you will notice that the application menu bar does not display the group name. Instead of the group name, Microsoft CRM displays a horizontal line to graphically divide the groups.

Important Editing the site map updates the Web client's application navigation pane, the wunderbar, and the Go To menu in the application menu bar all at the same time.

We also want to show you how the site map references screen regions in the context of the Outlook client. Although the Outlook client uses some of the same screen region names as the Web client, it also includes a few unique region names. Figure 6-30 shows the Microsoft CRM desktop client for Outlook, and the region names are identified in the subsequent list.

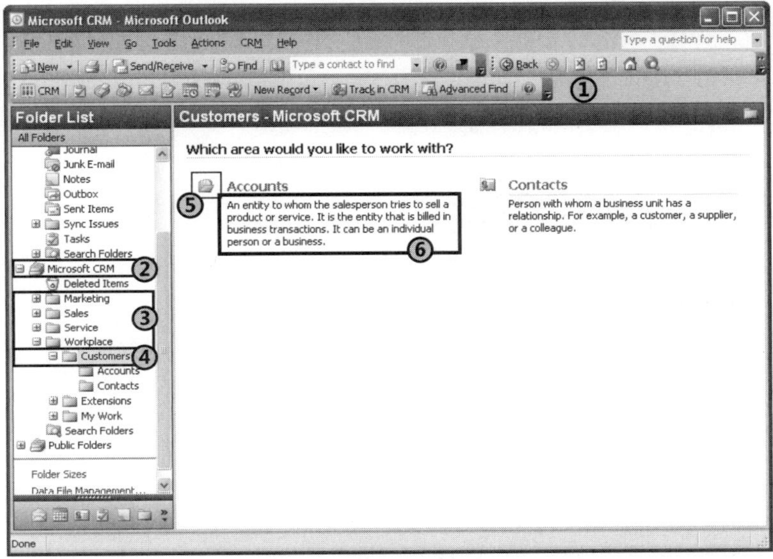

Figure 6-30 Screen regions in the Microsoft CRM desktop client for Outlook

1. Application toolbar
2. Microsoft CRM folder
3. Areas
4. Groups
5. Icon
6. Description

You can see that the Outlook client displays areas and subareas in the Outlook navigation pane as folders instead of as the buttons and links that the Web client uses.

Important Remember that the Web client and the Outlook client share the same site map to configure the application navigation. Therefore, you should always consider how changes you make in the site map will appear to Web and Outlook users.

Sitemap.xml

Now that you understand the terminology that Microsoft CRM uses for the site map, we'll show you how to modify it to meet your needs. As we explained earlier, the site map is simply an .xml configuration file that you manually edit. To get a copy of the current site map of your deployment to edit, you must export it from Microsoft CRM. As with any customization, you export the site map by browsing to Settings, clicking Customization, and then clicking Export Customizations. Select the Site Map record, click More Actions in the grid toolbar, and then click Export Selected Customizations. Microsoft CRM prompts you to open or save the file, as shown in Figure 6-31.

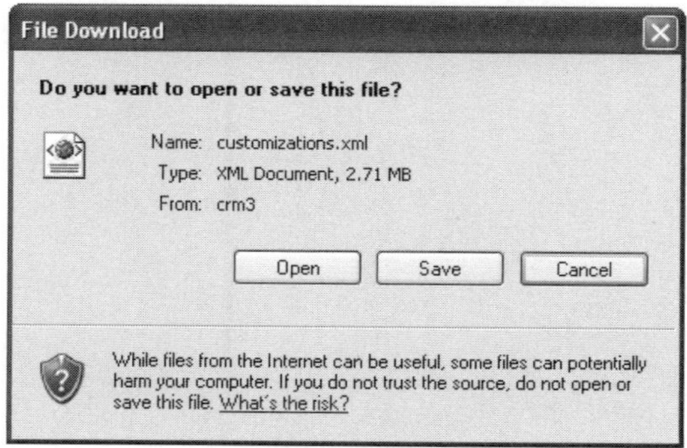

Figure 6-31 File download message for exporting customizations

Because you want to edit the site map file, you should save a copy to your local drive.

Best Practices Microsoft CRM uses customizations.xml as the default file name for all exported customizations. When you export the site map customizations, a best practice is to rename the customizations.xml file to Sitemap.xml. Although it is not required, using this naming convention makes the contents of the file obvious to you and others.

You can edit .xml files by using any text editor, such as Notepad or WordPad, but using an XML-specific editor such as Microsoft Visual Studio .NET 2005 makes the editing process much easier because you can expand and collapse the different XML elements. You can use Microsoft Internet Explorer to view an .xml file (as shown in Figure 6-32), but you won't be able to edit it there.

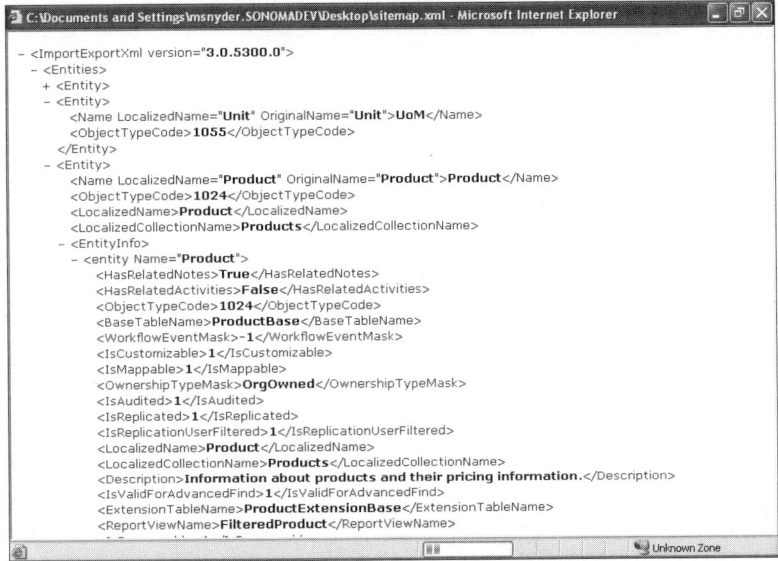

Figure 6-32 Viewing a sample Sitemap.xml file with Internet Explorer

Microsoft CRM creates a sitemap.xml file with the XML structure shown in Figure 6-33.

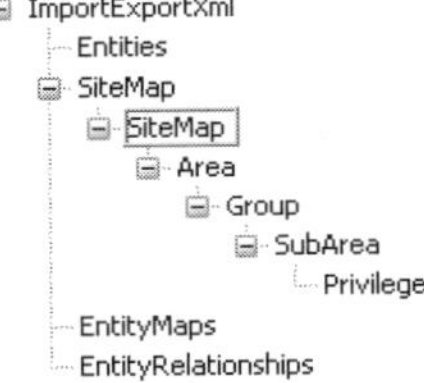

Figure 6-33 Sitemap.xml XML element structure

Only the *SiteMap* element in the Sitemap.xml file will contain any data. The *Entities*, *EntityMaps*, and *EntityRelationships* elements should be empty. Let's discuss each of the *SiteMap* elements and its attributes in detail.

SiteMap It might seem a little confusing initially, but Microsoft CRM uses the name SiteMap as the root node of the *SiteMap* element (illustrated in Figure 6-33). Your Sitemap.xml file can include only one occurrence of the SiteMap node under the *SiteMap* elements. Table 6-7 lists the only attribute for the SiteMap node.

Table 6-7 *SiteMap* Attribute

Name	Description	Data type	Required?	Applies to Web client?	Applies to Outlook clients?
Url	Specifies a URL that Microsoft CRM will display in the Outlook clients when users click the Microsoft CRM folder Valid values: Any valid URL	String	No	No	Yes

The SiteMap *Url* attribute lets you display the Web page of your choice when users click the Microsoft CRM folder in the Outlook client. Figure 6-34 shows an example in which we specified the URL *http://sharepoint* to display a Microsoft SharePoint intranet Web site.

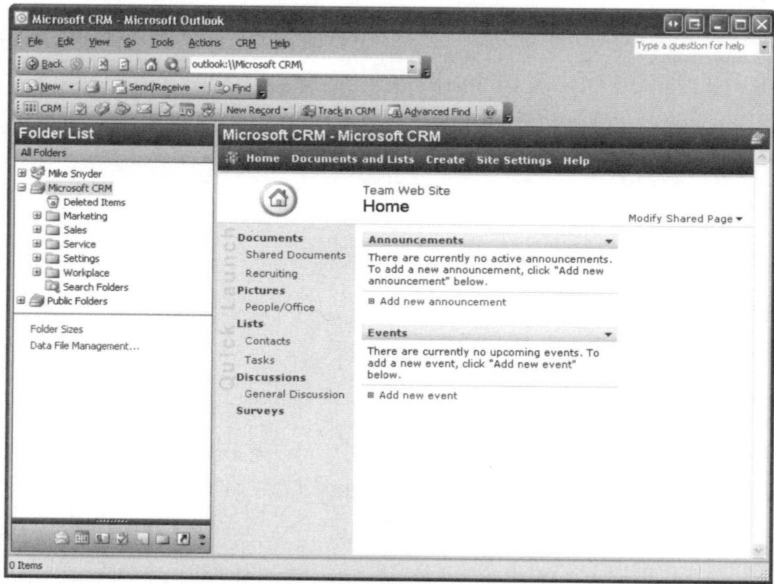

Figure 6-34 Using the *Url* attribute of SiteMap to change the default Web page in Outlook

To implement the example in Figure 6-34, you would change the SiteMap node from the default value.

```
<SiteMap>
```

Simply add the *Url* attribute to the node so that it looks like the following sample.

```
<SiteMap Url="http://sharepoint">
```

In the real world, you might want to display a custom Web page that you created, or perhaps some other intranet site. Note that changing this attribute affects both the laptop and desktop Outlook clients, but it does not affect users who access Microsoft CRM through the Web client.

Area The default sitemap.xml file includes five area elements (*Workplace*, *Sales*, *Marketing*, *Service*, and *Settings*), and you can modify, reorder, or remove any of these areas. You can also add entirely new areas to the Microsoft CRM navigation by adding new area elements to sitemap.xml. Remember, Microsoft CRM displays areas in the wunderbar, the application menu bar, and in the Outlook client folders.

> **Caution** Although you can technically remove the Settings area from the application navigation by removing it from the site map, you might accidentally lock yourself out of the customizations section by doing so. Therefore, we strongly recommend that you *never* remove the Settings area from the site map. If you do not want users to see this area in the application navigation, you should change their security role settings instead of modifying the site map.

Table 6-8 lists the attributes for the *Area* node.

Table 6-8 *Area* Attributes

Name	Description	Data type	Required?	Applies to Web client?	Applies to Outlook clients?
Description	Text that Microsoft CRM displays in the Outlook client when users click the parent folder	String	No	No	Yes
DescriptionResourceID	For internal use only	String	No	Yes	Yes
Icon	Specifies a URL to an image; allows you to display a different icon for the area	String	No	Yes	Yes
ID	Specifies a unique identifier in ASCII; spaces are not allowed. Valid values: a-z, A-Z, 0-9, and underscore (_)	String	Yes	Yes	Yes

Table 6-8 *Area* Attributes

Name	Description	Data type	Required?	Applies to Web client?	Applies to Outlook clients?
License	Specifies the user license requirement that determines whether the area is displayed Valid values: All, Professional, SmallBusiness	String	No	Yes	Yes
ResourceId	For internal use only	String	No	Yes	Yes
ShowGroups	Specifies whether Microsoft CRM will display an area's groups in the navigation pane Valid values: true false	Boolean	No	Yes	Yes
Title	Allows you to enter a different text label for the area	String	No	Yes	Yes
Url	Specifies a URL that Microsoft CRM will display in the Office Outlook clients when users click the folder that represents the area	String	No	No	Yes

Group Within each area of the site map, you can specify multiple groups (or no groups at all). Groups allow you to categorize the subareas in a manner that makes the most sense for your end users. The *Group* element in Sitemap.xml uses the attributes listed in Table 6-9.

Table 6-9 *Group* Attributes

Name	Description	Data type	Required?	Applies to Web client?	Applies to Outlook clients?
Description	Text that Microsoft CRM displays in the Outlook client when users click the parent folder	String	No	No	Yes
DescriptionResourceID	For internal use only	String	No	Yes	Yes
Icon	Specifies a URL to an image; allows you to display a different icon for the area	String	No	No	Yes
ID	Specifies a unique identifier in ASCII; spaces are not allowed. Valid values: a-z, A-Z, 0-9, and underscore (_)	String	Yes	Yes	Yes
IsProfile	Controls whether this group represents a user-selectable profile for the workplace Valid values: true, false	Boolean	No	Yes	No
License	Specifies the user license requirement that determines whether the subarea is displayed Valid values: All, Professional, SmallBusiness	String	No	Yes	Yes

Table 6-9 *Group* Attributes

Name	Description	Data type	Required?	Applies to Web client?	Applies to Outlook clients?
ResourceId	For internal use only	String	No	Yes	Yes
Title	Allows you to enter a different text label for the group	String	No	Yes	Yes
URL	Specifies a URL that Microsoft CRM will display in the Outlook clients when users click the folder that represents the group	String	No	No	Yes

Most of these attributes behave in exactly the same way as the *Area* element's attributes. We want to highlight one attribute unique to the group element: *IsProfile*.

When users navigate to the Workplace area, they can click a Personalize Workplace link in the navigation pane. Microsoft CRM displays the dialog box shown in Figure 6-35.

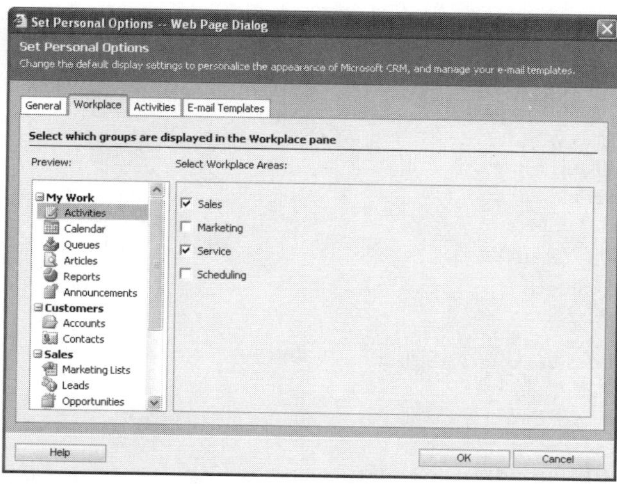

Figure 6-35 Set Personal Options dialog box

In this dialog box, users can select the groups that they want to see in their personal workplaces. Changing the groups displayed affects what they will see, but it does not affect what other users see.

Tip The Microsoft CRM user interface uses the phrase "Select Workplace Areas," but users actually select which workplace *groups* they want to display.

Microsoft CRM does not display all of the groups in the Personalize Workplace area; it shows only groups with an *IsProfile* attribute value of *true*. So if you want a particular group in the Workplace area to always appear for all users, set the *IsProfile* attribute of the group to *false* so that Microsoft CRM won't allow users to deselect the group in the Personalize Workplace area.

Tip Although users can personalize their workplace only by using the Web client, their changes will also appear in their Outlook client.

SubArea Each group element in the sitemap.xml file can contain multiple *SubArea* elements (or no *SubAreas* elements at all). *SubArea* elements possess the attributes shown in Table 6-10.

Table 6-10 *SubArea* Attributes

Name	Description	Data type	Required?	Applies to Web client?	Applies to Outlook clients?
AvailableOffline	Specifies whether to display a subarea when the user is offline in Office Outlook client Valid values: true, false	Boolean	No	No	Yes (laptop client only)
Client	Specifies whether to display the subarea depending on the type of client the user is accessing Microsoft CRM with Valid values: All (the default value) Outlook OutlookLaptopClient OutlookWorkstationClient Web	String	No	Yes	Yes
Description	Text that Microsoft CRM displays in the Outlook client when users click the parent folder (group)	String	No	No	Yes

Table 6-10 *SubArea* Attributes

Name	Description	Data type	Required?	Applies to Web client?	Applies to Outlook clients?
DescriptionResourceID	For internal use only	String	No	Yes	Yes
Entity	Allows you to enter the schema name of the entity you want to display when users click the subarea link	String	No	Yes	Yes
Icon	Specifies a URL to an image; allows you to display a different icon for the subarea	String	No	Yes	Yes
ID	Specifies a unique identifier in ASCII, with no spaces Valid values: a-z, A-Z, 0-9, and underscore (_)	String	Yes	Yes	Yes
License	Specifies the user license requirement that determines whether the subarea is displayed Valid values: All, (the default value) Professional, SmallBusiness	String	No	Yes	Yes
OutlookShortcutIcon	Specifies the icon to display in the Outlook client	String	No	No	Yes
ResourceId	Used internally to address a localized label to display Valid values: a-z, A-Z, 0-9, and underscore (_)	String	No	Yes	Yes
Title	Allows you to enter a different text label for the subarea	String	No	Yes	Yes

Table 6-10 *SubArea* Attributes

Name	Description	Data type	Required?	Applies to Web client?	Applies to Outlook clients?
URL	Specifies a URL that Microsoft CRM will display in the Outlook client when users click the folder that represents the subarea; overrides the schema name if you specify both a schema name and a *Url* attribute	String	No	Yes	Yes

Privilege The last element of the sitemap.xml document is the *Privilege* element. Each *SubArea* element can include only one *Privilege* element, and using the *Privilege* element within a *SubArea* element is optional. The *Privilege* element allows you to specify security criteria that Microsoft CRM evaluates to determine whether it will display a subarea to a user.

It's important to note that the *Privilege* element does not override the Microsoft CRM security settings for custom and system entities. Therefore, even if you tried to assign display (read) rights to a user by adding a site map privilege, the Microsoft CRM security settings would not display the subarea to a user who did not have read rights to that entity.

So if the Microsoft CRM security settings always make the final determination on whether to display a subarea to a user, you might wonder why anyone would ever need to use a *Privilege* element. We think the most obvious benefit of the *Privilege* element is that you can use it to configure security display rights for custom Web pages that you integrate with Microsoft CRM (which you cannot do by using the native Microsoft CRM security settings).

The *Privilege* element has the attributes listed in Table 6-11.

Table 6-11 *Privilege* Attributes

Name	Description	Data type	Required ?	Applies to Web client?	Applies to Outlook clients?
Entity	Allows you to enter the schema name of the entity that you want to reference for the privilege check	String	Yes	Yes	Yes

Table 6-11 *Privilege* Attributes

Name	Description	Data type	Required?	Applies to Web client?	Applies to Outlook clients?
Privilege	Specifies the privileges needed to display this subarea Valid values: A comma-separated list with no spaces, made up of these possible values: All, Append, AppendTo, Assign, Create, Delete, Read, (the default value) Share, Write	String	No	Yes	Yes

Let's look at an example that uses the *Privilege* element.

```
<SubArea Id="test_subarea" Title="Test Subarea" Url="custompage.aspx">
   <Privilege Entity="account" Privilege="Delete, Write"/>
</SubArea>
```

In this example, if the user had Delete or Write privileges for the account entity, Microsoft CRM would display the subarea in the application navigation pane. Conversely, if you added the custom Web page Custompage.aspx to your system and you didn't want a particular user to see this page, you would simply use the *Privilege* element in your site map to specify a security privilege that you knew the user didn't have. If you don't specify a *Privilege* attribute, Microsoft CRM defaults to the Read privilege of the entity.

```
<SubArea Id="test_subarea" Title="Test Subarea" Url="custompage.aspx">
   <Privilege Entity="account"/>
</SubArea>
```

In this example, if the user had Read rights to the Account entity, Microsoft CRM would display the subarea.

Site Map Editing Tips and Tricks

Editing the sitemap.xml file might initially appear as a very straightforward process, but here are a few tips and tricks that might save you some time:

- **Editing the order of elements in the site map works only in the Web client** The Microsoft CRM Web client displays navigation elements (such as subareas) in the order that you specify in the site map. However, the Microsoft CRM Outlook clients use folders to display the navigation. Outlook always displays folders in alphabetical order, not in the order that you specified in the site map.

- **Don't confuse the *Title* and *Description* attributes** It's easy to confuse what the *Title* and *Description* attributes do. The *Description* attribute appears only in the Microsoft CRM Outlook client; the *Title* attribute appears in both the Web and Outlook clients.
- **The site map is case-sensitive** Because the site map uses XML, which is case-sensitive, you must ensure correct casing for all of your attributes.
- **Watch out for default attributes** When we first opened the Sitemap.xml file to edit the name of a group or area (such as Sales), we looked for the text "Sales" so that we could change it. However, that text does not appear in the default sitemap.xml file. Instead, the *Area* element for sales looks like the following.

```
<Area Id="SFA" ResourceId="Area_Sales" Icon="/_imgs/sales_24x24.gif"
 DescriptionResourceId="Sales_Description">
```

  It isn't obvious what text you need to change because the word that we want to update ("Sales") does not appear anywhere in this element. To change the text to a new value, you must add a *Title* attribute to the *Area* element.

```
<Area Id="SFA" ResourceId="Area_Sales" Icon="/_imgs/sales_24x24.gif"
 DescriptionResourceId="Sales_Description" Title="New Sales Title">
```

  Because the *Title* attribute does not appear in any of the default elements, Microsoft CRM uses a behind-the-scenes translation to display the titles of the default entities. In this example, we would describe the *Title* attribute as defaulted from Microsoft CRM because it doesn't exist in the site map. So if you're looking in the site map and you can't find the correct attribute to update in the Sitemap.xml file, it's probably a default attribute that you'll need to explicitly add.
- ***Id* attributes must be unique** Each element requires an *Id* attribute. Remember that it must be unique from all of the other *Id* attributes in the site map.
- **Beware of conditionally required attributes** Earlier in this chapter, we outlined the attributes of each element and identified whether Microsoft CRM requires them. In some cases, an attribute might become required depending on the settings of other elements. For example, Microsoft CRM does not require you to enter a title for *Group* elements. However, if you want to display groups for a particular area (ShowGroups = "true"), the *Title* attribute becomes required for the groups nested under that area. Microsoft CRM usually prompts you with a good description of the error, but you should know that these conditional requirement possibilities exist.
- **How to recover from a site map error** Although Microsoft CRM validates the sitemap.xml file before the import, you might accidentally import a sitemap.xml file that modifies the navigation so that you cannot access the import customizations tool. If you cannot access the import tool, you obviously can't import a corrected site map file! Microsoft CRM allows you to directly access the import customizations tool at the following URL: *http://<crmserver>/tools/systemcustomization/ImportCustomizations/importCustomizations.aspx*.

- **Refreshing site map changes** When you import a new site map, sometimes clicking the Refresh button in Internet Explorer does not update Microsoft CRM with your changes. This depends on the type of change you made. If you don't see the changes you expect, we recommend closing the Web browser window and launching a new one. If that does not work, we have occasionally needed to restart Internet Information Services (you can use *iisreset*) on the Microsoft CRM Web server to get your navigation changes to appear.
- **Do not change the home page of Microsoft CRM Outlook folders** You might think that you can also customize the Microsoft CRM clients for Outlook by changing the home page of a folder in Outlook.

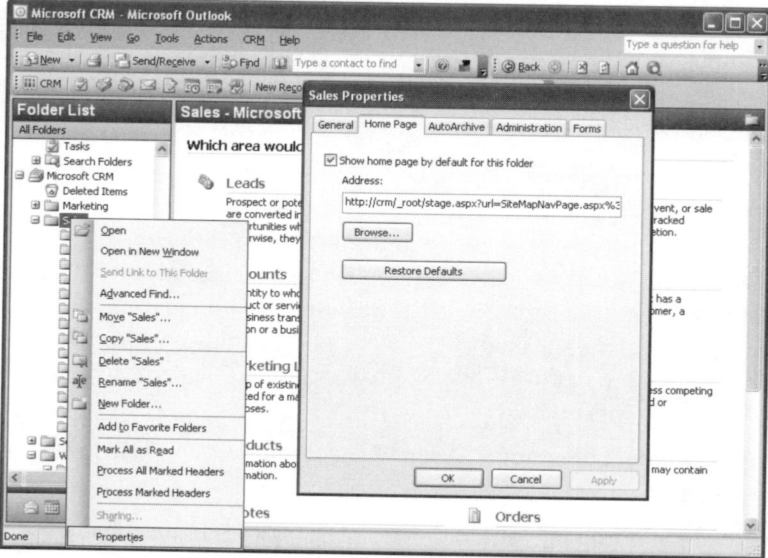

Although making this change is technically possible, it might adversely affect how the Microsoft CRM client for Outlook interacts with the site map, so we strongly discourage you from trying this.

- **Consistent attribute ordering will save editing time** You can put the attributes in any order you want, but putting them in a consistent order will save you time later when you want to edit them.

Entity Display Areas

As you learned earlier in this chapter, custom entities allow you to select the areas where you want Microsoft CRM to display your custom entities. You select or clear the appropriate areas by using the entity editor in the Web client, as shown in Figure 6-36.

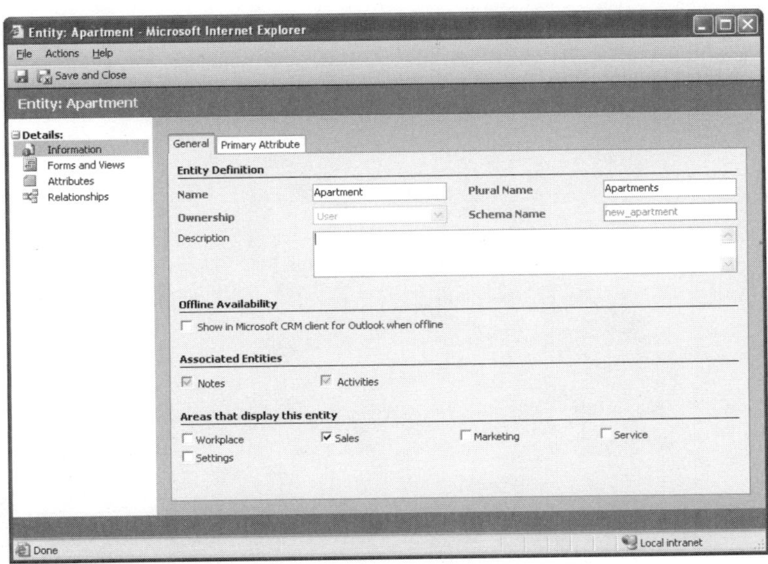

Figure 6-36 Editing display areas for a custom entity

When you select new areas or remove existing areas with the entity editor, Microsoft CRM automatically edits the site map for you. Because of this nuance, you should *always* export the site map before you edit it to make sure that you are working with the latest version.

Conversely, editing the different areas of the site map to include different entities and then importing the new file will automatically update the custom entity in Microsoft CRM. Therefore, the display area check boxes will update accordingly the next time you access this Web page.

Summary

Microsoft CRM includes many powerful features, but we think that the ability to create custom entities and custom data relationships through a Web-based administration tool ranks as one of the more important features. Custom entities allow you to easily track additional types of information related to your customers, and they behave almost identical to the default system entities. Understanding how Microsoft CRM structures entity relationships will help you plan and map your system to ensure a smooth implementation. The site map in Microsoft CRM lets you reconfigure almost every area of the application navigation (Web client and Outlook client) to hide or show the entities and links that make the most sense for your users.

Chapter 7

Reporting and Analysis

In this chapter:

CRM systems capture data about your customers' interactions, and your database will quickly grow to thousands (or millions) of data records about your customers. Although it's beneficial to capture these customer interactions in a database, this customer data provides real value only if you can easily extract it and present it to your users in a simple and easy-to-read format. Microsoft Dynamics CRM 3.0 offers multiple reporting and analysis options, and you can decide which tool to use based on factors such as the desired output format and the type of user who will create the analysis.

One thing we've learned from implementing Microsoft CRM at various companies is that not everyone defines the expression *report* the same way. When people in information technology departments hear the term, most of them immediately think of powerful report writing tools such as Microsoft SQL Server Reporting Services. However, most non-technology users such as managers and executives think of reports as simply *getting their data*; they typically don't care how they get it, as long as they get it on time and accurately. The Microsoft CRM user interface uses the term *report* to refer any type of data analysis file, regardless of its origin and type. Therefore, a report might be a Microsoft Office Excel file, a SQL Server Reporting Services report, a third-party reporting file, or a link to an external Web page report.

Note Although Microsoft CRM does not explicitly refer to entity views and the Advanced Find feature as reports, we consider them important data reporting and analysis tools because of their flexibility and ease of use. Therefore, we'll discuss their use as a reporting tool in this chapter.

Reporting and Analysis Tools

Microsoft CRM offers several reporting and analysis tools:

- Entity views and the Advanced Find feature
- Dynamic Excel files
- SQL Server Reporting Services
- Filtered views
- Third-party reporting tools

Each of these tools provides a unique set of benefits and drawbacks, so you should determine the most appropriate tool for each type of analysis. As you can see from the list of reporting tools, Microsoft CRM even allows you to integrate third-party reporting tools into the user interface. Table 7-1 summarizes the reporting tools and their features.

Table 7-1 Reporting and Analysis Tools in Microsoft CRM

	Entity views and Advanced Find	Dynamic Excel files	SQL Server Reporting Services	Filtered views	Third-party reporting tools
Report output	Microsoft CRM grids	Excel PivotTables and PivotCharts	Web-based reports that can be exported to additional formats such as Excel, PDF, and CSV	SQL Server database view	Varies
Skill level required to create or modify reports	Beginner	Beginner	Advanced	Advanced	Varies
Can schedule reports for e-mail delivery	No	No	Yes	No	Varies
Supports charts and graphs	No	Yes (with Excel charts or PivotCharts)	Yes	No	Varies
Report results can be cached for better performance	No	No	Yes	No	Varies
Supports sub-reports and drill-through reports	No	No	Yes	No	Varies

Table 7-1 Reporting and Analysis Tools in Microsoft CRM

	Entity views and Advanced Find	Dynamic Excel files	SQL Server Reporting Services	Filtered views	Third-party reporting tools
Can include data from multiple entities in results	No	No	Yes	Yes	Yes
Can include data from multiple entities in the report query	Yes	Yes	Yes	Yes	Yes
Supports report snap-shots	No	No	Yes	No	No
Can prompt users to enter parameters before running reports	No	No	Yes	No	Varies
Allows for user access restrictions	Yes	Yes	Yes	Does not apply	Varies
Respects Microsoft CRM security settings by default	Yes	Yes	Yes	Yes	No
Reports can run con-textually from an entity list or form	No	No	Yes	No	No
Users can access from Reports list	No	Yes	Yes	Yes	Yes

SQL Server Reporting Services reports clearly offer the most benefits and functionality, but they also typically require an advanced user to author new reports. In addition, Reporting Services reports might take additional time to configure and manage compared to the simpler reporting tools. The entity views and dynamic Excel tools offer less functionality than Reporting Services, but any beginner user can quickly and easily author new reports. Let's review each of these reporting tools in more detail.

Entity Views and Advanced Find

We explained how to set up and configure entity views in Chapter 5, "Forms and Views," but we want to emphasize that you can use entity views in conjunction with the Advanced Find feature as an entry-level reporting and analysis tool. Entity views and the Advanced Find feature offer the following reporting benefits:

- Users of all skill levels can set up and configure views by using the Advanced Find feature, but Advanced Find also offers powerful query features such as Group AND and Group OR that more sophisticated report writers will want.

- Users can save any views that they create using the Advanced Find feature so they can quickly run that report later.
- By default, only the user who creates an Advanced Find view can access it. However, Microsoft CRM allows you to share Advanced Find views with other users or with a team. Therefore, you can explicitly control access to a view so that only a select group of users has access.
- Entity system views (but not saved Advanced Find views) can be imported or exported along with the other system customizations.
- Users can sort the records in their views in ascending or descending order by clicking the column headers.
- Users can export the records in their views to Excel, and they can create dynamic worksheets that link to the Microsoft CRM database.

However, using entity views for reporting and analysis involves the following restrictions:

- Although you can query on attributes of related entities, you cannot display columns of related entities in your view. For example, you cannot display columns from the Contact entity in an Opportunity view, but you can use columns from Contact as part of the view filter criteria.
- You have very little control over output formatting because Microsoft CRM displays the data in a grid. You can't include charts, graphs, or subtotals when using views, but of course you can export the view data to Excel for further analysis.
- You can't schedule reports or deliver them via e-mail when using views.

Remember, although Microsoft CRM doesn't refer to entity views and the Advanced Find feature as *reports*, they're still powerful reporting and analysis tools.

Dynamic Excel Files

Many people consider Excel to be the world's most popular reporting and analysis tool, and we wholeheartedly agree with that statement. With its broad range of features and ease of use, we expect that your users leverage Excel for a lot (or most) of their data analysis needs. Fortunately, Microsoft CRM provides excellent integration with Excel so that your users can create reports and perform analysis of CRM data with a tool that they're already comfortable using.

To export data from Microsoft CRM to Excel, users can simply click the Export to Excel button in the grid toolbar and Microsoft CRM will export the data from the current view. When users export data to Excel, Microsoft CRM provides three types of export options:

- Export to static worksheet
- Export to dynamic PivotTable
- Export to dynamic worksheet

Let's review the difference between static and dynamic exports.

Static vs. Dynamic Exports

If you choose one of the dynamic export options, Microsoft CRM creates a live link between the data in your Excel file and the view data in Microsoft CRM. When the data in Microsoft CRM changes, you can automatically update the data in your dynamic Excel file by simply refreshing the external data. Exporting data to a static worksheet takes a snapshot of data at the time that you export it, but you can't automatically update the data in Excel like you can with a dynamic export.

> **Important** Dynamic Excel files update Microsoft CRM data only when Excel refreshes external data. When you export a dynamic Excel file from Microsoft CRM, Excel prompts you about whether you want to enable automatic data refresh for this file.

In addition to creating a live link between the Excel file and the Microsoft CRM database, the dynamic Excel files also respect the Microsoft CRM security settings. This means that each user sees only the data that he or she is allowed to see in the dynamic Excel file. For example, let's assume that we have two customer support representatives named Scott Bishop and Eli Bowen. If Scott exports a dynamic worksheet of the view My Active Cases, the Excel file shows the cases that Scott owns. Now imagine that Scott creates several additional customizations and additions to the Excel file and then e-mails the modified Excel file to Eli. When Eli opens the spreadsheet, Excel refreshes the Microsoft CRM view data to show only the cases that Eli owns. Although both Scott and Eli are using the same Excel file, Microsoft CRM automatically displays the correct data to each of them based on their security settings. Because static Excel files don't maintain a link to the Microsoft CRM database, they don't update the data based on the user's security settings.

> **More Info** If you choose to disable automatic refresh, and multiple users share the same file (such as via e-mail or a network share, for example), it's possible for users to view records that they should not have access to. In our example, if Scott disabled the automatic refresh option and then e-mailed the file to Eli, Eli would see all of Scott's active cases upon opening the file because the data would not refresh with Eli's credentials. Excel would show the appropriate data the next time that Eli refreshed external data, but this clearly isn't an ideal scenario. Because of this potential issue, we recommend that you enable the automatic refresh option if multiple users might access the same Excel file.

At first, you might wonder why anyone would want to export a static worksheet. We can think of several instances in which you might prefer a static export over a dynamic export:

- If you want to capture data at a specific time, you should use a static worksheet. For example, you might want to run a weekly report every Monday and compare the results to the previous week. With a dynamic Excel file, the numbers in the report constantly change because it's always pulling live data.
- If you want to share an Excel file exported from Microsoft CRM with a non–Microsoft CRM user, you should use a static worksheet. When a user opens a dynamic Excel file, Excel retrieves the latest data from Microsoft CRM based on the user's security settings. If the person opening the file (such as an external vendor or partner) doesn't have an active account, he or she encounters a login error.

- Similarly, if the person viewing the report isn't logged on to the computer with the same credentials used for his or her Microsoft CRM user account, that user also receives a login error message. Microsoft CRM uses integrated authentication, passing the domain and user name that the user logs on to the machine with, to retrieve the appropriate dynamic data. Even if the person has a Microsoft CRM license, he or she might be logged on under a different name or domain. This could happen if a user tried to open a dynamic Excel file from a personal computer at home if that computer were not part of the user's work domain.

Now that you understand the differences between static and dynamic exports, we'll explain how to use the Export to Excel feature in the user interface.

Caution Remember that when users export dynamic Excel files, they are running their reports on your *live* production database. Therefore, it's possible for a user to unknowingly create a complex query that seriously degrades the performance of your server. Because all Microsoft CRM users share the server, a renegade query or report could destroy the performance of Microsoft CRM for all of your users. If you're concerned about this scenario, you can disable the Export to Excel security privilege for certain roles in Security Settings as explained in Chapter 3.

Refreshing External Data in Excel

When you export data to a dynamic Excel file, Microsoft CRM automatically creates a link in the Excel file to Microsoft CRM SQL Server database. The process of refreshing external data in Excel isn't unique to Microsoft CRM, but we want to briefly explain some tips on how to do it. Here are three methods for refreshing external data in Excel:

1. Right-click the dynamic data range, and then click Refresh Data.

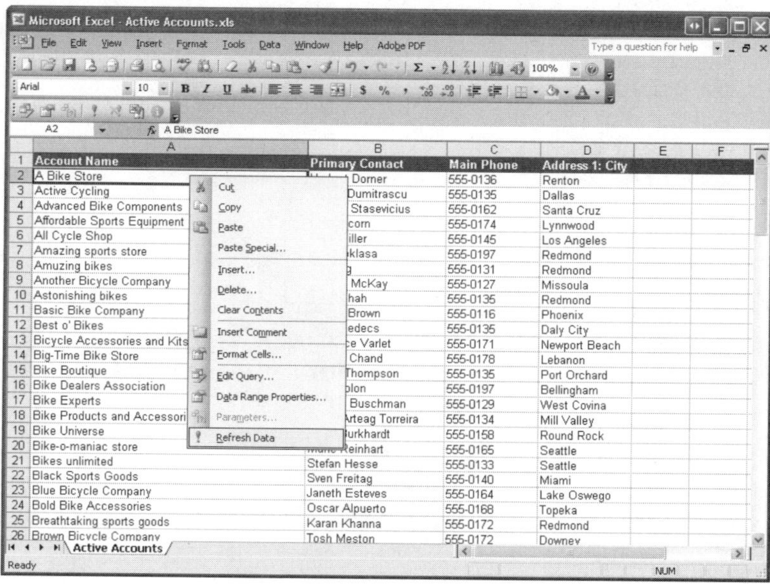

2. Select a cell within the dynamic data range, click Data in the menu bar, and then click Refresh Data.

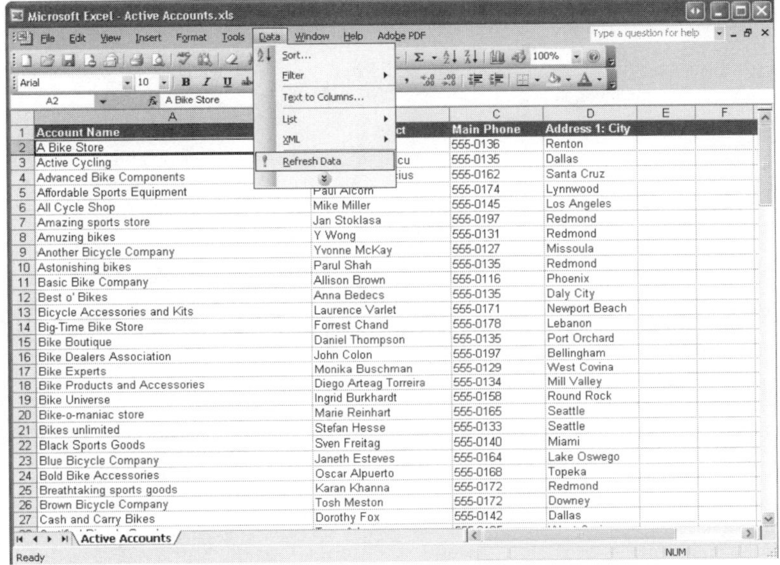

3. Display the External Data toolbar by clicking View in the menu bar, selecting Toolbars, and then clicking External Data. Click Refresh All, and Excel refreshes the external data for all of the dynamic ranges in your workbook.

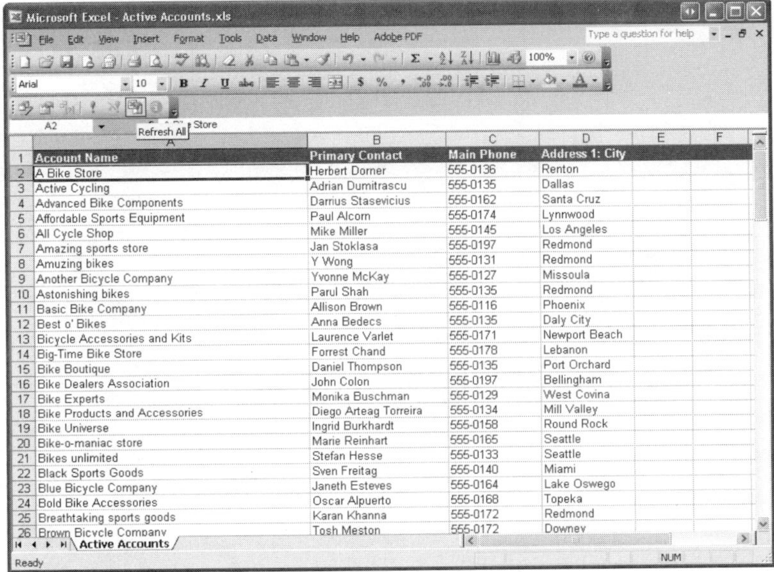

In addition to manually refreshing the external data, you can also configure the automatic refresh control by editing the data range properties. You access the data range properties by selecting a cell within the dynamic data range, clicking the Data menu, pointing to Import External Data, and then clicking Data Range Properties.

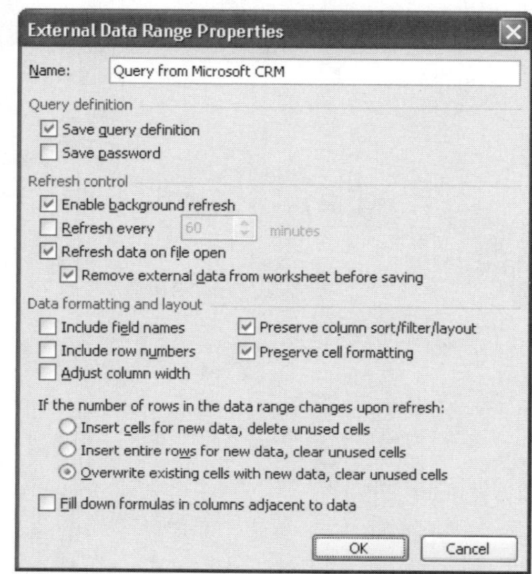

In the External Data Range Properties dialog box, you can enable an auto-refresh at a specified time interval or force a data refresh every time someone opens the Excel spreadsheet.

Exporting

To export data from Microsoft CRM to Excel, you simply click the Excel button on the grid toolbar, shown in Figure 7-1.

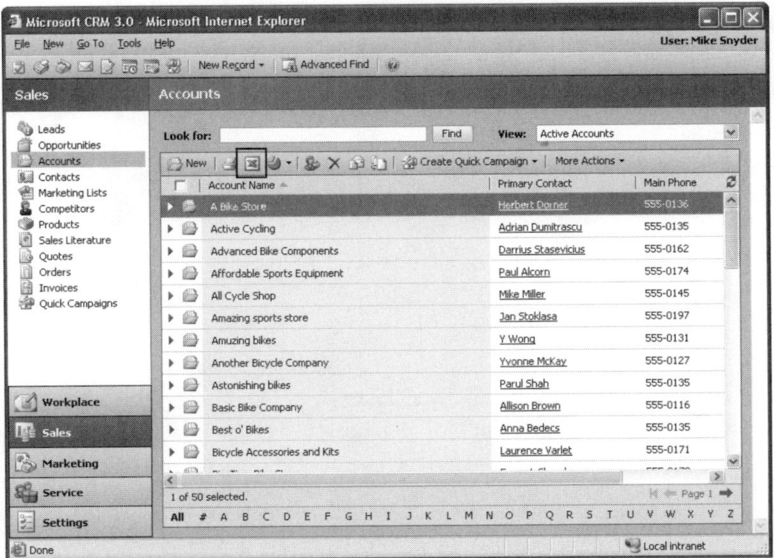

Figure 7-1 Excel button on the grid toolbar

Note To access the Excel button in the grid toolbar, users must have the Export to Excel security privilege enabled for at least one of their assigned security roles.

After you click the Excel button, Microsoft CRM prompts you to select the type of Excel file that you want to export. As we reviewed, you can choose to export data into Excel with one of the following methods:

- Static worksheet (one page or all pages)
- Dynamic PivotTable
- Dynamic worksheet

Static Worksheet

This option exports a snapshot of the CRM data at the time the user created the export. If data changes in Microsoft CRM after the export, the new data will not be reflected in the user's Excel file.

If you view a grid with multiple pages, you are prompted with the additional option of exporting to a static worksheet with records from all pages in the current view (see Figure 7-2). You can then determine whether you want all the records in the view, or just the records displayed on the current page.

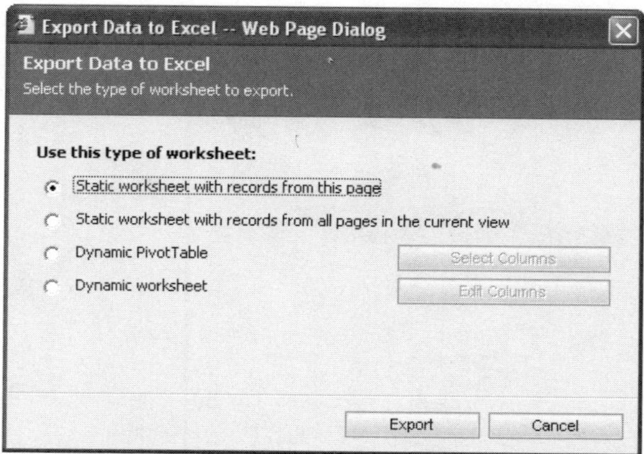

Figure 7-2 Exporting records from one page or all pages

When you export a static worksheet, Microsoft CRM automatically creates a column in Excel for each column in your view.

Dynamic PivotTable

If you choose to export data as a dynamic PivotTable, Microsoft CRM automatically creates a blank PivotTable using the view's data as its source data. By default, Microsoft CRM includes all of the view's columns in the PivotTable source data, but you can add or remove these columns by clicking the Select Columns button before you click the Export button. Figure 7-3 shows a sample PivotTable created by exporting the All Opportunities view.

Microsoft Excel - Open Opportunities.xls

Sum of Est. Revenue	Owner				
Potential Customer	Alan Jackson	Gail Erickson	Jose Curry	Mike Snyder	Grand Total
Front Sporting Goods			$275,044		$275,044
World Bike Discount Store	$188,988				$188,988
Active Cycling	$153,385				$153,385
Cash and Carry Bikes	$106,421				$106,421
Year-round Sports			$103,535		$103,535
Wide World Importers			$94,801		$94,801
Rugged Bikes		$94,679			$94,679
Vast Bike Sales and Rental			$93,434		$93,434
Racing Bike Outlet		$87,289			$87,289
Margie's Travel		$85,599			$85,599
The Cycle Store			$78,459		$78,459
Metropolitan Sports Supply	$68,436				$68,436
Friendly Neighborhood Bikes	$62,748				$62,748
The Cracker Box			$52,230		$52,230
Bike Universe			$42,568		$42,568
Fun Toys and Bikes	$40,201				$40,201
Major Sport Suppliers	$36,891				$36,891
Solid Bike Parts	$29,028				$29,028
New and Used Bicycles			$27,495		$27,495
Litware Inc.	$25,852				$25,852

Open Opportunities

Figure 7-3 Sample dynamic PivotTable using the All Opportunities view

As you can see, PivotTables allow you to sort, summarize, and group data into meaningful reports. From any PivotTable in Excel, you can easily create a chart by right-clicking the PivotTable and clicking PivotChart on the resulting menu. Figure 7-4 shows the sample chart created with one click from the dynamic PivotTable in Figure 7-3.

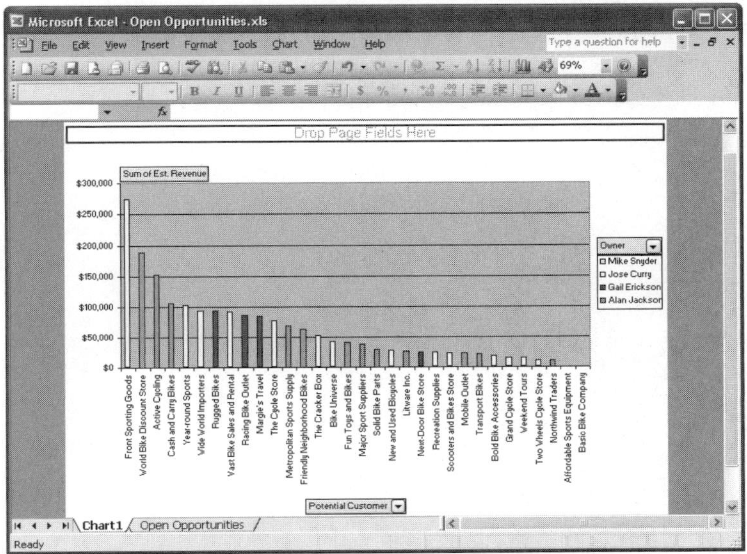

Figure 7-4 Sample chart created with one click from a PivotTable

> **Tip** PivotTables might appear intimidating to new users, but they're actually quite easy to use, and they provide excellent data analysis and charting options. The Microsoft Office Web site (*http://office.microsoft.com*) offers several excellent free tutorials that introduce PivotTables. We highly recommend these online tutorials if you're not comfortable using PivotTables as a data analysis tool.

Dynamic Worksheet

Exporting a view to Excel as a dynamic worksheet creates a worksheet of rows and columns in Excel similar to a static worksheet export. However, the dynamic worksheet allows you to select additional data columns to include in your Excel worksheet before you click the Export button. And, of course, it automatically creates the live link to the Microsoft CRM database. By exporting a dynamic worksheet, you can use the data in that dynamic worksheet to create your own PivotTables, charts, and additional calculations as necessary.

A Closer Look at Exported Excel Files

When you export an Excel file from Microsoft CRM, the file is saved with an .xls extension. However, the file that Microsoft CRM exports is *not* a typical Excel file. Microsoft CRM actually exports an *XML file* that it saves with an .xls extension to maintain correct file associations. Just like any .xml file, you can open and edit the exported Excel file with any text editor or XML editor. If you tried to open a regular (non-XML) Excel file in a text editor, you would see a bunch of strange characters.

For example, if you exported the default My Active Accounts view as a dynamic worksheet and opened the exported file in an XML editor, you would see something like this.

```
<?xml version="1.0"?>
<?mso-application progid="Excel.Sheet"?>
<Workbook xmlns="urn:schemas-microsoft-com:office:spreadsheet" xmlns:o="urn:schemas-microsoft-com:office:office" xmlns:x="
urn:schemas-microsoft-com:office:excel" xmlns:ss="urn:schemas-microsoft-com:office:spreadsheet" xmlns:html="http://www.w3.org/TR/REC-html40">
  <DocumentProperties xmlns="urn:schemas-microsoft-com:office:office">
    <Author>Microsoft Business Solutions</Author>
    <LastAuthor>Microsoft Business Solutions</LastAuthor>
    <Created>2005-03-15T21:41:01Z</Created>
    <Company>Microsoft Corporation</Company>
    <Version>11.6360</Version>
  </DocumentProperties>
  <ExcelWorkbook xmlns="urn:schemas-microsoft-com:office:excel">
    <WindowHeight>9090</WindowHeight>
    <WindowWidth>13260</WindowWidth>
    <WindowTopX>480</WindowTopX>
    <WindowTopY>45</WindowTopY>
    <ProtectStructure>False</ProtectStructure>
    <ProtectWindows>False</ProtectWindows>
  </ExcelWorkbook>
  <Styles>
    <Style ss:ID="Default" ss:Name="Normal">
      <Alignment ss:Vertical="Bottom"/>
      <Borders/>
      <Font/>
      <Interior/>
      <NumberFormat/>
      <Protection/>
    </Style>
    <Style ss:ID="s21">
      <Font x:Family="Swiss" ss:Size="10" ss:Bold="1" ss:Color="#FFFFFF"/>
      <Interior ss:Color="#333399" ss:Pattern="Solid"/>
    </Style>
    <Style ss:ID="s22">
      <Font x:Family="Swiss" ss:Size="10"/>
    </Style>
    <Style ss:ID="s23">
      <Font x:Family="Swiss" ss:Size="10"/>
      <NumberFormat ss:Format="Short Date"/>
```

From here, you could manually edit various properties of the Excel XML file as you saw fit. You probably won't ever have to edit the XML of an exported Excel file, but it's nice to know that the option exists.

Caution Only advanced users should attempt to manually edit an Excel XML file. You could very easily make a change that prevents Excel from opening the file correctly, so be very careful. If you do edit the file, make sure that you have a backup in case something goes wrong.

One instance in which you might want to edit the Excel XML file is if you need to change the connection string information of the Excel file. Exporting a dynamic worksheet or PivotTable creates a live link to the originating Microsoft CRM database, but there's no user interface in Excel 2003 to change the SQL database that the file references. However, you can change the connection string by editing the Excel XML file. If you examine the XML nodes, you'll see a node called *<Worksheet>* with a child element called *<QueryTable>*.

Under the *<QueryTable>* node, you will see a node called *<QuerySource>*. *<QuerySource>* contains an element called *<Connection>* that will look similar to this.

```
<Connection>DRIVER=SQL Server;APP=Microsoft Office 2003;Network=DBMSSOCN;Trusted_Connection=Yes;SERVER=sqlserver;DATABASE=organizationname_MSCRM</Connection>
```

Simply enter your updated SERVER and DATABASE values, save the file, and then open it in Excel. Voilà! You just changed the connection string.

Microsoft CRM also exports static worksheets as XML, but manually editing those files obviously won't provide as much benefit as editing the dynamic files because the data in a static worksheet won't change.

The ability to export Microsoft CRM data directly into Excel is a powerful reporting and analysis option for your end users to quickly create ad hoc analyses. We want to share two advanced techniques for working with dynamic Excel files:

- Using Microsoft Query to edit columns in exported dynamic Excel files
- Running Excel as a different user

Using Microsoft Query to edit columns in exported dynamic Excel files

1. After you export your dynamic worksheet or PivotTable to Excel, you might realize that you want to add columns to your file, but you want to save the work you've already done in Excel. If you're comfortable manually editing SQL syntax, you can follow these steps to add (or remove) the columns that Excel queries from Microsoft CRM in your dynamic files. The Microsoft Query Excel component must be installed on your machine to perform these steps. Excel 2003 can automatically install this component for you.
2. In your dynamic Excel file, right-click the data range, and then click **Edit Query**.

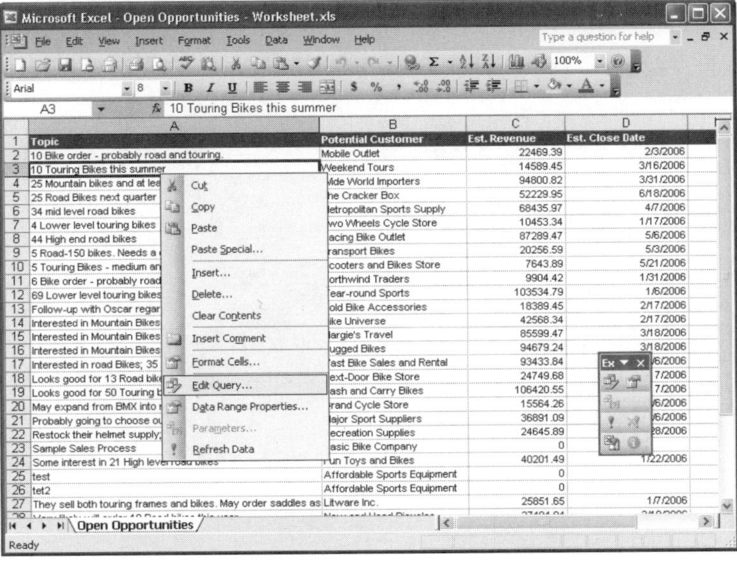

3. A message appears that says, "If you modify the query, columns that you deleted from the Excel external data range will reappear as new columns, unless you also eliminate those columns from the query." Click **OK**.
4. A message appears that says, "This query cannot be edited by the Query Wizard." Click **OK**.
5. In the Microsoft Query editor, click the SQL button on the toolbar.
6. In the SQL editor, you will see the data query and all of the columns that Excel pulls from Microsoft CRM. From here you can manually add or remove the columns that you want to appear in your Excel file.

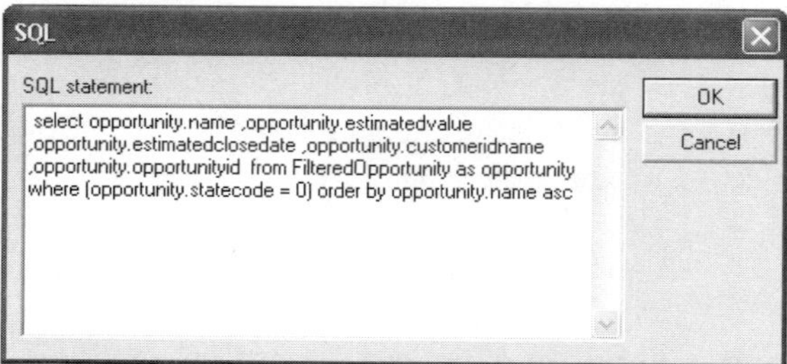

7. After editing the columns in SQL, click **OK**. You might see another message that says, "SQL Query can't be represented graphically. Continue anyway?" Click **OK**.
8. On the **File** menu, click **Return Data to Microsoft Office Excel**. Excel returns the modified columns in your data set.

Running Excel as a different user

1. The dynamic Excel files exported from Microsoft CRM connect to the database using integrated Microsoft Windows authentication. This means that Excel uses your current user credentials to query the Microsoft CRM database when you open dynamic Excel files. This works great for your end users, but as an administrator you might want to run dynamic Excel files as if you're a different user to confirm the data that your users will see. If you used the default Windows authentication, you would have to log off from your computer and then log on as the user whom you want to impersonate. If you have to do this frequently, the process might take too much time. Fortunately, you can follow these steps to impersonate a different user when running Excel 2003.
2. Navigate to C:\Program Files\Microsoft Office\Office11 and locate EXCEL.EXE in the file list.

3. Right-click **EXCEL.EXE**, and then click **Run as**.

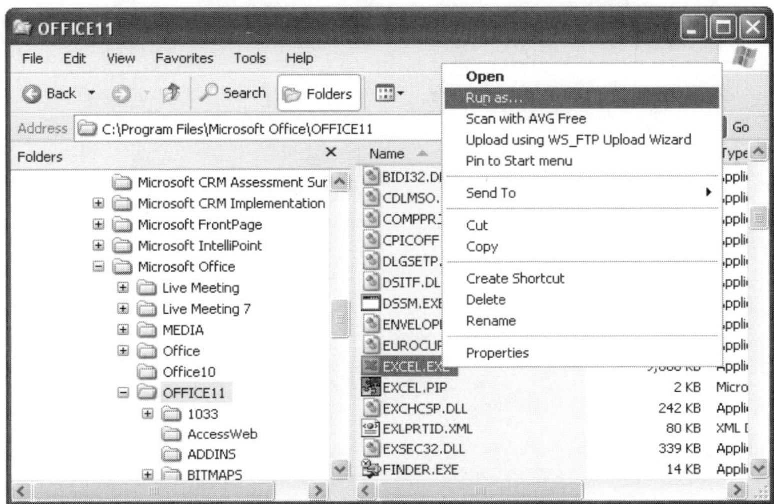

4. Select **The following user**, and then enter the credentials of the user whom you want to impersonate when Excel runs.

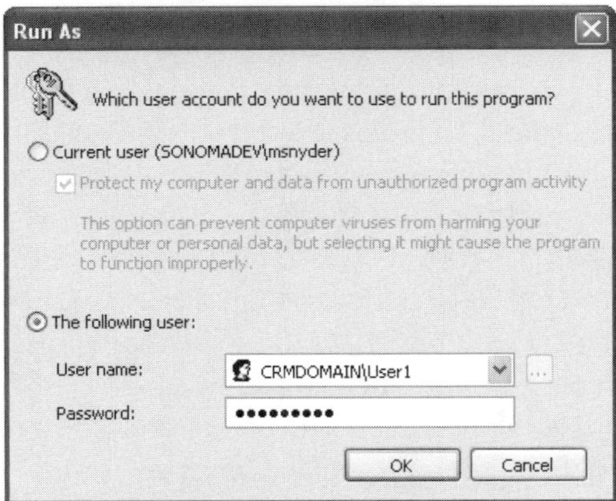

5. When you refresh external data, Excel retrieves data from Microsoft CRM using the user credentials that you just supplied.

Important The first time you run an Office application (such as Excel or Microsoft Office Word) as a user on your machine, you are prompted to set up your profile. You won't be able to do this correctly if you're impersonating another user the first time you run an Office application. Therefore, if you want to use this technique, you might need to log on to the computer one time as the impersonated user and then launch Excel to set up your profile. Then you can log back on as yourself and use the technique previously described.

Filtered Views

At this point, you've heard us warn you many times about not interacting with the SQL Server database directly. Now we'll tell you about the one (just one) time it's permitted to directly retrieve data from the SQL Server database.

If you were to browse the Microsoft CRM SQL database (with a tool such as SQL Server Enterprise Manager or SQL Query Analyzer), you might notice multiple data objects related to Accounts, including:

- AccountBase table
- AccountExtensionBase table
- AccountLeads table
- Account view
- FilteredAccount view

When you want to write your own custom report about Accounts, you might wonder which of these database objects includes the information you're looking for. In addition to the Account entity, the Microsoft CRM database has a similar setup for all of its entity data. The CRM database stores all of the data in highly normalized and efficient layout, but that doesn't necessarily simplify your reporting and analysis needs.

Fortunately, instead of forcing you to spend hours investigating what types of entity data Microsoft CRM stores in these various database objects, Microsoft CRM greatly simplifies reporting and analysis by offering you filtered views. *Filtered views* perform the cumbersome task of denormalizing multiple tables and relationships into a streamlined view of entity and system data. In addition, filtered views respect the Microsoft CRM security settings so that users who query filtered views (or run reports that query filtered views) will see only the data that they're allowed to see. Also, filtered views translate lookup fields and picklist values, and they calculate all datetime values in both Coordinated Universal Time (UTC) and the user's localized value. For example, the createdon field will display the user's local time and the createdonutc field will display the field with the Coordinated Universal Time.

When you create reports that leverage integrated Windows authentication (such as SQL Server Reporting Services), the filtered views will automatically filter the data that the report displays to users based on their logged on credentials, their business units, and their security roles. Two different users viewing the same report might see entirely different results depending on the Microsoft CRM security settings. This feature will save you hours by trying to manually determine the security and data settings of each custom report.

> **Important** Filtered views simplify the complex Microsoft CRM data model for use with reporting and analysis while maintaining user security and access to data. All of your custom reports should read data from the database filtered views exclusively. You should *never* write reports that query any other database table or view.

You can easily recognize filtered views in the database because their name always starts with the text "Filtered." Usually you can also determine which entity each filtered view relates to by simply looking at its name. Every entity has a filtered view, but Microsoft CRM also includes some filtered views that do not map directly to an entity. Table 7-2 shows some examples of filtered views.

Table 7-2 Sample Filtered View Names

Filtered view name	Entity name	Entity schema name
FilteredAccount	Account	account
FilteredActivityPointer	Activity	activitypointer
FilteredIncident	Case	incident
FilteredAnnualFiscalCalendar	n/a	n/a
FilteredAccountLeads	n/a	n/a

More Info The Report Writer's Guide in the Microsoft CRM software development kit (SDK) lists all of the filtered views and the type of data stored in each view.

As you customize your system by adding custom attributes to the system entities, Microsoft CRM automatically updates the filtered views for you. It also creates entirely new filtered views for each custom entity that you add to your installation.

Another important note about filtered views is that Microsoft CRM automatically configures all of the filtered view permissions to allow only SELECT (read-only) operations against them. Even though it's technically possible for a database administrator to change the default permissions, you should *never* change the filtered view permissions to allow INSERT, DELETE, or UPDATE operations. Attempting to perform any non-SELECT operation against a filtered view might cause irrevocable damage to your Microsoft CRM database.

SQL Server Reporting Services

SQL Server Reporting Services provides a complete server-based platform for the delivery, creation, and administration of reports. Microsoft CRM uses SQL Server Reporting Services as its reporting engine, and Microsoft CRM takes advantage of many built-in features of Reporting Services, such as e-mail delivery, report scheduling, exporting reports to multiple formats, report snapshots, and report caching.

This chapter will cover many aspects of Reporting Services and how it pertains to Microsoft CRM. However, Reporting Services is far too complex to cover adequately in this text, and we encourage you to review the Reporting Services Online Help installed with the product and the following links for additional information:

- Product overview: *http://www.microsoft.com/sql/technologies/reporting/overview.mspx*
- Report Definition Language: *http://msdn.microsoft.com/library/default.asp?url=/library/en-us/RSRDL/htm/rsp_ref_rdl_52g5.asp*

One of the most important concepts about Reporting Services and Microsoft CRM is that the reports also use integrated Windows authentication and filtered views to determine which data to display in the report to the user.

Architecture

SQL Server Reporting Services manages all parts of reporting, including report authoring, data source management, report security, output formats, and multiple delivery mechanisms. Figure 7-5 outlines the Reporting Services architecture and its various reporting components.

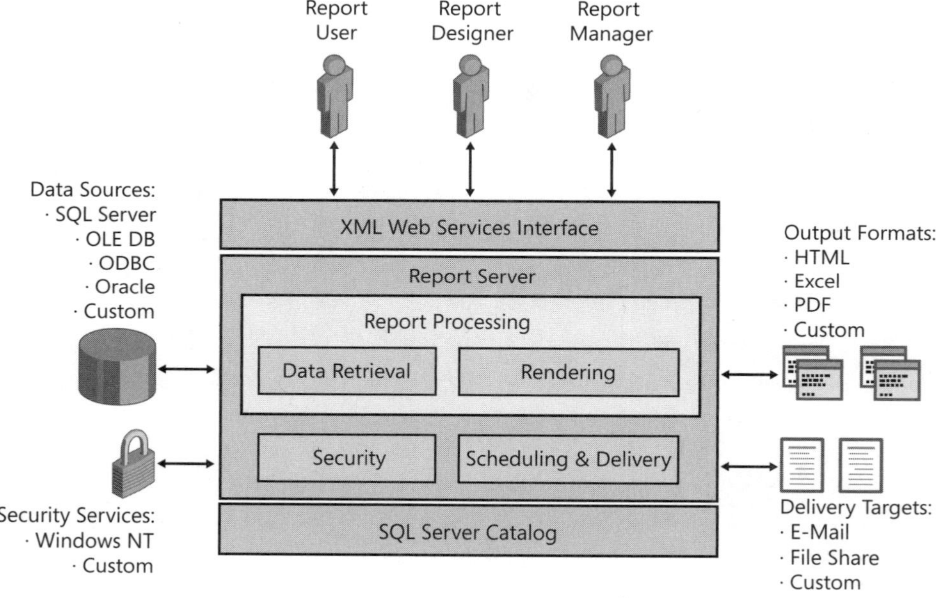

Figure 7-5 Reporting Services architecture

In addition to SQL Server, Reporting Services supports other data source types such as OLE DB and ODBC. This book will focus exclusively on SQL Server data sources because Microsoft CRM uses SQL Server to store its data.

Important Because Reporting Services supports multiple data sources, you can create a single report that combines Microsoft CRM data with other non–Microsoft CRM data (assuming Reporting Services supports the data type that you want to combine in the report).

Reporting Services report files use an .rdl file extension. RDL stands for Report Definition Language, an open-schema XML language definition that defines the data retrieval and display layout of a report. You can use Microsoft Visual Studio .NET to create report .rdl files, but you can also use any other report authoring tool that supports the RDL schema.

In addition to the report authoring flexibility created by using open-schema .rdl files, Reporting Services offers a programming model that allows developers to further customize and enhance the Reporting Services functionality. Please reference the previously listed resources if you're interested in learning more about the Reporting Services programming model and extensibility options.

Licensing and Installation

Reporting Services is a component of SQL Server, so there is no charge for the Reporting Services software if you have a valid SQL Server license and you install the Reporting Services web on the same server as SQL Server.

When you install Microsoft CRM, you can choose to have it install Reporting Services for you, or you can direct the Microsoft CRM installation program to use an existing server running Reporting Services. Installing Reporting Services can be tricky, but the Microsoft CRM Implementation Guide provides excellent troubleshooting information if you experience a problem. You can also reference the RSSetup.chm Help file located in the SRS directory of your Microsoft CRM installation CDs for more detailed instructions on installing Reporting Services.

More Info In high-volume Microsoft CRM deployments, we would recommend that you use a dedicated server running Reporting Services. By splitting the reporting load from the Microsoft CRM SQL Server, both machines will perform better for users' requests. Microsoft published a short white paper titled "Improving Performance of Microsoft CRM 3.0 by Using a Dedicated Report Server" that defines how to set up a dedicated report server with Microsoft CRM. You can download it here: *http://www.microsoft.com/downloads/details.aspx?FamilyID=c82dfbe2-db8f-4a78-92b2-7c866057cde6&DisplayLang=en*.

Reporting Services Reports in the Microsoft CRM User Interface

You access Reporting Services reports from the Microsoft CRM user interface by using one of three methods:

- Reports list
- Entity list
- Entity form

Reports List

The default Microsoft CRM installation creates a subarea called Reports in the My Work group of the Workplace area (see Figure 7-6). In addition to listing all of the available reports, you can use this Reports list to administer the reports, assuming that you have the Manage Reports security privilege. By default, the System Customizer and System Administrator security roles have the necessary permissions to edit reports.

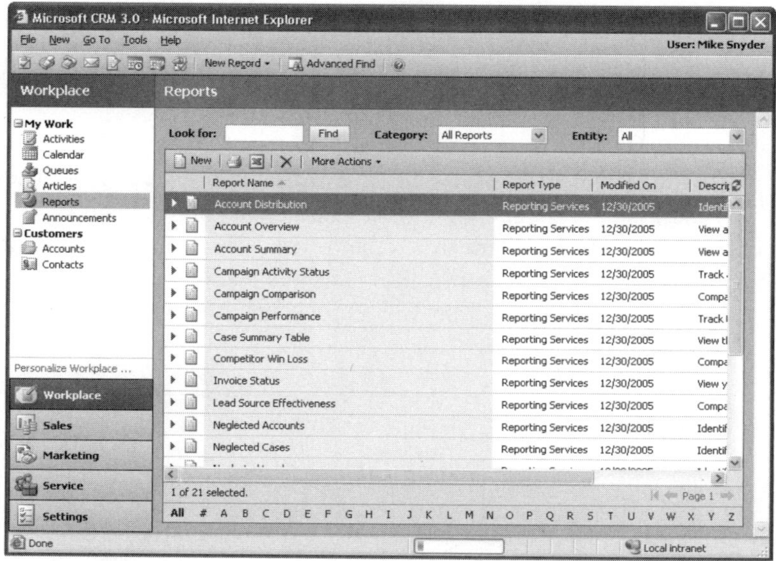

Figure 7-6 Reports list in the My Work group

Tip Remember that you can modify the site map to make the Reports list appear wherever you want in the application navigation, such as creating a new area called Reports in the wunderbar. The URL to use in the Site Map for the Reports list is Url="/CRMReports/home_reports.aspx".

Entity List

In addition to the reports list, you can allow users to run reports from the toolbar of an entity's grid by clicking the Report button, as shown in Figure 7-7 for the Account entity.

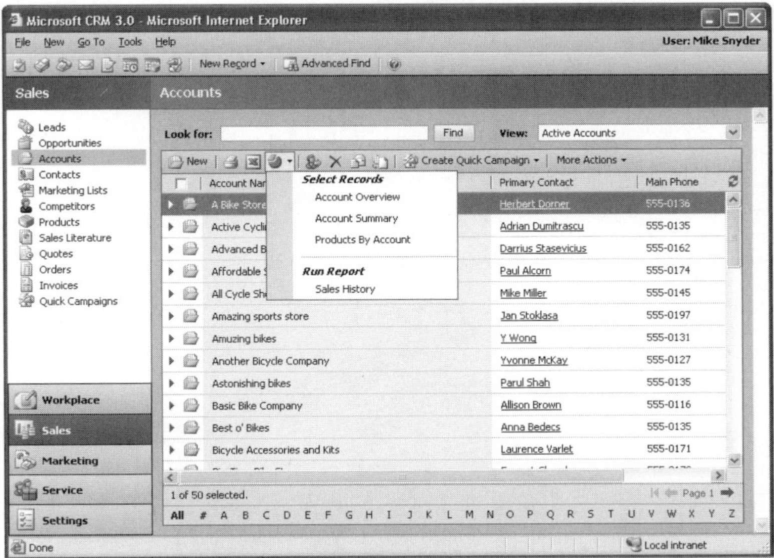

Figure 7-7 Accessing reports from an entity's grid toolbar

This figure shows reports listed under one of two groups: Select Records or Run Report. If the user chooses to run one of the reports listed under Select Records, Microsoft CRM prompts them to select which records they want to apply to the report. The three options are:

- All applicable records
- The selected records (10 maximum)
- All records on all pages in the current view

By selecting one of these three options, users can pre-filter the records that they want Microsoft CRM to include in the report results.

If the user selects a report listed under the Run Report group, Microsoft CRM will run the report independent of the selected records or the records that appear in the view.

Important We refer to reports that run for Select Records as *contextual reports* because they run within the context of particular records. You must create the report query using the correct technique to create your own custom contextual reports. We explain this technique later in this chapter.

Entity Form

Similar to running reports from the entity list, you can also run reports directly from the entity form by clicking the Reports button on the menu bar (Figure 7-8).

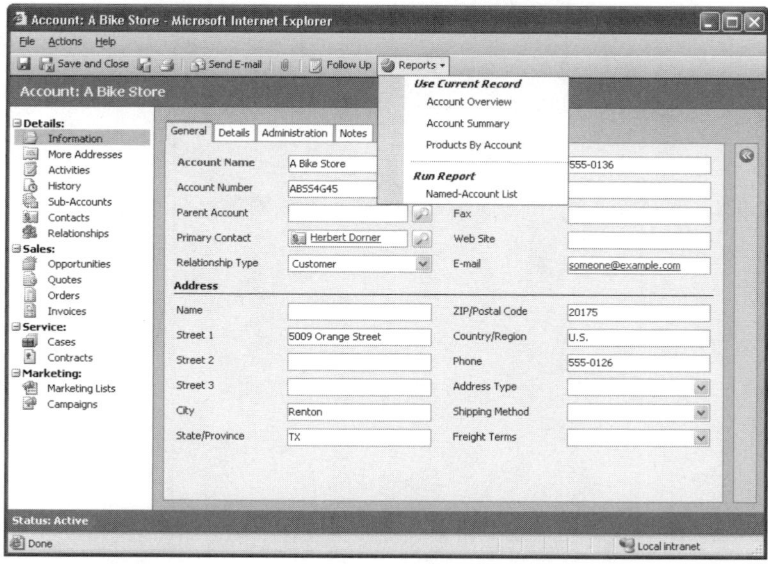

Figure 7-8 Accessing reports from the entity form

And just like running reports from the entity list, you can choose to run a contextual report or a non-contextual report. On the entity form, Microsoft CRM lists contextual reports under the Use Current Record grouping and the non-contextual reports under the Run Report grouping. If you choose to run a contextual report from the entity form, Microsoft CRM will not prompt you (like the entity list report) to further refine the record set because there is only one record to run the report for. Figure 7-9 shows the output if you run the contextual Account Overview report.

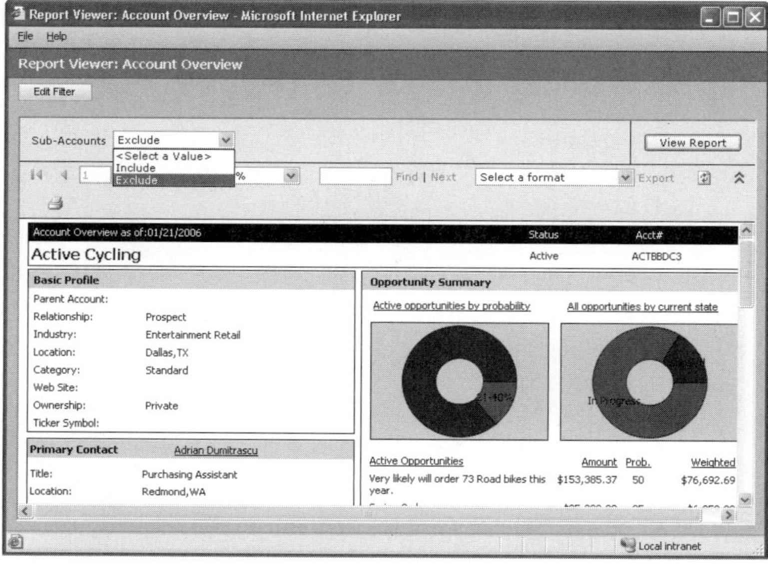

Figure 7-9 Sample Account Overview report

Without the contextual report feature, if you wanted to run the Account Overview report for a single Account, you would have to navigate to the Reports list, pick the report you wanted to run, and then manually specify an Account. Instead, Microsoft CRM allows you to launch a contextual report directly from the entity menu bar for the Account you're currently viewing to save users approximately 10 to 15 clicks every time they run a report.

Tip Create contextual reports whenever possible for your custom reports to save your users extra clicks in the application navigation.

We'll explain later in this chapter how to configure contextual reports and specify where you want them to appear in the application navigation.

Running a Reporting Services Report

Regardless of where you want to access the report from, running the report is straightforward. From the Reports list, simply double-click the name of the report that you want to run. You can run contextual reports by clicking the report name in the form or grid toolbar.

Now let's examine what your users see when they run Reporting Services reports:

- Report pre-filtering
- Results navigation
- Export options

You'll need to understand these parts of the report output to properly administer and manage your reports.

Report Pre-filtering

Microsoft CRM allows you to create Reporting Services reports with a pre-filtering option. *Pre-filtering* gives users the opportunity to set up and modify filter criteria before running the report. By pre-filtering a report, users can drastically reduce the number of records that

Reporting Services must manipulate, which will provide an increase in the report's performance. When users run a report with pre-filtering enabled, they see the report filtering criteria on the Report Viewer page. Figure 7-10 shows the default pre-filter page for the Account Distribution report.

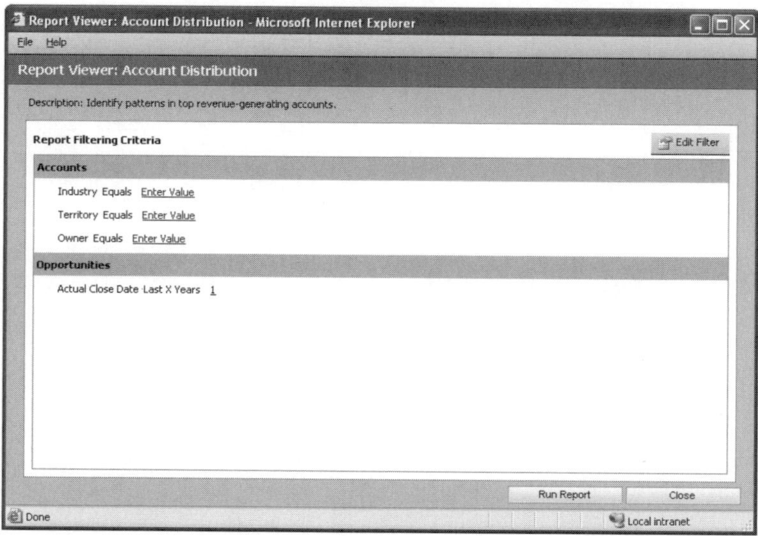

Figure 7-10 Report filtering criteria for pre-filtering report results

As you can see, this report pre-filtering allows the user to enter values for four default filters before running the report. If the user does not enter values where prompted by the Enter Value text (Industry, Territory, and Owner), the report will run as if that filter does not exist.

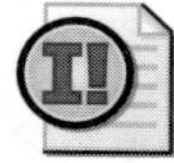

> **Important** The report pre-filtering functionality is unique to Microsoft CRM, so users can access pre-filtering only when they run reports within Microsoft CRM. If they navigate directly to the Web server running Reporting Services and run a report from there, the pre-filtering option is not available. Likewise, you must upload reports through Microsoft CRM to include the pre-filtering feature. You should not upload the reports directly to Reporting Services.

In addition to the default pre-filter parameters that appear on the Report Viewer page, users can further modify the pre-filter by clicking the Edit Filter button. The report pre-filter uses the same user interface as the Advanced Find feature (as shown in Figure 7-11), so users should be able to easily manipulate the pre-filter settings.

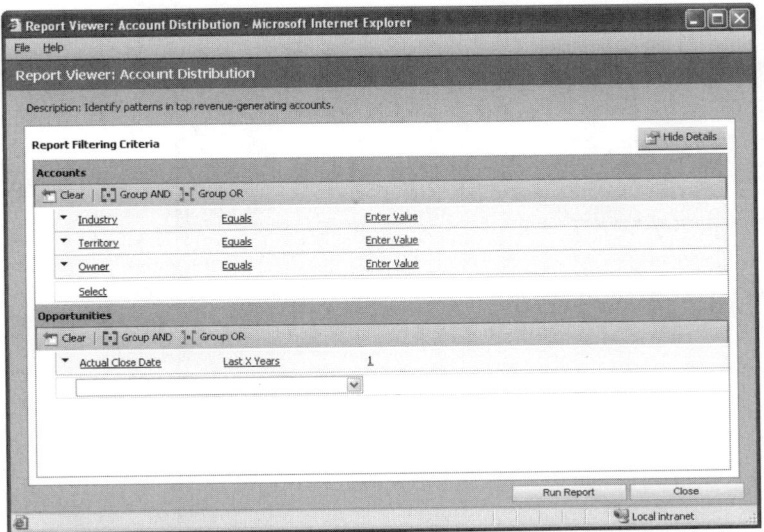

Figure 7-11 Modifying the default filters, using the same interface as the Advanced Find feature

Just as with the Advanced Find feature, you can create highly complex report filters to search for the exact type of results that interest you.

Results Navigation

After you set the pre-filter criteria for your reports, click the Run Report button to execute the report. Microsoft CRM displays a status message to the user while it creates the report

After executing the report, Microsoft CRM updates the Report Viewer page with the completed report. Figure 7-12 shows the output for the Account Distribution report.

In Figure 7-12, we highlighted two areas of the report output. The report navigation bar allows you to navigate records, change the zoom level, find text in the report output, export the results, and refresh and print the data. The navigation bar is common to all Reporting Services reports.

Above the report navigation bar are the report parameters unique to this report. By using report parameters, you can further refine the results in your report. Reporting Services supports many types of parameters, including text fields and drop-down lists, as shown in the Account Distribution example.

Important Report parameters are not the same as the pre-filter criteria. Microsoft CRM lets you use pre-filter criteria to reduce the number of records returned in your report. After Reporting Services generates the report, you can use report parameters to filter the report records in the result set. You define report parameters in the report .rdl file; you define pre-filter criteria in Microsoft CRM.

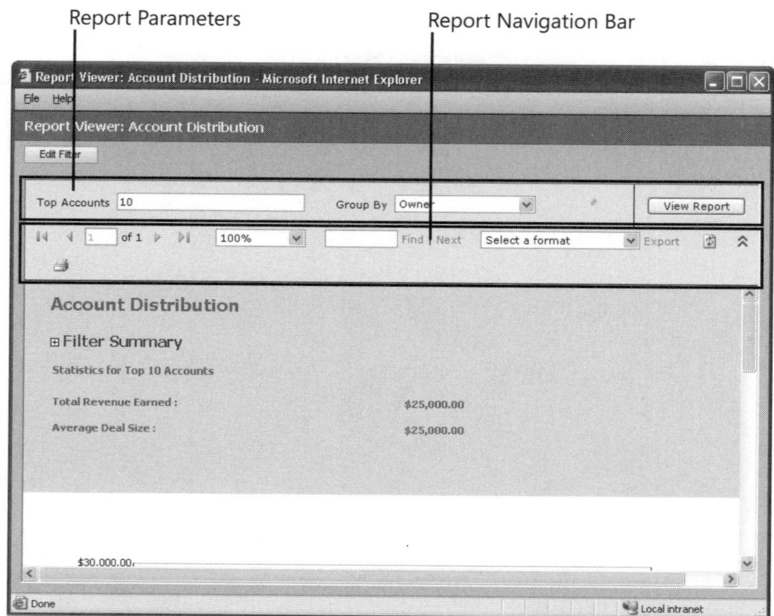

Figure 7-12 Reporting Services Account Distribution report output

If you double-click any of the columns in the Account Distribution chart, a new report appears on the Report Viewer page. Reporting Services refers to this nested report as a *sub-report*. Sub-reports allow you to link reports together so that users can examine a specific area of a report to get more detailed information. You can configure a sub-report to dynamically accept parameters from its parent report.

Tip Creating sub-reports and drill-throughs on your custom reports takes more work to develop and test, but users absolutely love this feature. Consider adding this drill-through feature on some of the most popular or important custom reports in your deployment.

Export Options

After you manipulate the report results to display the records that you want, Reporting Services allows you to export the report data to multiple formats easily. To export a report, simply choose a format from the Select A Format list in the report navigation bar, and then click Export, as shown in Figure 7-13.

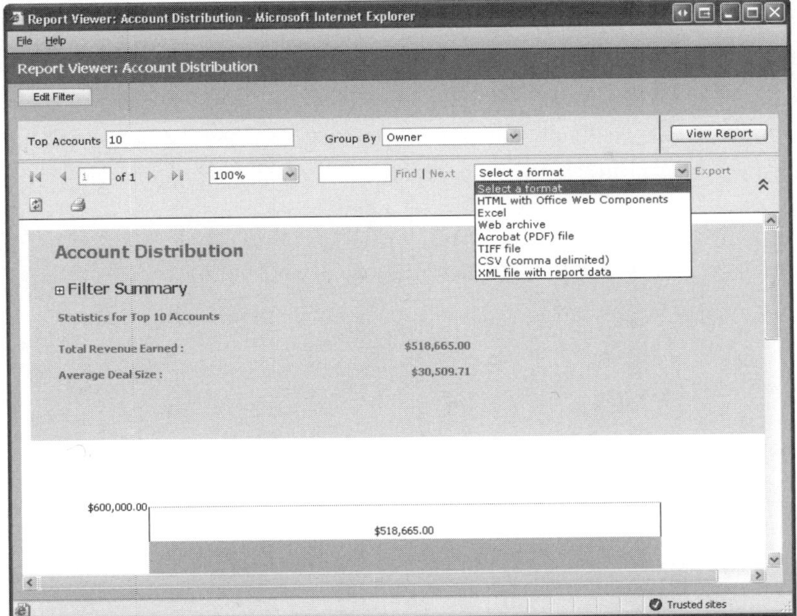

Figure 7-13 Exporting a report

You can export the report in any of the formats described in the following sections.

HTML with Office Web Components

- Converts the report to a Web page that can be opened with Microsoft Office products using the Office Web Components tools.
- Useful for the interactive tools available with Office Web Components.
- Requires Office Web Components version 10 (Office XP) on the client computer.
- This export option was deprecated from SQL Server Reporting Services 2005.

Excel

- Opens the report data in Excel.
- Ideal for additional manipulation or analysis of the data and for storing the data offline.
- Requires Excel version 10 (Office XP) or version 11 (Office 2003) on the client computer.
- Exporting to Excel can be an intensive process for the server, especially for large or complex reports.

Web Archive

- Renders output as a self-contained Web-based file (MHTML) and opens in Microsoft Internet Explorer. It will also embed any images directly into the file format.
- Advantageous if you need a portable, offline format. However, this format can be rendered accurately with Internet Explorer only.

Acrobat (PDF) File

- Saves the report as a .pdf file that can be opened with Adobe Acrobat Reader.
- Optimal choice for paginated reports, reports that will be printed, or reports that will be delivered to a broad range of client machines.

TIFF File

- Saves the report as an image file that opens with an application associated with this file type (such as Microsoft Windows Picture and Fax Viewer).
- Generally used for printing or graphics purposes.
- Not recommended for reports with large amounts of data.

CSV (Comma Delimited)

- Saves the report data in a comma separated value (CSV) format that can be opened with any application that handles .csv files, such as Excel.
- Smallest file size of any export option.
- Typically used when integrating the report data with other applications. It is also useful for opening within Excel for additional analysis.

XML File with Report Data

- Saves the report as raw.
- Typically used when programmatically integrating reporting data with other applications.

Authoring Reporting Services Reports

Microsoft CRM includes 20 Reporting Services reports in the default installation, and these 20 reports include 23 additional sub-reports. However, you will definitely want to create new reports (or modify the default reports) as you customize your Microsoft CRM database with new entity attributes and custom entities.

As we explained earlier in this chapter, Reporting Services includes the most powerful reporting features and functionality in Microsoft CRM, but the tradeoff is that creating or modifying Reporting Services reports typically requires an experienced report writer. Therefore, we don't expect to tell you everything you need to know about Reporting Services in this chapter, but we do want to demonstrate a few simple examples and highlight some unique areas of Microsoft CRM that relate to Reporting Services.

Report Authoring Tools

Although you can use any RDL-compliant report authoring tool, most Microsoft CRM customers will use Visual Studio .NET with the Reporting Services Report Designer add-in to author Reporting Services reports.

> **More Info** When you install Microsoft CRM, you can choose to install SQL Server 2000 Reporting Services, but not SQL Server 2005 Reporting Services. However, you can point a Microsoft CRM installation to an existing SQL Server 2005 Reporting Services installation for use with Microsoft CRM. Because Microsoft CRM installs SQL Server 2000 Reporting Services, all of our examples will show SQL Server 2000 Reporting Services and Visual Studio .NET 2003.

The Microsoft CRM installation discs include the Reporting Services Report Designer add-in, so you can easily install it if you have Visual Studio .NET on your computer.

Installing the Report Designer add-in for Visual Studio .NET

1. Navigate to the SRS folder of the Microsoft CRM installation disc 1 on your client computer.
2. Double-click **Setup.exe** and follow the installation wizard.
3. Complete the wizard, accepting all of the default settings. The installation wizard might tell you that it can't install the server running Reporting Services components.

   Because you want to install only the Report Designer add-in (a client component), you can ignore this warning and click **Next**.

   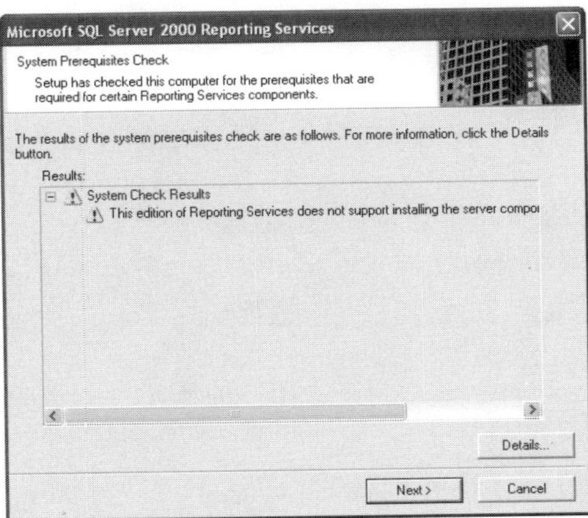

4. After installation is complete, confirm that the Report Designer installed correctly. Open Visual Studio .NET 2003.
5. On the **File** menu, point to **New**, and then click **Project**.

6. Under **Project Types**, look for a project type called Business Intelligence Projects. If you see this project type, the Reporting Services Report Designer installed successfully.

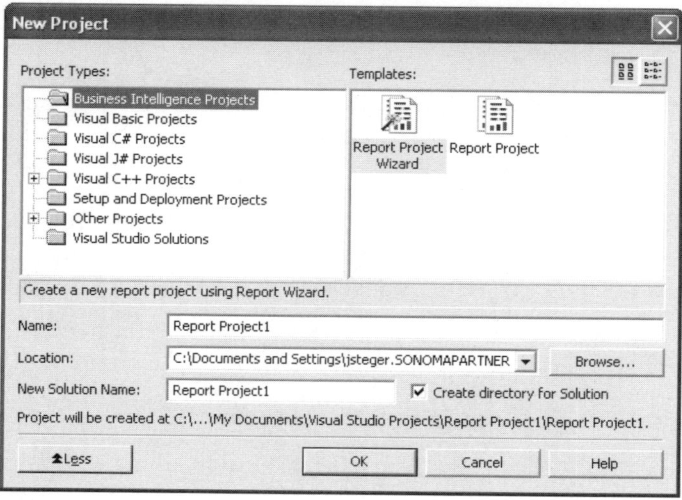

Important You should not install the Report Designer on the server running Microsoft CRM or Reporting Services. Rather, you should always edit the report .rdl files on a client computer and then upload the files to the server when you're finished.

For additional resources regarding developing reports in Reporting Services, you can install the Reporting Services Books Online.

Editing a Reporting Services Report

We will now show you how to use Visual Studio .NET 2003 and the Report Designer to edit one of the Microsoft CRM default reports and then upload the modified report back to Microsoft CRM. You might need to edit the default Microsoft CRM reports if you add custom attributes and you want to modify the report layout to include these new fields.

Tip The default Reporting Services reports in Microsoft CRM use complex data sets and advanced reporting features. You should edit these reports only if you're extremely comfortable authoring Reporting Services reports. Beginner or intermediate report writers might feel more comfortable creating new reports from scratch instead of trying to edit the default Microsoft CRM repots.

In the following example, we will show you how to modify the Account Overview report. Let's assume we would like to add the number of employees as a field in the Basic Profile section of the report. Figure 7-14 shows the final report with the field added.

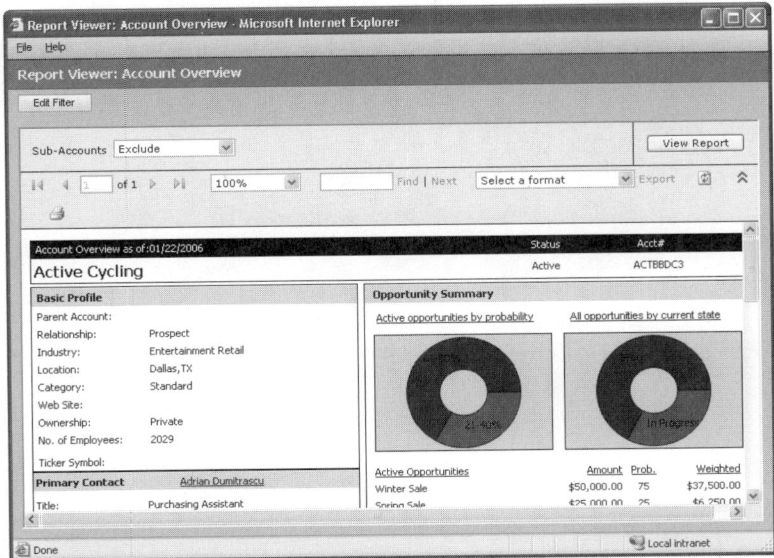

Figure 7-14 Modified Account Overview report

Almost all of the default Microsoft CRM reports use a sub-report to display the report details, and the Account Overview report is no different. Therefore, we need to modify the Account Overview Sub-Report to add the number of employees field to the report layout.

> **Warning** Whenever you update a report, make sure that you save a backup of the original. This will allow you to roll back to the original version should you have any problems.

Modifying the Account Overview report

1. Click the **Reports** subarea in the **Workplace** area.
2. Change the **Category** to **Hidden Reports**, and then select the **Account Overview** sub-report.
3. Click **More Actions**, and then click **Download Report**. Save the report to your desktop, making sure that the file you download has an .rdl file extension instead of an .xml file extension. You can do this by changing the Save as Type drop-down from XML Document to All Files.
4. In Visual Studio .NET 2003, click the **File** menu, point to **New**, and then click **Project**.
5. In the **Project Types** section, select **Business Intelligence Projects**, and in the **Templates** section, select **Report Project**.
6. Give your Visual Studio project a name like "CRM Reports," and then click **OK**. Visual Studio creates a Reporting Services project with two empty folders: Shared Data Sources and Reports.

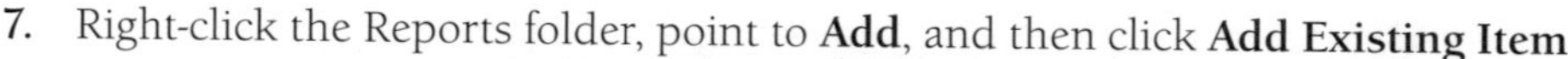

7. Right-click the Reports folder, point to **Add**, and then click **Add Existing Item**.

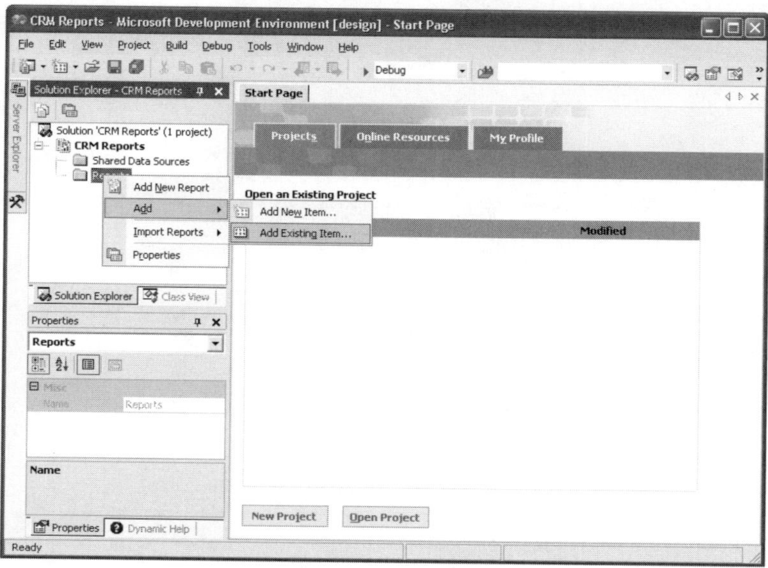

8. In the **Look in** list, click **Desktop**. Select the Account Overview Sub-Report.rdl file, and then click **Open**.
9. Visual Studio adds the report to your project. Double-click the report to open it in Layout mode.
10. Click the **Data** tab to verify your data connection. If your data connection does not work, you will receive the following error.

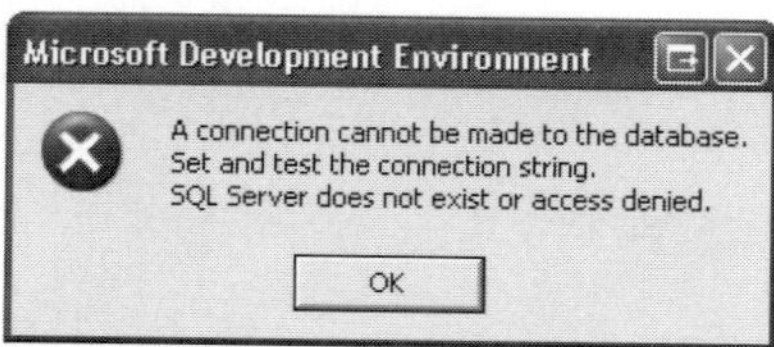

11. If your preview does not generate an error, you do not need to edit your data connection, and you can skip to step 14. To edit your data connection, click the **Data** tab, and then click the ellipsis (...) button on the toolbar.

12. In the **Dataset** dialog box, click the ellipsis (...) button next to **Data Source: CRM** to open the **Data Source** dialog box.

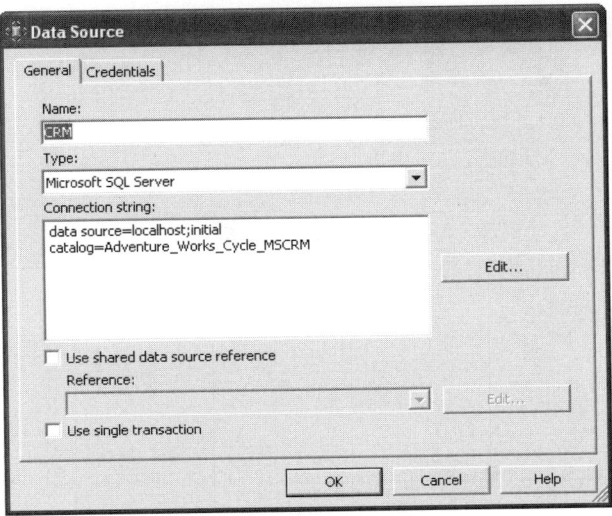

13. Make sure that the data source and initial catalog values in the Connection String are correct for your environment. When you download reports, sometimes Microsoft CRM will set the data source to localhost and the initial catalog to Adventure_Works_Cycle_MSCRM. Change these default values to the correct values for your deployment. The data source should be the name of your Microsoft CRM SQL Server. The initial catalog should be the name of the Microsoft CRM database. The initial catalog name should appear as *organizationname*_MSCRM, where *organizationname* is the organization name used when Microsoft CRM was installed. After you edit these values, click **OK** to close the **Data Source** dialog box, and then click **OK** in the **Dataset** dialog box. If you click the **Preview** tab, it should display a blank Account Overview report. If you still receive an error, review your data source settings.

14. Before you can add the number of employees field to the report, you must modify the report's dataset so that the report query includes the number of employees field in the result set. As we mentioned earlier, most of the default Microsoft CRM reports include multiple data sets, so you'll need to know which data set to edit. We already determined that you want to add the number of employees field to the ds_BasicProfile data set. To edit the query, click the **Data** tab and select **ds_BasicProfile** from the **Dataset** list. The SQL query text can sometimes look awkward in the **Generic Query** window.

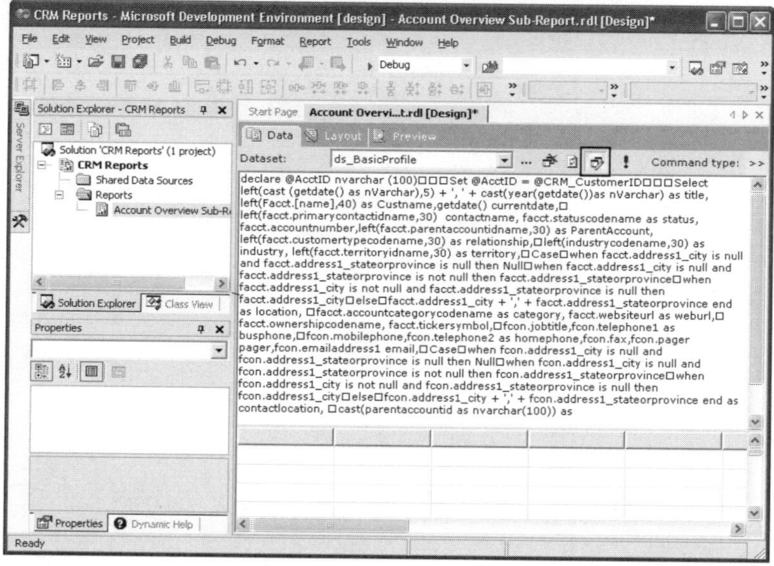

15. To convert the SQL query text to a format that's easier to read, you can click the Generic Query Designer button (outlined in the screen shot) and then click it again. Visual Studio will format the query a little more cleanly, but it will still have some inconsistent spacing.

16. To add the number of employees field to the query, you need to know the schema name of the attribute. Remember that one method to look up attribute schema names is to browse to http://*<crmserver>*/sdk/list.aspx. You'll find that the schema name we're looking for is *numberofemployees*. To add this field to the query, add the following text after the SELECT keyword in the query:

```
facct.numberofemployees,
```

This is a complex query that we won't explain in detail; however, *facct* is an alias that the query uses to reference the FilteredAccount database view. A snippet of the final code with the new field added would look like the following.

```
DECLARE @AcctID nvarchar(100)
SET @AcctID = @CRM_CustomerID
  SELECT
               facct.numberofemployees,
               LEFT(cast(getdate() AS nVarchar), 5) + ', ' + cast(year(getdate())
 AS nVarchar) AS title, LEFT(Facct.[name], 40) AS Custname, getdate()
 ...
```

17. After you add the field to the query, click the **Save** button in the Visual Studio .NET toolbar. Make sure you save before you click on the Layout or Preview tab again; otherwise, you might receive a warning message.

18. Now that the report query results include the number of employees data field, we can add that field to the report output in the Layout section. Click the Layout tab, and then click the text box that contains **Ownership**.

19. In the table outline, right-click the icon with the three horizontal lines next to **Ownership**, and then click **Insert Row Below** to insert a new row between **Ownership** and **Ticker Symbol**.

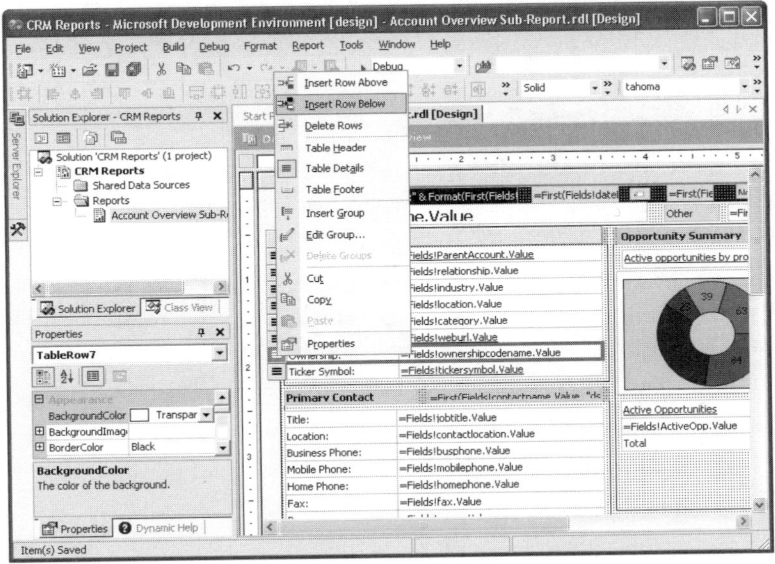

20. Click the text box under **Ownership** and type **No. of Employees:**.

21. Right-click the box to the right of the **No. of Employees** field, and then click **Properties**.

22. In the **Texbox Properties** dialog box, do the following:

    a. In the **Name** box, type **numberofemployees**.

    b. In the **Value** list, select **=Fields!numberofemployees.Value**. This should be at the top of the list because you added it as the first field in the query. If this field doesn't appear automatically, you can manually type it into the Value box.

    c. Click **OK**.

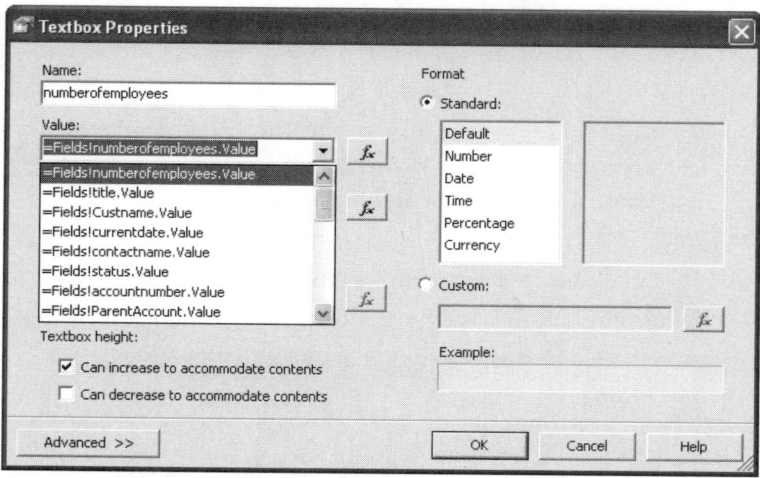

23. Click the **=Fields!numberofemployees.Value** field and then select the text alignment for this field to the left to remain consistent with the other fields in this column. You can set the text alignment from the toolbar or by modifying the TextAlign property in the Properties window.

24. Save your report by clicking **Save All** on the **File** menu. If you try to preview the report, you won't see any data because the report needs an Account ID value to run correctly. You must upload the report to Microsoft CRM to see it work.

25. In the Web client, navigate to the Microsoft CRM Reports list.

26. Select the **Account Overview** sub-report (in the **Hidden Reports** category), click **More Actions**, and then click **Edit Report**.

27. In the **Source** section, click **Browse**, select the **Account Overview** sub-report that you just edited, and then click **Save and Close**.

> **Note** Do not select the file you downloaded to your desktop. You must select the updated .rdl file from the directory in which Visual Studio stores your project files.

28. Run the Account Overview report, and you'll see **No. of Employees** in the **Basic Profile** section of the report.

As you can see, even though the default Microsoft CRM reports are complex, an inexperienced report author can make simple modifications to add custom attributes, make minor formatting changes, and so on. You can imagine how to carry this same concept through to adding additional fields to a report or modifying where fields appear in the report layout.

Creating a New Reporting Services Report

As you saw with the Account Overview report example, the default Microsoft CRM Reporting Services reports use complex queries, multiple data sets, and sub-reports, so you might not feel comfortable making significant changes to those reports. Therefore, we recommend that beginner report writers create entirely new reports. We'll walk you through this process.

Let's walk through a quick example of creating a new report from scratch. Our sample report will create a list of all the Activity records for an Account. This report will help users because it will display both open and closed Activities for an Account on a single page. We will also show you how to use some of the special reporting fields such as the pre-filter field that Microsoft CRM provides to include additional functionality in your report.

> **Tip** When creating a new report, you might be able to find an existing report to use as a template. This allows you to create a report with the same formatting as the default reports.

Creating a new report

1. Using the same CRM Reports project you created in the Account Overview example, right-click the **Reports** folder, and then click **Add New Report**.
2. If this is your first time creating a new report, you will see the Report Wizard. Click **Next**.
3. The first step of a new report is to create a new data source:
    a. In the **Name** box, type **CRM**.
    b. In the **Type** list, select **Microsoft SQL Server**.
    c. To enter the **Connection String**, click the **Edit** button, which opens the **Data Link Properties** dialog box.
        i. On the **Connection** tab, enter or select the name of the computer running SQL Server on which you installed Microsoft CRM.
        ii. Select the **Use Windows NT Integrated security** option button.
        iii. Select your database (<*organizationname*>_MSCRM).
        iv. Click **OK**.
    d. If you select the **Make this a shared data source** check box, you can reuse this data source for additional reports in the Visual Studio Report Designer. However, you cannot deploy a report to Reporting Services through Microsoft CRM with a shared data source, so you must manually reset the data source for each report before you deploy it.
    e. Click **Next**.

4. On the **Design the Query** page, enter the following SQL statement and click **Next**.

```
SELECT     FilteredActivityPointer.activitytypecodename, FilteredActivityPointer.
subject, FilteredActivityPointer.modifiedonutc,
                      FilteredActivityPointer.modifiedbyname, FilteredActivityPoi
nter.statecodename, FilteredActivityPointer.statuscodename,
                      FilteredActivityPointer.owneridname, FilteredAccount.name
FROM         FilteredAccount INNER JOIN
                      FilteredActivityPointer ON FilteredAccount.accountid = Filt
eredActivityPointer.regardingobjectid
ORDER BY FilteredActivityPointer.modifiedonutc DESC
```

5. You can continue through the Report Wizard to adjust the report formatting, or just click **Finish** to accept the default formatting.
6. For the report name, type **Account Activities**, and then click **Finish**. You will see the report in Layout mode. You can adjust the report column widths by dragging the columns to the left or right. You can also click the **Preview** tab to see what your report will look like.
7. On the **File** menu, click **Save** to save your new report. Now you are ready to add it to Microsoft CRM.
8. In the Web client, navigate to the Microsoft CRM Reports list and click **New** on the grid toolbar.
9. In the Location field, select your new Account Activities.rdl and give the report a name. Remember that the report name must be unique.
10. Click **Save and Close**, and then run your new report. Here is the report output if you accept the default layout formatting for the Adventure Works Cycle sample database.

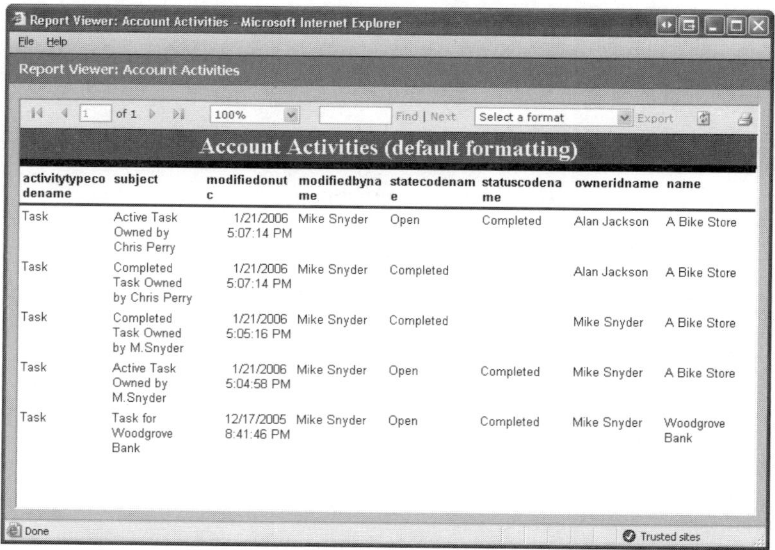

activitytypecodename	subject	modifiedonutc	modifiedbyname	statecodename	statuscodename	owneridname	name
Task	Active Task Owned by Chris Perry	1/21/2006 5:07:14 PM	Mike Snyder	Open	Completed	Alan Jackson	A Bike Store
Task	Completed Task Owned by Chris Perry	1/21/2006 5:07:14 PM	Mike Snyder	Completed		Alan Jackson	A Bike Store
Task	Completed Task Owned by M.Snyder	1/21/2006 5:05:16 PM	Mike Snyder	Completed		Mike Snyder	A Bike Store
Task	Active Task Owned by M.Snyder	1/21/2006 5:04:58 PM	Mike Snyder	Open	Completed	Mike Snyder	A Bike Store
Task	Task for Woodgrove Bank	12/17/2005 8:41:46 PM	Mike Snyder	Open	Completed	Mike Snyder	Woodgrove Bank

The default Reporting Services formatting looks pretty bad, so we would never deploy a report that looked like this to end users. However, we wanted this example to demonstrate how quickly and easily you can create a custom report for Microsoft CRM. Our example used the default Reporting Services formatting, but you would obviously want to edit the report formatting (fonts, colors, and so on) to match all of the other reports used in Microsoft CRM.

Tip The Microsoft CRM Software Development Kit (SDK) includes a Report Style Guide document that lists all of the fonts and colors that you should use to match the formatting of the default Microsoft CRM reports. You could build your reports by using an existing report as a template, which will save you from extra formatting steps.

Reporting Parameters

In the example report we just finished, we created a simple standalone report that didn't use any report parameters. Reporting Services uses *parameters* to allow you to dynamically alter the report query and output based on incoming variables. In addition to the standard parameter functionality that Reporting Services supports, Microsoft CRM offers a few additional special report parameters, listed in Table 7-3.

Table 7-3 Microsoft CRM Reporting Parameters

Parameter	Description	Usage
CRMAF_<*filteredentityview*>	Adds pre-filtering to the report	Add to query expression (Data tab)
CRM_FilterText	Passes any filtered values to a text box in your report	Add to report layout
CRM_URL	Tells Microsoft CRM the path to the Web server Important to set when using drill-through capabilities	Add to report layout
CRM_Locale	Sets the language of the report	Add to report layout
CRM_SortField	Defines the attribute to use for custom sorting within the report	Add to report layout
CRM_SortDirection	Defines the direction of the sort	Add to report layout
CRM_FormatDate	Formats date	Add to report layout
CRM_FormatTime	Formats time	Add to report layout

As you can see from this table, the CRMAF_ parameter is unique because it's the only one you use in the query of your report. You use the other parameters in the report layout mostly to help format data. Explaining how to use the report layout Microsoft CRM report parameters would require detailed explanations of how to use the Reporting Services Report Designer and is therefore beyond the scope of this book. However, we'll review using the CRMAF_ parameter because of its power and ease of use.

Pre-Filters and Contextual Reports

To use the CRMAF_ parameter, you simply need to modify your report query by pre-pending CRMAF_ to the name of the filtered view your report references. So instead of using this query syntax:

```
Select industry, numberofemployees from FilteredAccount
```

you would use this syntax in your query:

```
Select CRMAF_FilteredAccount.industry,
CRMAF_FilteredAccount.numberofemployees from FilteredAccount as
CRMAF_FilteredAccount
```

When you include the CRMAF_*<filteredentityview>* parameter in your SQL query, you're telling Microsoft CRM that you want to display the pre-filter option to users before it runs the report. As you learned earlier, the pre-filter option allows your users to modify the filter criteria before they run the report. If you don't include this parameter in your query, Microsoft CRM will skip the pre-filter option and immediately run the report for all of the records in the query.

In addition to displaying the pre-filter option, you also use the CRMAF_ parameter in your queries to create contextual reports that users can run from the entity form or the entity list.

> **Note** When users run a report contextually, Microsoft CRM won't display the pre-filter criteria to the users, but it will include the pre-filter criteria as part of the report results. Users can modify the pre-filter criteria by clicking the Edit Filter button after they run a report. Or they can modify the default pre-filter criteria for the report as explained later in this chapter.

The criteria to create a contextual report include:

1. Creating a report that queries data from filtered views using the alias CRMAF_*<filteredentityview>* and then joining your related filtered views (entities) in the report query.
2. Making sure you include the CRMAF_ alias name on all of the fields in your query.
3. Incorporating the filtered entity and the other filtered entities from your query in the Related Record Types when you upload the report to Microsoft CRM.
4. Displaying the report using the Lists and the Forms for related record types.

The following procedure shows the steps for creating a custom report that uses the CRMAF_ parameter to create contextual reports and reports that use the pre-filter.

Adding pre-filtering to your custom Activity report

1. Open the Account Activities report that we created in the previous example.
2. On the Data tab, change your query to add the CRMAF_ <*filteredentityview*> parameters as shown.

```
SELECT     CRMAF_FilteredActivityPointer.activitytypecodename,
CRMAF_FilteredActivityPointer.subject,
CRMAF_FilteredActivityPointer.modifiedonutc,
CRMAF_FilteredActivityPointer.modifiedbyname,
CRMAF_FilteredActivityPointer.statecodename,
CRMAF_FilteredActivityPointer.statuscodename, CRMAF_FilteredActivityPointer.owner
idname, CRMAF_FilteredAccount.name
FROM         FilteredAccount AS CRMAF_FilteredAccount INNER JOIN
                      FilteredActivityPointer AS CRMAF_FilteredActivityPointer ON
 accountid = CRMAF_FilteredActivityPointer.regardingobjectid
ORDER BY CRMAF_FilteredActivityPointer.modifiedonutc DESC
```

3. Save the report file, and then upload it to Microsoft CRM using the Reports manager we showed earlier. Make sure that you select the Related Record Types and the Display In areas so that users can run this report contextually.

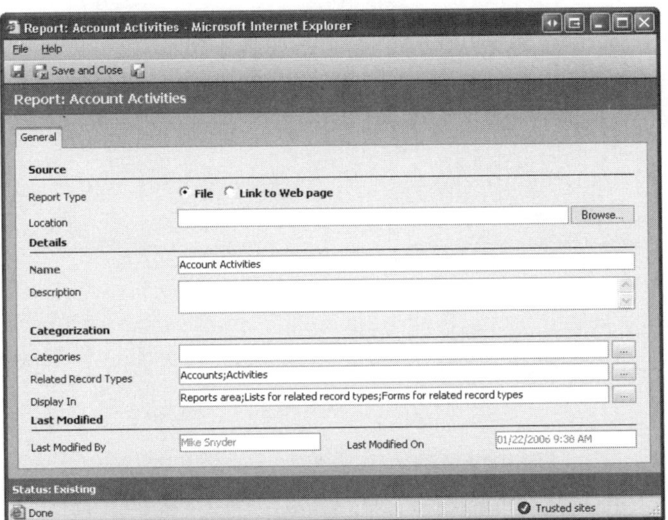

4. Now when you run your report from the Reports list, you will see the pre-filter option.

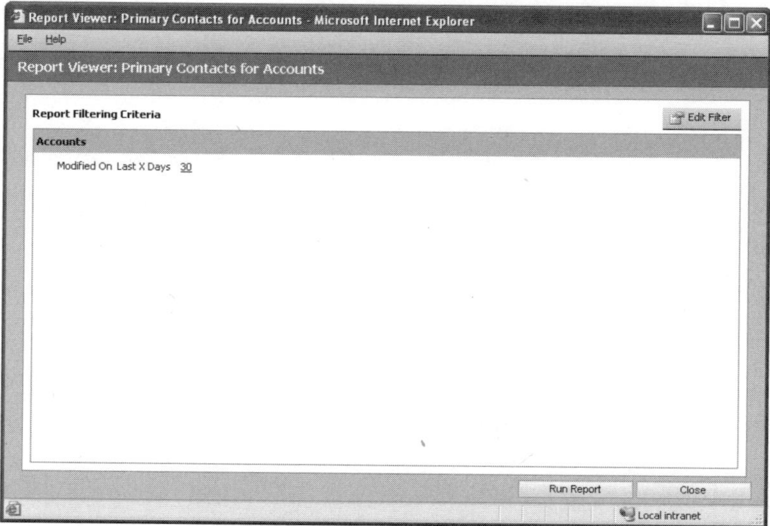

5. When you open an Account record, users will see this report listed under the Use Current Record grouping on the Reports button in the toolbar. Therefore, when they run this report from the Account form, Microsoft CRM will run the report contextually for just the Account record that the user is working with.

> **Note** If your custom report appears under the Run Report grouping, you did not configure the report or the query to run correctly contextually. Double check your query and report configuration.

By default, Microsoft CRM creates a pre-filter of Modified in the Last 30 Days for each entity in your report with the CRMAF_prefix. We'll explain later in this chapter how you can modify the default pre-filter options to include additional variables and change the default values.

> **Best Practices** Using contextual reports will save your users time and provide powerful reports and analysis options as they work with various records in Microsoft CRM. By using the CRMAF_ parameter, you can easily create custom reports to take advantage of this feature. Therefore, as a best practice, you should try to make your custom reports available to run contextually from their related entities.

Using Reporting Services Manager

Until now, we've discussed only administering reports using the Microsoft CRM Reports list. However, some of the report administration functions and tasks require you to access the Reporting Services Report Manager Web site at http://<*reportserver*>/reportmanager. You use the Reporting Services Report Manager for the following tasks:

- Scheduling report execution for performance and snapshots
- Scheduling reports for e-mail delivery

Scheduling Report Execution for Performance

Running complex reports might drastically reduce the performance of your reporting server. If you install Microsoft CRM and Reporting Services on the same server, these complex reports might negatively affect performance for all of your Microsoft CRM users. Therefore, it's ideal to install Reporting Services on a dedicated computer separate from Microsoft CRM. If that's not possible, you can use Reporting Services report execution settings to reduce the impact of report execution on the performance of the server running Microsoft CRM. This technique allows you to execute a report and cache the results, providing a performance boost at run time when viewing the report. In addition to caching report results, this execution setting also lets you take a report *snapshot* that freezes a copy of the report results as of a specific time (useful for quarterly progress reports, monthly quotas, and so on).

To configure report caching and snapshots, you need to browse to the report you want to modify with the Reporting Service Report Manager (installed by default at *http://<crmserver>/reports*), click the Properties tab, and then click the Execution link in the left column. From this page, you can turn caching off/on, schedule caching intervals, schedule automatic report snapshots, and set up report timeouts.

> **Note** Just before we sent this book to the publisher, Microsoft released a utility called the Microsoft CRM 3.0 Report Scheduling Wizard that allows users to schedule and create report snapshots directly within the Microsoft CRM user interface (instead of within the Reporting Services Report Manager). After you download and install this tool, a Schedule Report option will appear under the More Actions button in the Reports list toolbar. The wizard walks you through all the steps you need to create, schedule, and even share report snapshots. Because of its ease of use and power, we recommend that every Microsoft CRM customer download and use this tool. You can download it here: *http://www.microsoft.com/downloads/details.aspx?FamilyID=a101d4d9-6463-4a45-899b-3c3ee979c4d0&DisplayLang=en.*

When you configure report caching or snapshots, you must run the report from the context of a specific user. If you run the report in the context of a user with higher privileges (such as a system administrator), every person who views that report would see the same data that the system administrator would see regardless of their individual business unit and security roles. Consequently, a lower-level user might see data in the report that he or she would not be able to see through the Microsoft CRM user interface.

Conversely, if you choose to cache a report or take a snapshot with a user who has lower-level privileges, a higher-level user might miss data that he or she should be able to view. Therefore, you must consider carefully which user credentials you want to specify when you configure report caching and snapshots.

Scheduling Reports for E-Mail Delivery

Reporting Services allows you to schedule reports (hourly, daily, weekly, and so on) and deliver the report results via e-mail by using a notification list. You can send the reports to any valid e-mail address in any of the output formats that Reporting Services supports. As with report caching and snapshots, when you deliver reports through e-mail, you must run them from the context of a single user.

> **Caution** All e-mail recipients will see identical reports results, so make sure that you don't accidentally send confidential information to an inappropriate user.

We will walk through a simple example of scheduling a report that Reporting Services will deliver via e-mail. To deliver reports via e-mail, you must first configure an e-mail server for the server running Reporting Services. If Microsoft CRM installed Reporting Services for you, the e-mail server value will be blank, and you'll have to configure it manually.

Configuring an e-mail server running SQL Reporting Services 2000

1. Log on to the Reporting Services server.
2. Click **Start**, and then click **My Computer**.
3. Navigate to C:\Program Files\Microsoft SQL Server\MSSQL\Reporting Services\ReportServer (assuming a default installation of Reporting Services).
4. Open RSReportServer.config in Notepad, and then scroll to the <*Extensions*> node.
5. Under the <*Delivery*> node, a child <*Extension*> node appears with the attribute Name="Report Server Email".
6. In the <RSEmailDPConfiguration> node, a variety of properties appears that can be set to configure your e-mail server. At a minimum, you must enter valid values for the following nodes:
    a. <SMTPServer> </SMTPServer> Enter a valid SMTP (e-mail) server either by its DNS name or IP address.
    b. <SMTPServerPort></SMTPServerPort> Enter the port that the SMTP service uses. Most SMTP servers use port 25.
    c. <From> </From> Enter an e-mail address that Reporting Services will use as the From address in the e-mail reports.
7. Save the RSReportServer.config file and log off of the server.

Now that you have configured the e-mail server for the Reporting Services server, you can schedule a report for e-mail delivery. Let's walk through an example of configuring the Neglected Leads report for scheduled e-mail delivery.

More Info Refer to the Reporting Services Help or the following article for more information about configuration of e-mail services: *http://msdn.microsoft.com/library/default.asp?url=/library/en-us/rsadmin/htm/arp_configserver_v1_4bzl.asp*

Scheduling an e-mail report

1. Open Reporting Services Manager (http://*<reportserver>*/reportmanager).
2. Click the *<organizationname>*_MSCRM folder.
3. Click the Neglected Leads report.

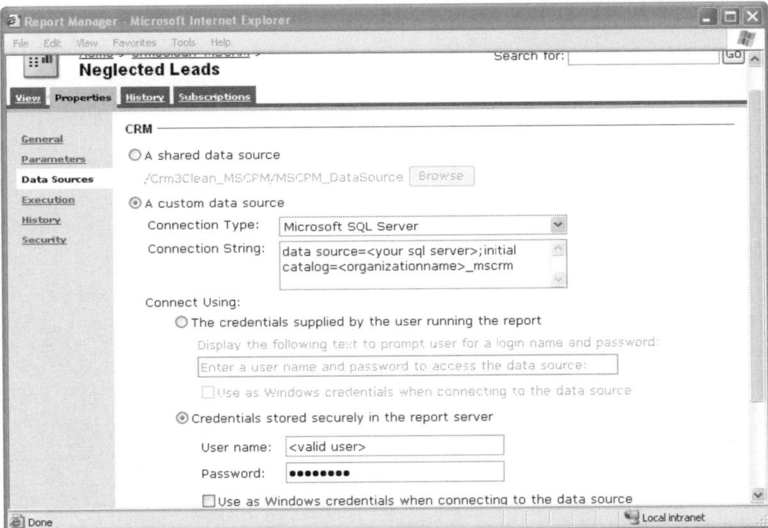

4. On the **Properties** tab, click **Data Sources**. To schedule the report, you must specify a user under which Reporting Services will execute the report. To do this, create a new data source and store the credentials securely with the report.
5. Click **A custom data source**.
   a. In the **Connection Type** box, select **Microsoft SQL Server**.
   b. In the **Connection String** box, enter **data source=**<your sql server>**;initial catalog=**<organizationname>**_MSCRM**.
   c. In the **Connect Using** section, select **Credentials stored securely in the report server**, enter a valid user name and password, and clear the **Use as Windows credentials when connecting to the data source** check box.
6. Click **Apply**.

7. To test the credentials you just entered, click the **View** tab and confirm that the report renders correctly. If it does not, you must modify the data connection settings until the report renders correctly.

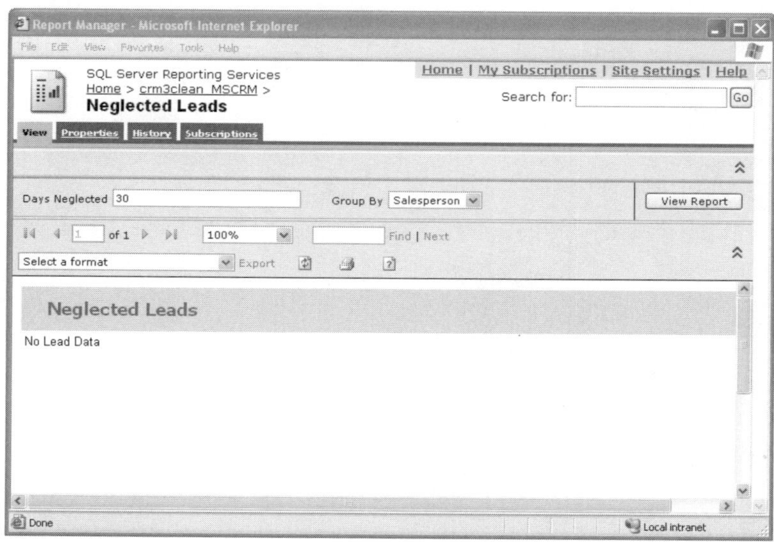

8. On the **Subscriptions** tab, click the **New Subscription** button to begin creating the subscription for this report.

> **Note** You can create subscriptions only for reports in which the data source is set to use stored credentials or no credentials.

9. Change the **Delivered By** option to **Report Server E-Mail**. If this option does not appear, you must properly configure Reporting Services with an e-mail server (see the preceding procedure).
10. Enter valid e-mail addresses in the **To**, **Cc**, and **Bcc** boxes. Separate multiple e-mail addresses with a semicolon.
11. Enter a subject for the e-mail.

> **Tip** @ReportName and @ExecutionTime are special tokens that Reporting Services will replace with the report name and the time the report was generated before sending the e-mail. We recommend that you leave these tokens in the Subject field.

12. For this example, select **Web archive** for the render format (although you can pick different formats), and leave the **Include Report** and **Include Link** options selected. The **Include Report** option tells Reporting Services to include the report as an attachment. The **Include Link** option allows for a link back to the report on the server running Reporting Services in the body of the e-mail. The render formats include the same options as exporting a report from the report viewer.

13. To select a schedule, click the **Select Schedule** button.

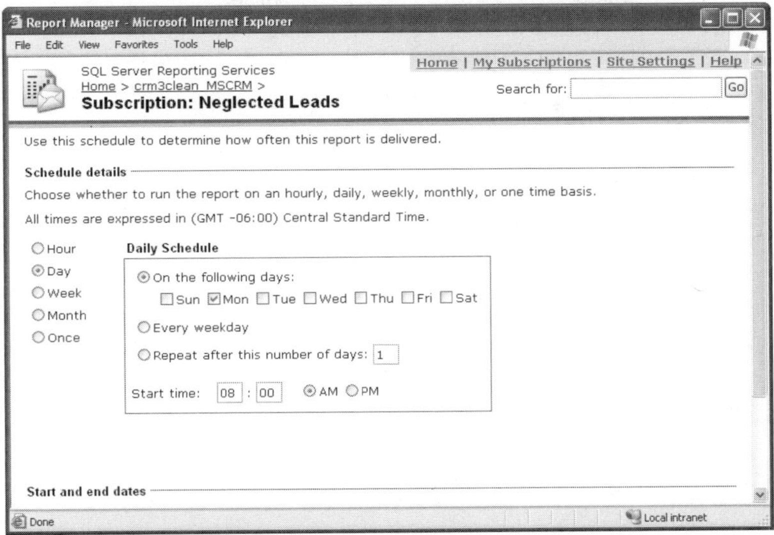

14. On the schedule page, enter the day, time, and recurrence that you would like for delivery of this report, and then click **OK**.

15. You now have the option to alter the query and report parameters for this scheduled report. For this example, we will leave everything as is. Click **OK**.

16. Click the **Subscriptions** tab to see your new e-mail report.

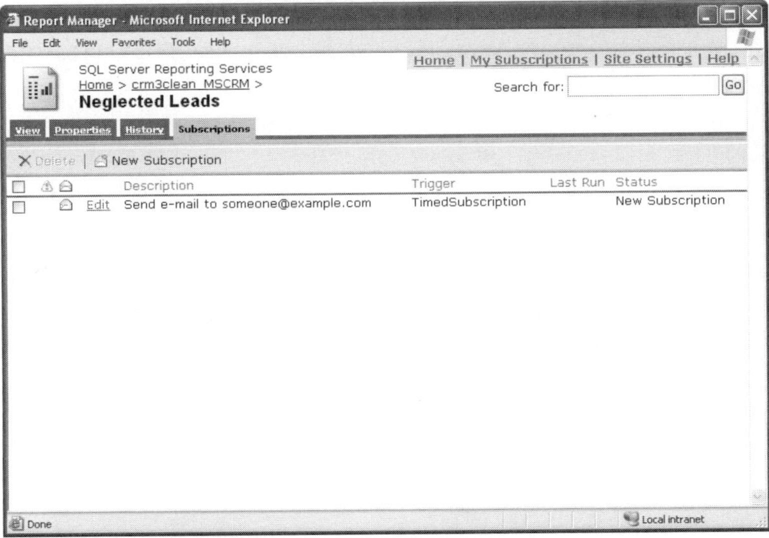

When the report is sent, you will receive an e-mail resembling the one shown in Figure 7-15.

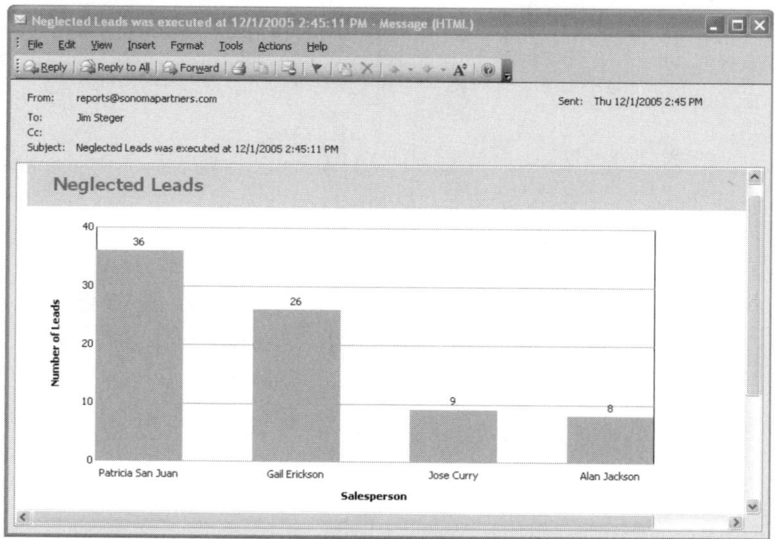

Figure 7-15 E-mailed report

> **Note** The Web archive option for rendering will display the report within the context of the e-mail for HTML-capable browsers. Other rendering options, such as Acrobat (PDF) and Excel, will arrive as e-mail attachments.

Third-Party Reporting Tools

If you must use a third-party reporting tool for your reporting and analysis needs instead of the tools bundled with Microsoft CRM, you can easily extend Microsoft CRM's reporting features to integrate new report types. By extending reporting to include new report types, you allow your users to run the third-party reports directly within the Microsoft CRM user interface, rather than having to leave Microsoft CRM and launch an entirely new application to get the information they're looking for.

When you extend Microsoft CRM to recognize new report types, you edit the Report.config file located in the C:\Inetpub\wwwroot_Resources\ folder on the server running Microsoft CRM (assuming a default installation). When you edit Report.config, you must specify three attributes:

- Report file extension
- Report handler
- Report type name

The sample Reports.config file that ships with Microsoft CRM includes the following information.

```
<?xml version="1.0" encoding="utf-8" ?>
<viewers>
    <viewer extension="xyz" handler="/Specialviewer.aspx" name="Special Report Type"/>
    <viewer extension="abc" name="Client Rendered Report"/>
</viewers>
```

The *extension* attribute refers to the file extension of your report file. For example, Reporting Services reports are .rdl files, so their file extension would be *"rdl"*. If your third-party report file used the extension .rpt, for example, you would set up the attribute to look like *extension="rpt"*.

The *handler* attribute tells Microsoft CRM how it should render the report when a user runs a report with that file extension.

The *name* attribute changes the Report Type value that appears in the Reports list.

We can't go into too much detail about using the Reports.config file to integrate third-party reporting tools because its usage will vary depending on the reporting tool that you're using, but if your company is already commited to a different reporting platform than SQL Server Reporting Services, you can still integrate those third-party reports directly into the Microsoft CRM user interface.

Custom Reporting

In addition to all of the reporting options we've already covered, you can create your own custom Web pages for reporting on Microsoft CRM data. Then you can integrate these custom Web page reports directly into the Microsoft CRM user interface. This reporting option might appeal to companies that have strong Web development skills but not a lot of experience with writing reports using SQL Services Reporting Services.

In the following example, we will show you how to tie a custom Web-based report in to Microsoft CRM. This example consists of a simple .NET Web page that displays data from Microsoft CRM using the security credentials of the user viewing the report. Because we will be using the filtered views and integrated Windows authentication in our Web page, the report security will be conveniently handled by Microsoft CRM.

Best Practices Although a Microsoft ASP.NET Web reporting approach might help companies without expertise in creating SQL Server Reporting Services reports, you will miss out on powerful features such as pre-filtering, report caching, snapshots and e-mail delivery. Therefore, we recommend that you create your custom reports using SQL Server Reporting Services whenever possible.

Creating a custom external report

1. Start Visual Studio .NET 2003.
2. On the **File** menu, point to **New**, and then click **Project**.
3. In the **Project Types** list, select **Visual C# Projects**, and in the **Templates** list, select **ASP.NET Web Applications**.
4. In the **Location** box, type **http://localhost/crmreports**.

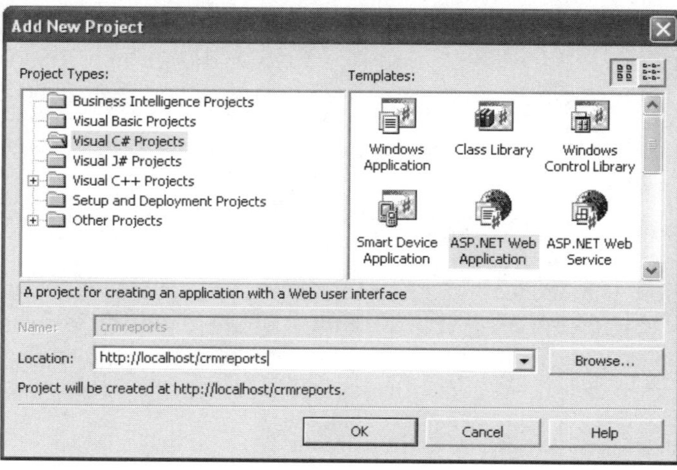

5. Click **OK**.
6. Enter the following code in WebForm1.aspx HTML view. Be sure to enter your SQL Server database and Microsoft CRM organization name as indicated.

```
<%@ Page language="c#" %>
<%@ Import Namespace="System.Data" %>
<%@ Import Namespace="System.Data.SqlClient" %>

<html>
<script language="C#" runat="server">

 protected void Page_Load(Object sender, EventArgs e)
 {
        string sql =
"select fullname as 'Full Name', address1_telephone1 as 'Business Phone', owneridname
as 'Owner' from FilteredLead";
 SqlConnection conn = new SqlConnection("server=<yourcrmdatabaseserver>;database=<orga
nization>_mscrm; Integrated Security=SSPI");
 SqlDataAdapter myCommand = new SqlDataAdapter(sql, conn);

 DataSet ds = new DataSet();
 myCommand.Fill(ds, "Leads");

 report.DataSource = ds.Tables["Leads"].DefaultView;
 report.DataBind();
 }
```

```
</script>

<body>

 <h3><font face="Verdana">Lead Report</font></h3>

 <asp:datagrid id="report" runat="server"
 width="700"
 backcolor="#ccccff"
 bordercolor="black"
 showfooter="false"
 cellpadding=3
 cellspacing="0"
 font-name="Verdana"
 font-size="8pt"
 headerstyle-backcolor="#aaaadd"
 enableviewstate="false"
 autogeneratecolumns="True"
 />

</body>
</html>
```

Now we have to deploy our report to the Web server running CRM. To do this, we must first create a virtual Web on the Microsoft CRM server and then deploy the file to that new Web. For our virtual directory, we use the *workingwithcrm* virtual Web. (You can find instructions on creating this in the book Introduction.)

After you create the workingwithcrm virtual Web, copy the Webform1.aspx, the Global.asax, and the Web.config files from your project directory to the C:\Inetpub\workingwithcrm directory on the server running Microsoft CRM.

Because we created this virtual directory underneath the Microsoft CRM Web site, our virtual Web site will inherit the Web.config settings of Microsoft CRM. This could generate some errors as Microsoft CRM loads assemblies not necessarily available to your Web site. To prevent this problem, you might have to update your Web.config file and remove the extra assemblies. In your default Web.config, locate the compilation node.

```
<compilation
    defaultLanguage="c#"
    debug="true"
/>
```

In the Microsoft CRM Web.config file, you will see the following lines in the Reporting Services section. Simply replace the compilation node of the Web.config in your example virtual Web with the following code.

```
<compilation defaultLanguage="C#" debug="true">
   <assemblies>
    <remove assembly="Microsoft.Crm, Version=3.0.5300.0, Culture=neutral, PublicKeyToken=31b
f3856ad364e35"/>
    <remove assembly="Microsoft.Crm.Entities, Version=3.0.5300.0, Culture=neutral, PublicKey
```

```
Token=31bf3856ad364e35"/>
    <remove assembly="Microsoft.Crm.ManagedInterop, Version=3.0.5300.0, Culture=neutral, Pub
licKeyToken=31bf3856ad364e35"/>
    <remove assembly="Microsoft.Crm.MetadataHelper, Version=3.0.5300.0, Culture=neutral, Pub
licKeyToken=31bf3856ad364e35"/>
    <remove assembly="Microsoft.Crm.MetadataService, Version=3.0.5300.0, Culture=neutral, Pu
blicKeyToken=31bf3856ad364e35"/>
    <remove assembly="Microsoft.Crm.NativeInteropProxy, Version=3.0.5300.0, Culture=neutral,
 PublicKeyToken=31bf3856ad364e35"/>
    <remove assembly="Microsoft.Crm.ObjectModel, Version=3.0.5300.0, Culture=neutral, Public
KeyToken=31bf3856ad364e35"/>
    <remove assembly="Microsoft.Crm.Platform.ComProxy, Version=3.0.5300.0, Culture=neutral,
PublicKeyToken=31bf3856ad364e35"/>
    <remove assembly="Microsoft.Crm.Platform.Proxy, Version=3.0.5300.0, Culture=neutral, Pub
licKeyToken=31bf3856ad364e35"/>
    <remove assembly="Microsoft.Crm.Platform.Server, Version=3.0.5300.0, Culture=neutral, Pu
blicKeyToken=31bf3856ad364e35"/>
    <remove assembly="Microsoft.Crm.Platform.Sdk, Version=3.0.5300.0, Culture=neutral, Publi
cKeyToken=31bf3856ad364e35"/>
    <remove assembly="Microsoft.Crm.Platform.Types, Version=3.0.5300.0, Culture=neutral, Pub
licKeyToken=31bf3856ad364e35"/>
    <remove assembly="Microsoft.Crm.Scheduling, Version=3.0.5300.0, Culture=neutral, PublicK
eyToken=31bf3856ad364e35"/>
    <remove assembly="Microsoft.Crm.Tools.ImportExportPublish, Version=3.0.5300.0, Culture=n
eutral, PublicKeyToken=31bf3856ad364e35"/>
  </assemblies>
</compilation>
```

Caution The actual version numbers might change, so be sure to check the Microsoft CRM Web.config file for the actual values used.

Now that we have our custom report developed, we want to add it to Microsoft CRM. Although technically you could upload it through the Reporting Services Manager, we recommend that you always add your reports through the Microsoft CRM interface. Let's do that now.

Adding a custom external report to Microsoft CRM

1. In the **Workplace** area, select the **Reports** subarea, and then click **New**.
2. Select **Link to Web page** as the report type.
3. In the **Location** box, type **http://<*crmserver*>/workingwithcrm/webform1.aspx**.
4. In the **Name** box, type **Custom Lead Report**.
5. In the **Categories** box, select **Sales Reports**.
6. In the **Related Record Types** box, select **Leads**.
7. In the **Display In** box, select **Reports area**, **Forms for related record types**, and **Lists for related record types**. We will explain these options later in this chapter.

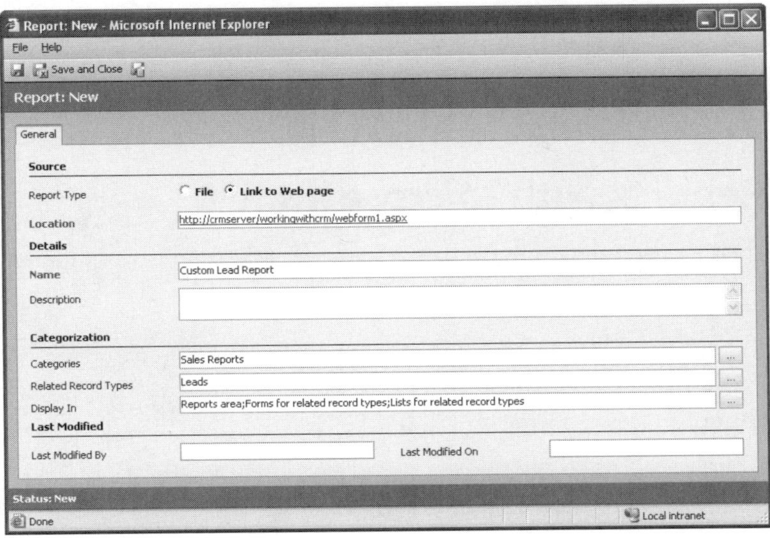

8. Click **Save**.

Now that you've added the custom Web report to Microsoft CRM, your users can run this report directly within the Microsoft CRM user interface.

Accessing the custom external report

1. In the **Workplace** area, select the **Reports** subarea.
2. Double-click **Custom Lead Report**.

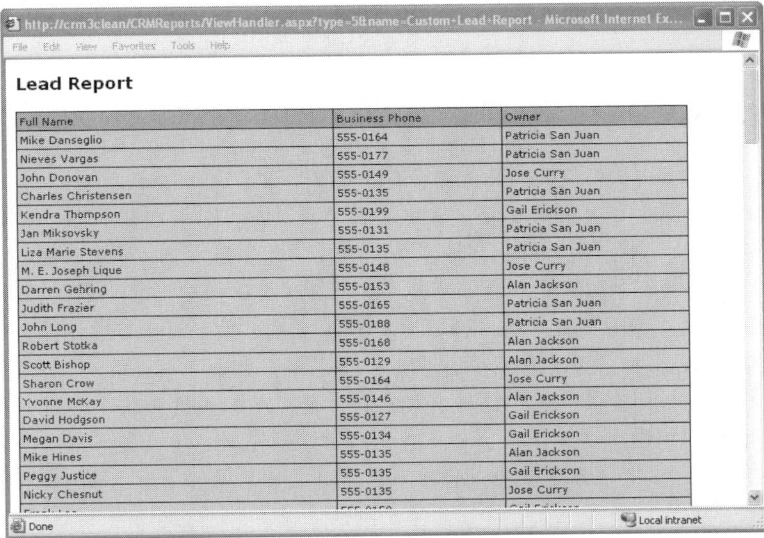

Full Name	Business Phone	Owner
Mike Danseglio	555-0164	Patricia San Juan
Nieves Vargas	555-0177	Patricia San Juan
John Donovan	555-0149	Jose Curry
Charles Christensen	555-0135	Patricia San Juan
Kendra Thompson	555-0199	Gail Erickson
Jan Miksovsky	555-0131	Patricia San Juan
Liza Marie Stevens	555-0135	Patricia San Juan
M. E. Joseph Lique	555-0148	Jose Curry
Darren Gehring	555-0153	Alan Jackson
Judith Frazier	555-0165	Patricia San Juan
John Long	555-0188	Patricia San Juan
Robert Stotka	555-0168	Alan Jackson
Scott Bishop	555-0129	Alan Jackson
Sharon Crow	555-0164	Jose Curry
Yvonne McKay	555-0146	Alan Jackson
David Hodgson	555-0127	Gail Erickson
Megan Davis	555-0134	Gail Erickson
Mike Hines	555-0135	Alan Jackson
Peggy Justice	555-0135	Gail Erickson
Nicky Chesnut	555-0135	Jose Curry

This example showed how you can create your own custom Web-based reports using ASP.NET. Remember to create your Web pages so that they use integrated Windows authentication and reference the Microsoft CRM filtered views, and the Web reports will automatically display the correct data to users based on their security settings.

Managing Reports with Microsoft CRM

As you learned earlier, the term reports in Microsoft CRM can refer to different types of files, including:

- Any type of report files (such as Excel, Word, or Microsoft Office Access) that you upload to the server
- Reporting Services reports
- Third-party report files
- Links to Web pages (categorized as reports)

Regardless of the report type, Microsoft CRM stores all uploaded reports in the SQL Server Reporting Services database. Consequently, you might have to perform some report management tasks in Microsoft CRM and some in the Reporting Services Report Manager. Table 7-4 summarizes some common report administration tasks and the tools that you should use to perform them.

Table 7-4 Report Management Tools for Various Tasks

Administrative task	Microsoft CRM Reports list	Reporting Services Report Manager	Microsoft CRM Organization Settings
Upload a new report	Yes	Not recommended (won't support pre-filters)	No
Download a report for editing	Yes	Not recommended	No
Delete a report	Yes	Not recommended	No
Edit a report name or description	Yes	No	No
Specify where a report appears in the user interface	Yes	No	No
Schedule reports (configure caching)	No	Yes	No
Schedule reports (configure snapshots)	No (Yes – with Report Scheduling Wizard utility installed)	Yes	No

Table 7-4 Report Management Tools for Various Tasks

Administrative task	Microsoft CRM Reports list	Reporting Services Report Manager	Microsoft CRM Organization Settings
Manage report subscriptions (delivery by e-mail)	No	Yes	No
Specify which users can view specific reports	No	Yes	No
Edit the report categories	No	No	Yes

You can access the Microsoft CRM Reports list by navigating to the Reports subarea of the Workplace area.

Report Security

To add, edit, or download a report, users must have the Manage Reports privilege assigned to at least one of their user roles. The System Administrator and System Customizer roles include this privilege by default.

Tip If you need to allow a specific user to manage reports but you don't want to assign him or her a System Administrator or System Customizer role, you can create a special security role that includes just the Manage Reports privilege. Because security permissions are additive, adding this Manage Reports role will allow the user to edit reports. This tactic allows you to assign the Manage Reports privilege to users without modifying the default security roles.

When you upload a report to Microsoft CRM, all users can access the report by default. However, this isn't a security concern because when users run the report, the Microsoft CRM security settings will display only the data that each user should see. However, if you do need to restrict access to certain reports, you can configure unique security settings for each report in the Reporting Service Report Manager. The Microsoft CRM Implementation Guide explains this process in detail. In addition you can also download and use the Report Scheduling Wizard to define which users can view specific report snapshots.

Report Categories

Reporting categories allow you to group similar reports together so that users can filter the Reports list based on these categories, as shown in Figure 7-16.

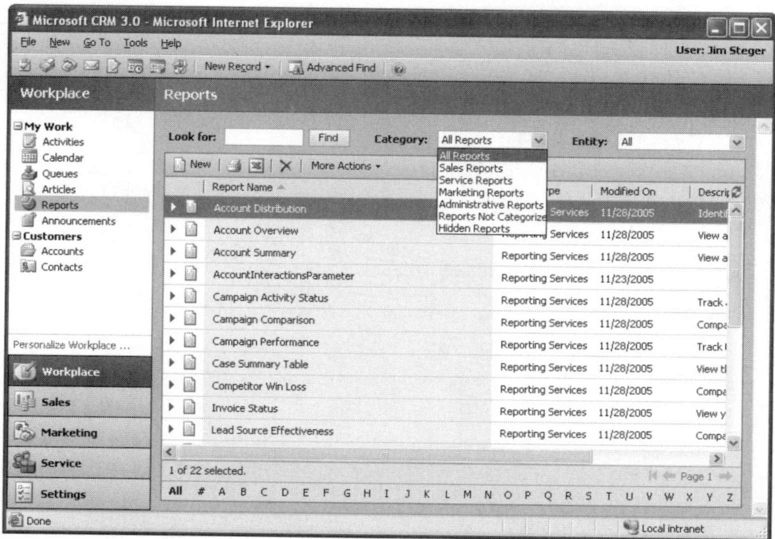

Figure 7-16 Filtering reports by report categories

You can assign a report to a single category, or you can assign a report to multiple categories if necessary. Microsoft CRM includes four report categories in the default installation:

- Sales reports
- Service reports
- Marketing reports
- Administrative reports

Of course, you can add, modify, or delete these report categories to fit your business needs. Let's review how to manage report categories.

Managing report categories

1. Browse to the **Settings** area of Microsoft CRM, and then click **Settings** and **Organization Settings**.
2. Now click **System Settings,** and Microsoft CRM will launch the System Settings dialog box.
3. On the **Report Categories** tab, you will see the familiar list for editing the categories. From here you can add, modify, delete, sort, and move the various report categories.

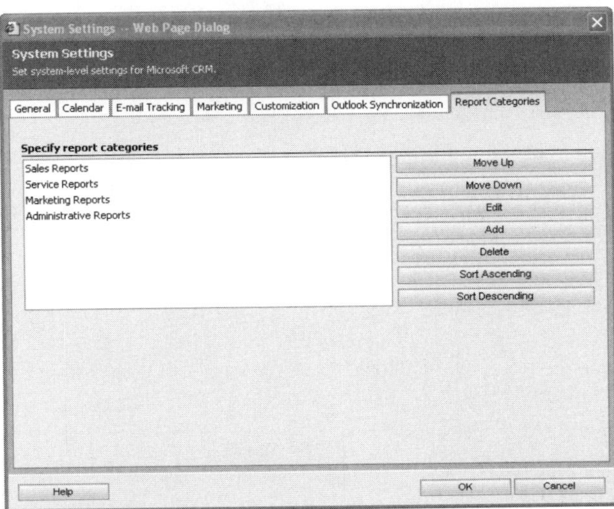

Remember the following when you edit report categories:

- Your changes will appear immediately in the user interface; you don't need to publish your changes.
- If a report belongs to just one category and you delete that category, you can still access the report by using the All Reports and Reports Not Categorized filters.
- The order you set in the list is the order in which Microsoft CRM will display the report categories in the category filter.

Reports List Management

In this section, we will discuss the following management tasks that you can perform from the Reports list:

- Downloading a report
- Editing report properties
- Editing the default filter
- Remember that you can access the Reports list by browsing to the Workplace area and clicking on Reports.

Downloading a Report

To edit a report, first download the report file from Microsoft CRM. You can download individual report files from the Report list in the Microsoft CRM user interface.

Downloading a report file

1. Navigate to the **Reports** subarea in the **Workplace** area to view the Reports list.
2. Select the report that you would like to download.
3. On the **More Actions** menu, click **Download Report**.
4. When the **File Download** dialog box appears, click **Save** and save the file to a location on your computer.

Tip When you download a Reporting Services report, you should change the selection in the Save As Type list from XML Document to All Files before you save. If you don't change this selection, the file will be saved as <*reportname*>.rdl.xml, and you'll have to manually remove the .xml file extension later.

Editing Report Properties

For every report in Microsoft CRM, you can configure the report properties to set up how you want the report to appear in the user interface. To access a report's properties, select a report name in the Reports list, and then click Edit Report on the More Actions menu. Figure 7-17 shows the properties editor.

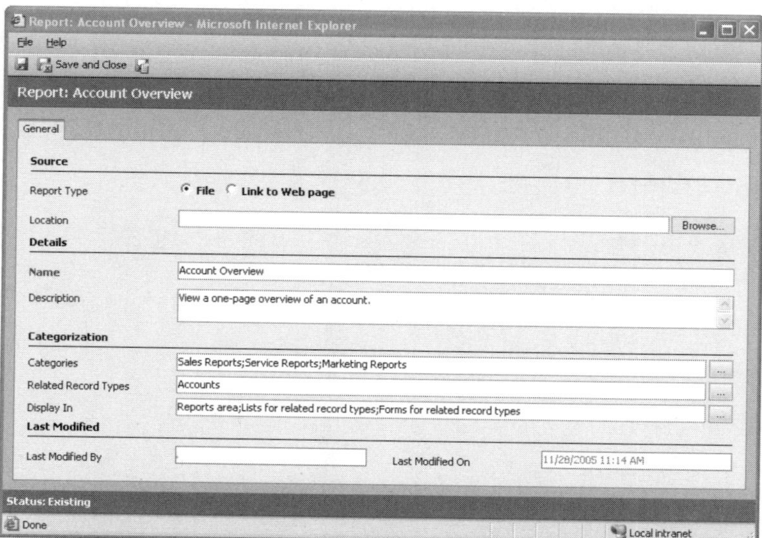

Figure 7-17 Report properties editor

More Info The Reports list grid behaves differently than the other grids in Microsoft CRM. Normally, if you double-click a record, you open the form to edit. With reports, double-clicking a record opens the Report Viewer and allows you to run the report. You must click Edit Report on the More Actions menu to edit the properties of any report.

You may alter the following properties when adding or editing a report:

- **Report Type** Microsoft CRM includes two report types: File and Link to Web page. The file option uploads the report to Microsoft CRM. The Link to Web page option stores a link pointing to a Web address. The Web page address can be either an internal or external URL.
- **Location** This is an upload dialog box or a simple text box, depending on the report type that you specify.
- **Name** This is your report name. The report name appears in the navigation and the Reports lists, so try to be as descriptive as possible. If you enter the name of an existing report, Microsoft CRM will ask if you want to overwrite the existing report file.
- **Description** This optional field allows you to enter more information about what the report does. The description information appears in the Reports list.
- **Categories** Select one or more report categories that the report will belong to.
- **Related Record Types** This attribute allows you to associate the report with system and custom entities. For example, the Account Overview displays information about an Account record, so you would select Account in the Related Record Types field. You must configure this property in conjunction with the Display In property. Adding related record types to a report also determines which entities you can use to edit a report's pre-filter for Reporting Services reports.
- **Display In** After you specify the related record types for a report, you can choose how you want the report to display for those entities. You can select any combination of Reports Area, Lists For Related Record Types, and Forms For Related Record Types. Reports Area displays the report on the general reporting tab list for access. Lists For Related Record Types allows the report to be run against the entity list (grid). Forms For Related Record Types displays the report as an option from an individual entity's form page.

Note The Display In settings apply to all of a report's related record types. For example, you can't specify to display a report on entity A's form and list but only display the report on entity B's list. The Display In settings apply to all of the related record types.

In addition to the editable report properties, Microsoft CRM displays information about the last time a user modified the report. You cannot edit these fields because Microsoft CRM automatically populates them for you.

Editing the Default Filter

You learned that Microsoft CRM allows users to pre-filter their results when they run Reporting Services reports. If you upload a new Reporting Services report, Microsoft CRM creates a default pre-filter of "Modified in the last 30 days" for that report. You can edit the default pre-filter to include additional default parameters that will automatically display to your users. Of course, users can still edit the pre-filter on the fly when they run the report, but you can save them clicks by editing a report's default filter to include the parameters that users will likely want.

Editing the default filter

1. Navigate to the **Reports** subarea in the **Workplace** area to view the Reports list.
2. Select the report that you would like to edit.
3. On the **More Actions** menu, click **Edit Default Filter**.
4. The **Report Viewer** page appears with the current pre-filter settings in Detail mode. Simply edit the filter values to fit your needs.
5. Click **Save Default Filter**.

The next time a user runs this report, he or she will see the report pre-filter that you just configured.

> **Note** Report pre-filters apply only to Reporting Services reports, so you can edit the default filter only for reports of this type.

Batch Transferring Reports

If you have a large number of reports that you want to transfer from one server to another, Microsoft CRM provides two tools to download and publish reports in a batch.

- **DownloadReports.exe** Downloads all of the reports from a server running Microsoft CRM to a specific folder
- **PublishReports.exe** Allows you to upload multiple reports from a folder at one time

Typically, you would use these tools to develop your reports in a development environment and then easily deploy them to a production server.

> **Note** The download and publish batch tools don't have a Web-based user interface; you must run them from a command prompt on the CRM server.

The batch tools are installed on the Web server running Microsoft CRM during the installation process. You must have the following permissions to run these commands:

- Report Manager System Administrator security role
- Content Manager role on the root folder of Reporting Services Report Manager

Caution You should use extreme caution when you run the PublishReports.exe tool. After you start the process, Microsoft CRM will not provide you with additional prompts or warnings if reports with conflicting names exist in the system. The batch tool will simply replace any existing report with the same name, so you might accidentally replace a report that you did not plan on updating. The best use for the PublishReports.exe tool is to update *all* of the reports on the server running Microsoft CRM. We do not recommend using PublishReports.exe to insert a handful of reports; you should use the Reports list interface for this type of task.

For detailed instructions on how to use these batch report tools, please refer to the Microsoft CRM Implementation Guide.

Report Formatting

Maintaining a consistent user interface helps improve usability and user acceptance, and this rule applies to reports too. When you create custom reports, format your reports so that they have a look and feel that is consistent with your other reports. You saw earlier in this chapter that just accepting the default formatting of a Reporting Services report can turn out a visually unappealing report.

Fortunately Microsoft provides detailed style and formatting specifications in a Report Style Guide document if you want your custom reports to match the default reports in Microsoft CRM. We have included a few sample specifications from that document in Table 7-5 and Table 7-6, but you can get the entire style guide by downloading the Microsoft CRM SDK.

Table 7-5 Report and Page Header Formats

Attribute	Report and page header	Report header summary text
Background color (RGB/Hex)	222,221,207 / #DEDDCF	222,221,207 / #DEDDCF
Foreground color (RGB/Hex)	Black	102,102,102 / #666666
Font	Tahoma 14-point bold	Verdana 8-point bold italic
Border	None	None
Height	.5 inches	Varies

Table 7-6 Page Footer Format

Attribute	Page footer
Background color (RGB/Hex)	222,221,207 / #DEDDCF
Foreground color (RGB/Hex)	102,102,102 / #666666
Font	Tahoma 8-point bold
Border	None
Height	.28125 inches

You don't have to spend a lot of time guessing about which fonts and colors Microsoft CRM uses in the default reports. You can find all of the information and specifications you need for consistent report formatting in the Report Style Guide.

Tips

Your users will love their Microsoft CRM system if they have quick access to all of the reports they need. Unfortunately, most people wait until just before going live with Microsoft CRM to start thinking about and creating reports. Consequently, reports frequently get rushed and shortchanged on development and testing. So our first and most important tip is don't ignore reports until the end of your implementation process. Reports always take longer than you expect to develop and test!

Here are a few other tips to keep in mind when you're working with Microsoft CRM reports.

General

- Always keep backups of your report files, and never edit the live reports. If possible, save your reports in a version-control mechanism such as Microsoft Visual SourceSafe so that you can roll back to previous versions if necessary.
- Adding images or logos to your report will help improve their appearance, but adding too many can slow down the report's performance. Therefore, be mindful of the number of images used and their file sizes. Embedding images in the report or database (instead of referencing an external URL) provides for better portability.
- If you run a report with a graphic and a red X displays where the graphic should be, you're probably experiencing a problem in which Internet Explorer blocks a cookie from Reporting Services. You can explicitly allow cookies from the server running Reporting Services by modifying the Privacy settings within Internet Explorer (explained in Microsoft Knowledge Base article 908672).
- When using the Reporting Services Designer, be sure you are in the layout or data view if you click the Save button on the toolbar. If you click Save on the Preview tab, Visual Studio tries to save the output of the report instead of the report itself.
- If you create custom stored procedures or views for your reports, you should not add them in the Microsoft CRM databases. Remember, Microsoft does not support modifying or altering the SQL Server databases directly; you should create a separate database for this type of situation.

- Microsoft CRM conveniently creates two columns for each lookup and picklist field in the filtered view. You can reference the lookup or picklist value, or just reference the name directly. Make sure that your report writers know this so that they don't waste time trying to join filtered views to display the names.
- Two additional views (FilteredStringMap and FilteredStatusMap) provide the picklist and status reasons, respectively. You might need to reference these views for custom parameter lists.

Performance

- If possible, you should try to use an entirely separate server for your reporting needs instead of the live production database. Keeping reporting on a separate database server is absolutely critical for larger organizations, databases with large amounts of data, and companies with complex, time-consuming report queries. Moving reporting to a separate database server provides the following benefits:
    - You can add indices specific to the needs of the report queries without adverse effects on the transactional database.
    - If any particular report or load creates a performance bottleneck, you won't affect other Microsoft CRM users when the report runs. Data caching and snapshots might also help alleviate this problem.
    - You can create custom stored procedures and views as necessary.
    - You can configure refined security for report authors. For instance, you can limit which stored procedures and views a particular report author can access.
- When creating queries in your reports, do not use select * (to return all of the columns in your query). You will get better performance by selecting only the columns you need returned.
- Make sure that you modify the default pre-filters for each custom Reporting Services report you create to further limit the amount of data returned (thus improving performance).
- Perform filtering, calculations, and grouping in SQL Server rather than in Reporting Services where possible. SQL Server performs grouping operations more efficiently and quickly than Reporting Services.
- Because filtered views return a UTC and a local date for each date field, make sure that you also reference the UTC date when comparing dates in a report.

Summary

Microsoft CRM offers many different reporting and analysis tools to choose from. The tools range from simple options such as views and Excel exports to a sophisticated enterprise-class reporting tool such as SQL Server Reporting Services. And, of course, you can extend the reporting options even further to include your own third-party reporting tool if necessary. Add all of these options together and you have almost unlimited flexibility to get your customer data out of Microsoft CRM.

Microsoft CRM includes 20 different Reporting Services reports as part of the default installation, and you can modify all of these reports as necessary. You can also create entirely new reports by using the Report Designer add-in for Visual Studio .NET. You can deploy your new reports seamlessly into the Microsoft CRM user interface. Reporting Services also allows you to configure report scheduling tasks such as caching results, taking report snapshots, or delivering reports via e-mail.

Chapter 8
Workflow

In this chapter:

We were recently speaking with a prospect who had been using the Microsoft CRM 1.2 software for several months. He asked us to create custom code to automatically create follow-up activities and other similar automation processes. We asked him, "Why not use workflow?" and a blank look developed on his face. He didn't know what we were talking about. It turns out that this Microsoft CRM administrator, like many others we suspect, didn't know that Microsoft CRM includes an incredibly powerful workflow engine to help automate and standardize business processes!

You might wonder how this could be possible. Well, the workflow tools are not included in the user interface of the Web client or the Microsoft CRM clients for Microsoft Office Outlook. Instead, the workflow tools are separate applications that run on the Microsoft CRM Web server. Because you can access the workflow tools only by logging on to the server, some people never even know that they exist. This is quite a shame because the Microsoft CRM workflow tools give you some of the most powerful customization functionality available.

Of course you know that Microsoft Dynamics CRM 3.0 includes workflow features, so let's discuss the benefits and details of setting up and using these features in the following topics:

- Overview
- Events
- Conditions
- Actions
- Sales process management

- Dynamic values in workflow
- Custom assemblies
- Workflow Monitor tool
- Importing and exporting workflow
- Workflow examples

Overview

Many companies try to adopt and implement standardized business processes to help their operations run more consistently and smoothly. For example, the CEO might say, "All customer service cases must be resolved within 24 hours," or, "We're implementing a new sales process for all deals over $100,000." However, the communication of these business processes often gets delivered to employees in an ad hoc and unregulated manner. A process document might exist on a network file share, but people don't know that it's there. And some employees might rely on word-of-mouth information from co-workers to learn the processes for their jobs. Consequently, standardizing business processes can prove challenging for some companies, particularly larger organizations. So what benefit does workflow offer for these scenarios? Microsoft CRM workflow provides a tool to help you set up and define business process activities (including the proper sequencing) that employees should use when working with Microsoft CRM data.

> **Important** Conceptually, you can think of Microsoft CRM workflow as an application or service that runs in the background 24 hours a day, 7 days a week, constantly evaluating your Microsoft CRM data and the multiple workflow rules in your deployment. When the workflow service sees a trigger event, it fires the appropriate workflow rules to run the workflow actions. Typical workflow actions include sending an e-mail message, creating a task, and updating a data field.

We'll cover the following workflow basics in this section:

- Running workflow rules in the user interface
- Types of workflow
- Workflow utilities
- Securing workflow rules

Running Workflow Rules in the User Interface

We'll explain how to create workflow rules shortly, but first we want to show you how workflow rules appear in the Microsoft CRM user interface. Let's assume that you've already created multiple workflow rules for the Opportunity entity. When users look at a view of Opportunity records, they can select one or more records and then click Apply Rule on the More Actions menu, located on the grid toolbar, as shown in Figure 8-1.

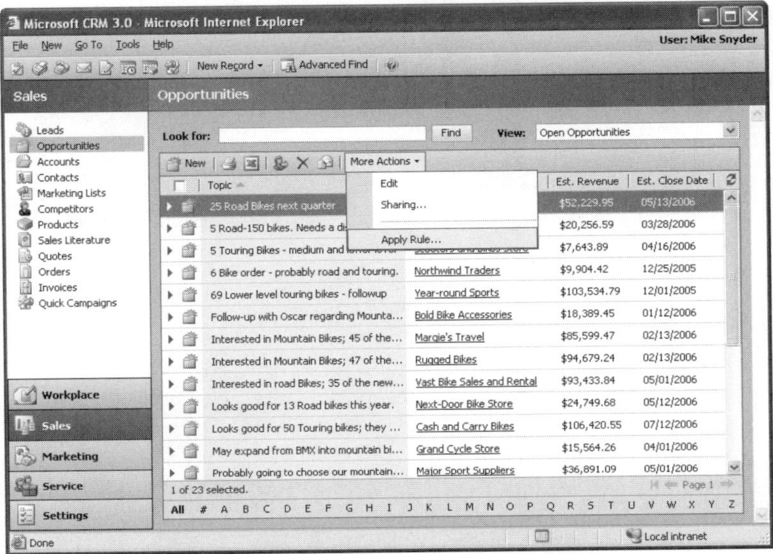

Figure 8-1 Accessing workflow rules from the grid toolbar

A dialog box appears, as shown in Figure 8-2.

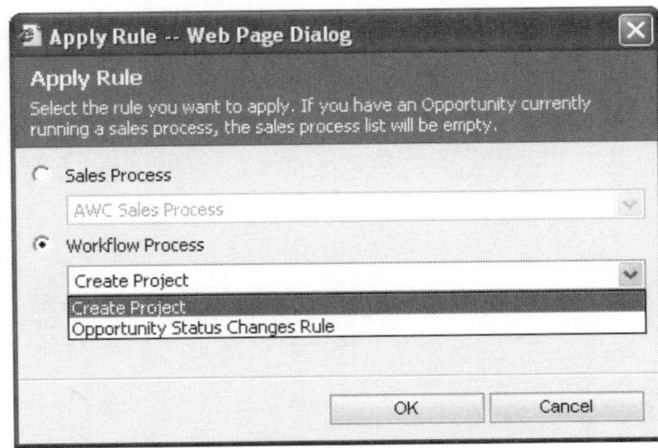

Figure 8-2 Apply Rule dialog box

As you can see, you choose to apply either a workflow process rule or sales process rule to the records selected in the Opportunity view. After you select the rule that you want to apply and click OK, Microsoft CRM runs that rule for each of the selected records and takes the actions that the rule specifies.

> **Note** You can apply sales process rules to Opportunity records only.

We've just described how to apply workflow rules manually by using the user interface. Of course, the real benefit comes from when you set up workflow rules that trigger automatically based on the events that you specify.

Caution The Workflow service responsible for executing rules does not respond immediately to new rules. You might experience a slight delay between the time that you apply a rule and the time that the rule is implemented. Depending on the workflow action, you might also have to refresh the record you're viewing to see new or updated values.

Types of Workflow

As you just saw, Microsoft CRM includes two types of workflow rules:

- **Workflow process** Actions that Microsoft CRM executes based on the trigger events and conditions that you specify
- **Sales process** Logical phases of a sales process defined by stages and actions within each sales stage

Because sales processes apply only to the Opportunity entity, you'll usually work with workflow process rules. Table 8-1 shows the entities for which you can create workflow process rules, grouped by their functional areas in the software.

Table 8-1 Entities That Support Workflow Process Rules

Common	Sales	Marketing	Customer service
Account	Lead	Campaign	Case
Contact	Opportunity	Campaign Activity	Contract
Appointment	Invoice	Campaign Response	Service Activity
E-mail	Order	Marketing List	
Fax	Quote		
Letter			
Phone Call			
Task			

As you can see, Microsoft CRM does not support workflow rules for organization-owned entities such as Products, Subjects, and Territories.

Important You can also create workflow process rules for any custom entity with user-owned records. You specify user ownership (versus organization ownership) at the time that you create a custom entity.

If you need to create many very similar workflow or sales process rules, you can create a workflow template. To create a new workflow rule from a template in Workflow Manager (explained later in this chapter), change the view to Rule Template, and then click Create Rule From Template on the Actions menu. Users can't see or apply workflow templates through the user interface; they're designed to help administrators quickly create new rules and sales processes. This same template technique works for both workflow and sales process rules.

Tip You can also create a copy of a workflow or sales process rule by clicking Create Copy on the Actions menu or the Create Copy button on the toolbar.

Workflow Utilities

Microsoft CRM workflow offers several utilities to help you design, manage, and administer workflow rules. The four workflow utilities are:

- **Workflow Manager** Use this tool to create, modify, delete, activate, and deactivate workflow rules and sales processes.
- **Workflow Monitor** Use this tool to view and troubleshoot all of the current workflow rules running in your deployment.
- **Export Workflow Wizard** Use this tool to export one or more workflow or sales process rules so that you can import them into a different Microsoft CRM deployment.
- **Import Workflow Wizard** Use this tool to import workflow and sales process rules into your current deployment.

All of these utilities offer a simple and clean interface that any power user can quickly learn. You do not need programming skills or complex code to create powerful workflow rules. As we mentioned earlier, you access and run all of these workflow utilities by logging on to the Microsoft CRM Web server (you can use Remote Desktop or Terminal Services). You'll find shortcuts to the workflow utilities by clicking Start, pointing to All Programs, and then clicking Microsoft CRM. We'll discuss the use of each of these utilities in detail in this chapter.

Securing Workflow Rules

Just like the other features in Microsoft CRM, you can set up and configure detailed security settings for your workflow rules. Let's cover securing workflow rules from two different perspectives:

- Creating workflow rules
- Running workflow rules

Creating Workflow Rules

You learned that you create workflow rules by using Workflow Manager on the Microsoft CRM Web server. So before anyone can even launch Workflow Manager, the user must have permission to log on to the server. Most of the time, users with the System Administrator role will be responsible for creating and managing workflow rules. However, this is not a requirement. If you decide to allow other users or managers to create workflow rules, you'll have to give them permission to log on to the Microsoft CRM Web server.

After a user logs on to the server, he or she may launch Workflow Manager. Workflow Manager will run only for users assigned a security role with Create, Read, Write, and Delete privileges for both the Process and Process Instance entities.

Important The Microsoft CRM security roles refer to workflow as the Process and Process Instance entities. You can find these entities on the Customization tab when you're editing a security role.

Only the System Administrator and the System Customizer default security roles include the security privileges necessary to launch Workflow Manager, but you can add these privileges to other roles. You can also assign users a security role that includes different access levels for the Process and Process Instance entities; you do not have to assign the Organization-level rights to use workflow.

When a user creates a workflow rule, Microsoft CRM assigns the rule to the same business unit as the owner who created the rule. If someone later updates an existing rule, Microsoft CRM updates the rule owner and the rule's business unit to reflect the last user who modified it.

Important The workflow rule's business unit and owner are critically important, because workflow rules run in the security context of the user who created the rule, not the security privileges of the user running the rule. However, if a user manually applies a workflow rule through the user interface, the rule will run under the context of that user's security privileges (not under the security privileges of the rule owner).

If you experience a scenario in which the workflow rule doesn't run correctly when kicked off automatically but it does work correctly when you run it manually, 9 times out of 10 this problem can be fixed by making sure that the workflow rule has the security privileges necessary to execute all of the actions contained in the rule.

> **Tip** Because workflow rules can run in the security context of the rule owner, you should not create workflow rules with a Restricted Access Mode user. If a Restricted Access Mode user creates a workflow rule, Microsoft CRM will never execute the rule correctly, because such users by definition cannot modify Microsoft CRM records.

Running Workflow Rules

To manually apply a workflow rule through the user interface, a user must have a security role that includes the Read privilege for the Process entity. By default, all of the security roles in Microsoft CRM include the Organization access level for the Read privilege of the Process and Process Instance entities. Therefore, all of your users can manually run all of the workflow rules. We assume that, sooner or later, you'll want to restrict or hide certain workflow rules so that some of your users cannot run them.

You already learned that each workflow rule includes an owner and a business unit. However, when you're configuring the security roles and access levels for your users in regards to workflow, you need to know that workflow security behaves differently than the regular entities like Account and Contact. Consider the sample business unit hierarchy in Figure 8-3.

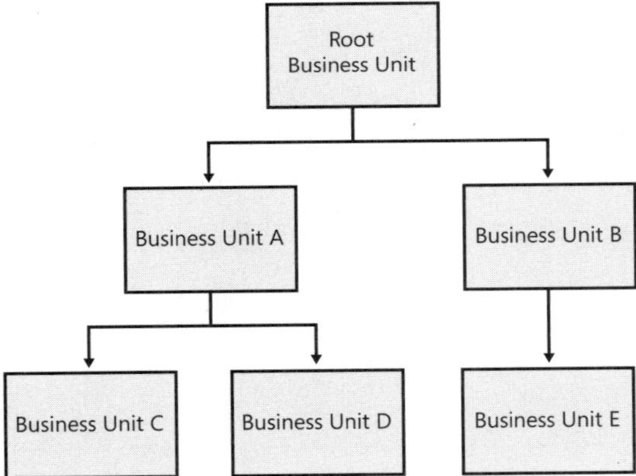

Figure 8-3 Sample business unit hierarchy

If you create a workflow rule as the System Administrator, you probably belong to the Root Business Unit, and therefore the workflow rule will belong to the Root Business Unit. Unlike its treatment of the other entities, such as Account and Contact, Microsoft CRM propagates workflow rules down the business unit hierarchy to make the workflow rule available to the child business units. Therefore, this workflow rule would be available to users in all of the child business units (A, B, C, D, and E). So even if a user in Business Unit D only had Business Unit Access Level for the Read privilege of the Process entity, he or she could run a workflow rule created and owned by a user in the Root Business Unit. In regards to the other entities like Accounts or Contacts, a user in Business Unit D would need Organization Access Level to view records owned by someone in the Root Business Unit.

If you logged on as a user from Business Unit B and created a workflow rule, that rule would belong to Business Unit B. If you then modified the default security roles so that users have Business Unit access levels (instead of the default access level of Organization) for the Read privilege of the Process entity, only users who belonged to Business Unit B and Business Unit E could see and apply this rule.

Because users can manually apply workflow rules of any event type (including Create, Assign, and Change Status) if they have security privileges to read the workflow rule, someone might accidentally wreak havoc on your system by manually running a rule that is not designed to be executed manually! To prevent this scenario, you can try using a naming convention with your workflow rules that warns users about potential trouble. For example, you could prefix the rule name with "DO NOT USE -." However, the safest solution for restricting user access is to create workflow rules that belong to a business unit that no users belong to. Then replace Organization-level access with Business Unit–level access for the Process Read privilege for all security roles. By using this technique, you can effectively "hide" complex or sophisticated workflow rules that you don't want users to accidentally apply manually.

Events

When you create a workflow rule, you must define the event that will trigger it. You can specify only one event per workflow rule, so carefully consider which event will achieve your desired results. Workflow rules offer four trigger events:

- **Manual** Manual events are applied manually by using the user interface. You can also include Manual rules as a subprocess in a different workflow rule (subprocesses are explained later in this chapter).
- **Assign** Changing the owner of a record in Microsoft CRM triggers the Assign event.
- **Create** Creating a new record of an entity triggers the Create event.
- **Change Status** Changing the status of a record triggers the Change Status event.

More Info Only the Manual and Create events apply to sales process workflow rules.

The Assign event sometimes causes confusion, because people expect that assigning a record to a queue will trigger this event, but actually it does not. The Microsoft CRM user interface uses the word *assign* in regard to queues, so it's easy to understand why people might expect this behavior. However, Microsoft CRM triggers the Assign event only when you change the owner of a record. Queues cannot own records, so assigning a record to a queue really just adds it to a queue; it does not change the record's owner.

We also want to add some clarification about the Change Status event. We've been working with Microsoft CRM for years, but sometimes we still get confused between the state of a record and the status of a record. So don't worry if you need to look this up, too! The Change

Status event refers to the status (schema name of statecode) of an entity but not the status reason (schema name of statuscode). Table 8-2 displays some sample status and status reason values to illustrate the differences.

Table 8-2 Status and Status Reason Values for Select Entities

Entity	Status values	Status reason values
Account	Active Inactive	Active Inactive
Case	Active Resolved Cancelled	In Progress On Hold Waiting for Details Researching Problem Solved Canceled
Lead	Open Qualified Disqualified	New Contacted Qualified Lost Cannot Contact No Longer Interested Canceled
Phone Call	Open Completed Canceled	Open Sent Received Canceled

Many people assume that changing the status reason of a record will trigger the Change Status event. However, only changing the status value will trigger workflow.

To create a workflow rule and specify the workflow event, log on to the Microsoft CRM Web server and open the Microsoft CRM Workflow Manager (click Start, point to All Programs, point to Microsoft CRM, and then click Workflow Manager). A dialog box prompts you to enter the name of the Microsoft CRM server for which you want to manage workflow rules. You can select the https:// secured connection option if necessary. After you enter the server name and click OK, the Workflow Manager appears, as shown in Figure 8-4.

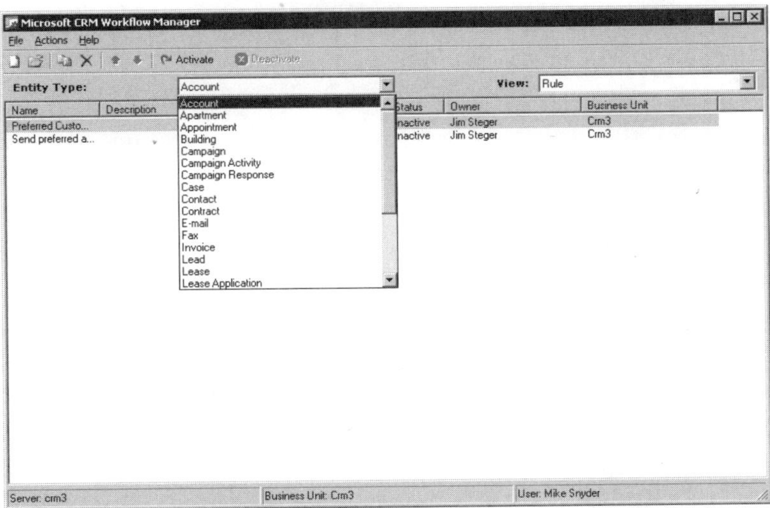

Figure 8-4 Microsoft CRM Workflow Manager

In Workflow Manager, you can select an entity and display all of the current workflow rules attached to it by using the Entity Type list. After you find the entity for which you want to create the workflow rule, click the New button on the toolbar to open the page shown in Figure 8-5.

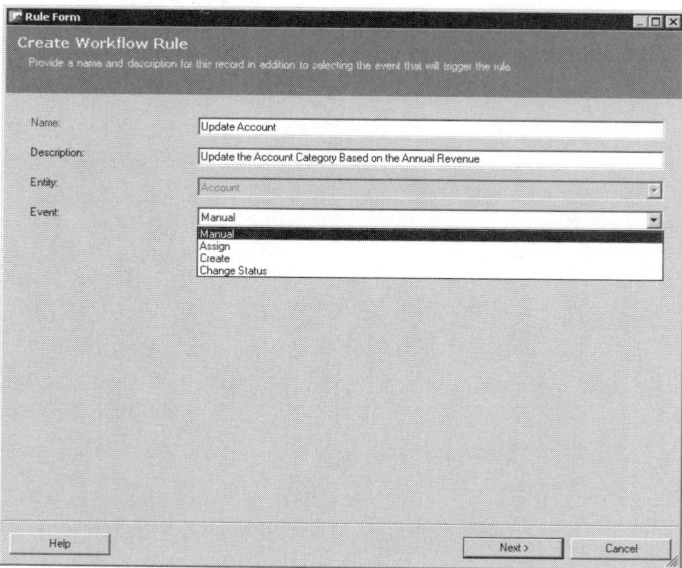

Figure 8-5 Create Workflow Rule page

On this page, you'll enter the name of the workflow rule, add a short description, and select the workflow event for the rule. Keep in mind that users will see the only name of the workflow rule when they apply it manually, so try to be as descriptive as possible about what the rule does.

Workflow Conditions

Conditions allow you to add business logic to manage the actions of your workflow rule. You have the ability to create simple or complex logical statements that control when actions should be taken. Typical scenarios might include sending an e-mail message a month before a service contract expires, creating different sets of activities based on potential revenue of an opportunity, or updating a sales stage when all activities are completed.

After you name the workflow rule and select a workflow event, Microsoft CRM opens the Select Behavior page, on which you can edit the workflow. You can insert a condition by clicking Insert Condition in the Common Tasks section, as shown in Figure 8-6.

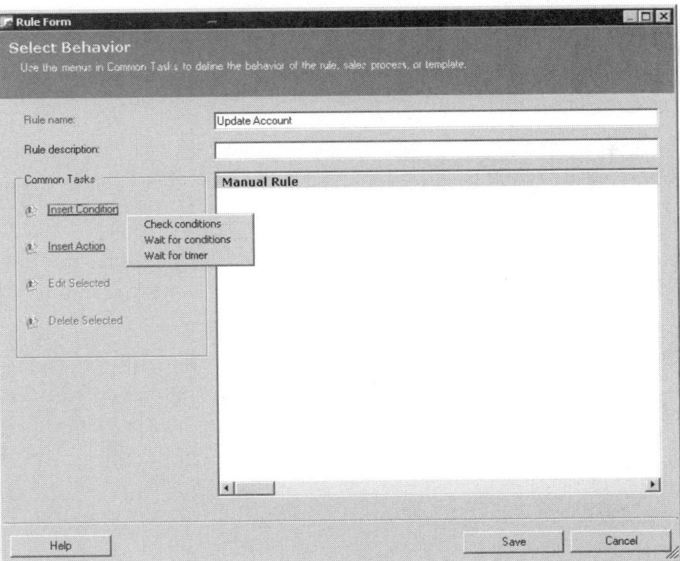

Figure 8-6 Inserting a condition

Microsoft CRM automatically determines which conditions you can insert into a workflow rule, depending on which part of the rule you select in the statement box. For instance, you can use the Else If option (shown in Figure 8-7) only within an existing Check condition.

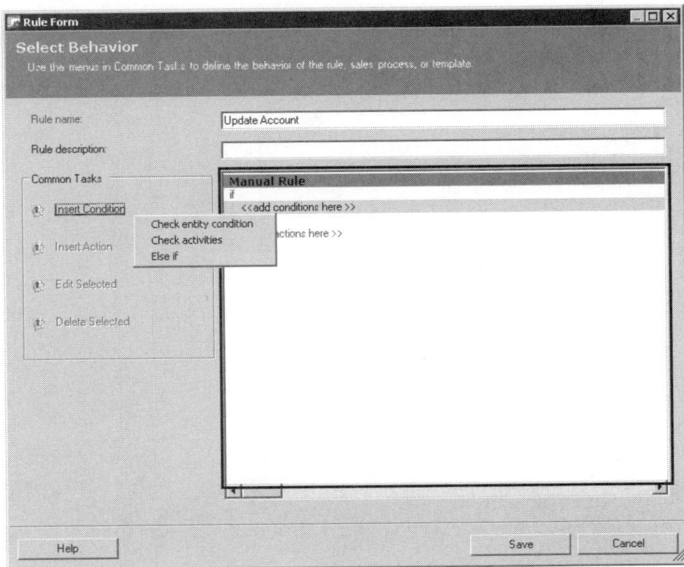

Figure 8-7 Subconditions available based on the context of the statement box

Let's discuss the options available when adding conditions to your workflow rules. Conditions can be broken into the following high-level categories, in which each has possible subconditions available:

- Check conditions
- Wait for conditions
- Wait for timer

Check conditions

Check conditions provides you with a logical if-then-else arrangement for use in your workflow rules: *If* the defined conditions are met, *then* perform the actions listed. Additionally, you can nest conditions within other conditions to create more sophisticated evaluation criteria. Figure 8-8 shows a rule that first checks if the Account is a standard customer AND has an annual revenue greater than $10,000,000. If both conditions are true, then it updates the Account's category to a preferred customer.

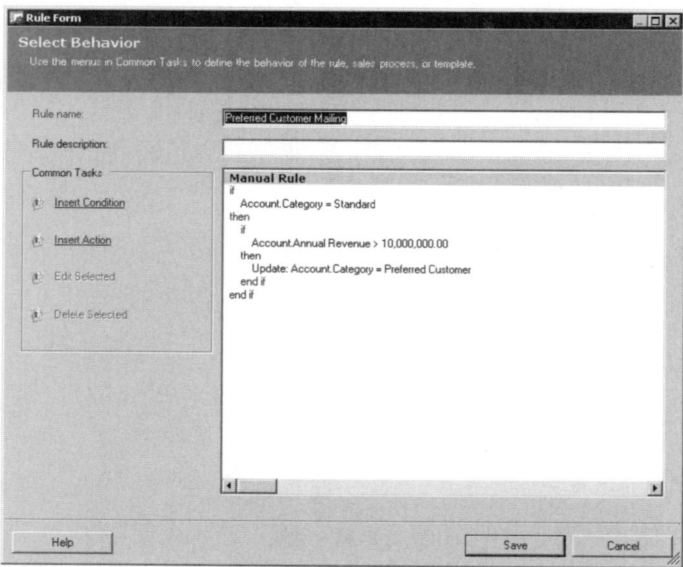

Figure 8-8 Grouped conditions

> **Note** Nested conditions are always evaluated with an AND operator. The OR operator is not available for grouped conditions. You would have to create separate conditions to accomplish an OR.

After you insert a check condition and select it, workflow offers you the following subconditions:

- **Check entity condition** Evaluates the value of a specific attribute (field) of the entity. The operators available are based on the data type of the field chosen.

- **Check activities** Returns a value of true if any activities exist for the entity. You can only include activities created by a workflow rule. This condition is not applicable to rules created for Activity entities.
- **Else if** Continues the conditional logic only if the first condition returns false.

Figure 8-9 shows the page for adding a new check entity condition statement.

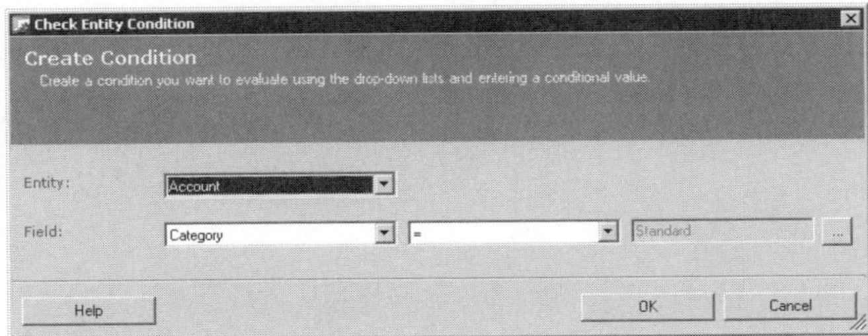

Figure 8-9 Adding a check entity condition

Wait for conditions

Wait for conditions pauses a workflow rule until the conditions specified within the wait statement are completed. Figure 8-10 shows a workflow rule for the Account entity trigged by the Create event. It waits until the Account entity's category equals Preferred Customer and then sends a welcome e-mail message to the account.

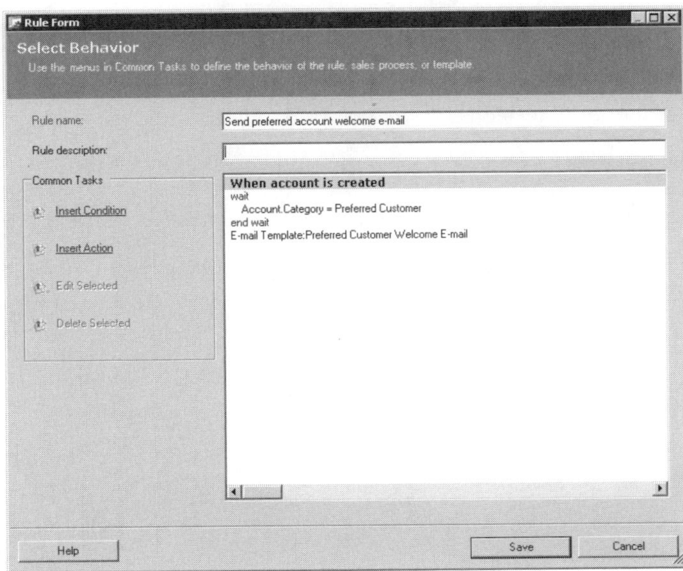

Figure 8-10 Wait for condition

Two subconditions exist for the Wait for conditions statement. Both prevent the continuation of the rule until their conditions are met:

- **Wait entity condition** Evaluates the value of a specified field before continuing
- **Wait activity condition** Checks to determine whether an activity from a previous step in the rule reaches a specified value of Completed, Cancelled, or Either before continuing

Caution Wait activity condition can only check for activities created by workflow.

Wait for timer

Similar to Wait for conditions, Wait for timer allows you to suspend your rule until a chosen amount of time elapses. A few scenarios that benefit from this condition include:

- Sending reminder e-mail messages before the expiration of a contract, an opportunity closing, or the start date of an appointment.
- Changing ownership of a Lead or Case record one day after creation if someone has not addressed the record.
- Checking the status or the activities of an opportunity one month after initial creation.

The following three settings determine the starting point for your timer:

- **From now on** Waits for the amount of time specified from when the condition step is executed.
- **After** Starts the timer after a selected value from the referenced entity.
- **Before** Begins the timer before a selected value from the referenced entity.

Figure 8-11 shows how to configure a timer condition to wait one month after the actual close date of an opportunity.

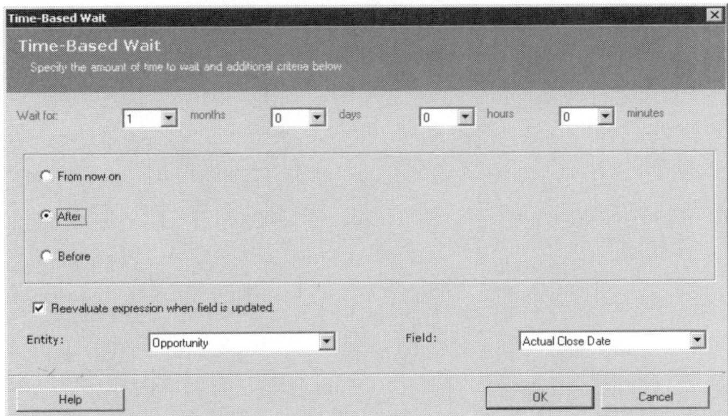

Figure 8-11 Wait for timer condition

Note You can set up your rule to wait from 1 minute to 24 months!

Workflow Actions

Now that you understand workflow conditions, we'll explain the workflow actions that you can insert into conditions. After all, using conditions without any actions wouldn't really provide any benefits. If you click Insert Action, Microsoft CRM lists the workflow actions available, as shown in Figure 8-12.

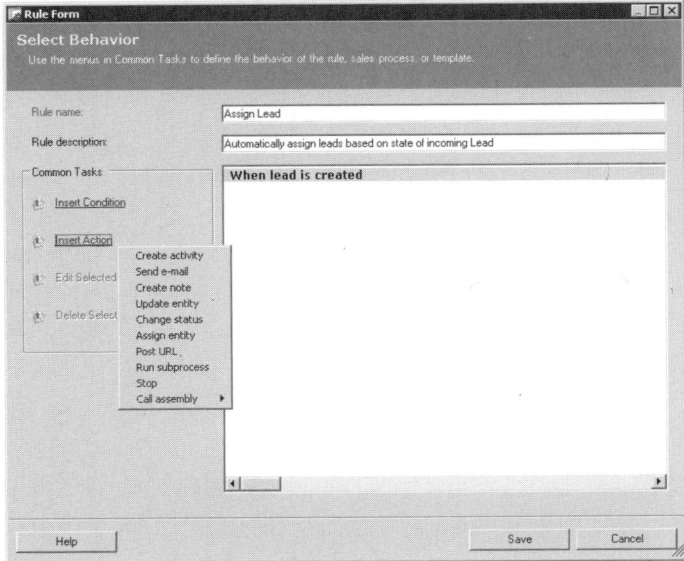

Figure 8-12 Workflow actions

You'll use the workflow editor to set up and manage the conditions and actions for this workflow rule. The following workflow actions are available when you're creating workflow rules:

- Create activity
- Send e-mail
- Create note
- Update entity
- Change status
- Assign entity
- Post URL
- Run subprocess
- Stop
- Call assembly

Create Activity

You can obviously use the create activity action to create a Task, Phone Call, Fax, or Letter activity. When you click Create Activity, the dialog box shown in Figure 8-13 appears, allowing you to specify additional parameters related to the activity, such as due date, owner, and priority.

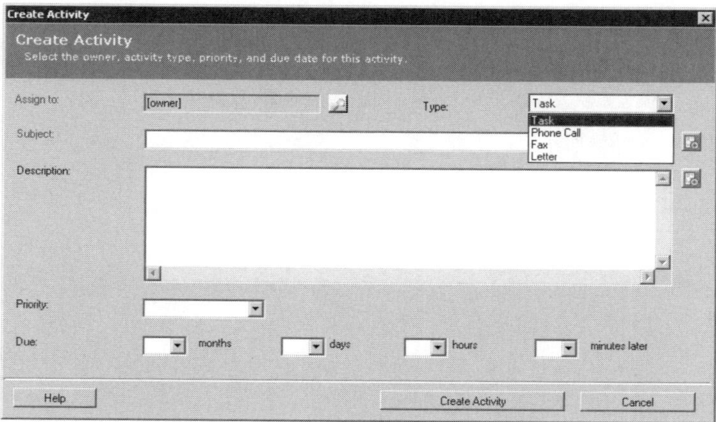

Figure 8-13 Create Activity dialog box

Send E-Mail

Use this action when you want to automatically send an e-mail message as part of your workflow rule. When you select the send e-mail action, the dialog box shown in Figure 8-14 appears.

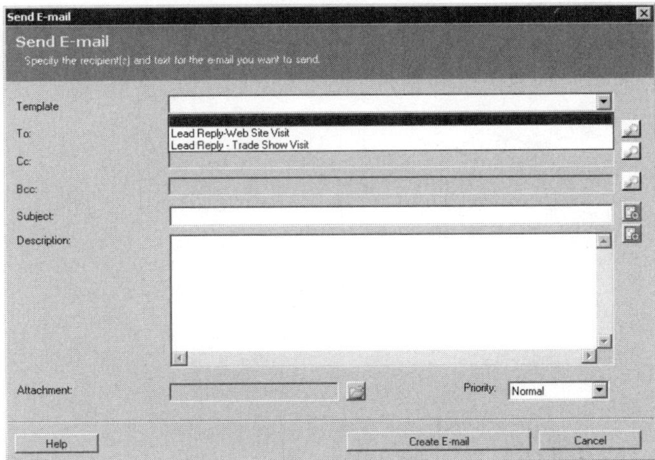

Figure 8-14 Send E-mail dialog box

From here, you can configure the key attributes of the message, such as the recipients, the subject, and the body. The following are some of the key details and constraints related to sending e-mail messages with workflow:

- You can select an E-mail template if the entity of the workflow rule offers a template. However, you cannot specify the recipient of the E-mail template. Microsoft CRM automatically sends the E-mail template to the customer record.
- You can select only one recipient for the To line, but you can select multiple recipients for the Cc and Bcc lines.
- Although Microsoft CRM sends the message as HTML (instead of plain text), you cannot include images or hyperlinks in the Description box (body) of the message, like you can with an E-mail template. However, you can send images and hyperlinks in an e-mail created in workflow by selecting an E-mail template.
- If you enable e-mail tracking, Microsoft CRM automatically appends the tracking code to the Subject line of your workflow messages.
- You can specify one file attachment per e-mail message. Note that you aren't uploading the file to the Microsoft CRM server; instead, you're specifying a path where the workflow engine can locate the file. Make sure that this file remains accessible via the network based on the security credentials of the workflow rule when it executes (for either the rule owner or the user who manually applied the rule).

Create Note

Use this action when you want to append a note to the entity record. You can specify the note subject and description, and you can add an attachment, just as you can with the send e-mail action. Figure 8-15 shows the Create Note dialog box.

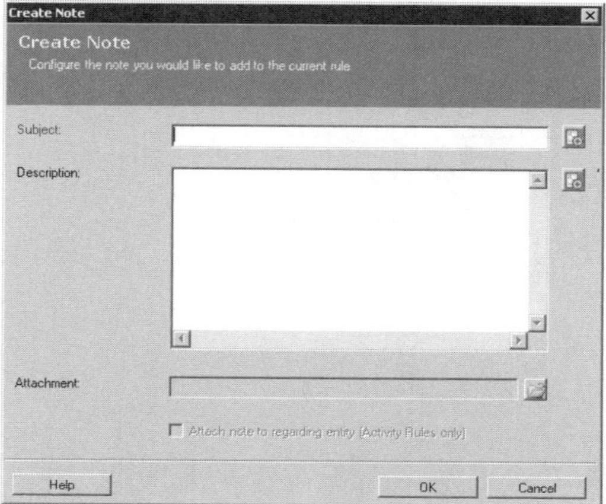

Figure 8-15 Create Note dialog box

If you're creating a workflow rule for an activity, you also have the option to attach the note to the regarding record of the activity (instead of adding a note to the activity record) by selecting the check box at the bottom of the dialog box.

Update Entity

The update entity action allows you to update data in the fields of records related to the workflow entity. For example, you might create an opportunity workflow rule that automatically changes the priority attribute to High if the estimated value of the deal is greater than $100,000. To change the value of the record's priority attribute, you must use the update entity action. When you select the update entity action, a dialog box like the one shown in Figure 8-16 appears.

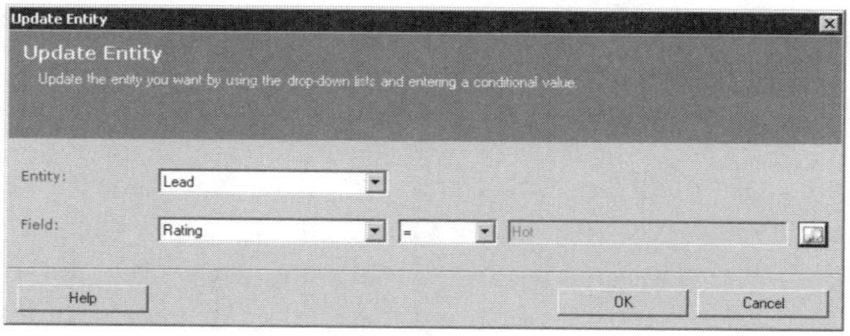

Figure 8-16 Update Entity dialog box

In addition to selecting the entity of the workflow rule, Microsoft CRM automatically determines which related entities you can include in the rule. After you select an entity, you can select the field that you want to update and then set the new value. You should consider the following points when you use the update entity action:

- You can update any attribute of an entity by using this technique, even if the attribute does not appear on the entity's form. So, you can update data on "hidden" attributes to track and manage behind-the-scenes data.
- Microsoft CRM prevents you from entering invalid data types into fields (you can't enter text in an integer field), but the update entity action bypasses any client-side validation that might exist, such as the *onChange* or *onSave* events. Consequently, you want to make sure that you don't accidentally configure an update entity action that will insert invalid data into your system.
- Updating an entity with this action triggers any post-callouts related to the entity.

Change Status

The change status action changes the status of the entity. Again, don't confuse this with the status reason (as we explained earlier in this chapter); you can think of this as changing the state of the entity.

Assign Entity

Use this action to change the assignment of the workflow entity. Figure 8-17 shows that you can assign the workflow entity to the Manager, User, or Queue.

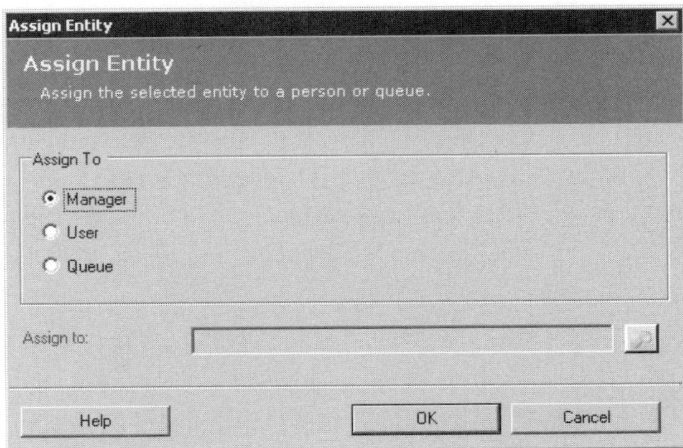

Figure 8-17 Assign Entity dialog box

To assign an entity to the Manager, you must specify a user as the Manager in the user record. If a Manager isn't specified, workflow will generate an error when it tries to complete the assignment.

If you assign the entity to the Manager or to a User, Microsoft CRM actually changes the owner of the entity. However, if you assign the entity to a Queue, Microsoft CRM does not change the owner—it just adds the record to the queue. You can only assign certain types of entities to a queue, such as cases and activities, so this option is disabled for non-queue-supported entities.

Post URL

This action sends data from the workflow entity to a URL address that you specify. Although this action does work for very simple scenarios, it involves a couple of critical shortcomings:

- It sends data only; it cannot determine whether the recipient system actually received the transmission. The post URL action cannot receive data from the other application.
- It might pause the workflow rule if the post URL address is not available, requiring a manual restart of the workflow rule.

Because of these issues, Microsoft replaced the post URL action with the greatly enhanced call assembly action in Microsoft CRM 3.0. However, the post URL action remains in the user interface to support customers who developed post URL workflow rules in Microsoft CRM 1.2.

Important Use the post URL action only if you need to reuse workflow rules that you created in previous versions of Microsoft CRM. You should not create any new workflow rules through the post URL action; use the call assembly action instead. Microsoft announced that the post URL action will not be supported in future releases of Microsoft CRM (after Microsoft CRM 3.0).

Run Subprocess

The run subprocess action allows you to insert an entirely separate workflow rule as an action in the original workflow rule. When the subprocess rule completes, it returns the record back to the original workflow rule so that it can complete its process. You can reference a workflow rule as a subprocess only if it uses a Manual workflow event trigger. Figure 8-18 shows how to use one workflow rule to reference a second workflow rule as a subprocess.

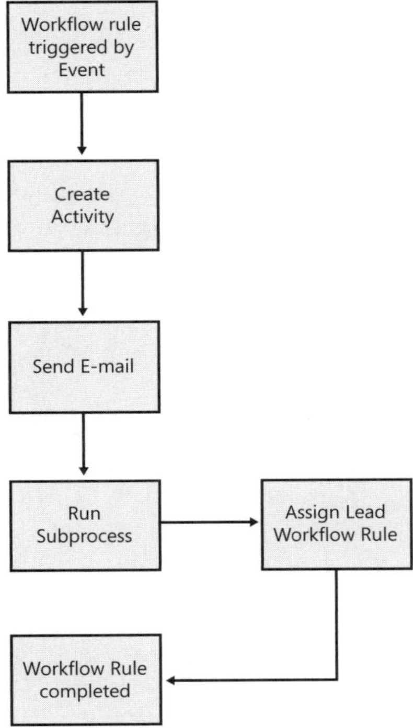

Figure 8-18 Sample workflow subprocess flow

When you start to develop a large number of workflow rules, you might find that multiple rules perform the same subset of actions. To help make workflow rules easier to manage, you could create a manual workflow rule that performs this subset of actions and then have all other rules run this subset workflow rule as a subprocess. Then if you need to change the subset of actions, you only have to edit the subset workflow rule in order for the new logic to be immediately applied to all of the workflow rules that reference this rule as a subprocess.

Caution When you use subprocesses, you might accidentally create a situation in which a workflow rule can't ever complete because it's stuck in a loop. If a workflow rule gets stuck in an infinite loop, it will have a negative impact on your server's performance. If you experience this, immediately cancel all of the looping rules in Workflow Monitor and deactivate the rule stuck in the loop. You should always carefully examine your business logic and test your complex workflow rules in a development environment—you don't want to be the person who accidentally sends 1,000 copies of the same e-mail message to all of your customers because a workflow rule got stuck in an infinite loop!

Stop

A workflow rule processes all of the conditions and actions that you configure, and then it considers the rule finished. However, you might face a situation in which you want to stop a workflow rule somewhere in the middle of its process (typically based on a condition evaluation).

You would use the stop action for such situations. When you insert a stop action, you can select from one of four options:

- **Complete** Immediately stops the workflow rule with a status of Finished.
- **Cancel** Immediately stops the workflow rule with a status of Canceled.
- **Complete and stop processing other rules** Immediately stops the workflow rule with a status of Finished. This action also stops any other workflow rules that were triggered by the same workflow event.
- **Cancel and stop processing other rules** Immediately stops the workflow rule with a status of Canceled. This action also stops any other workflow rules that were triggered by the same workflow event.

Let's look at an example scenario with the complete and stop processing other rules action. Assume that you have two workflow rules for the Lead entity based on the Create event. When you create a new lead record, Microsoft CRM runs both workflow rules in the order specified within Workflow Manager.

Tip Microsoft CRM processes workflow rules for an entity in the order in which they're listed in Workflow Manager. You can move rules up and down in the order process by clicking Move Up or Move Down on the Actions menu in Workflow Manager.

If you used the stop action within the first rule, workflow would still process the second rule for the Create event. However, if you used the complete and stop processing other rules action within the first rule, workflow would not run that second rule (or any other subsequent rules).

Call Assembly

If none of the previous workflow actions accomplishes what you want, Microsoft CRM allows you to call your own Microsoft .NET assembly directly within workflow. So what could you do within workflow by calling an external assembly? Well, just about anything, really. You might create a simple assembly that performs a mathematical calculation, or perhaps you would use an assembly that calls a Web service hosted on an external Web site that integrates directly with your financial system.

Important The call assembly action opens the door to almost unlimited customization and integration options within workflow, because you can reference your own .NET assemblies. We even heard a member of the Microsoft CRM product team describe the call assembly action as your "Get Out of Jail Free card," and we like that analogy!

We'll explain more about using the call assembly action in this chapter. Chapter 9, "Server-Side SDK," also includes a detailed explanation of how to build and deploy your own .NET assemblies for use in workflow.

Sales Process Management

Microsoft CRM offers a unique type of workflow called a sales process just for the Opportunity entity. The sales process workflow allows you to define the various sales stages that an opportunity should progress through before completion of the sale. Within each sales stage, you can define the activities that the salespeople should complete before workflow automatically advances the opportunity to the next sales stage.

By implementing sales processes, you can assist your salespeople by clearly defining the standardized business processes recommended by your organization. You can set up multiple sales processes, because different types of opportunities might require different types of sales processes (or no sales process at all). For example, you might not use any sales process on smaller opportunities, but you want to configure a specific sales process for opportunities greater than a specific dollar amount. Using sales processes and sales stages also provides additional reporting and analysis parameters for your company to evaluate. Microsoft CRM includes a Sales Pipeline report that allows you to quickly view your opportunities grouped by their sales stages (Figure 8-19).

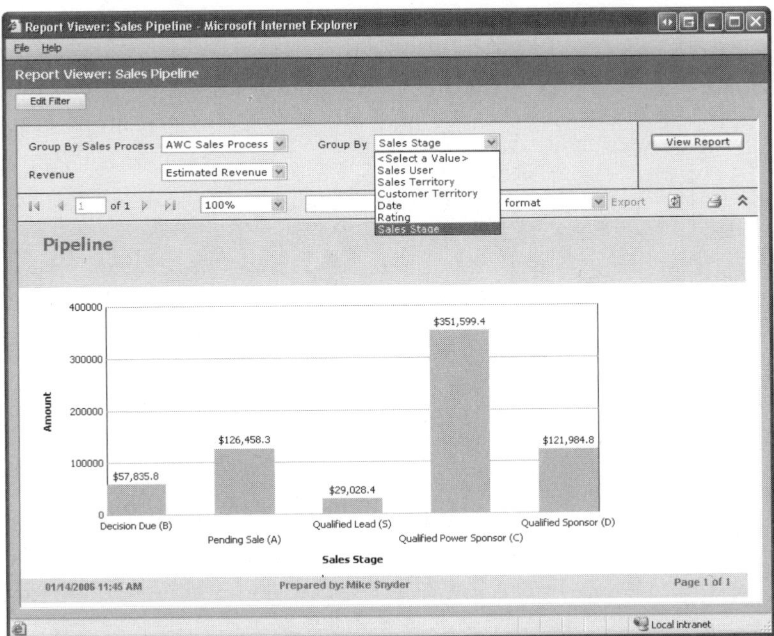

Figure 8-19 Sample Sales Pipeline report grouped by sales stage

Keep in mind that you can assign only one sales process to each opportunity, and you can't "undo" or change the sales process after it's been applied to an opportunity.

Working with Sales Processes

You can trigger sales processes with either the Create or the Manual workflow event. Figure 8-20 shows a sample of what salespeople see when viewing an Opportunity record with a sales process.

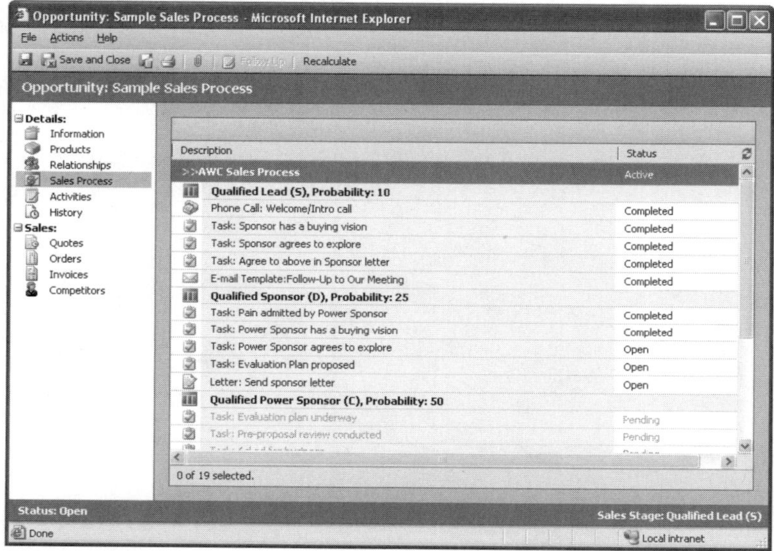

Figure 8-20 Sample sales process attached to an Opportunity record

You can see that Microsoft CRM groups activities within each sales stage and shows users which activities they should complete for their current stage. In the Workflow Manager, you can define which activities the salesperson must complete before automatically advancing the opportunity to the next sales stage.

> **Important** By using a sales process, Microsoft CRM will "hold" the future activities as Pending until the opportunity advances to the next stage. After the opportunity advances to a new sales stage, workflow automatically creates the next batch of activities for that stage.

In addition to letting workflow automatically advance an opportunity to the next stage, users can manually jump forward in the sales process by clicking Change Stage on the Actions menu. The following are three important points that you should know about manually setting a sales stage:

- If you move forward in the sales process (to a later stage), Microsoft CRM does not automatically close any currently open activities. Therefore, users should manually mark those activities as closed.
- Workflow does not create activities for any sales stages that you skipped. Instead, it leaves activities from skipped stages as Pending.
- If you move backward in the sales process (to a previous stage), workflow no longer automatically advances sales stages for the user. He or she must manually set the sales stage to move forward again. Likewise, if you move backward, workflow does not re-create any activities that you already completed.

Tip You can always see the current sales stage for an opportunity in the lower-right corner of the record.

Configuring a Sales Process

You will use Workflow Manager to create and edit your sales process by using the same tools that you use to create a workflow rule. Figure 8-21 shows a sample sales process in the workflow editor.

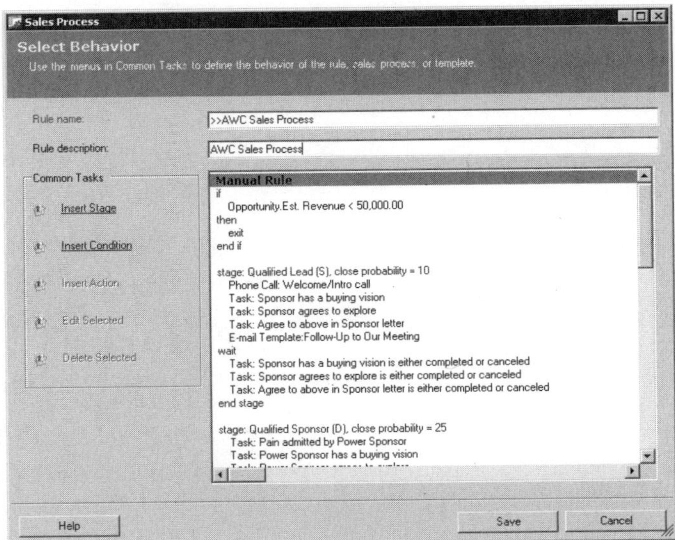

Figure 8-21 Editing a sales process in workflow

You can see in the Common Tasks section that you can still insert conditions and actions, but now you can also insert the sales stages. Within each sales stage, you can specify the actions that you want to include. One thing you can't do is include a condition within a sales stage anywhere other than in the wait section. However, you can specify a condition at the beginning of a sales process. In Figure 8-21, we created a condition in which Microsoft CRM would not apply this sales process to any opportunity with an estimated revenue value of less than $50,000.

Tip If you want to include a condition within a sales stage, you can insert a subprocess action that references another workflow rule (a non–sales process rule) that includes your conditional logic.

You can also see that within each stage you can specify the wait conditions that must be met before workflow will advance the opportunity to the next sales stage. You can configure this so that the user must complete or cancel all (or just some) of the activities in the sales stage to progress forward.

Dynamic Values in Workflow

Now that you understand the concepts involved with using, creating, and managing workflow, let's get into some of the details related to actually creating rules and actions. One of the most important workflow features that you'll use (probably in every single rule that you create) is dynamic values. Conceptually, *dynamic values* in workflow are almost identical to the data fields concepts that you learned in regard to E-mail templates. You can use dynamic values in your workflow rules to populate information specific to the workflow entity into your conditions, actions, assemblies, and so on. As a matter of fact, you'll even use data fields in conjunction with dynamic values within a workflow rule.

To help illustrate the benefits of dynamic values, let's consider a common business scenario. For every new case created, your company wants the following processes to happen automatically:

- Send an e-mail message to the customer acknowledging that you received the request; include the case number in the message so that the customer can reference it later.
- Send a notification e-mail message to the case owner about the new case, including data about the customer.

Because we want this process to run for every new case created, we'll obviously create a workflow rule for the Case entity and select the Create workflow event. Next, we'll insert a send e-mail action to send the case acknowledgement message to the customer. Fortunately, Microsoft CRM includes an E-mail template called New Case Acknowledgement that we'll use for this rule, shown in Figure 8-22.

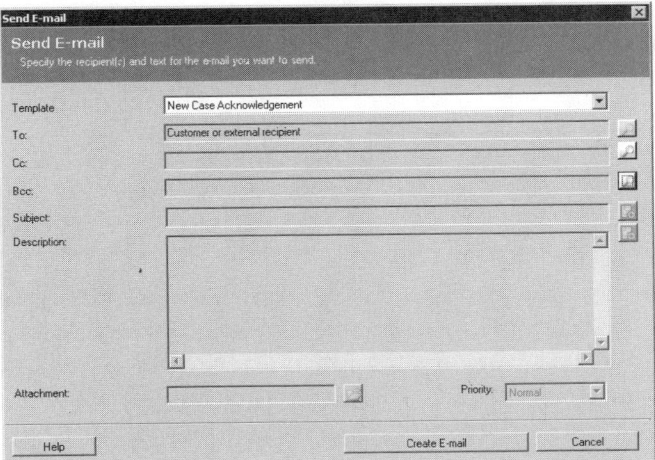

Figure 8-22 Using the New Case Acknowledgement E-mail template

You'll notice that when you select an E-mail template, Microsoft CRM disables all of the fields except for the Cc and Bcc fields. That's because all of the data for these disabled fields is defined by the E-mail template. If you examined the E-mail template, you would see that it contains the information shown in Figure 8-23.

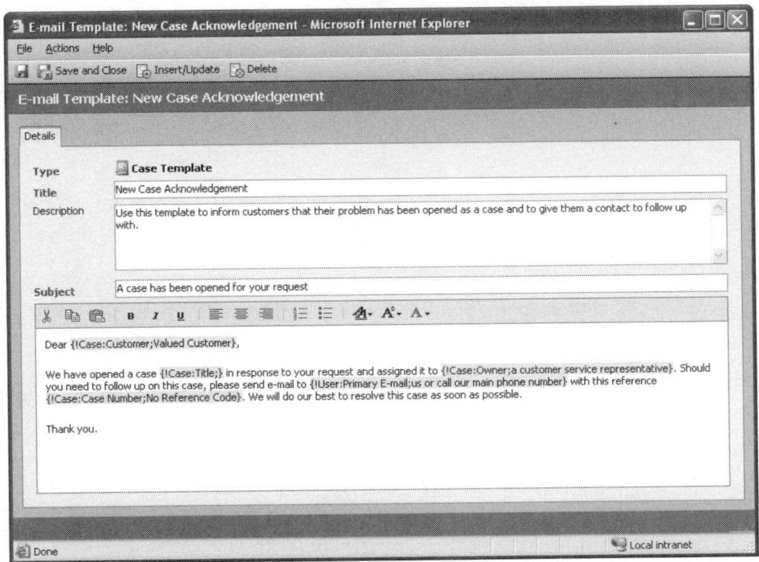

Figure 8-23 New Case Acknowledgement E-mail template

This E-mail template already includes the case number as a data field ({!Case:Case Number;No Reference Code}), so we can use the template with no modifications. Since this send e-mail action does not require any further modification, all we need to do is click Create E-mail. We could have added the case owner as a Bcc recipient, and he or she would receive a copy of the message. However, we want the message to the case owner to include additional information about the case and the customer that this E-mail template doesn't include. So for our next step, we'll insert another send e-mail action in the workflow rule.

Tip You can't specify the recipient in the To line when you use an E-mail template in workflow. Microsoft CRM sends the e-mail message to the customer related to the record. So, if you need to be able to set the recipient in the To field, you cannot use an E-mail template.

For the internal message to our customer service representative (the Case owner), we'll set the To recipient as the owner of the case. In the Subject line, we want to include the case number and the customer name. To get those two values to appear in the message, we'll insert a data field that references a dynamic value. For our e-mail Subject line, we entered the following text: Case # for customer was assigned to you.

Now we'll insert the data fields where we want them to appear, starting with the case number. Place the cursor to the right of the # symbol, and then click the button that appears to the right of the Subject field. The data field dialog box shown in Figure 8-24 appears.

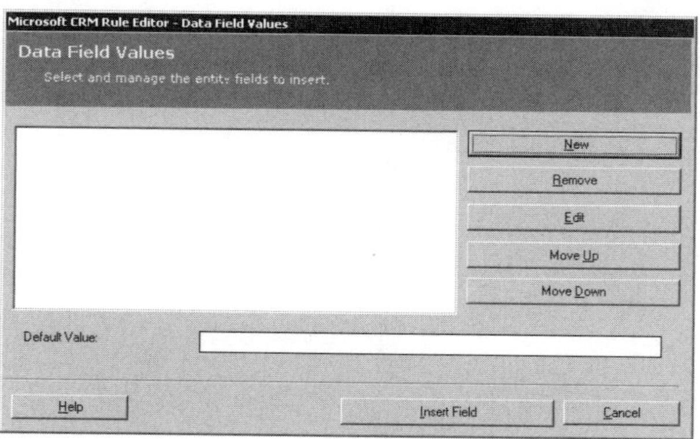

Figure 8-24 Data Field Values dialog box

This dialog box is almost identical to the data field dialog box for E-mail templates (see Chapter 2, "Setting Up Your System," for details). When we click the New button, the Select Value dialog box appears, as shown in Figure 8-25.

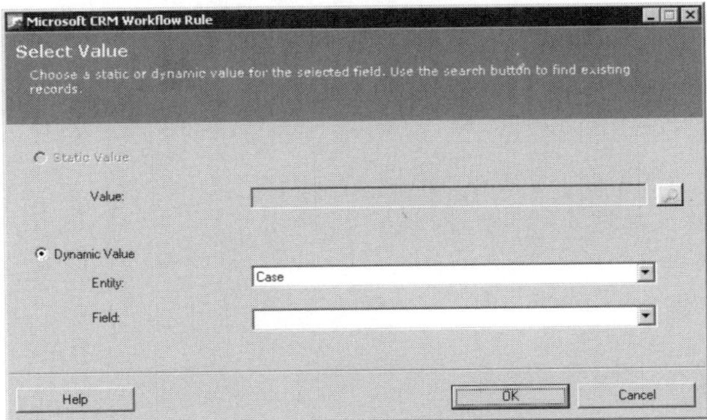

Figure 8-25 Select Value dialog box

In the Select Value dialog box, you can insert a static or dynamic value in the data field:

- **Static value** Inserts a fixed value in the data field. This static value will appear on every single record that references the rule.
- **Dynamic value** Inserts a data value that varies depending on the current record running the workflow rule.

In this example, we obviously don't want to insert a static value for the case number, because each case includes a unique number. Therefore, we'll insert a dynamic value of Case Number in our data field.

> **Important** Using dynamic values in workflow rules allows you to insert data specific to the entity running the workflow rule. In addition, you can insert dynamic values from entities related to the workflow entity.

If you click the Entity picklist, you'll see that we can insert dynamic values from the Case entity in addition to entities related to the case, such as Case, Owner, Account, Contact, Contract, and Subject. Because we want the case number, we'll select the Case entity and then click Case Number in the Field picklist. When we click OK, Microsoft CRM returns us to the data field editor. We click Insert Field and then click OK, acknowledging that we didn't set a default value (because every case includes a case number by default). You should try to always include a default value when you insert data fields.

In the Send E-mail dialog box, you'll notice that Microsoft CRM inserted the data field {!Case:Case Number;} in our Subject line. When Microsoft CRM executes this rule, it will retrieve the case number and automatically drop that dynamic value into our Subject line! Now we'll repeat that process to add more dynamic values that we want to include in our message. Figure 8-26 shows our e-mail message, complete with dynamic values from multiple entities such as Case, Account, Contract, and Subject.

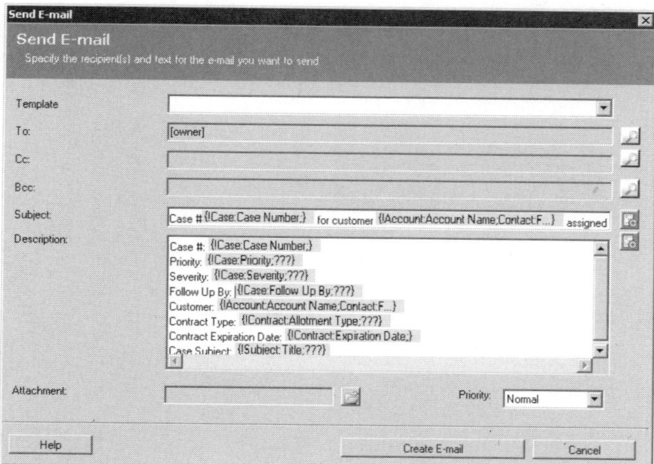

Figure 8-26 New case e-mail message with multiple dynamic value data fields

Important You can use data fields with dynamic values with almost all of the workflow actions, such as create activity, send e-mail, create note, update entity, and so on. You can also reference dynamic values within conditions to evaluate expressions in workflow.

Now that our e-mail message is complete, we've satisfied the two requirements that our business process wanted for new case creation. At this point, you should save your new workflow rule, and don't forget to activate it. As you can imagine, dynamic values provide you with a lot of flexibility in designing and creating your workflow rules. They also benefit your users and customers, because you can include very specific and individualized data in the actions that your workflow rules execute.

Calling Assemblies in Workflow

You already know that you can call a .NET assembly as an action within a workflow rule. A typical .NET assembly would accept one or more parameters as input, and then it would return some values as output. Of course, you could pass static values as inputs for your workflow assembly, but we know that you'll want to pass data specific to a record in to your assembly. More importantly, you will want to reference the data that your assembly outputs within your workflow conditions and actions. You'll use the dynamic value techniques that we just explained to pass data in to your workflow assemblies as input, and then you can reference the assembly output as a dynamic value with your conditions and actions.

Let's walk through a simple example using one of the workflow assemblies that Microsoft CRM includes with the default installation: Add date and time. We want to further expand our customer service case example to make sure that we automatically set a follow up by date equal to 24 hours after the case is created. If you try to use the update entity action to set the follow up by date field in your workflow rule, you'll notice that the static value gives you only two options:

- Execution time
- Static date and time

Neither of these will work because we want to set the case follow-up date to be 24 hours after the case created on date, and each case has a different created on date and time value. Therefore, we'll have to use a workflow assembly to perform the date manipulation (add 24 hours to the case create date) that we want to determine the correct value for the follow up by field. Conceptually, we're going to follow the process outlined in Figure 8-27.

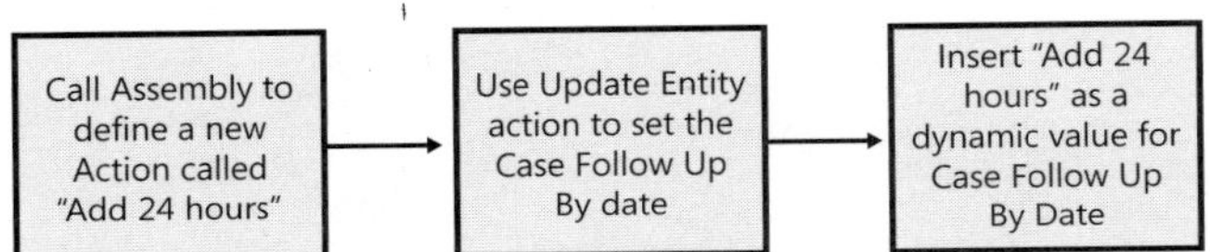

Figure 8-27 Process flow to reference assembly with dynamic values

First, we will define a new workflow action by using the Add date and time assembly. In the workflow rule editor, click Insert Action in the Common Tasks section, point to Call Assembly, point to Date And Time Functions, and then click Add Date And Time. The Create Assembly Call dialog box appears, where we'll enter the new action name and specify the input parameters for the Add date and time assembly. Let's enter a name of "Add 24 hours" for this action.

Now we must specify the input parameters for this assembly, so we'll double-click the Date and Time parameter. In the Select Value dialog box, we'll select Dynamic Value and choose the Case Entity and the Created On date because that's the value that we want to add 24 hours to. Back in the Create Assembly Call dialog box, we'll double-click the Hours parameter and then, in the Select Value dialog box, enter 24 as the static value. Finally, we'll click OK in the Create Assembly Call dialog box, shown in Figure 8-28.

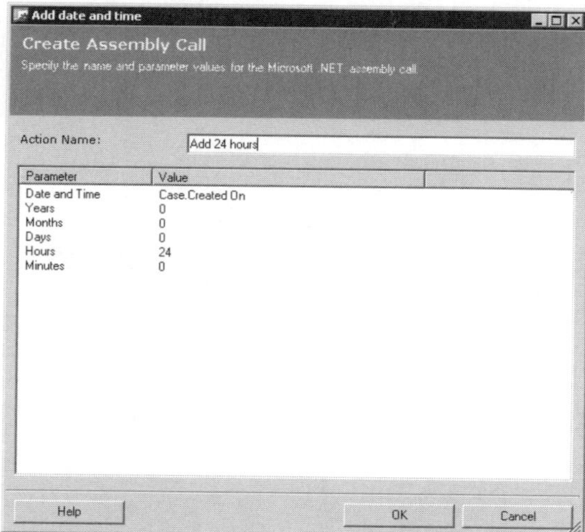

Figure 8-28 Settings for the Add 24 hours action referencing an assembly

We just defined our custom workflow action that will accept a dynamic input value of Case Created On and then add 24 hours. Now we want to use this action to update the follow up by date of new cases in our workflow rule. Click Insert Action, and then click Update Entity. In the Update Entity dialog box, select the Case entity and the Follow Up By field. Set the expression to = and click the look-up button to open the Select Value dialog box. Now for the impressive part: when you select Dynamic Value and click the Entity list, you'll see that our custom-defined action appears, as shown in Figure 8-29.

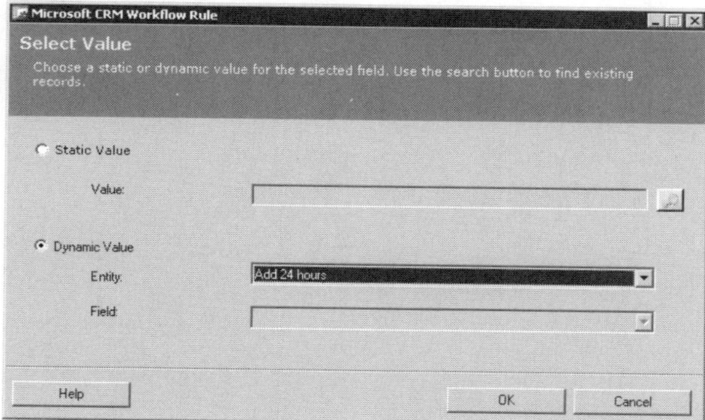

Figure 8-29 Referencing the output of an assembly as a dynamic value

Caution It might not be intuitive, but you reference your custom actions (defined through workflow assembly output) as an entity in the Dynamic Value selection.

Select Add 24 Hours, and then click OK twice to return to the workflow rule editor and save your updated workflow rule. That's it, you just implemented a call to an assembly that will update the case follow up by date to a value 24 hours later than the case created on date.

As we mentioned, there's almost no limit to the types of customization and integration that you can perform by combining your custom .NET assemblies with workflow and dynamic values. Chapter 9 includes more technical information about

- Creating custom code for a workflow assembly.
- Deploying a workflow assembly.
- Modifying the Workflow.config file.

Workflow Monitor

As we explained, the workflow service runs constantly behind the scenes, evaluating your rules and Microsoft CRM data. The Workflow Monitor utility allows you to view all of the workflow rules running in your system, in addition to a log of previously executed rules. Workflow Monitor should be your primary resource when you're troubleshooting or debugging any issues with workflow.

Definitions

Workflow process defines an activated workflow rule. A *workflow process instance* identifies a workflow process that has been executed. Table 8-3 describes the utility used to manage both types of workflow data.

Table 8-3 Workflow Tools

Term	Entity	Utility
Workflow process	Process	Workflow Manager
Workflow process instance	Process Instance	Workflow Monitor

As with all of the workflow utilities, you access Workflow Monitor from the Microsoft CRM Web server. When you launch the application, you first enter your Microsoft CRM Web server. The Workflow Monitor displays two tabs, Process and Log, as shown in Figure 8-30.

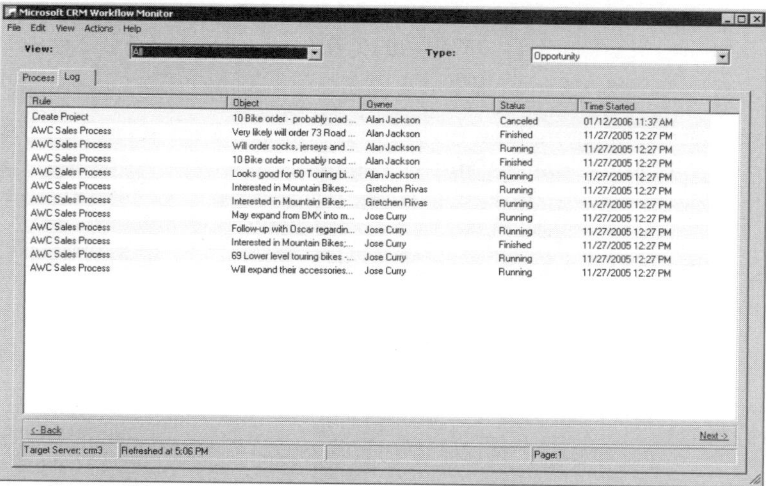

Figure 8-30 Workflow Monitor

Process Tab

The Process tab displays all running workflow process instances for all entity types. You filter the information on this tab with the Type and View lists. The Type list contains all entities available for workflow rules in alphabetical order. The View list displays the following options:

- **Summary** Lists all of the entities and the number of active, paused, and total process instances attached to each entity. When the view is set to Summary, the type selection is ignored.
- **All** Shows all running instances for the entity selected in the Type list.
- **Active** Shows all running instances that are either currently running or waiting to be run. Rules that are in the waiting status will have a wait condition.
- **Paused** Shows rules that have an error and must be reviewed and acted upon.

The information on the Process tab is refreshed every 300 seconds by default. You can change the refresh rate and number of records to retrieve in the grid by clicking Options on the Edit menu. You may perform maintenance actions on the instances in the grid from the Process tab by using the Actions menu. You may also individually manage any given instance from the instance's properties page.

Workflow Monitor maintenance actions include:

- **Pause** Lets you manually pause an instance at any time.
- **Resume** Resumes a paused instance. If the Workflow service paused the instance because of an error, you must correct the error before resuming.
- **Cancel** Allows you to terminate an instance. No further steps will be executed, and the instance will move from the Process tab to the Log tab.

In addition to performing these actions, you also can view the properties of any running instance by clicking Properties on the View menu or by double-clicking the process instance in the grid.

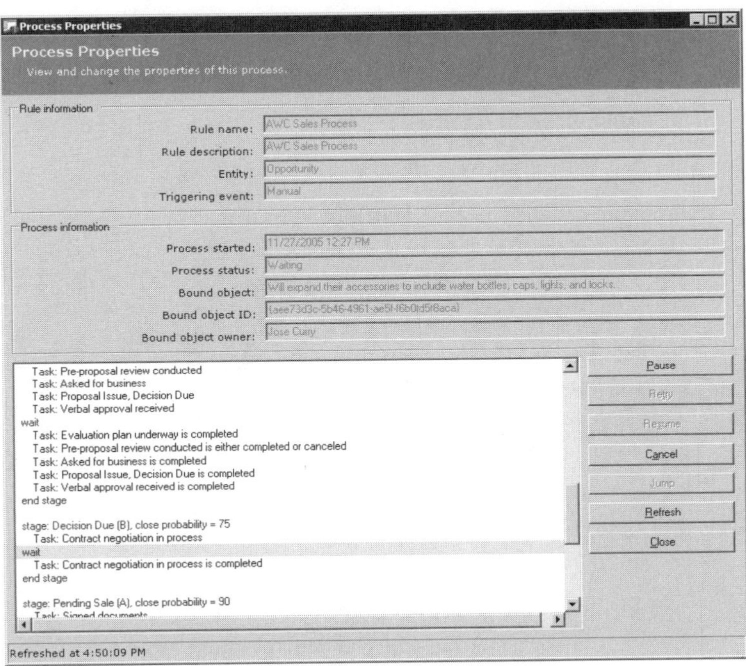

As you can see, Microsoft CRM provides quite a bit of information concerning the instance selected, including the originating rule and event, the status, the time the process started, and the entity (object) that it is executing against. Even more useful, you can see each step in the rule, with the current step highlighted in yellow.

In this dialog box, you can perform the three actions previously mentioned, in addition to the following two actions:

- **Retry** Attempts to execute the current step again. You might use this when trying to repair a failed subprocess or assembly step.
- **Jump** Allows you to skip to a future step in the rule by clicking a new step and then clicking the Jump button.

> **Caution** If you jump ahead of the current step, a warning states that unexpected results might occur.

Log Tab

The Log tab displays all finished workflow processes and also allows you to access the step execution history of any finished process. The Type box contains the same entity list as the Process tab. The View box provides filters for the following statuses:

- **All** Shows all completed and running instances for the entity selected in the Type box
- **Running** Shows all instances that are still running but have completed some steps
- **Finished** Shows instances that have completed their final steps
- **Canceled** Shows instances that have been manually canceled

You can access the log details for a process instance by selecting a record and clicking Properties from the View menu or double-clicking a process instance. The log details show a complete history of each step, the status, and the time at which it executed, as shown in Figure 8-31.

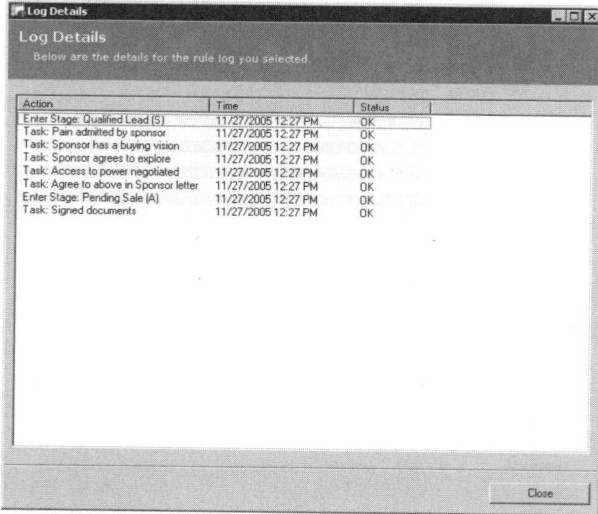

Figure 8-31 Workflow log properties

The actions available on the Log tab are purge and export. As it sounds, purging the log removes entries from the grid. Exporting the log saves the information to an XML file, which you can archive or import into another application for analysis.

> **Note** You will only purge or export the records currently shown in the grid. If you have multiple pages, you must repeat this process for each page. Also, you can purge or export individually selected records.

Import/Export

Just as with entity customizations, you can import and export your workflow rules from one Microsoft CRM system to another. Therefore, you can create and test all of your workflow rules on a development system and deploy them to your production environment.

Microsoft CRM workflow includes two utilities for these processes: the Export Workflow Wizard and the Import Workflow Wizard. Let's explore how both applications function and discuss some actions that you might have to take after importing a set of workflow rules.

Export Workflow Wizard

You can access the Export Workflow Wizard on the Microsoft CRM Web server. On the Start menu, point to All Programs, point to Microsoft CRM, and then click Export Workflow Wizard.

Like all wizards, this tool walks you through some simple steps to export your information. Select your Microsoft CRM server, and then select the Use Secured Connection check box if you require Secure Sockets Layer (SSL) to access your server. When you reach the Select Workflow Type And Rules page, you have the option to selectively choose the rules that you want to export.

Tip Click the column headers to sort on a particular column. Click the blank column header above the check boxes to select or clear all displayed rules.

Choose a path to store the resulting XML file, including a name for your file, on the Save Export File page. Finally, the wizard allows you to review your export summary. Clicking Export on the Review Export Summary page saves all of the selected rules to the file specified.

Warning If you are selectively choosing rules for export, don't forget to export any subprocess rules that your rules might reference.

Import Workflow Wizard

The Import Workflow Wizard can also be found on the Microsoft CRM Web server. The process you will follow when importing a workflow file is:

1. Open the Import Workflow Wizard application from the Microsoft CRM Web server, and then import your saved XML file.
2. If the wizard notes any dependencies, you must correct them after import by using Workflow Manager.
3. Activate your rules.

The Import Workflow Wizard validates the XML document for any errors or dependencies. You are notified of its findings on the Review XML File Validation page before import begins. Workflow allows you to correct some dependencies after import in Workflow Manager. Those conditions and actions are marked with "MISSING DETAILS," as shown in Figure 8-32. Other errors will prevent you from performing the import.

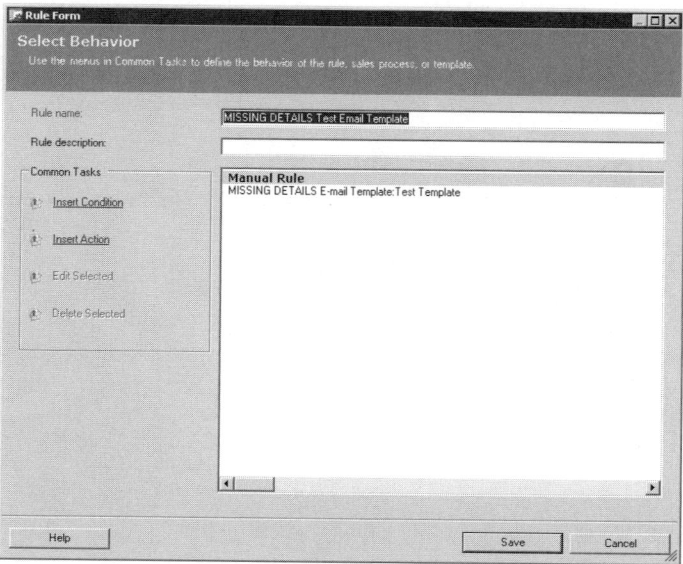

Figure 8-32 Example of a rule that must be reset after import

The following are two common errors that will prevent you from successfully importing the file:

- **Malformed XML document** If the XML document has been altered or does not conform to the import schema, you will receive an error, so you cannot complete the import.
- **Attribute references** When you reference an attribute from the update entity action or from a condition, the Import Workflow Wizard first validates that the attribute exists in the target system. If the attribute does not exist, you will not be able to continue.

If your workflow rule contains the following references, you will receive dependency warnings and must correct them after import before your rules will be successfully activated:

- **Entity references** If the workflow rule that you import references a specific object such as a user, you might need to reselect the object after you import the rule.
- **E-mail templates** Any E-mail templates used in an imported rule must be reselected. Unlike missing entity fields, you only receive a warning from the wizard if the template does not exist on the destination server. Therefore, you could add the template to Microsoft CRM after the rule is imported.

- **Subprocess** Workflow Manager must reconnect any subprocess calls. Edit each step that contains a run subprocess action, and then reset the process.
- **Assembly calls** External assembly parameters are dependent on the Workflow.config file on the target server. Each call assembly action must be reset, and parameters must be reselected.

> **Important** Each step that contains "MISSING DETAILS" in its name must be reset for your rule to successfully run. Also, don't forget to activate your rules!

Workflow Examples

Now that you understand the concepts and details related to Microsoft CRM workflow, let's look at a few examples that will show you how to pull everything together in real-world workflow scenarios.

Creating a Business Process for Each New Lead

Let's assume that your company would like to use a standardized process to handle each lead that is entered into the system. However, your business process varies depending on the lead source and the location of the prospective client. In this example, we will demonstrate:

- Using conditions to create different sets of activities.
- Using the send e-mail action to send a template response for leads generated from the Web.
- Using the create activity action to generate activity records for the lead owner.
- Using the Wait for timer command to automatically close any stale leads.

Creating the rule

1. Log on to the Microsoft CRM Web server, and then open Workflow Manager.
2. Select **Lead** from the **Entity Type** list, and leave **Rule** selected in the **View** list.
3. On the **File** menu, click **New**.
4. In the Create Workflow Rule wizard, enter **New Lead Process** in the **Name** box, and leave **Create** selected in the **Event** list. Click **Next**.

Sending the response for Web site leads

1. Click **Insert Condition**, and then click **Check conditions**.
2. Click **<< add conditions here >>** in the statement window, click **Insert Condition**, and then click **Check entity condition**.

3. In the **Check Entity Condition** dialog box, select the options shown in the following image.

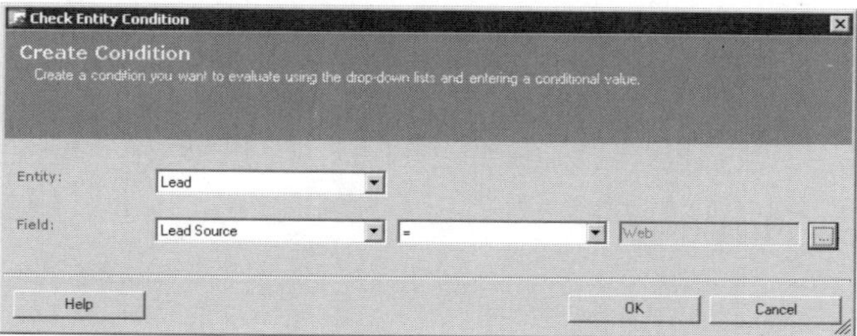

4. Click **<< add actions here >>**, click **Insert Action**, and then click **Send e-mail**.
5. To use one of the default templates provided by Microsoft CRM, select **Lead Reply-Web Site Visit** in the **Template** list, and then click **Create E-mail**.

Your rule should now look like Figure 8-33.

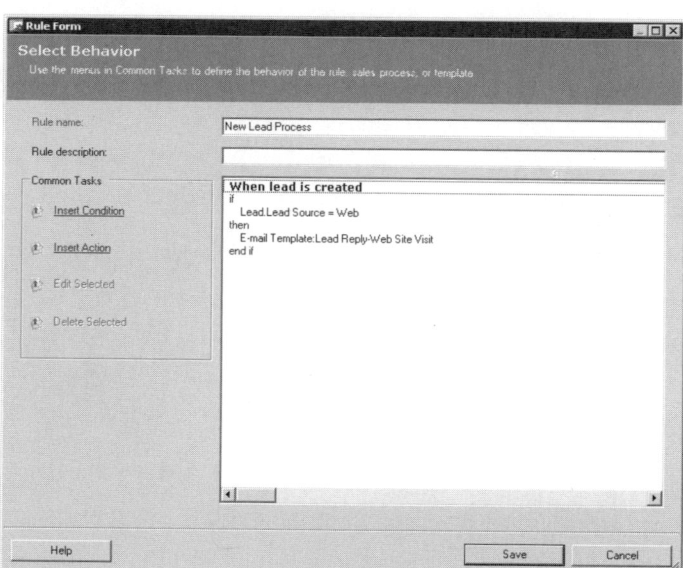

Figure 8-33 Workflow rule after Web lead condition and actions are entered

Our next step is to add the common actions that our new lead process expects. We want to create a Phone Call activity so that someone from our company will contact and attempt to qualify the lead.

Creating phone call actions

1. To add a Phone Call activity, click the end if statement, click **Insert Action**, and then click **Create activity**.
2. In the **Type** list, select **Phone Call**. In the **Subject** box, type **Follow up on new web lead -** . Then click the **Insert Fields** button to the right of the **Subject** box. When the **Data Field Values** dialog box appears, click **New**.
3. For **Dynamic Value**, select **Lead** in the **Entity** list and **Topic** in the **Field** list. Click **OK**.
4. Type **No topic** in the **Default Value** box, and then click **Insert Field**.
5. Select **1** days for the due date, and then click **Create Activity**.

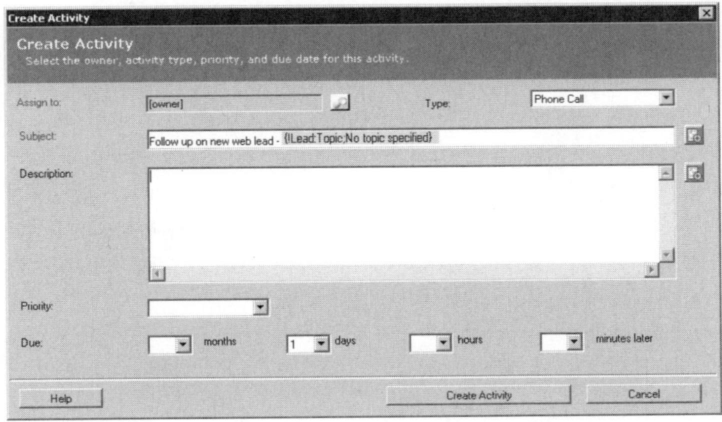

In our last sequence of steps, we will add some follow-up and clean-up steps. We will add a Wait for timer step to pause the rule for 14 days. Then we'll check to see whether it is still an open lead and log a task to the owner to try to reconnect with the lead. We'll add a final Wait for Timer command for one month. If the lead is still open after one month, we will send an e-mail message to the manager and close the lead.

Adding the follow-up steps

1. Click the **Phone Call** activity.
2. Click **Insert Condition**, and then click **Wait for timer**.
3. In the **Time-Based Wait** dialog window, set the **Wait for** selection boxes to 14 days. Select **From now on**, and then click **Ok**.
4. Click **Insert Condition** back in the **Common Tasks** section, and then click **Check Conditions**. Click **<< add conditions here>>**, click **Insert Condition**, and then click **Check entity condition**. Select Entity: **Lead**, Field: **Status,** =, and Static Value: **Open**.
5. Click **<< add actions here>>**, and then create a final Task activity to determine whether the lead still has any interest in our products. For the **Subject**, enter **Follow up with**, and enter dynamic text to choose the topic. Choose **1** day for the due date.

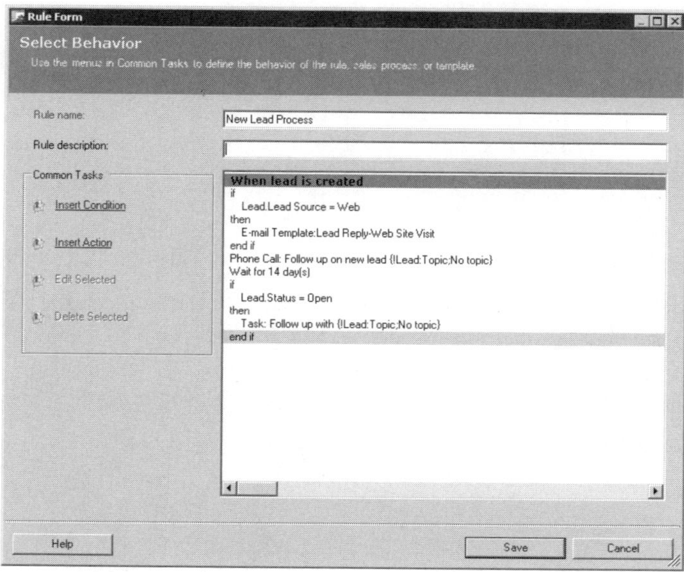

6. For the clean-up step, make sure that you click the **Follow Up** task because we want to execute it only if the lead is still open. Add another Wait for timer condition for 1 month from now.

> **Note** If we added our timer outside of the *if-then-end if* statement, the last Wait for Timer statement will execute regardless of whether the lead was closed in the first 14 days. Although this doesn't necessarily harm anything, it forces the process instance to stay in a running state longer than necessary.

7. Click **Insert Condition**, and then click **Check Conditions**. Click **<< add conditions here>>**, click **Insert Condition**, and then click **Check entity condition**. Select Entity: **Lead**, Field: **Status**, **=**, and Static Value: **Open**.
8. Click **<< add actions here>>**, and then create a change status action. Change the state to **Disqualified**, click **Save**, and then activate your new rule.

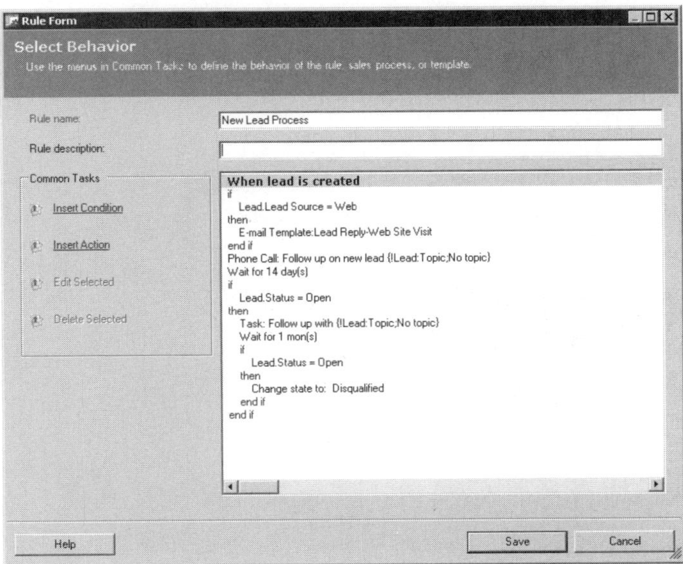

Escalating Overdue Cases

A common goal for customer service organizations is to have a quick turnaround time when responding to and resolving support cases. Our example organization would like to ensure that they react to all cases within one day. After one day, we will check to see whether the case is still open. If it is, we will e-mail the owner's manager. We will then wait another day to see whether the status has changed. If not, we will send another e-mail message to the manager and route the case to the Level 2 support. We will then create a loop until the case is resolved. Figure 8-34 shows the process graphically.

In addition to creating conditionals and actions that you are already familiar with, we will cover the following key points:

- Using the stop action
- Using the run subprocess action
- Creating a looping process
- Simulating an update event
- Using the call assembly to return a value to your rule

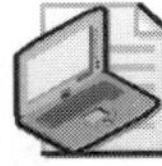

Note We will only show the code for the assembly and how to use it within the Rule Form editor. For more details on how to implement your own custom assemblies, see Chapter 9.

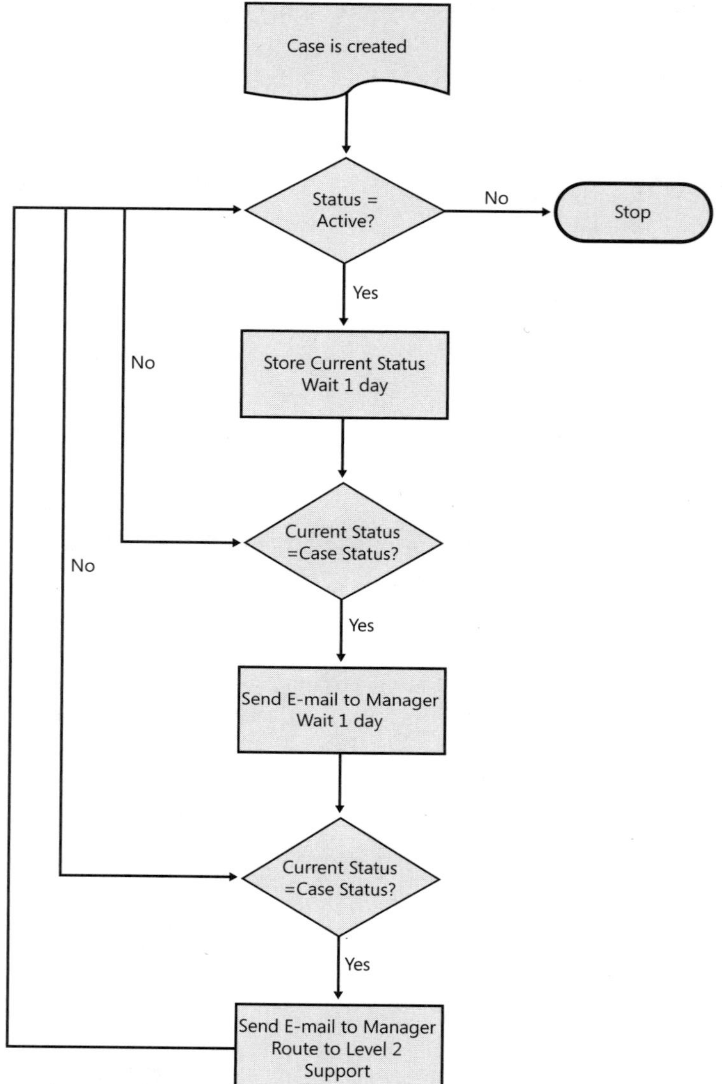

Figure 8-34 Case escalation logic

By now you are familiar with Workflow Manager, so we will focus only on the new actions used for this example. We will be creating three workflow rules for the case entity, in the following order:

- **E-mail rule** A manual rule that will simply e-mail the owner's manager.
- **Escalating logic rule** A manual rule that will contain the logic for the case escalation. This rule will be calling itself, creating a looping situation.
- **Create rule** A rule that will be triggered from the Create event and will simply call our escalating logic process.

An E-mail template won't allow us to specify the owner's manager in the To line, so we will manually create the e-mail message in workflow. We chose to create a separate rule for the e-mail message that we will reference as a subprocess so that we will be able to use this e-mail message in our parent rule without having to configure it multiple times; a separate rule also allows us to make changes to the message in one centralized place.

Creating the e-mail rule

1. In Workflow Manager for the Case entity, create a Manual rule called Send Escalation Email that looks like the following image.

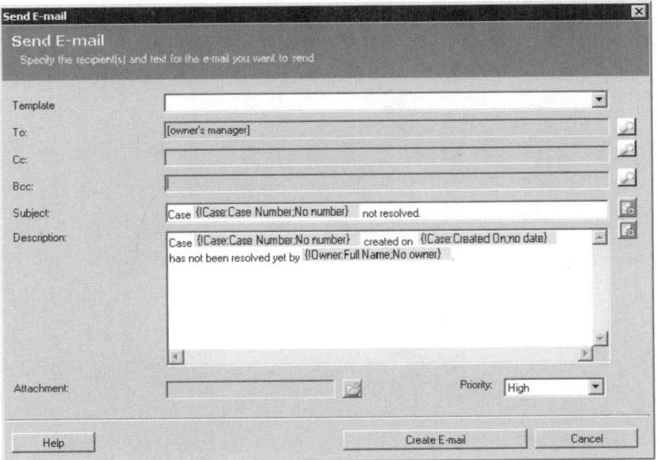

2. Save and activate the rule.

The next step is to create the main escalating logic. We will use the flowchart from Figure 8-34 as our blueprint. This rule will highlight a few key points when working with workflow. The first is the notion of an update event. As you saw, an update doesn't exist when you create a new rule. However, because the workflow engine is constantly evaluating active rules, you can simulate an update event by doing the following:

- Storing the value of the field you want to check for updates on in a dynamic value by using a custom assembly
- Creating a recursive loop (or having the process call itself) with a subprocess and wait command to evaluate the stored value with the existing value from the entity

Use extreme care when creating a loop, especially one that calls additional subprocesses. You always have the potential to create a situation that causes an infinite loop. Such a situation will create a performance bottleneck and will have to be manually terminated in Workflow Monitor. If you find yourself in an infinite loop, immediately terminate the step, deactivate the rule, and correct the problem.

> **More Info** The workflow update technique we are about to show has many useful advantages. However, if you truly need to respond to an update event, you should consider using a callout. See Chapter 9 for more information and a discussion of when to use workflow versus callouts.

Finally, we have included the custom assembly code at the end of this example for reference. For the purpose of this exercise, we will assume that it is already installed and available to Workflow Manager. See Chapter 9 for more details on developing and deploying custom workflow assemblies.

The final rule should look like Figure 8-35.

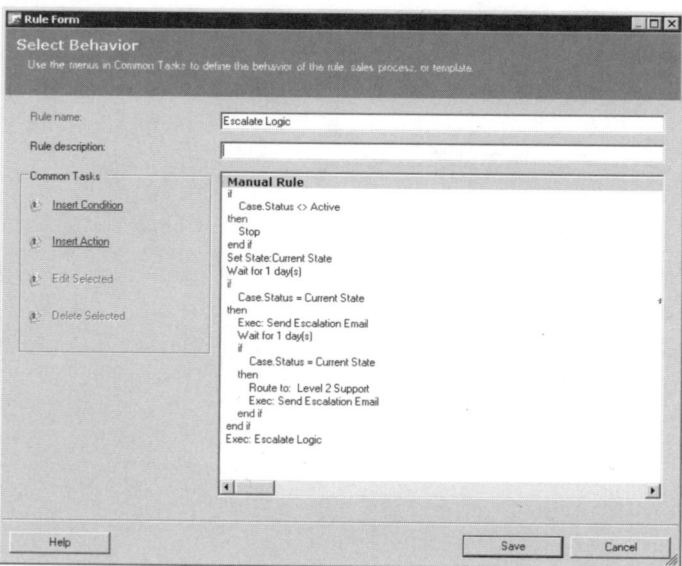

Figure 8-35 Escalating logic rule final steps

Creating the escalate logic rule

1. In Workflow Manager for the Case entity, create a Manual rule called Escalate Logic.
2. Add your initial condition, checking the status of case. If it is not active (meaning that it has been resolved or canceled), we want to immediately exit with a stop command, marking the process as Complete.
3. Use a custom assembly function to store the current status (state) of our case. To do this, click **Insert Action**, point to **Call assembly**, point to **Custom Assemblies**, and then click **Set State**. A custom dialog box appears that is based on the configuration settings of the custom assembly. Type **Current State** in the **Action Name** box. Double-click the **Status** parameter, and then choose **Status** from the **Field** list for the **Dynamic Value**.

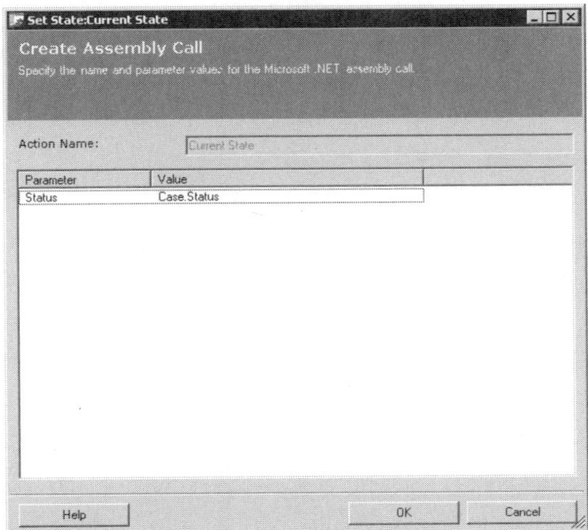

4. Add your Wait for timer condition, setting it for 1 day, and a Check Conditions condition immediately after. For the conditions, compare the **Case.Status** field against a **Dynamic Value**, and then select **Current State** in the **Entity** list.
5. For the actions of this condition, we will add our subprocess. Click **Insert Action**, and then click **Run subprocess**. Choose **Send Escalation Email** in the **Subprocess** list.

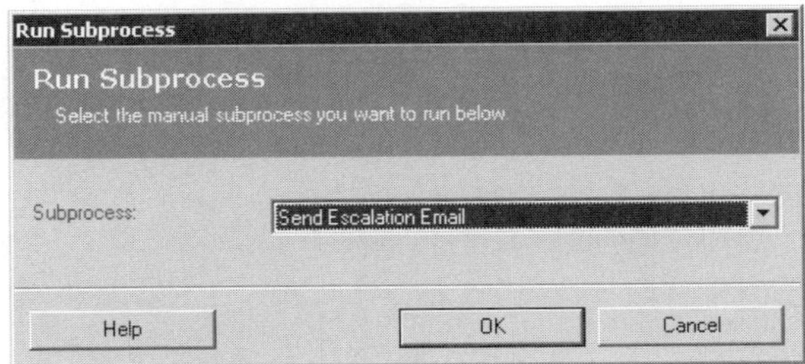

6. Continue to add the logic as shown back in Figure 8-35.
7. At the end, we want to create a recursive loop, so we will add one more subprocess action. This time, though, we will call the Escalate Logic rule.
8. Save and activate your rule.

The last step is to initiate the Escalate Logic rule each time a new case is created. We will build a rule based on the case's Create event that simply calls the Escalate Logic rule through the subprocess action.

Creating the create rule

1. In Workflow Manager for the Case entity, add a create rule called Escalate Case that looks like the following.

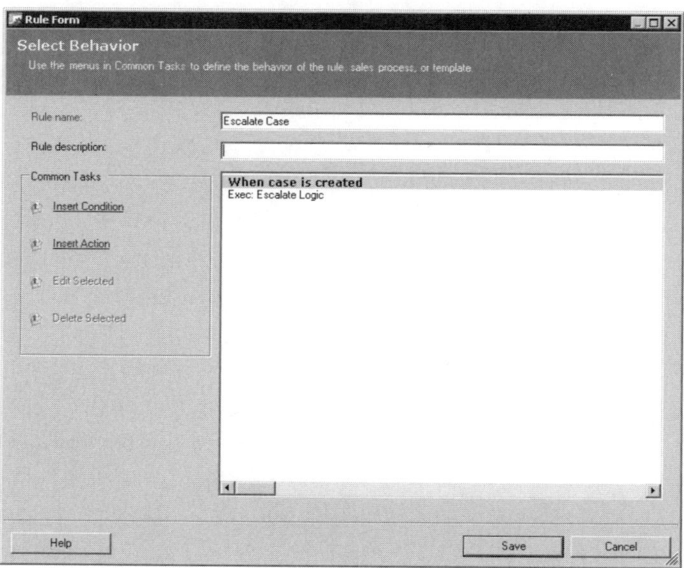

2. Save and activate the rule.

For reference, Listing 8-1 shows the code for our simple routine used to return the value of our status code. If you download the sample code, we have already compiled this code into a .dll, so you just need to copy WorkingWithCrm.Workflow.dll from <*Code Installation Directory*>\WorkingWithCrm.Workflow\Utils to C:\Program Files\Microsoft CRM\Server\bin\assembly on the CRM server.

Listing 8-1 Custom Assembly Code

```
using System;
using System.Reflection;
using System.Runtime.CompilerServices;

namespace WorkingWithCrm.Workflow
{
 public class CustomAssembly
 {
   public int SetInteger(int Value)
   {
     return Value;
   }
 }
}
```

To register your custom assembly with Workflow Manager, you must add the code from Listing 8-2 to your workflow.config file. The default location for the workflow.config file is C:\Program Files\Microsoft CRM\Server\bin\assembly. You will need to add the *allowunsignedassemblies="true"* attribute to the <*workflow.config*> node and then add Set Status <*method*> node, as shown below.

Listing 8-2 Custom Assembly Configuration Settings

```
<workflow.config xmlns="http://microsoft.com/mscrm/workflow/"
allowunsignedassemblies="true">
    <methods>
    <method name="Set Status"
      assembly="WorkingWithCrm.dll"
      typename="WorkingWithCrm.CustomAssembly"
      methodname="SetInteger"
      group="Custom Assemblies"
      isvisible="1"
      timeout="7200">
      <parameter name="Status" datatype="picklist" entityname="incident"
attribute="statecode" />
      <result datatype="picklist" entityname="incident" attribute="statecode" />
    </method>
    ... existing method nodes ...
  </methods>
</workflow.config>
```

Summary

Microsoft CRM includes powerful workflow functionality that you can set up and configure to implement standardized business processes in an automated fashion. Workflow includes several administration utilities–Workflow Manager, Workflow Monitor, the Export Workflow Wizard, and the Import Workflow Wizard–that any power user can quickly learn without any programming knowledge. You can create workflow rules for many different entities, in addition to a special kind of workflow called a sales process for opportunities. Workflow rules allow you to specify criteria and business logic about how Microsoft CRM should execute the rule. In addition to configuring the workflow trigger event, you can insert conditions and actions within each rule. Workflow rules follow the Microsoft CRM security model, so you can configure the rules and security roles for your organization to restrict user access.

Part III
Extending Microsoft CRM

When we work with prospects considering a Microsoft Dynamics CRM 3.0 purchase, we hear lots of stories about complex business rules and sophisticated programming requirements. Usually at least one time in the sales process the prospect will ask a question along the lines of "Is this even possible to program in Microsoft CRM?" That's when big smiles cross our faces as we say "Of course!" This isn't just tough talk to win a deal, we mean it when we say that you can program almost anything with Microsoft CRM.

Part III of the book goes into the details of how you can use the Microsoft CRM Software Development Kit (SDK) to create your own custom code. By working within the SDK framework, your custom solutions stand a very good chance of upgrading smoothly when Microsoft releases new versions and updates of Microsoft CRM. The Microsoft CRM SDK opens all sorts of programming interfaces into the software, so any experienced Web developer can be up and running with custom solutions in very little time. The last chapter in this part will also show you how to integrate Microsoft CRM with SharePoint Products and Technologies.

We printed all of the examples in this part of the book so that you can download the sample code and deploy the software to your organization if you wish. The Introduction explains how you can download the sample code off of the companion Web site.

Chapter 9

Server-Side SDK

In this chapter:

In addition to all of the Web-based configuration and customizations tools we've discussed so far, Microsoft Dynamics CRM 3.0 provides a programming interface that allows you to create even more complex and sophisticated customizations. Information about accessing the Microsoft CRM programming interface is published in a document called the "Microsoft CRM 3.0 Software Development Kit (SDK)." To create customizations and integrations by using the information in the SDK, you must be comfortable developing applications with tools such as Microsoft Visual Studio .NET. We will assume you have working knowledge of Visual Studio .NET and Web application configuration using Microsoft Internet Information Services (IIS). If you're not a developer, we still recommend that you read the chapters in this part of this book to gain an understanding of the types of customizations that the Microsoft CRM programming model makes possible.

The SDK defines all of the supported interaction points, also known as application programming interfaces (APIs), that you can access when writing code that integrates with Microsoft CRM. Using the APIs for your customizations provides several significant benefits:

- **Ease of use** The APIs include hundreds of pages of documentation complete with real-world examples, code samples, and helper classes to help you write code that works with Microsoft CRM.
- **Supportability** If you encounter technical problems or issues using the APIs, you can contact Microsoft technical support or use the Microsoft CRM public newsgroup for assistance.

- **Upgrade support** Microsoft makes every effort to ensure that the code you create for Microsoft CRM 3.0 using the APIs will upgrade smoothly with future versions of the product, even if the underlying SQL Server database changes radically. This is also true for any hotfixes that Microsoft might release for Microsoft CRM 3.0.
- **Certification** By following the documented APIs, you can submit your customizations to a third-party testing vendor to certify that your application works within the confines of the SDK. This certification provides comfort and reassurance for people evaluating your customizations.

> **Caution** As we discussed in Chapter 4, "Entity Customization: Concepts and Attributes," it is technically possible for you to create programming customizations that bypass the Microsoft CRM APIs and interact directly with the SQL Server database. However, we strongly discourage anyone from attempting to do this for all of the reasons just listed.

The Microsoft CRM SDK Help file is divided into three main components:

- **Server Programming Guide** Explains how to write customizations that you deploy on the Microsoft CRM server. Server-related customizations include pre- and post-callouts, workflow assemblies, system integration, and so on.
- **Client Programming Guide** Explains how to customize the Web and Microsoft Outlook that users use to access Microsoft CRM. Client-related customizations include form and field event scripts, IFrames, and so on.
- **Report Writer's Guide** Describes how to interact with Microsoft SQL Server Reporting Services to create, customize, and manage reports.

> **More Info** When you download the Microsoft CRM SDK, in addition to the SDK Help file, you will also find an SDKReadme.htm file. This document contains many known issues regarding the SDK, and we recommend that you review it before working with the SDK.

This chapter will cover the following server-side SDK topics:

- Architecture
- CRMService Web services
- MetadataService Web services
- Queries
- Callouts
- Workflow plug-in assemblies
- ISV.configs
- Development environments
- Sample code

Chapter 10, "Client-Side SDK," will cover the client-side programmatic customizations in detail. Don't forget that all of our sample code is available for download. (The book's Introduction specifies the download URL.)

Architecture

As you learned in Chapter 1, "Microsoft CRM 3.0 Introduction and Architecture," Microsoft CRM uses a metadata and server platform layer to abstract the application and extensibility points from the Microsoft SQL Server database tier. The platform layer also controls security, event management, and extensibility points (such as callouts and workflow) while enforcing the proper constraints for interacting with the underlying schema of the database. By providing a supported API, Microsoft CRM allows developers to customize the application and continue to use those customizations after future upgrades.

Figure 9-1 shows a graphical representation of the Microsoft CRM architecture.

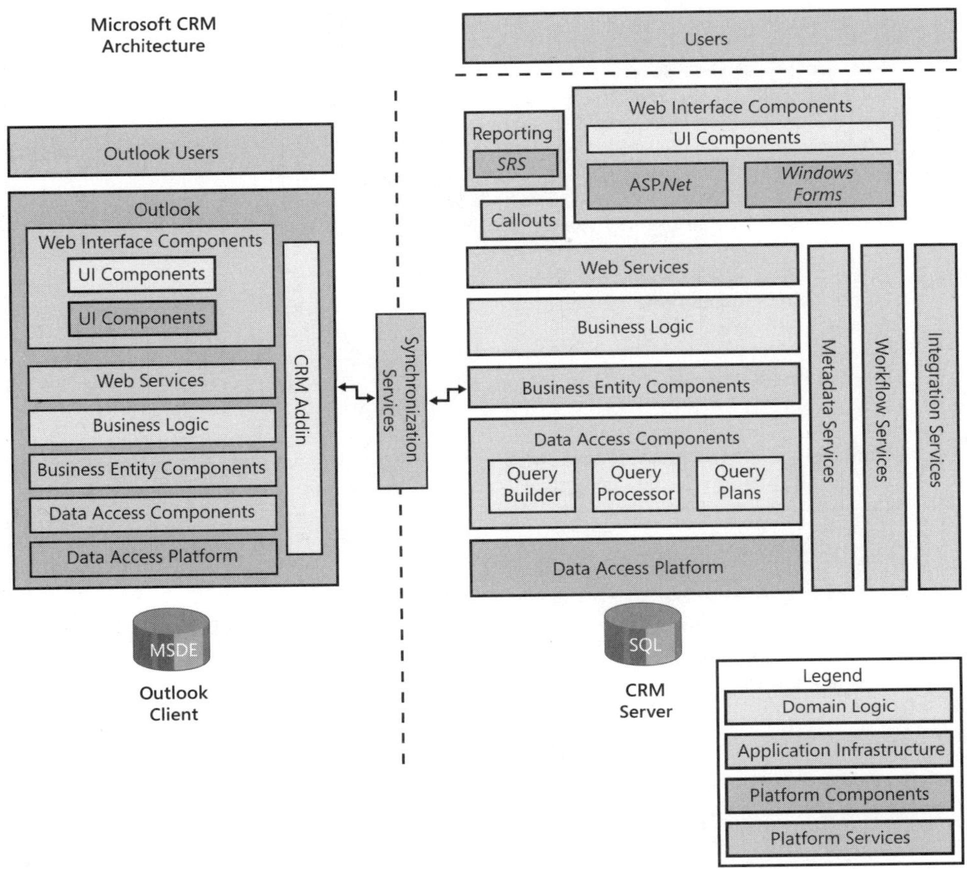

Figure 9-1 Microsoft CRM technical architecture

Comparing the Microsoft CRM 3.0 SDK with the Version 1.2 SDK

Microsoft CRM has always allowed system developers to interact with the software. Although the APIs of Microsoft CRM versions 1.0 and 1.2 were adequate for a wide range of customizations, the Microsoft CRM 3.0 APIs provide even more functionality with a drastically simplified programming model. The Microsoft CRM 3.0 APIs reduce the overall number of methods and offer a strongly typed, WSDL-compliant Web service approach.

More Info The Web Services Description Language (WSDL) is an XML format published for describing Web services. People typically pronounce WSDL as "wiz-dull."

Table 9-1 outlines a few of the key differences between the Microsoft CRM 3.0 SDK and the Microsoft CRM 1.2 SDK.

Table 9-1 SDK Version Differences

Microsoft CRM 3.0 SDK	Microsoft CRM 1.2 SDK
Microsoft .NET Web services with a dynamically generated WSDL	Pre-compiled proxy DLLs and C++ Active Template Library (ATL)–based .srf files
Strongly typed objects and attributes	XML strings used for all entities, parameters, and so on
IntelliSense available within Visual Studio .NET, including custom entities and attributes	No SDK integration with Visual Studio .NET
Unnecessary to pass user authentication for each method call	User authentication is a required parameter for all methods
QueryExpression available as a fast, ad hoc way to retrieve data	Only the string-based FetchXml available
Metadata Web service available for querying details about the data structure	No APIs available to retrieve system metadata

This table clearly illustrates that, in addition to providing a more robust programming interface than Microsoft CRM 1.2, the Microsoft CRM 3.0 SDK also provides several significant improvements designed to increase developer productivity so that customizations are easier to write, test, and deploy.

Microsoft CRM uses a service-oriented approach for its APIs, making use of two WSDL-compliant Web services (CrmService and MetadataService). As you can see from Figure 9-2, Microsoft CRM controls data access for the application interfaces, reports, and extensibility through the use of these two Web services. As you learned in Chapter 7, "Reporting and Analysis," Microsoft CRM also allows for direct and secure retrieval of data from SQL Server through the use of filtered views. Filtered views provide read-only access of data directly to the database layer, but they still honor the security privileges of the calling user.

The shaded, rounded rectangles in Figure 9-2 denote the business logic extension areas available to you.

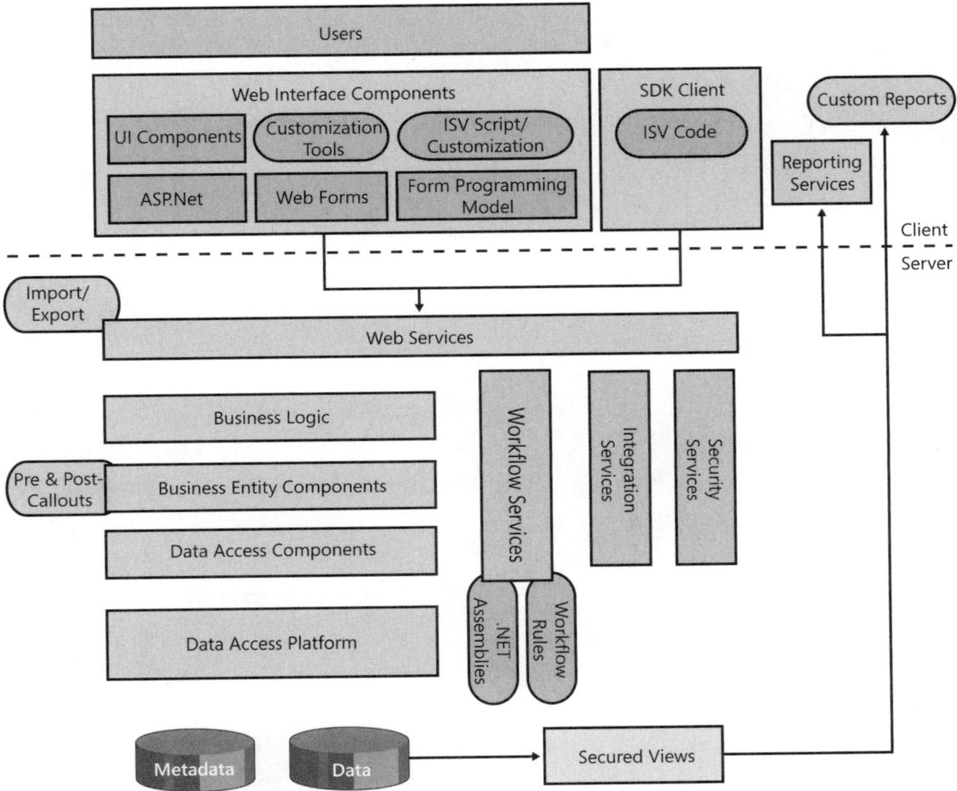

Figure 9-2 Microsoft CRM extensibility architecture

This chapter will focus on the server-side API services and server-based customization points available to you for custom integration and application development in Microsoft CRM.

CrmService Web Service

The CrmService Web service is the core API mechanism for programmatically interacting with all entities within Microsoft CRM. This service contains six common methods that work on all entities, and an *Execute* method that is available for all other needs. The service is strongly typed and WSDL compliant and will also update with any changes to the schema.

Important Microsoft CRM automatically updates its API interfaces as you add custom entities and custom attributes using the Web-based administration tools. Therefore, if you add multiple custom attributes to the Account entity, you will be able to reference these new attributes programmatically through the API and even with IntelliSense updates to reflect these new attributes in Visual Studio .NET.

The CrmService Web service is located at *http://<crmserver>/mscrmservices/2006/crmservice.asmx*.

You must add a Web reference in your Visual Studio project to programmatically access its methods. We recommend using the same naming convention that Microsoft uses for its examples, as you will see in the following procedure.

Adding a CrmService Web reference to your project

1. Open a project in Visual Studio .NET.
2. Right-click the project and then click **Add Web Reference**.
3. In the **Add Web Reference** dialog box, add the CrmService reference:
   a In the **URL** box, type **http://**<crmserver>**/mscrmservices/2006/crmservice.asmx**.
   b In the **Web reference name** box, type **CrmSdk.** (Note that this is case-sensitive.)
   c Click **Add Reference**.

In addition, we recommend instantiating the service *Url* property in your code, as shown below.

```
// Standard CRM Service Setup
CrmService service = new CrmService();
service.Credentials = System.Net.CredentialCache.DefaultCredentials;
service.Url = "http://<crmserver>/mscrmservices/2006/crmservice.asmx";
```

The *Url* property allows you access to the Web service URL that may be different from the URL specified in your project's Web reference. In the "Coding and Testing Tips" section of this chapter, we will explain how to use configuration settings that allow you to set the *Url* property of service, which allows you to deploy to different Microsoft CRM environments without having to recompile your code.

Warning Both the CrmService and MetadataService Web services offer a *PreAuthenticate* property. This property should cache the credentials of the calling user, but the Microsoft sdkreadme.htm document notes that this behavior might cause sporadic HTTP status 401: Unauthorized errors. Therefore, Microsoft recommends avoiding the *PreAuthenticate* property in your code at this time.

When used within the context of Web pages, code executes under the security credentials of the user browsing the Web page. At times, you might want to execute your code using different security credentials than those of the user browsing the Web page. You can change the calling user the service uses by adding the following lines of code after your standard service setup. You would replace the string of zeros (also referred to as an empty GUID) with an actual systemuserid GUID of the user whom you wish to impersonate).

```
service.CallerIdValue = new CallerId();
service.CallerIdValue.CallerGuid = new Guid("00000000-0000-0000-0000-000000000000");
```

> **Note** The calling user will need to be part of the PrivUserGroup in Active Directory. This group is created during the installation of Microsoft CRMMicrosoft CRM will ignore an empty GUID and just use the security credentials of the user browsing the web page. If you specify a GUID that does not exist, no data will return.

Now that you have a little background on the CrmService Web Service, let's review these additional topics related to the CrmService:

- Service naming conventions
- Common methods
- *Execute* methods
- *Request* and *Response* classes
- *DynamicEntity* class
- Attributes

Service Naming Conventions

Microsoft CRM uses a strict naming convention for its classes, and Table 9-2 lists them for you. You can also find this information in the SDK or by using the Visual Studio IntelliSense – another excellent benefit of using a strongly typed service!

Table 9-2 Naming Conventions

Class, type, enumeration	Naming convention	Example
Core *BusinessEntity* names	All lowercase. This is the schema name or logical name in the metadata.	`account myaccount = new account();`
Custom *Business-Entity* names	All lowercase with an underscore after the prefix defined in customization settings.	`new_bankaccount myEntity = new new_bankaccount();`
BusinessEntity attributes	All lowercase. This is the schema name or logical name in the metadata.	`account.name` `new_bankaccount.name`

Message names	Pascal case.	`CreateRequest`
		`CreateResponse`
		`SendEmailRequest`
		`SendEmailResponse`

State enumerations	Pascal case.	`Account.State`
References to entity names in *Fetch* and *QueryExpression*	All lowercase. This is the schema name or _logical name in the metadata.	`QueryExpression accountQE = new QueryExpression ("account");` `"<fetch mapping='logical'> <entity name='account'> <all-attributes/> </entity></fetch>";`

Common Methods

The following six methods provide the basic CRUD (create, read, update, delete) operations for entities, including custom entities:

- ***Create*** Creates a new record for a given entity.
- ***Retrieve*** Returns a single record based on the entity ID passed in.
- ***RetrieveMultiple*** Returns multiple records based on a query expression.
- ***Update*** Edits an existing record.
- ***Delete*** Removes a record.
- ***Fetch*** Returns multiple records based on a FetchXML query. The FetchXML query syntax mirrors that of Microsoft CRM versions 1.x.

Let's consider a simple example to show you how you would use one of the common methods. This example will retrieve the topic, first name, last name, and industry for a single Lead record and then display it on a Web page. We will work with the Lead record shown in Figure 9-3.

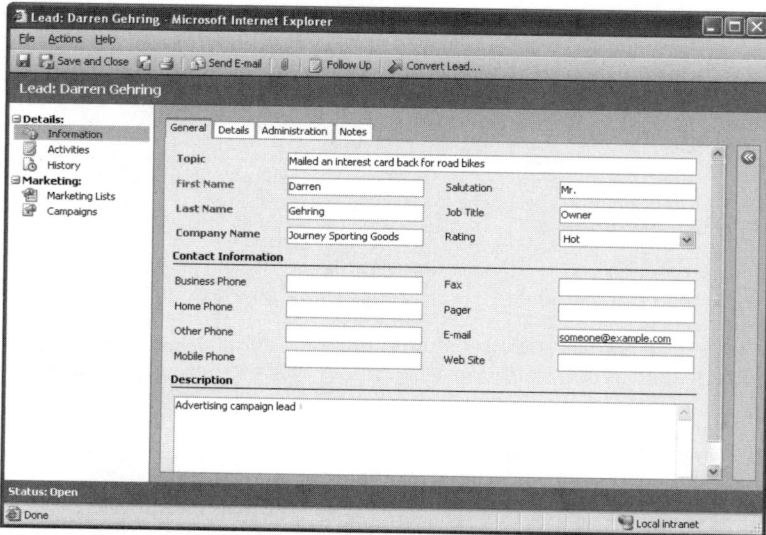

Figure 9-3 Lead form

Since this is our first SDK example, we will walk through the process of creating a basic Web application project in Visual Studio .NET 2003. We will then use and refer to this project for many of our examples in this chapter. You can also find a copy of it with our sample code download.

Creating a Web application project

1. Open Visual Studio .NET 2003.
2. On the **File** menu, navigate to **New**, and select **Project**.

3. Under **Project Types**, select **Visual C# Projects,** and then click **ASP.NET Web Application** under **Templates**.
4. In the **Location** box, enter **http://localhost/WorkingWithCrm** (assuming you have IIS installed on your development computer).
5. Using the procedure in the previous "CrmService Web Service" section, add a Web reference to the CrmService Web service, calling it **CrmSdk**.

Retrieving a Lead record from Microsoft CRM

1. On the **File** menu, select **Add New Item**.
2. In the resulting **Add New Item** dialog window, select **Web Form** and enter **leadretrieve.aspx** in the **Name** box.
3. Replace the default text on the page with the code shown in Listing 9-1.
4. **Save** your **Web form** page.
5. From the **Build** menu, select **Build Solution**.

Listing 9-1 shows the Web page code for retrieving our lead record. If you were to run this sample, you would need to update the namespace of your CrmSdk reference update the path for the *Url* attribute.

Listing 9-1 Retrieving a Lead Record

```
<%@ Page Language="C#" %>
<%@ Import Namespace="WorkingWithCrm.CrmSdk" %>

<!doctype html public "-//w3c//dtd xhtml 1.0 transitional//en"
"http://www.w3.org/tr/xhtml1/dtd/xhtml1-transitional.dtd">

<script runat="server">
 protected void Page_Load(object sender, EventArgs e)
 {
  // Standard CRM Service Setup
  CrmService service = new CrmService();
  service.Credentials = System.Net.CredentialCache.DefaultCredentials;
  service.Url = "http://<crmserver>/mscrmservices/2006/crmservice.asmx";

  // We are using a known lead GUID. In practice, this will be passed in to your routines.
  Guid leadId = new Guid("2EFAB039-2543-428E-95B8-10EA13D58198");

  // Set the columns to return.
  ColumnSet cols = new ColumnSet();
  cols.Attributes = new string [] {"subject", "firstname", "lastname", "industrycode"};

  try
  {
   // Retrieve the record, casting it as the correct entity.
   lead oLead = (lead)service.Retrieve(EntityName.lead.ToString(), leadId, cols);

   // Display the results.
   // Since we have a strongly typed response, we can just access the properties of our object.
   Response.Write("Topic: " + oLead.subject + "<br>");
```

```
    Response.Write("First Name: " + oLead.firstname + "<br>");
    Response.Write("Last Name: " + oLead.lastname + "<br>");
    Response.Write("Industry: " + oLead.industrycode.Value);
   }
   catch (System.Web.Services.Protocols.SoapException ex)
   {
    // Handle error.
   }
  }
</script>

<html>
<head runat="server" id="Head1">
 <title>Retrieve Lead</title>
 <style>body { font-family:Tahoma;font-size:9pt; }</style>
</head>
<body>
 <form id="crmForm" runat="server">
 </form>
</body>
</html>
```

When you add this code to your Web and execute it in Internet Explorer, you might receive the following error.

```
Object reference not set to an instance of an object.
Line: Response.Write(oLead.industrycode.Value);
```

This error occurs because Microsoft CRM does not return an object reference for any attribute that has a value of null. We received this error because our sample Lead does not have an Industry value selected in the picklist; hence, its value is null in the database. Therefore, when your code tries to access the industrycode value property, you get an exception.

Important Microsoft CRM will not return a requested field if it is null in the database.

To account for the possibility that Microsoft CRM might not return a field that your code is expecting, you should ensure that the attribute you want to access is not null. This code snippet shows how to check for null values.

```
Response.Write("Industry: ");
if (oLead.industrycode != null)
      Response.Write(oLead.industrycode.Value);
```

After the code in Listing 9-1 is updated to check for a null value and refreshed, you'll receive the following output:

```
Topic: Mailed an interest card back for road bikes
First Name: Darren
Last Name: Gehring
Industry:
```

The SDK contains many more examples that demonstrate how to use each of these common methods.

Execute Method

The *Execute* method is provided to run any special commands or business logic not available from the common methods. Unlike the common methods, the *Execute* method works on a Request and Response classes. You pass a request class as a parameter to the *Execute* method, which then processes the request and returns a response message. Though the *Execute* method can perform all of the actions of the common methods, its real purpose is to provide the functionality that the common methods lack. Typical actions you might use the *Execute* method for are retrieving the current user, assigning and routing records, and sending e-mails through Microsoft CRM. For instance, the code snippet below shows how to retrieve the current user using the *Execute* method.

```
// Standard CRM Service Setup
CrmService service = new CrmService();
service.Credentials = System.Net.CredentialCache.DefaultCredentials;
service.Url = "http://<crmserver>/mscrmservices/2006/crmservice.asmx";

// Get current user object.
WhoAmIRequest userRequest = new WhoAmIRequest();
WhoAmIResponse user = (WhoAmIResponse) service.Execute(userRequest);
```

Note You must always cast the returning message to the appropriate instance of the *Response* class.

Request and *Response* Classes

Microsoft CRM uses a *Request* and *Response* message class model for the *Execute* method, as shown in Figure 9-4. You must create a *Request* class message, set the properties that you require, and pass the request a target message. You then send the request object to the platform by using the *Execute* method. The platform will run the request and send back an instance of a *Response* class message.

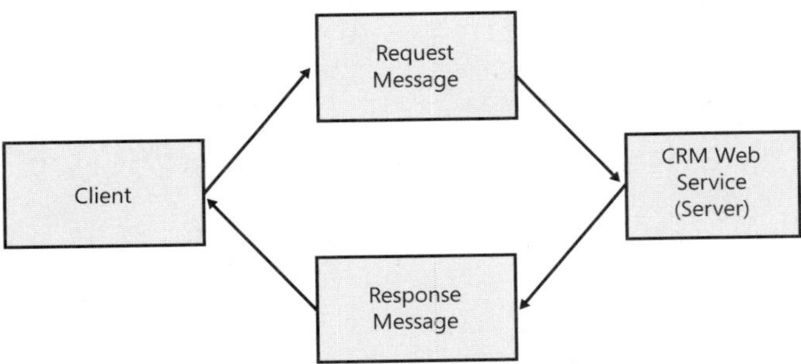

Figure 9-4 Request/Response model for the *Execute* method

Microsoft CRM *Requests* and *Responses* classes support generic, targeted, specialized, and dynamic entity requests. These request classes always end in the word *Request*, such as *WhoAmIRequest*, *CreateRequest*, and *SendEmailRequest*. Generic requests are not dependent on a specific entity and will not contain an entity name in its class name. Generic requests can work across multiple entities (such as the *AssignRequest*) in addition to sometimes working with no entities (such as the *WhoAmIRequest*).

Generic requests that apply to entities require a target message class to specify which entity should receive the action. A target class will begin with the word *Target*, and once instantiated and configured, it will then be applied to the *target* property of a generic class. This code example shows how a *TargetQueuedIncident* could apply to the *RouteRequest* to send a case to a support queue.

```
// Standard CRM Service Setup
CrmService service = new CrmService();
service.Credentials = System.Net.CredentialCache.DefaultCredentials;
service.Url = "http://<crmserver>/mscrmservices/2006/crmservice.asmx";

// Create the Target object (case or incident for this example)
TargetQueuedIncident target = new TargetQueuedIncident();

// EntityId is the Guid of the case record being routed
// We are using a known case GUID. In practice, this will be passed in to your routines.
target.EntityId = new Guid("D5F7CAE8-D51E-40EF-9EFC-592B484BCCFF");

// Request object
RouteRequest route = new RouteRequest();
route.Target = target;
route.RouteType = RouteType.Queue;

// EndPointId is the GUID of a non-work
 in progress queue or user the case is being routed to.
// We are using a known case GUID. In practice, this will be passed in to your routines.
route.EndpointId = new Guid("922F63E8-6585-DA11-8D43-0003FF12CD51");


// SourceQueueId is the Guid of the queue the case is coming from
// We are using a known case GUID. In practice, this will be passed in to your routines.
route.SourceQueueId = new Guid("E8B77049-13C1-41FE-93B0-B3B8031F089C");

try
{
 // Execute the Request
 RouteResponse routed = (RouteResponse)service.Execute(route);
}
catch(System.Web.Services.Protocols.SoapException ex)
{
 // Handle error.
}
```

Specialized requests are similar to targeted requests except that they work only on a specific entity to perform a distinct action. Their naming convention will always be

<Action><EntityName>Request. Good examples of these requests are the *SendEmailRequest* or the *LoseOpportunityRequest*.

The dynamic entity request permits you to use requests at runtime for any entity. By setting the parameter *ReturnDynamicEntities* to True, your results will be returned as a *DynamicEntity* class instead of the *BusinessEntity* class. Not all requests permit the *DynamicEntity* option, and you should refer to the SDK for the complete list. We will go into more detail about the *DynamicEntity* class next.

DynamicEntity Class

The *DynamicEntity* class, derived from the *BusinessEntity* class, provides runtime access to entities and attributes even if those entities and attributes did not exist when you compiled your assembly. The *DynamicEntity* class contains the logical name of the entity and a property-bag array of the system attributes. In programming terms, this can be thought of as using a variant for a variable type. The class allows you to access entities and attributes created in Microsoft CRM, even though you may not have the actual entity definition from the WSDL.

The *DynamicEntity* class must be used with the *Execute* method, and it contains the following properties:

Name Sets the entity schema name

Properties Array of type *Property* (which is a name/value pair)

Let's review the syntax of the *DynamicEntity* class to create a Lead. We will create a string property to store our subject text, which we will pass into the *DynamicEntitydynLead* object. After we create our *DynamicEntity* object and set its name to *lead*, we create the *TargetCreate-Dynamic* class to serve as our target message for the *CreateRequest* call. Note that we must explicitly set the owner for the *DynamicEntity*, because it is not assumed.

```
// Standard CRM Service Setup
CrmService service = new CrmService();
service.Credentials = System.Net.CredentialCache.DefaultCredentials;
service.Url = "http://<crmserver>/mscrmservices/2006/crmservice.asmx";

// Get current user ID.
WhoAmIRequest userRequest = new WhoAmIRequest();
WhoAmIResponse user = (WhoAmIResponse) service.Execute(userRequest);

// Set up dynamic entity.
DynamicEntity dynLead = new DynamicEntity();

// Set entity name and specify array of properties.
dynLead.Name = "lead";
dynLead.Properties = new Property[] {
CreateStringProperty("subject","New Lead Using Dynamic Entities"),
CreateStringProperty("lastname","Steen"),
CreateStringProperty("firstname","Heidi"),
CreateOwnerProperty(user.UserId),
};
```

```
// Standard target request, passing in the dynamic entity.
TargetCreateDynamic target = new TargetCreateDynamic();
target.Entity = dynLead;
CreateRequest create = new CreateRequest();
create.Target = target;
CreateResponse response = (CreateResponse)service.Execute(create);

// Helper method that creates a string property based on passed-in values
private Property CreateStringProperty(string Name, string Value)
{
 StringProperty prop = new StringProperty();
 prop.Name = Name;
 prop.Value = Value;
 return prop;
}

// Helper method that creates an owner property based on a passed-in GUID
private Property CreateOwnerProperty(Guid UserId)
{
 Owner ownerid = new Owner();
 ownerid.Value = UserId;
 ownerid.type = EntityName.systemuser.ToString();;

 OwnerProperty prop = new OwnerProperty();
 prop.Name = "ownerid";
 prop.Value = ownerid;
 return prop;
}
```

Obviously, you would not use the dynamic entity approach to create a Lead record, because it's not as efficient and it requires more code. However, Microsoft CRM provides this class for run-time situations in which you might not know the entity or for when you want to add new attributes to an existing entity. You will see that this class is extremely handy when you want to deserialize unknown XML into an entity class, as we will demonstrate in our Data Auditing example in the "Sample Code" section later in this chapter.

We also want to mention the helper methods, shown in this example, which we use for creating the properties that we want to set. In this particular example, we know that we are working with string and owner properties, but in some scenarios, you might not know the property type. To address this, you must query the metabase and determine the data types of your desired attributes at run time. Microsoft CRM allows you to do this with the MetadataService Web service, as you will see shortly.

Attributes

In earlier versions of Microsoft CRM, you passed all attributes to the API methods as strings. However, Microsoft CRM 3.0 API uses strongly typed classes, so you must create typed attributes when setting values for an entity. The SDK documentation lists examples of each type and how to use them, so we won't list them here. However, you will see examples of this throughout our sample code.

MetadataService Web Service

In addition to the CrmService Web service, the Microsoft CRM API includes a MetadataService Web service that allows you to programmatically access the metadata. With the MetadataService Web service, you can query entities and their attributes. You can also retrieve picklist and status values from the string map table.

The Metadata Web service is located at *http://<crmserver>/mscrmservices/2006/metadataservice.asmx*

As with the CRMService Web service, you will need to add a Web reference in your project to access the methods and properties available.

However, unlike the CRMService Web service, the MetadataService Web service allows for retrieve (read-only) requests only. Therefore, you can use this service to retrieve information, but you cannot manipulate the underlying metadata. You must use the Web-based customization tools to add, modify, or delete the metadata.

Adding a MetadataService Web reference to your project

1. Open the WorkingWithCrm project you created earlier in this chapter in Visual Studio .NET.
2. Right-click the project, and then click **Add Web Reference**.
3. In the **Add Web Reference** dialog box, add the MetadataService reference:
   a. In the **URL** box, type ***http://<crmserver>/mscrmservices/2006/metadataservice.asmx***.
   b. In the **Web reference name** box, type **MetadataServiceSdk**. (Note that this is case-sensitive.)
   c. Click **Add Reference**.

The Metadata Web service offers four key methods:

- ***GetTimeStamp*** Returns the date and time of the last metadata update
- ***RetrieveAttributeMetadata*** Returns all information regarding a specific entity's attribute
- ***RetrieveEntityMetadata*** Returns all information regarding a specific entity
- ***RetrieveMetadata*** Returns all of the metadata

When using the *RetrieveEntityMetadata* and *RetrieveMetadata* methods, you must pass in a flag to tell the platform how much data you would like to return. Microsoft CRM refers to this as *MetadataFlags*, and you can specify one of five values:

- ***All*** Returns all metadata
- ***EntityOnly*** Retrieves metadata referring to the entity only

- ***IncludeAttributes*** Retrieves entity metadata, including attribute information
- ***IncludePrivileges*** Retrieves entity metadata, including the security privileges
- ***IncludeRelationships*** Retrieves entity metadata, including data relationship information

You should choose your flag based on the needs of your application, keeping in mind that Microsoft CRM provides these different options for performance reasons. The more data you request from the metabase, the longer it will take to process and return the results.

Listing 9-2 shows how you would use the Metadata Web service to access information about a picklist attribute. This example also shows some of the information that you can retrieve about this attribute that you can use in your own application.

Listing 9-2 Retrieving Metadata Information

```
<%@ Page Language="C#" %>
<%@ Import Namespace="WorkingWithCrm.MetadataServiceSdk" %>

<script runat="server">
 protected void Page_Load(object sender, EventArgs e)
 {
  MetadataService service = new MetadataService();
  service.Credentials = System.Net.CredentialCache.DefaultCredentials;
  service.Url = "http://<crmserver>/mscrmservices/2006/metadataservice.asmx";

  try
  {
   AttributeMetadata attMetaData = service.RetrieveAttributeMetadata("account",
     "accountcategorycode");
   PicklistAttributeMetadata picklist = (PicklistAttributeMetadata)attMetaData;

  System.Text.StringBuilder results = new System.Text.StringBuilder();

   results.Append(@"<table width=""600"">");
  results.Append(WriteRow("<b>Property</b>","<b>Value</b>"));
  results.Append(WriteRow("DisplayName: ",attMetaData.DisplayName.ToString()));
  results.Append(WriteRow("DefaultValue: ",attMetaData.DefaultValue.ToString()));
  results.Append(WriteRow("DisplayMask: ",attMetaData.DisplayMask.ToString()));
  results.Append(WriteRow("IsCustomField: ",attMetaData.IsCustomField.ToString()));
  results.Append(WriteRow("Name: ",attMetaData.Name.ToString()));
  results.Append(WriteRow("RequiredLevel: ",attMetaData.RequiredLevel.ToString()));
  results.Append(WriteRow("Type: ",attMetaData.Type.ToString()));
  results.Append(WriteRow("ValidForCreate: ",attMetaData.ValidForCreate.ToString()));
  results.Append(WriteRow("ValidForRead: ",attMetaData.ValidForRead.ToString()));
  results.Append(WriteRow("ValidForUpdate: ",attMetaData.ValidForUpdate.ToString()));

  string optionList = string.Empty;
  foreach(Option o in picklist.Options)
  {
   optionList += o.OptionValue.ToString() + "=" + o.Description + "<br>";
  }

  results.Append(WriteRow("Options",optionList));
  results.Append("</table>");
  Response.Write(results.ToString());
 }
```

```
catch (System.Web.Services.Protocols.SoapException ex)
 {
  // Handle error.
 }
}

// Helper method to write out a table row of output
private string WriteRow(string Label, string Value)
{
 return @"<tr style=""font-family:tahoma;font-size:8pt;""><td valign=""top"">"
+ Label + "</td><td>" + Value + "</td></tr>";
}
</script>

<html>
<head runat="server" id="Head1">
 <title>Metadata Attribute</title>
 <style>body { font-family:Tahoma;font-size:9pt; }</style>
</head>
<body>
 <form id="crmForm" runat="server">
 </form>
</body>
</html>
```

Figure 9-5 shows the output if you were to run this Web form page in Visual Studio .NET.

Property	Value
DisplayName:	Category
DefaultValue:	-1
DisplayMask:	ValidForAdvancedFind, ValidForForm, ValidForGrid
IsCustomField:	False
Name:	accountcategorycode
RequiredLevel:	None
Type:	Picklist
ValidForCreate:	True
ValidForRead:	True
ValidForUpdate:	True
Options	1=Preferred Customer 2=Standard

Figure 9-5 Picklist metadata

Again, we won't list all of the properties and methods of the MetaData WebService because of space considerations, but you can use the SDK or the Visual Studio IntelliSense feature to discover all of its available properties and methods.

Queries

With any custom code that you create, of course you'll need to programmatically query data from Microsoft CRM. Microsoft CRM offers three data retrieval mechanisms: *QueryExpression*, FetchXML, and filtered views.

QueryExpression Class

Microsoft CRM provides a powerful, typed *QueryExpression* class. You initialize *QueryExpression* like all other classes.

```
QueryExpression query = new QueryExpression();
```

You then set the entity that you want to query plus any other query parameters required for your search. Table 9-3 lists the main fields (each with their own properties) that are available with this class. For more details on the *QueryExpression* fields, consult the SDK.

Table 9-3 *QueryExpression* Fields

Field	Description
ColumnSet	Property that contains an array of columns to return. Use *AllColumns()* to return all possible fields for an entity. If left null, only the primary key is returned.
Criteria	Contains the filters of your query.
Distinct	Determines whether duplicate records should be returned.
EntityName	Sets the name of the entity to search.
LinkEntities	Joins an entity to other entities.
Orders	Specifies the order of the results.
PageInfo	Sets the number of pages and number of records per page for the result set.

We will now create a sample query that you can execute against the sample database. This query starts by retrieving all Leads created this week. The results should be identical to the Leads Opened This Week view on the Leads grid. We have sorted this grid by the Name (*fullname*) column, as shown in Figure 9-6.

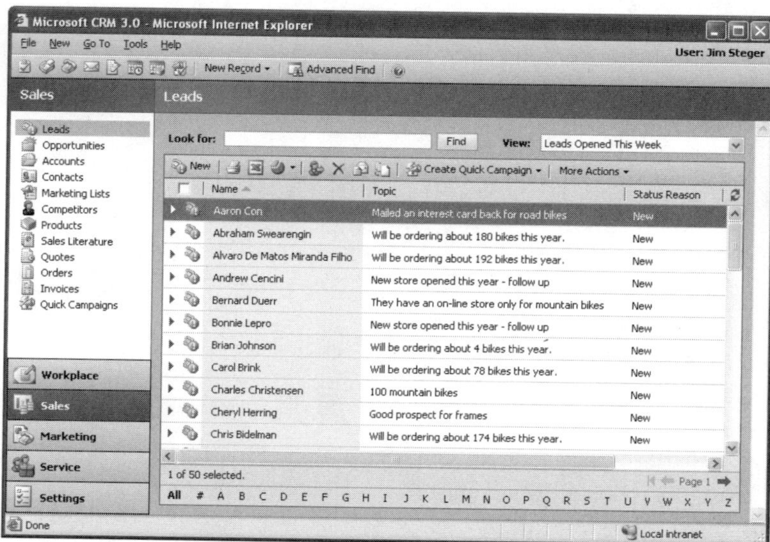

Figure 9-6 Leads Opened This Week

```
// Standard CRM Service Setup
CrmService service = new CrmService();
service.Credentials = System.Net.CredentialCache.DefaultCredentials;
service.Url = "http://<crmserver>/mscrmservices/2006/crmservice.asmx";

try
{
 QueryExpression query = new QueryExpression();

 // Set the query to retrieve Lead records.
 query.EntityName = EntityName.lead.ToString();

 // Create a set of columns to return.
 ColumnSet cols = new ColumnSet();
 cols.Attributes = new string [] {"subject", "fullname", "createdon"};

 // Create the ConditionExpression.
 ConditionExpression condition = new ConditionExpression();
 condition.AttributeName = "createdon";
 condition.Operator = ConditionOperator.ThisWeek;

 // Builds the filter based on the condition
 FilterExpression filter = new FilterExpression();
 filter.FilterOperator = LogicalOperator.And;
 filter.Conditions = new ConditionExpression[] {condition};

 OrderExpression order = new OrderExpression();
 order.OrderType = OrderType.Ascending;
 order.AttributeName = "fullname";

 query.ColumnSet = cols;
 query.Criteria = filter;
 query.Orders = new OrderExpression[] {order};

 // Retrieve the values from Microsoft CRM.
 BusinessEntityCollection retrieved = service.RetrieveMultiple(query);

 Response.Write("<table>");
 for( int i=0; i<retrieved.BusinessEntities.Length; i++)
 {
  lead leadResult = (lead)retrieved.BusinessEntities[i];

  Response.Write("<tr>");
  Response.Write("<td style=\"font-family:tahoma;font-
size:8pt;\">" + leadResult.fullname.ToString() + "</td>");
  Response.Write("<td style=\"font-family:tahoma;font-
size:8pt;\">" + leadResult.subject.ToString() + "</td>");
  Response.Write("<td style=\"font-family:tahoma;font-
size:8pt;\">" + leadResult.createdon.date.ToString() + "</td>");
  Response.Write("</tr>");
 }
 Response.Write("</table>");
}
catch (System.Web.Services.Protocols.SoapException ex)
{
 // Handle error.
}
```

If you parsed the results in a Web page (shown in Figure 9-7), you would see the same data returned by the grid view.

Aaron Con	Mailed an interest card back for road bikes	12/11/2005
Abraham Swearengin	Will be ordering about 180 bikes this year.	12/11/2005
Adrian Dumitrascu	May order 75 Road bikes this year.	12/11/2005
Alan Brewer	Contact in 30 days	12/11/2005
Alvaro De Matos Miranda Filho	Will be ordering about 192 bikes this year.	12/11/2005
Alvin Torre	32 bikes of all types.	12/11/2005
Andrew Cencini	New store opened this year - follow up	12/11/2005
Barry Johnson	10 mountain bikes	12/11/2005
Bernard Duerr	They have an on-line store only for mountain bikes	12/11/2005
Bonnie Lepro	New store opened this year - follow up	12/11/2005
Brannon Jones	Very likely will order 18 Road bikes	12/11/2005
Brian Johnson	Will be ordering about 4 bikes this year.	12/11/2005
Carol Brink	Will be ordering about 78 bikes this year.	12/11/2005
Caroline Vicknair	Mountain bikes and road bikes; maybe clothing.	12/11/2005
Charles Christensen	100 mountain bikes	12/11/2005
Cheryl Herring	Good prospect for frames	12/11/2005
Chris Bidelman	Will be ordering about 174 bikes this year.	12/11/2005
Cindy Dodd	4 touring bikes.	12/11/2005
Connie Coffman	31 less expensive road bikes	12/11/2005
Daniel Thompson	Mailed an interest card back for road bikes	12/11/2005
Darren Gehring	Mailed an interest card back for road bikes	12/11/2005
David Hodgson	Mailed an interest card back for road bikes	12/11/2005
David Johnson	Will be ordering about 34 bikes this year.	12/11/2005
Deanna Meyer	50 mountain bikes	12/11/2005
Donald Thompson	Will be ordering about 10 bikes this year.	12/11/2005
Doris Traube	Good prospect for frames	12/11/2005

Figure 9-7 Leads returned from *QueryExpression*

> **Tip** You could also perform simple queries with the *QueryByAttribute* class. See the SDK for sample code.

FetchXML

If you used the Microsoft CRM 1.x SDK, you're probably familiar with FetchXML. Using the FetchXML syntax, you can create a string containing your query statement. You then pass that string using the common method *Fetch*.

We generally recommend that you use *QueryExpression* over FetchXML for better performance, in addition to the fact that the *QueryExpression* results will be strongly typed. However, the FetchXML option still exists to ease the upgrade path for users of earlier versions of Microsoft CRM.

The following code snippet shows an example of a FetchXML call that uses the *Fetch* method.

```
CrmService service = new CrmService();
service.Credentials = System.Net.CredentialCache.DefaultCredentials;
service.Url = "http://<crmserver>/mscrmservices/2006/crmservice.asmx";

// Retrieve the full name of any contact whose first name equals "Alan".
string fetch = @"
 <fetch mapping=""logical"">
```

```
  <entity name=""contact"">
   <attribute name=""fullname""/>
    <filter>
     <condition attribute=""firstname"" operator=""eq"" value=""Alan""/>
    </filter>
  </entity>
 </fetch>";

try
{
 // Retrieve the results.
 string result = service.Fetch(fetch);
}
catch (System.Web.Services.Protocols.SoapException ex)
{
 // Handle error.
}
```

The resulting string of this query when run against the Microsoft CRM sample database would be the similar to the following:

```
<resultset morerecords='0' paging-cookie='$1$$contact$contactid$1$0$38${688676F1-19D7-46BB-
96AB-5D764BE0180B}$!$contact$contactid$1$0$38${AAE5EADD-A358-470C-9E6B-7E4FFDF773E1}$'>
<result><fullname>Alan Waxman</fullname></result><result><fullname>Alan Brewer</fullname>
</result></resultset>
```

Filtered Views

In addition to *QueryExpression* and FetchXML, you can also use SQL filtered views to retrieve data from Microsoft CRM. We introduced filtered views in Chapter 7, "Reporting and Analysis," so we won't review them in detail again. In the context of creating custom code that reads data from Microsoft CRM, you can connect to the filtered view tables in SQL Server directly instead of using the API.

Important Accessing data in filtered views is the only case in which your code should ever connect directly to SQL Server. For all other calls, you should use the methods provided in the Microsoft CRM API.

Remember that you must connect to SQL Server by using Windows authentication, not SQL Server authentication, because the views join the systemuser base table based on the domain credentials of the calling user. This requirement prevents you from using a filtered view from a callout or workflow assembly, because the calling context will be the server's system account. Therefore, for those types of assemblies, you should use *QueryExpression* or FetchXML to retrieve the data that you require.

Callouts

Callouts, also referred to as Business Logic Extensions in the SDK, provide a synchronous mechanism to run custom logic or spawn custom processes both before and after Microsoft CRM executes a request against the platform layer. Figure 9-8 shows the callout integration approach.

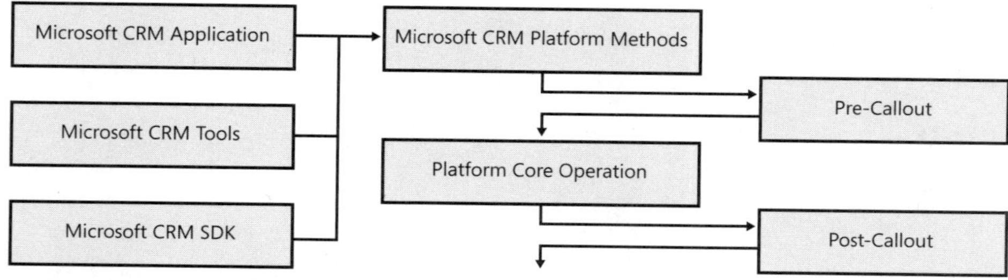

Figure 9-8 Callout architecture

Microsoft CRM 3.0 supports both pre-callouts (events that fire before an action is taken against the platform) *and* post-callouts. Further, the Microsoft CRM 3.0 callout architecture is fully .NET-compliant, which means it uses a simple configuration file registration to solve the COM+ installation woes.

> **Tip** When developing integration to and from other applications, you will typically make heavy use of the Microsoft CRM pre- and post-callout model.

Available Events

As users work within the application, their actions cause Microsoft CRM to trigger callout assemblies. Table 9-4 lists the events available for both pre- and post-calls.

Table 9-4 Pre- and Post-Callout Events

Event	Event names	Description
Create	*PreCreate PostCreate*	Fired when a new record is created
Update	*PreUpdate PostUpdate*	Fired when an existing record is modified
Delete	*PreDelete PostDelete*	Fired when a record is deleted
Assign	*PreAssign PostAssign*	Fired when a record is assigned to a new owner
Set state	*PreSetState PostSetState*	Fired when a record's state value is changed
Merge	*PreMerge PostMerge*	Fired when the merge command is executed against two records

Configuration File

The callout configuration file defines the callout events and registers custom assemblies against those events. The configuration file must be named Callout.config.xml and deployed to the assembly directory located on the Web server <*crm install drive*>\Program Files\Microsoft CRM\server\bin\assembly by default. An example configuration file does not exist on the Web server, but examples do exist with the sample code of the SDK.

> **Tip** Add the configuration file to your project to keep it under version control so that multiple developers can easily access it.

We will now discuss the key elements that the configuration file contains. The main node is the <*callout*> node, which takes an entity and an event as attributes. The entity will be the entity schema name, and the event will be one of the twelve events listed in Table 9-4. The following is an example of registering a post-callout routine to fire when a user modifies an Account record.

```
<callout entity="account" event="PostUpdate">
```

The <*callout*> node has a child node called <*subscription*>. Subscriptions define the assembly, class, and parameters of your event. The assembly and class attributes do just as you would expect. A sample callout subscription is shown here.

```
<callout.config version="2.0">
 <callout entity="account" event="PostUpdate">
 <subscription assembly="CalloutAssembly.dll"
 class="MyCallouts.PostUpdateAccount">
  <prevalue>name</prevalue>
  <postvalue>name</postvalue>
 </subscription>
 </callout>
</callout.config>
```

The <*prevalue*> and <*postvalue*> child nodes denote which entity schema attribute values Microsoft CRM should pass in to the callout assembly. In the preceding sample, the *PostUpdate* event will send the Account's original *name* value (prevalue) as well as the submitted value (postvalue). These prevalue and postvalue nodes are optional, but if you do not include them, Microsoft CRM will not pass any values to your callout method. Again, Microsoft CRM will pass only non-null values into your callout code, so make sure that your code won't error if it doesn't receive a data value that it expects.

> **Note** Microsoft CRM will ignore the <*prevalue*> and <*postvalue*> nodes depending on the event. For instance, the <*postvalue*> node is ignored for the pre-callout events.

Lastly, do not include nodes that you do not need in your assemblies. You will just hinder performance by sending a larger XML stream than required, and you will also put more processing on your methods, as you will have to filter through the extraneous elements.

> **Tip** If necessary, you can pass all the fields using the keyword *@all*, as in *<prevalue>@all </prevalue>* or *<postvalue>@all</postvalue>*. Remember that Microsoft CRM returns only non-null values to the callout, even if you use the *@all* setting.

The SDK contains additional examples of the callout assemblies and configuration files.

Development

When you develop a callout assembly, you must add a reference to Microsoft.Crm.Platform .Callout.Base.dll in your project file. This file is located on the Microsoft CRM server CD (Disk 1) at <*server CD*>\GAC\Microsoft.Crm.Platform.Callout.Base.dll. Copy this file to a directory on your development client, and add a reference to it in Visual Studio .NET. As always, update the Url parameter with your Microsoft CRM server. Also update the default record GUIDs per the comments in the code.

After you reference the Callout.Base.dll file in your project, you can build a custom callout assembly. Simply create a standard class library and add a class file. Your class file must inherit from *CrmCalloutBase*, as the following snippet shows.

```
using Microsoft.Crm.Callout;

namespace MyCompany.Callout
{
 public class CalloutExample : CrmCalloutBase
 {
 }
}
```

> **Important** You should not reference any of the Microsoft CRM .dll files other than Microsoft.Crm.Platform.Callout.Base.dll in your projects.

Deployment

Because of its .NET architecture, deploying your custom Microsoft CRM 3.0 callout requires minimal effort. You simply copy your assemblies and the callout configuration file to the Microsoft CRM Web server in the following directory: <*crm install drive*>\Program Files\Microsoft CRM\server\bin\assembly.

After you put the files in this folder, you must restart Internet Information Services (IIS), which you can do with an *iisreset* of the Microsoft CRM Web server. If you already have a callout installed and you try to update the folder, you might get the error shown in Figure 9-9, because IIS already has an instance of the .dll file in memory.

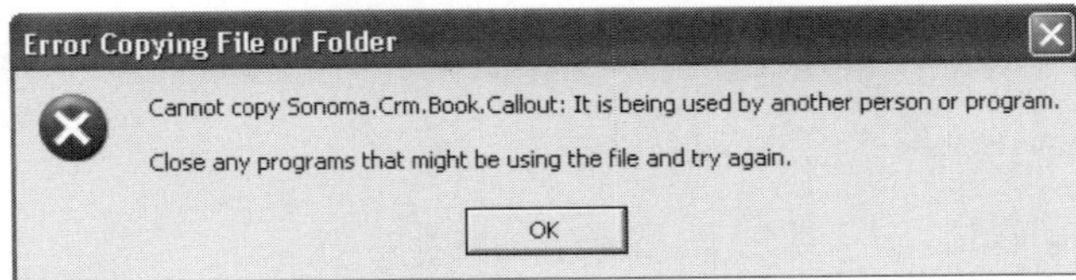

Figure 9-9 Error deploying a callout

To avoid this problem, perform an *iisreset* before copying the assembly files. Remember that you should try to deploy only when users are not accessing Microsoft CRM, because running the *iisreset* command restarts the Web server.

> **Note** You do not have to deploy Microsoft.Crm.Platform.Callout.Base.dll. Microsoft CRM automatically installs this file to the global assembly cache (GAC) of the Web server during the installation process, which makes it available to your assemblies.

We will demonstrate coding examples of the callout at the end of the chapter.

Workflow Plug-in Assemblies

As you learned in Chapter 8, the Microsoft CRM workflow module allows you to create powerful business rules that help automate your sales, marketing, and customer service processes. In addition to the default workflow actions, you can also reference custom assemblies directly within a workflow rule. This feature drastically opens a wide array of extensibility possibilities.

Plug-in assemblies can accept values from a workflow rule and then return values back to the workflow logic to be used in other actions, or they can execute actions on their own. You define the workflow assemblies with a configuration file that the Workflow Manager uses to display the appropriate helper screens to the user.

Custom Assembly Development

Like you did with the callout, you will create a class library for your custom workflow assembly. However, unlike with the callout, you do not have to inherit from a specific base class. You simply create a class and add the methods that you need. The signature of the method should match the parameters that you set in your configuration file. Also, any method that you want to access from the workflow must be declared as public.

```
using System;
using System.Reflection;
using System.Runtime.CompilerServices;

namespace WorkingWithCrm.Workflow
{
 public class CustomAssembly
```

```
    {
      public string GetFullName(string FirstName, string LastName)
      {
        return FirstName + " " + LastName;
      }
    }
  }
```

Configuration File

Upon installation, Microsoft CRM creates a workflow configuration file (Workflow.config) in the <*crm install drive*>\Program Files\Microsoft CRM\server\bin\assembly directory.

Microsoft CRM includes three workflow plug-in assemblies (one of which isn't visible in the Workflow Manager), and you should not remove these assemblies. A default Workflow.config file is also installed. We recommend that when you develop a new workflow plug-in assembly, you should just add your customizations into the existing Workflow.config file and leave the default workflow assemblies alone.

The default Workflow.config file looks like Figure 9-10.

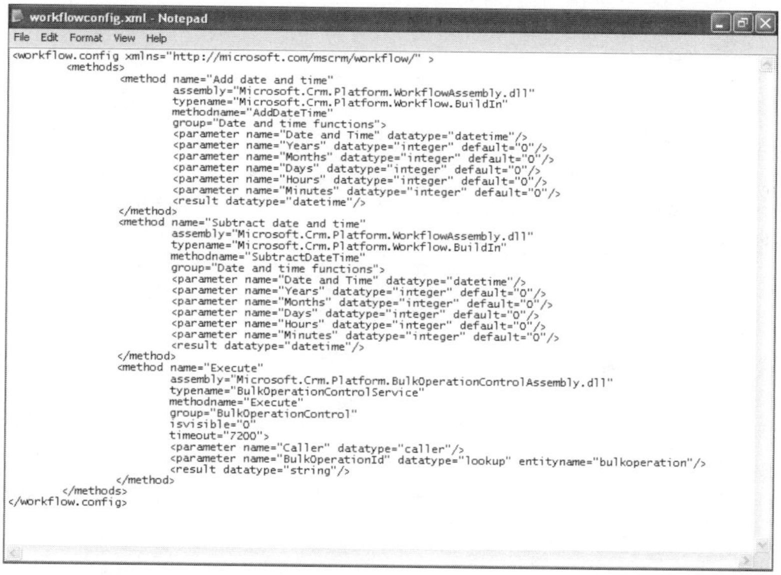

```
workflowconfig.xml - Notepad
File Edit Format View Help
<workflow.config xmlns="http://microsoft.com/mscrm/workflow/" >
        <methods>
                <method name="Add date and time"
                        assembly="Microsoft.Crm.Platform.WorkflowAssembly.dll"
                        typename="Microsoft.Crm.Platform.Workflow.BuildIn"
                        methodname="AddDateTime"
                        group="Date and time functions">
                        <parameter name="Date and Time" datatype="datetime"/>
                        <parameter name="Years" datatype="integer" default="0"/>
                        <parameter name="Months" datatype="integer" default="0"/>
                        <parameter name="Days" datatype="integer" default="0"/>
                        <parameter name="Hours" datatype="integer" default="0"/>
                        <parameter name="Minutes" datatype="integer" default="0"/>
                        <result datatype="datetime"/>
                </method>
                <method name="Subtract date and time"
                        assembly="Microsoft.Crm.Platform.WorkflowAssembly.dll"
                        typename="Microsoft.Crm.Platform.Workflow.BuildIn"
                        methodname="SubtractDateTime"
                        group="Date and time functions">
                        <parameter name="Date and Time" datatype="datetime"/>
                        <parameter name="Years" datatype="integer" default="0"/>
                        <parameter name="Months" datatype="integer" default="0"/>
                        <parameter name="Days" datatype="integer" default="0"/>
                        <parameter name="Hours" datatype="integer" default="0"/>
                        <parameter name="Minutes" datatype="integer" default="0"/>
                        <result datatype="datetime"/>
                </method>
                <method name="Execute"
                        assembly="Microsoft.Crm.Platform.BulkOperationControlAssembly.dll"
                        typename="BulkOperationControlService"
                        methodname="Execute"
                        group="BulkOperationControl"
                        isvisible="0"
                        timeout="7200">
                        <parameter name="Caller" datatype="caller"/>
                        <parameter name="BulkOperationId" datatype="lookup" entityname="bulkoperation"/>
                        <result datatype="string"/>
                </method>
        </methods>
</workflow.config>
```

Figure 9-10 Default Workflow.config file

As you can see, you have multiple parameter and configuration options available within this file. Some of the key concepts related to configuring the workflow file include:

- Use the *Group* attribute to create submenus in the Workflow Manager. You can then neatly categorize your custom assembly functions.
- You can pass in parameters to your methods by using the <*parameter* /> element. The Workflow Manager will allow you to select values based on the *datatype* attribute.

- You may also optionally return values from your methods back to the workflow rule.
- Use the *allowunsignedassemblies* attribute if you want to deploy a .dll file that is not digitally signed, as shown here.

```
<workflow.config xmlns="http://microsoft.com/mscrm/workflow/
" allowunsignedassemblies="true">
```

- Be sure to review the configuration schema located in the SDK. This schema is used by the workflow engine to validate your configuration file. If you are unsure of a location of an attribute or element, review this schema for the actual definition.

Deploying the Assembly

You deploy your custom workflow assembly just as you would a callout assembly. The workflow engine runs from a service on the Microsoft CRM Web server, so you must shut off the service named Microsoft CRM Workflow Service. You can then copy the assemblies and workflow configuration file to the Microsoft CRM Web server in the <*crm install drive*>\Program Files\Microsoft CRM\server\bin\assembly directory.

Deploying a workflow plug-in assembly

1. On the Microsoft CRM Web server, click **Start**, click **Run**, type **cmd** in the **Open** box, and click **OK**.
2. At the command prompt, run the following commands, pressing **Enter** after each command:
   a. net stop mscrmworkflowservice
   b. iisreset
3. Copy assembly and configuration files.
4. Back at the command prompt, run **net start mscrmworkflowservice** and press **Enter**.

Digitally Signing Your Assembly

We mentioned the concept of digitally signing an assembly when we discussed the configuration file. Digital signing creates a strong name for your assembly and will further strengthen its identity to the server. Microsoft CRM Workflow Manager assumes that assemblies will be signed unless you specify otherwise by setting the *allowunsigned-assemblies* attribute to True. If you don't set this attribute to True in the Workflow.config file and you deploy an unsigned assembly, the Microsoft CRM workflow service will generate an error and will not process the request.

Review the Building Secure Assemblies section on MSDN for more information about digitally signing assemblies: *http://msdn.microsoft.com/library/default.asp?url=/library/en-us/secmod/html/secmod80.asp*

Creating a Workflow Assembly

Now that you know how to create, deploy, and configure a custom assembly in workflow, let's review a real-world example of using an assembly in workflow. Assume that your company uses a support queue that receives e-mail messages sent to support@example.com, and you configured Microsoft CRM to create E-mail activities for this queue. You want to automatically create a Case for every e-mail message sent to the support@example.com queue address, and using a workflow assembly is a great method to accomplish this.

Conceptually, we'll create a workflow rule for the Activity entity based on the create event. However, we can't use the native Microsoft CRM workflow actions to create a new Case. Therefore, we'll use our custom assembly to create the new Case record for us. We don't want a new Case record for every Activity created in Microsoft CRM; we just want a new Case for e-mails sent to the support queue address.

The sample will cover the following steps:

- Creating a custom workflow assembly
- Updating the Workflow.config file
- Deploying the files to the server
- Creating and configuring the workflow rule

Creating a Custom Workflow Assembly

First, we will create a custom workflow plug-in assembly that contains a method called *CreateCaseFromEmail*. The *CreateCaseFromEmail* method will accept an activity ID, a subject, an e-mail address, and a description.

Building a workflow assembly project

1. Create a new **C# Class Library** project in Visual Studio .NET 2003 called **WorkingWithCrm.Workflow**.
2. Add a new **Class** file called **Incident**.
3. Be sure check for the System.Web.Services reference. If it doesn't exist, add a reference to the System.Web.Services namespace.
4. Add a **Web Reference** to the **CrmService** Web service, calling it **CrmSdk**.
5. Enter the code shown in Listing 9-3.

Listing 9-3 Incident Workflow Class

```
using System;
using System.Reflection;
using System.Runtime.CompilerServices;
using WorkingWithCrm.Workflow.CrmSdk;
```

```
namespace WorkingWithCrm.Workflow
{
 public class Incident
 {
  public Incident() {}

  public void CreateCaseFromEmail( Guid ActivityId, string Subject, string EmailAddress, str
ing Description )
  {
   // Set these default values in a configuration file.
   // defaultContactId will be the default customer for the case, if the e-mail
is not matched in the system.
   Guid defaultContactId = new Guid("4517E3AC-EE78-DA11-9375-0003FF12CD51");

   // defaultOwnerId will be used as the owner of the case.
   Guid defaultOwnerId = new Guid("7CC5B172-5659-DA11-8FFF-0003FF12CD51");

   // serviceUserId is a user that at least has the following privileges:
   // case: organization create & read; activity: organization write & read
   Guid serviceUserId = new Guid("7CC5B172-5659-DA11-8FFF-0003FF12CD51");

   CrmService service = new CrmService();
   service.Credentials = System.Net.CredentialCache.DefaultCredentials;
   service.Url = "http://<crmserver>/mscrmservices/2006/crmservice.asmx";

   service.CallerIdValue = new CallerId();
   service.CallerIdValue.CallerGuid = serviceUserId;

   // Attempt to retrieve a contact record from the e-mail
address, using the QueryByAttribute class.
   ColumnSet cols = new ColumnSet();
   cols.Attributes = new string [] {"contactid"};

   QueryByAttribute query = new QueryByAttribute();
   query.ColumnSet = cols;
   query.EntityName = EntityName.contact.ToString();

   // The query will retrieve all contacts who match this e-mail address.
   query.Attributes = new string [] {"emailaddress1"};
   query.Values = new string [] {EmailAddress};

   // Execute the retrieval.
   BusinessEntityCollection retrieved = service.RetrieveMultiple(query);

   // If we find a match, use the first one we find. Otherwise, leave the default.
   Guid contactId = defaultContactId;
   if (retrieved.BusinessEntities.Length > 0)
   {
    contact oContact = new contact();
    oContact = (contact)retrieved.BusinessEntities[0];
    contactId = oContact.contactid.Value;
   }

   incident oIncident = new incident();
   oIncident.title = Subject;
   oIncident.description = Description;
```

```
    Customer customerId = new Customer();
    customerId.Value = contactId;
    customerId.type = EntityName.contact.ToString();
    oIncident.customerid = customerId;


    // Set the owner to be the passed-in queue.
    oIncident.ownerid = new Owner();
    oIncident.ownerid.Value = defaultOwnerId;
    oIncident.ownerid.type = EntityName.systemuser.ToString();

    try
    {
     // Create the case.
     Guid incidentId = service.Create(oIncident);

     // Set the regarding value of the E-mail activity to our new incident ID.
     email oEmail = new email();

     Lookup regarding = new Lookup();
     regarding.Value = incidentId;
     regarding.type = EntityName.incident.ToString();
     oEmail.regardingobjectid = regarding;

     oEmail.activityid = new Key();
     oEmail.activityid.Value = ActivityId;

     service.Update(oEmail);
    }
    catch (System.Web.Services.Protocols.SoapException ex)
    {
     // Handle error.
    }
   }
  }
 }
```

Updating the Workflow.config File

Now we need to add a new method to the Workflow.config file to register our new assembly method. To better organize our assemblies in the Workflow Manager, we will add a value to the *group* attribute and name it Custom Assemblies. The *isvisible* and *timeout* attributes are optional, but we will go ahead and explicitly specify values for them. We will also configure the Workflow.config file to allow this unsigned assembly to execute by setting the *allowunsignedassemblies* attribute to True on the Workflow.config node.

To edit the Workflow.config file, we recommend that you copy it into your project file so that you can edit it without overwriting the existing values. Make the following additions to the file:

```
<workflow.config xmlns="http://microsoft.com/mscrm/workflow/"
allowunsignedassemblies="true">
 <methods>
   <method name="Create Case From Email"
    assembly="Sonoma.Crm.Book.Workflow.dll"
```

```
    typename="Sonoma.Crm.Book.Workflow.Incident"
    methodname="CreateCaseFromEmail"
    group="Custom Assemblies"
    isvisible="1"
    timeout="7200">
    <parameter name="ActivityId" datatype="lookup" entityname="email" />
      <parameter name="Subject" datatype="string" />
      <parameter name="EmailAddress" datatype="string" />
      <parameter name="Description" datatype="string" />
    </method>

 ...existing method nodes...

 </methods>
</workflow.config>
```

Deploying the Files to the Server

Now that you have the assembly file built and the configuration file updated, you must deploy them to your Web server. Perform the following steps on the Web server:

1. Log on to the Microsoft CRM Web server. Click **Start**, click **Run**, type **cmd**, and then press Enter.
2. At the command prompt, type **net stop mscrmworkflowservice**, and then press Enter.
3. At the command prompt, type **iisreset**, and then press Enter.
4. Copy the .dll file and Workflow.config file to *<crm install drive>*\Program Files\Microsoft CRM\server\bin\assembly.
5. At the command prompt, type **net start mscrmworkflowservice**, and then press Enter.

Creating and Configuring the Workflow Rule

Now that we've deployed our workflow assembly, we will create a workflow rule that takes advantage of the assembly's functionality. After you have deployed your assembly and restarted the workflow service, log on to the Microsoft CRM Web server and launch the Workflow Manager.

1. To open the Workflow Manager, click **Start**, point to **All Programs**, point to **Microsoft CRM**, and then click **Workflow Manager**.
2. Select **E-mail** as the entity type and create a new rule for the *Create* event, calling it **Create Case**.
3. We will create a conditional that will first check to see if the To address is Support Queue. Click **Insert Condition**, and then click **<<Check conditions>>**. Click **Insert Condition**, and then select **Check Entity Condition**.
4. In the **Check Entity Condition** dialog box, leave **E-mail** selected as the entity. For the field, select **To**, then **contain**, and then click the ellipsis button (. . .).

5. In the **Select Value** dialog box, choose **Static Value**. Click the lookup button and choose **Queue** for the type. Then change the destination of the queue you set up to receive the incoming e-mails from **Available** to **Selected**. Our example uses **Support Queue.** Click **OK** three times.

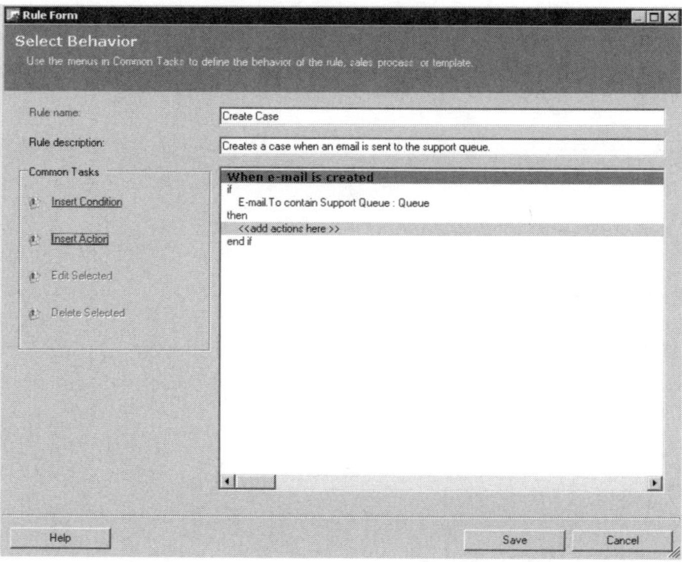

6. Now create a new action that will call our custom assembly. Click **<<add actions here>>**. Then click **Insert Action**, point to **Call assembly**, point to **Custom Assemblies**, and then click **Create Case From Email**.

7. The following dialog box appears. In the **Action Name** box, type **Create Case**.

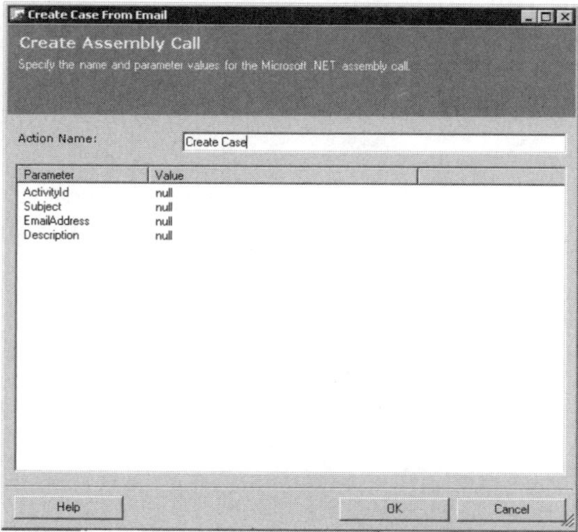

8. Double-click **ActivityId** and select **Dynamic Value**. Click **OK**.
9. Double-click **Subject** and select **Dynamic Value**. Leave **Email** for the entity, and choose **Subject** in the **Field** box. Click **OK**.
10. Double-click **EmailAddress** and select **Dynamic Value**. Leave **Email** for the entity, and choose **Sender** in the **Field** box. Click **OK**.
11. Double-click **Description** and select **Dynamic Value**. Leave **Email** for the entity, and choose **Description** in the **Field** box. Click **OK**.

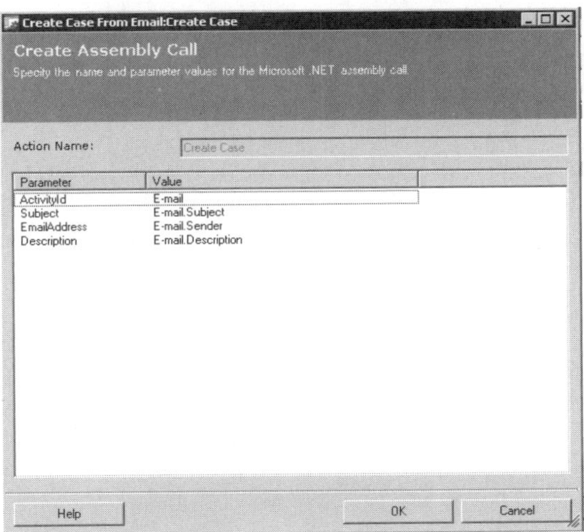

12. Click **OK**, and then click **Save**.

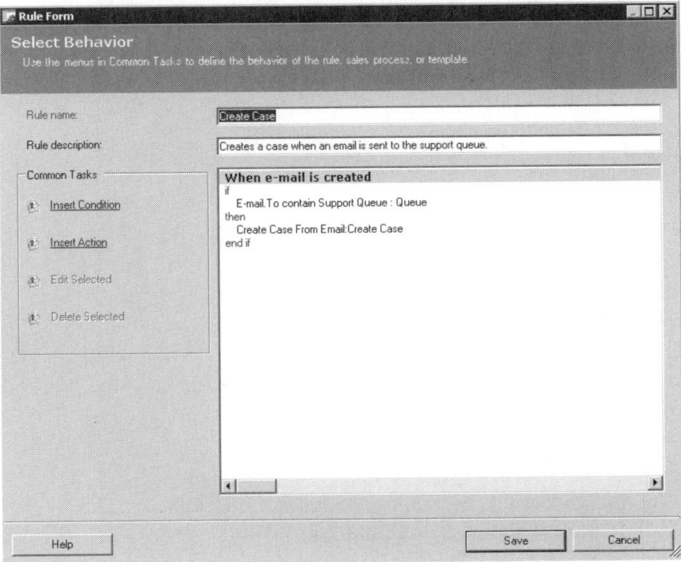

13. Activate your new workflow rule.

Now send an e-mail message to your support queue. Microsoft CRM triggers the workflow rule when the E-mail activity is created in Microsoft CRM. The rule will run and create our case for us, as shown in Figure 9-11.

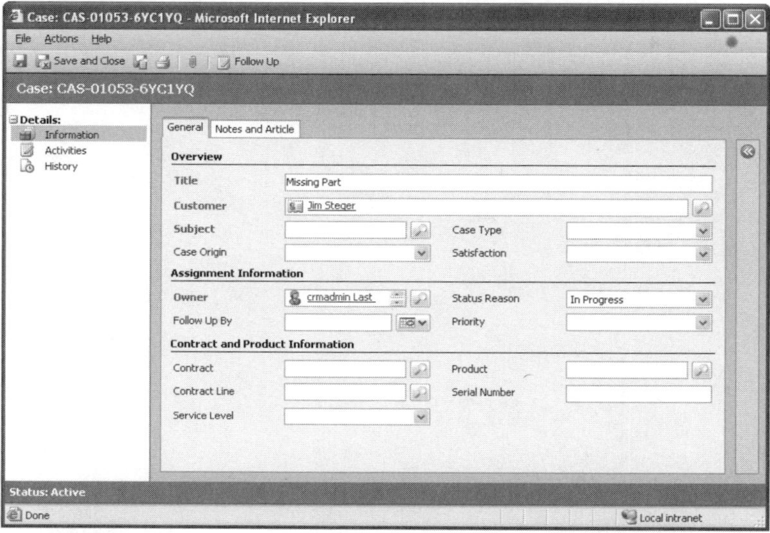

Figure 9-11 New Case record created from support e-mail message

Figure 9-12 shows that our e-mail activity is also properly associated with the case!

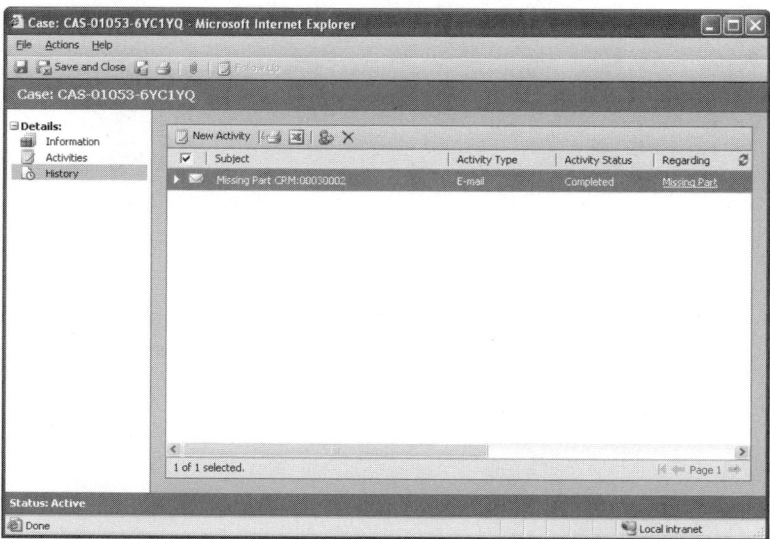

Figure 9-12 E-mail activity associated with new case record

Callout vs. Workflow

You might find yourself wondering when you should use a pre- or post-callout versus when you should use a workflow rule. As you would expect, the answer depends on your situation. For instance, if you need to take an action before the data reaches the platform, you will have to use a callout (pre-callout in this case). If you would like the user to manually instantiate the action, a manual workflow rule would be used.

Remember that any action or event available in workflow can be done with the callout and the SDK. However, the reverse is not true. In general, keep your callout routines as simple and fast as possible. When processes become long, see whether you can transfer them to a workflow assembly for asynchronous processing.

We would recommend the following guidelines to help you decide when to use a callout versus a workflow assembly:

Use callouts

- To alter data prior to submission to the platform.
- To take action after an update to an entity. (Workflow does not provide an easy trigger mechanism for the update event.)
- When you need a synchronous transaction and an immediate response.
- To take action before or after the merging of two records or the deletion of a record.
- When accessing custom entities that are organization-owned. Workflow can be used only on entities that have user ownership.

Use workflow

- For all asynchronous actions–transactions that can be completed without having the user wait for their completion. A typical asynchronous action might be to send an e-mail message after some condition is met. The user usually wouldn't have to wait until the system created and sent the message.
- For simple common tasks. The Workflow Manager has a list of actions, already built and available for use, that require no custom application development. Available actions include creating new records (such as Activities or Notes), sending e-mail messages, and updating values on related entities.
- To allow more configuration options to the user who is creating the workflow logic. Because the user builds the workflow rule with the rule editor, he or she can also alter it without necessarily requiring programmatic interaction.
- When you need a user to manually execute the necessary logic.

Development Environment

Now that we've reviewed the key server-side integration points within the server SDK, we hope that you're excited to actually create your own code that will work with Microsoft CRM. However, even if you're an expert developer, setting up and configuring a development environment for Microsoft CRM requires you to know a trick or two unique to the software. We've consolidated some of the key points into three categories:

- Configuring multiple Microsoft CRM installations
- WSDL reference
- Coding and testing tips

Configuring Multiple Microsoft CRM Installations

When you're creating custom code with the SDK, you obviously don't want your development coding to interfere with your Microsoft CRM users when they're using the system. Therefore, you should plan on creating at least two Microsoft CRM installations to minimize the impact of any coding development on your users. We'll refer to the system that your users are on as the *production* environment, and you'll write your code in the *development* environment. If possible, we recommend creating a third Microsoft CRM environment, commonly known as *staging*, for testing your changes before you push them live to production. Figure 9-13 shows one possible implementation of development, staging, and production environments.

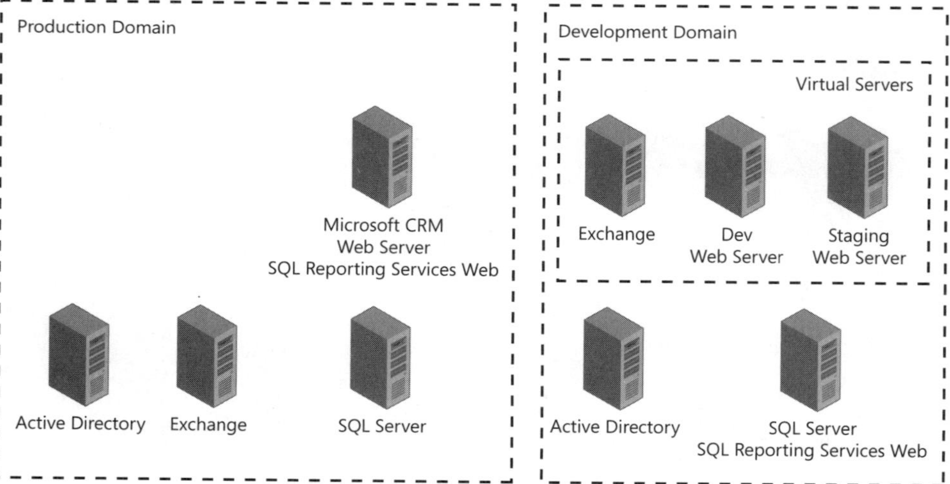

Figure 9-13 Microsoft CRM environments

We recommend that you create at least two domains, one for production and one for development and staging. When planning your Microsoft CRM environments, be sure to keep the following in mind:

- You need a dedicated Web server for each of the staging and development environments, but these two environments can share the same Microsoft Active Directory domain and the same server running SQL Server between them. Virtual servers work well for your development and testing Web server environments, but try to avoid putting SQL Server on a virtual server, because you might experience mediocre performance.
- When Microsoft CRM creates the SQL Server databases, it uses the organization name that you entered in the installation wizard. However, you can enter any organization name you want, because it's not tied to the license key. This allows you to use the same server for multiple environments.
- Create organizational units (OUs) in your development Active Directory domain for each installation (one for staging, and one for development in our example). We recommend using the same OU name that you used for your database name so that it is easier to keep track of your installations.
- Although it's possible to share a SQL Server Reporting Services server across staging and development, we recommend that you create a dedicated Reporting Services server for each environment. This will allow you to manage the reports for each environment independently.
- Use the redeployment tools (provided for free by Microsoft) to synchronize your data between Microsoft CRM deployments on different domains. You will not be able to simply restore the databases, because the system GUIDs will not match between domains.

Note If you set up your production, staging, and development environments in the same domain, you could expedite migrations by simply restoring the SQL Server databases from one environment to another. Despite this potential benefit, we generally recommend against the single-domain setup. By using two different domains, you minimize the chances of accidentally damaging the production environment during your testing and development. However, if you're a risk-taker, maybe the single-domain installation fits you better!

WSDL Reference

After you set up your project file, you must add Web references to the two Web services. For simplicity, we recommend that you keep the naming convention of the Web references Microsoft uses for its sample code.

We showed you how to add the CrmService and MetadataService Web references to Visual Studio .NET one at a time. However, instead of adding the CrmService and Metadata Web references individually, you can also create a common assembly that contains both the CrmService and Metadata Web references. Then you can reference the common assembly in your other projects, which allows you to update the CrmService and Metadata Web services in a single place if you ever need to update this information.

Another tip related to the WSDL reference includes using a configuration file to set the *Url* property. You might have noticed in our code samples that we explicitly set the *Url* property of the *CrmService* and *MetadataService* classes. Here's an example.

```
service.Url = "http://<crmserver>/mscrmservices/2006/crmservice.asmx";
```

But what would happen to our code when we have multiple CRM environments such as production, staging, and testing? Because each environment would have its own unique URL to the Web service APIs, we would have to update the URL, recompile, and then deploy. Obviously, that approach is not a good strategy.

So, instead of hard-coding the URL address in our web reference, we prefer to specify the *Url* property of the service by using a configuration setting so that each environment setting depends on simply updating a configuration file. Using a configuration setting technique will help you develop against one environment and compile your assemblies just once. You can then quickly deploy your solution to separate staging or production environments.

You could access this value from the registry or the Web.config file. The following code snippet shows one example of how to call a routine and use a configuration setting the *Url* property. We create a *ConfigSettings* class, which simply accesses two application-setting keys in your Web.config file. Then when you deploy your solution, you need only update the Web.config settings to point to the correct server. The code lists a simple class that contains two static strings that retrieve the *Url* values from the Web.config file. You would add the following class to the appropriate place in your project.

```
public class ConfigSettings
{
 public static string CrmServiceUrl = System.Configuration.ConfigurationSettings.AppSettings
["CrmServiceUrl"];
 public static string CrmMetadataUrl = System.Configuration.ConfigurationSettings.AppSetting
s["CrmMetadataUrl"];
}
```

Add the following two keys in your Web.config file. If your Web.config file already contains an *<appSettings>* node, just include *<add>* nodes.

```
<appSettings>
 <!-- Crm web service url -->
 <add key="CrmServiceUrl" value="http://
<crmserver>/mscrmservices/2006/crmservice.asmx"/>>
 <!-- Crm metadata web service url -->
 <add key="CrmMetadataUrl" value="http://
<crmserver>/mscrmservices/2006/metadataservice.asmx"/>
</appSettings>
```

Make sure you reference the *ConfigSettings* class assembly, and then set the *Url* property as follows.

```
CrmService service = new CrmService();
service.Credentials = System.Net.CredentialCache.DefaultCredentials;
service.Url = ConfigSettings.CrmServiceUrl;
```

> **Tip** Are your custom entities or new attributes not appearing in IntelliSense in Visual Studio? Make sure that you have published your changes *and* updated your Web reference in Visual Studio. You can update the Web reference by right-clicking it and then clicking Update Web Reference.

Coding and Testing Tips

This section contains development and testing tips that we use when working on Microsoft CRM projects. We hope you find them as useful as we do. We'll review the following topics:

- Microsoft .NET Framework version 2.0 versus version 1.1
- Application Mode and Loader.aspx
- Enabling the default Internet Explorer context menu
- Accessing query string parameters
- Referencing the Microsoft CRM assemblies or files
- Authentication and coding with filtered views
- Web.config file considerations
- Server assembly impersonations
- Authentication to test different users and roles
- Enabling platform-level tracing
- Enabling development errors

Microsoft .NET Framework Version 2.0

As documented in the SDK, Microsoft CRM 3.0 does support writing client-side code using Visual Studio .NET 2005 and the .NET Framework version 2.0 that accesses the *CRMService* and *MetadataService* Web services. However, Microsoft CRM 3.0 **does not support** callout or workflow assemblies written in Visual Studio .NET 2005 and the .NET Framework version 2.0. You should still continue to use Visual Studio .NET 2003 and the .NET Framework Version 1.1 when creating custom assemblies for callouts and workflow.

Please review the latest SDK for the most up-to-date information on the support for .NET Framework Version 2.0.

Application Mode and Loader.aspx

Of course you've noticed that Microsoft CRM launches into a special Internet Explorer window that does not have the menu bar, address bar, toolbar, and so on. Microsoft CRM refers to this as the *Application Mode*, and it runs in this mode by default. Often, developers need these additional Internet Explorer features that application mode hides. You can launch Microsoft CRM in a standard Internet Explorer window by browsing to http://<*crmserver*>/loader.aspx.

Using the Loader.aspx page disables application mode for that single Web session. You can also permanently disable application mode for *all* users and *all* sessions by updating the Web.config file.

Disabling application mode

1. On the Microsoft CRM Web server, navigate to <*web installation path*>\ (typically C:\Inetpub\wwwroot\).
2. Open the Web.config file in Notepad (or any text editor).
3. Look for the AppMode key, and change its value to Off.
4. Save the Web.config file.

Enabling the Default Internet Explorer Context Menu

In addition to running in Application Mode, Microsoft CRM modifies the standard Internet Explorer behavior by displaying its own context menu when you right-click in the application. Right-clicking a grid gives you options unique to Microsoft CRM, such as Open, Print, and Refresh List. However, right-clicking a form won't display a context menu like you would see on a normal Web page. When you're troubleshooting and debugging, you might find that you want to access the standard Internet Explorer context menu so that you can use features such as View Source, Properties, or Open In New Window. You can re-enable the Internet Explorer context menu by editing the Global.js file.

Re-enabling the Internet Explorer standard context menu

1. On the Microsoft CRM Web server, navigate to <*web installation path*>_common\scripts (typically C:\Inetpub\wwwroot_common\scripts).
2. Open the Global.js file in Notepad (or any text editor). Note: Do not double-click this file because it will attempt to execute the JavaScript file.
3. Right-click the file, and then click **Edit**.
4. Use your text editor's Find feature to locate the *document.oncontextmenu()* function.
5. Comment out the existing code in this function by adding /* and */ as shown in the following code. You can undo this change later by simply removing event.returnValue = true; line and the comment characters.

```
function document.oncontextmenu()
{
 event.returnValue = true;

 /*
 var s = event.srcElement.tagName;
 (!event.srcElement.disabled &&
 (document.selection.createRange().text.length > 0 ||
    s == "TEXTAREA" ||
 s == "INPUT" && event.srcElement.type == "text"));
 */
}
```

6. Save the file.
7. Open a page in Microsoft CRM and right-click it. You will see the familiar Internet Explorer context menu.

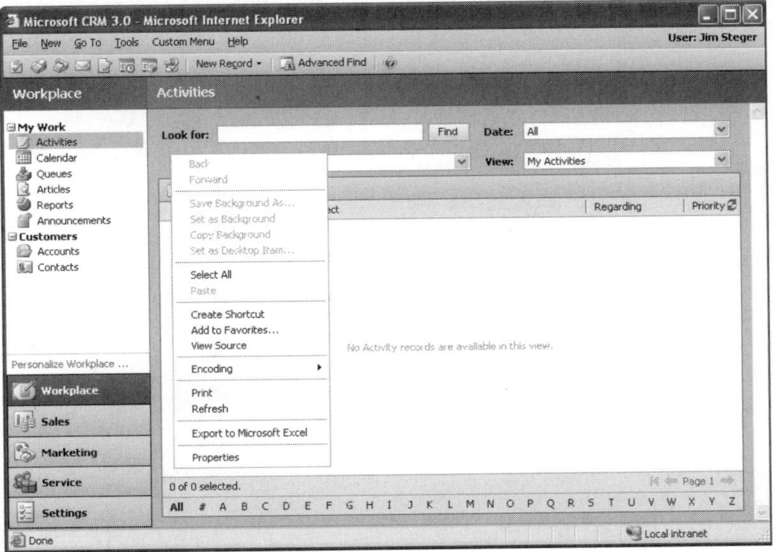

> **Caution** Use this technique on development servers only. Do not modify the Global.js file in a production or staging environment; this unsupported change might cause unpredictable behavior. Microsoft CRM prevents use of the right-click context menu for the user's benefit and also to maintain a predictable navigation structure in the application interface.

Accessing Query String Parameters

When testing or debugging your code, you will frequently need the GUID of an entity record or want to see the query string parameters that Microsoft CRM passed to the window. You can access the URL of any page and view its GUID by pressing Ctrl+N on your keyboard. Internet Explorer opens a new window, and the address bar displays its query string parameters. You can also press the F11 key when viewing a record to toggle the display so that the URL address bar appears.

If you have re-enabled the Internet Explorer context menu, you can also get this information by right-clicking the page and selecting Properties. You can then copy the URL from the Properties dialog box.

Referencing the Microsoft CRM Assemblies or Files

You should never reference any Microsoft CRM assemblies other than Microsoft.Crm.Platform .Callout.Base.dll. You also should not import any of the JavaScript, style sheets, or behavior files into your project. Microsoft will not support this type of code reuse, and you will probably experience significant code problems when Microsoft CRM releases hotfixes, updates, or patches.

> **Caution** Because you're not supposed to even *reference* any of the Microsoft CRM assemblies other than Microsoft.Crm.Platform.Callout.Base.dll, it should also be pretty obvious that you shouldn't attempt to *modify* any of the Microsoft CRM .dll files, either.

If you want to mimic any look or functionality of Microsoft CRM, you must re-create it yourself. The SDK provides a sample style sheet and a UI Style Guide, but if you want to review and understand the native script files, you can find most of them in < *web installation path*>_common. If you want to review styles or code, copy these files to your own directory.

Authentication and Coding with Filtered Views

The SQL filtered views provide an excellent method for you to quickly and easily retrieve Microsoft CRM data by using standard SQL Server connections. However, because the filtered views rely on Integrated Windows authentication for data security, you must pay attention to how your code connects to the filtered views.

If you were to go under the hood of a filtered view in SQL and look at its script, you would see that it uses a custom function to enforce the security settings.

```
create function dbo.fn_FindUserGuid ()
returns uniqueidentifier
as
begin
 declare @userguid uniqueidentifier
 select @userguid = s.SystemUserId
 from SystemUserBase s
 where s.DomainName = SUSER_SNAME()
 return @userguid
end
```

SUSER_SNAME() is a special function in SQL that returns the currently authenticated user, and the preceding function uses it to find the *systemuserid* identifier. If your code doesn't authenticate to SQL Server by using Windows authentication, your queries will never return any data, because all of the filtered views perform an inner join using *systemuserid*.

To connect to the database by using Windows authentication instead of SQL Server authentication, your connection string should include the following parameter: *Integrated Security=SSPI*. The full string would look something like this.

```
server=databaseserver;database=yourcustomdatabase;Integrated Security=SSPI
```

More Info Remember that you should never alter the Microsoft CRM databases by adding your own routines or stored procedures. Microsoft doesn't support this type of alteration, and it will probably result in the loss of your routines upon upgrades or hotfixes. Instead, you should create your own database to store your custom routines.

If you're calling your custom SQL routines from a Web page, you must configure additional settings to make sure that your Web page passes the integrated Windows credentials to SQL Server. First, the user should belong to the SQLAccessGroup, which will happen automatically when you add users to Microsoft CRM. Second, you must ensure that your Web application does not permit anonymous access by disabling anonymous access in IIS for your virtual directory or Web site. Finally, you must add or update the Web.config file in your custom web with the following nodes located in the *<system.web>* node set.

```
<authentication mode="Windows" />
<authorization><deny users="?" /></authorization>
<identity impersonate="true" />
```

These keys ensure that IIS uses the Windows credential set when accessing a page in your virtual web.

As we explained earlier, another consequence of the integrated security features in filtered views is that you can't use filtered views in callouts or in workflow assemblies. The callout and workflow engine runs under the security context of the user, and, because you cannot impersonate to SQL Server from your connection string, you cannot retrieve data by using the filtered views. In these cases, we recommend that you use the *QueryExpression* class because the Web service does allow impersonation.

Web.config File Considerations

If you create custom pages that work with Microsoft CRM, you should deploy them to a directory outside of the Microsoft CRM root and create a new Web site or a new virtual directory. The easiest way to leverage cross-site scripting (see Chapter 10 for more details) is to set up a virtual directory underneath the Microsoft CRM web. When you create a virtual directory, you will inherit the Web.config settings of the parent web, which in this case would be settings from the Microsoft CRM Web.config file.

If you add your custom web files to a virtual directory underneath the Microsoft CRM web, you might receive an error similar to this one when accessing your custom pages:

"File or assembly name Microsoft.Crm.Tools.ImportExportPublish, or one of its dependencies, was not found."

You have a couple of options for getting around this error. One is to register each of the assemblies that fail in the global assembly cache (GAC). The other is to remove these entries in your custom Web.config file. To remove the assemblies from your Web.config file, add the *<remove>*

node for each Microsoft CRM assembly that fails to load in your custom application. Here's an example of how this looks.

```
<compilation defaultLanguage="C#" debug="true">
 <assemblies>
  <remove assembly="Microsoft.Crm.Tools.ImportExportPublish, Version=3.0.5300.0, Culture=
neutral, PublicKeyToken=31bf3856ad364e35"/>
 </assemblies>
</compilation>
```

Warning Make sure that you add this to *your* Web.config file. Do not alter these values in the Microsoft CRM Web.config file.

Server Assembly Impersonation

You might find that you need to use the credentials of the user making the request in your callouts or workflow assemblies. The SDK documents this numerous times, but, because it is such a useful technique, we want to mention here, too. This code snippet shows how to accomplish impersonation.

```
CrmService service = new CrmService();
service.Credentials = System.Net.CredentialCache.DefaultCredentials;
service.Url = "http://<crmserver>/mscrmservices/2006/crmservice.asmx";

// Get the current user ID.
WhoAmIRequest userRequest = new WhoAmIRequest();
WhoAmIResponse userResp = (WhoAmIResponse) service.Execute(userRequest);

service.CallerIdValue = new CallerId();
service.CallerIdValue.CallerGuid = userResp.UserId;
```

When you are using impersonation from a callout, the user context already contains the user ID for you. So, instead of making an additional request, you could simply use the following.

```
CrmService service = new CrmService();
service.Credentials = System.Net.CredentialCache.DefaultCredentials;
service.Url = "http://<crmserver>/mscrmservices/2006/crmservice.asmx";

service.CallerIdValue = new CallerId();
service.CallerIdValue.CallerGuid = userContext.UserId;
```

Authentication to Test Different Users and Roles

When testing, you will often need to review users with different roles to validate security and custom functionality. Because Microsoft CRM uses your logon information for its authentication credentials, by default you will access the application under the Windows account that you used to access your computer. If you wanted to check the functionality of a different role, you would have to change the role of your account or log on with a different account.

Chapter 3, "Managing Security and Information Access," showed you in detail how to force the browser to prompt for credentials. This technique allows you to authenticate as different users without having to log off of your computer. Remember that this will affect all intranet web applications that you currently access. Another approach is to use the run as command to launch Internet Explorer. In a DOS prompt, you could execute the following: runas /user:domain\user "C:\Program Files\Internet Explorer\iexplore http://<crmserver>". You will then be prompted for a valid password and then Internet Explorer will launch under the specified user context.

Enabling Platform-Level Tracing

You might need to track down issues at the platform level to debug callouts, workflow, or even the Outlook client. Enabling this type of tracing requires a registry change. The locations of the registry settings are listed in Table 9-5.

Table 9-5 Registry Settings Locations

Web server	HKEY_LOCAL_MACHINE\Software\Microsoft\MSCRM
Outlook client	HKEY_CURRENT_USER\Software\Microsoft\MSCRMClient

To enable tracing, you must create the registry values listed in Table 9-5 in the appropriate key, as specified by Table 9-6.

Table 9-6 Registry Values

Name	Type	Data
TraceEnabled	dword	1
TraceDirectory	string	Enter a directory (such as C:\MSCRM\Tracing). Note that this directory must exist; Microsoft CRM will not create it for you.
TraceCategories	string	*:Verbose
TraceCallStack	dword	Off
TraceRefresh	dword	1
TraceSchedule	string	Hourly

Remember that tracing will negatively affect performance, so be sure to turn it off when it is no longer required. To do this, change TraceEnabled to 0.

Caution We would be remiss if we didn't provide the obligatory warning from Microsoft when editing the registry: *"Using Registry Editor incorrectly can cause serious, system-wide problems that may require you to re-install Windows to correct them. Microsoft cannot guarantee that any problems resulting from the use of Registry Editor can be solved. Use this tool at your own risk."*

Enabling Development Errors

By default, Microsoft CRM displays a nice, user-friendly error message if it encounters a problem trying to execute a request. However, as you develop and troubleshoot your code, you'll want to see more descriptive information about any errors. You can enable detailed development errors (Figure 9-14) with a setting in the Web.config file.

Enabling development errors in the Web.config file

1. On the Microsoft CRM Web server, navigate to <web installation path>\ (typically C:\Inetpub\wwwroot\).
2. Open the Web.config file in Notepad (or any text editor).
3. Look for the DevErrors key, and change its value to On.
4. Save the Web.config file.

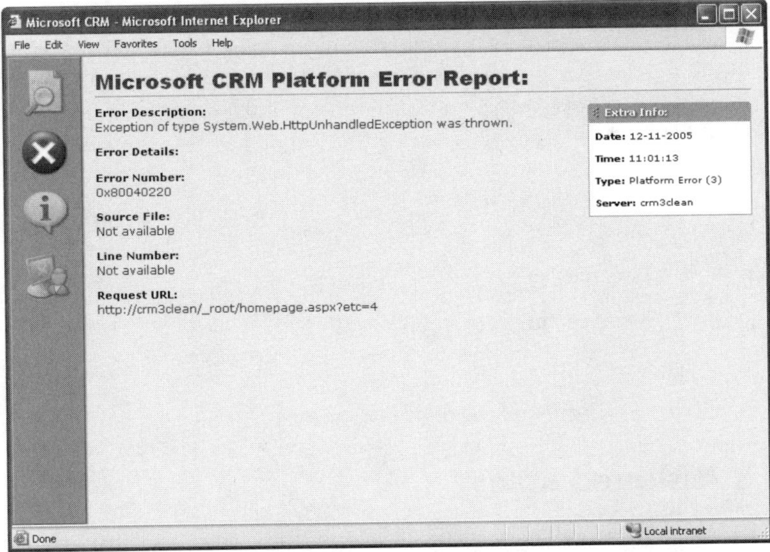

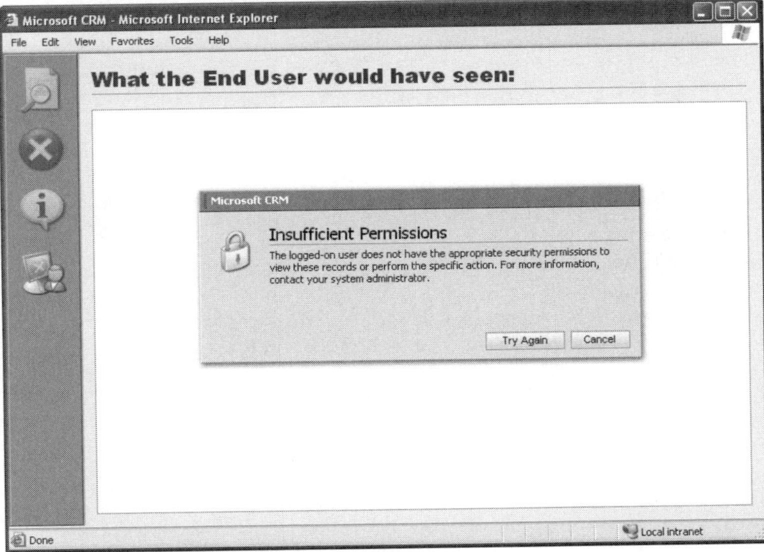

Figure 9-14 Development errors enabled

Sample Code

The Microsoft CRM SDK includes great code samples and examples that you can reference when you develop your own solution. You should definitely use them as a resource, but we wanted to include additional code samples in this book that address common requests. We will demonstrate how to:

- Retrieve a user's assigned roles
- Create an auto number field
- Validate a field when converting an Opportunity
- Add data auditing
- Create a Project record from converted Opportunities

Retrieving a User's Assigned Roles

The Microsoft CRM security model allows you to assign one or more security roles to each user. The native classes help you retrieve a user's actual privileges associated with the combination of the user's roles, but you might find that you need to retrieve just the roles for custom security or business logic. For example, your code might take some action if the user has a Salesperson role, but not if he or she has a Customer Service role.

Listing 9-4 shows the code for the *QueryExpression* class to retrieve the assigned roles of the calling user. Note that this query uses an extra join to retrieve the roles for the user.

Listing 9-4 Retrieving Assigned Roles

```
// Standard CRM Service Setup
CrmService service = new CrmService();
service.Credentials = System.Net.CredentialCache.DefaultCredentials;
service.Url = "http://<crmserver>/mscrmservices/2006/crmservice.asmx";

// Retrieve user information.
WhoAmIRequest userRequest = new WhoAmIRequest();
WhoAmIResponse user = (WhoAmIResponse) service.Execute(userRequest);

// We will create two link entities.
// One will be between role and systemuserroles entities.
LinkEntity roleXuserroles = new LinkEntity();
roleXuserroles.LinkFromEntityName = EntityName.role.ToString();
roleXuserroles.LinkFromAttributeName = "roleid";
roleXuserroles.LinkToEntityName = "systemuserroles";
roleXuserroles.LinkToAttributeName = "roleid";

// The second will be between the systemuser and systemuserroles entities.
LinkEntity userXuserroles = new LinkEntity();
userXuserroles.LinkFromEntityName = "systemuserroles";
userXuserroles.LinkFromAttributeName = "systemuserid";
userXuserroles.LinkToEntityName = EntityName.systemuser.ToString();
userXuserroles.LinkToAttributeName = "systemuserid";
```

```
// Create a condition filtering the systemuserid from the systemuserroles entity.
ConditionExpression condition = new ConditionExpression();
condition.AttributeName = "systemuserid";
condition.Operator = ConditionOperator.Equal;
condition.Values = new object[]{user.UserId};

// Add the filter.
userXuserroles.LinkCriteria = new FilterExpression();
userXuserroles.LinkCriteria.Conditions = new ConditionExpression[] {condition};

// Connect the user link to the role link.
roleXuserroles.LinkEntities = new LinkEntity[] {userXuserroles};

// Build a query expression.
QueryExpression query = new QueryExpression();
query.EntityName = EntityName.role.ToString();
query.ColumnSet = new AllColumns();

// Add the join back to the role query.
query.LinkEntities = new LinkEntity[] {roleXuserroles};

try
{
 // Retrieve the values from Microsoft CRM.
 BusinessEntityCollection retrieved = service.RetrieveMultiple(query);
}
catch (System.Web.Services.Protocols.SoapException ex)
{
 // Handle error.
}
```

Creating an Auto Number Field

Microsoft CRM uses a GUID to uniquely identify each record in the database, and Microsoft CRM also gives you the ability to add custom attributes. However, Microsoft CRM does not provide a way to create an automatically incrementing field (typically referred to as an *Identity* field in SQL Server). Although some objects (such as Cases, Invoices, and Quotes) include a numbering scheme that neatly identifies a unique record to the user, entities such as Lead, Account, and Contact do not include a numbering method. If your users want to reference records by a simple integer number instead of the unfriendly looking GUID, you can create custom code that manages a numbering scheme for the entities that you want to uniquely identify with a number.

This example code will simulate the SQL Server Identity concept to give our end users a Lead entity numbering scheme using the pre-callout. We will first create a new integer attribute on the Lead form. Then we will develop a query to get the maximum Lead number and use that method within a pre-callout routine to set the value of the Lead number before saving a new Lead record to the database.

> **Real World** This example demonstrates the power and usefulness of impersonation. Since we want the lead number to be unique across all Leads, it's critical that we execute our *QueryExpression* method under the context of a user who has read access to all lead records.

Configure the Lead form

1. Add a new integer attribute to the Lead form called *new_leadnumber*.
2. Add this field to the form, and make sure that it is disabled to the user because we will be populating the value automatically.

Building a callout assembly project

1. Create a new **C# Class Library** project in Visual Studio .NET 2003 called **WorkingWithCrm.Callout**.
2. Be sure check for the System.Web.Services reference. If it doesn't exist, add a reference to the System.Web.Services namespace.
3. Add a **Web Reference** to the **CrmService** Web service, calling it **CrmSdk**.
4. Add a reference to the Microsoft.Crm.Platform.Callout.Base.dll.
5. Add a new **Class** file called **LeadCallout**.
6. Enter the code shown in Listing 9-5.

Listing 9-5 Creating an Auto Number Field

```
using System;
using System.Diagnostics;
using System.IO;
using System.Xml;
using WorkingWithCrm.Callout.CrmSdk;
using Microsoft.Crm.Callout;


namespace WorkingWithCrm.Callout
{
 /// <summary>
 /// This Sample shows how to log various events with callouts
 /// </summary>
 public class LeadCallout: CrmCalloutBase
 {
  public LeadCallout()
  {
  }
```

```
// This Sample shows how to log an object creation using a precallout
public override PreCalloutReturnValue PreCreate(CalloutUserContext userContext, CalloutEnt
ityContext entityContext, ref string entityXml, ref string errorMessage)
{
 // Call the helper function NextLeadNumber() to return the next highest lead number value
 string nextLeadNumber = NextLeadNumber();

 // Create an xml document in order to work with the xml stream
 XmlDocument entityDoc = new XmlDocument();
 entityDoc.LoadXml(entityXml);

 // Create the appropriate xml node
 XmlNodeList propertyList = entityDoc.GetElementsByTagName("Property");
 XmlElement leadNumberValue = null;
 XmlElement properties = (XmlElement) entityDoc.GetElementsByTagName("Properties")[0];
 XmlElement leadNumberElement = entityDoc.CreateElement("Property");
 XmlAttribute typeAttrib = entityDoc.CreateAttribute("type");

 // Set the values for our new_leadnumber field
 leadNumberElement.SetAttribute("type", "http://www.w3.org/2001/XMLSchema-
instance", "StringProperty");
 leadNumberElement.SetAttribute("Name", "new_leadnumber");
 leadNumberValue = entityDoc.CreateElement("Value");
 leadNumberValue.InnerText = NextLeadNumber();
 leadNumberElement.AppendChild(leadNumberValue);
 properties.AppendChild(leadNumberElement);

 // Add back to the entityXml
 StringWriter output = new StringWriter();
 entityDoc.Save(output);
 entityXml = output.ToString();

 // Remove the extra XML that will confuse CRM
 entityXml = entityXml.Replace("xmlns=\"\"", "");
 entityXml = entityXml.Replace("<?xml version=\"1.0\" encoding=\"utf-16\"?>", "");

 return PreCalloutReturnValue.Continue;
}

#region Helpers
public bool IsTextIncluded( string InputString, string ValueToCheck )
{
 return (InputString.IndexOf(ValueToCheck) > -1);
}

public string NextLeadNumber()
{
 // Standard CRM Service Setup
 CrmService service = new CrmService();
 service.Credentials = System.Net.CredentialCache.DefaultCredentials;
service.Url = "http://<crmserver>/mscrmservices/2006/crmservice.asmx";

 // We need a user that has global read access to the lead record so that we
 // have the absolute maximum lead number. If all roles have global read privileges to
 // the read value of the Lead, then this wouldn't be necessary.
```

```
    // For production, access this guid in a config file.
    Guid callerid = new Guid("0686EE2A-FC46-DA11-B935-0003FF07CD51");

    // Impersonate our global read user
    service.CallerIdValue = new CallerId();
    service.CallerIdValue.CallerGuid = callerid;

    // Create a set of columns to return
    ColumnSet cols = new ColumnSet();
    cols.Attributes = new string [] {"leadid", "new_leadnumber"};

    // Set the order of the bring back the highest new_leadnumber value at the top
    OrderExpression order = new OrderExpression();
    order.AttributeName = "new_leadnumber";
    order.OrderType = OrderType.Descending;

    // To improve performance, we will only pass back the top record
    // This will return only 1 page with 1 record per page
    PagingInfo pages = new PagingInfo();
    pages.PageNumber = 1;
    pages.Count = 1;

    // Create a query expression and set the query parameters
    QueryExpression query = new QueryExpression();
    query.EntityName = EntityName.lead.ToString();
    query.ColumnSet = cols;
    query.Orders = new OrderExpression[] {order};
    query.PageInfo = pages;

    // Retrieve the values from CRM
    BusinessEntityCollection retrieved = service.RetrieveMultiple(query);

    string nextNumber = "1";

    // Check to see if we have any records
    if (retrieved.BusinessEntities.Length > 0)
    {
     // Cast to results lead object and only retrieve first record
     lead results = (lead)retrieved.BusinessEntities[0];

     // Return the next value lead number. If there are records, but none have a number
(the result will be null), so just pass back 1
     nextNumber = (results.new_leadnumber != null) ? (results.new_leadnumber.Value + 1).ToStr
ing() : "1";
    }

   return nextNumber;
  }
  #endregion
 }
}
```

After you build your assembly, you must update the Callout.config.xml file to include your new method. Replace the assembly and class names with the ones from your project. Note that we do not need any values from Microsoft CRM for this routine to function, so you don't need to specify a *<prevalue>*. The Callout.config.xml file code is shown below:

```
<?xml version="1.0" encoding="utf-8" ?>
<callout.config version="2.0">
 <callout entity="lead" event="PreCreate">
  <subscription assembly="WorkingWithCrm.Callout.dll" class="WorkingWithCrm.Callout.LeadCall
out"></subscription>
 </callout>
</callout.config>
```

Next you will deploy the Callout.config.xml file and your .dll file to *<crm install drive>*\Program Files\Microsoft CRM\Server\bin\assembly. And don't forget to do an *iisreset* on the server after deploying the files.

Validating a Field When Converting an Opportunity Record

Let's imagine that as part of your sales process, you want every sales person to enter the start date of a project (a custom Opportunity attribute) before the sales person can close an Opportunity as won. However, you don't want to make the project state date field required on the Opportunity form because that would force the sales person to enter a value before he or she could save a record. In this example the user won't know the project start date until the customer agrees to the purchase, so it doesn't make sense to configure this as a required field. However, your business requirement dictates they must enter this project start date field before they can close the Opportunity as won. This example will walk through all the steps necessary to develop a customization that will perform this type of check.

At first, you might think that the pre-callout would be the obvious choice for implementing this solution because we do not recommend using the pre-callout for data validation when users create or modify records. Although the pre-callout allows you to pass back an error message to the client, the client will lose any data that the user entered. So, in this example, if the user updated 10 fields on the Opportunity and then saved it, the pre-callout could check to make sure the user completed it according to your business rules. However, if there is a problem, the user will see an error and lose all of the data from the 10 fields that he or she just updated. Obviously, this would make for some unhappy users, so we won't go down this path. For regular form validation, we recommend using client-side methods, as demonstrated in Chapter 10, instead of the pre-callout.

However, this particular example is a unique case in which we need to use the pre-callout for validation. In our example, we want to perform a validation when the user interacts with a Web dialog page. As you will learn in Chapter 10, Microsoft CRM does not include client-side events such as Converting Leads or Closing Opportunities on Web dialog pages. Fortunately, the pre-callout provides the appropriate hook for us to perform this type of Web dialog page validation. If the user tries to close an Opportunity without entering a project start date, we will return a simple error message (shown in Figure 9-15) that instructs him or her to correct it.

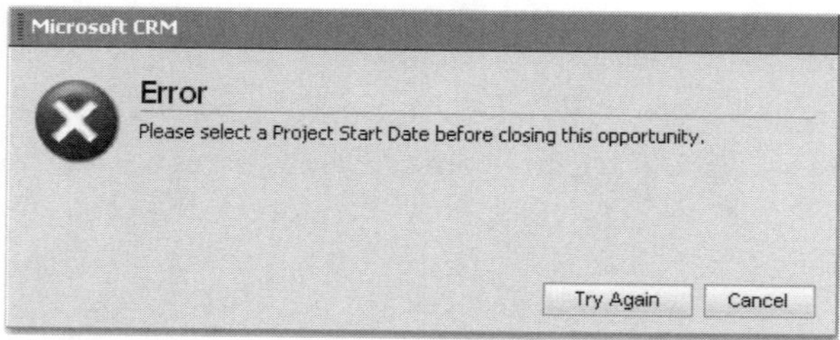

Figure 9-15 Custom callout error returned to the user

Configure the Opportunity form

1. Add a new *datetime* attribute to the Opportunity form called *new_projectstartdate*..
2. Leave the default value as Unassigned.
3. Add this field to the form and select the **Lock field on the form** check box.
4. Publish the Opportunity entity.

> **Caution** When you deploy the pre-callout assembly in this example, the user must enter a value in this field. If someone accidentally removes this field from the form, no one will be able to close an Opportunity. We recommend that you lock any fields that you reference in a custom event, callout, or workflow assembly so that other users who might edit the form know to leave that field on the form.

Next we must create the pre-callout code. The pre-callout offers us six events to choose from (*PreCreate*, *PreUpdate*, *PreDelete*, *PreAssign*, *PreSetState*, and *PreMerge*), but we need to know which one is appropriate for our solution. We know that we need to check the value of the new_projectstartdate field. We also need to have access to the statecode because we don't want to validate unless the user is closing the Opportunity record. Let's brainstorm some options.

Microsoft CRM handles closing an Opportunity record differently than most other entities. When an Opportunity record is closed (marked as inactive), a special activity record is created and logged with the Opportunity record. Due to this, we could attempt to configure a pre-callout method against the OpportunityClose activity. Upon inspection of the sdkreadme.htm, we find a known issue detailing that callout events are not fired for the OpportunityClose activity records when closed through the application.

Since the OpportunityClose activity callout event does not work in this instance, we have to accomplish our task with one of the Opportunity events. Your next inclination might be to use the *PreSetState* event for the opportunity, checking for the statecode and new_projectstartdate field. Unfortunately, the entity XML is not passed in to the *PreSetState* event; see the method signature in the following code.

```
public override PreCalloutReturnValue PreSetState(CalloutUserContext userContext,
 CalloutEntityContext entityContext, ref int newStateCode, ref int newStatusCode,
 ref string errorMessage)
```

What about using the opportunity *PreUpdate* event and doing the statecode and new_projectstartdate field checks? We did a quick test to output a sample entity XML using the *PreUpdate* event after we closed an Opportunity so that we could review the information available to us.

```
PreUpdate - 12/9/2005 12:05:11 PM
ObjectType: 3
ObjectId: b2dd35ea-1b5a-da11-ba15-0003ff12cd51
CreatorId: a1195f86-995a-da11-ba15-0003ff12cd51
entityXml: <BusinessEntity xsi:type="DynamicEntity" Name="opportunity" xmlns:xsi=
  "http://www.w3.org/2001/XMLSchema-instance" xmlns="http://schemas.microsoft.com/crm/2006/
  WebServices"><Properties><Property xsi:type="CrmDateTimeProperty"
  Name="new_projectstartdate">
<Value>2005-12-09T00:00:00</Value></Property></Properties></BusinessEntity>
```

As you can see, the *entityXml* line doesn't include the state and status reasons as properties, which prevents us from easily checking the statecode value.

Obviously, the remaining pre-callout events, *PreCreate*, *PreDelete*, *PreAssign*, and *PreMerge*, don't apply to our scenario.

Because it doesn't appear that any of the native options will get us exactly what we want in one step, we will have to make an extra SDK call to get the information that we need. We decided to go back and use the *PreSetState* method and add an additional call to retrieve the value of the project start date field. The *PreSetState* method fires only when a statecode change is made, which occurs when you close an Opportunity.

We will look at the statecode and determine whether it is being marked as Won. If it is being changed to any other state, we will not validate that the Project Start Date field contains data. After we know that the user is closing the Opportunity and marking it as Won, we will make a separate call to retrieve the saved value of the project start date.

Using our WorkingWithCrm.Workflow callout project, add a new class file called Validate-Opportunity. Add the pre-callout code shown in Listing 9-6.

Listing 9-6 Using a Pre-Callout to Validate a Form Field

```
using System;
using System.Xml;
using WorkingWithCrm.Callout.CrmSdk;
using Microsoft.Crm.Callout;


namespace WorkingWithCrm.Callout
{
 /// <summary>
 /// This callout class will log all data changes for the entities specified.
 /// </summary>
 public class ValidateOpportunity : CrmCalloutBase
 {
  public ValidateOpportunity()
  {
  }

  public override PreCalloutReturnValue PreSetState(CalloutUserContext userContext,
 CalloutEntityContext entityContext, ref int newStateCode, ref int newStatusCode,
 ref string errorMessage)
  {
   // Standard CRM Service Setup
   CrmService service = new CrmService();
   service.Credentials = System.Net.CredentialCache.DefaultCredentials;
   service.Url = "http://<crmserver>/mscrmservices/2006/crmservice.asmx";

   // Create the Column Set Object indicating the fields to be retrieved.
   ColumnSet cols = new ColumnSet();
   cols.Attributes = new string [] {"new_projectstartdate"};

   // Retrieve the Opportunity record.
   opportunity opp = (opportunity)service.Retrieve(EntityName.opportunity.ToString(),
 entityContext.InstanceId, cols);

   bool isValid = true;

   // Only check this if the new state code is won (1).
   // Otherwise, we would be validating when a user reopened an Opportunity, and there
might be existing data that would always force this error.
   if (newStateCode == 1)
```

```
  {
   // If the new_projectstartdate field is null, then no data exists for it.
   if (opp.new_projectstartdate == null)
    isValid = false;
  }

  if (isValid)
  {
   return PreCalloutReturnValue.Continue;
  }
  else
  {
   // Set the error message and abort the transaction.
   errorMessage = "Please select a Project Start Date before closing this opportunity.";
   return PreCalloutReturnValue.Abort;
  }
 }
}
}
```

Next we update the Callout.config.xml file to register this new routine and deploy our assemblies. After an *iisreset*, you now have custom validation when closing an Opportunity record!

```
<?xml version="1.0" encoding="utf-8" ?>
<callout.config version="2.0">
 <callout entity="opportunity" event="PreSetState">
  <subscription assembly="WorkingWithCrm.Callout.dll" class="WorkingWithCrm.Callout.Validate
Opportunity">
  </subscription>
 </callout>
</callout.config>
```

Note Are you having problems getting your callout to work? Your first troubleshooting step should be to double-check the configuration file. Callout errors are typically caused by incorrectly setting up the configuration file or forgetting to include the entity that you want to register. Be sure to check the Microsoft CRM Web server Event Viewer for any errors that Microsoft CRM might log. You can also add your own trace logging for further analysis.

Data Auditing

Microsoft CRM automatically records the date, the time, and the user who last modified a record. However, it does not record the specific values that the user changed in the record. This lack of detailed data auditing might cause some concern for your management and executives in today's intense Sarbanes-Oxley world. Fortunately, you can save the day for management by using the SDK and this code sample to add a data auditing feature that uses the post-update callout method and custom entities.

We mentioned earlier that you must explicitly tell Microsoft CRM which fields you want passed in to your routine in the Callout.config.xml file. Therefore, you can choose to audit a specific set of fields or you can audit changes to all fields by using the *@all* keyword. Because Microsoft CRM passes the before and after data on any changes to the post-update callout method, you can leverage this to add your own custom data logging.

Before we begin coding, we must first create a custom entity called Data Audit that will store our auditing information. We will use this custom entity to record the field level changes. For this example we will audit changes to the Contact entity, so we'll add a one-to-many relationship from the Contact entity to the Data Audit entity. Our final result will resemble Figure 9-16.

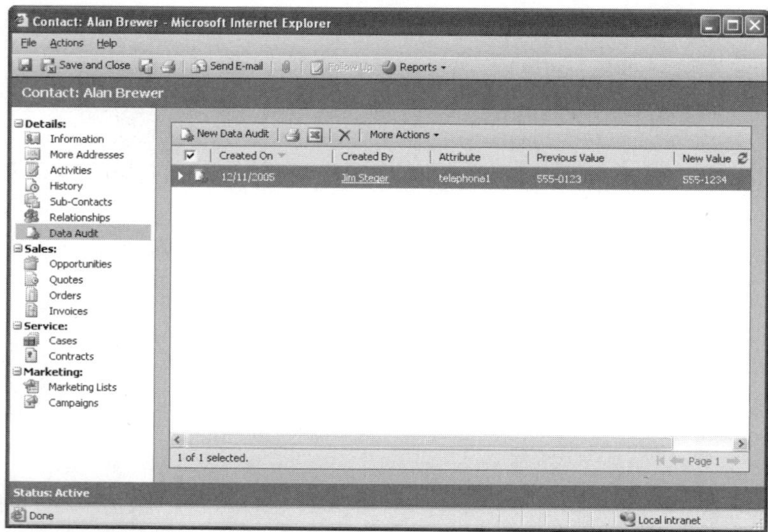

Figure 9-16 Data Audit grid

If a user double-clicked one of the Data Audit records in this grid, Microsoft CRM will launch the form for the Data Audit entity. We decided to just remove all the fields from that form and display a message to the user by labeling a section with the following text: "This information is generated by the system."

Finally, as with all new custom entities, you must update your security roles to allow the appropriate access to our Data Audit entity. At a minimum, you will have to allow for Create and Read privileges for all users so that all of their changes are properly logged in our Data Audit entity. To maintain the integrity of the data audit records, you should not grant Delete privileges on the Data Audit entity to any role except the System Administrator role, which has access to all entities and privileges by default.

To summarize, we will do the following:

1. Create a new entity called Data Audit, which includes a relationship to the Contact entity.
2. Customize the Form, Preview, and Associated views of our new entity.

3. Use the **WorkingWithCrm.Callout** project created in the "Creating an Auto Number Field" example and add a reference to the Microsoft.VisualBasic namespace.
4. Add a new class file called **DataAudit** and enter the code in Listing 9-7.
5. Add an entry to the Callout.config.xml file to run the callout each time a user updates a Contact record.
6. Deploy the callout assembly and configuration file to the Microsoft CRM Web server.

Creating and customizing a custom Data Audit entity

1. Create a new entity called Data Audit, as shown in the following graphic. Be sure to change the Ownership to Organization. Also, change the primary attribute's maximum length to 25 characters, change the requirement level to No Constraint, and clear the **Notes** and **Activities** check boxes.

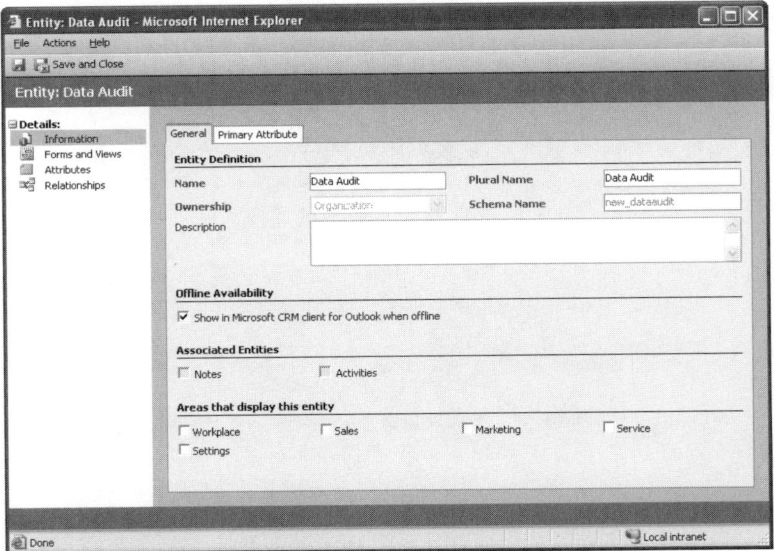

2. Click **Attributes**, and add the custom attributes shown in Table 9-7. You do not need to add an attribute for the dates or for the person who made the change because you will be using the fields (*createdby* and *createdon*) that are automatically created with the entity.

Table 9-7 Audit Entity Attributes

Display name	Schema name	Type
Previous Value	*New_PreviousValue*	ntext (2,000)
New Value	*New_NewValue*	ntext (2,000)
Attribute	*New_Attribute*	Nvarchar (150)

3. Click **Relationships** and add a many-to-one, referential relationship to the Contact entity.

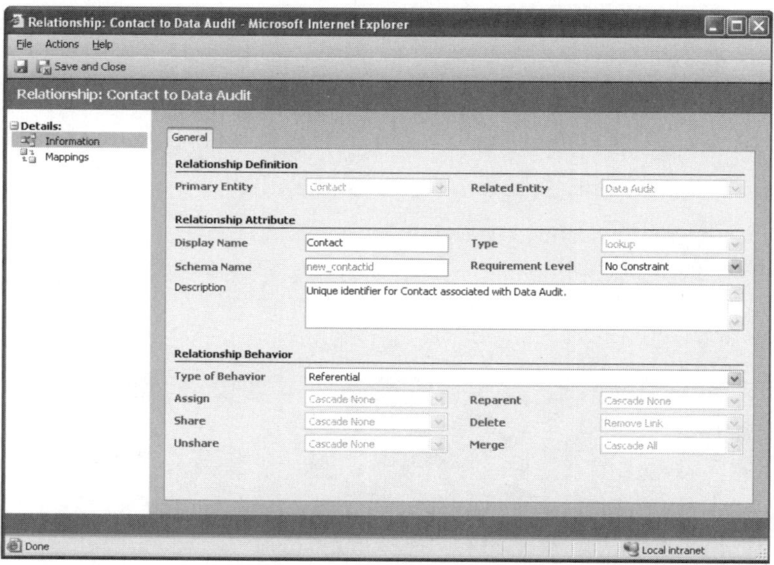

4. Click **Forms and Views**, click **Form**, and then remove all of the fields. Click **Add a Section**, and then type **This information is generated by the system.** in the **Name** box. Select the check box to show the name on the form. Click **Save and Close** in the toolbar.

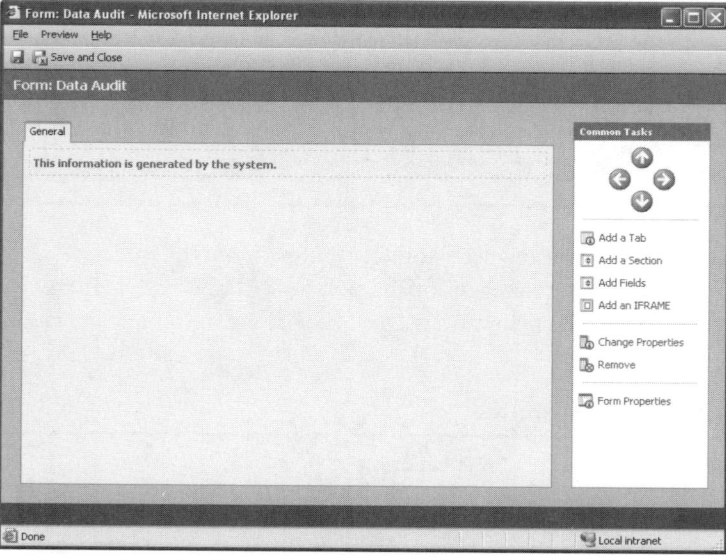

5. Double-click **Preview**, and then add the fields shown here.

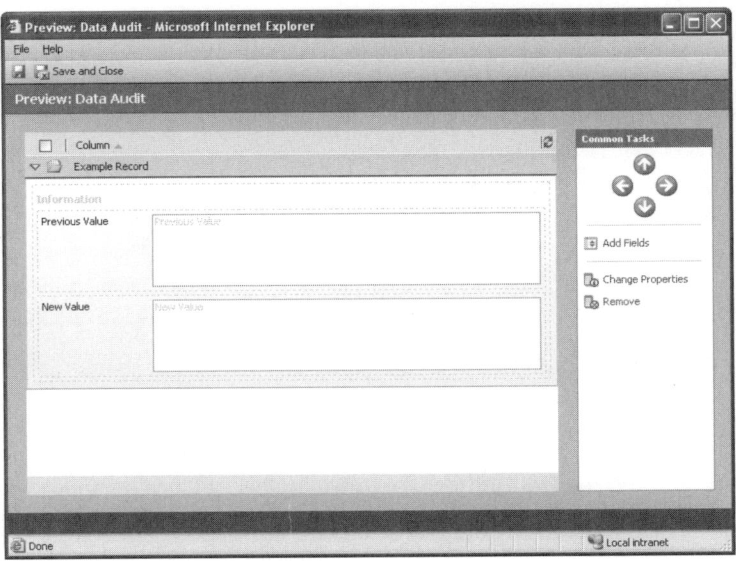

6. Double-click **Data Audit Associated View**, and then change the columns and default sort to the following.

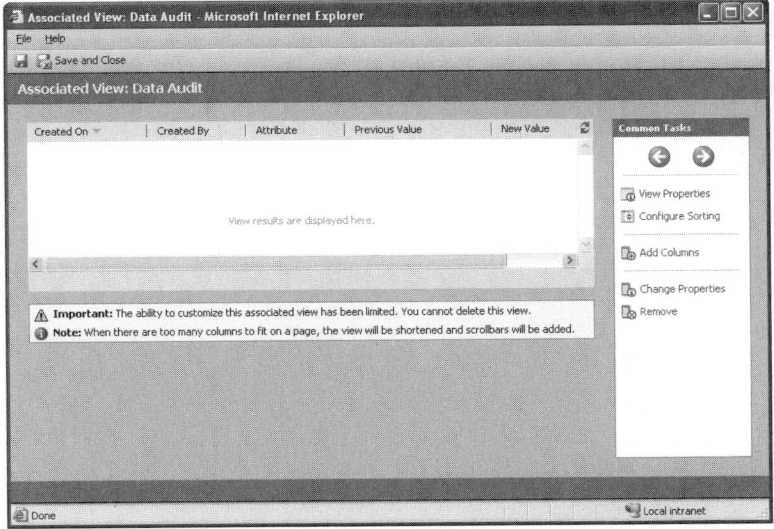

7. Publish this entity.

> **Important** Don't forget to add the appropriate security settings for this new entity in your system. By default, only the System Administrator role has access to newly created custom entities.

We will use the *PostUpdate* callout method and pass in all the columns to handle our data auditing. The incoming data will be passed in as XML snippets, so we could then use XPath or even string techniques to analyze each property to determine whether an attribute was changed. However, we chose to deserialize the resulting input XML strings into two separate *DynamicEntity* classes to demonstrate that technique.

> **Note** You will find a performance impact when using this the deserialize code. In high volume environments, you may find that an alternate another approach may provide performance.

This example brings to light an interesting situation in which Microsoft CRM passes data to the callout. We mentioned earlier that null values are not passed to the callout, even if you specify that a specific field should be passed in the callout configuration file. To help clarify what this means, consider this example: You enter "James" for a contact record that previously had no middle name, and you leave the gender field unchanged. When you save, the *PostUpdate* callout fires. The following are two snippets of pre- and post-XML data passed to the *PostUpdate* callout method.

```
PreImageXml Snippet:
<BusinessEntity xsi:type="DynamicEntity" Name="contact" xmlns:xsi="http://www.w3.org/2001/
XMLSchema-instance"  xmlns="http://schemas.microsoft.com/crm/2006/WebServices">
 <Properties>
   <Property xsi:type="PicklistProperty" Name="gendercode">
    <Value>1</Value>
   </Property>
 </Properties>
</BusinessEntity>

PostImageXml Snippet:
<BusinessEntity xsi:type="DynamicEntity" Name="contact" xmlns:xsi="http://www.w3.org/2001/
XMLSchema-instance"
xmlns="http://schemas.microsoft.com/crm/2006/WebServices">
 <Properties>
  <Property xsi:type="StringProperty" Name="middlename">
   <Value>James</Value>
  </Property>
  <Property xsi:type="PicklistProperty" Name="gendercode">
<Value>1</Value>
  </Property>
 </Properties>
</BusinessEntity>
```

As you can see, the PreImageXml data does not contain a node for *middlename*, because it was originally blank (null). So the number of properties for the pre- and post-*DynamicEntity* objects will vary depending on the passed-in data.

Therefore, we can't simply try to perform one loop through the submitted properties and compare the differences, because we could have nodes. We will instead loop through the pre- and post-*DynamicEntity* objects individually and add the attribute name and values to a *NameValueCollection*. We chose to use the *NameValueCollection* because it automatically concatenates the values for keys with the same name. However, on null fields, only one value will be added, so we will need to know whether it was pre- or post-data. For simplicity, we will append a pipe character (|) on the pre-data and prepend a pipe character on the post-data to delineate our data. We will then loop through the resulting *NameValueCollection*, split the value string, and compare the values from there. When we find that the new value doesn't match the previous one, we will call an insert method to update the audit entity for the contact record.

The code for our DataAudit class file is shown in Listing 9-7. Be sure to add the Microsoft .VisualBasic reference to your callout project file.

Listing 9-7 Updating the Audit Entity

```
using System;
using System.Collections.Specialized;
using System.IO;
using System.Xml;
using System.Xml.Xsl;
using System.Xml.Serialization;
using WorkingWithCrm.Callout.CrmSdk;
using Microsoft.Crm.Callout;


namespace WorkingWithCrm.Callout
{
  /// <summary>
  /// This callout class will log all data changes for the entities specified.
  /// </summary>
  public class DataAudit : CrmCalloutBase
  {
    public DataAudit()
    {
    }

    public override void PostUpdate(CalloutUserContext userContext, CalloutEntityContext
 entityContext, string preImageEntityXml, string postImageEntityXml)
    {
      // Standard CRM Service Setup
      CrmService service = new CrmService();
      service.Credentials = System.Net.CredentialCache.DefaultCredentials;
      service.Url = "http://<crmserver>/mscrmservices/2006/crmservice.asmx";
      service.CallerIdValue = new CallerId();
      service.CallerIdValue.CallerGuid =  userContext.UserId;

      // Only execute if the contact record is updated
      if (entityContext.EntityTypeCode == 2)
      {
        // Deserialize entityxml looking for the values we need
        if ( (preImageEntityXml != null && preImageEntityXml.Length > 0) && (postImageEntity
Xml != null && postImageEntityXml.Length > 0 ) )
        {
        // Deserialize the pre and post data
        DynamicEntity dePre = DeserializeXmltoDynamicEntity(preImageEntityXml);
        DynamicEntity dePost = DeserializeXmltoDynamicEntity(postImageEntityXml);
```

```
            NameValueCollection prop = new NameValueCollection();
            AddPropertiesToCollection(prop,dePre,false);
            AddPropertiesToCollection(prop,dePost,true);

            foreach (string key in prop)
            {
            // Using the Visual Basic split method in order to split on a string, instead of a
            character
                  string[] arr = Microsoft.VisualBasic.Strings.Split(prop[key],"|,|",-1,
                    Microsoft.VisualBasic.CompareMethod.Text);

            if (arr.Length > 1)
            {
                  // If the values do not match, then insert a record into our audit table
                  if (arr[0] != arr[1]) InsertAuditRecord(service,entityContext.InstanceId,key,
                    arr[0],arr[1]);
            }
            else
            {
                  // If the array length is 1, then we have a case where a text value was
changed to or from  a blank value.
                  // Need to split on just the resulting string
                  string[] arrBlankText = prop[key].Split('|');

                  if (arrBlankText.Length > 1)
InsertAuditRecord(service,entityContext.InstanceId,key,arrBlankText[0],arrBlankText[1]);
                  }
               }
         }
      }
   }

    /// <summary>
    /// This helper method will loop through the properties and add them to the passed
in name/value collection.
    /// If the DynamicEntity is pre data, it will append a pipe (|) character. If it is
post data, then it will prepend
    /// a pipe (|) character. This will allow us to easily split the resulting the
collection when checking for any changed values.
    /// </summary>
    /// <param name="prop">Name/value collection to store the resulting values.</param>
    /// <param name="EntityData">DynamicEntity of properties to loop through.</param>
    /// <param name="PostData">Boolean to determine if the DynamicEntity contains pre or
post Xml data.</param>
    public void AddPropertiesToCollection( NameValueCollection prop, DynamicEntity EntityDat
a, bool PostData )
    {
      Property currentProperty;
      string attributeName;
      string attributeValue;
      string attributeModValue;

      // Loop through entities
      for (int i=0; i<EntityData.Properties.Length; i++)
      {
```

```
// Reset the variables
currentProperty = EntityData.Properties[i];
attributeValue = string.Empty;
attributeModValue = string.Empty;

// Get the attribute name
attributeName = currentProperty.Name;
attributeValue = GetValueFromProperty(currentProperty);

// Add a pipe character after the value if we are looping through the pre data or
// before the value if we are looping through the post data.
attributeModValue = (PostData) ? "|" + attributeValue : attributeValue + "|";

// Skip these values, since they change on every update
if ( (attributeName != "modifiedon") && (attributeName != "modifiedby") )
{
 prop.Add(attributeName,attributeModValue);
}
}
}

/// <summary>
/// This function will return the value from a property based on its property type.
/// </summary>
/// <param name="InputProperty"></param>
/// <returns></returns>
public string GetValueFromProperty( Property InputProperty )
{
  Type propType = InputProperty.GetType();
  string propValue = string.Empty;

  // Returning the values will depend on the attribute's property type
  if (propType == typeof(CustomerProperty))
  {
    // Return the name, not the Guid
    propValue = ((CustomerProperty)InputProperty).Value.name.ToString();
  }
  else if (propType == typeof(CrmBooleanProperty))
  {
   propValue = ((CrmBooleanProperty)InputProperty).Value.Value.ToString();
  }
  else if (propType == typeof(CrmDateTimeProperty))
  {
   propValue = ((CrmDateTimeProperty)InputProperty).Value.Value.ToString();
  }
  else if (propType == typeof(CrmDecimalProperty))
  {
   propValue = ((CrmDecimalProperty)InputProperty).Value.Value.ToString();
  }
  else if (propType == typeof(CrmFloatProperty))
  {
    propValue = ((CrmFloatProperty)InputProperty).Value.Value.ToString();
  }
  else if (propType == typeof(CrmMoneyProperty))
  {
    propValue = ((CrmMoneyProperty)InputProperty).Value.Value.ToString();
  }
```

```
        else if (propType == typeof(CrmNumberProperty))
        {
         propValue = ((CrmNumberProperty)InputProperty).Value.Value.ToString();
        }
        else if (propType == typeof(LookupProperty))
        {
          // Return the name, not the Guid if one exists
          // Note that the owningbusinessunit lookup does not provide a name, so will skip it.
          if (InputProperty.Name.ToString() != "owningbusinessunit")
            propValue = ((LookupProperty)InputProperty).Value.name.ToString();
        }
        else if (propType == typeof(OwnerProperty))
        {
          // Return the name, not the Guid
          propValue = ((OwnerProperty)InputProperty).Value.name.ToString();
        }
        else if (propType == typeof(PicklistProperty))
        {
          propValue = ((PicklistProperty)InputProperty).Value.Value.ToString();
        }
        else if (propType == typeof(StringProperty))
        {
          propValue = ((StringProperty)InputProperty).Value.ToString();
        }
        else if (propType == typeof(StatusProperty))
        {
          // Return the name, not the Guid
          propValue = ((StatusProperty)InputProperty).Value.ToString();
        }

      return propValue;
    }

    /// <summary>
    /// Inserts a new record in the audit table.
    /// </summary>
    /// <param name="service"></param>
    /// <param name="ContactId"></param>
    /// <param name="AttributeName"></param>
    /// <param name="PreviousValue"></param>
    /// <param name="NewValue"></param>
    private void InsertAuditRecord( CrmService service, Guid ContactId, string
AttributeName, string PreviousValue, string NewValue )
    {
      Lookup contactId = new Lookup();
      contactId.Value = ContactId;
      contactId.type = EntityName.contact.ToString();

      new_dataaudit audit = new new_dataaudit();
      audit.new_attribute = AttributeName;
      audit.new_contactid = contactId;
      audit.new_previousvalue = PreviousValue;
      audit.new_newvalue = NewValue;

      service.Create(audit);
    }
```

```
    /// <summary>
    /// Translates a xml string from the callout into a DynamicEntity object.
    /// </summary>
    /// <param name="XmlString"></param>
    /// <returns></returns>
    public DynamicEntity DeserializeXmltoDynamicEntity (string XmlString)
    {
      TextReader sr = new StringReader(XmlString);
      XmlRootAttribute root = new XmlRootAttribute("BusinessEntity");
      root.Namespace = "http://schemas.microsoft.com/crm/2006/WebServices";
      XmlSerializer xmlSerializer = new XmlSerializer(typeof(BusinessEntity), root);
      BusinessEntity entity = (BusinessEntity)xmlSerializer.Deserialize(sr);
      DynamicEntity myDE = entity as DynamicEntity;
      return myDE;
    }
  }
}
```

Finally, we update the Callout.config.xml file to register our DataAudit routine, passing in all (non-null) values.

```
<?xml version="1.0" encoding="utf-8" ?>
<callout.config version="2.0">
 <callout entity="contact" event="PostUpdate">
  <subscription assembly="WorkingWithCrm.Callout.dll" class="WorkingWithCrm.Callout.DataAudit">
   <prevalue>@all</prevalue>
   <postvalue>@all</postvalue>
 </subscription>
 </callout>
</callout.config>
```

This data audit example shows how to pull together the various Microsoft CRM customization options to solve a real business need. Our example works for Contact records only, but of course you could modify and extend this example to perform a similar data audit on other entities such as Lead, Opportunity, Account, and Case.

Creating a Project Record from Converted Opportunities

When you convert a Lead, you can create new Account, Contact, and Opportunity records with values mapping from the originating lead. Likewise, you can convert an Opportunity by marking it as Won or Lost, but are not able to natively create new entity records. We've had several customers who need to automatically create new records triggered from these convert actions. For this example, we will create a new "Project" record (a custom entity) upon each successfully converted Opportunity. To accomplish this, we will do the following:

1. Create a new entity called **Project**.
2. Customize the Opportunity entity to include a field called **Project Name**.
3. Create a custom workflow assembly that will create a new Project entity based on the information from the Opportunity closing it.
4. Create a new workflow rule that uses this custom assembly.

Creating the Project entity

1. Create a new entity called Project, and leave the default values for the primary attribute.
2. Create a many-to-one, referential relationship to the Account entity as shown.

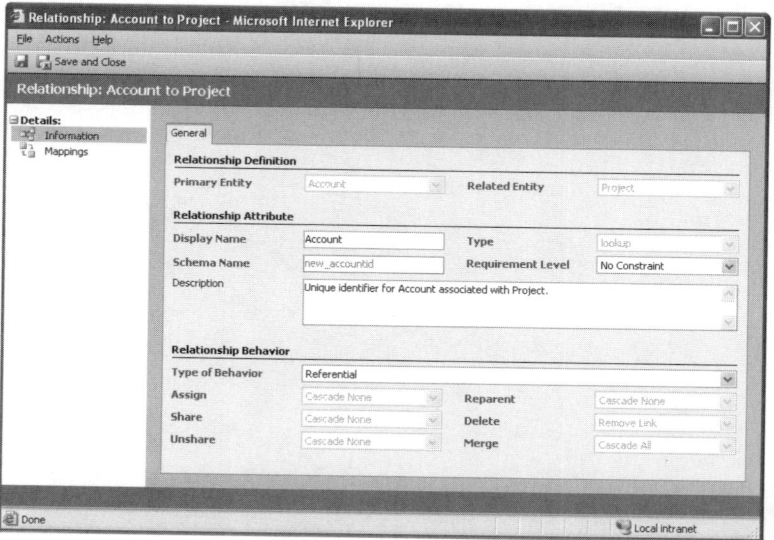

3. Create another many-to-one, referential relationship to the Opportunity entity. This will allow us to track which Opportunity created the Project record.
4. Add the Account and Opportunity lookup fields to the Project form.

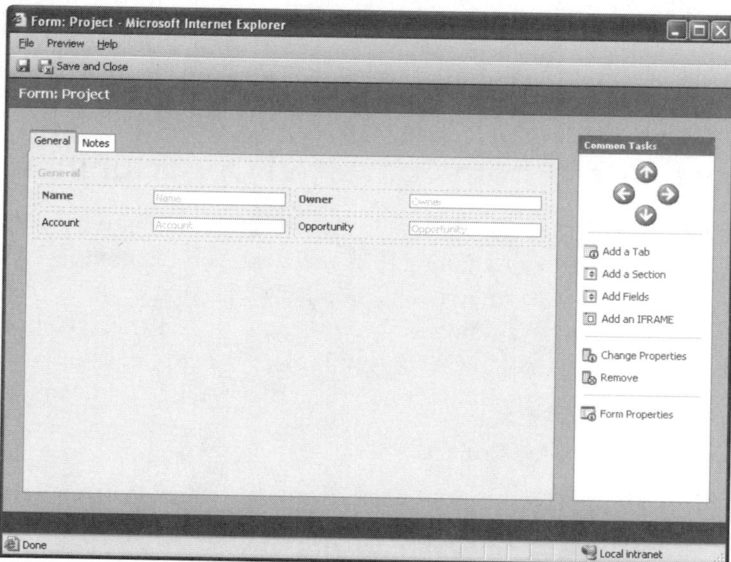

5. Save and publish the Project entity.
6. Update the security roles to provide access to this new entity.

Next we will develop a routine that creates an account based on some passed-in parameters. For this example, we want to have all of our projects relate to Account records. However, the Opportunity allows for either an Account or a Contact for its customer reference. We decided to handle this by creating two methods. The main method, *CreateProjectRecord*, will take in the project name, an account ID, and an opportunity ID. This method will be used when the Opportunity customer is an account. We then create a second method called *CreateProjectRecordFromContact*, which will take in a project name, a contact ID, and an opportunity ID when our customer is a contact. Then we will retrieve the parent account for the Contact record and pass that as our account ID. If no parent account is found, we will simply leave the account ID blank for the project.

Use the WorkingWithCrm.Workflow assembly you created back in the "Creating a Workflow Assembly" section of this chapter. Add a new class file named CustomProject to the Visual Studio .NET project with the code displayed in Listing 9-8.

Listing 9-8 Creating the Project Record

```
using System;
using System.Reflection;
using System.Runtime.CompilerServices;
using WorkingWithCrm.Workflow.CrmSdk;

namespace WorkingWithCrm.Workflow
{
  public class CustomProject
  {
    public void CreateProjectRecordFromContact( string ProjectName, Guid ContactId, Guid Opp
ortunityId )
    {
      // If the customer is a contact record, we will try to retrieve the parent account to
use for the project
      CrmService service = new CrmService();
      service.Url = "http://<crmserver>/mscrmservices/2006/crmservice.asmx";
      service.Credentials = System.Net.CredentialCache.DefaultCredentials;
      WhoAmIRequest userRequest = new WhoAmIRequest();
      WhoAmIResponse userResponse = (WhoAmIResponse) service.Execute(userRequest);
      service.CallerIdValue = new CallerId();
      service.CallerIdValue.CallerGuid = userResponse.UserId;

      // Retrieve the record, casting it as the correct entity
      ColumnSet cols = new ColumnSet();
      cols.Attributes = new string [] {"parentcustomerid"};
      contact oContact = (contact)service.Retrieve(EntityName.contact.ToString(), ContactId,
 cols);

      // If we find a parent account for this contact, use that as our project account
      Guid accountId = Guid.Empty;
      if (oContact.parentcustomerid != null)
        accountId = new Guid(oContact.parentcustomerid.Value.ToString());

      // Call the CreateProjectRecord method passing in the accountid (if one was found)
      CreateProjectRecord( ProjectName, accountId, OpportunityId );
    }
```

```
    public void CreateProjectRecord( string ProjectName, Guid AccountId, Guid OpportunityId )
    {
      // Standard CRM Service Setup
      CrmService service = new CrmService();
      service.Url = "http://<crmserver>/mscrmservices/2006/crmservice.asmx";
      service.Credentials = System.Net.CredentialCache.DefaultCredentials;
      WhoAmIRequest userRequest = new WhoAmIRequest();
      WhoAmIResponse userResponse = (WhoAmIResponse) service.Execute(userRequest);
      service.CallerIdValue = new CallerId();
      service.CallerIdValue.CallerGuid = userResponse.UserId;

      // Create the new_project object
      new_project project = new new_project();

      // Set properties
      project.new_name = ProjectName;

      // Check to see if there is a valid account
      if ( (AccountId.ToString() != string.Empty) && (AccountId != Guid.Empty) )
      {
        Lookup accountId = new Lookup();
        accountId.Value = AccountId;
        accountId.type = EntityName.account.ToString();
        project.new_accountid = accountId;
      }

      // Check to see if there is a valid opportunity
      if ( (OpportunityId.ToString() != string.Empty) && (OpportunityId != Guid.Empty) )
      {
        Lookup oppId = new Lookup();
        oppId.Value = OpportunityId;
        oppId.type = EntityName.opportunity.ToString();
        project.new_opportunityid = oppId;
      }

      // Set the project owner
      project.ownerid = new Owner();
      project.ownerid.Value = userResponse.UserId;
      project.ownerid.type = EntityName.systemuser.ToString();

      // Creates the record in crm
      Guid entityGuid = service.Create(project);
    }
  }
}
```

You must update the Workflow.config file to register your new assembly with the following code.

```
<method name="Create Project Record From Contact"
  assembly="Sonoma.Crm.Book.Workflow.dll"
  typename="Sonoma.Crm.Book.Workflow.CustomProject"
  methodname="CreateProjectRecordFromContact"
  group="Custom Assemblies"
  isvisible="1"
```

```
  timeout="7200">
  <parameter name="ProjectName" datatype="string"/>
  <parameter name="ContactId" datatype="lookup" entityname="contact" />
  <parameter name="OpportunityId" datatype="lookup" entityname="opportunity" />
</method>

<method name="Create Project Record From Account"
  assembly="Sonoma.Crm.Book.Workflow.dll"
  typename="Sonoma.Crm.Book.Workflow.CustomProject"
  methodname="CreateProjectRecord"
  group="Custom Assemblies"
  isvisible="1"
  timeout="7200">
  <parameter name="ProjectName" datatype="string"/>
  <parameter name="AccountId" datatype="lookup" entityname="account" />
  <parameter name="OpportunityId" datatype="lookup" entityname="opportunity" />
</method>
```

Note the use of lookup parameters. This tells the Workflow Manager that you want to pass a GUID identifier for that identity, as you will see shortly. You will now deploy the assembly to the Web server, using the same process you have used before. Then you must create a workflow rule to create a new account when the Opportunity status is closed and marked as Won.

1. To open the Workflow Manager, click **Start**, point to **All Programs**, point to **Microsoft CRM**, and then click **Workflow Manager**.
2. Select **Opportunity** as the entity type, and then create a new rule for the Change Status event, calling it **Create Project**.
3. Using the techniques you learned in Chapter 8, create a workflow rule as shown here.

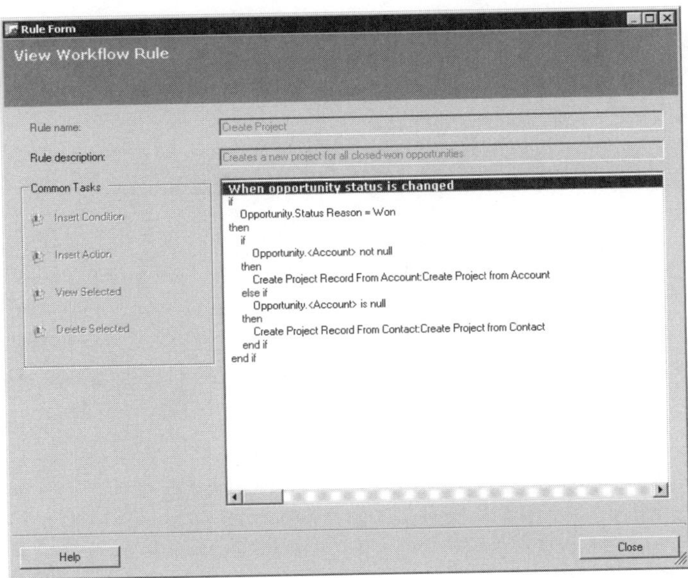

4. When you create the custom assembly actions, you must set the parameters to the following:
   a. **Create Project Record from Account** Project Name: Use the dynamic opportunity Topic field. Use the Dynamic setting for both Account and Opportunity.
   b. **Create Project Record from Contact** Project Name: Use the dynamic opportunity Topic field. Use the Dynamic setting for both Account and Opportunity.
5. Activate your new workflow rule.

After you activate the workflow rule, go back to your Microsoft CRM application and create a new Opportunity, selecting an Account as your potential customer. After you have saved it, click Close Opportunity on the Actions menu, and then mark the Opportunity as Won. You should see a Projects subarea in the navigation pane, as shown in Figure 9-17. Click it to see your new project.

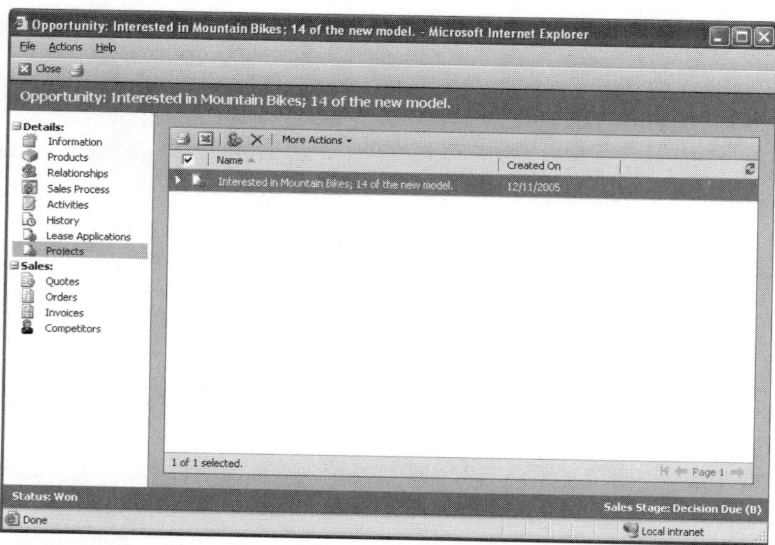

Figure 9-17 Project list

Remember that the workflow rule will run asynchronously, so it's possible that you could click the Projects tab and not see anything because the rule hasn't completed processing yet. In that case, click the Refresh icon to check for new data. If it still doesn't appear, you should log back on to the server and use the Workflow Monitor tool to make sure that the rule processed correctly.

> **Note** We could have also implemented this feature by using a post-callout. We decided to use a workflow assembly because we don't need the project to be created synchronously. This also allows for tweaks to the workflow rule without requiring development changes (such as changing the values passed in to the routine to default the account fields, or adding conditions for when you want to create a new record).

Summary

You should now have a firm understanding of the touch points available to you when working with the Microsoft CRM server-side SDK. As you saw, you can create and include custom processes and logic at various points in the application, notably through the use of callouts and by extending the workflow capabilities with custom assemblies.

The Microsoft CRM API provides a clear, scalable method for accessing entities and manipulating data in the system without the need to understand the underlying mechanisms of the platform. By using these techniques, you have almost unlimited possibilities for customizing Microsoft CRM to your specific business needs.

Chapter 10

Client-Side SDK

In this chapter:

In Chapter 5, "Entity Customization: Forms and Views," we explained how to perform basic form customizations on each entity. You can easily add fields, tabs, and sections to a form by using the Web-based administration tool, without having to do any programming. However, if you want to set up more complex form customizations than the Web-based administration tool allows, Microsoft Dynamics CRM 3.0 offers a rich, client-side programming model.

In the context of Web-based applications, *client-side* refers to code that executes on the user's Web browser. For Microsoft CRM specifically, the client-side customizations take place primarily on an entity's form. Microsoft CRM includes a software development kit (SDK) that explains the supported methods you can use to create custom client-side scripts that tap into form and field events, such as *onLoad*, *onSave*, and *onChange*. This chapter examines these advanced form programming techniques. We will also review the use of IFrames within the Microsoft CRM forms and the ISV.Config file and how you can use these two features to extend the Microsoft CRM interface with your own custom Web pages. In addition, we'll supply numerous examples on how you might implement some customizations that these powerful client-side customizations allow.

Because of the nature of the client-side programming model, this chapter contains a significant amount of dynamic HTML (DHTML) and scripting code. However, even if you're not an expert with these technologies, hopefully this chapter will help you understand the types of client-side customizations possible within Microsoft CRM.

We created the samples in this chapter so that you could deploy them to your own Microsoft CRM deployment. You can download all of the sample code directly from the download site mentioned in the book's Introduction. We will also provide references to additional information regarding client-side scripting syntax and methods later in this chapter.

Client-Side SDK Overview

After reading Chapter 9, "Server-Side SDK," you should be familiar with the Microsoft CRM API and general architecture. We will now focus on the many events and programmatic possiblilities available to you by using client-side techniques. We'll cover the following topics in the client-side SDK overview:

- Definitions
- Understanding client-side scripting with Microsoft CRM
- Referencing CRM elements
- Available events

Definitions

Before we get too deep in the client-side SDK and examples, let's review a few key expressions and their definitions.

- **Client-side scripting** Code that executes on a user's Internet browser, instead of a centralized Web server.
- **Hypertext Markup Language (HTML)** A tag-based language used to render content in an Internet browser.
- **Cascading style sheet** A definition document that describes how a Web document should display formats and styles to the user.
- **Document Object Model (DOM)** An application programming interface designed to access HTML documents, representing elements in the document in an object-oriented model.
- **Dynamic HTML (DHTML)** A technology that extends regular HTML with client-side scripting and cascading style sheets, exposing the elements on an HTML document so that you can manipulate them programmatically by using the DOM.
- **Globally unique identifier (GUID)** A string that represents a unique value. Microsoft CRM uses a GUID as the unique identifier for each record.

Understanding Client-Side Scripting with Microsoft CRM

Client-side scripting helps distribute the application processing load between the client computer and the Web server. Because Microsoft CRM uses a Web-based architecture, it displays all of its data on Web pages. However, the Microsoft CRM pages don't appear as typical Web pages that users see when browsing the Internet. Rather, Microsoft CRM relies heavily on DHTML to achieve a more advanced and functional user interface. Because the DOM treats each HTML element as an object, a developer may use traditional DHTML programming techniques to access the Microsoft CRM forms to create even more customized and sophisticated Web pages within Microsoft CRM.

Microsoft CRM supports a specialized subset of DOM methods and events as defined in the client-side SDK. We will examine many of the available properties and methods here, but refer to the Microsoft CRM SDK for a complete list of supported methods.

Referencing CRM Elements

The "Client Programming Guide" section of the Microsoft CRM SDK provides information regarding the client methods, properties, and events available to a programmer. In the following tables, we highlight a few of the key actions that you will probably use frequently in your own scripts.

Table 10-1 Global Methods

Property	Description
IsOnline	Gets a Boolean value indicating whether the form is currently online.
IsOutlookClient	Gets a Boolean value indicating whether the form is currently being displayed in one of the Microsoft Office Outlook clients.
IsOutlookLaptopClient	Gets a Boolean value indicating whether the form is currently being displayed in the full, offline-capable Microsoft CRM client for Outlook, also known as the Microsoft CRM laptop client for Outlook.
IsOutlookWorkstationClient	Gets a Boolean value indicating whether the form is currently being displayed in the online-only Microsoft CRM client for Outlook, also known as the Microsoft CRM desktop client for Outlook.

Table 10-2 *crmForm* Properties

Property	Description
all	A collection of CRM fields on the form.
IsDirty	Gets or sets a value indicating whether any of the fields on the form have been modified.
FormType	Gets an integer value designating the mode of the form. Possible values are: 0 = Undefined Form Type 1 = Create Form 2 = Update Form 3 = Read Only Form 4 = Disabled Form 5 = Quick Create Form 6 = Bulk Edit Form
ObjectId	Gets the entity GUID that the form is displaying. This property returns null if the form is in Create mode.
ObjectTypeCode	Gets the integer code of the entity that the form is displaying (1 = Account, 2 = Contact, and so on).

Table 10-3 *crmForm* Methods

Method	Description
Save()	Executes the save function (simulates a user clicking Save).
SaveAndClose()	Executes the save and close function (simulates a user clicking Save And Close).
SetFieldReqLevel(sField, bRequired)	Sets a field as required. Note that this is unsupported and may change or not be available in future releases.

Table 10-4 *crmForm.all* Field Collection Properties

Property	Description
Precision	Gets the number of digits to display for *currency*, and *float* data types.
DataValue	Gets or sets the value of the field.
Disabled	Gets or sets a value indicating whether the field is available for user entry.
ForceSubmit	Gets or sets a value indicating whether the field should be submitted to the database on a save. By default, any enabled, modified field will be submitted. This property is useful when you need to submit a disabled field.
IsDirty	Gets a value indicating whether the field has been modified.
Min	Gets the minimum allowable value for *currency*, *float*, and *integer* data types.
Max	Gets the maximum allowable value for *currency*, *float*, and *integer* data types.
MaxLength	Gets the maximum length of a string or memo field.
RequiredLevel	Gets the required status of the field. Possible values are: 0 = No Constraint 1 = Business Recommended 2 = Business Required

Table 10-5 *crmForm.all* Collection Methods

Method	Description
SetFocus()	Moves the mouse cursor to the field, making it active on the form.
FireOnChange()	Executes the Microsoft CRM OnChange event for the attribute specified.

The lookup and picklist field types differ from the other fields, because they act as arrays (a collection of name/value pairs). The value that Microsoft CRM stores in the database (a GUID for lookup fields and an integer for picklist fields) is not the value that the user will see on the form. Because you probably don't want to reference the GUID or integer value, Microsoft CRM includes the following additional attributes of the *DataValue* property for displaying the translated value as shown in the next three tables.

Table 10-6 *crmForm.all.<lookupfield>.DataValue* Attributes

Attribute	Description
id	Gets or sets the GUID identifier. Required for set.
type	Gets or sets the object type code. Required for set.
name	Gets or sets the name of the record to be displayed in the lookup field on the form. Required for set.

Table 10-7 *crmForm.all.<picklistfield>* Properties and Methods

Syntax	Description
DataValue	Gets or sets the currently selected option, returning an integer.
SelectedText	Gets the text displayed with the currently selected option.
GetSelectedOption	Gets a picklist.
Options	Returns an array of picklist objects and sets new options for a drop-down list by specifying an array of picklist objects.
AddOption(option)	Adds a new option at the end of the picklist collection. *DataValue* and *Name* must have valid values.
DeleteOption(value)	Removes a picklist option based on the integer value passed in.

Table 10-8 *crmForm.all.<picklistfield>.DataValue* Attributes

Attribute	Description
Name	Gets or sets the text displayed in the picklist.
Data	Gets or sets the data.

Available Events

Microsoft CRM supports three client-side events that you can reference within your custom scripts:

- **Form *onLoad* event** Executes immediately before the form loads in the browser. This event allows you to manipulate the form before displaying it to the user.
- **Form *onSave* event** Triggered when the user clicks the Save, Save and Close, or Save and New buttons. This event happens before the form is submitted and can be used to cancel the save. Also, this event always fires, even if the user did not change any of the fields on the form.
- **Field *onChange* events** Fires when the user navigates away from a form field (clicks elsewhere or presses the Tab key) in which he or she changed the value.

Note The form *onSave* event for Microsoft CRM does not correspond to the standard DTHML *onSave* event. If you want to cancel the save, use the following syntax: *event.returnValue = false;*

We introduced adding client-side scripts to an entity form in Chapter 5, but we'll go through a quick refresher anyway.

Adding event code

With a System Administrator or System Customizer role, you will navigate to the **Settings** section, click **Customizations**, and then click **Customize Entities**.

1. In the **Customize Entities** section, double-click the entity that you want to customize.
2. In the navigation pane, click **Forms and Views**.
3. Double-click **Form** from the resulting list.

The form editor page will now display and show all of the tabs and fields that the form will display to the user, as shown in Figure 10-1 for the Account entity.

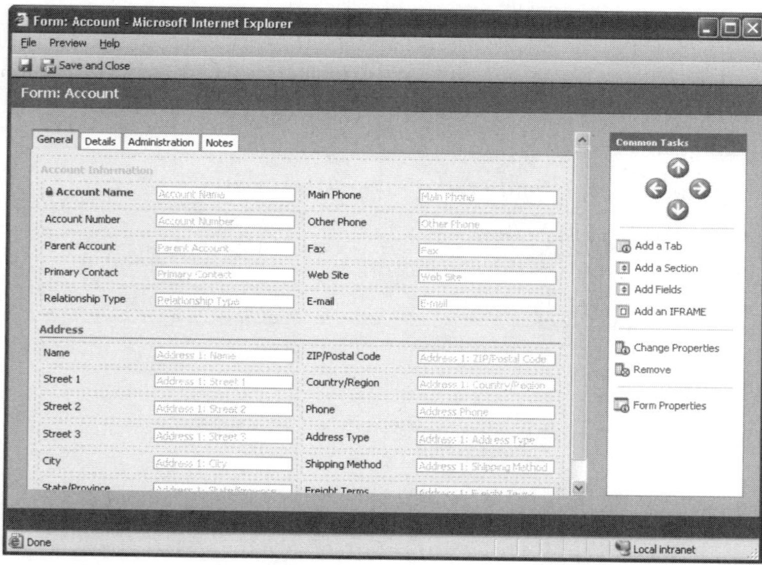

Figure 10-1 The form editor page

Customizing form events

To customize the form events (*onLoad* and *onSave*), follow these steps:

1. Click **Form Properties** in the **Common Tasks** area. A dialog box appears that lists the *onLoad* and *onSave* events.
2. Select the event that you want to add code to, and then click **Edit**.
3. Enter your custom script in the **Event Detail Properties** dialog window (shown in Figure 10-2), select the **Event is enabled** check box, and then click **OK**.

Adding steps to the field event

Adding scripts to the field event (*onChange*) works the same way as it does for form events:

1. In the form editor, double-click the field where you will add your code. Or you can select a field and then click **Change Properties**.
2. The Field Properties dialog will launch. Click to the **Events** tab.
3. Click **Edit**. You will see the **Event Detail Properties** dialog box, as shown in Figure 10-2.

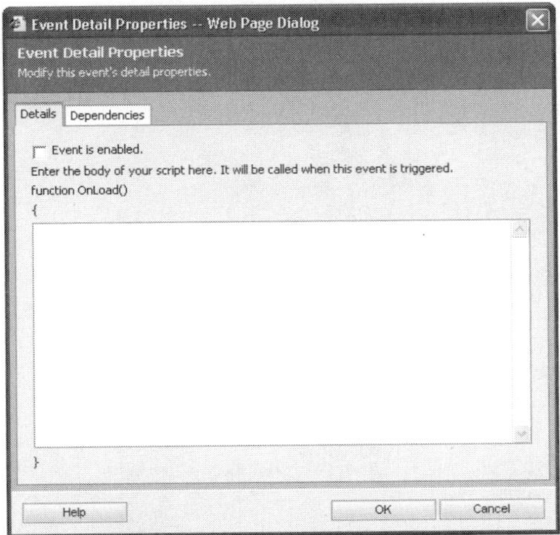

Figure 10-2 The Event Detail Properties dialog box

Remember these key points related to configuring your client-side scripts on the entity forms:

- You must enable your script by selecting the Event Is Enabled check box on the Event Properties dialog. This check box tells Microsoft CRM to run the script the next time the event triggers.
- Although not required, it's a good practice to specify the fields your script uses on the Dependencies tab. Specifying dependent fields will block users from accidentally removing fields from the form that your script requires.
- You can test and debug your scripts by using one of the form preview options: Create, Update, and Read-Only.
- Microsoft CRM provides a Simulate Form Save button on the preview that will trigger the *onSave* event. You can use this button to test your *onSave* custom scripts.
- Of course you need to remember to publish your customizations when you're done.

We'll show lots of examples of client-side customizations later in this chapter. We just wanted to give you a quick background on the customization process and terminology.

IFrames and Scripting

Microsoft CRM allows you to add an IFrame (also known as an *inline frame*) to the form of an entity. Chapter 5 introduced IFrames and described how to set up a simple IFrame within a form, but now we'll go into the details of how to really take advantage of this powerful feature with client-side customization techniques. The IFrame feature creates tremendous integration and customization opportunities for a developer within Microsoft CRM. Because you can programmatically access an IFrame document from the Microsoft CRM form through the DOM, your enhancements can appear seamless to the user. Figure 10-3 shows a sample IFrame that references a Windows SharePoint Services Web site.

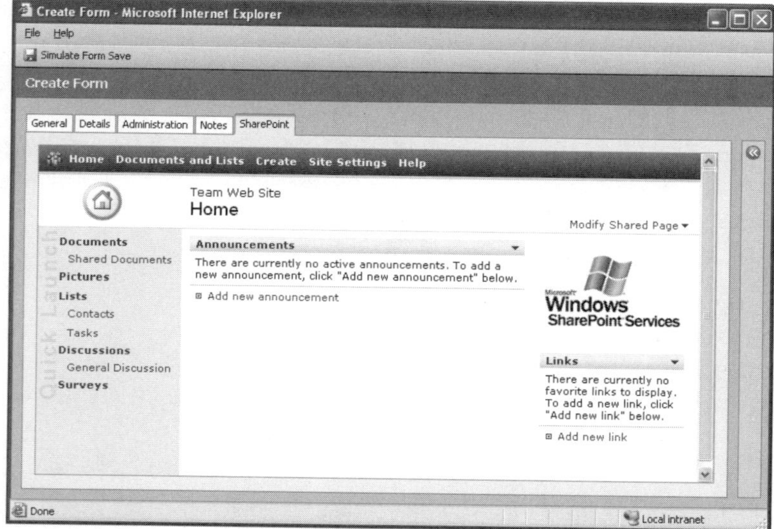

Figure 10-3 IFrame sample

IFrames can reference any URL or Web page, whether they are hosted on your Web server or any other any Web server. Common uses might include displaying SharePoint sites, adding mapping functionality through external Web sites, and custom application integration.

Caution Remember that Microsoft CRM laptop client for Outlook users can work offline, so they might experience an issue with a form if the IFrame references a Web page that they can't access offline. Therefore, don't include any key functionality that offline users will require within an IFrame.

Security

We couldn't possibly provide a comprehensive analysis on Web application security within the scope of this book, but we want to briefly touch upon the notion of Microsoft CRM cross-site scripting and its IFrame-related security issues. Cross-site scripting provides a powerful (and potentially dangerous) feature within Web applications, including Microsoft CRM. In most cases, DHTML and the user's browser settings permit scripting access to and from IFrame documents that reside on the same domain and reference matching protocols (such as FTP, HTTP, or HTTPS).

For example, consider an HTML document called Main.htm located on the *www.adatum.com* domain (*http://www.adatum.com/main.htm*). The Main.htm page includes an IFrame that references a second Web page named Frame.htm. The protocol in this example is HTTP for both pages, and because they both reside on the same domain, the browser will permit the scripts from the Frame.htm page to access and manipulate content on the Main.htm document. Internet Explorer will disable scripting access to IFrame URLs that refer to a page on another domain or reference the page through a different protocol. So if the IFrame source was *https://www.adatum.com/frame.htm* (accessed by using the SSL protocol) or *http://www.contoso.com/frame.htm* (located on another domain), Internet Explorer will prevent script access between the pages. Figure 10-4 shows a graphical representation of this.

Cross-Site Scripting Allowed

Same domain (www.adatum.com) and protocol (http)

Host Page

http://www.adatum.com/main.htm

IFrame Page

http://www.adatum.com/frame.htm

Cross-Site Scripting Denied

Same domain (www.adatum.com), but different protocols (http for main page, https for fram page)

Host Page

http://www.adatum.com/main.htm

IFrame Page

https://www.adatum.com/frame.htm

Same protocol (http), but different domains (www.adatum.com and www.contoso.com)

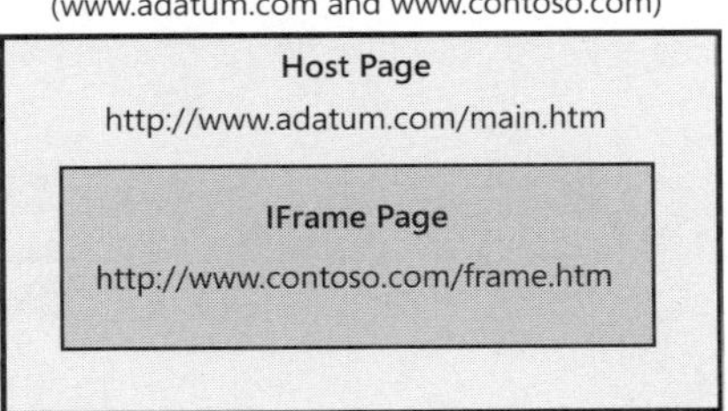

Figure 10-4 Default Internet Explorer IFrame security

In addition to the default Internet Explorer security behavior, Microsoft CRM allows you to add another layer of security with its *Restrict cross-frame scripting* setting. This option will set the value of the *security* attribute of the IFrame tag to *restricted*. Under default conditions, this setting will have the following affects:

- Restricts JavaScript and VBScript from executing on the IFrame page
- All hyperlinks will open in a new browser window

So even if Internet Explorer would have allowed cross-frame scripting, you can disable this for a specific IFrame in Microsoft CRM. By default, Microsoft CRM restricts cross-frame scripting on new IFrame pages. So if you want your scripts to run, you must uncheck the cross-frame scripting setting. Obviously, we recommend that you leave the default setting of not allowing cross-frame scripting for security purposes unless you have a specific need for this feature.

CRM IFrame Scripting Example

We will now demonstrate how the domain and Microsoft CRM IFrame property settings affect the form's display and scripting capabilities between the IFrame document and the Microsoft CRM Contact form. In this example, we will integrate a custom Web page that calculates monthly mortgage payments. The custom Web page within the IFrame will take values entered by a user, calculate the correct mortgage payment, and then populate that payment value back into a native Microsoft CRM field.

The resulting form should look like Figure 10-5.

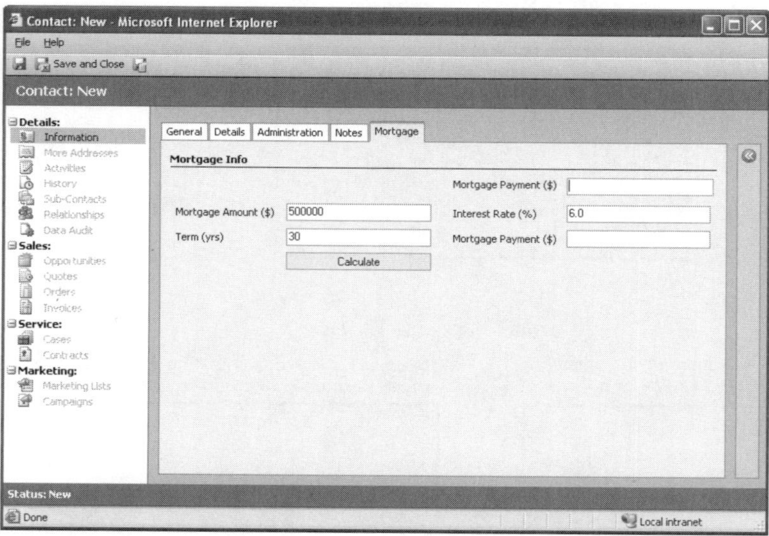

Figure 10-5 Contact form with custom mortgage Web page

Adding attributes

For this example, we need to add a new attribute (Mortgage Amount) to the Contact entity.

1. Browse to the Customization area of Microsoft CRM and double-click the Contact entity. Click **Attributes** in the navigation pane.
2. Add a **money** attribute called mortgagepayment (the schema name will be **new_mortgagepayment**, provided that you haven't changed your default schema name prefix).
3. Type **Mortgage Payment** in the **Display Name** box.

4. Change the **Type** field to **money**. Leave the money value defaults and click **Save and Close**.

Modifying the form

1. In the navigation pane, click **Forms and Views,** and then click **Form** to open the **Form Editor** window.
2. Add a new tab called **Mortgage** on the Contact form. This tab will contain an automatically expanding IFrame that points to a custom HTML page and two currency fields.
3. Add a section called **Mortgage Info**. Select both the label and the divider line options.
4. Add the new **Mortgage Payment** field that you just created.
5. Add a section called **iframe**. This section will contain an automatically expanding IFrame.
6. Select the newly created section, and then click the **IFrame** link. We will vary the properties of the IFrame to see the impact that they have on the form. Initially, set the following properties:
    a. **Name**: test
    b. **URL**: *http://*<crmserver>*/workingwithcrm/mortgage.htm*. (Note that *<crmserver>* should be replaced with the name of the server on which CRM is installed. We will explain how to deploy the mortgage.htm file next.)
    c. **Label**: Leave blank.
    d. **Security**: Clear the **Restrict cross-frame scripting** check box. We will start by allowing the two pages scripting access, so that the IFrame page can update a field on the Microsoft CRM form.
7. Switch to the **Formatting** tab, and set the following properties:
    a. Number of Rows: Select **Automatically expand to use available space**.
    b. Scrolling: Select **Never**. We have created a form to mirror the existing Microsoft CRM form. If we allow scrollbars, Internet Explorer will allocate space for this, shifting our IFrame form, as shown in Figure 10-6.
    c. Border: Clear **Display Border**. As with scrolling, we don't want to alert users that they are looking at a different page. We want to create the illusion that they are working on the native Microsoft CRM form.
8. Switch to the **Dependencies** tab, select **Mortgage Amount** and **Mortgage Payment**, and make them dependent.

Blending an IFrame Web Page with the Microsoft CRM Form

In our mortgage calculator example, we want the users to believe they are using one form. We don't want (or need) them to know that some of the fields on the Mortgage tab are actually hosted within an IFrame. Therefore, it's important that we modify the IFrame settings to make our page blend in as much as possible.

Figure 10-6 shows how the IFrame page would look with the border enabled and scrolling set to As Necessary. If you look to the right, Microsoft CRM automatically allotted space for a scrollbar should it need it. Therefore, the Interest Rate and Mortgage Payment fields in our IFrame shift to the left and they don't line up with the native Mortgage Payment form field. In addition, with the border enabled, a blue outline frames our IFrame page.

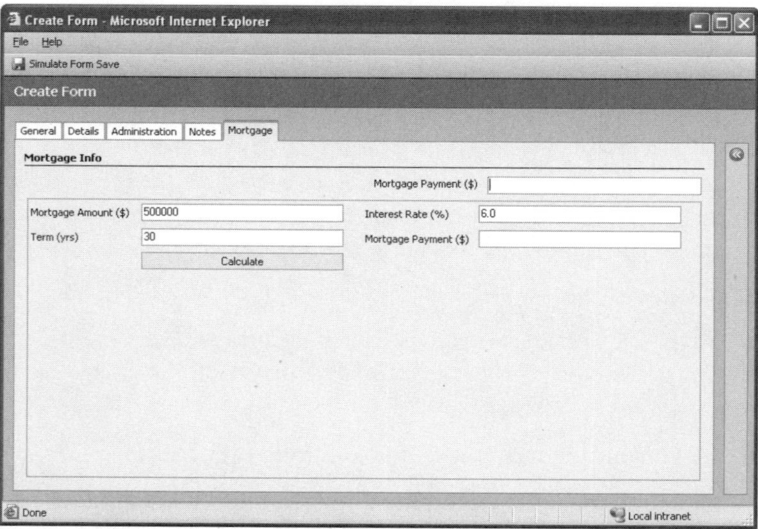

Figure 10-6 IFrame with automatic scrolling enabled and a border displayed

Since we like our Web pages and forms neat and tidy with all of the fields lined up correctly, we're going to tweak the IFrame configuration options. By setting the scrollbars to Never and disabling the border, we can then format our custom IFrame Web page to blend in with the Microsoft CRM form, creating the illusion of one page and a consistent interface to the user, as shown back in Figure 10-5.

Custom HTML Page

Now we need to create the custom Mortgage.htm Web page that contains the mortgage calculator within the IFrame. The Web page takes three financial inputs and then it calculates a monthly mortgage payment by using a custom JavaScript method. It then attempts to write the value back to the CRM form, allowing it to be saved with the Contact record.

You should take note of the following in regards to the Mortgage.htm file:

- The styles of the custom Web page mirror those of the native Microsoft CRM form. This allows us to seamlessly integrate our IFrame page into the form.
- This example includes a simple JavaScript page, but you can create much more sophisticated Web pages within an IFrame.
- Our custom page will also contain a Mortgage Payment field to demonstrate the interaction between the Microsoft CRM form and the custom Web page.
- The script attempts to send the monthly payment result back to the Microsoft CRM form. The Microsoft CRM form is unnamed, but it will always be the first item in the forms collection. So, you can reference it with the following syntax:

  ```
  parent.document.forms[0]
  ```

- For this example, we use a submit button on the custom page. In the "Client-Side Code Examples" section later in this chapter, the "Saving an IFrame Form from Microsoft CRM" sample shows how you can also use cross-frame scripting to force a submit event of your custom page.

The code for the Mortgage.htm page is shown in Listing 10-1.

Listing 10-1 mortgage.htm HTML Code:

```
<html>
<head>
 <title>Mortgage Calculator</title>
 <script type="text/javascript" language="javascript">
 /// <summary>
 /// calculate() takes a mortgage amount, an interest rate, and a term in years
 /// and calculates what the monthly mortgage payments will be
 /// </summary>
 function calculate()
 {
  // Gather inputs from form
  var mortgageamount = document.crmForm.mortgageamount.value;
  var interestrate = document.crmForm.interestrate.value;
  var term = document.crmForm.term.value;

  // Calculate payment and assign to field on form
  var mortgagepayment = calculatePMT( interestrate, term * 12, mortgageamount)
  document.crmForm.mortgagepayment.value = mortgagepayment;

  // Also assign back to the Microsoft CRM form
  parent.document.forms[0].all.new_mortgagepayment.DataValue = mortgagepayment;
 }

 /// <summary>
 ///
 calculatePMT() simulates the financial PMT routine and is used to determine monthly payments
 /// </summary>
 /// <param name="rate">Annual interest rate</param>
 /// <param name="nummonths">Length of term in months</param>
 /// <param name="presentvalue">Amount to finance</param>
```

```
 function calculatePMT(rate, nummonths, presentvalue)
 {
  var intRate = rate /100 / 12;
  var pmt = Math.floor((presentvalue*intRate)/(1-Math.pow(1+intRate,(-1*nummonths)))*100)/100;
  return pmt;
 }
 </script>

<style type="text/css">
 body { font-size:11px; font-family:"Tahoma,Verdana"; margin:0px; border:0px; background-
color:#eef0f6; cursor:default; }
 td { font-size:11px; font-family:"Tahoma,Verdana"; }
 td.sec { width:100%; color:#000000; font-weight:bold; padding-left:0px; padding-
bottom:2px; text-overflow:ellipsis; overflow:hidden; }
 td.bar { border-bottom:1px solid #000000; }
 td.req { font-weight:bold; color:#9f2409; overflow:hidden; text-overflow:ellipsis;
padding-top:5px; }
 td.rec { font-weight:bold; color:#466094; overflow:hidden; text-overflow:ellipsis;
padding-top:5px; }
 table.layout { table-layout:fixed; width:100%; }
 input { font-size:8pt; width:100%; height:19px; border:1px solid #7b9ebd; }
 button { filter:progid:DXImageTransform.Microsoft.Gradient(GradientType=0, StartColorStr=
#ffffff, EndColorStr=#cecfde); cursor:hand; font-size:11px; padding-left:5px; padding-right:
5px; border:1px solid #7b9ebd; }
</style>
</head>

<body>
<form id="crmForm" name="crmForm" action="iframe-example.htm" method="get">
<div style="padding:0px;">
<table class="layout" cellspacing="0" cellpadding="3" border="0" ID="Table1">
 <col width="115"/><col/><col width="135" style="padding-left:20px;"/><col/>
 <tr>
  <td>Mortgage Amount ($)</td>
  <td><input type="text" id="mortgageamount" name="mortgageamount" value="500000" /></td>
  <td>Interest Rate (%)</td>
  <td><input type="text" id="interestrate" name="interestrate" value="6.0" /></td>
 </tr>
 <tr>
  <td>Term (yrs)</td>
  <td><input type="text" id="term" name="term" value="30" /></td>
  <td>Mortgage Payment ($)</td>
  <td><input type="text" id="mortgagepayment" name="mortgagepayment" value="" /></td>
 </tr>
 <tr>
  <td> </td>
  <td><input type="button" id="btnSubmit" name="btnSubmit" value="Calculate" onclick=
"calculate();" /></td>
 </tr>
</table>
</div>
</form>

</body>
</html>
```

For this example, we will reuse the *workingwithcrm* virtual Web. (Instructions on creating this can be found in the Introduction.) After you complete the page, you must deploy it to the location specified by the IFrame URL property (the <*crmserver*>/workingwithcrm/ directory). Copy the Mortgage.htm file to C:\Inetpub\workingwithcrm on your Microsoft CRM Web server, using whatever method is easiest (such as xcopy or FTP).

After you save the form, you can preview it to see the results. Using the Create Form preview functionality, we can also test how the *Restrict cross-frame scripting* setting works. Enter some values into the mortgage calculator and click Calculate. You will see that both Mortgage Payment ($) fields on the custom page and the native Microsoft CRM form update, as shown in Figure 10-7.

Also, notice that with the border turned off and the scrolling set to Never, the form looks as if it is part of the native page. Because we allowed cross-frame scripting in our IFrame properties, we can execute the custom page's JavaScript routines. Also, since we deployed and referenced the page using the same domain and protocol as the Microsoft CRM server, we will be able to access elements on the Microsoft CRM form and populate our monthly payment results back to Microsoft CRM.

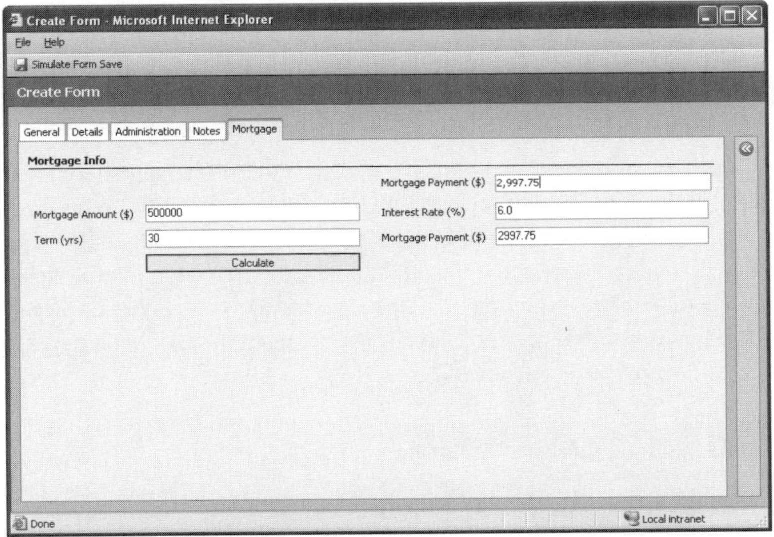

Figure 10-7 Mortgage tab preview

What would happen if we restricted cross-frame scripting? Figure 10-8 shows that when the Calculate button is clicked, the IFrame's monthly payment field was not populated. The Microsoft CRM form also remains blank, and no error message is displayed. All scripting on the custom IFrame page was disabled and prevented from executing.

Figure 10-8 Mortgage tab with cross-frame scripting disabled

Important Remember that when you disable cross-site scripting in Microsoft CRM, your referenced IFrame page will also be restricted from running any scripts (even if those scripts don't try to go cross-frame into Microsoft CRM).

Let's enable cross-frame scripting again but move the IFrame form to another server and access it in a different URL domain. We will update the URL property of the IFrame to *http://crmserver2/workingwithcrm/iframe-example.htm*. Then we preview the form and try the mortgage calculation again. The mortgage payment field correctly populates, but a script error appears in the browser (similar to the one shown in Figure 10-9). Internet Explorer displays the access denied message because it doesn't allow scripting across two Web pages hosted on different domains: crmserver and crmserver2.

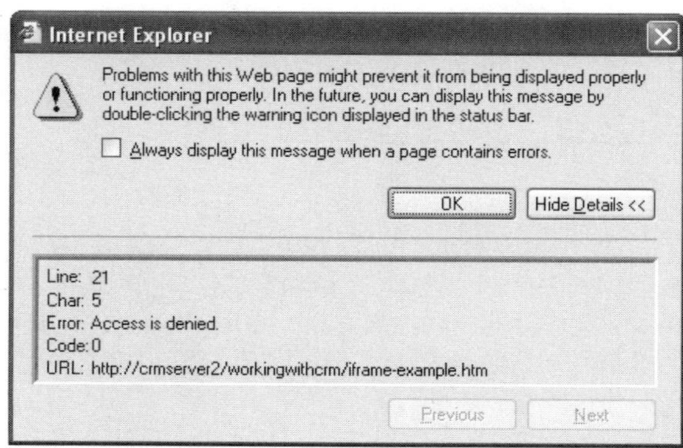

Figure 10-9 Scripting access denied error

Of course, you could accomplish this particular mortgage calculation example by using alternate methods. For example, you could simply add the mortgage fields from the IFrame to the native Contact form and use the *onChange* event to do the same calculations. Another option would be to add the fields to the native form and call a Web service or Web page from the *onChange* event. With simple business logic, you really don't need the overhead of a custom IFrame, but you can see that with more complex situations, the IFrame element with cross-frame scripting can be a valuable tool.

Dynamic IFrame URLs

Even though you enter a URL address for an IFrame when you add it to a form, you can still programmatically change this URL on the fly. For example, you might need to change the IFrame URL based on user form selections, or even update the protocol of the URL based on the protocol of Microsoft CRM. To do this, you can update the *src* property of the IFrame from either the *onLoad*, *onSave*, or *onChange* events. The code would look like:

```
crmForm.all.<iframe_name>.src = <URL reference>
```

ISV.config

The ISV.config.xml file allows you to integrate custom Web pages into the Microsoft CRM application. By editing the ISV.config file in conjuction with the site map functionality you learned about in Chapter 6, "Entity Customization: Relationships and Custom Entities," you can create a highly customized application navigation for your Microsoft CRM users. Some exciting enhancements in Microsoft CRM 3.0 ISV.config file include the ability to add buttons and action menu links to the grid toolbar, JavaScript code support for menus and buttons, and access to the parent window. Microsoft CRM includes a default ISV.config.xml file in the *<web installation path>*_Resources\ folder, but the ISV.config features are disabled by default.

More Info You can get more information about the ISV.config in the Client Programming Guide of the SDK.

Integration Areas

Figure 10-10 shows the areas in the main application window that you can customize with the ISV.config file. As you can see in this figure, we added some sample buttons and menu items to illustrate how the ISV.config customizations will appear in the user interface. You may add custom buttons or menus to the following areas of the application navigation:

1. Application menu bar
2. Application toolbar
3. Grid toolbar
4. Grid actions menu

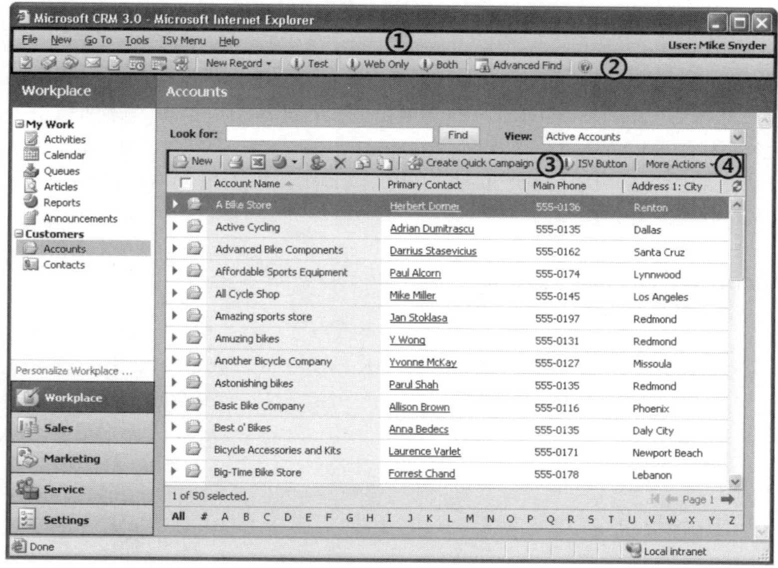

Figure 10-10 Application integration points

In addition to the application navigation, you can also customize the entity form. Figure 10-11 displays the integration areas that the ISV.config offers in an entity form window. You may customize the following:

1. Detail form menu bar
2. Toolbar
3. Navigation pane

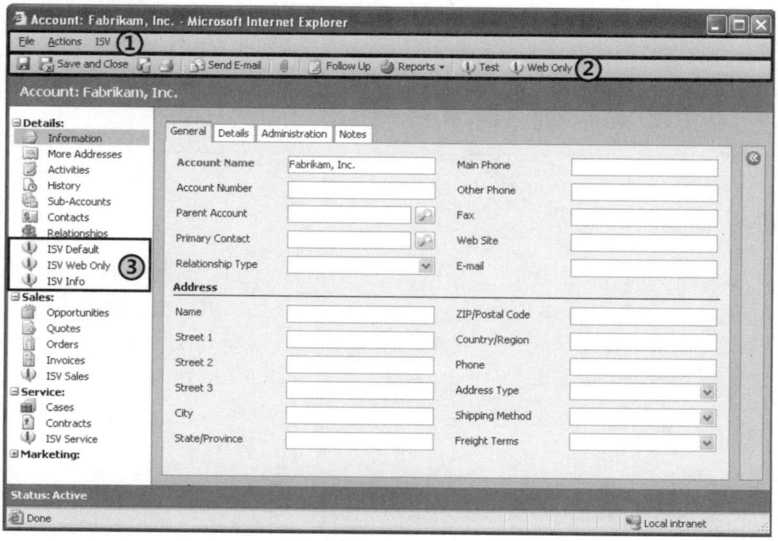

Figure 10-11 Entity form integration points

> **Note** You can't customize the *application* navigation pane by using the ISV.config file, but you can customize the *entity* navigation pane. Chapter 6 explains how to customize the application navigation pane by using the site map.

The following code snippet is from the ISV.config.xml file that ships with Microsoft CRM. We will discuss the meaning of the elements available in this file next.

```
<configuration version="3.0.0000.0">
 <Root>
  <MenuBar>
   <CustomMenus>
    <Menu Title="ISV">
     <MenuItem Title="New Window" Url="http://www.microsoft.com" />
   </CustomMenus>
  </MenuBar>
  <ToolBar>
   <Button Title="Test" ToolTip="Info on Test" Icon="/_imgs/ico_18_debug.gif"
JavaScript="alert('test');" />
   <ToolBarSpacer />
  </ToolBar>
 </Root>

 <!-- Microsoft Customer Relationship Management Entities (Objects) -->
 <Entities>
  <Entity name="account">
   <MenuBar>
    <CustomMenus>
     <Menu Title="ISV">
      <MenuItem Title="Coming Soon..." Url="http://www.microsoft.com"
PassParams="0" WinMode="1" />
      <MenuSpacer />
      <SubMenu Title="Sub Test">
       <MenuItem Title="Test Sub 1" Url="http://www.microsoft.com" PassParams="1" />
       <MenuSpacer />
       <MenuItem Title="Test Sub 2" />
      </SubMenu>
     </Menu>
    </CustomMenus>
   </MenuBar>
   <ToolBar ValidForCreate="0" ValidForUpdate="1">
    <Button Title="asdf" ToolTip="Info on Test" Icon="/_imgs/ico_18_debug.gif" Url="http://
www.microsoft.com" PassParams="1" WinParams="" WinMode="0" />
    <ToolBarSpacer />
    <Button Title="Test" ToolTip="Info on Test" Icon="/_imgs/ico_18_debug.gif" Url="http://
www.microsoft.com" PassParams="1" WinParams="" WinMode="1" />
    <Button Title="Web Only" ToolTip="Web client only. This will not show up in any outlook
pages." Icon="/_imgs/ico_18_debug.gif" JavaScript="alert('test');" Client="Web" />
    <Button Title="Outlook Only" ToolTip="Outlook Only -
 This is available offline also." Icon="/_imgs/ico_18_debug.gif" JavaScript="alert('Test');"
Client="Outlook" AvailableOffline="true" />
   </ToolBar>
   <NavBar>
```

```
    <NavBarItem Icon="/_imgs/ico_18_debug.gif" Title="ISV Default" Url="http://
www.microsoft.com" Id="navItem" />
   </NavBar>
   <Grid>
    <MenuBar>
     <ActionsMenu>
      <MenuItem Title="Coming Soon..." Url="http://www.microsoft.com" WinMode="1" />
      <MenuSpacer />
     </ActionsMenu>
     <Buttons>
      <Button Title="Test" ToolTip="Info on Test" Icon="/_imgs/ico_18_debug.gif"
Url="http://www.microsoft.com" WinParams="" WinMode="2" />
      <ToolBarSpacer />
    </MenuBar>
   </Grid>
  </Entity>
</configuration>
```

Menu Bar

As you just saw, editing the ISV.config.xml file allows you to add menu links to the main application, the entity form, and a grid's Actions menu. As the sample configuration file shows, adding a *<MenuBar>* node beneath the *<Root>* node will add custom menus to the application. To create a custom menu on the entity's form, you would need to place a *<MenuBar>* directly beneath the *<Entity>* node.

The *<MenuBar>* node requires a *<CustomMenu>* node. The *<CustomMenu>* node can contain *<MenuItem>* nodes that have the attributes listed in Table 10-9 to further define your custom menu links.

Table 10-9 *<MenuItem>* Attributes

Attribute	Availability	Description
AvailableOffline	Entity and grid only	Defines whether the link should appear in the Outlook client if the client is offline. Valid options are True and False.
Client	All	Defines which client applications the link should appear in. Valid options are Web and Outlook. If you leave this blank or ignore the node, the menu item will display in both client applications.
JavaScript	All	If populated, Microsoft CRM will execute the JavaScript. If populated, the *Url* attribute will be ignored.

Table 10-9 *<MenuItem>* Attributes

Attribute	Availability	Description
PassParams	Entity and grid only	If set to 1, Microsoft CRM will pass the *entityid* and *enititytypecode* of the entity form to the new window. Valid options are 0 (don't pass parameters) and 1 (pass parameters).
Title	All	Displays the label that appears to the user.
Url	All	Microsoft CRM will open a window to the path specified in this attribute. If the *JavaScript* attribute is populated, the *Url* attribute will be ignored.
ValidForCreate	Entity and grid only	Displays menu item when the entity form is in create mode. Valid options are 0 (don't display) and 1 (display).
ValidForUpdate	Entity and grid only	Displays menu item when the entity form is in update mode. Valid options are 0 (don't display) and 1 (display).
WinMode	All	Determines the type of window to open. Valid options are: ■ 0 (normal window) ■ 1 (modal dialog box) ■ 2 (modeless dialog box)

The following code snippet from the ISV.config.xml file shows how to add a custom menu that would display within the main application window.

```
<Root>
 <!-- The main Global Menu Bar located at the top of all root level areas -->
 <MenuBar>
  <CustomMenus>
   <Menu Title="Custom Menu">
   <MenuItem Title="Corporate Web Site" Url="http://www.fabrikam.com" />
   <MenuSpacer />
   <!-- A horizontal drop down menu spacer -->
   <SubMenu Title="Sub Menu">
    <MenuItem Title="Sub Menu 1" Url="http://www.fabrikam.com/submenu1.aspx" WinMode="2" />
    <MenuItem Title="Sub Menu 2" Url="http://www.fabrikam.com/submenu2.aspx" WinMode="1" />
   </SubMenu>
  </Menu>
  </CustomMenus>
 </MenuBar>
</Root>
```

Figure 10-12 displays the result of this configuration.

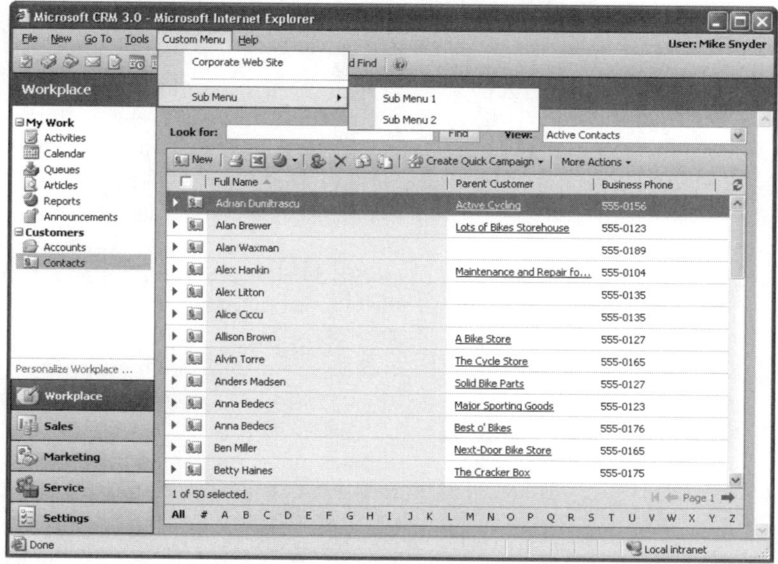

Figure 10-12 Custom Menu

Likewise, you could add a custom menu to an entity menu bar (instead of the application menu bar) by adding code such as the following under the *<Entity>* node:

```
<Entities>
 <Entity name="account">
  <MenuBar>
   <CustomMenus>
    <Menu Title="Custom Menu">
     <MenuItem Title="Custom Application Window" Url="http://www.fabrikam.com/
customwindow.aspx" ValidForUpdate="1" ValidForCreate="0" AvailableOffline="false" /> />
     </Menu>
    </CustomMenus>
   </MenuBar>
 </Entity>
</Entities>
```

Navigation Pane

You can also use the ISV.config.xml file to add links in the entity navigation pane. The *<NavBar>* node of the ISV.config.xml file controls the entity navigation pane, which resides under the *<Entities><Entity>* nodes. Table 10-10 describes the *<NavBarItem>* attributes available to you.

Note Remember that to add links to the application's navigation pane, you will have to use the site map.

Table 10-10 *<NavBarItem>* Attributes

Attribute	Description
AvailableOffline	Defines whether the link should appear in the Outlook client if the client is offline. Valid options are True and False.
Client	Defines which client applications the link should appear in. Valid options are Web and Outlook. If you leave this blank or ignore the node, the menu item will display in both client applications.
Id	Defines the HTML ID of the link. This string value must be unique and is required.
Icon	Defines a path to an image file. Image size should be 16 x 16.
Title	Displays the label that appears to the user.
Url	Microsoft CRM will open a window to the path specified in this attribute. If the *JavaScript* attribute is populated, the *Url* attribute will be ignored.
ValidForCreate	Displays menu item when the entity form is in create mode. Valid options are 0 (don't display) and 1 (display).
ValidForUpdate	Displays menu item when the entity form is in update mode. Valid options are 0 (don't display) and 1 (display).

Toolbar

The *<ToolBar>* node contains the *<Button>* and *<ToolBarSpacer />* nodes. These buttons are available from the main application toolbar as well as from an entity form's toolbar. Here's an example of a *<ToolBar>* node:

```
<ToolBar ValidForCreate="0" ValidForUpdate="1">
 <Button Title="Custom Button 1" ToolTip="Use this to open a custom window." Icon="/_imgs/
ico_18_debug.gif" Url="http://www.fabrikam.com/intranet/customwindow.aspx" Client="Web"
PassParams="1" WinParams="height=350,resizable=0" WinMode="0" />
 <ToolBarSpacer />
</ToolBar>
```

The *<ToolBar>* node also contains the *ValidForCreate* and *ValidForUpdate* attributes. Just as with menu items, you can apply these attributes selectively at the button level. The *<Button>* element contains the same attributes as *<MenuItem>*, plus the *Icon* and *WinParams* attributes. The *Icon* attribute defines an image that will appear with the button. This image size should be 16 x 16 pixels. The *WinParams* attribute allows you to define additional JavaScript window.open options (see Table 10-11 and Table 10-12) and it's dependent on the WinMode selected. You add options and their values in a comma-separated string, such as the following:

```
WinParams="height=350,width=600,toolbars=0,menubar=0,location=0"
```

Note You have to specify parameters only if you want specify different values than the Microsoft CRM default settings.

Table 10-11 WinMode = 0 Parameters

Parameter	Valid options	Description
Height	Number in pixels	Determines the height of the window
Left	Number in pixels	Determines the horizontal placement of the window relative to the upper-left corner of the screen
Location	Yes or no 1 or 0 Default: yes	Displays the Microsoft Internet Explorer address bar in the browser window
Menubar	Yes or no 1 or 0 Default: yes	Displays the Internet Explorer topmost menu bar in the browser window
Resizable	Yes or no 1 or 0 Default: yes	Allows the window to be resized and will display the corner handles at the bottom of the window
Scrollbars	Yes or no 1 or 0 Default: yes	Allows for the vertical and horizontal scrollbars to appear
Status	Yes or no 1 or 0	Displays the status bar at the bottom of the browser window
Toolbar	Yes or no 1 or 0	Displays the Internet Explorer toolbar in the browser window
Top	Number in pixels	Determines the vertical placement of the window relative to the upper-left corner of the screen
Width	Number in pixels	Determines the width of the window

Table 10-12 WinMode = 1 or 2 Parameters

Parameter	Valid options	Description
dialogHeight	Number in pixels	Determines the height of the window
dialogLeft	Number in pixels	Determines the horizontal placement of the window relative to the upper-left corner of the screen
Center	Yes or no 1 or 0 Default: yes	Determines whether the window should open in the center of the screen
Edge	Sunken or raised Default: raised	Determines the type of window edge style to use
Help	Yes or no 1 or 0 Default: yes	Determines whether the Help icon should appear
Resizable	Yes or no 1 or 0 Default: yes	Allows the window to be resized and will display the corner handles at the bottom of the window
Scroll	Yes or no 1 or 0 Default: yes	Allows for the vertical and horizontal scrollbars to appear
Status	Yes or no 1 or 0	Displays the status bar at the bottom of the browser window
Toolbar	Yes or no 1 or 0	Displays the Internet Explorer toolbar in the browser window
dialogTop	Number in pixels	Determines the vertical placement of the window relative to the upper-left corner of the screen
dialogWidth	Number in pixels	Determines the width of the window

Grid Toolbar

You can also use the ISV.config to add links to the Actions menu and add buttons to the grid toolbar. The grid configuration merges both the *<MenuBar>* and *<Button>* elements, so we won't repeat all the available attributes. You customize the grid toolbar by adding a *<Grid>* to an *<Entity>* node, as shown here:

```
<Grid>
 <MenuBar>
  <ActionsMenu>
   <MenuItem Title="Custom Grid Action" Url="http://www.fabrikam.com/
customgridwindow.aspx" WinMode="1" />
   </ActionsMenu>
   <Buttons>
    <Button Title="Custom Grid Button" ToolTip="This displays a custom button on a grid tool
bar." Icon="/_imgs/ico_18_debug.gif" Url="http://www.fabrikam.com/customgridbutton.aspx"
WinParams="" WinMode="2" />
  </Buttons>
 </MenuBar>
</Grid>
```

For custom Web pages accessed from a grid toolbar button or menu, you can programmatically access the selected records in the grid by using the *windows.dialogArguments* method. For example, the following Web page will display the GUIDs of the selected records in a grid back to the user when accessed from the *<Grid>* node of an entity.

```
<!DOCTYPE HTML PUBLIC "-//W3C//DTD HTML 4.0 Transitional//EN">
<html>
<head>
<title>Custom Grid Page</title>
<script language="javascript">
function window.onload()
{
  if(window.dialogArguments != null)
  {
    var arr = new Array(window.dialogArguments.length -1);
    arr = window.dialogArguments;

    for(i=0; i< arr.length; i++)
    {
      alert(arr[i]);
    }
  }
  else
  {
    alert("No records were selected");
  }
}
</script>

</head>
<body>

</body>
</html>
```

Appointment Book

The final area of customization within the ISV.config.xml file relates to the scheduling module. Microsoft CRM allows you to change and customize the colors of the appointment book. Table 10-13 lists the attributes related to the <*TimeBlock*> attribute within the *AppointmentBook* node.

Table 10-13 <*TimeBlock*> Attributes

Attribute	Description
AvailableOffline	Determines whether the link should appear in the Outlook client if the client is offline. Valid options are True and False.
Client	Defines which client applications the link should appear in. Valid options are Web and Outlook. If you leave this blank or ignore the node, the menu item will display in both client applications.
CssClass	Defines the style for the given entity and status. The cascading style sheet is located at: <*web installation path*>\SM\Gantt\style\ganttcontrol.css.
EntityType	Defines the entity used in the time block. Valid values are 4201 (Appointment) and 4214 (Service).
StatusCode	Refers to the status code of the entity in the appointment book.

Deploying the ISV.config.xml File

To deploy the ISV.config.xml file, simply copy the file to the Microsoft CRM Web server in the <*web installation path*>_Resources directory. You can also import and export the ISV.config file via the Web client interface in the Customization area under Import and Export Customizations.

> **Tip** Remember to back up the default ISV.config.xml file before you deploy your version. The default ISV.config.xml file created on installation contains examples of the various nodes. Of course, you can retrieve all the information that you need from the SDK, but sometimes it is useful to review the default example when adding new and unfamiliar node.

Enabling the ISV.config.xml File

After you copy the ISV.config.xml file to the _Resources folder (or import it through the user interface), you must enable it by editing the Web.config file. You can choose from one of the following possible values:

- **All** Display the customizations in all of the clients (Web client, the Microsoft CRM desktop client for Outlook, and the Microsoft CRM laptop client for Outlook).
- **None** Disable all customizations. This is the default value.
- **Outlook** Enable customizations for both versions of the Microsoft CRM client for Outlook, but not the Web client.

- **OutlookLaptopClient** Enable customizations for the Microsoft CRM laptop client for Outlook (offline-capable).
- **OutlookWorkstationClient** Enable customizations for the Microsoft CRM desktop client for Outlook (online-only).
- **Web** Enable customizations for the Web client only.

Updating the Web.config file

1. On the Microsoft CRM Web server, navigate to *<web installation path>*\ (typically *C:\Inetpub\wwwroot*).
2. Open the Web.config file in Notepad (or any text editor).
3. Look for the ISVIntegration key, and change its value to the setting that you need.
4. Save the Web.config file.

> **Note** The ISVIntegration key allows you to enter multiple values by entering the values with commas (no spaces), such as "OutlookWorkstationClient,Web" or "OutlookLaptopClient,Web". Including None with any of these values disables ISV.config for all of the clients.

After you enable the ISVIntegration key, you must also make sure that you enable the ISV Extensions privilege for the user's security role so that he or she can see the extensions, as shown in Figure 10-13. The ISV Extensions privilege is listed on the Customizations tab as a miscellaneous privilege.

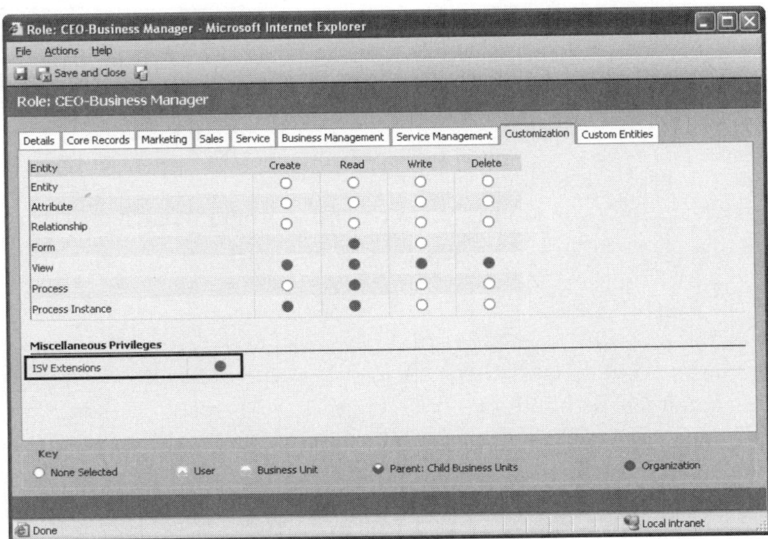

Figure 10-13 Enabling the ISV Extensions privilege

Caution If you configure your extensions for the Microsoft CRM laptop client for Outlook (offline mode), make sure that your users can access those links when they're offline.

CRM Client-Side Scripting Tips

In this section, we will review some useful tips we've discovered when working with client-side scripts. These topics include:

- Development environment
- Languages
- Testing and debugging
- Additional resources

Development Environment

We recommend that you create your scripts in an external editor instead of attempting to write code directly in the Microsoft CRM Event Detail Properties dialog window. Common script editor choices would be Microsoft Visual Studio .NET, Microsoft Office FrontPage, and Notepad. We recommend that you write your scripts in an external editor for the following reasons:

- The Enter and Tab keys do not function as expected in the Microsoft CRM text area. This makes it extremely difficult to write well-formatted and easy-to-read code.
- External editors provide a myriad of tools to assist in development (such as Microsoft IntelliSense, color coding, and integrated debugging). The Microsoft CRM form is simply an HTML form text area that doesn't provide any of these development features.
- An external editor allows you to use a version control program (such as Microsoft Visual SourceSafe) to archive and back up your scripts.

Languages

Microsoft CRM renders event scripts on the client-side of the browser, so you must use a scripting language compatible with Internet Explorer (such as Microsoft JScript or JavaScript). Microsoft CRM provides no validation of your script; it merely renders the script out to the resulting HTML page. Therefore, you can use the scripting language that you're most comfortable with or that your business logic requires.

Testing and Debugging

Any developer who has received an emergency call on the weekend about a coding or system problem knows the importance of thoroughly testing your code! Because Microsoft CRM does not validate any script code, you are responsible for ensuring that your scripts will work with Microsoft CRM. We recommend the following test techniques when developing your custom scripts:

- Always test your scripts on a development Microsoft CRM environment and not on production servers.
- Where possible, set up a simple Web page with a test form, and test your JavaScript outside of Microsoft CRM. This will provide for faster development and debugging. Then copy and paste the final code into the appropriate Microsoft CRM event.
- Use the Preview command to test your client-side scripts before publishing.
- If it appears that your code doesn't work as expected, first ensure that you enabled your event. Then, use the *alert()* method to output various logic points, and try to first eliminate the interaction with Microsoft CRM. In many cases, the flaw may be contained within the code logic itself, independent of the integrated properties of Microsoft CRM.
- Add an external script reference. You can inject a reference to an external script file from the form's *onLoad()* event (refer to the examples in this chapter for syntax). This allows you to update the JavaScript directly and test against the actual CRM form on a development server, instead of constantly launching the preview form. We only recommend referencing an external script during the development phase of your project, don't do this in production environments because Microsoft does not support using this technique.
- When making updates to your script and reviewing them in a preview form, you must close and launch a new preview form with each script change. Microsoft CRM caches the form, so simply refreshing your existing preview form will not show your changes.
- Always export a backup copy of the entity that you are updating. This allows you to roll back if your updates cause an irreversible error.
- Be sure to keep backups of your scripts and store them with source control.

Tip If you are new to scripting languages, you should be aware that both JavaScript and Jscript are case-senstive. So, <*field*>.SetFocus() will properly move the mouse cursor to the field, while <*field*>.setfocus() will do nothing!

Additional Resources

The following list provides some additional information regarding the topics discussed in this chapter:

- Microsoft CRM SDK: Available with Microsoft CRM and includes detailed information regarding the client-side integration options, as well as additional coding examples

- DHTML overview: *http://msdn.microsoft.com/library/default.asp?url=/workshop/author/dhtml/dhtml_node_entry.asp*
- DHTML object reference: *http://msdn.microsoft.com/library/default.asp?url=/workshop/author/dhtml/reference/objects.asp*
- JScript User's Guide: *http://msdn.microsoft.com/library/default.asp?url=/library/en-us/script56/html/e4fb1cc7-15e0-43e9-bf2e-469fe7b2050c.asp*
- Regular expressions: *http://msdn.microsoft.com/library/default.asp?url=/library/en-us/jscript7/html/jsreconintroductiontoregularexpressions.asp*

Client-Side Code Examples

Now that you understand the framework and the details about the Microsoft CRM client-side SDK, we want to get into the fun of coding examples and real-world usage of these features. We have included a variety of script samples for reference and to provide a starting point for your own customization needs. The following examples are just a sampling of the many ways in which you can integrate custom logic by using the information in the client-side SDK:

- Formatting and translating U.S. phone numbers
- Referencing an external script file
- Dynamically changing picklist values
- Setting a default phone call subject
- Allowing multi-select lists
- Adding custom validation
- Saving an IFrame form from Microsoft CRM
- Automatically populating a phone number on the Phone Call activity

Formatting and Translating U.S. Phone Numbers

You can add the following script to the *onChange* event of any field used for a phone number. The script will automatically format any 7- or 10-digit number as 555-1212 or (312) 555-1212. In addition, it will translate a phone number entered as letters to its numeric equivalent; for example, if the user entered 866-555CODE the script would convert the letters in the phone number to (866) 555-2633.

Figure 10-14 shows an example phone number entered by a user.

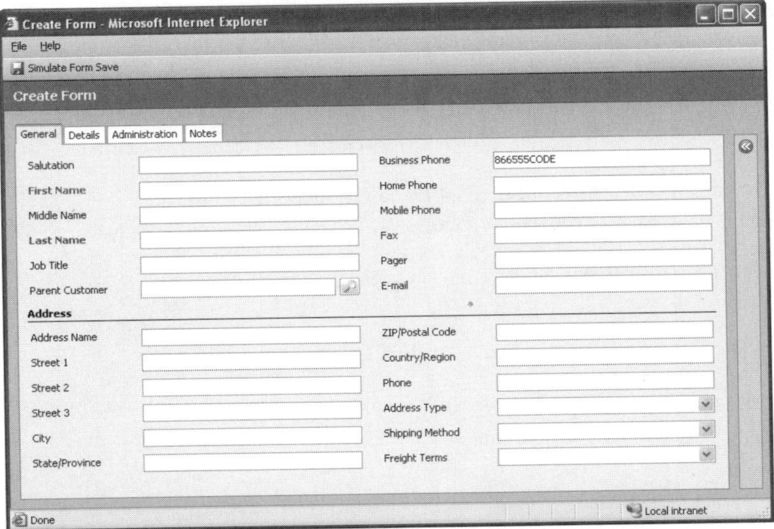

Figure 10-14 A phone number on the Contact form as entered by a user

Figure 10-15 shows how the script will translate the Business Phone entry as soon as the user changes focus on the phone number field.

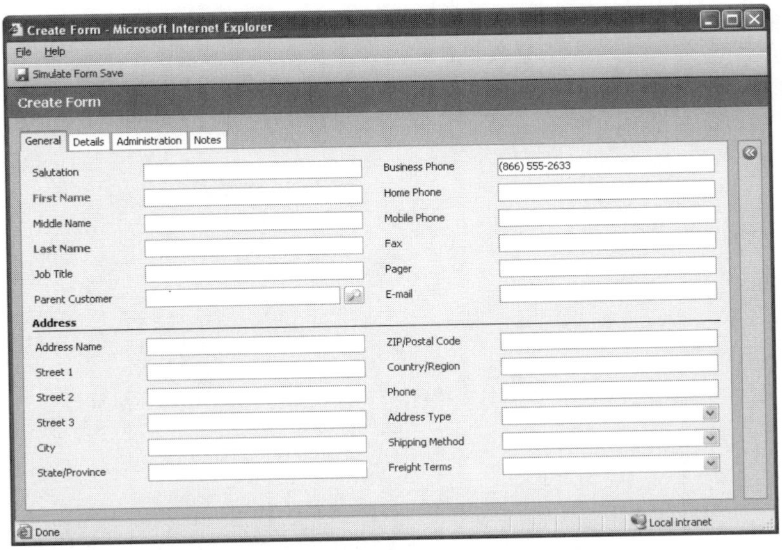

Figure 10-15 The translated and formatted phone number

The script fires as soon as the user enters a phone number and their cursor exits the field (either by clicking elsewhere on the form or by pressing the Tab key). This is referred to as losing focus, or changing focus. When fired, the script first takes the entered text and removes any special characters. It then passes the first 10 characters of the modified text through a translation function that exchanges any letters for their equivalent phone digits. Finally, it takes that result, formats it, and assigns it back to the field. To account for the possibility of people entering extensions, the script will just output any characters after the 10th digit as they were entered. Listing 10-2 shows the phone number formatting script.

Listing 10-2 Formatting and Translating U.S. Phone Numbers

```
/*
Installation:
Add this script to onChange event of any phone number field.

Description:
This method will auto-format basic 7 and 10 digit US phone numbers,
  while leaving any extensions.
It will also translate any letters in the input to its equivalent phone digit.

Example: (800) 555-1212
*/


// Get the field that fired the event
var oField = event.srcElement;

// Verify that the field is valid
if (typeof(oField) != "undefined" && oField != null)
{
  if (oField.DataValue != null)
  {
    // Remove any special characters
    var sTmp = oField.DataValue.replace(/[^0-9,A-Z,a-z]/g, "");

    // Translate any letters to the equivilant phone number, if method is included
    try
    {
      if (sTmp.length <= 10)
      {
      sTmp = TranslateMask(sTmp);
      }
      else
      {
        sTmp = TranslateMask(sTmp.substr(0,10)) + sTmp.substr(10,sTmp.length);
      }
    }
    catch(e)
    {
    }

    // If the number is a length we expect and support,
    // format the translated number
    switch (sTmp.length)
    {
    case 1:
    case 2:
    case 3:
```

```
    case 4:
    case 5:
    case 6:
    case 8:
    case 9:
      break;
    case 7:
      oField.DataValue = sTmp.substr(0, 3) + "-" + sTmp.substr(3, 4);
      break;
    case 10:
      oField.DataValue = "(" + sTmp.substr(0, 3) + ") " + sTmp.substr(3, 3) +
"-" + sTmp.substr(6, 4);
      break;
    default:
      oField.DataValue = "(" + sTmp.substr(0, 3) + ") " + sTmp.substr(3, 3) +
"-" + sTmp.substr(6, 4) + " " + sTmp.substr(10,sTmp.length);
      break;
    }
  }
}


/// <summary>
/// TranslateMask() will step through each character of an
/// input string and pass that character to the
/// TranslatePhoneLetter() helper method
/// </summary>
/// <param name="s">Input string to translate</param>
function TranslateMask( s )
{
  var ret = "";

  //loop through each char, and pass it to the translation method
  for (var i=0; i<s.length; i++)
  {
    ret += TranslatePhoneLetter(s.charAt(i))
  }

  return ret;
}

/// <summary>
/// TranslatePhoneLetter() takes a character and returns the
/// equivalent phone number digit if it is alphanumeric
/// </summary>
/// <param name="s">Character to translate</param>
function TranslatePhoneLetter( s )
{
 var sTmp = s.toUpperCase();
 var ret = s;

 switch( sTmp )
 {
 case "A":
 case "B":
```

```
    case "C":
     ret = 2;
     break;
    case "D":
    case "E":
    case "F":
     ret = 3;
     break;
    case "G":
    case "H":
    case "I":
     ret = 4;
     break;
    case "J":
    case "K":
    case "L":
     ret = 5;
     break;
    case "M":
    case "N":
    case "O":
     ret = 6;
     break;
    case "P":
    case "Q":
    case "R":
    case "S":
     ret = 7;
     break;
    case "T":
    case "U":
    case "V":
     ret = 8;
     break;
    case "W":
    case "X":
    case "Y":
    case "Z":
     ret = 9;
     break;
    default:
     ret = s;
     break;
   }

   return ret;
  }
```

Referencing an External Script File

As we discussed earlier, you can add code against the form's *onLoad* event that references an external script file. The main reason to do this would be for ease of script administration and code reuse. For example, if we added the phone number formatting script from the previous example to 20 or 30 different phone number fields in the Lead, Account, and Contact entities and then we needed to modify the script, we would have to manually update the script in all 20 to 30 locations. Referencing an external script will save you this headache because you would only need to make one update. However, we only recommend using this technique in your development environment. Microsoft doesn't support referencing an external script for the following reasons:

- **No offline capabilities** If a user goes offline, the reference to the script file will be severed, breaking any routines that use the functions in the reference script.
- **Deployment difficulties** Script code added directly to the events can be deployed with the built-in import/export mechanisms. By referencing an external file, you will be responsible for deployment and updating the references in the Microsoft CRM form events.
- **Access issues** When referencing a file on an external Web site, if that site is not available or if there is a delay in loading the file, the required methods might not be available to your code and cause errors.

> **Note** Adding files to the Microsoft CRM Web site file structure is prohibited and unsupported by Microsoft. Instead, you should create a virtual Web that accesses a file system directory outside the installation root of Microsoft CRM, as shown in the previous IFrame example. This allows you to add custom files to the Microsoft CRM Web server.

The code shown in Listing 10-3 will allow you to use DHTML to add an external script reference. You will need to update the *url* variable with the proper path to your script file and then add the script to the form's *onLoad* event.

Listing 10-3 Referencing an External Script File

```
/*
Installation:
Update the url variable with the correct path to your script file.
Add this script to the form's onLoad() event.

Description:
This will add the defined URL as an external script reference within the head tag of the page.
*/

// Define your script URL
var url = "http://<crmserver>/custom/lib/script.js";

// Create the script element
var obj = new Object();
obj = document.createElement("<script src='" + url + "' language='javascript'>");


// Get the head node from the document stream
var arr = new Array();
```

```
arr = document.getElementsByTagName("head");

// Insert our new script element into the node set
arr[0].insertAdjacentElement("beforeEnd",obj);
```

Note Adding the following snippet directly to the *onLoad* event will not work:

<script language="JavaScript" src="http://<*crmserver*>/custom/lib/script.js"></script>

The manner by which Microsoft CRM injects the *onLoad* script code to the form's output prevents this line from executing.

Dynamically Changing Picklist Values

The default behavior of picklist attributes in Microsoft CRM is that each field operates totally independent of other values on the form. In reality, you might want to dynamically alter the picklist values of a record based on other values selected in the record. For example, if the user selects that a Contact's shipping method is Will Call, it doesn't make sense to let the user select FOB (Freight on Board) as the Freight Terms for that Contact.

This example will show how you can dynamically change values of the Freight Terms picklist field based on the selection of the Shipping Method picklist. If the user selects Will Call as the shipping method, we will use the client-side SDK to programmatically remove the FOB (Freight on Board) option from the Freight Terms list and automatically set the option to Free of Charge. If the user then changes the Shipping Method to a new value, we must programmatically add the FOB (Freight on Board) option back to the Freight Terms list.

Tip You can use the code and concepts from this example to extend your company's Microsoft CRM deployment to dynamically update different sets of picklist values depending on the needs of your organization.

As you saw earlier, Microsoft CRM provides two routines for managing picklist options: *AddOption()* and *DeleteOption()*. We will use *DeleteOption()* to remove the FOB option when Will Call is selected. When any other value is selected, we will add the FOB option (if it has been removed). This example will demonstrate how you would access and work with picklist fields. Figure 10-16 shows the results on the form.

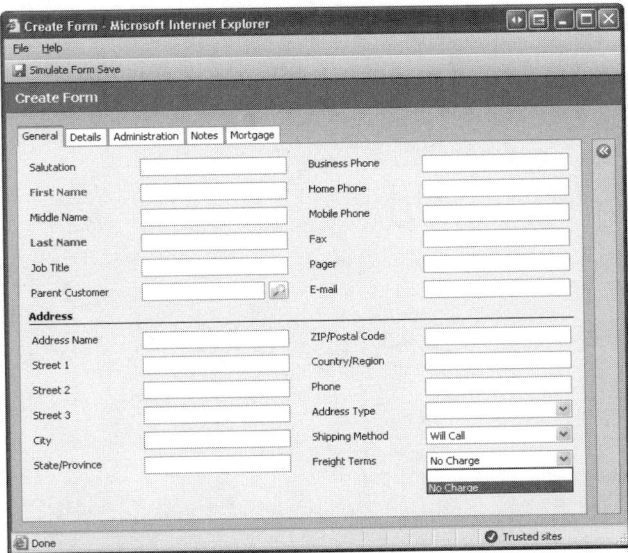

Figure 10-16 Form preview of Shipping Method picklist script

> **Caution** You should not programmatically add options to a picklist that do not exist in Microsoft CRM. Technically, you can add any name/value option with the *AddOption()* method, but if the value has not been configured through the form customization, Microsoft CRM will not be able to display it correctly on the form.

For this example, you will need to add code to the address1_shippingmethodcode field's *onChange* event. You must also add similar to code to the contact form's *onLoad* event for the form's update mode, to address update situations in which Will Call is already selected. The script for this example can be found in Listing 10-4.

Listing 10-4 Dynamically Changing Picklist Values

```
/*
Installation:
Add this script to the contact address1_shippingmethodcode field's onChange() event.

Description:
This script will remove the FOB option from the Freight Terms picklist if shipping method is
 Will Call.
*/

// Set up our picklist constants
// Ensure that these match the codes in CRM
var SHIPPINGMETHODCODE_WILLCALL = 7;
var FREIGHTTERMSCODE_FOB = 1;
var FREIGHTTERMSCODE_NOCHARGE = 2;

// Gather our field references
var oShipMethod = event.srcElement;
var oFreightTerms = crmForm.all.address1_freighttermscode;
```

```
var freightTerms = oFreightTerms.Options
var fobExists = false;

// Loop through existing options and determine whether the FOB option exists
for (var i=0; i<freightTerms.length; i++)
{
 if (freightTerms[i].DataValue == FREIGHTTERMSCODE_FOB)
 fobExists = true;
}

if (oShipMethod.DataValue == SHIPPINGMETHODCODE_WILLCALL)
{
 // Default to No Charge
 oFreightTerms.DataValue = FREIGHTTERMSCODE_NOCHARGE;

 // Remove FOB as an option
 oFreightTerms.DeleteOption(FREIGHTTERMSCODE_FOB);
}
else
{
 // Default to blank
 oFreightTerms.DataValue = null;

 // If the FOB option is missing, add it back
 if (! fobExists)
 oFreightTerms.AddOption("FOB",FREIGHTTERMSCODE_FOB);
}

/* ------------------------------------------------------ */

/*
Installation:
Add this script to the contact form's onLoad() event.

Description:
This script will remove the FOB option if shipping method is Will Call.
*/

// Set up our constants
var CRM_FORM_TYPE_CREATE = "1";
var CRM_FORM_TYPE_UPDATE = "2";

// Set up our picklist constants
// Ensure that these match the codes in CRM
var SHIPPINGMETHODCODE_WILLCALL = 7;
var FREIGHTTERMSCODE_FOB = 1;
var FREIGHTTERMSCODE_NOCHARGE = 2;

// Only check if form is in update mode
if (crmForm.FormType == CRM_FORM_TYPE_UPDATE)
{
 if (document.crmForm.all.address1_shippingmethodcode.DataValue == SHIPPINGMETHODCODE_WILLCALL)
 {
 // Remove FOB as an option

 document.crmForm.all.address1_freighttermscode.DeleteOption(FREIGHTTERMSCODE_FOB);
 }
}
```

Tip When you need to find the value of a picklist item, navigate to the entity's Attributes page. Double-click the picklist attribute. On the right, you will see the list of options. Double-click an option name, and a dialog box displays the corresponding value, as shown in Figure 10-17.

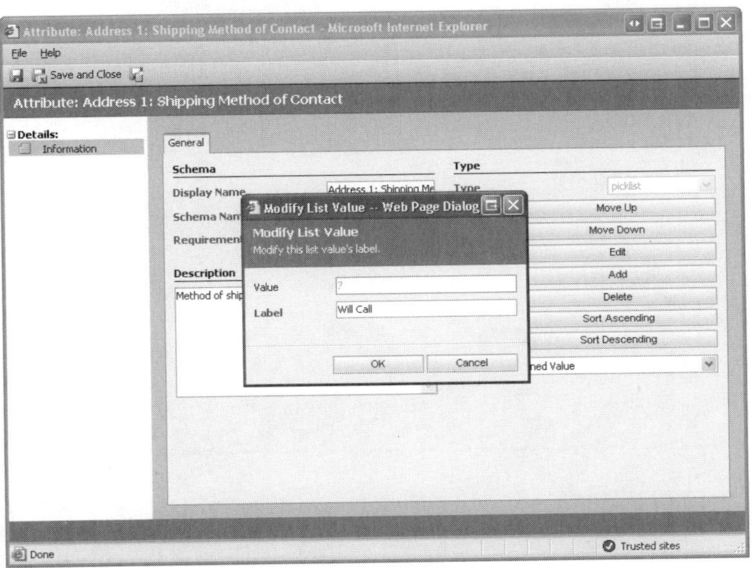

Figure 10-17 Retrieving picklist values

Setting a Default Phone Call Subject

Another clever use of the client-side SDK and picklists allows users to select a picklist value that will automatically update another field (or fields) with predefined values. This type of customization would save sales people time if you applied it to the Phone Call activity form. When the sales person needs to make a large number of phone calls, they could just select a picklist value that will update the subject of the Phone Call activity, instead of having to manually type it for each call they make.

To implement this, we will create a new picklist attribute on the Phone Call entity called Call Type, and our client-side script will automatically populate the Subject and Category boxes with default values based on the Call Type value the user selects in the picklist. We will also use client-side script to set the Duration field to blank (instead of the default 30 minutes).

This script will also demonstrate how you can programmatically access lookup fields such as the Recipient field on the Phone Call activity form. In addition to populating the Phone Call subject with the Call Type text, the script will automatically append the name(s) of the call recipient(s) after the Call Type text (Figure 10-18). We will retrieve the call recipient values from the *to* (Recipient) field. Since a Phone Call can include multiple recipients, Microsoft CRM passes the data from the lookup *DataValue* property as an array of values.

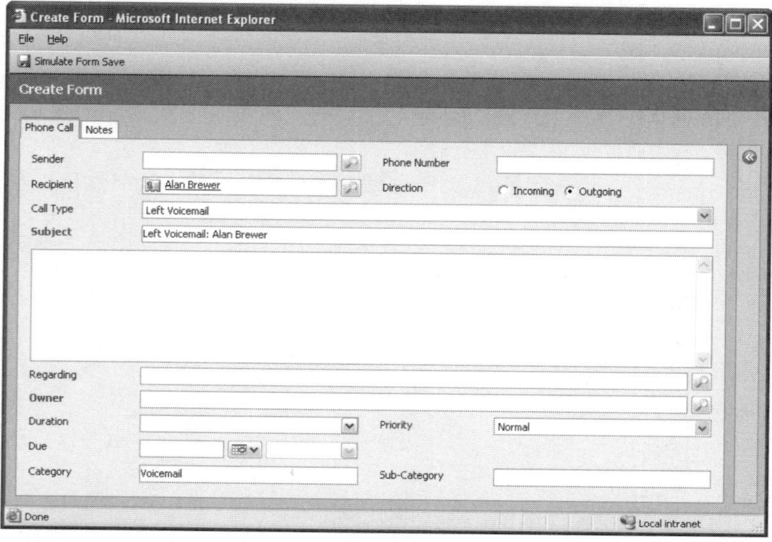

Figure 10-18 Phone Call form

As you have now done numerous times, you must first create the new Call Type picklist attribute.

Setup

1. Browse to the Customizations section of Microsoft CRM and double-click the Phone Call entity. Click **Attributes** in the navigation pane.
2. Create a picklist attribute called **calltype** (new_calltype).
3. Enter **Call Type** for the display name.
4. Add the following values in order:
   a. Left Voicemail
   b. No Answer
   c. Requested Information
   d. Wrong Number
   e. Requested Call Back
   f. Left Message with Operator
5. Leave the default value as **Unassigned Value**.

After you create the new attribute, you must add it to the form, as shown in Figure 10-18. Then you'll need to apply two scripts in Listing 10-5 to the Phone Call entity; the first will be applied to the *new_calltype onChange* event, and the second will be applied to the form's *onLoad* event.

Listing 10-5 Setting a Default Phone Call Subject

```
/*
Installation:
Add this script to the new_callresult field's onChange() event.

Description:
This script will populate the subject and category based on the selection of the
new_callresult selection.
*/

// Set up our constants
/*
new_callresult picklist values:
1 Left Voicemail
2 No Answer
3 Requested Information
4 Wrong Number
5 Requested Call Back
6 Left Message with Operator
*/

var aCategory = ["","Voicemail","No Answer","Info Request","Wrong Number","Call Back",
"Message"];


// Gather our field references
var oCallResult = event.srcElement;
var oRecipient = document.crmForm.all.to;
var oCategory = document.crmForm.all.category;
var oSubject = document.crmForm.all.subject;

// Ensure that we have a valid, populated element
if (typeof(oCallResult) != "undefined" && oCallResult != null)
{
 var toName = "";


 if (oRecipient.DataValue != null)
 {
 // The lookup field contains an array of values
 var aTo = new Array();
 aTo = oRecipient.DataValue;

 // Loop through and create a user list
 for (var i=0; i<aTo.length; i++)
 {
  // Create a comma separated list of receipient names
  toName += (i==0) ? aTo[i].name : ", " + aTo[i].name;
 }
 }

 // Set defaults based on call result selection
 oCategory.DataValue = aCategory[oCallResult.DataValue];
 oSubject.DataValue = oCallResult.SelectedText + ": " + toName;
}
```

```
/* ---------------------------------------------------------- */

/*
Installation:
Add this script to the Phone Call form's onLoad() event.

Description:
This script will default the Duration field to blank.
*/

document.crmForm.all.actualdurationminutes.DataValue = null;
```

Allowing Multi-Select Lists

Microsoft CRM does not natively allow for multi-select lists. Picklist values allow you to select one value only. However, we can enhance the previous picklist example to create a simple workaround for this situation.

We will use the Case entity form for this example. We will create two new attributes called Problem Category (a read-only ntext field) and Problem Category List (a picklist containing different problem types). When a user selects a picklist value from the Problem Category List, we will append that value in the Problem Category box. This will allow our service representative to classify a case's problem under multiple pre-set categories. Because we want only our predefined categories to be selected, we will disable the Problem Category field on the form, preventing users from entering text. Figure 10-19 shows what the resulting form looks like when filled with multiple categories.

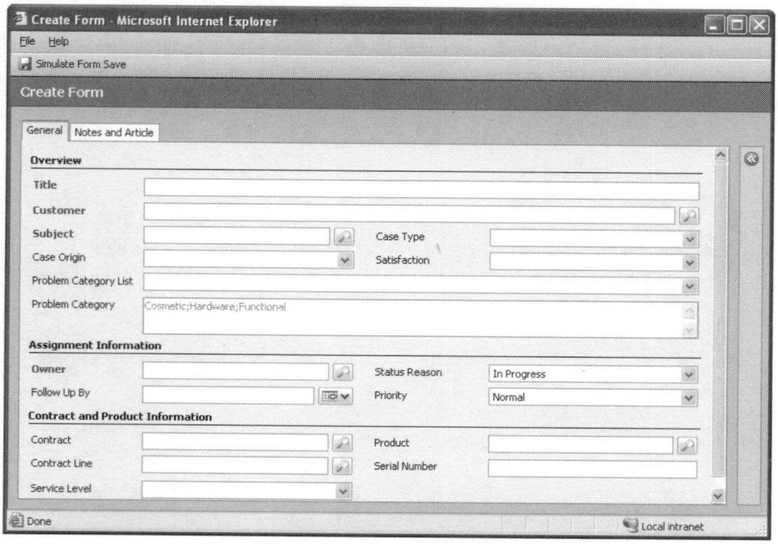

Figure 10-19 Multiple problem categories selected

Since this field is read-only, we will also create a custom picklist value called Clear Selections that removes any entries from the list. The prompt to clear selections is shown in Figure 10-20.

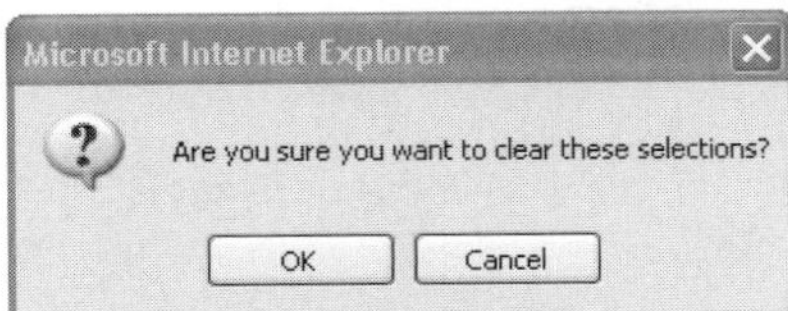

Figure 10-20 Prompt to clear selections

> **Note** You might think adding problem categories to a Case is somewhat redundant because the default Case form requires you to choose a subject. However, Microsoft CRM doesn't allow you to select multiple subjects for a single Case so this solution is a decent workaround if you need to track multiple problem categories. Even if you don't need this particular feature, the request to select multiple values from a picklist is something we hear often from customers, so hopefully you can imagine how to extend it to other areas. You might also recognize that storing and reporting on string values is not a preferred programmatic method, because those values can change and then adversely affect your report groupings. However, while this solution isn't perfect, this workaround is clearly better for reporting than using a free-form text field.

Setup

1. Browse to the Customizations section of Microsoft CRM and double-click the Case entity. Click **Attributes** in the navigation pane.
2. Create a picklist attribute called **problemcategorylist** (new_problemcategorylist) for the Case entity.
3. Enter **Problem Category List** for the display name.
4. Add the following values in order:
    a. -- Clear Selections --
    b. Cosmetic
    c. Functional
    d. Hardware
    e. User Error
5. Leave the default value as **Unassigned Value**.
6. Create an **ntext** attribute called *problemcategory (new_ problemcategory)*.
7. Enter **Problem Category** for the display name.
8. Add both fields to the form.
9. Add the code from Listing 10-6 to the new_problemcategorylist field's onChange event.
10. Select the **Disabled on form** check box on the **Problem Category** field after you add it to the form. This prevents users from entering their own categories so that the field can be used for reporting.
11. **Save** the form, and then publish the Case entity.

Listing 10-6 Allowing Multi-Select Lists

```
/*
Installation:
Add this script to the Case new_problemcategorylist field's onChange() event.

Description:
This script will concaten ate any values in the category list to the Category textarea. If
"-- Clear Selections --" is chosen, it will blank out any existing selections.
*/


// Set up our constants
var NEW_PROBLEMCATEGORYLIST_CLEAR = 1;

// Gather our field references
var oProblemCategoryList = event.srcElement;
var oProblemCategory = crmForm.all.new_problemcategory;


// If the "-- Clear Selections --" option is selected
if (oProblemCategoryList.DataValue == NEW_PROBLEMCATEGORYLIST_CLEAR)
{
  // Ask the user if they want to clear their selections
  var bConfirm = false;
  bConfirm = confirm("Are you sure you want to clear these selections?");

  if (bConfirm)
  {
    // Set the category field to blank, and null out the picklist
    oProblemCategory.DataValue = "";
    oProblemCategoryList.DataValue = null;

    // Since the field is disabled, force a new submission on updates
    oProblemCategory.ForceSubmit = true;
  }
}
else
{
  // If valid
  if (typeof(oProblemCategory) != "undefined" && oProblemCategory != null)
  {
    // Get the current category text
    var categoryText = (oProblemCategory.DataValue == null) ? "" : oProblemCategory.DataValue;

    // Get the current picklist option and determine whether it already exists in the
    selected text var selectedCategory = oProblemCategoryList.SelectedText;
    var testStr = new RegExp(selectedCategory, "g");
    var isIncluded = categoryText.match(testStr);

    // If not, append it to the value
    if (! isIncluded )
      categoryText += (categoryText.length == 0) ? selectedCategory : ";" + selectedCategory;

    // Reset the category list, add string back to the category field
    oProblemCategoryList.DataValue = null;
```

```
    oProblemCategory.DataValue = categoryText;

    // Since the field is disabled, force a new submission on updates
    oProblemCategory.ForceSubmit = true;
  }
}
```

Adding Custom Validation

For each attribute in Microsoft CRM, you specify a data type and a requirement level of No Constraint, Business Recommended, or Business Required. Microsoft CRM will automatically validate required fields and make sure that the user input matches the data type for each field (for example, it ensures that numbers are entered in an integer field). However, you will probably run across scenarios where you want to include additional input validation such as conditionally requiring a field based on the selection of another field, or you might want to validate the formatting of an e-mail address. Let's examine these scenarios.

Conditionally Setting Required Fields

We will use our updated Case form for this example. If a user selects Problem for the Case Type, we want to make the Case Origin field and our new Problem Category required. But since we don't always want these fields required, we could not just modify the Requirement Level of those two attributes. The easiest way to accomplish our business goal is to programmatically set the requirement level of the fields to Business Required by using the CRM form's *SetFieldReqLevel* method. This method will change the field label to red and provide automatic validation on enabled fields (see Figure 10-21).

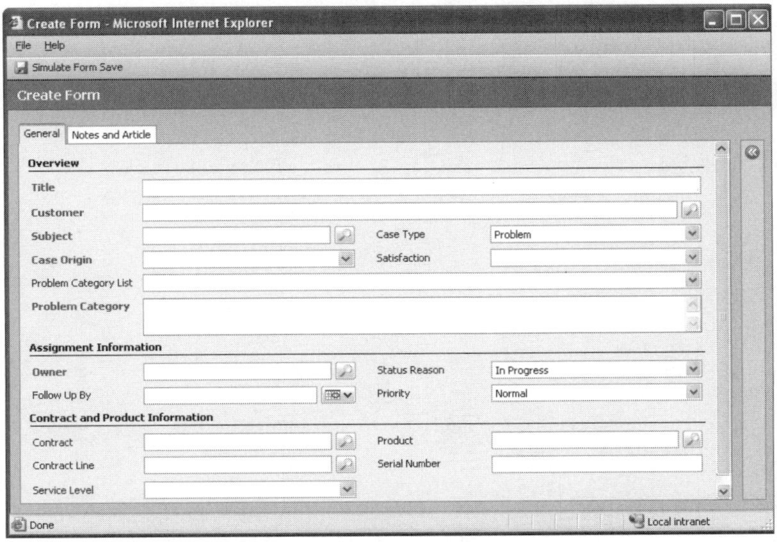

Figure 10-21 Required fields set from code

However, the Microsoft CRM Requirement Level validation does not apply to disabled fields. So even though we set the Problem Category field to a Requirement Level of Business Required, Microsoft CRM won't check this field on save since it's disabled. Therefore, we must implement our own field validation. Figure 10-22 displays the custom error prompt that users will see if they attempt to save without selecting a problem category.

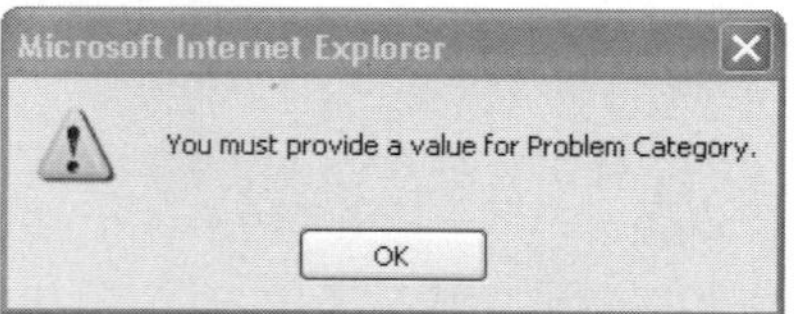

Figure 10-22 Custom error prompt

This example requires the custom code in Listing 10-7 to be applied appropriately to all of the available events (*onLoad*, *onSave*, and *onChange*) to properly accomplish this task. Note the following key points from this sample:

- Use *crmForm.SetFieldReqLevel* to programmatically set the requirement level of a field.
- *crmForm.SetFieldReqLevel* is not currently supported and may not be available in future releases.
- Microsoft CRM does not validate disabled fields. You must do this manually in the *onSave* event.
- If you want to cancel a save in the *onSave* event, use the following: *event.returnValue = false;*

Listing 10-7 Conditionally Setting Required Fields

```
/*
Installation:
Add this script to the Case casetypecode field's onChange() event.

Description:
This script will determine whether "Problem" is selected as the case type,
and if so, force the Problem Category and Case Origin fields to be required.
*/

// Set up our constants
var CASETYPECODE_PROBLEM = "2";

// Gather our field references
var oCaseTypeCode = event.srcElement;

// Set up a switch statement to allow for additional options to be added
switch (oCaseTypeCode.DataValue)
{
 case CASETYPECODE_PROBLEM:
 crmForm.SetFieldReqLevel("new_problemcategory", true);
 crmForm.SetFieldReqLevel("caseorigincode", true);

 break;
```

```
 default:
 crmForm.SetFieldReqLevel("new_problemcategory", false);
 crmForm.SetFieldReqLevel("caseorigincode", false);
 break;
}

/* ------------------------------------------------------ */

/*
Installation:
Add this script to the Case form's onLoad() event.

Description:
This script will determine whether "Problem" is selected as the case type,
and if so, force the Problem Category and Case Origin fields to be required.
*/

// Set up our constants
var CASETYPECODE_PROBLEM = 2;

// Gather our field references
var oCaseTypeCode = document.crmForm.all.casetypecode;

// Set up a switch statement to allow for additional options to be added
switch (oCaseTypeCode.DataValue)
{
 case CASETYPECODE_PROBLEM:
 crmForm.SetFieldReqLevel("new_problemcategory", true);
 crmForm.SetFieldReqLevel("caseorigincode", true);

 break;
 default:
 crmForm.SetFieldReqLevel("new_problemcategory", false);
 crmForm.SetFieldReqLevel("caseorigincode", false);
 break;
}

/* ------------------------------------------------------ */

/*
Installation:
Add this script to the Case form's onSave() event.

Description:
This script will determine whether "Problem" is selected as the case type,
and if so, force the Problem Category and Case Origin fields to be required.

Since the Problem Category field is a disabled field, we need to manually validate the field.
*/

// Set up our constants
var CRM_REQUIRED_LEVEL_REQUIRED = 2;

// Gather our field references
var oProblemCategory = document.crmForm.all.new_problemcategory;
```

```
// Catch if Problem Category is null and required
if ( (oProblemCategory.RequiredLevel == CRM_REQUIRED_LEVEL_REQUIRED) && (oProblemCategory
.DataValue == null) )
{
 // Display error message to user
 alert("You must provide a value for Problem Category.");

 // Return false, preventing the form from saving
 event.returnValue = false;
}
```

Validating an E-Mail Address Format

The custom validation script in this sample ensures that an e-mail address is entered in the proper format. (It will not check to determine whether it is a valid e-mail address, although that could be done, too.) We will pass the text entered into the e-mail address field through a simple regular expression, alerting the user that the entry does not appear to be valid. We will also add a check to the *onSave* routine to prevent the form from being saved if the user does not correct the e-mail address. For this sample, we will use the Account form, checking the emailaddress1 field with the routine shown in Listing 10-8.

Listing 10-8 Validating an E-Mail Address Format

```
/*
Installation:
Add this script to the onChange event of any e-mail address field.

Description:
This script will ensure that an e-mail address is in a proper format.
*/

// Gather our field references
var oEmailAddress1 = document.crmForm.all.emailaddress1;

// Remove any non-e-mail address characters
var sCleanedEmailAddress = oEmailAddress1.DataValue.replace(/[^0-9,A-Z,a-z,\@,\.]/g, "");
var regexEmail = /^.+@.+\..{2,3}$/;

// Test the cleaned email string against the email regular expression
if ( (regexEmail.test(sCleanedEmailAddress)) )
{
 oEmailAddress1.DataValue = sCleanedEmailAddress;
}
else
{
 // Display error message to user
 alert("The Email Address appears to be invalid. Please correct.");
}

/* ------------------------------------------------------- */

/*
```

```
Installation:
Add this script to the onSave event of any form containing an e-mail address field.

Description:
This script will ensure that an e-mail address is in a proper format.
*/

// Gather our field references
var oEmailAddress1 = document.crmForm.all.emailaddress1;

// Ensure that we have a value
if (oEmailAddress1.DataValue != null)
{
 // Remove any non-e-mail address characters
 var sCleanedEmailAddress = oEmailAddress1.DataValue.replace(/[^0-9,A-Z,a-z,\@,\.]/g, "");
 var regexEmail = /^.+@.+\..{2,3}$/;

 // Test the cleaned email string against the email regular expression
 if ( ! (regexEmail.test(sCleanedEmailAddress)) )
 {
 // Display error message to user
 alert("The Email Address appears to be invalid. Please correct.");

 // Return false, preventing the form from saving
 event.returnValue = false;
 }
}
```

Saving an IFrame Form from Microsoft CRM

Earlier in this chapter, you saw how to add a custom Web page to the Microsoft CRM form though the IFrame element. This sample will show you how to initiate (or submit) a postback on your custom page inside the IFrame with the save buttons of the Microsoft CRM form by using the new *onSave* event.

In earlier versions of Microsoft CRM, which lacked the *onSave* event, developers were forced to create separate navigation pages. This resulted in a less-than-ideal user interface experience for end users. The technique demonstrated in this example allows for your custom pages to write data to different systems (or even Microsoft CRM through the provided Web services, if needed) from within the main Microsoft CRM form. This simplified user experience allows the user to just click Save once, and then the code will automatically transmit the appropriate submissions to the various Web pages.

In this example, we will take a basic .NET Web Form and reference it from the Case form by using an IFrame, as shown in Figure 10-23.

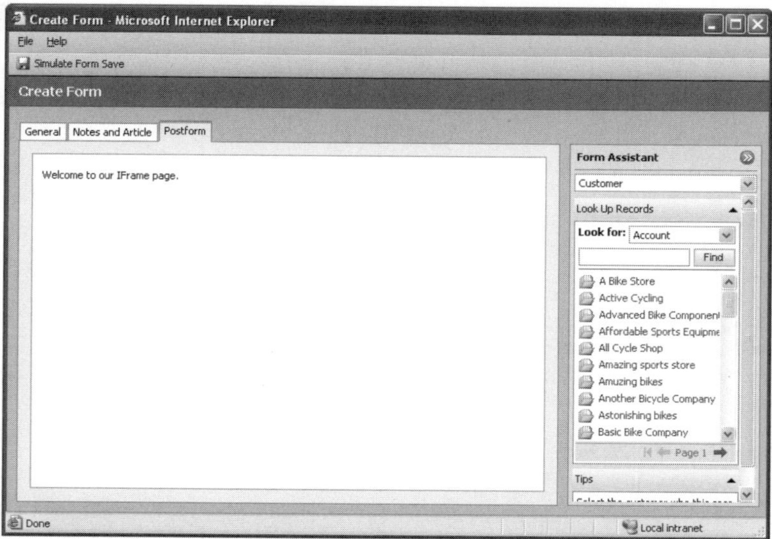

Figure 10-23 Custom .NET page referenced from Microsoft CRM

Then we will use the *onSave* event to initiate a postback to the .NET form when the user clicks one of the native CRM save buttons. For the purposes of this example, we will simply display text stating that the custom page was submitted, as shown in Figure 10-24.

> **Important** For this to work, you must enable cross-frame scripting and have the target page on the same domain and referenced with the same protocol as the user accessing Microsoft CRM. For more information, see the discussion earlier in this chapter regarding IFrame security.

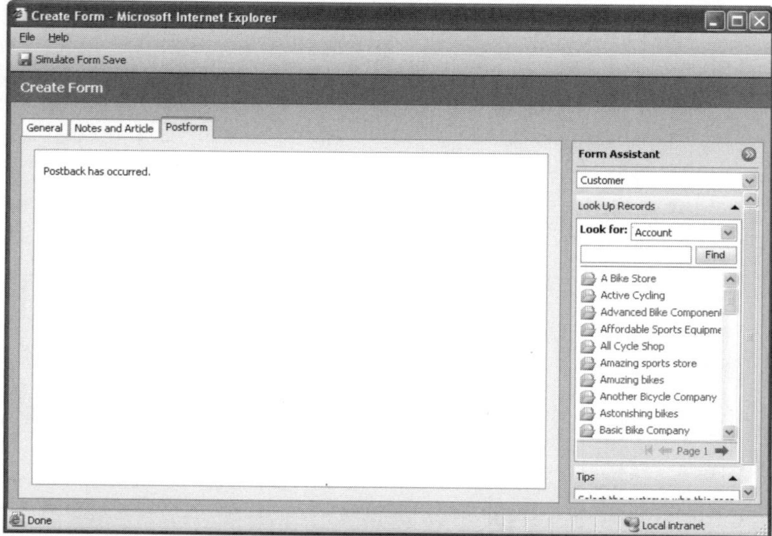

Figure 10-24 Successful postback of custom .NET page from Microsoft CRM

Server-side setup

1. Create the **postform.aspx** page, shown in the following code:

```
<%@ Page Language="C#"  %>
<!doctype html public "-//w3c//dtd xhtml 1.0 transitional//en" "http://www.w3.org/tr/
xhtml1/dtd/xhtml1-transitional.dtd">

<script runat="server">
  protected void Page_Load(object sender, EventArgs e)
  {
    if (Page.IsPostBack)
    {
      lblDisplay.Text = "Postback has occurred.";
    }
    else
    {
      lblDisplay.Text = "Welcome to our IFrame page.";
    }
  }
</script>

<html>
<head runat="server" id="Head1">
  <title>Postback Page</title>
  <style>body { font-family:Tahoma;font-size:8pt; }</style>
</head>
<body>
  <form id="crmForm" runat="server">
  <asp:Label id="lblDisplay" runat="server" />
  </form>
</body>
</html>
```

2. Copy this page to your *workingwithcrm* virtual directory on the Microsoft CRM Web server. Note that we are reusing the *workingwithcrm* virtual Web explained in the book's Introduction.

Client-side setup

1. Add a new tab and section to the case form called **Postform**.
2. Using the same steps from the IFrame section, add an IFrame called **postform** and, for the **Url** field, enter the Web path to your **postform.aspx** page. Don't forget to uncheck the **Restrict cross-frame scripting** check box.
3. Add the following code to the form's **onSave** event:

```
document.frames("IFRAME_postform").document.crmForm.submit();
```

Automatically Populating a Phone Number on the Phone Call Activity

When you are creating a new Phone Call activity from scratch, it would be helpful to have the phone number of the sender or recipient, depending on the call direction, automatically populated in the phone number field; this would save you the effort of having to click the record to retrieve it. Microsoft CRM does not provide this feature natively, but it can easily be added by clever use of code from both the client and server APIs. This example will use both the client-side scripting techniques demonstrated in the previous samples and a C# Web service using the Microsoft CRM CrmService Web service. Our Web service will interact with Microsoft CRM to retrieve the phone number of the first person selected (recipient for outgoing calls and sender for incoming calls) and pass the result back to our client script for display, as shown in Figure 10-25. Please refer to Chapter 9 for detailed information regarding the use of server-side code with Microsoft CRM.

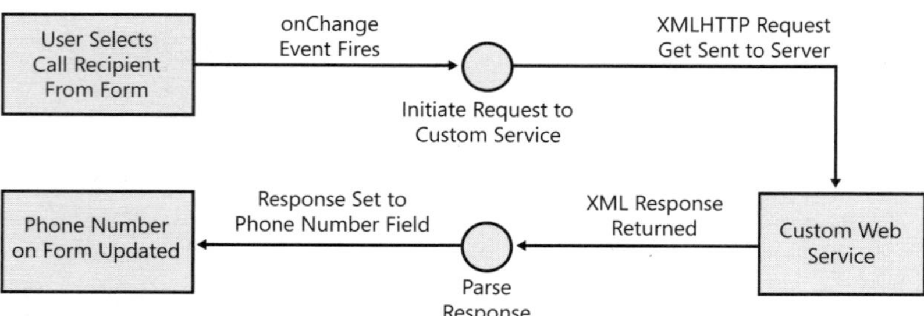

Figure 10-25 Diagram of a Web service call

This example also introduces the XMLHTTP commands, which will call the Web service and parse its results. This technique provides an excellent mechanism for allowing your client scripts to communicate with outside services and systems. To allow these commands, we need to allow the virtual Web to accept the Get and Post protocols for a Web service. This can be done by updating the Web.config file's *<system.web>* node located in your *workingwithcrm* virtual Web with the following:

```
<webServices>
  <protocols>
   <add name="HttpGet"/>
   <add name="HttpPost"/>
 </protocols>
</webServices>
```

Similar to the IFrame, this example will not work off-line. The user will need to be online when accessing the phone call activity page in order for the auto-populating phone number to work. The next code sample (Listing 10-9) shows the client side script you will apply to the *onChange* event of the *Recipient* and *Sender* attributes on the phone call activity form.

Listing 10-9 Automatically Populating a Phone Number on the Phone Call Activity

```
/*
Installation:
Update the url variable with the appropriate path to the web service.
Add this script to the onChange() event for the phone call Recipient and Sender fields.

Description:
This script will use the first recipient selected and auto-populate the phone number.
*/
```

```
// Update with the path to your web service
var url = "http://<crmserver>/workingwithcrm/phonenumber.asmx/RetrieveContact";


// Set up our bit constants
// Ensure that these match the codes in CRM
var DIRECTIONCODE_INCOMING = 0;

// Gather our field references
var oSender = document.crmForm.all.from;
var oRecipient = document.crmForm.all.to;
var oPhoneNumber = document.crmForm.all.phonenumber;
var oDirection = document.crmForm.all.directioncode;

// Determine whether the phone call is incoming or outgoing
// Incoming (0): use sender; Outgoing (1): use recipient;
var oField = (oDirection == DIRECTIONCODE_INCOMING) ? oSender : oRecipient;

if (oField.DataValue != null)
{
 // The lookup field contains an array of values
 var aPerson = new Array();
 aPerson = oField.DataValue;

 // Get the values from the first record
 var sId = aPerson[0].id;
 var sObjectTypeCode = aPerson[0].type;

 // Remove the braces from the GUID
 sId = sId.replace(/[{,}]/g, "");
}

// Leave the phone number blank if there are any errors from our service call
try
{
 // Use XMLHTTP connection to Web server containing SDK code to retrieve the phone number
 var oXmlHTTP = new ActiveXObject("Msxml2.XMLHTTP");

 // Open connection to Web service
 oXmlHTTP.Open("POST", url, false);

 // Set a header to tell the browser we are sending posted data
 oXmlHTTP.setRequestHeader("Content-Type", "application/x-www-form-urlencoded")

 // Send request, passing in the GUID and object type code
 oXmlHTTP.Send("id=" + sId + "&ObjectTypeCode=" + sObjectTypeCode);

 // Parse the response to the phoneNumber variable
 var phoneNumber = "";

 // Check to see if we have a valid response
 if ((oXmlHTTP.responseXML.xml) != null && (oXmlHTTP.responseXML.xml.toString().length > 0))
 {
 // The service will return the phone number back in a string node
 phoneNumber = oXmlHTTP.responseXML.selectSingleNode("string").text;
 }

 // Assign response back to Phone Number field
```

```
 oPhoneNumber.DataValue = phoneNumber;
}
catch(e)
{
}
```

Listing 10-10 shows our Web service for returning a Contact record. We added this service to our WorkingWithCrm Web application project. We will deploy the service to the *workingwith-crm* virtual Web on the Microsoft CRM Web server and update the Web.config to allow the Web service protocols, as previously mentioned.

Listing 10-10 Phonenumber.asmx/RetrieveContact

```
using System;
using System.Collections;
using System.ComponentModel;
using System.Data;
using System.Diagnostics;
using System.Web;
using System.Web.Services;

using WorkingWithCrm.CrmSdk;

namespace WorkingWithCrm
{
  public class phonenumber : System.Web.Services.WebService
  {
    public phonenumber () {}

    [WebMethod]
    public string RetrieveContact(string Id, int EntityTypeCode)
    {
      // Standard CRM service setup
      CrmService service = new CrmService();
      service.Credentials = System.Net.CredentialCache.DefaultCredentials;

      // Create the Column Set object indicating the fields to be retrieved
      ColumnSet cols = new ColumnSet();

      string ret = string.Empty;

      // Ensure that we have a string that can be converted to a GUID
      if (ValidGuid(Id))
      {
        // oGuid is the GUID of the record being retrieved
        Guid oGuid = new Guid(Id);

        try
        {
          // The EntityName indicates the EntityType of the object being retrieved
        switch (EntityTypeCode)
          {
            case 1:
              cols.Attributes = new string[] { "telephone1" };
              account account = (account)service.Retrieve(EntityName.account.ToString(),
oGuid, cols);
```

```
                ret = account.telephone1;
                break;
              case 2:
                cols.Attributes = new string[] { "telephone1" };
                contact contact = (contact)service.Retrieve(EntityName.contact.ToString(),
oGuid, cols);
                ret = contact.telephone1;
                break;
              case 4:
                cols.Attributes = new string[] { "telephone1" };
                lead lead = (lead)service.Retrieve(EntityName.lead.ToString(), oGuid, cols);
                ret = lead.telephone1;
                break;
              case 8:
                cols.Attributes = new string[] { "address1_telephone1" };
                systemuser systemuser = (systemuser)service.Retrieve(EntityName.systemuser.
ToString(), oGuid, cols);
                ret = systemuser.address1_telephone1;
                break;
              default:
                ret = string.Empty;
                break;
            }
          }
          catch(System.Web.Services.Protocols.SoapException ex)
          {
            ret = "Error: " + ex.Detail.InnerXml;
          }
        }
        else
        {
          ret = "no phone";
        }

        return ret;
      }

      /// <summary>
      /// Determines whether the given string is a valid GUID (enclosed brackets are optional).
      /// </summary>
      /// <remarks>
      /// This method will return true if the string is in a 8-4-4-4-12 format, optionally
      /// enclosed in brackets; otherwise it will return false.
      /// </remarks>
      /// <param name="guid"></param>
      /// <returns></returns>
      public static bool ValidGuid(string Guid)
      {
        return ((System.Text.RegularExpressions.Regex) new System.Text.RegularExpressions.Rege
x(@"^\{?[a-fA-F\d]{8}-([a-fA-F\d]{4}-){3}[a-fA-F\d]{12}\}?$", System.Text.RegularExpressions
.RegexOptions.Singleline | System.Text.RegularExpressions.RegexOptions.Compiled)).IsMatch(Guid);
      }
    }
  }
```

Summary

This chapter discussed the methods and options available to a script developer attempting to enhance and extend the application forms. In addition to the new events available in Microsoft CRM 3.0, the addition of the IFrame element further enhances the ability to add custom functionality without requiring the user to leave the form. Hopefully you have seen that, by using scripts and the new touch points opened by Microsoft CRM, you can easily create user-friendly and complex application integration.

Chapter 11

Integration with External Applications

In this chapter:

If you've read this far, you should have a good understanding of the different customization and integration capabilities that Microsoft Dynamics CRM 3.0 offers. However, your organization probably uses multiple applications to manage different parts of your operation. Maybe your corporate Web site generates new incoming leads for your salespeople, or perhaps your department makes heavy use of document libraries in Microsoft SharePoint Products and Technologies. By leveraging Microsoft CRM customization and integration tools, you can integrate the data stored in Microsoft CRM with these other types of business applications to enhance your users' productivity and efficiency.

You already know that Microsoft CRM provides out-of-the-box integration with different applications, such as:

- Microsoft Office Outlook
- Microsoft Office Excel
- Microsoft SQL Server Reporting Services
- Microsoft Exchange Server

Although integration with these applications provides great benefits, these systems represent only a fraction of the integration opportunities available to your organization. Microsoft CRM can integrate with almost any application that offers a method to extract or retrieve data programmatically, so the integration possibilities are almost endless. Some common Microsoft CRM integration requests that we hear include:

- Microsoft SharePoint Products and Technologies
- Custom Web sites (intranets or extranets)
- Microsoft Office products, such as Microsoft Word, Microsoft Access, Microsoft OneNote, and Microsoft Visio

- Microsoft Dynamics products, such as Microsoft Dynamics GP and Microsoft Dynamics SL
- Custom applications
- Third-party applications

Of course, we couldn't possibly explain the integration details for all of these systems in the book, so this chapter focuses on the following two common integration scenarios:

- Integrating external Web site data with Microsoft CRM
- Integrating Microsoft CRM with Microsoft Windows SharePoint Services

We will explain how you can quickly integrate these applications to work with Microsoft CRM.

Integration with an External Web Site

Frequently, one of the first questions we hear from prospects and customers is, "Can my company's Web site integrate with Microsoft CRM?" Hopefully you realize that the answer is yes, but many customers and prospects don't know how to approach this project. This question is a little tricky: There is no one way to set up a Web site for Microsoft CRM integration because the recommended solution architecture varies depending on the location of your servers, your network configuration, and the access protocols allowed between them. However, we'll talk you through a common customer configuration and then show you how to create code that converts a Web site form request into a Microsoft CRM Lead record.

Our Web site integration explanation will cover the following topics:

- Integration architecture
- The External Connector license
- Sample integration code

Integration Architecture

Most companies install Microsoft CRM on their local network, and it's pretty typical to use a third-party hosting provider to host corporate Web sites. In this scenario, the actual code for integrating Microsoft CRM with your Web site isn't too complex, but you might face some hurdles getting all of the network configurations correct. Figure 11-1 shows a sample network layout for a company hosting its corporate Web site with a third party.

Let's assume that you want to create a contact request form on your corporate Web site that potential customers fill out with basic information about themselves to request more information about your products and services. When prospects submit the form, most Web sites capture the data in a database or send a notification e-mail, and then salespeople must retype the information in their company's CRM system. However, instead of having to manually retype these leads in Microsoft CRM, you want the Web site requests to automatically flow into the Microsoft CRM database as Lead records.

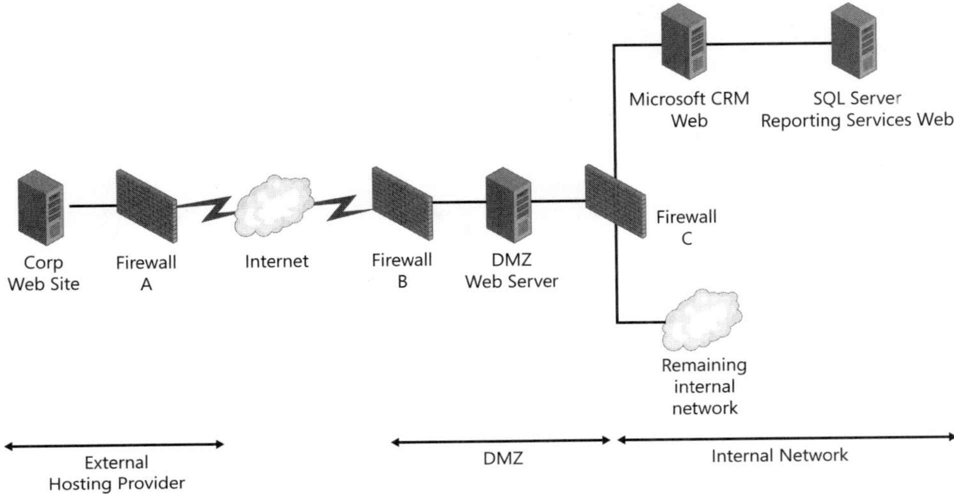

Figure 11-1 Typical network topology for a corporate Web site

Again, you have plenty of programming options available to accomplish this integration, but we'll just discuss one potential implementation. We recommend using a Web service–based approach for this integration example, using the following process:

1. A customer submits a request on a corporate Web site form.
2. The form calls a custom Web service that is installed on the same server as the corporate Web site (running on its own Web site).
3. The Web service receives data from the Web site form and calls the Microsoft CRM Web service.
4. The Microsoft CRM Web service inserts the new record in the database as a Lead record.

Figure 11-2 shows the programming flow for this process.

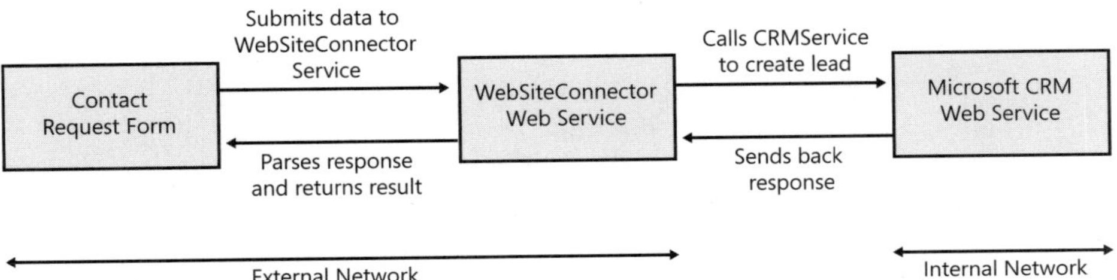

Figure 11-2 Architecture of sample Web site and Microsoft CRM integration

This Web service–based approach offers the following benefits:

- You can call the Web service client-side from an XMLHTTP call or by using standard server-side techniques. So, even if your Web site form is a simple HTML page, you can still easily communicate with the Web service.
- Using the Web service eliminates data latency between the Web site request and the record's insertion into Microsoft CRM. After record creation, the Microsoft CRM software can immediately take additional actions, such as sending a confirmation e-mail message.
- You can reuse the Web service for other applications that must insert Lead records into Microsoft CRM. For example, you might allow your partners to register their leads into your Microsoft CRM system by granting them programmatic access to the Web service.
- Because Web services can use HTTP or Secure Sockets Layer (HTTPS) for communication, they can traverse firewalls without additional network hardware and minimal (if any) changes to your network infrastructure.
- A Web service–based approach follows the Web service–based architectural model used by Microsoft CRM.

Although this design offers many benefits, you should consider some of the potential downfalls related to using a Web service–based integration mechanism. Ask yourself these questions:

- What will happen if the Web service temporarily cannot connect to the Microsoft CRM Web service? What type of error feedback should you display to the prospect who is submitting the Web form?
- What types of traffic do the firewalls in this scenario allow? For example, your network administrator might block incoming traffic on the firewall port needed (port 443 for HTTPS connections) to allow the Web service to connect to Microsoft CRM.

If you're concerned that you might temporarily lose the connection between your corporate Web site and Microsoft CRM, a queuing mechanism might work better for your situation. Such a design is more complex to code and test, but it would solve any issues related to intermittent connectivity.

If your network administrator blocks incoming traffic on the firewall ports that you need, you will probably have to consider an alternate design in which Microsoft CRM "pulls" lead data from the corporate Web site. In our example design, the corporate Web site "pushes" data to Microsoft CRM whenever new leads submit a request.

The External Connector License

You already learned that Microsoft CRM software licensing is based on named users. Therefore, when you're implementing integration solutions such as the one in our corporate Web site example, you must consider the licensing ramifications of extending Microsoft CRM data to third parties and external users. Sometimes, purchasing a license for each external named user can be difficult (or impossible) to execute in Web site portal scenarios, because the external users are constantly changing. Fortunately, Microsoft CRM offers an External Connector license for just these types of integration scenarios. The External Connector license gives you the rights to push and pull data from Microsoft CRM without requiring a separate user license for each user. Chapter 1, "Microsoft Dynamics CRM 3.0 Overview," explains the details related to Microsoft CRM licensing.

Sample Integration Code

Now let's see how the code for this Web site integration example works! To accomplish our goal of inserting Lead data directly into Microsoft CRM from a Web site form (via a custom WebSiteConnector Web service), we must follow these steps:

1. Determine which parameters (fields) you want to capture from your Web site Lead form.
2. Create a Web service that accepts the parameters you want to capture and then calls the Microsoft CRM Web service to insert that information as a new Lead record.
3. Deploy this Web service to your Web site's server.
4. Update and deploy your contact request form on your corporate Web site to use this new Web service.

We recommend that you configure the WebSiteConnector Web service to communicate with the Microsoft CRM API Web service through HTTPS.

Creating the Web service

1. Create a new **C# ASP.NET Web Application** project in Microsoft Visual Studio .NET 2003 called **WebSiteConnector**. See Chapter 9 for more details on creating a Web application project in Visual Studio .NET 2003.
2. Add a **Web Reference** to the Microsoft CRM CRMService Web service called **CrmSdk**. The reference should be *http://<crmserver>/mscrmservices/2006/crmservice.asmx*. See Chapter 9 for more details.
3. Add a **Web Service** file called **InsertLead.asmx**.
4. Switch to code view, and replace the default code with the following code. Be sure to add a *using* statement with the correct reference to the CrmSdk service, and replace *<externalcrmserverdomain>* with a domain name that maps to your Microsoft CRM server. For the service *Credentials* property, be sure to use a licensed Microsoft CRM user that has the ability to create a new lead record.

> **Important** Unlike previous examples, the Web service call to the Microsoft CRM server will be coming from outside your network. Therefore, you will need to use a domain name that will resolve to the public IP address of the Microsoft CRM Web server. You could do this by registering a domain name or using an IP address (depending on your network configuration and preferences) that points to your network. Then you must configure your firewalls to direct traffic from that domain to your Microsoft CRM Web server.

```
using System;
using System.Collections;
using System.ComponentModel;
using System.Data;
using System.Diagnostics;
using System.Web;
using System.Web.Services;
using WebSiteConnector.CrmSdk;


namespace WebSiteConnector
{
  /// <summary>
  /// Summary description for InsertLead.
  /// </summary>
  public class InsertLead : System.Web.Services.WebService
  {
    public InsertLead()
    {
      //CODEGEN: This call is required by the ASP.NET Web Services Designer
      InitializeComponent();
    }

    #region Component Designer generated code
    //Required by the Web Services Designer
    private IContainer components = null;

    /// <summary>
    /// Required method for Designer support - do not modify
    /// the contents of this method with the code editor.
    /// </summary>
    private void InitializeComponent()
    {
    }

    /// <summary>
    /// Clean up any resources being used.
    /// </summary>
    protected override void Dispose( bool disposing )
    {
      if(disposing && components != null)
      {
        components.Dispose();
      }
      base.Dispose(disposing);
    }

    #endregion

    [WebMethod]
    public string InsertLeadFromWebForm(string Token, string FirstName, string LastNam
e, string Company, string EmailAddress, string Comments)
    {
      string ret = string.Empty;
```

```
// Ensure that only valid users use the service by checking for the proper Key value.
if (Token == "some long string")
{
  // Validate we have required fields
  if (LastName == string.Empty)
  {
    ret = "Last name must be entered.<br>";
  }
  else if (Company == string.Empty)
  {
    ret += "Company must be entered.<br>";
  }

  // If our return value is empty, we passed our validation, so submit to CRM.
  if (ret == string.Empty)
  {
    CrmService service = new CrmService();

    // Replace https://<externalcrmserverdomain> with a URL that will resolve
    // to the external IP address of the Microsoft CRM server.
    // Change https: to http: if you do not have SSL installed.
    service.Url = "https://<externalcrmserverdomain>/mscrmservices/2006/
crmservice.asmx";

    // We need to set the Web service authentication to a user with the ability
to create a Lead record.
    //
 This user should have only enough privileges to perform the task required.
    // For production, please encrypt this information.
    service.Credentials = new System.Net.NetworkCredential("crmuser", "password"
, "domain");

    lead oLead = new lead();
    oLead.firstname = FirstName;
    oLead.lastname = LastName;
    oLead.companyname = Company;
    oLead.emailaddress1 = EmailAddress;
    oLead.description = Comments;
    oLead.subject = LastName + ", " + FirstName;
    oLead.leadsourcecode = new Picklist();
    oLead.leadsourcecode.Value = 8; // Web

    try
    {
      // Create the lead
      Guid leadId = service.Create(oLead);
      ret = "Success";
    }
    catch (System.Web.Services.Protocols.SoapException ex)
    {
      ret = ex.Detail.InnerXml;
    }
  }
}
else
```

```
                {
                    ret = "Unauthorized";
                }
                return ret;
            }
        }
    }
```

> **Tip** Store the Web service URL and the Microsoft CRM user credentials securely in a configuration file. See Chapter 9, "Microsoft CRM Server-Side SDK," for more information on how to do this.

5. Build your assembly.
6. Create a new virtual directory on your corporate Web site server called **WebSiteConnector**, and then deploy your files.

After we deploy our Web service to the corporate Web server, we must either update our Web site's lead form to pass the information to our service or create a new form. For this example, we will create a simple new form to demonstrate how to connect with the WebSiteConnector Web service and pass the user-entered data into it. Figure 11-3 displays our sample information request form.

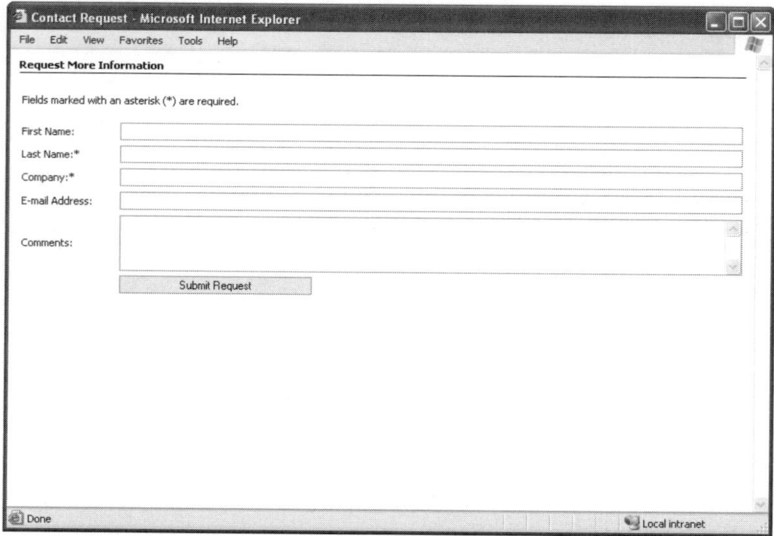

Figure 11-3 Information request Web form

You will deploy this contact request Web page to your corporate Web site. Because we don't have a sample corporate Web site, we will simply deploy this file to the root of the WebSite-Connector virtual directory.

Creating a sample contact request form Web page

Because we will create an HTML page, you can use any tool to create this page. For this example, we will reuse our WebSiteConnector project in Visual Studio .NET.

1. Create a new **HTML Page** called ContactRequest.htm.
2. Add the following code, replacing the *url* variable with the path to your **WebSiteConnector** virtual Web site.

```
<!doctype html public "-//w3c//dtd html 4.0 transitional//en" >
<html>
<head>
<title>Contact Request</title>

<script language="JavaScript">

function submitForm()
{
  // Set the url variable to the URL where the Web service is installed.
  var url = "/WebSiteConnector/insertlead.asmx/InsertLeadFromWebForm";

  // Validate our required fields. We will also validate on the server.
  if (document.all.crm.lastname.value == "")
  {
    alert('Please enter a last name.');
    document.all.crm.lastname.focus();
    return;
  }
  else if (document.all.crm.company.value == "")
  {
    alert('Please enter a company name.');
    document.all.crm.company.focus();
    return;
  }

   try
   {
    // Use xmlhttp connection to web server containing SDK code to retrieve the phone
    number var oXmlHTTP = new ActiveXObject("Msxml2.XMLHTTP");

    // Open connection to web service
    oXmlHTTP.Open("POST", url, false);

    // We set a header to tell the browser we are sending posted data
    oXmlHTTP.setRequestHeader("Content-Type", "application/x-www-form-urlencoded")

    // Build query string based on entered values
    var qs = "token=some long string";
    qs += "&firstname=" + document.all.crm.firstname.value;
    qs += "&lastname=" + document.all.crm.lastname.value;
    qs += "&company=" + document.all.crm.company.value;
    qs += "&emailaddress=" + document.all.crm.emailaddress.value;
    qs += "&comments=" + document.all.crm.comments.value;

    // Send request, passing in the request string
    oXmlHTTP.Send(qs);
```

```
        var result = "";

        // Check to see if we have a valide response
        if ((oXmlHTTP.responseXML.xml) != null && (oXmlHTTP.responseXML.xml.toString()
.length > 0))
        {
          // The service will return the result in a string node.
          result = oXmlHTTP.responseXML.selectSingleNode("string").text;
        }

        // Check to see if our service returns a success.
        if (result == "Success")
        {
          // Let the user know their submission was a success.
          msg = "<br><br>Thank you for your request. A representative will contact you
shortly.";

          // Hide the form
          document.all.formtable.style.display = "none";
        }
        else
        {
          msg = "There was an error with your submission. Please try again. <br>Error: " +
 result;
        }
}
  catch(e)
  {
    msg = "There was an error with your submission. Please try again. Error: <br>" +
e.message;
  }

  // Display our results back to the user.
  document.all.div_results.innerHTML = msg;
}
</script>

<style>
  body{ font-size:11px; margin:10px; border:0px; cursor:default; }
  table.layout { table-layout:fixed; width:100%; height:auto; }
  td, div {font-size:11px; font-family:tahoma, verdana; }
  .bar { border-bottom:1px solid #000000; }
  td.req { font-weight:bold; color:#9f2409; overflow:hidden; text-
overflow:ellipsis; padding-top:5px; }
  textarea { font-size:8pt; width:100%; border:1px solid #7b9ebd; }
  input { font-size:8pt; width:100%; height:19px; border:1px solid #7b9ebd; }
  .sec
  {
  font-size:11px;
  font-family:tahoma, verdana;
  width:100%;
  color:#000000;
  font-weight:bold;
  padding-left:0px;
  padding-bottom:2px;
  text-overflow:ellipsis;
  overflow:hidden;
  }
```

```
  button
  {
  filter:progid:DXImageTransform.Microsoft.Gradient(GradientType=0, StartColorStr=
#ffffff, EndColorStr=#cecfde);
  cursor:hand;
  font-size:11px;
  padding-left:5px;
  padding-right:5px;
  border:1px solid #7b9ebd;
  }
</style>


</head>

<body>
<div class="sec bar">Request More Information</div>
<div id="div_results"></div>

<form name="crm" id="crm" method="post">
<div id="formtable">
<table class="layout">
  <col width="100"><col/>
  <tr><td colspan="2">Fields marked with an asterisk (*) are required.<br><br></td></
tr>
  <tr>
    <td>First Name:</td>
    <td><input name="firstname" type="text" id="firstname" maxlength="50" /></td>
  </tr>
  <tr>
    <td>Last Name:*</td>
    <td><input name="lastname" type="text" id="lastname" maxlength="50" /></td>
  </tr>
  <tr>
    <td>Company:*</td>
    <td><input name="company" type="text" id="company" maxlength="100" /></td>
  </tr>
  <tr>
    <td>E-mail Address:</td>
    <td><input name="emailaddress" type="text" id="emailaddress" maxlength="100" /></td>
  </tr>
  <tr>
    <td>Comments:</td>
    <td><textarea id="comments" rows="4" cols="40"></textarea></td>
  </tr>
  <tr>
    <td> </td>
    <td><input type="button" name="btnsubmit" value="Submit Request" id="btnsubmit" on
click="submitForm();" style="width:200px;" /></td>
  </tr>
</table>
</div>
</form>
</body>
</html>
```

3. Deploy this file to your **WebSiteConnector** Web site.

When users submit the contact request Web page, they see a confirmation page indicating that their information was received, shown in Figure 11-4.

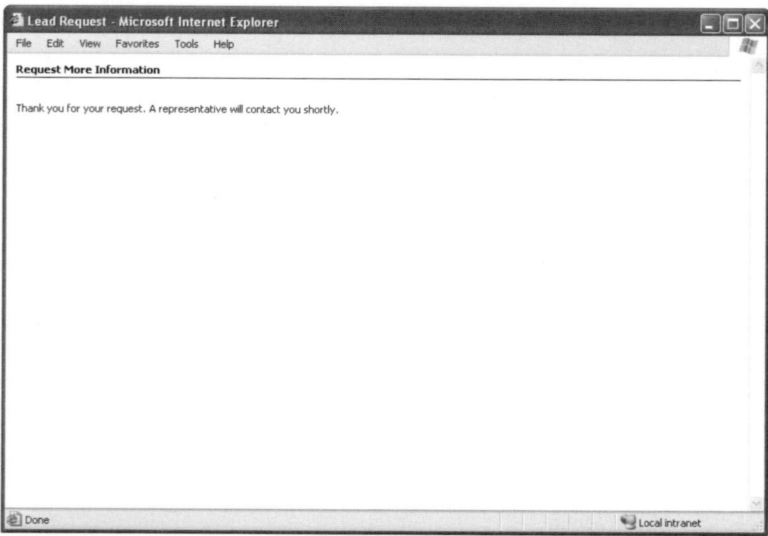

Figure 11-4 Web page result displayed to a prospect after a successful transaction

Meanwhile, our code takes the user-entered values from the form and passes them to our Web service, which attempts to insert a Lead record into Microsoft CRM through the Microsoft CRM Web service. Figure 11-5 shows a sample Lead record created using this code.

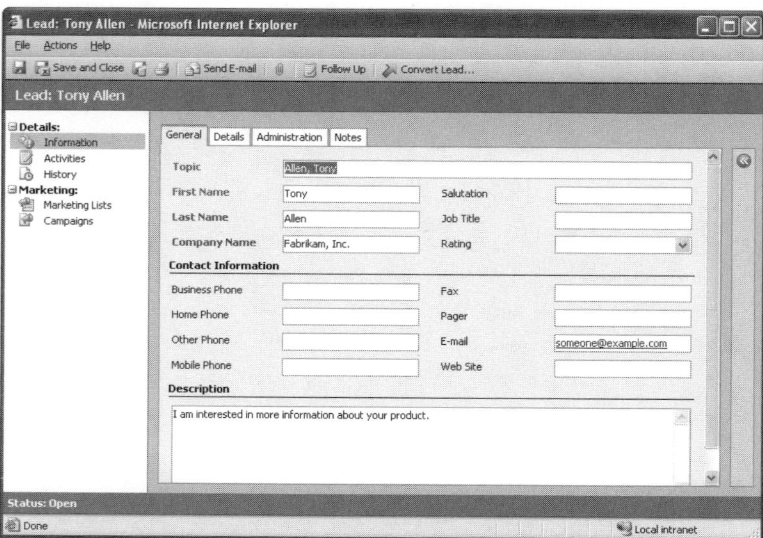

Figure 11-5 Lead record created from our Web page

That's it! You now have fully functioning integration between your corporate Web site and your Microsoft CRM system.

Web Service Security Considerations

When you deploy your Web service on a server over the Internet, you should consider how you will prevent unauthorized users from accessing your Web service and inserting records into your Microsoft CRM application. To keep our sample code simple, we merely forced the request to pass in a valid string token. Although this approach is better than nothing, it certainly isn't sufficient for a production, Internet-exposed service.

Because this book is about Microsoft CRM and not Web service security, we won't go further into this topic. However, when you're ready to design and implement your Web service on your production Web site, you should review the Web Service Security article on MSDN at *http://msdn.microsoft.com/library/default.asp?url=/library/en-us/dnpag2/html/wssp.asp*.

Additional Integration Considerations

In addition to considering Web service security, keep these additional points in mind whenever you design and implement Microsoft CRM integration code:

- As mentioned earlier, exposing Microsoft CRM data to external users and third-party systems requires an External Connector license.
- You should try to only allow SSL connections for your Web services.
- You must authenticate as a licensed user with the appropriate security privileges to communicate with the Microsoft CRM Web service. In our example, we used a user who only had the rights to create and read Lead records. By leveraging a user with limited roles, you will limit your exposure should a malicious program compromise your Web service or user account. And always remember to encrypt the Microsoft CRM user information.
- Remember to check your data types. Make sure that each field you're inserting will not exceed the maximum length for that field, and verify that it conforms to the data type requirements of the corresponding Microsoft CRM field.
- When working with picklists (drop-down lists), make sure that your source integer values match the values in Microsoft CRM. Alternately, you could create a mapping file between the two systems to keep the values in sync.
- Always validate your input on the server side, in addition to any client-side validation you choose to add. If you only use client-side validation, a malicious user could modify the Web page, remove your client-side validation, and submit data.

Extending the Example

Hopefully this sample showed you how easily you can create integration between your company Web site and Microsoft CRM. The following is a list of additional ways in which you could extend this simple example by using the techniques you learned in previous chapters:

- Update the Web service to check Microsoft CRM for duplicates based on some of the entered parameters. Then, instead of creating an additional record, you could add a note to the previously created Lead record.
- After a Lead record is created, set up a workflow rule to send an automated response to the user confirming that you received the request.
- Create a workflow rule that creates activities specific to your business process when a new Lead record is created from the Web site.
- Use a pre-create callout routine before you create the Lead record in Microsoft CRM to validate the address information entered by the prospect.
- Create a Web service that retrieves a customer's account information (such as cases or quotes) from Microsoft CRM and displays it to the customer on your company Web site.
- Publish your Knowledge Base articles to your company Web site so that your customers can troubleshoot their own issues.

Really, there's almost no limit to the types of integrations you can create between Microsoft CRM and your company Web site.

Integration with Windows SharePoint Services

SharePoint Products and Technologies is a server-based collaboration infrastructure designed to organize and deliver information across your organization. In just the last year, we've seen companies of all sizes rapidly adopt SharePoint Products and Technologies as their tool of choice for company intranets, department Web sites, and team-based collaboration projects. If you've never used it before, you should set up a demo site to see how quickly and easily you can create and manage Web sites. Because more and more companies are using SharePoint Products and Technologies, they of course want to know if they can integrate their Microsoft CRM data with their SharePoint sites. By now, you already know what our answer will be. Of course you can! This section will give you two detailed examples on how to use Windows SharePoint Services to create a customer service dashboard and how to access SharePoint document libraries from the Microsoft CRM user interface.

SharePoint Products and Technologies consists of SharePoint Portal Server 2003 and Windows SharePoint Services 2003. Both offer great functionality, but because Windows SharePoint Services 2003 comes free with Microsoft Windows Server 2003, we'll use that technology for our integration examples.

Note If you are using SharePoint Portal Server 2003, the examples and their concepts still apply, but the steps you follow will vary slightly.

We will cover the following topics related to integrating with Windows SharePoint Services:

- Creating a dashboard of Microsoft CRM data
- Simple document library integration
- Additional references

Creating a Dashboard of Microsoft CRM Data

Users love dashboards. Managers love dashboards. Executives love dashboards. Dashboards are great and everybody loves them, but in the past, creating nice, graphically pleasing Web-based dashboards required quite a bit of fancy programming and, potentially, the use of third-party charting components. Fortunately, Microsoft CRM and Windows SharePoint Services combine to make it incredibly easy for any administrator (even non-developers) to create amazing dashboards in literally minutes. This section will show you how easily you can display Microsoft CRM data in a dashboard by using the free Microsoft Office Web Parts and Components. Office Web Parts and Components is a collection of controls that allow you to publish database-driven spreadsheets and charts directly to a SharePoint site.

Note Explaining how to install and create SharePoint sites is beyond the scope of this book, so we'll assume that you already have a simple SharePoint site up and running. For more information, please visit: *http://www.microsoft.com/windowsserver2003/technologies/sharepoint/default.mspx.*

In addition to creating a dashboard page in Windows SharePoint Services, we can leverage the Microsoft CRM site map feature to display the same dashboard in the Microsoft CRM user interface. The final output of this sample is shown in Figure 11-6.

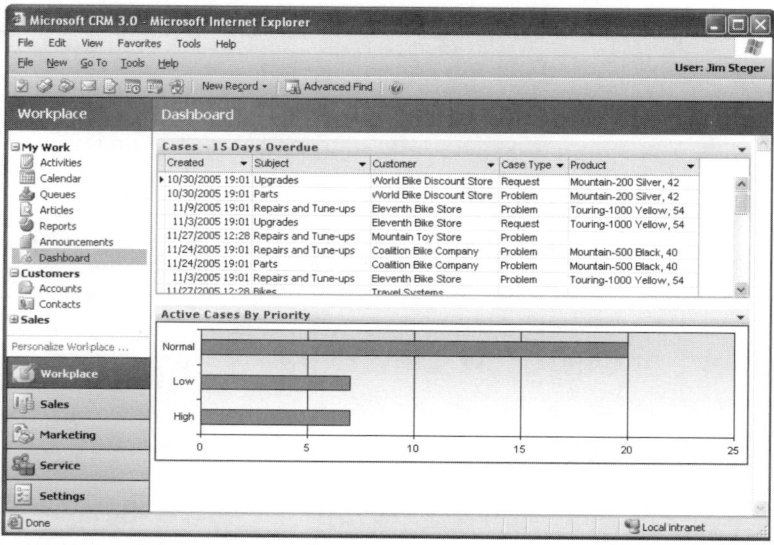

Figure 11-6 Dashboard in Microsoft CRM

To complete this sample, we will follow these steps:

1. Download and install the Office Web Parts and Components to our SharePoint site.
2. In Windows SharePoint Services, create a new document library, and then add a Web Part Page to it.
3. On that page, add and configure three Web Parts to create our dashboard:
   a. A PivotChart showing the number of active cases, grouped by priority
   b. A datasheet listing the cases that have been open for longer than 15 days
   c. A hidden Web Part that helps us format the page
4. Update the site map in Microsoft CRM with a link pointing to our SharePoint site.

Prerequisites

1. For the server, you need Microsoft CRM 3.0 and Windows SharePoint Services 2003.
2. On the client computer, you need Microsoft Office 2003. Earlier versions of Office will not display these Web Parts.
3. On the client computer, you must have Microsoft Internet Explorer 6 Service Pack 1 (SP1) or later and the Microsoft Office 2003 Web Components add-in installed. Visit the following for more information: *http://www.microsoft.com/downloads/details.aspx?familyid=7287252C-402E-4F72-97A5-E0FD290D4B76&displaylang=en*
4. You must install the Office Web Parts and Components Web Part on the Windows SharePoint Services server.

Office Web Parts and Components doesn't install with Windows SharePoint Services by default, so follow these steps to acquire the software:

Setting up Office Web Parts and Components

1. Download Microsoft Office Web Parts and Components from *http://www.sharepointcustomization.com/resources/webparts.htm*, and save it to a directory on your server running Windows SharePoint Services.
2. Log on to your server running Windows SharePoint Services and go to the directory where you saved the Microsoft Office Web Parts and Components executable file. Double-click the downloaded executable, **STSTPKPL.EXE**.
3. Click **Run** at the next prompt, and then select the check box to accept the terms. Click **Next**.
4. Click **Install**.

After you have satisfied the prerequisites, you're ready to create your dashboard. The steps include:

1. Create a new document library.
2. Create a Web Part Page (the dashboard page).
3. Add a PivotChart Web Part.
4. Format the PivotChart.
5. Format the Web Part.
6. Add an Office Datasheet Web Part.
7. Add a Content Editor Web Part.
8. Add the dashboard to the Microsoft CRM interface.

When we build our Web Part dashboard page, we must decide where to add it within Windows SharePoint Services. You could simply create your dashboard page in the default Shared Documents document library. However, because we want to display the dashboard in Microsoft CRM, we don't want the Windows SharePoint Services navigation toolbar or header to contain the page title. We'll show you a technique to hide the toolbar and header that comes with all pages in Windows SharePoint Services. Consequently, if a user browsed to dashboard our page directly from Windows SharePoint Services (instead of through the Microsoft CRM user interface), he or she could not access the Windows SharePoint Services toolbar and header. To help mitigate this confusion, we will create a special document library to store the pages that we plan to integrate into the Microsoft CRM interface, separate from other document libraries. Of course, there's no technical requirement to hide the toolbar and header from our dashboard page, but we think this is an important step to keep the user interface as consistent as possible.

Caution Perform any changes on a development or test environment first!

Let's get started by creating our new document library.

Creating a new document library

1. In Microsoft Internet Explorer, browse to your SharePoint site.
2. On the main toolbar, click **Document and Lists**.
3. On the **Document and Lists** toolbar click **Create**. Then click **Document Library** from the **Create Page** Web page.

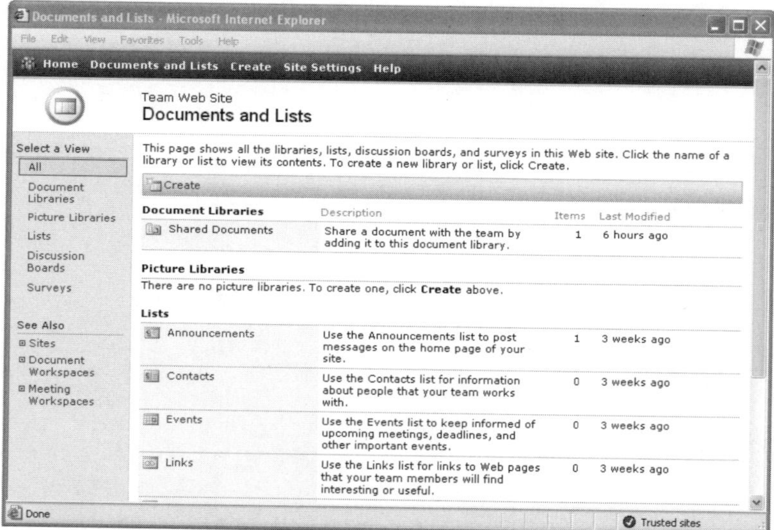

4. On the **New Document Library** page, type **CRM Integration** in the **Name** box. Select **No** for the questions in the **Navigation** and **Document Versions** sections. In the **Document Template** section, select **Web Part Page**. Click **Create**.

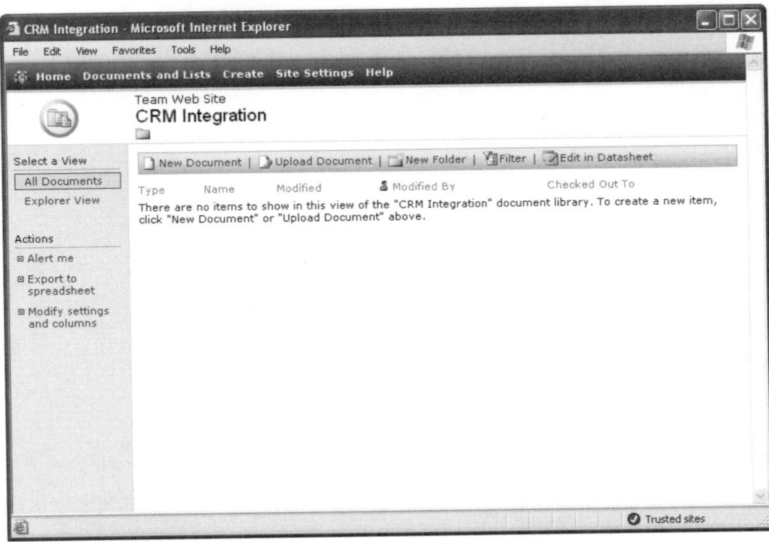

You now have a document library that will contain Web pages. The next step is to create a new Web Part Page that will be our dashboard page.

Creating a Web Part Page

1. On the **CRM Integration** document library page, click **New Document** on the document library toolbar.
2. On the **New Web Part Page** page, type **CRM Dashboard** in the **Name** box, and then select **Full Page, Vertical** in the **Layout** section.

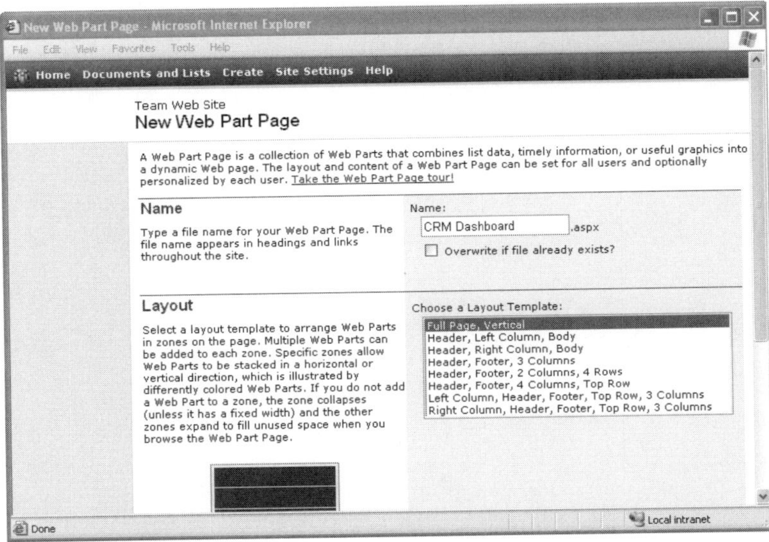

3. Click **Create**.

Now that you have the basic dashboard page (shown in Figure 11-7) in place, we will add the Web Parts to our dashboard.

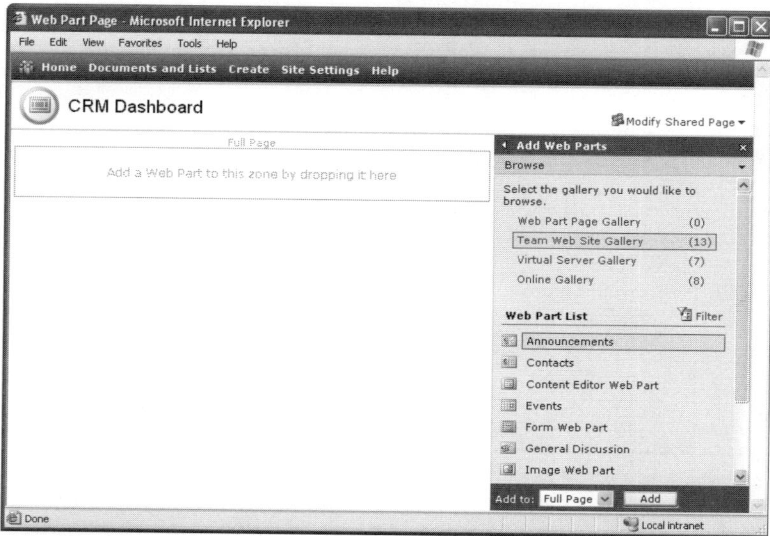

Figure 11-7 Web Part Page

To populate this page with data, we will add two Office Web Parts. The first will be a PivotChart that displays the number of active cases organized by priority. The second will be a spreadsheet that shows a list of cases that have been open (unresolved) for more than 15 days. Let's begin with the PivotChart Web Part.

Adding a PivotChart Web Part

1. On the Web Part Page, click **Virtual Server Gallery** in the tool pane.
2. Drag **Office PivotChart** from the **Web Part List** section into the body of the Web Part Page.
3. In the Web Part, click **Connect to an external data source**.

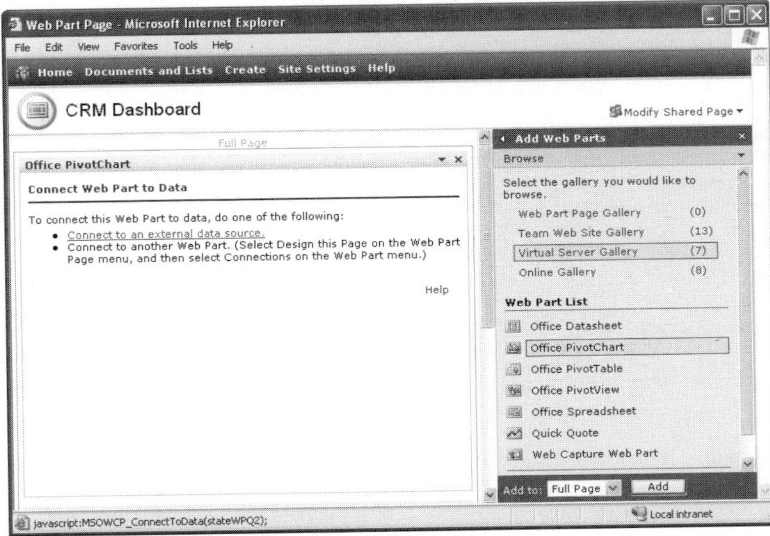

4. In the **Select Data Source** dialog page, create a new SQL Server connection to the Microsoft CRM database:

   a. Click **+New SQL Server Connection.doc**, and then click **Open**.

   b. In the **Server Name** box, enter the name of your Microsoft CRM SQL Server computer, and then select **Use Windows Authentication** for **Log on Credentials**. Click **Next**.

   c. In the **Select the database that contains the data you want** list, choose your Microsoft CRM database in the form <*organization name*>_mscrm.

   d. Clear the **Connect to a specific table** check box, click **Next**, and then click **Finish**.

5. When you have a connection to the Microsoft CRM database, a dialog box shows all of the available tables and views. We're going to connect to one of the Microsoft CRM filtered views, called FilteredIncident. Select **FilteredIncident**, and then click **OK**.

6. You might see the following two warnings. Click **OK** for both.

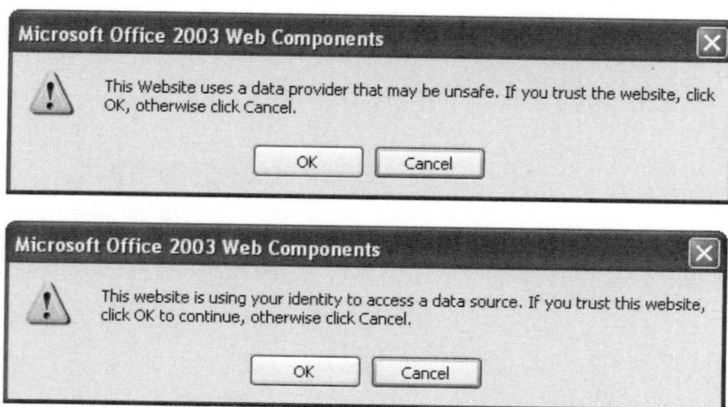

Note These two warnings will continue to appear every time you or any users try to access this page until you adjust your Internet Explorer security settings. To permanently eliminate these warnings, add your SharePoint site to the list of trusted sites in Internet Explorer.

7. Your page should look similar to the following graphic.

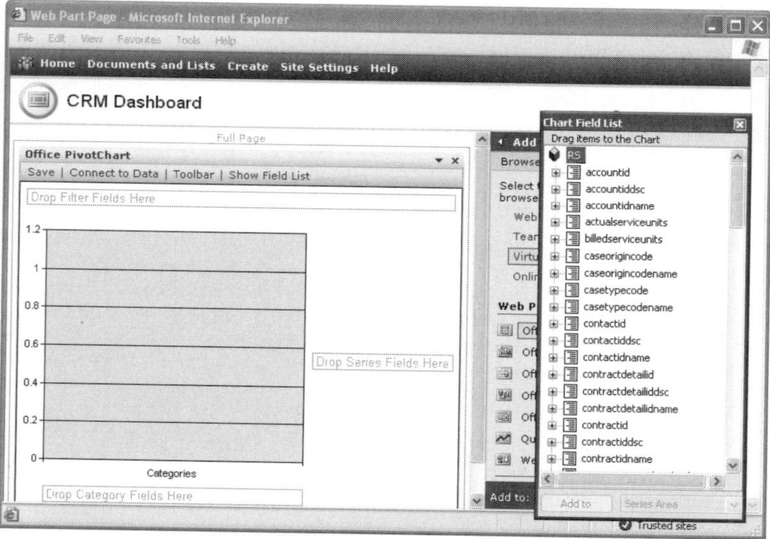

8. To start adding data fields, drag the **statecodename** field from the **Chart Field List** to the top of the chart, where it says **Drop Filter Fields Here**.

Tip If the field list disappears, you can always bring it back into focus by clicking the Show Field List on the PivotChart toolbar or by clicking the chart.

9. Drag the **prioritycodename** field to the bottom of the chart in the **Drop Category Fields Here** area. Drag the **prioritycodename** field again, but place it on top of the chart this time, to provide a total count.

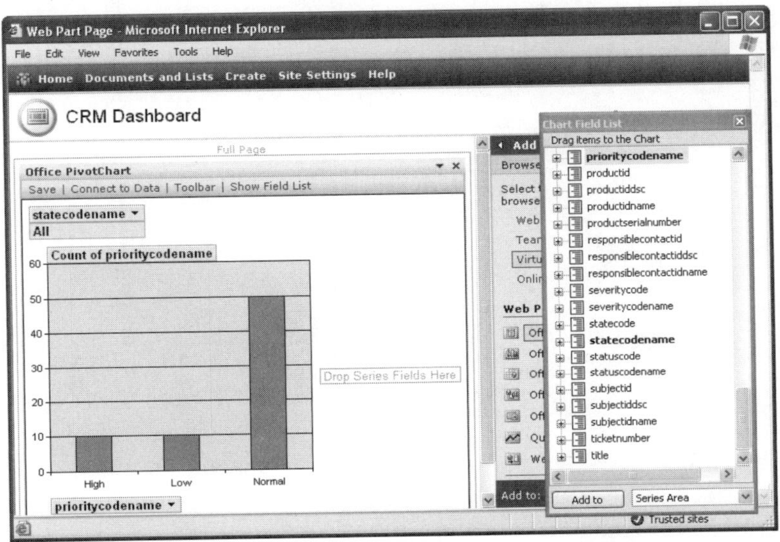

Believe it or not, you now have a working PivotChart that pulls dynamic data from Microsoft CRM. From here, we will clean up the chart's format.

Note We are using the basic PivotChart functionality contained within Excel. See the Excel Help documentation for additional information regarding the use of PivotCharts.

Formatting the PivotChart

1. First change the chart type. On the PivotChart toolbar, click **Toolbar** to see the available tools for your chart. Click the chart, and then click the **Chart Type** button on the toolbar.

2. In the **Commands and Options** dialog box, click the **Type** tab, and then click **Bar** in the list on the left. Select **Clustered Bar** as the chart type, and then click **Save** on the PivotChart toolbar.

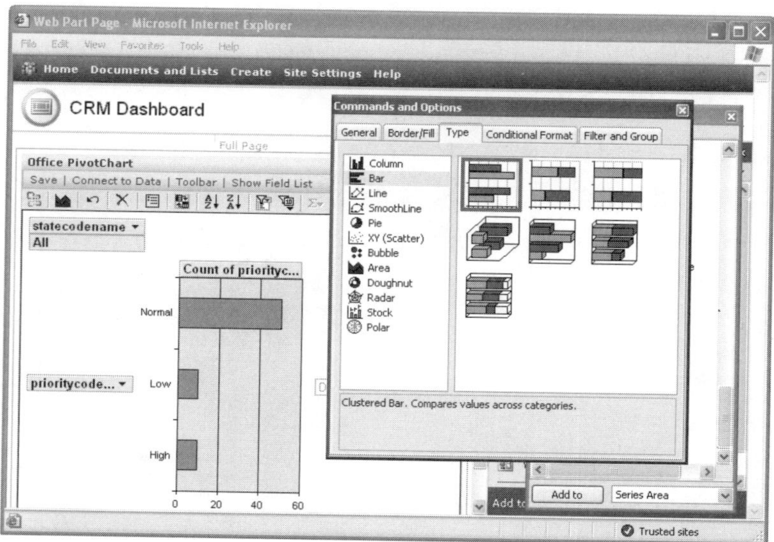

3. In the **Commands and Options** dialog box, click the **Border/Fill** tab, and in the **Fill** section, select **Gradient** in the **Fill Type** list. Move the **Amount** slider to the far right for a nice, light gray gradient.

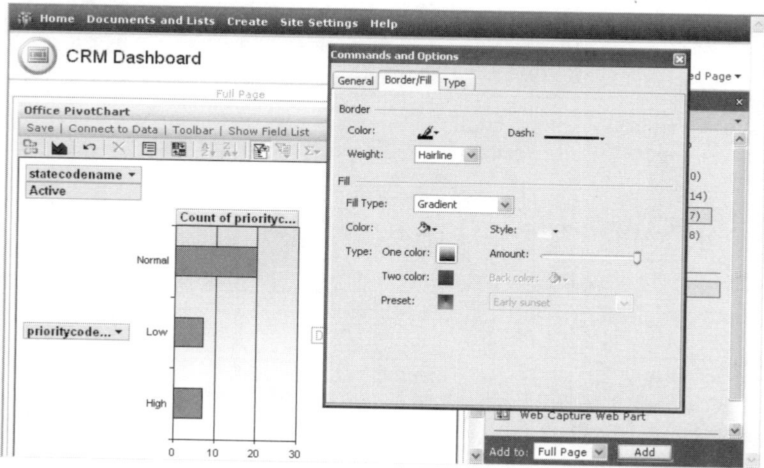

4. To display only active cases, update the statecodename filter by clicking the down arrow next to **statecodename** and leaving only **Active** selected. Click **Save**.

> **Tip** Remember to save your work often!

We now have our PivotChart working as we want. Our final step is to clean up the format of the Web Part.

Formatting the Web Part

1. To open the **Web Part Properties** pane, click **Modify Shared Page**, point to **Modify Shared Web Parts**, and then click **Office Pivot Chart**.

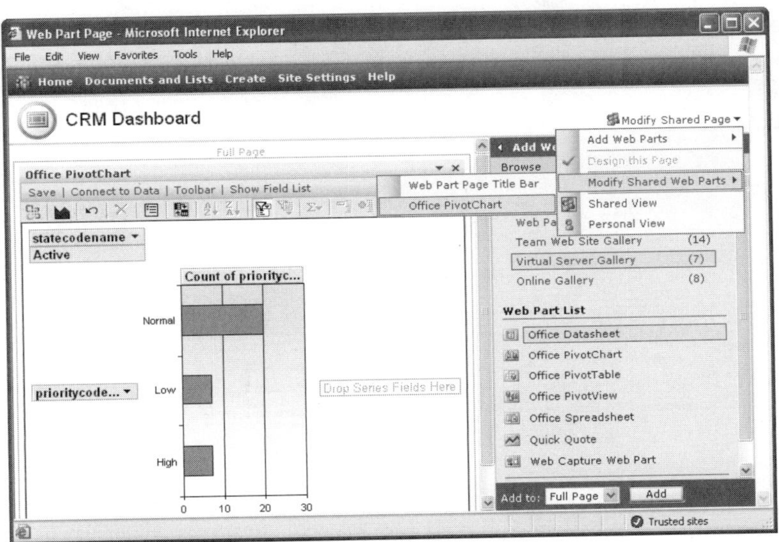

2. In the **Office PivotChart** pane in the **Appearance** section, change the title to **Active Cases By Priority**.
3. In the **Height** section, click **Yes**, enter **150** in the text box, and then select **Pixels**.
4. Scroll down to the **PivotView** section, and then clear the **Show Toolstrip** check box to hide the Web Part toolbar.
5. Right-click the chart, and then clear the **Toolbar** checkmark to turn off the PivotChart toolbar.
6. Right-click the chart, and then clear the **Drop Areas** check box to hide the drop areas outlines from the user.
7. Click **OK** in the **Web Part Properties** pane. An Internet Explorer dialog box might ask if you want to save your changes. Click **OK**.

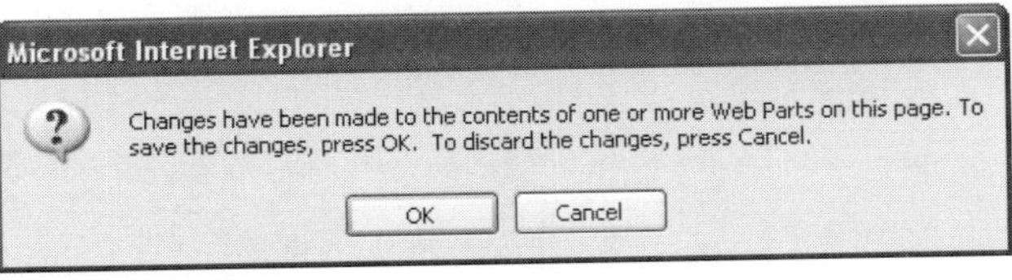

Congratulations, you have finished your Web page! Your page should look similar to the one shown in Figure 11-8; of course, the chart will display Case data from your Microsoft CRM system.

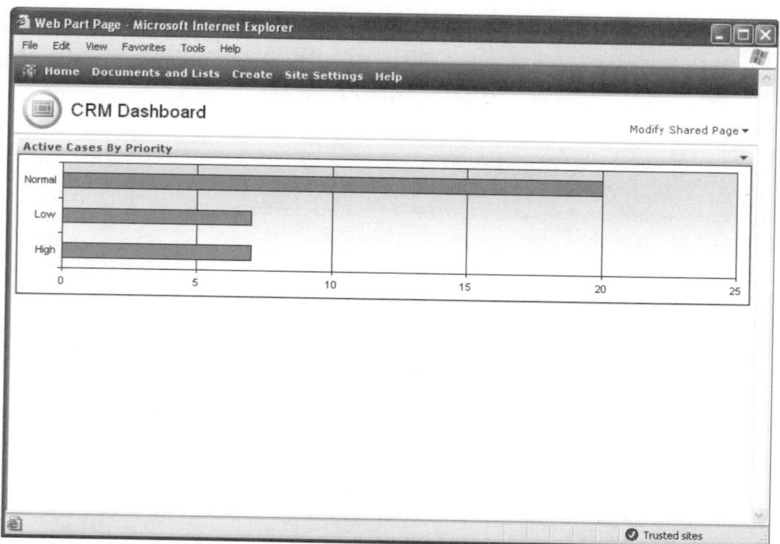

Figure 11-8 Windows SharePoint Services page after adding the Office PivotChart Web Part

Now that we've completed the PivotChart on our dashboard, our next task is to add a datasheet Web Part that lists all active cases with a created date of 15 days or older.

Adding an Office Datasheet Web Part

1. Click **Modify Shared Page**, point to **Add Web Parts**, and then click **Browse**. The **Add Web Parts** pane appears, and the page appears in design mode.
2. In the **Browse** section, click **Virtual Server Gallery**, and then drag **Office Datasheet** onto the body of the Web Part Page above the PivotChart.
3. Click **Connect to an external data source** in the Web Part, and then select the data source that you used for the PivotChart. In the **Select Table** dialog box, select the **FilteredIncident** view again. Click **OK**, and then click **Save**.
4. All of the records and columns from the Microsoft CRM Incident table appear. However, we want to update the default query to return only the records that are older than 15 days and still active. Click the down arrow on the **Office Datasheet** Web Part, and then click **Modify Shared Web Part**.

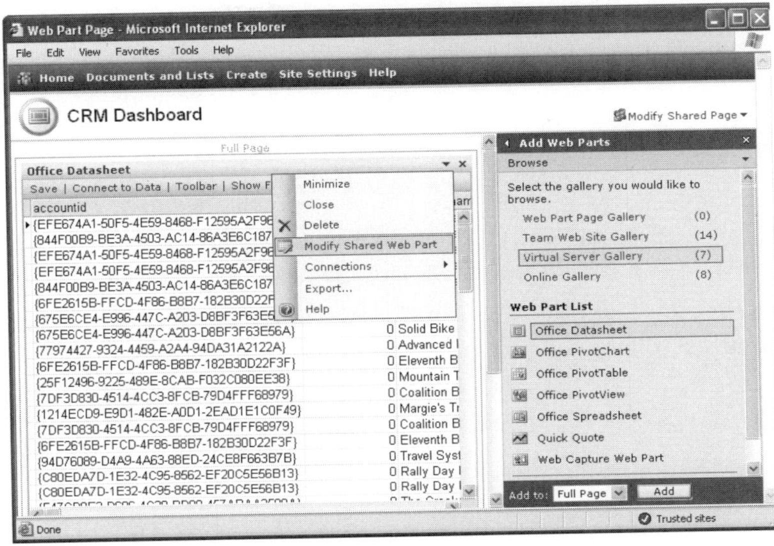

5. To alter the properties of the Web Part, in the **Appearance** section, type **Cases - 15+ Days Overdue** in the **Title** box. In the **Height** section, click **Yes**, enter **150** in the text box, and select **Pixels**.

6. In the **PivotView** section, change the connection type to **SQL Command Text**. Then click in the **Query Text** box to enable the ellipsis (...) button.

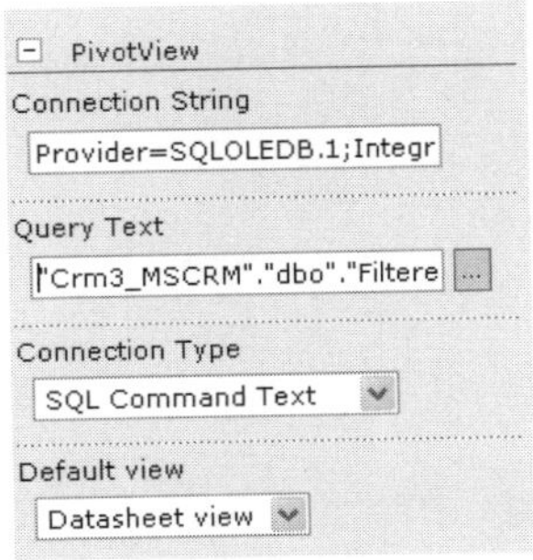

7. Click the ellipsis button to launch the **Text Entry** dialog box. Remove the existing query, and then add the following code.

```
select
 customeridname as [Customer],
 subjectidname as [Subject],
 casetypecodename as [Case Type],
 owneridname as [Owner],
 productidname as [Product],
 createdon as [Created]
from
 filteredincident
where
 statecode = 0
 and createdon < dateadd(d,-15,getdate())
```

8. Click **Apply**. Your table of data will probably disappear. If so, you will have to add back the columns that you want to display.
9. Click **Show Field List** in the Web Part toolbar and drag the following columns onto the Web Part in order: **Created**, **Subject**, **Customer**, **Product**, **Case Type**, and **Owner**. Click **Save**.
10. To format the datasheet and remove the toolbar, click **Toolbar** on the Web Part toolbar. Click the **Commands and Options** button on the toolbar, and then change the font to **Tahoma 8** to update the font of the column headings. Click **Save**.
11. Right-click the **Created** column, and then click **Commands and Options**. Select **Tahoma** and **8** for the font. Repeat for each column. Click **Save**.
12. Click **Toolbar** again in the Web Part toolbar to remove the toolbar. Click **Save**. Then clear **Show Tool strip** in the **PivotView** section of the properties pane. Click **OK**.

Your page should now resemble Figure 11-9.

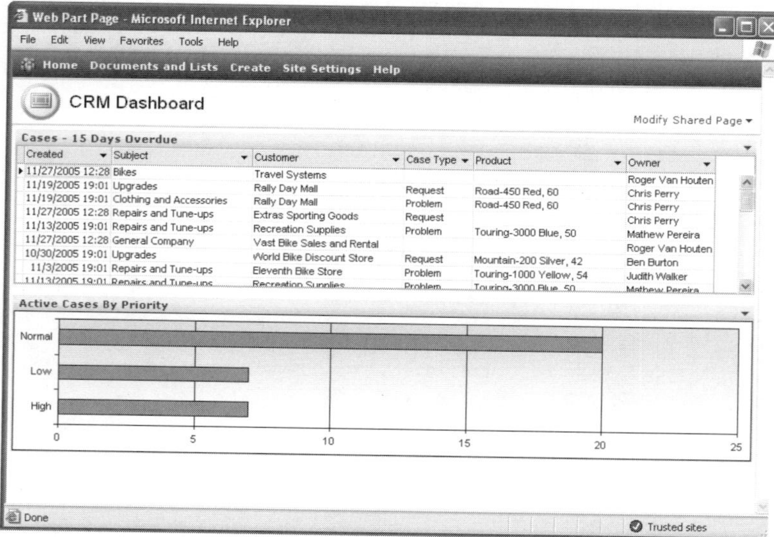

Figure 11-9 Windows SharePoint Services page after adding the Office Datasheet Web Part

The last step we will perform is optional, but we feel it's worth knowing. If we were to add this page to Microsoft CRM as it is currently constructed, it would look similar to Figure 11-10. Notice that it includes the Windows SharePoint Services navigation and title bar.

Because users will access this dashboard from the Microsoft CRM interface, the Windows SharePoint Services navigation and title bar might cause confusion. We'll show you how to hide it or remove it from the dashboard page. One method to accomplish this would be to open the Web page in Microsoft Office FrontPage 2003 and change the page layout directly. We will discuss editing with FrontPage in the next example. A second method (our recommendation) is to simply hide the toolbar and header using the technique we describe next.

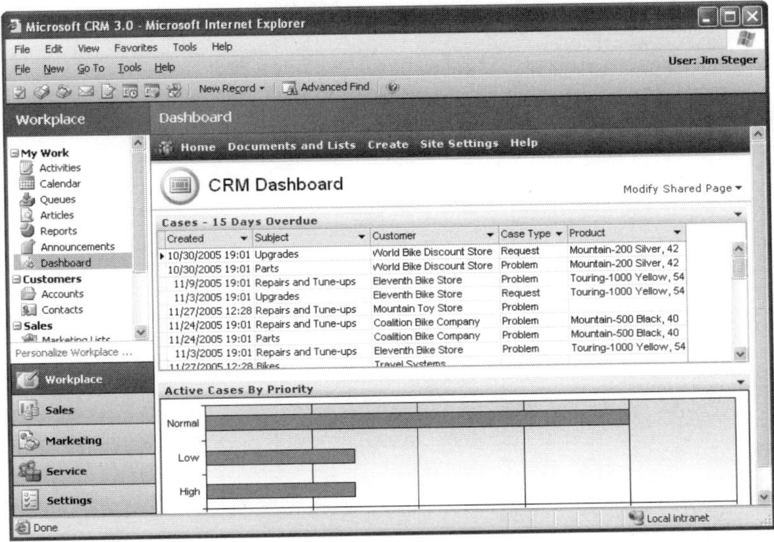

Figure 11-10 Microsoft CRM dashboard page with Windows SharePoint Services navigation

Windows SharePoint Services doesn't provide a user interface option for turning off the header or top navigation menu. However, because SharePoint sites use cascading style sheets styles, we can take advantage of cascading style sheets and simply hide these items. To modify the cascading style sheets, we will use a Content Editor Web Part. This Web Part allows us to add custom content and code that Windows SharePoint Services will render on the page.

Adding a Content Editor Web Part

1. From your dashboard page in Internet Explorer, click **Modify Shared Page**, point to **Add Web Parts**, and then click **Browse**.
2. In the **Team Web Site Gallery** section, drag the **Content Editor** Web Part from the **Web Part List** and place it above the **Cases - 15 Days Overdue** Web Part.
3. Click the **open the tool pane** link in this Web Part, and then click **Source Editor**.
4. In the **Text Entry** dialog box, enter the following code, and then click **Save**.

```
<style>
.ms-bannerframe
{
display:none;
}

.ms-titleareaframe
{
display:none;
}
</style>
```

5. To add just the cascading style sheets styles to the page, and not the Web Part itself, expand the **Layout** section and clear the **Visible on Page** check box. Click **OK.** The following graphic shows the dashboard with the top navigation and header hidden.

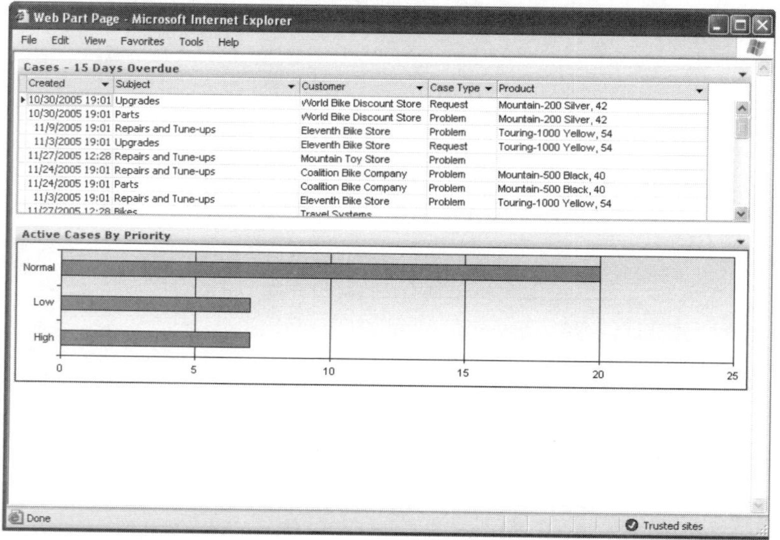

Tip After you hide the header, you will no longer see the Modify Shared Page menu that you have been using to edit the page. To open the page in edit mode and display the hidden Content Editor Web Part, click the down arrow on the Web Part itself, and then click Modify Shared Web Part.

Our dashboard is now ready to be integrated into Microsoft CRM. We will add a link to the dashboard from the Workplace area in the application navigation pane. As you remember from Chapter 6, "Relationships and Custom Entities," you do this by editing the site map.

Adding the dashboard to the Microsoft CRM interface

1. Export the site map and create a backup copy, in case you need to roll back.
2. Open the site map in your favorite XML editor, look under the *<Group Id="MyWork" ResourceId="Group_MyWork" DescriptionResourceId="My_Work_Description">* node, and add the following new *<SubArea>* code. Be sure to change <yoursharepointserver> to your Windows SharePoint Services server.

```
<SubArea Id="nav_dashboard" Title="Dashboard" Icon="/_imgs/ico_18_miscReports.gif"
Url="http://<yoursharepointserver>/CRM%20Integration/CRM%20Dashboard.aspx" />
```

3. Add a *Title* attribute in the workplace *Area* node to get our custom subarea to display. We will add a title called *Workplace.*

```
<Area Id="Workplace" ResourceId="Area_Workplace" ShowGroups="true"
Icon="/_imgs/workplace_24x24.gif" DescriptionResourceId=
"Workplace_Description" Title="My Work">
```

4. Save the file, and then import your new site map into Microsoft CRM by using the Import Customizations feature.

After you update the site map, refresh your Microsoft CRM window (if you had it open) and you should see Dashboard under the My Work group. Clicking the Dashboard link opens your new dashboard in Microsoft CRM, as shown in Figure 11-11.

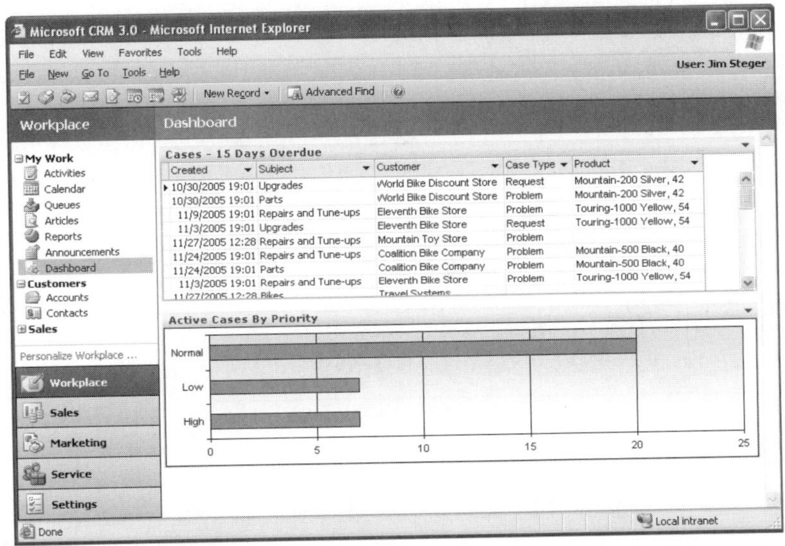

Figure 11-11 Dashboard using Windows SharePoint Services in Microsoft CRM

Obviously, you can expand on this concept and add multiple Web Parts to this dashboard page or even create multiple dashboard pages for each functional role at your organization.

> **Important** Just like Microsoft CRM, Windows SharePoint Services uses Integrated Windows authentication so that users don't have to explicitly log on. Therefore, the data that each user sees in the dashboard is unique to his or her Microsoft CRM user security privileges! Remember that users can add the SharePoint site to their list of trusted sites in Internet Explorer to permanently eliminate the security prompts and warnings.

Simple Document Library Integration

One of the great features of Windows SharePoint Services is the document libraries that let your organization's employees share and collaborate on documents in a centralized location. Windows SharePoint Services also offers additional document management functionality, such as check in and check out, e-mail alerts, discussions, approvals, and direct integration with Microsoft Office. Many companies like using document libraries to store important documents related to their customers. You're already using Microsoft CRM to store data about customers; wouldn't it be great to link a customer's SharePoint document library to his or her

Microsoft CRM Account record, so that users could access both types of information within the Microsoft CRM user interface? You can see where we're going with this, and we're going to show you how to integrate Windows SharePoint Services document libraries with the Microsoft CRM Account form.

Conceptually, we will create a single document library that stores documents for all of our accounts, and then we'll add an Account Number attribute to the document in Windows SharePoint Services to link it to a Microsoft CRM record. By linking the documents with an Account Number, our integration code will automatically filter the records from the document library to display only the documents relevant to the account currently being accessed in Microsoft CRM. To accomplish the integration of the documents and the Account record, we will require users to include an Account Number for each document that they add to the document library.

More Info We chose to link documents from Windows SharePoint Services to Microsoft CRM via an Account Number attribute in this example, but we could have linked them by using other methods, such as the GUID. As a reminder, Chapter 9 includes sample code to implement an auto-Account Number feature in Microsoft CRM.

The final result of our integration is shown in Figure 11-12.

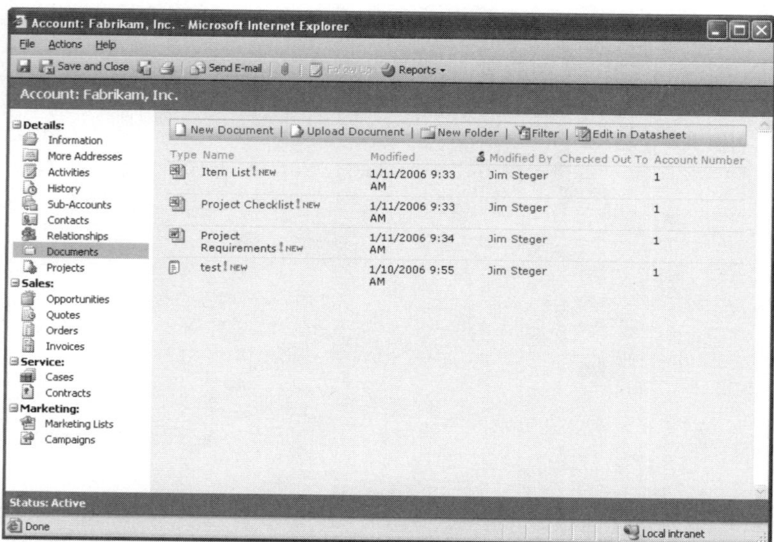

Figure 11-12 Account document library using Windows SharePoint Services

This example will cover the following topics:

- Creating a new SharePoint site
- Creating the document library
- Developing a redirect page
- Configuring Microsoft CRM
- Using the document library
- Editing the SharePoint site with FrontPage
- Additional enhancements

Creating a New SharePoint Site

If you're familiar with Windows SharePoint Services, you know that a single installation includes one site by default but it can support many different sites. For our document integration, we will want to have more design control over the pages within the site, and because of this, we recommend creating a new site.

Creating a SharePoint site

1. Use Internet Explorer to browse to your SharePoint site.
2. Click **Site Settings** on the main toolbar.
3. In the **Administration** section, click **Manage sites and workspaces**. On the **Sites and Workspaces** page, click **Create** on the toolbar.
4. On the **New SharePoint Site** page, enter the following:
   a. In the **Title** box, enter **Microsoft CRM Integration**. In the **Description** box, type **SharePoint site used for integration with Microsoft CRM.**
   b. In the **URL name** box, Type **crm**. Your final URL should be *http://<yoursharepointserver>/crm*.
   c. For **User Permissions** options, select **Use same permissions as parent site**.
   d. Click **Create**.
5. On the **Template Selection** page, select **Blank Site**, and then click **OK**.

   Your page should resemble the page shown in Figure 11-13.

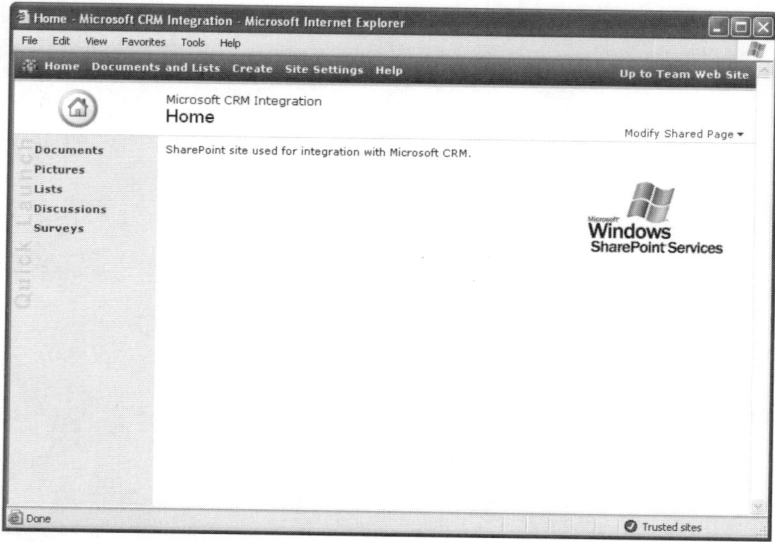

Figure 11-13 New SharePoint site

Creating the Document Library

Now that your new site is in place, we will add a document library to the site to contain all of our Account documents. We will then add a column (Account Number) to this document library. To integrate the data between Microsoft CRM and SharePoint, we will link the Microsoft CRM account number attribute and the newly created Account Number column in the document library.

After we configure our document library, we will configure a filter on the Account Number column. Then, when Windows SharePoint Services filters the page based on the account number, we will examine the URL of the filtered page and reverse engineer it to determine the URL that we need to reference within Microsoft CRM.

Creating a document library

1. Click **Create** on the main toolbar, and then on the **Create Page** page, click **Document Library**.
2. On the **New Document Library** page, enter the following:
   a. In the **Title** box, enter **Account Documents**. In the **Description** box, type **Documents related to Microsoft CRM Account records**.
   b. Select **No** for the question in the **Navigation** section.
   c. In the **Document Versions** section, select **Yes**.
   d. For **Document Template**, choose **Microsoft Office Word document**. This selection identifies Word as the default document type.
   e. Click **Create**.

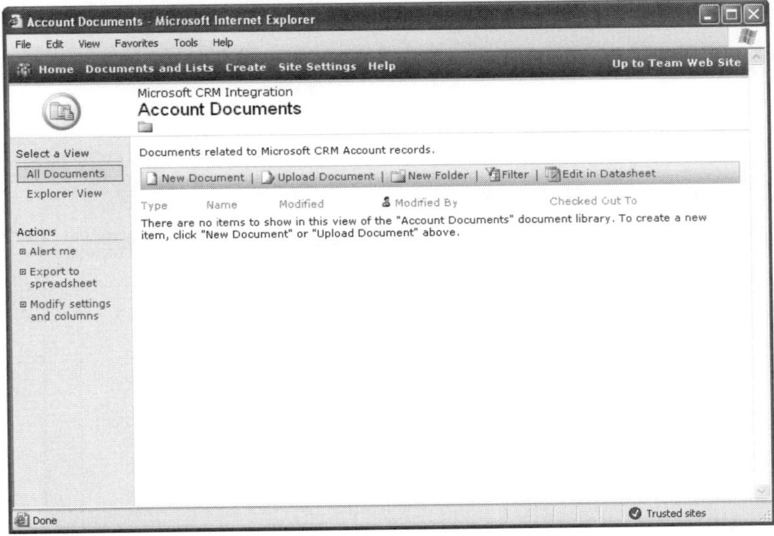

3. In the **Actions** list, click **Modify settings and columns**.
4. On the **Customize Account Documents** page, in the **Columns** section, click **Add a new column**.
5. On the **Add Column** page, enter the following:
    a. In the **Column name** box, type **Account Number**.
    b. For **The type of information in this column is**, select **Single line of text**. This data type matches the attribute type of the Microsoft CRM field.
    c. In the **Optional Settings for Column** section, select **Yes** for the **Require that this column contains information** option. Leave the other default settings and click **OK**.
6. On the **Customize Account Documents** page, click the link next to Web address to return to the document library.

> **Important** Be sure to match the data type of your new column with the attribute of the Microsoft CRM column. Because the account number is a string (nvarchar), we will use a single line of text for our new column. Remember, if you need to find the attribute information for Microsoft CRM, you can use this link: *http://<crmserver>/sdk/list.aspx*.

We now want to find the URL that Windows SharePoint Services creates for a filtered view based on the Account Number. The easiest way to determine the URL is to add a test document to the document library.

Finding the URL for a filtered view

1. Click **Upload Document** on the document library toolbar.
2. Select any document from your computer as a test. Type **1** in the **Account Number** box. Click **Save and Close**.

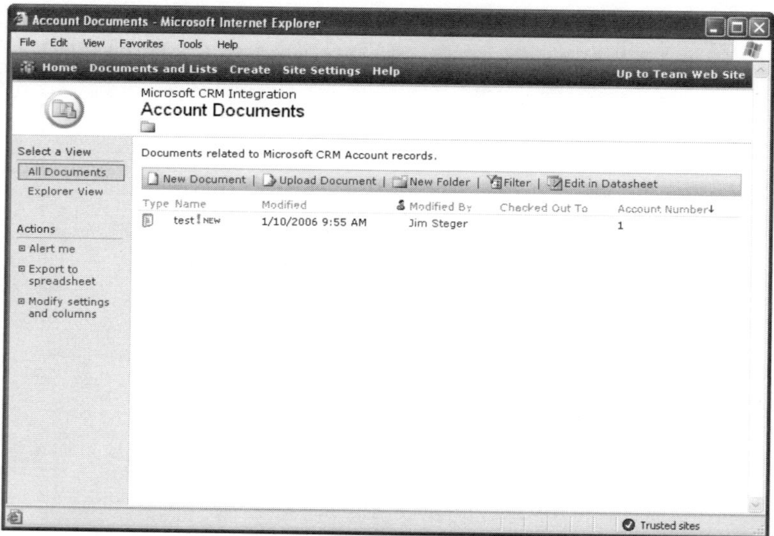

3. In the Account Documents document library, click **Filter** on the document library toolbar. Drop-down lists appear above each column. Select **1** in the drop-down list above the **Account Number** column.

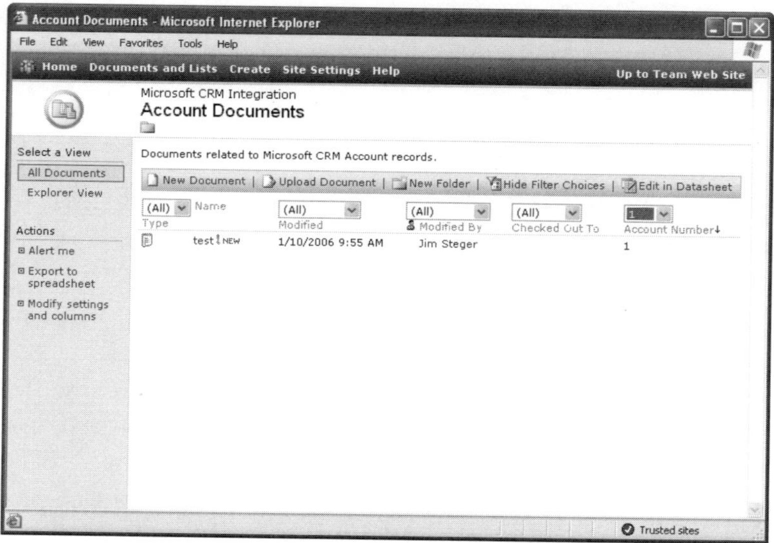

4. Copy the URL from the Internet Explorer address bar and save it. We will be using it shortly. It should look something like this.

```
http://<yoursharepointserver>/crm/Account%20Documents/Forms/AllItems.aspx?View=
%7b443D4E24%2d9229%2d48A4%2d9EF9%2dB6C9810F836F%7d&FilterField1=Account%5fx0020%5fNumb
er&FilterValue1=1
```

As you can see from this URL, Windows SharePoint Services uses the query string parameters to set the view of its page. We will take this URL and dynamically set the *FilterValue1* parameter in our .NET redirect page. Let's see how.

Developing a Redirect Page

To display documents on the Account form, we will add a link in the Account navigation pane using the ISV.config. Microsoft CRM will automatically append the GUID of the account to the query string for all links in the navigation. As we just learned, Windows SharePoint Services filters the document library by including the account number in the query string but Microsoft CRM only includes the GUID of the account. Therefore, we must create an interim redirect page that will translate the URL into the format that we need for Windows SharePoint Services to display the correct documents. We will use an ASP.NET page for the redirect page. It will use the GUID of the account to retrieve the account number from Microsoft CRM, and then it will append that number to the query string *FilterValue1* parameter of the Windows SharePoint Services URL.

The page is conceptually quite simple. Microsoft CRM will pass the *entityid* in the query string, and we will use that to retrieve the record's account number. We will then append that value to the URL that we discovered in the last section. However, we must remove the last 1 from the URL, because we want to determine what that value will be. The URL that you will use should look similar to this:

```
http://<yoursharepointserver>/crm/Account%20Documents/Forms/AllItems.aspx?View=
%7b443D4E24%2d9229%2d48A4%2d9EF9%2dB6C9810F836F%7d&FilterField1=Account%5fx0020%5fNumber&Fil
terValue1=
```

Finally, we perform a Web redirect to the document library.

Creating a redirect page

1. Open the WebSiteConnector project that you created earlier in this chapter, or create a new C# Web Application project.
2. Add a Web Form page called DocumentRedirect.aspx.
3. Copy the code in Listing 11-1 to the page and build it. Note that you must replace *<crmserver>* with the actual name of your Microsoft CRM Web server. Also, use the URL that you discovered earlier from your SharePoint site for your *url* variable (step 4 of the Finding the URL of a filtered view procedure).

4. Since this page will be deployed on the Microsoft CRM Web server, we will reuse our standard *workingwithcrm* virtual web that we created earlier for deployment. Copy the assembly to the bin folder of the workingwithcrm folder on your Microsoft CRM Web server. Copy the DocumentRedirect.aspx page to the root of the WebSiteConnector virtual directory.

The code for DocumentRedirect.aspx is shown in Listing 11-1.

Listing 11-1 DocumentRedirect.aspx

```
<%@ Page Language="C#" %>
<%@ Import Namespace="WorkingWithCrm.CrmSdk" %>

<script runat="server">
protected void Page_Load(object sender, EventArgs e)
{
  string entityId = Request.QueryString["oId"];

  CrmService service = new CrmService();
  service.Credentials = System.Net.CredentialCache.DefaultCredentials;
  service.Url = "http://<crmserver>/mscrmservices/2006/crmservice.asmx";

  ColumnSet cols = new ColumnSet();
  cols.Attributes = new string [] {"accountnumber"};

  try
  {
    // Retrieve the record, casting it as the correct entity
    account oAccount = (account)service.Retrieve(EntityName.account.ToString(), new Guid(ent
ityId), cols);
    string acctNumber = (oAccount.accountnumber == null) ? string.Empty : oAccount.accountnu
mber.ToString();

    string url = "http://<yoursharepointserver>/crm/Account%20Documents/Forms/
AllItems.aspx?View=%7bCE73E44C%2d0622%2d48B2%2dBC88%2d414B5EC8277F%7d&FilterField1=Account%5
fx0020%5fNumber&FilterValue1=";
    url += acctNumber;

    Response.Redirect(url, true);
  }
  catch (System.Web.Services.Protocols.SoapException ex)
  {
    // Handle error
  }
}
</script>
```

Configuring Microsoft CRM

After we deploy our redirect file, we just have to add a link to it from the Microsoft CRM interface. Because we want this link to display on the Account entity's navigation pane, we must update the ISV.config file.

Update the ISV.config file with the following code.

```
<Entity name="account">
 <!-- The Account Left Nav Bar -->
 <NavBar>
 <NavBarItem Icon="/_imgs/ico_18_queue.gif" Title="Documents" Url="/websiteconnector/
documentredirect.aspx" Id="navItem1" />
 </NavBar>
</Entity>
```

Replace the *Url* attribute with the appropriate path to your custom page.

> **Note** Remember to make sure that Microsoft CRM enables ISV integration by checking the ISVIntegration setting in the Web.config file. The user accessing the account record must also belong to a role with the ISV Extensions privilege enabled. Review Chapter 3, "Managing Security and Information Access," for more information regarding setting up security and Chapter 10, "Client-Side SDK," for information regarding the ISV.config file.

Next, open Microsoft CRM and browse to an Account record. You should see the new Documents link in the Details section of the navigation pane. Type **1** in the Account Number box, and then click Save. Click the Documents link to see the document library, as shown in Figure 11-14.

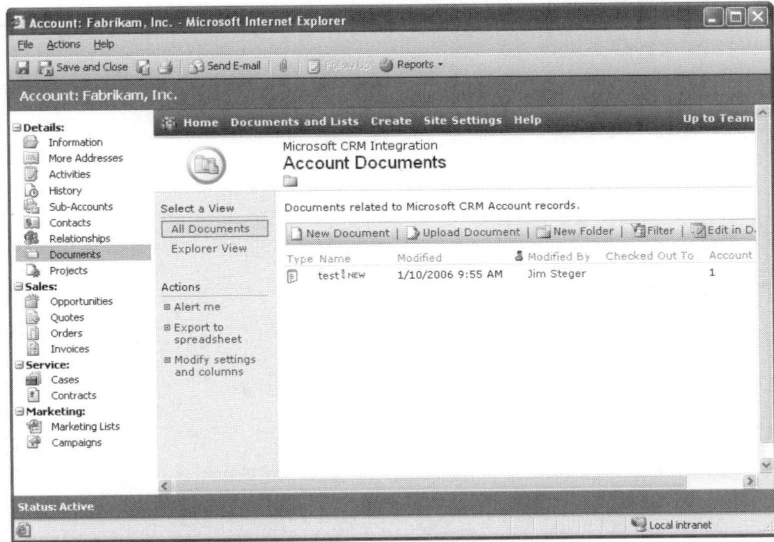

Figure 11-14 Account Documents page in Microsoft CRM

And, because this Account's account number is now 1, you will see that the document library is correctly returning our original test document.

Using the Document Library

To ensure that our system integration is working, try out a couple of documents. From your current account, upload another document with an account number of 2, and you will see that the document will not appear in the list, but will appear with an account whose account number is 2.

Here are few additional items of interest regarding Microsoft CRM and Windows SharePoint Services:

- Remember that Microsoft CRM caches the Web pages linked from the left navigation pane. If you need to refresh, either right-click the Windows SharePoint Services page and then click Refresh, or close and re-open the Account record.
- When you click New Document in the document library, a Word document appears that is linked to Windows SharePoint Services. Remember selecting Word as your default document when you created the document library? That setting is what drives this functionality. Even better, when you save your document, you will be prompted for an account number, and your document will be automatically saved in your document library. Pretty cool!
- When you click the document, Windows SharePoint Services gives you a menu of options that allows you to edit the document properties, check the document in and out, review version history, and set up e-mail alerts. You get all of this functionality from Windows SharePoint Services without writing any custom code.
- Unfortunately, this example has the same user interface problem as our dashboard. As we currently have it constructed, users could browse to the SharePoint site from within Microsoft CRM. We will show you how that can be improved in the next section.

Editing the SharePoint Site with FrontPage

Performing a simple integration between Microsoft CRM and a Windows SharePoint Services document library requires very little code and can be accomplished in a matter of hours, not weeks. However, although this implementation is serviceable, we can make a few more quick improvements that will enhance the user interface even further.

In our dashboard example, we showed you how to add some simple style code in a Content Editor Web Part to remove the site toolbar and page header. This approach worked well for that instance, because we were working with a single Web Part Page.

In this example, we have a document library, not a Web Part Page, so we must consider the layout of additional pages (such as a document upload page, properties pages, and so on). For this example, we will use FrontPage 2003 to edit the SharePoint site.

Important Many professional developers use Visual Studio exclusively. However, FrontPage and Windows SharePoint Services are very tightly integrated, making adjustments simple. Therefore, we strongly recommend that you use FrontPage for this type of modification.

Changing the page layout with FrontPage 2003

1. Open FrontPage 2003.
2. On the **File** menu, click **Open Site**. In the **Open Site** dialog box, type **http:// <*yoursharepointserver*>/crm** in the **Site name** box.
3. In the **Folder List**, click **Account Documents**, and then click **Forms**. You will see several .aspx pages and a Word template.

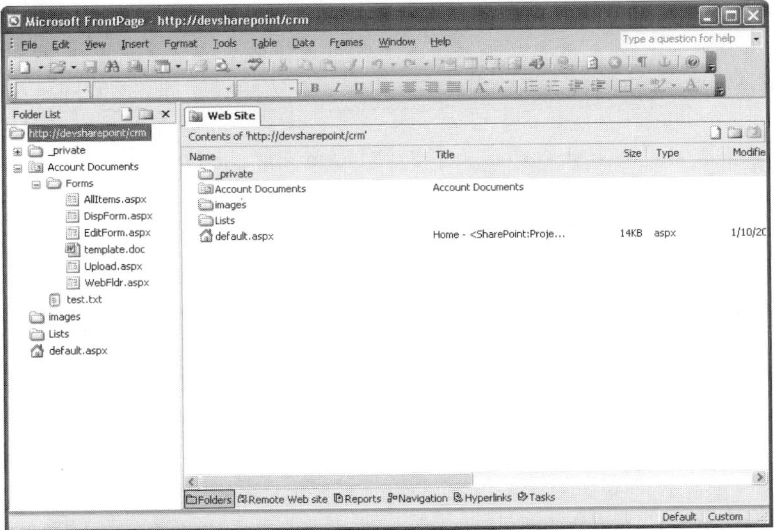

4. Double-click **AllItems.aspx** to open the main document library page for editing. From here, you can use the design or code view to make changes to this page.

Warning You will be changing the Windows SharePoint Services files directly on the server! Use caution when editing any of these files, as you could break functionality. Always test your changes on a development server first.

5. Remove the navigation and title elements; the Microsoft CRM interface will provide those for us. Note that some elements might be required for the page to render (such as the *SharePoint:ListProperty* element). Test the page in your browser or in the FrontPage Preview mode after each change. When you are finished removing these elements, your page should resemble the following graphic:

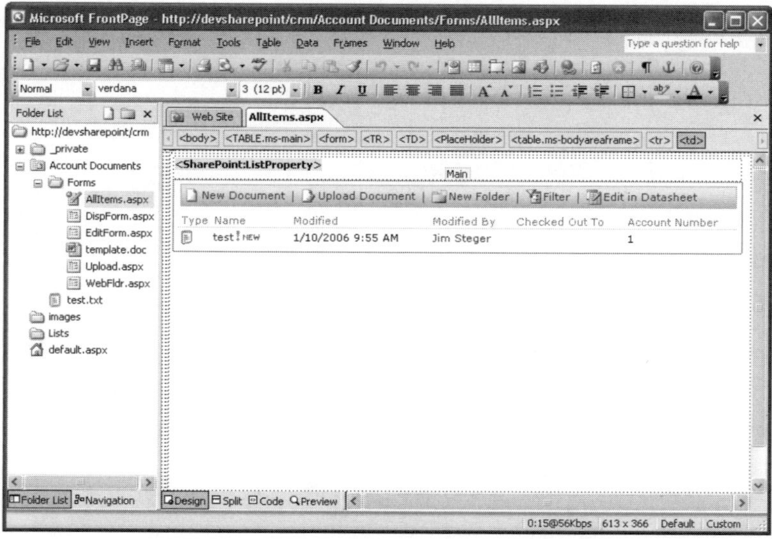

6. To change the background color, click **Theme** on the **Format** menu.

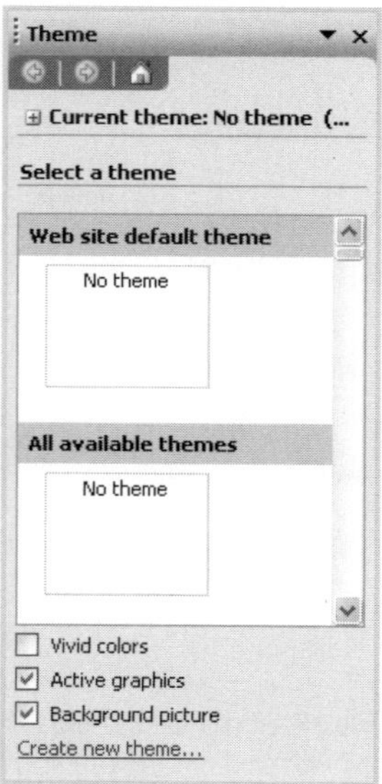

7. At the bottom of the **Theme** pane, click **Create new theme** to open the **Customize Theme** dialog box.

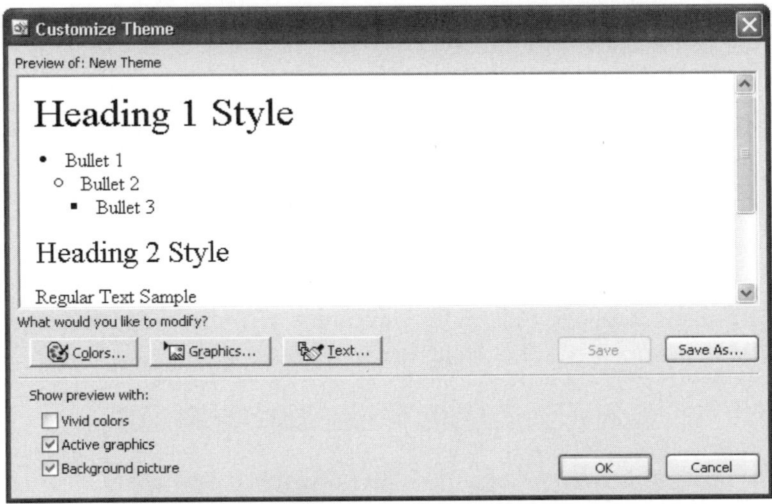

8. Click the **Colors** button, and then click the **Custom** tab. For the **Background** item, click the **Color** drop-down list, and then click **More Colors**.

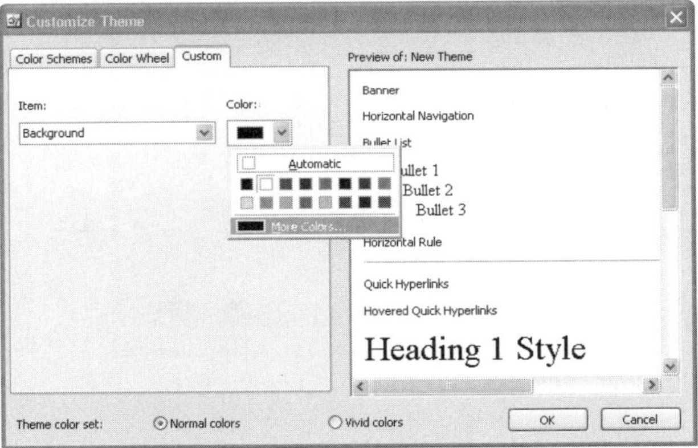

9. Enter the following hex value: **Hex={EE,F0,F6}**. This corresponds to the light blue color of an entity's form tab. Click **OK** twice.

> **Note** The actual background color in CRM is a darker blue (#ACC0E9), but the document library Web Part didn't show as well on it, so we chose the lighter color for this example. The SDK comes with a handy UI Style Guide, which is a PDF document that details all of the colors and user interface specifications for the whole application. It is an excellent reference if you are creating custom pages!

10. Click **Save As**, and then enter **Microsoft CRM** in the **Enter new theme title** box. Click **OK** to close the **Save Theme** dialog box, and click **OK** again to close the **Customize Theme** dialog box.
11. In the **Theme** pane, **Microsoft CRM** appears as an available theme. If you click the icon, you can choose to apply the theme to the selected pages or the entire site (apply as default theme). For this example, click **Apply as default theme** on the menu. Click **Yes** in the warning message.
12. Save your page.

So what did this accomplish? Well, go back to your Account record in Microsoft CRM and look at the Documents link. Figure 11-15 shows the results.

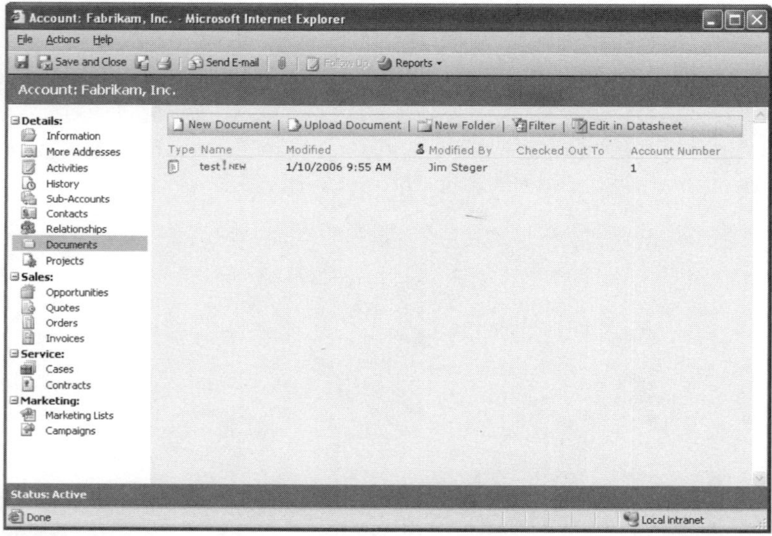

Figure 11-15 Updated Account Documents page in Microsoft CRM

Obviously, the Web Part style is a bit different, but the cleaner user interface already makes the page appear more integrated. In addition, by removing the navigation, you prevent users from accidentally browsing to areas of Windows SharePoint Services.

You should repeat the preceding steps for the other files to clean up their look. You will be able alter the upload document (Upload.aspx), view document (DispForm.aspx), and update document (EditForm.aspx) properties pages.

You can also edit the default Word document that appears when users add new documents to your document library. Typical customizations to this might include adding your company header and logo and changing the styles of the document to match your corporate policies.

FrontPage and Ghosting

As we create new sites and begin to modify the Windows SharePoint Services files in FrontPage, we want to take a moment to mention the concept of *ghosting*. When we created our new Microsoft CRM site, Windows SharePoint Services did not copy all of the pages and files to a server directory or database. Instead, it created a link to the core files in a database along with the definition of the site. That process is referred to as *ghosting*. Ghosting improves the site's overall performance and saves disk space.

However, ghosting requires that all pages in the site use the same definition. Editing a page in FrontPage removes the link for that page and all dependent pages, instead of creating a link to the core site pages in the database. You lose the performance gains of ghosting as a result, because Windows SharePoint Services has to make a database call to retrieve the page. In addition, global changes to the site might not always apply, because the edited pages are now stored separately.

For small sites or a limited number of users, this effect might be negligible, but you should understand the impact as you begin to alter your site's pages with FrontPage.

Additional Enhancements

Obviously, forcing the user to provide the link between the document records in Windows SharePoint Services and Microsoft CRM, and with a text variable at that, is not ideal. We concede that the document integration is simplistic in its implementation. The main point of the example is that with minimal code and effort, you can use the power of Windows SharePoint Services in conjunction with Microsoft CRM to provide a quick and serviceable solution for your business.

For a more robust solution, you might prefer to use your own document Web Part, which would allow you to control the menu links, toolbar actions, styles, and so on. You might also decide to provide the integration with the document automatically, using the account's GUID instead of a user-entered number. Clearly, you can develop more elegant and robust solutions, but those solutions are probably more appropriate for Windows SharePoint Services SDK discussions.

Additional References

The following are some additional SharePoint Products and Technologies references that you might find useful:

- *http://www.microsoft.com/sharepoint*
- *http://msdn.microsoft.com/library/default.asp?url=/library/en-us/odc_2003_ta/html/sharepoint.asp*
- *http://www.microsoft.com/resources/documentation/wss/2/all/adminguide/en-us/stsh01.mspx*

Summary

Hopefully you saw some useful examples of how you can connect your external applications to Microsoft CRM. By leveraging the events and touch points that Microsoft CRM provides, you can incorporate complex, real-time integration with your existing legacy systems and additional third-party applications. Often, Web developers get tunneled into constantly adding a new custom Web page to solve a particular use case, forgetting that more intuitive solutions for the user might exist with other known applications, such as Office, Reporting Services, or Windows SharePoint Services.

Our primary goal is to highlight how the customization capabilities and interoperability of Microsoft CRM allow you to use it as the core platform for your line-of-business applications. You can then customize and extend Microsoft CRM to create a truly unique, user-friendly, and powerful application tool set for your business.

Index

B

C

D

E

F

G

H

I

N

O

P

Q

R

T

X-Z

Mike Snyder

Mike Snyder is cofounder and principal of Sonoma Partners, a Chicago-based consulting firm that specializes in Microsoft CRM implementations. Microsoft awarded Sonoma Partners as the Global Microsoft CRM Partner of the Year in both 2003 and 2005. Recognized as one of the industry's leading CRM experts, Mike authors several popular newsletters and blogs about Microsoft CRM.

Prior to Sonoma Partners, Mike led multiple product development teams at Motorola and Fortune Brands. Mike graduated with honors from Northwestern's Kellogg Graduate School of Management with a Masters of Business Administration degree, majoring in Marketing and Entrepreneurship. He has a bachelor's degree in engineering from Notre Dame. Mike lives in Chicago, IL with his wife and three children. He enjoys ice hockey and playing with his kids in his free time.

Jim Steger

Jim Steger is also a cofounder and principal of Sonoma Partners. He architected and led multiple award-winning Microsoft CRM deployments, including complex enterprise integration projects. He's been developing solutions and writing code for Microsoft CRM since the version 1.0 beta. Jim also contributed to the Microsoft CRM 3.0 Technology Adoption Program and provided input for several of the Microsoft CRM 3.0 certification courses.

Prior to Sonoma Partners, Jim designed and led various global software development projects at Motorola and Acco Office Products. Jim earned his bachelor's degree in engineering from Northwestern University. He currently lives in Chicago, IL with his wife and son. In his free time, Jim enjoys playing beach volleyball and watching football with his son.

Additional Resources for Developers: Advanced Topics and Best Practices

Published and Forthcoming Titles from Microsoft Press

Code Complete, Second Edition

Steve McConnell • ISBN 0-7356-1967-0

For more than a decade, Steve McConnell, one of the premier authors and voices in the software community, has helped change the way developers write code—and produce better software. Now his classic book, *Code Complete*, has been fully updated and revised with best practices in the art and science of constructing software. Topics include design, applying good techniques to construction, eliminating errors, planning, managing construction activities, and relating personal character to superior software. This new edition features fully updated information on programming techniques, including the emergence of Web-style programming, and integrated coverage of object-oriented design. You'll also find new code examples—both good and bad—in C++, Microsoft® Visual Basic®, C#, and Java, although the focus is squarely on techniques and practices.

More About Software Requirements: Thorny Issues and Practical Advice

Karl E. Wiegers • ISBN 0-7356-2267-1

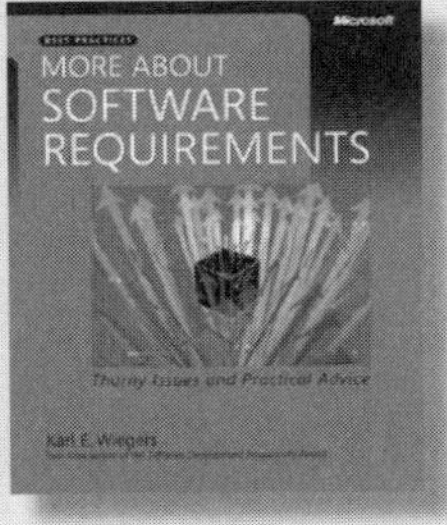

Have you ever delivered software that satisfied all of the project specifications, but failed to meet any of the customers expectations? Without formal, verifiable requirements—and a system for managing them—the result is often a gap between what developers think they're supposed to build and what customers think they're going to get. Too often, lessons about software requirements engineering processes are formal or academic, and not of value to real-world, professional development teams. In this follow-up guide to *Software Requirements*, Second Edition, you will discover even more practical techniques for gathering and managing software requirements that help you deliver software that meets project and customer specifications. Succinct and immediately useful, this book is a must-have for developers and architects.

Software Estimation: Demystifying the Black Art

Steve McConnell • ISBN 0-7356-0535-1

Often referred to as the "black art" because of its complexity and uncertainty, software estimation is not as hard or mysterious as people think. However, the art of how to create effective cost and schedule estimates has not been very well publicized. *Software Estimation* provides a proven set of procedures and heuristics that software developers, technical leads, and project managers can apply to their projects. Instead of arcane treatises and rigid modeling techniques, award-winning author Steve McConnell gives practical guidance to help organizations achieve basic estimation proficiency and lay the groundwork to continue improving project cost estimates. This book does not avoid the more complex mathematical estimation approaches, but the non-mathematical reader will find plenty of useful guidelines without getting bogged down in complex formulas.

Debugging, Tuning, and Testing Microsoft .NET 2.0 Applications

John Robbins • ISBN 0-7356-2202-7

Making an application the best it can be has long been a time-consuming task best accomplished with specialized and costly tools. With Microsoft Visual Studio® 2005, developers have available a new range of built-in functionality that enables them to debug their code quickly and efficiently, tune it to optimum performance, and test applications to ensure compatibility and trouble-free operation. In this accessible and hands-on book, debugging expert John Robbins shows developers how to use the tools and functions in Visual Studio to their full advantage to ensure high-quality applications.

The Security Development Lifecycle

Michael Howard and Steve Lipner • ISBN 0-7356-2214-0

Adapted from Microsoft's standard development process, the Security Development Lifecycle (SDL) is a methodology that helps reduce the number of security defects in code at every stage of the development process, from design to release. This book details each stage of the SDL methodology and discusses its implementation across a range of Microsoft software, including Microsoft Windows Server™ 2003, Microsoft SQL Server™ 2000 Service Pack 3, and Microsoft Exchange Server 2003 Service Pack 1, to help measurably improve security features. You get direct access to insights from Microsoft's security team and lessons that are applicable to software development processes worldwide, whether on a small-scale or a large-scale. This book includes a CD featuring videos of developer training classes.

Software Requirements, Second Edition
Karl E. Wiegers • ISBN 0-7356-1879-8

Writing Secure Code, Second Edition
Michael Howard and David LeBlanc • ISBN 0-7356-1722-8

CLR via C#, Second Edition
Jeffrey Richter • ISBN 0-7356-2163-2

For more information about Microsoft Press® books and other learning products, visit: **www.microsoft.com/mspress** *and* **www.microsoft.com/learning**

Microsoft® Press

Additional Resources for C# Developers

Published and Forthcoming Titles from Microsoft Press

Microsoft® Visual C#® 2005 Express Edition: Build a Program Now!

Patrice Pelland • ISBN 0-7356-2229-9

In this lively, eye-opening, and hands-on book, all you need is a computer and the desire to learn how to program with Visual C# 2005 Express Edition. Featuring a full working edition of the software, this fun and highly visual guide walks you through a complete programming project—a desktop weather-reporting application—from start to finish. You'll get an unintimidating introduction to the Microsoft Visual Studio® development environment and learn how to put the lightweight, easy-to-use tools in Visual C# Express to work right away—creating, compiling, testing, and delivering your first, ready-to-use program. You'll get expert tips, coaching, and visual examples at each step of the way, along with pointers to additional learning resources.

Microsoft Visual C# 2005 *Step by Step*

John Sharp • ISBN 0-7356-2129-2

Visual C#, a feature of Visual Studio 2005, is a modern programming language designed to deliver a productive environment for creating business frameworks and reusable object-oriented components. Now you can teach yourself essential techniques with Visual C#—and start building components and Microsoft Windows®–based applications—one step at a time. With *Step by Step*, you work at your own pace through hands-on, learn-by-doing exercises. Whether you're a beginning programmer or new to this particular language, you'll learn how, when, and why to use specific features of Visual C# 2005. Each chapter puts you to work, building your knowledge of core capabilities and guiding you as you create your first C#-based applications for Windows, data management, and the Web.

Programming Microsoft Visual C# 2005 Framework Reference

Francesco Balena • ISBN 0-7356-2182-9

Complementing *Programming Microsoft Visual C# 2005 Core Reference*, this book covers a wide range of additional topics and information critical to Visual C# developers, including Windows Forms, working with Microsoft ADO.NET 2.0 and Microsoft ASP.NET 2.0, Web services, security, remoting, and much more. Packed with sample code and real-world examples, this book will help developers move from understanding to mastery.

Programming Microsoft Visual C# 2005 *Core Reference*

Donis Marshall • ISBN 0-7356-2181-0

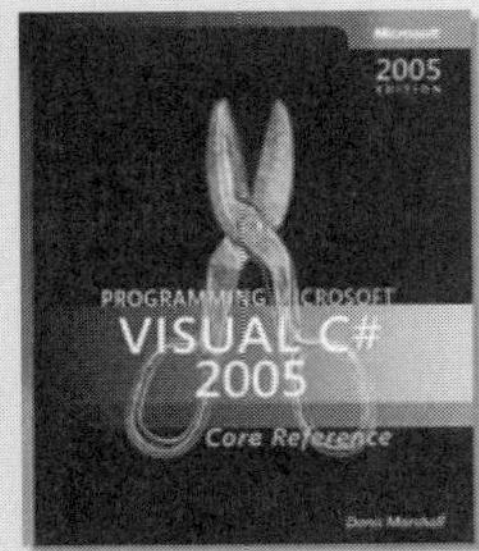

Get the in-depth reference and pragmatic, real-world insights you need to exploit the enhanced language features and core capabilities in Visual C# 2005. Programming expert Donis Marshall deftly builds your proficiency with classes, structs, and other fundamentals, and advances your expertise with more advanced topics such as debugging, threading, and memory management. Combining incisive reference with hands-on coding examples and best practices, this *Core Reference* focuses on mastering the C# skills you need to build innovative solutions for smart clients and the Web.

CLR via C#, Second Edition

Jeffrey Richter • ISBN 0-7356-2163-2

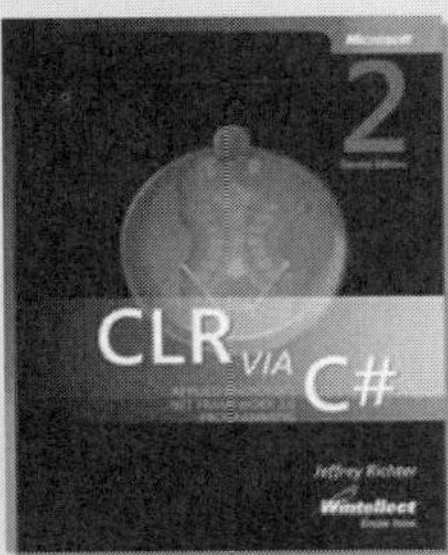

In this new edition of Jeffrey Richter's popular book, you get focused, pragmatic guidance on how to exploit the common language runtime (CLR) functionality in Microsoft .NET Framework 2.0 for applications of all types—from Web Forms, Windows Forms, and Web services to solutions for Microsoft SQL Server™, Microsoft code names "Avalon" and "Indigo," consoles, Microsoft Windows NT® Service, and more. Targeted to advanced developers and software designers, this book takes you under the covers of .NET for an in-depth understanding of its structure, functions, and operational components, demonstrating the most practical ways to apply this knowledge to your own development efforts. You'll master fundamental design tenets for .NET and get hands-on insights for creating high-performance applications more easily and efficiently. The book features extensive code examples in Visual C# 2005.

Programming Microsoft Windows Forms
Charles Petzold • ISBN 0-7356-2153-5

CLR via C++
Jeffrey Richter with Stanley B. Lippman
ISBN 0-7356-2248-5

Programming Microsoft Web Forms
Douglas J. Reilly • ISBN 0-7356-2179-9

Debugging, Tuning, and Testing Microsoft .NET 2.0 Applications
John Robbins • ISBN 0-7356-2202-7

For more information about Microsoft Press® books and other learning products, visit: **www.microsoft.com/books** *and* **www.microsoft.com/learning**

Microsoft Press products are available worldwide wherever quality computer books are sold. For more information, contact your book or computer retailer, software reseller, or local Microsoft Sales Office, or visit our Web site at **www.microsoft.com/mspress**. To locate your nearest source for Microsoft Press products, or to order directly, call 1-800-MSPRESS in the United States. (In Canada, call **1-800-268-2222**.)

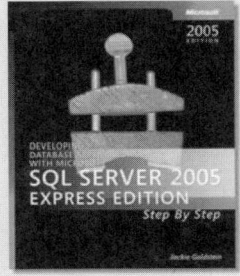

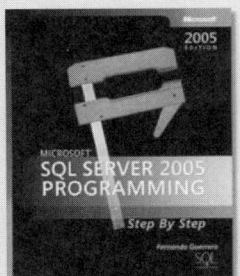

Additional Resources for Visual Basic Developers

Published and Forthcoming Titles from Microsoft Press

Microsoft® Visual Basic® 2005 Express Edition: Build a Program Now!

Patrice Pelland • ISBN 0-7356-2213-2

Featuring a full working edition of the software, this fun and highly visual guide walks you through a complete programming project—a desktop weather-reporting application—from start to finish. You'll get an introduction to the Microsoft Visual Studio® development environment and learn how to put the lightweight, easy-to-use tools in Visual Basic Express to work right away—creating, compiling, testing, and delivering your first ready-to-use program. You'll get expert tips, coaching, and visual examples each step of the way, along with pointers to additional learning resources.

Microsoft Visual Basic 2005 *Step by Step*

Michael Halvorson • ISBN 0-7356-2131-4

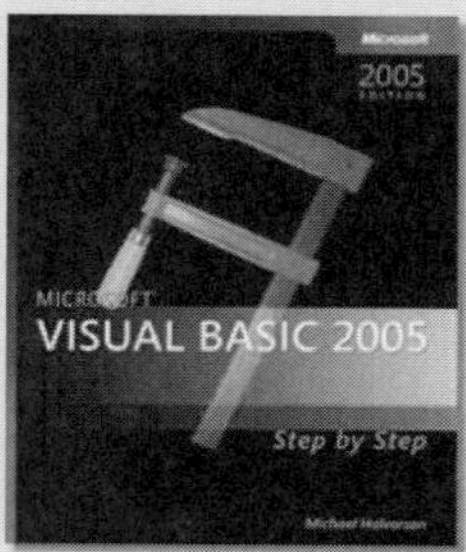

With enhancements across its visual designers, code editor, language, and debugger that help accelerate the development and deployment of robust, elegant applications across the Web, a business group, or an enterprise, Visual Basic 2005 focuses on enabling developers to rapidly build applications. Now you can teach yourself the essentials of working with Visual Studio 2005 and the new features of the Visual Basic language—one step at a time. Each chapter puts you to work, showing you how, when, and why to use specific features of Visual Basic and guiding as you create actual components and working applications for Microsoft Windows®. You'll also explore data management and Web-based development topics.

Programming Microsoft Visual Basic 2005 *Core Reference*

Francesco Balena • ISBN 0-7356-2183-7

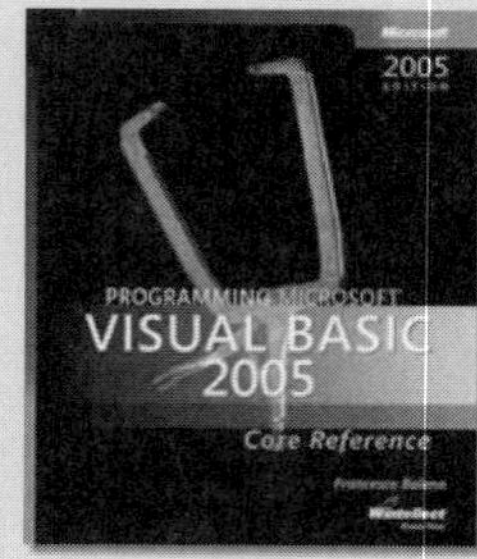

Get the expert insights, indispensable reference, and practical instruction needed to exploit the core language features and capabilities in Visual Basic 2005. Well-known Visual Basic programming author Francesco Balena expertly guides you through the fundamentals, including modules, keywords, and inheritance, and builds your mastery of more advanced topics such as delegates, assemblies, and My Namespace. Combining in-depth reference with extensive, hands-on code examples and best-practices advice, this *Core Reference* delivers the key resources that you need to develop professional-level programming skills for smart clients and the Web.

Programming Microsoft Visual Basic 2005 Framework Reference

Francesco Balena • ISBN 0-7356-2175-6

Complementing *Programming Microsoft Visual Basic 2005 Core Reference*, this book covers a wide range of additional topics and information critical to Visual Basic developers, including Windows Forms, working with Microsoft ADO.NET 2.0 and ASP.NET 2.0, Web services, security, remoting, and much more. Packed with sample code and real-world examples, this book will help developers move from understanding to mastery.

Programming Microsoft Windows Forms
Charles Petzold • ISBN 0-7356-2153-5

Programming Microsoft Web Forms
Douglas J. Reilly • ISBN 0-7356-2179-9

Debugging, Tuning, and Testing Microsoft .NET 2.0 Applications
John Robbins • ISBN 0-7356-2202-7

Microsoft ASP.NET 2.0 *Step by Step*
George Shepherd • ISBN 0-7356-2201-9

Microsoft ADO.NET 2.0 *Step by Step*
Rebecca Riordan • ISBN 0-7356-2164-0

Programming Microsoft ASP.NET 2.0 *Core Reference*
Dino Esposito • ISBN 0-7356-2176-4

For more information about Microsoft Press® books and other learning products, visit: **www.microsoft.com/books** *and* **www.microsoft.com/learning**

Microsoft Press products are available worldwide wherever quality computer books are sold. For more information, contact your book or computer retailer, software reseller, or local Microsoft Sales Office, or visit our Web site at **www.microsoft.com/mspress**. To locate your nearest source for Microsoft Press products, or to order directly, call 1-800-MSPRESS in the United States. (In Canada, call **1-800-268-2222**.)

Additional Resources for Web Developers

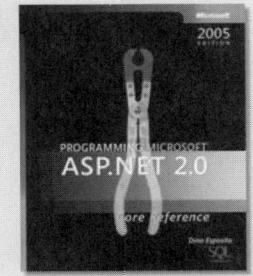

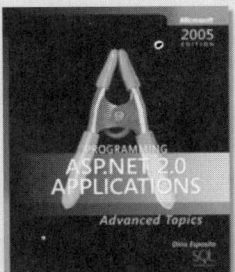

Published and Forthcoming Titles from Microsoft Press

1/07

What do you think of this book?
We want to hear from you!

Do you have a few minutes to participate in a brief online survey? Microsoft is interested in hearing your feedback about this publication so that we can continually improve our books and learning resources for you.

To participate in our survey, please visit:

www.microsoft.com/learning/booksurvey

And enter this book's ISBN, 0-7356-2259-0. As a thank-you to survey participants in the United States and Canada, each month we'll randomly select five respondents to win one of five $100 gift certificates from a leading online merchant.* At the conclusion of the survey, you can enter the drawing by providing your e-mail address, which will be used for prize notification *only*.

Thanks in advance for your input. Your opinion counts!

Sincerely,

Microsoft Learning

Learn More. Go Further.

To see special offers on Microsoft Learning products for developers, IT professionals, and home and office users, visit: *www.microsoft.com/learning/booksurvey*

* No purchase necessary. Void where prohibited. Open only to residents of the 50 United States (includes District of Columbia) and Canada (void in Quebec). Sweepstakes ends 6/30/2006. For official rules, see: *www.microsoft.com/learning/booksurvey*